CORPORATE
FINANCE
AND THE
SECURITIES
LAWS

Second Edition

Charles J. Johnson, Jr.

Joseph McLaughlin

ASPEN LAW & BUSINESS
A Division of Aspen Publishers, Inc.

This publication is designed to provide accurate and authoritative information in regard to the subject matter covered. It is sold with the understanding that the publisher is not engaged in rendering legal, accounting, or other professional services. If legal advice or other professional assistance is required, the services of a competent professional person should be sought.

—From a *Declaration of Principles* jointly adopted by a Committee of the American Bar Association and a Committee of Publishers and Associations.

Third Printing—1999

Copyright © 1997

by
Aspen Law & Business
A Division of Aspen Publishers, Inc.
A Wolters Kluwer Company

Permissions
Aspen Law & Business
1185 Avenue of the Americas
New York, NY 10036

Printed in the United States of America.

ISBN 1-56706-354-3

About Aspen Law & Business

Aspen Law & Business—comprising the former Prentice Hall Law & Business and Little, Brown's Professional Division—is a leading publisher of authoritative treatises, practice manuals, services, and journals for attorneys, financial and tax advisors, corporate and bank directors, and other business professionals. Our mission is to provide practical solution-based how-to information keyed to the latest legislative, judicial and regulatory developments.

We offer publications in the areas of banking and finance; bankruptcy; business and commercial law; corporate law; pensions, benefits, and labor; insurance law; securities; taxation; intellectual property; government and administrative law; matrimonial and family law; environmental and health law; international law; legal practice and litigation; and criminal law.

Aspen Law & Business is a division of Aspen Publishers, Inc., a Wolters Kluwer Company.

Other Aspen Law & Business products treating corporate and securities law issues include:

The Business Judgment Rule
Corporation, A Service
The Corporate Governance Advisor, a bimonthly journal
Delaware Law of Corporations and Business Organizations
Folk on The Delaware General Corporation Law
Fundamentals of Securities Regulation
Insights, a monthly corporate and securities journal
The Investment Lawyer, a monthly journal
Meetings of Stockholders
Raising Capital
Regulation of Corporate Disclosure
The Regulation of Money Managers
Securities Regulation
Securitization: Structured Financing, Financial Asset Pools,
  and Asset-Backed Securities
Takeover Defense
U. S. Regulation of the International and Securities and
  Derivatives Markets
Venture Capital and Public Offering Negotiation
Securitization of Financial Assets

ASPEN LAW & BUSINESS
A Division of Aspen Publishers, Inc.
A Wolters Kluwer Company

For Chris
and
to the memory of
J. Courtney Ivey

C.J.J., Jr.

For
Joseph Nicholas McLaughlin
and
Genevieve Lardiere McLaughlin

J.McL.

TABLE OF CONTENTS

Chapter 1

Chapter 3

Chapter 4

MANIPULATIVE PRACTICES AND MARKET ACTIVITIES DURING DISTRIBUTIONS

Chapter 9

Chapter 12

Chapter 13

Chapter 14

ABOUT THE AUTHORS

Charles J. Johnson, Jr. is one of the country's most experienced securities lawyers. A graduate of Yale College and Harvard Law School, he began the practice of law at Brown & Wood in 1956 and became a partner in 1967. He is now of counsel to Brown & Wood LLP. During his last ten years as a member of the firm, he was the head of its corporate and securities practice.

Mr. Johnson has acted as counsel to issuers and investment banking firms in hundreds of major financial transactions, including public offerings of debt and equity securities, leveraged buyouts, issuer tender offers, underwritten calls and institutional private placements. Among the transactions in which he has played a major role are the initial public offering by Communications Satellite Corporation and numerous first mortgage bond financings by Duke Power Company and Public Service Electric and Gas Company. He represented Merrill Lynch, Pierce, Fenner & Smith Incorporated when it went public in 1971 and subsequently worked on the public offerings of several other securities firms. He has represented the underwriters in a large number of securities offerings by money center banks and bank holding companies.

The author has written many articles for legal journals, including "Application of Federal Securities Laws to International Securities Transactions," which appeared in the *Albany Law Review*. He contributed a chapter on legal considerations in the establishment of a United States commercial paper program for a book published by *Euromoney*. The *Review of Securities & Commodities Regulation* has published articles by him on former Rules 10b-6 and 10b-7, on underwritten calls, and on Rule 415 and the integrated disclosure system.

Mr. Johnson has been an active participant in continuing legal education programs, including Practicing Law Institute seminars on the mechanics of underwriting, international finance transactions, and the 10b series of rules. He has also been a regular speaker at the Practicing Law Institute's *Annual Institute on Securities Regulation* where he has lectured on such matters as the regulations of the National Association of Securities Dealers, Inc., innovative financial products, and special disclosure problems. He has spoken at conferences sponsored by the Institute for International Research on Law in the Euromarkets and on Eurocommercial paper.

Mr. Johnson also has presented papers or participated in programs sponsored by the American Bar Association, the Southwest Legal Foundation, the Securities Industry Association, the New York Society of Securities Analysts, and the Fordham Corporate Law Institute.

Mr. Johnson is an elected member of the American Law Institute. He served a three-year term as a member of the Committee on Securities Regulation of The Association of the Bar of The City of New York, the final year as Chairman of its Subcommittee on the Issue and Distribution of Securities.

Joseph McLaughlin is a partner of Brown & Wood LLP in New York City, where he has one of the country's most diversified securities practices. A graduate of Columbia College and Columbia Law School, he was also a Jervey Fellow of the Parker School of Foreign and Comparative Law at Columbia Law School and did post-graduate work at the University of Munich. He practiced with Sullivan & Cromwell for seven years, where he worked on a wide variety of securities transactions.

Mr. McLaughlin became general counsel of Goldman, Sachs & Co. in 1976. He worked closely for many years with the firm's investment banking departments, as well as with its equity and fixed-income research, sales and trading areas. He was active in securities industry matters, including the Federal Regulation Committee of the Securities Industry Association, the Corporate Financing Committee of the National Association of Securities Dealers, Inc. and the Legal Advisory Committee of the New York Stock Exchange, Inc. During this period, Mr. McLaughlin contributed to industry and SEC initiatives involving securities research, trading practices, short sales, the net capital rule, margin regulations, underwriters' liability, the "Papilsky rules" and shelf registration. Many of these subjects are discussed in this book.

After experimenting with a teaching career, Mr. McLaughlin joined Brown & Wood LLP, where he is a member of the corporate and securities group. He works on domestic and international public offerings and private placements and spends a significant part of his time on regulatory and litigation matters for securities industry associations and more than 20 major broker-dealer clients. He also represented two of the leading groups responsible for the SEC and legislative initiatives that produced the Private Securities Litigation Reform Act of 1995.

Mr. McLaughlin is a leading writer and speaker on the subject of electronic communications and the securities laws, the listing of foreign securities on

U.S. exchanges, and the future of U.S. securities regulation. He also co-chaired an American Bar Association committee's Task Force on Sellers' Due Diligence and Similar Defenses Under the Federal Securities Laws and has recently chaired its Task Force on Rule 10b-6.

Mr. McLaughlin is an elected member of the American Law Institute. He is also a frequent speaker at programs sponsored by the Practicing Law Institute, the Securities Industry Association, PSA The Bond Market Trade Association, the New York Stock Exchange, the Securities Regulation Institute at the University of California at San Diego, the Conference Board and the Center for Strategic and International Studies.

PREFACE TO THE SECOND EDITION

As in the case of the first edition, this book is about doing deals—transactions in which business corporations raise funds in the U.S. and international capital markets. We do not intend the book as a complete treatise on the U.S. federal securities laws, nor do we intend it as an investor's or issuer's guide to the capital markets. Rather, we are trying to explain the legal environment in which capital markets transactions take place, just as we are trying to explain the capital markets transactions to which that environment is always trying to adapt. What we are describing in this book is in many ways just as much an ecosystem as a tropical rain forest—and, unfortunately, sometimes just as impenetrable.

There are some hopeful signs that the jungle canopy is thinning. In 1996 alone, the Securities and Exchange Commission initiated action on several fronts to reform the way it administers two of the most important federal securities laws. First, as a result in part of the revolution in information technology and communication, it requested public comment on possible fundamental changes under the Securities Act of 1933. Second, it completed the most important revision in more than 40 years of the way in which it regulates trading practices during the pendency of securities distributions.

We have tried to retain the book's practical orientation, which we believe was largely responsible for the first edition's considerable success. We caution, however, that the pace of change in the capital markets is still accelerating. Many of the topics discussed in this book may need to be revisited within a relatively short time.

As in the first edition, our focus has remained the raising of capital by business corporations. We have not discussed public finance—the sale of securities by federal or state governmental entities or their instrumentalities—or the corporate and specialized securities aspects of mergers and acquisitions. Nor do we focus on the parallel structure of SEC rules and forms that are designed specifically for the needs of "small business." Unlike the first edition, however, we have included a new chapter on asset-backed financing. Brown & Wood LLP was a pioneer in this field, which has become such an important source of funds for U.S. corporations that we could no longer justify a failure to discuss it.

As in the case of the first edition, we have had the full support of our colleagues at Brown & Wood LLP. Many of them provided us with valuable insights into their areas of special expertise.

A special debt is owed to Norman D. Slonaker, who is really one of the preeminent transactional lawyers in the United States. We also thank Renwick D. Martin, who prepared the chapter on asset-backed financing. Thomas R. Smith, Jr., John A. MacKinnon, Frank P. Bruno and Brian M. Kaplowitz were generous with their help on Investment Company Act issues, as were R.J. Ruble and Thomas A. Humphreys on tax issues, Michael S. Sackheim and A. Robert Pietrzak on matters relating to futures and William R. Goldman on bankruptcy law. Joseph W. Armbrust, Daniel M. Rossner, William R. Massey, John C. Maguire, Edward F. Petrosky, Christopher B. Mead, Howard G. Godwin, Jr., Steven A. Malsin and Taisa Markus read certain chapters and provided important suggestions.

Much expertise that used to be taken for granted at large Wall Street firms has migrated into the legal, compliance and capital markets departments of the investment banking firms. We are therefore grateful for the help of Richard N. Doyle, Jr., Wood Steinberg and Andrea L. Dulberg of Merrill Lynch & Co. and of John W. Curtis, Victoria Bridges and Michael Rogers of Goldman, Sachs & Co.

Any errors or omissions are, of course, the sole responsibility of the authors.

Joshua G. Grunat, who helped to cite-check the first edition, supervised a team of associates that performed the same task on the second edition. For their help in this regard, we are grateful to Tara H. Adams, John F. Haley, Amy E. Moorhus, Meaghan M. O'Toole, Vincent G. Bradley, Daniel A. McLaughlin, Rochelle M. Tarlowe, Carolyn D. Wember, Ron Scharf and Michael B. Robinson.

Charles J. Johnson, Jr.
Joseph McLaughlin
New York
May 1997

PREFACE TO THE FIRST EDITION

This book is about doing deals—structuring them, shepherding them through the regulatory process, keeping them out of trouble, and getting them closed. It is about the Federal securities laws, those laws and regulations administered by the Securities and Exchange Commission that have a direct impact on every aspect of corporate finance and that must be complied with if a deal is to get done.

A corporation that decides to go public or to raise additional funds to finance a growing business must comply with the Securities Act of 1933 and the applicable provisions of the Securities Exchange Act of 1934. If debt securities are being sold to the public, the Trust Indenture Act of 1939 will be applicable. If securities are being issued by a public utility holding company or one of its operating subsidiaries, then competitive bidding may be required under the Public Utility Holding Company Act of 1935. An obscure provision of the Investment Company Act of 1940 may come into play when least expected.

The securities laws regulate other types of financial transactions such as corporate restructurings, offers to exchange new securities for existing securities, and stock repurchase programs. At the same time, corporate financial officers and investment bankers must contend with regulations administered by state securities commissions, the National Association of Securities Dealers, Inc., and the Federal Reserve Board. In the case of a hybrid instrument—a security tied to the performance of a commodity, a stock or bond index, a foreign currency, or the rate of inflation—care must be taken to assure that the transaction does not run afoul of the Commodity Exchange Act.

Guiding their clients through this morass of regulation are lawyers of a special breed known as securities lawyers. I have been one for over 33 years, practicing in New York City with Brown & Wood. In writing this book, I have called upon my experiences as a securities lawyer to flesh out the descriptions of the statutes and rules with some practical observations on how they are applied in real-life situations and how they can best be coped with when a crisis arises in the course of a financial transaction. I have described the mechanics and practices of corporate finance in addition to the legal principles that govern them. I have not hesitated to insert editorial comment where I have thought it appropriate.

This book places securities regulation in an historical perspective. I believe that the law can be understood more fully and applied more effectively with a knowledge of its development over the years. Also, the history of the securities laws and the development of investment banking practices are a part of the culture of the financial community. A knowledge of the way that these laws and practices have evolved adds zest to an already fascinating business.

This book is directed primarily to lawyers working in the field of corporate finance, members of the "green goods" bar to use a Wall Street term. By discussing the law in the context of specific types of transactions, my objective is a book that will be useful to experienced securities lawyers as well as those just learning the law of corporate finance. Also, the lawyer whose practice is not devoted primarily to securities regulation may find it helpful to read through the relevant chapters if a client is about to engage in a financial transaction such as a public offering of convertible debentures or the establishment of a commercial paper program.

I hope this book will be useful to businessmen as well. I hope it will be read by corporate officers responsible for financial transactions—the chief executive officer, the chief financial officer, and those who assist them. It also can provide insights to investment bankers. The legal aspects of corporate finance are so intertwined with the business aspects that a businessman cannot fully perform his functions without some knowledge of securities regulation.

The practice of securities law is a fascinating occupation. Equally fascinating is the work of the corporate financial officer and the investment banker. The intellectual challenge of corporate finance is a source of constant stimulation to the securities lawyer and the financial experts that he represents. There is a camaraderie in the practice of securities law. I value the relationships that I have developed over the years with investment bankers, corporate financial officers, and members of the accounting profession, to say nothing of the scores of other securities lawyers with whom I have worked on hundreds of financial transactions. I have learned from all of them, and many have become my close friends.

There is some drudgery in the work, particularly for the younger lawyer. There is little to challenge the intellect in marking up an indenture for a "plain-vanilla" debenture offering. The work is hard. "All nighters" at the printer take their toll. But it is exciting to work on a deal, especially an important deal with national or worldwide visibility, and the feeling of satisfaction at the closing of a successful financing can be one of the securities lawyer's greatest rewards.

I have always believed that it is the job of the securities lawyer to get the deal done. Closing the deal should be the objective foremost in his mind, as it is in the mind of the businessman that he represents. Clients appreciate a "businessman's lawyer," one who can cut through to the core of a problem to accomplish the client's objective. In the thick of a deal, decisions must be made quickly. There are times when a lawyer must be willing to stick his neck out and take a position, even though the law and its application are less than clear. This is not to say that a financial transaction must not be approached with the greatest care. Someone once said that to be a good securities lawyer you don't have to be very smart, but you do have to be very very careful.

There are times when a lawyer simply must say "No," no matter how unhappy it may make his client. But there are real problems and manufactured problems, and it is the job of the securities lawyer to solve problems, not to create them. He must distinguish between the important issues and those that are more theoretical than real. The real problems should be raised early in the transaction and not at the eleventh hour. There are few legal problems that cannot be solved with the proper approach, but it is frustrating to a client for a legal issue to be raised on the eve of the closing when it should have been raised before the deal was put in motion.

There is nothing worse than over-lawyering on a deal, unless it is a combative approach to a transaction. Most financial transactions should be viewed as cooperative endeavors, not adversary proceedings, and the lawyer who attempts to score points for the sake of his ego renders a disservice to his client. Counsel for the underwriters in a public offering should always remember that the issuer is his client's client and that the managing underwriter has worked hard to secure this relationship. The issuer's officers and lawyers should be treated accordingly.

By working shoulder to shoulder, rather than nose to nose, the participants in a financial transaction can best accomplish the objective of getting the deal done. The aim of this book is to provide some help and guidance to the lawyers, corporate executives, and investment bankers who share this goal.

Charles J. Johnson, Jr.
New York
June 1990

ABBREVIATIONS AND TERMS
FREQUENTLY USED IN THIS BOOK

1933 Act	Securities Act of 1933
1934 Act	Securities Exchange Act of 1934
1939 Act	Trust Indenture Act of 1939
1940 Act	Investment Company Act of 1940
AAU	Agreement among underwriters
ADR	American depositary receipts
ADS	American depositary shares
ADTV	Average daily trading volume
AMEX	American Stock Exchange
CEA	Commodity Exchange Act
CFTC	Commodity Futures Trading Commission
DTC	The Depository Trust Company
ESOP	Employee stock ownership plan
IET	Interest equalization tax
Improvements Act	National Securities Markets Improvement Act of 1996
MD&A	Management's Discussion and Analysis of Financial Condition and Results of Operations
MJDS	Multijurisdictional disclosure system
MSRB	Municipal Securities Rulemaking Board

MTN	Medium-term notes
NASD	National Association of Securities Dealers, Inc.
NASDAQ	National Association of Securities Dealers Automated Quotation System
NASDR	NASD Regulation, Inc.
NRSRO	Nationally recognized statistical rating organization
NYSE	New York Stock Exchange, Inc.
OID	Original issue discount
PORTAL	Private Offering, Resale and Trading Through Automated Linkages
QIB	Qualified institutional buyer
Reform Act	Private Securities Litigation Reform Act of 1995
Reporting Issuer (or Reporting Company)	Issuer obligated to file periodic reports with the SEC
SEAQ	Stock Exchange Automated Quotation System
SEC	Securities and Exchange Commission
SPV	Special purpose vehicle
SRO	Self-regulatory organization
SUSMI	Substantial U.S. market interest
U.S. gaap	U.S. generally accepted accounting principles

Chapter 1

OVERVIEW OF THE SECURITIES ACT OF 1933 AND THE INTEGRATED DISCLOSURE SYSTEM

History of the 1933 Act

When Franklin Delano Roosevelt took the Presidential oath of office in March 1933, the country was still reeling from the impact of the 1929 market crash and its aftershocks. The nation was in the grips of a deep depression, and investor confidence was at an all-time low. Between September 1, 1929 and July 1, 1932, the aggregate market value of all stocks listed on the New York Stock Exchange (the "NYSE") had declined from an all-time high of close to $90 billion to less than $16 billion, a loss to which, in the words of the Senate Banking and Currency Committee, "the annals of finance present no counterpart."[1]

---

1. S. Rep. No. 1455, 73d Cong., 2d Sess., *Stock Exchange Practices, Report of the Senate Banking and Currency Committee Pursuant to S.Res. 84 (72d Cong.) and S.Res. 56 and S.Res. 97 (73d Cong.) (June 16, 1934)* at 7. There are two widely-used repositories of the legislative history of the Securities Act of 1933 and the Securities Exchange Act of 1934. The first, which is limited to the original legislation, is the 11-volume compilation prepared by J.S. Ellenberger and Ellen P. Mahar, librarians at Covington & Burling in Washington, D.C., and published in 1973 for the Law Librarians'

According to a House committee report, some $50 billion of new securities had been floated in the United States during the decade following World War I, of which fully half had proved to be worthless.[2] It was a crash "unique in financial history."[3] The House committee report placed much of the blame on the securities industry:

> The flotation of such a mass of essentially fraudulent securities was made possible because of the complete abandonment by many underwriters and dealers in securities of those standards of fair, honest, and prudent dealing that should be basic to the encouragement of investment in any enterprise. Alluring promises of easy wealth were freely made with little or no attempt to bring to the investor's attention those facts essential to estimating the worth of any security.[4]

Securities regulation had been the exclusive province of the states. This had been the case since 1911 when the first blue sky law was enacted in Kansas. In the aftermath of the crash, however, state securities laws were perceived to be inadequate, resulting in growing pressure for regulation on the Federal level.

In his speech accepting the Presidential nomination of his party, Franklin Roosevelt promised not only a "new deal" for the American people but also called for the "letting in of the light of day on issues of securities, foreign and domestic, which

Society of Washington, D.C. by Fred B. Rothman & Co., South Hackensack, N.J. The second, *Federal Securities Laws: Legislative History*, was prepared by the Securities Law Committee of the Federal Bar Association and is published by The Bureau of National Affairs, Inc. It covers each of the federal securities laws in four volumes and supplements and has been updated through 1990.

2. H.R. Rep. No. 85, 73d Cong., 1st Sess., at 2 (1933) [hereinafter *H.R. Rep. No. 85*].

3. J. Seligman, *The Transformation of Wall Street* 2 (Houghton Mifflin 1982) [hereinafter *Seligman*].

4. H.R. Rep. No. 85, *supra* note 2, at 2.

are offered for sale to the investing public."[5] As one of his first acts as President, Mr. Roosevelt delivered to the Congress on March 29, 1933 a message proposing remedial legislation:

> I recommend to the Congress legislation for Federal supervision of traffic in investment securities in interstate commerce.
>
> In spite of many State statutes the public in the past has sustained severe losses through practices neither ethical nor honest on the part of many persons and corporations selling securities.
>
> Of course, the Federal Government cannot and should not take any action which might be construed as approving or guaranteeing that newly issued securities are sound in the sense that their value will be maintained or that the properties which they represent will earn profit.
>
> There is, however, an obligation upon us to insist that every issue of new securities to be sold in interstate commerce shall be accompanied by full publicity and information, and that no essentially important element attending the issue shall be concealed from the buying public.
>
> This proposal adds to the ancient rule of caveat emptor, the further doctrine "let the seller also beware." It puts the burden of telling the whole truth on the seller. It should give impetus to honest dealing in securities and thereby bring back public confidence.[6]

The drafting of legislation to carry out this message had been assigned to Huston Thompson, a former member of the Federal Trade Commission.[7] The bill drafted by Thompson

---

5. Quoted in Seligman, *supra* note 3, at 19.

6. H.R. Rep. No. 85, *supra* note 2, at 1–2.

7. J. M. Landis, *The Legislative History of the Securities Act of 1933*, 28 Geo. Wash. L. Rev. 29 (1959) [hereinafter *Landis*]. The brief account that follows is taken principally from this article, which is required reading for anyone interested in the history of Federal securities regulation. *See also*

called for more than disclosure. It gave to the Federal government extensive powers to control the issuance of securities. Sam Rayburn, Chairman of the House Committee on Interstate and Foreign Commerce, became convinced that the Thompson bill did not provide a sound basis for Federal securities legislation. In response to Mr. Rayburn's concern, Raymond S. Moley, the head of the President's "brain trust," turned for help to Harvard professor Felix Frankfurter who, in turn, called upon the skills of James M. Landis, Benjamin V. Cohen and Thomas G. Corcoran.

This team determined to prepare a draft based on the English Companies Act, stressing the theme of disclosure expressed in the President's message. The first draft was completed over a weekend. It went through a number of revisions, with the assistance of Middleton Beaman, the chief legislative draftsman for the House of Representatives.

By the time the bill was ready to be reported to the full committee, agitation had built up on Wall Street, and Mr. Rayburn consented to a meeting between the draftsmen and a delegation of New York lawyers comprised of John Foster Dulles and Arthur H. Dean of Sullivan & Cromwell and A. I. Henderson of the Cravath firm. Landis reports that Dulles launched an inadequately prepared attack to the annoyance of Rayburn, but that Dean and Henderson were far better acquainted with the details of the bill and that their technical comments had merit. Ultimately, the Securities Act of 1933 (the "1933 Act") became law on May 27, 1933.

The essential elements of the 1933 Act consisted of (a) mandatory full disclosure in a registration statement filed with the Federal Trade Commission (later the SEC), (b) SEC review during a "waiting period," at the end of which sales could commence, (c) mandatory delivery of a prospectus at or before the delivery of the security, and (d) civil liabilities for untrue statements and for certain omissions.

Schlesinger, *The Coming of the New Deal* 440–42 (Houghton Mifflin 1959). For a detailed account of the drafting process, *see* Seligman, *supra* note 3, at 50–72.

Contemporaneous concern about the 1933 Act[8] focused primarily on the new civil liabilities which were to be imposed on "those who have participated in . . . [the] distribution either knowing of such untrue statement or omission or having failed to take due care in discovering it."[9] In this connection, Section 11(c) specified that the applicable standard of "due care" was to be "that of a person occupying a fiduciary relationship." The securities industry understandably opposed the application of a "fiduciary" standard of "due care" as a measure of underwriters' responsibility for an issuer's untrue statements or omissions. This opposition, which extended to other provisions of the new statute relating to underwriters' liabilities, led to amendments in 1934 that provided, among other things, that the standard of care was to be that of "a prudent man in the management of his own property." In addition, the new Securities Exchange Act of 1934 (the "1934 Act") created an agency to administer both statutes, the Securities and Exchange Commission (the "SEC").[10]

---

8. The reactions to the 1933 Act varied. Some thought that it would retard economic recovery and bring an end to firm commitment underwriting. A.H. Dean, *The Federal Securities Act: I,* Fortune 50, 106 (August 1933). Some felt that it was of secondary importance in a comprehensive program of social control over finance. A.A. Berle, Jr. *High Finance: Master or Servant,* 23 Yale Rev. 20 (1933). Others adopted a more positive attitude and, recognizing that the principles embodied in the 1933 Act "have become a permanent and integral part of our legal system," stressed the need to find "ways and means of accomplishing expeditiously and efficiently their avowed purposes." W.O. Douglas & G.E. Bates, *The Federal Securities Act of 1933,* 43 Yale L.J. 171, 173 (1933).

9. H.R. Rep. No. 85, *supra* note 2, at 9.

10. The SEC is an independent agency in the executive branch of the Federal government. It is made up of five commissioners appointed by the President of the United States with the advice and consent of the Senate. Commissioners hold office for a term of five years. No more than three may be members of the same political party.

The SEC is presided over by a chairman who has sole power to assign commission personnel to perform such functions as may have been delegated to them. The chairman sets the tone for the SEC during his tenure.

Operation of the 1933 Act

• *Disclosure Philosophy*

It cannot be emphasized too often that the 1933 Act is a disclosure statute. Its principal purpose, as set forth in its preamble, is to provide "full and fair disclosure of the character of securities sold in interstate and foreign commerce and through the mails. . . ." As explained in 1933 by Professor Frankfurter:

Unlike the theory on which state blue-sky laws are based, the Federal Securities Act does not place the government's imprimatur upon securities. It is designed merely to secure essential facts for the investor, not to substitute the government's judgment for his own.[11]

On the staff level, the SEC is organized into four divisions: Corporation Finance, which administers the 1933 Act and the Trust Indenture Act of 1939; Market Regulation, which administers the 1934 Act; Investment Management, which regulates investment companies, investment advisers and public utility holding companies; and Enforcement. In addition, there are the Offices of the General Counsel and the Chief Accountant as well as other staff offices, including Economic Analysis and the relatively new Compliance Inspections and Examinations.

The SEC accounting staff has for many years issued periodic Staff Accounting Bulletins, which are indispensable for the preparation of the financial statements included in a prospectus. More recently, the staff of the Division of Corporation Finance has introduced the publication of "staff legal bulletins."

The SEC staff also issues "no-action" letters that state that the staff will not recommend any enforcement action to the SEC if the requesting party proceeds with a described transaction. The courts are not bound by SEC staff no-action letters but may accord them significant respect. No-action letters are issued on a fact-specific basis, but securities lawyers frequently cite these letters as precedents.

The SEC's principal office is in Washington, D.C. It has regional offices that are located in major cities throughout the country.

11. Frankfurter, *The Federal Securities Act: II,* Fortune 53, 108 (August 1933). It cannot be denied that disclosure also has a prophylactic effect. For example, a chief executive officer is less likely to engage in self-dealing with his corporation if he knows that his conduct will be exposed to public scrutiny. As Louis Brandeis put it, "Publicity is justly commended as a rem-

• *Definition of Security*

An important threshold question under the 1933 Act is whether or not a financing vehicle is a "security." The term is broadly defined in Section 2(l) as well as in Section 3(a)(10) of the 1934 Act.[12]

According to the U.S. Supreme Court's leading decision in *Reves v. Ernst & Young*,[13] Congress "did not attempt precisely to cabin the scope of the Securities Acts" but rather "enacted a definition of 'security' sufficiently broad to encompass virtually any instrument that might be sold as an investment." In deciding what transactions are covered by the federal securities laws, "legal formalisms" are less important than "the economics of the transaction." Some instruments, on the other hand, are "obviously within the class Congress intended to regulate because they are by their nature investments." For example, "stock is, as a practical matter, always an investment if it has the economic characteristics traditionally associated with stock."

In *Reves*, the Court adopted a rebuttable presumption that all notes are "securities." To rebut the presumption would require a showing that the note bears a strong resemblance to those categories of notes held by lower courts not to be securities, e.g., notes delivered in consumer financing, notes secured by home mortgages, notes evidencing unsecured bank loans to individuals, short-term notes secured by business assets. The required "resemblance" would depend on four factors: the mo-

---

edy for social and industrial diseases. Sunlight is said to be the best of disinfectants; electric light the most efficient policeman." Brandeis, *Other People's Money* 92 (Frederick A. Stokes 1914).

12. The U.S. Supreme Court has consistently held that the scope of coverage of the 1933 Act and the 1934 Act, insofar as it depends on the two "virtually identical" definitions in the two statutes, "may be considered the same." *Reves v. Ernst & Young*, 494 U.S. 56, 61 note 1 (1990). In practice, however, attempts to characterize an instrument as a security are more likely to succeed where the effect is to preserve holders' federal antifraud remedies under the 1934 Act than where it would lead to rescission rights under the 1933 Act.

13. 494 U.S. 56 (1990).

tivations of the parties, whether the instrument is traded, the expectations of the investing public and the presence or absence of an alternative regulatory scheme for the public's protection.

The term "security" includes a guarantee of a security. If a subsidiary corporation makes a public offering of debentures guaranteed by its parent, the guarantee must therefore be registered under the 1933 Act along with the primary obligations.

Is an orange grove a security? Hardly. But the U.S. Supreme Court has held that a security was indeed involved in an offer of land sales contracts covering plots planted with citrus trees along with service contracts giving the promoter discretion and authority over the cultivation of the groves and the harvest and marketing of the crops.[14] The Section 2(l) definition includes among the types of securities subject to the 1933 Act a "certificate of interest or participation in any profit-sharing agreement," an "investment contract," and "any interest or instrument commonly known as a security." In *SEC v. Howey*, Justice Murphy said that an investment contract is "a contract, transaction or scheme whereby a person invests his money in a common enterprise and is led to expect profits solely from the efforts of the promoter or a third party . . . ."

The Supreme Court has held that a bank certificate of deposit is not a security.[15] However, the Court of Appeals for the Second Circuit, applying the *Howey* analysis, found that Merrill Lynch's then existing "CD Program" involving the sale of certificates of deposit selected by the firm, including some specifically created for the program, involved investment contracts because a significant portion of the customer's investment depended on Merrill Lynch's managerial and financial expertise.[16]

More recently, a corporation that was a party to certain interest rate and currency swaps argued that these were "securities" for purposes of the 1933 Act, the 1934 Act and a state's

---

14. *SEC v. W.J. Howey Company*, 328 U.S. 293 (1946).

15. *Marine Bank v. Weaver*, 455 U.S. 551 (1982).

16. *Gary Plastic Packaging Corporation v. Merrill Lynch, Pierce, Fenner & Smith Incorporated*, 756 F.2d 230 (2d Cir. 1985).

blue sky law. The court rejected the argument.[17] It held that the swaps were not investment contracts because they lacked the element of a "common enterprise." Even if viewed as notes, they fell outside each of the four parts of the *Reves* "family resemblance" test. Neither were they "evidences of indebtedness" because they lacked the essential element of an obligation to pay principal, and they were not "options" on securities because they did not give either counterparty the right to take possession of any security. The court was careful to point out that it was not holding that all swaps or leveraged derivative instruments were not securities.

• *Registration and Prospectus Delivery Requirements*

The basic operative provisions of the 1933 Act are the registration and prospectus delivery requirements set forth in Section 5. These are the only requirements of the 1933 Act that can be violated, except for the antifraud prohibitions of Section 17 and (in a loose sense) the disclosure-based remedies provided by Sections 11 and 12(a)(2). The remainder of the 1933 Act consists of definitions, exemptions and other provisions that implement Section 5.

Section 5 requires that its registration and prospectus delivery requirements be complied with in connection with any offer or sale of a security in interstate commerce or through the use of the mails. The SEC vigorously enforces Section 5 through administrative and court proceedings, but the primary reason for complying with Section 5 is that a violation entitles a buyer to return the security to the seller—no questions asked—at any time during the year following the sale. There is nothing wrong with selling "puts" to customers, but it is a major mistake to do so inadvertently and without getting paid for them!

Of course, not every transaction in securities must be registered with the SEC or be the subject of a prospectus. Important exemptions are available, based either on the nature of the security (Section 3) or the nature of the transaction (Section 4).

---

17. *Procter & Gamble Co. v. Bankers Trust Company*, 925 F. Supp. 1270 (S.D. Ohio 1996).

The burden of proving the availability of an exemption, however, is on the person who claims it.

• • *Registration for a Purpose.* Before considering in more detail the operation of the 1933 Act, a common misconception should be laid to rest—the misconception that there is something bad about securities that are not registered and something good about securities that are registered. A report appears in the business section of the morning newspaper to the effect that a broker has been sanctioned by the SEC for selling "unregistered securities." The reader thereby assumes that, on the one hand, there are nice registered securities with wings and halos and, on the other hand, there are bad unregistered securities with forked tails and horns. There are many people, even in the securities industry, who believe that if a person sells unregistered securities he will go to jail, but that if he can find some good registered securities to deliver in the transaction he will remain a free man. This is not the way that the 1933 Act operates.

Millions of shares of common stock are traded on the NYSE that have never been the subject of a registration statement. They may have been issued before the adoption of the 1933 Act; they may have been issued in a private placement and resold in accordance with Rule 144 (to be discussed below); they may have been sold in an offshore offering or issued as a stock dividend.

Conversely, if a company reacquires for its treasury shares that had once been the subject of a registration statement, it must register them again before it may sell them to the public. Similarly, if a person in a control relationship with a company acquires that company's registered securities in the open market, the securities must be registered again before they may be resold through a broker-dealer in a public offering outside of the limits of Rule 144.

A sale of securities in violation of the 1933 Act cannot be remedied by filing a registration statement after the fact, except for the purpose of a rescission offer. Securities issued in a private placement cannot be made freely tradable by registering them after the fact, except for the purpose of resale with the use of a current prospectus. (It is also possible under certain circumstances, as discussed in Chapter 7, to conduct a registered exchange offer that gives holders of privately-placed securities the opportunity to exchange them for registered securities.)

Although the 1933 Act speaks of registering securities, it is more accurate to think in terms of registering a transaction, or at least of registering securities for the purpose of sale in a particular transaction. A registration statement is filed and becomes effective not to place a stamp of approval on the securities but to provide persons being offered securities in a non-exempt transaction with sufficient information on which to base an informed investment decision. Part of the ambiguity must be laid to somewhat faulty draftsmanship. As one of the principal draftsmen of the 1933 Act acknowledged in 1959,

> The bill also came close to accurately carving out a differentiation between the registration of securities and the registration of offerings of securities. . . . It was, however, far from perfect on this point as well as in many of its other provisions.[18]

• • *Operation of the Registration Requirement.* Assume that a commercial or industrial corporation (not a bank or other issuer of exempted securities) proposes to sell to the public one million shares of common stock through an underwriting syndicate. The 1933 Act requires such an issuer to provide potential investors with extensive information concerning its business and finances. This information is made available to the public by filing a registration statement with the SEC, either in paper or electronic form.[19] Once filed, this is a public document available for examination at the SEC's office in Washington, D.C. or through various electronic databases.

• • • *Contents of the Registration Statement.* Section 7 of the 1933 Act requires that our hypothetical issuer's registration statement contain the information specified in Schedule A to the 1933 Act except as otherwise required by the SEC. The SEC has

---

18. Landis, *supra* note 7, at 36.

19. If debt securities are to be offered, in addition to filing under the 1933 Act, it will be necessary to qualify the indenture under the Trust Indenture Act of 1939.

adopted registration forms[20] that specify the required contents of the registration statement. These forms and the related SEC rules make Schedule A obsolete for all intents and purposes.[21]

Form S-1 is used for the registration of securities where no other form is authorized or prescribed. In practice, this form is used by issuers that have not previously filed periodic reports under the 1934 Act.[22] Form S-1 has been the basic 1933 Act registration form for many years and requires a full description of the business and finances of the issuer.

The 1933 Act did not contemplate a system of continuous reporting through the filing of periodic reports. Even after the passage of the 1934 Act, which required issuers of listed securities to file periodic reports, the two statutes operated independently. A 1933 Act registration statement and related prospectus

---

20. Rule 130 provides that the term "rules and regulations" as used in Section 7 includes the forms for registration of securities and the related instructions.

21. Registration statements filed by a foreign government, or a political subdivision thereof, are governed by Schedule B to the 1933 Act. No forms have been adopted for these registration statements. As described in Chapter 9, however, the disclosures have become fairly well standardized.

22. The 1934 Act also requires the "registration" of securities, but primarily for the benefit of persons who purchase securities in the secondary markets. Section 12(b) of the 1934 Act requires registration of securities listed on a national securities exchange. Section 12(g) extends the registration requirement to any securities traded in interstate commerce if the issuer has total assets exceeding $1 million (increased by SEC rule to $5 million) and a class of equity securities held of record by 500 or more persons. Application for registration under the 1934 Act is made on Form 10. Section 13 of the 1934 Act requires issuers of registered securities to keep their Form 10 current through the filing of annual reports on Form 10-K and quarterly reports on Form 1O-Q. Form 8-K is used for any current updating, including the disclosure of acquisitions. (There are corresponding reports for foreign private issuers.) Any issuer that has filed a 1933 Act registration statement that has become effective is required by Section 15(d) of the 1934 Act to file the same periodic reports as are required of an issuer with securities registered under the 1934 Act. An issuer can relieve itself of 1934 Act reporting requirements, generally by certifying to the SEC that fewer than 300 persons are holders of record of the registered security.

delivered the information considered necessary for persons buying a particular distribution of securities. Periodic reports filed under the 1934 Act delivered the information considered necessary for persons buying securities traded on securities exchanges. There was no good reason, however, for the differences between the forms and instructions that governed the content of periodic reports filed under the 1934 Act and those that governed registration statements filed under the 1933 Act. The information required for a decision to purchase or sell securities on an exchange or in the over-the-counter market is substantially the same as the information required for a decision whether or not to purchase securities being distributed in a registered public offering.

With the extension in 1964 of the periodic reporting requirements of the 1934 Act to substantial issuers of securities traded over-the-counter, the "efficient market hypothesis" began to gain recognition. The efficient market hypothesis is that information that an issuer disseminates by means of its 1934 Act reports, communications with shareholders or press releases is absorbed into the market through the activities of the financial press, securities analysts and other professionals, thereby causing the market price of the issuer's securities to reflect this information. Thus, it may be presumed in the case of an offering of new securities by a widely-followed public company that the prospective investors in the new securities have already received and discounted the information previously made public by the issuer. Accordingly, it should not be necessary to disclose it to them again. As Milton H. Cohen stated in his seminal article, *"Truth in Securities" Revisited,*[23] the combined disclosure requirements of the 1933 and 1934 Acts probably would have been quite different if they had been enacted in the opposite order.

The *Wheat Report,*[24] published in 1969, accepted the efficient market hypothesis. It recommended expanded periodic

---

23. 79 Harv. L. Rev. 1340 (1966).

24. This report, *Disclosure to Investors—A Reappraisal of Administrative Policies Under the '33 and '34 Acts,* was prepared under the direction of Commissioner Francis M. Wheat. It was transmitted to the SEC on March 27, 1969 and released to the public on April 14, 1969.

disclosure under the 1934 Act and coordination of the disclosure requirements of the 1933 Act and the 1934 Act. In accordance with the report's recommendations, the SEC adopted in late 1970 a short form of registration statement, called Form S-16, which provided for incorporation by reference of reports filed under the 1934 Act.[25] As originally adopted, Form S-16 was available only for securities issued on the conversion of convertible securities or the exercise of warrants as well as for securities being sold "in the regular way" on a national securities exchange by persons other than the issuer. The form was amended in 1972 to make it available for any kind of secondary offering[26] and in 1978 to make it available for primary offerings where the aggregate market value of the issuer's voting stock held by non-affiliates was $50 million or more and where underwriters were firmly committed to take and pay for all, or not less than 90%, of the securities being offered.[27]

In 1977, the SEC adopted Regulation S-K, then consisting of two items, "Description of Business" and "Description of Property." For the first time, the principal disclosure items were made uniform for annual reports on Form 10-K and 1933 Act registration statements. In time, full consistency was achieved, and the various registration and reporting forms under the 1933 Act and the 1934 Act now specify the required information by references to Regulation S-K.

In March 1982, the SEC announced significant changes in the forms and rules governing registration statements under the 1933 Act.[28] This action represented the final stage of the SEC's program to implement an integrated disclosure system under the 1933 Act and the 1934 Act. New Forms S-1, S-2 and S-3 were adopted to replace Forms S-1, S-7 and S-16, and the abbreviated Form S-3 (unlike its predecessor, Form S-16) was

---

25. SEC Release No. 33-5117 (December 23, 1970). Form S-16 had an antecedent in Form S-7, which for many years allowed qualified issuers to omit from their 1933 Act registration statements information relating to management compensation and transactions that was set forth in the issuer's 1934 Act filings.

26. SEC Release No. 33-5265 (June 27, 1972).

27. SEC Release No. 33-5923 (April 11, 1978).

28. SEC Release No. 33-6383 (March 3, 1982).

made available for primary offerings of securities even where there was no firm commitment underwriting.[29] Later in 1982, the SEC adopted an integrated disclosure system for foreign private issuers, with registration forms (Forms F-1, F-2 and F-3) that correspond to their domestic counterparts.[30]

• • • *Form S-1.* Form S-1 continues to be the general purpose form for U.S. issuers that do not qualify for either Form S-2 or Form S-3.[31]

• • • *Form S-2.* This second tier registration form is not used very often.

• • • *Form S-3.* Form S-3, like its predecessor Form S-16, is an abbreviated document containing information as to the securities being registered, the plan of distribution and similar matters. All other disclosures may be provided through incorporation by reference of the latest annual report on Form 10-K and any subsequent Form 10-Q and Form 8-K reports. Any 1934 Act reports or proxy statements filed after the effective date of the registration statement and prior to the termination of the offering are deemed to be incorporated by reference. The ability to amend and update the prospectus through subsequent 1934 Act filings (without the need to reprint or sticker the prospectus itself) is important for Rule 415 shelf registration programs.

Form S-3 may be used by any issuer meeting the following registrant requirements:

---

29. As discussed in Chapter 8, the availability of Form S-3 for primary offerings on a delayed or continuous basis was the driving force behind the growth of shelf registration.

30. SEC Release No. 33-6437 (November 19, 1982). See Chapter 9 for a discussion of registration forms for foreign private issuers.

31. Other forms are available for specialized types of issuers or transactions. For example, Form S-8 may be used for the registration of securities to be offered to employees (including consultants or advisers) under certain employee benefit plans. Registration statements on Form S-8 become effective automatically upon filing, and they can therefore be abused. The SEC has found it necessary to emphasize that Form S-8 is not intended to be used in connection with the offer or sale of securities in capital-raising transactions.

- The issuer is organized under the laws of the United States or any state or the District of Columbia and has its principal business operations in the United States or its territories.

- The issuer has a class of securities registered pursuant to Section 12(b) or Section 12(g) of the 1934 Act or is required to file reports pursuant to Section 15(d) of the 1934 Act.

- The issuer has been subject to the 1934 Act filing requirements and has filed all required 1934 Act material for a period of at least 12 months, and all filings during the immediately preceding 12 months have been made on a timely basis.

- Neither the issuer nor any of its subsidiaries has failed to make a required preferred stock dividend or sinking fund payment or defaulted on payment of any material indebtedness or long-term lease rentals since the end of the most recent fiscal year for which a Form 10-K annual report has been filed.

- A foreign private issuer satisfying all of the foregoing, other than the first condition, is eligible provided the 1934 Act reports filed were the same as those required of a domestic registrant.

The SEC increased the availability of Form S-3 in 1992 when it reduced the required 1934 Act reporting history from 36 months to 12 months.[32] It should also be noted that issuers of investment-grade asset-backed securities need not meet the 1934 Act registration or reporting history requirements.

Use of the form is also conditioned on the offering meeting at least one of the following transaction requirements:

- A primary or secondary offering of debt or equity securities for cash if the issuer has a "float" of at least $75 million (reduced in 1992 from $150 million). Float

---

32. SEC Release No. 33-6964 (October 22, 1992).

is computed by reference to the market value of the issuer's voting stock held by non-affiliates.[33]

— A primary offering for cash of non-convertible debt securities or preferred stock rated by a nationally recognized statistical rating organization in a generic rating category that signifies "investment grade" (typically one of the four highest rating categories but without regard to "subcategories or gradations indicating relative standing").

— Any secondary offering of a security that is either listed on a stock exchange or quoted on NASDAQ.

— Dividend reinvestment plans, rights offerings and securities offered on conversion of outstanding convertible securities or the exercise of outstanding warrants.

— Investment-grade asset-backed securities.

Several other important points should be noted about the Form S-3 transaction requirements. First, Form S-3 may be used to register nonconvertible debt securities or preferred stock rated investment grade even if the issuer does not meet the float test. Second, the form may be used for secondary offerings of listed or NASDAQ quoted securities even if the issuer does not meet the float or investment grade test. Third, because of the requirement that primary offerings be "for cash," Form S-3 may not be used for exchange offers.

Form S-3 may be used to register securities issued by a majority-owned subsidiary that does not itself meet the registrant and transaction tests if:

— the parent meets the registrant requirements and the subsidiary is registering straight debt or preferred stock rated investment grade; or

— the parent meets the registrant requirements and the applicable transaction requirement (e.g., the "float"

---

33. In 1997 the SEC amended Forms S-3 and F-3 to permit the inclusion of nonvoting stock in the computation of "float". SEC Release No. 33-7419 (May 8, 1997).

test) and fully and unconditionally guarantees the securities being registered (which may not be convertible securities).

• • • *Effectiveness of the Registration Statement.* By the terms of Section 8(a) of the 1933 Act, a registration statement becomes effective by operation of law on the 20th day after filing. In practice, it does not become effective until declared effective by the staff of the SEC under delegated authority. This works through the magic of a "delaying amendment" under Rule 473,[34] which prevents the registration statement from becoming effective until our hypothetical issuer has responded to any SEC comments on the contents of the registration statement and is ready to sell its securities. At that time, and upon request of the issuer and its underwriters, the staff "accelerates" the effectiveness of the registration statement by issuing the requisite order. One of the advantages of shelf registration (discussed in greater detail in Chapter 8) is that it eliminates the uncertainty and delays sometimes associated with SEC review on a transaction-by-transaction basis.

• • • *Offers and Sales of the Registered Securities.* In examining how the 1933 Act governs the offering process for our hypothetical offering, it is important to keep in mind the three stages of the registration process described above: (i) the period prior to the filing of the registration statement with the SEC, (ii) the period between the time the registration statement is filed and the time it

---

34. Under Section 8(a), if an amendment to a registration statement is filed prior to the effective date, the registration statement is deemed to have been filed at such time as the amendment is filed. Thus, the filing of an amendment has the effect of beginning a new 20-day period. At one time, it was the practice to delay the effective date to allow the SEC to complete its review of the registration statement by filing a telegraphic "delaying amendment" changing an insignificant word in the document. The convention was to change the word "possible" to "practicable" where it customarily appears on the facing sheet of the registration statement. Rule 473 now permits a legend to be set forth on the facing sheet that serves to delay the effectiveness of the registration statement until an SEC order is issued declaring it effective.

is declared effective, and (iii) the period after the registration statement is effective. It is also important to distinguish between sales, including contracts to sell, on the one hand, and offers, on the other hand. With respect to offers, it is important to distinguish between oral offers and written offers.

Prior to the time that the registration statement is filed, Section 5(c) prohibits any offer of the securities to be registered, whether written or oral. Once the registration statement is filed, the securities may be offered for sale, but an actual sale or a contract to sell is prohibited. During this so-called "waiting period," while the SEC staff may be reviewing the registration statement and the underwriters are marketing the issue, there is no restriction on oral offers, but no written offering material is permitted other than the preliminary or "red herring" prospectus[35] permitted by Rule 430, even if the material is accompanied by the preliminary prospectus.[36] Thus, during the period between filing and effectiveness, it would be a violation of Section 5(b)(1) for an underwriter to send a preliminary prospectus to a customer with a cover letter pointing out the merits of the proposed investment.[37]

There is considerable interest among underwriters in finding a way to permit their sales personnel to inform customers by means of e-mail of the availability of a new offering. While an e-mail message may consist of "magnetic impulses" within Rule 405's elaboration on Section 2(9)'s definition of "written" as including

---

35. So called for the legend (formerly required to be in red ink) that must be printed on the cover of every preliminary prospectus. Item 501(c)(8) of Regulation S-K.

36. Rule 482 permits investment companies to use certain limited supplemental selling literature during this period. Also, as discussed below, certain communications are deemed under SEC rules not to be offers or prospectuses.

37. In *Franklin, Meyer & Barnett*, 37 S.E.C. 47 (1956), a broker-dealer was sanctioned because, among other transgressions, a registered representative enclosed with a preliminary prospectus his business card upon which he wrote "Phone me as soon as possible as my allotment is almost complete on this issue." An oral statement to this effect would not have violated Section 5. *See also Diskin v. Lomasney & Co.*, 452 F.2d 871 (2d Cir. 1971).

any form of "graphic communication," it would seem more logical to analyze e-mail messages on the basis of whether or not they are being used as substitutes for oral (e.g., telephone) conversations. After all, voice mail messages also consist of "magnetic impulses," and no one has yet suggested that a voice mail message is a "prospectus." The use of e-mail for this purpose is discussed further below in connection with Rule 134.

There is no 1933 Act requirement that a preliminary prospectus be provided to investors; however, Rule 15c2-8(b) under the 1934 Act states that it is a deceptive practice for a broker-dealer participating in an issuer's initial public offering not to send copies of the preliminary prospectus to investors at least 48 hours prior to the expected time of mailing of confirmations. The 48-hour requirement does not apply to securities of reporting companies. The preliminary prospectus is distributed other than for Rule 15c2-8 purposes only to the extent that the underwriters believe it will be useful as a marketing tool for the offering.

Rule 15c2-8(b) has no further application once the final prospectus is available. In other words, an underwriter or dealer may confirm a sale immediately to a customer who turns up after the deal is priced.

Rule 15c2-8(e) requires a broker-dealer to take reasonable steps to make available a copy of the preliminary prospectus to each registered representative who is expected to solicit customers' orders and to make available to him a copy of any amended preliminary prospectus. The purpose of this requirement is to provide the salesman with a reasonable basis on which to advise his customers as to the investment merits of the security.

Once the registration statement is declared effective, the securities may continue to be offered and actual sales may be made. Written offers must take the form of the final prospectus, except that other offering material (sometimes referred to as "supplementary selling literature") may be used if preceded or accompanied by the final prospectus.

• • *Operation of the Prospectus Delivery Requirement*

• • • *Delivery with Confirmation.* Rule 10b-10 under the 1934 Act requires that broker-dealers send out a written confirmation of every purchase and sale of securities. In the case of an offering registered under the 1933 Act, the final prospectus must be "sent or given" to the customer before or at the same time as the sending or giving of the confirmation of sale. The statutory basis for this requirement is found in Section 5(b)(1), which provides that after a registration statement has been filed, it is unlawful to transmit a prospectus unless it meets the requirements of Section 10. In turn, Section 2(10) defines the term "prospectus" to include any communication "which offers any security for sale or confirms the sale of any security." On the other hand, Section 2(10)(a) excludes from the definition of "prospectus" a communication that is "sent or given" after the effective date of a registration statement if, prior to or at the same time as such communication, a prospectus meeting the requirements of Section 10(a) (i.e., the final prospectus) is "sent or given" to the person to whom the communication is made. Thus, the confirmation itself is a prospectus that does not meet the requirements of Section 10, and its transmittal would constitute a violation of Section 5(b)(1) unless the final prospectus is sent or given to the customer at the same time or earlier than the time that the confirmation is sent or given. The underwriter does not bear the risk of nondelivery of the prospectus; it is sufficient if he can prove that he sent the prospectus together with or earlier than the confirmation. The established practice, however, is to include a copy of the final prospectus in the same envelope as the confirmation.[38]

A copy of the final prospectus must therefore precede or accompany each confirmation of sale. However, except as provided in Rule 15c2-8, there is no requirement that a prospectus be given to an investor before he makes an investment decision. The result is that, except in the case of an initial public offering, a purchaser of securities may never see an offering document until he purchases the securities and subsequently receives a confirmation. If he makes a written request for a pre-

---

38. Chronic delays in printing the final prospectus and in delivering it to underwriters in sufficient quantities have frequently caused delays in the mailing of confirmations. See Chapter 3 for a discussion of this problem in the context of the introduction in 1995 of "T+3" settlements.

liminary prospectus, it must be furnished to him (if one has been prepared), but if he does not, it is likely that he will not see an offering document until after his purchase has been made.

If the purchaser reads the prospectus that he receives with his confirmation and decides that he does not want the security, he has no right to renege on his purchase. Although many securities firms will not attempt to hold a customer to his agreement under these circumstances, there is nothing in the 1933 Act that gives a purchaser a right to change his mind after reading the prospectus. If a securities salesman has made an oral statement to his customer that the final prospectus indicates is false or misleading, the customer can rescind his purchase commitment under Section 12(a)(2), which permits rescission where there has been an oral misrepresentation. There is nothing in the 1933 Act that affords a purchaser a reasonable time to read a prospectus before being bound.[39]

These conclusions may on the surface appear inconsistent with the statutory goal of full and fair disclosure as the basis for an informed investment decision. But this is the law, and the courts have so held. In *Byrnes v. Faulkner, Dawkins & Sullivan*,[40] Judge Werker had this to say on the matter:

> The defendant's Fifth Affirmative Defense is unique; Faulkner asserts the right to cancel the contract and re-

---

39. A customer's receipt of a confirmation is related to the possible availability to the customer of a statute of frauds defense under Section 8-319 of the former version of the Uniform Commercial Code, which requires a party to an oral contract for the purchase or sale of securities to object within ten days to the contents of the confirmation. As a practical matter, the statute of frauds defense has very seldom been asserted as a defense by customers or other participants in the organized securities markets, even in periods of abrupt moves in securities prices. Moreover, the 1994 revision of Article 8 of the Uniform Commercial Code, as approved by the National Conference of Commissioners on Uniform State Laws and the American Law Institute, deletes former Section 8-319 and specifically makes the statute of frauds inapplicable to such contracts.

40. 413 F. Supp. 453 (S.D.N.Y. 1976), *aff'd* 550 F.2d 1303 (2d Cir. 1977).

scind the purchase on the receipt of the prospectus. No authority has been cited for this proposition, and this court has been unable to find any. Acceptance of this defense would stretch the provisions of the [1933 Act] far beyond their intended scope.

The defendant argues that inherent in the prospectus delivery requirement is an implied right to rescind. Otherwise, so the argument goes, the purpose of the delivery requirement would be defeated. That reading flies in the face of the statute and ignores already far-reaching, remedial provisions.

Section 5(b)(2) of the 1933 Act makes it unlawful for anyone to send a registered security through the mail "for the purpose of sale or for delivery after sale, unless accompanied or preceded by a prospectus." It was clearly within the contemplation of the drafters of the statute that a purchaser might not see the prospectus covering the security he purchased until after the sale had been completed. Yet no provision of the statute either permits recission upon receipt of the prospectus or prevents the parties from binding themselves to the terms of a contract prior to that receipt.

Furthermore, Section 12 of the 1933 Act explicitly provides for recission in two specific circumstances: where a person offers or sells securities (a) in violation of Section 5 of the Act or (b) through the use of a material misrepresentation. The defendant would have this section judicially amended to include a third situation, i.e., where a person, in conformity with the statute[,] delivers a final prospectus and the purchased securities simultaneously. This the court refuses to do.[41]

• • • *Delivery with Registered Security.* Section 5(b)(2) prohibits the use of the mails or any means of interstate commerce to "carry" any 1933 Act-registered security for the purpose of sale or for delivery after sale unless the security is "accompanied or preceded" by a final prospectus. Unlike the requirement of Sec-

---

41. *Id.* at 472-73.

tion 5(b)(1) that the final prospectus be "sent or given" with or before the confirmation, Section 5(b)(2) appears to require that the prospectus "accompan[y] or precede" the delivery of the security. In more leisurely times, one could usually assume that the prospectus had been delivered to the customer (with the confirmation) prior to the settlement date on which the security was delivered to the customer's account. Under a T+3 settlement regime, such an assumption is more hazardous. This subject is discussed in more detail in Chapter 3.

• • • *After-Market Transactions.* In principle, all dealers must deliver final prospectuses to persons who buy in the after-market for a specified period of time after a registration statement becomes effective. The existence and duration of this obligation is the subject of a bold-face notice required by Item 502(e) of Regulation S-K to appear on the inside front or outside back page of the prospectus. The obligation extends to dealers who did not participate in the offering, and it also applies to underwriters who are no longer acting as such.

The obligation arises from the terms of the "dealer's exemption" in Section 4(3)(B) of the 1933 Act, which states in effect that the exemption is *not* available during a period of 40 or 90 days following the later of the effective date of the registration statement or the first bona fide offering of the security. It is therefore necessary for the dealer to deliver a prospectus in order to avoid its confirmation constituting an illegal prospectus violating Section 5(b)(1) of the 1933 Act.

The applicable period of time is generally 90 days, but the SEC's Rule 174(b) reduces the period to *zero* if immediately prior to the filing of the registration statement the issuer was subject to the reporting requirements of the 1934 Act. In the case of an initial public offering, Rule 174(d) terminates the delivery obligation "after the expiration of 25 calendar days after the offering date" if the securities are listed on an exchange or quoted in NASDAQ as of their offering date. For this purpose, the "offering date" is the later of the effective date of the registration statement or the date of the first bona fide offering of the security.

The prospectus delivery obligation applies to transactions between dealers, as well as between a dealer and a customer. In the case of "face-to-face" transactions between members of a national securities exchange on the floor of the exchange, Rule 153 permits a "constructive delivery" procedure by which a member firm is deemed to have received a copy of a prospectus that has been delivered to the exchange by the issuer or any underwriter. No such procedure exists for transactions between dealers in the over-the-counter market, despite suggestions that such a procedure should be adopted.[42]

As a practical matter, the expiration of the after-market period during which a prospectus must be delivered also determines when a broker-dealer may commence the publication of research reports on the security covered by the prospectus.[43] Confusion sometimes arises on this point because of the unfortunate wording of the legend prescribed by Item 502(e) of Regulation S-K, which requires the insertion of the "expiration date" of the prospectus delivery period into a sentence that states that dealers must deliver a prospectus "until" that date. In other words, if the prospectus delivery period "expires" on June 15, the legend will require delivery of a prospectus "until" June 15. A research analyst relying on the legend may therefore understandably assume that a report may be mailed on June 15, but this would be one day too early.

• • • *Unsold Allotments and Updating the Prospectus.* In any event, underwriters and dealers are required to comply with the prospectus delivery obligation with respect to their unsold allotments. If an issue is difficult to sell (a "sticky issue" in the vernacular of Wall Street), the underwriters and dealers may require a substantial period of time to complete the distribution. Indeed, it is not uncommon for the managing underwriter to take back all of the securities not sold by the syndicate, place

---

42. Joseph McLaughlin, *"Ten Easy Pieces" for the SEC,* 18 Rev. Sec. & Comms. Reg. 200, 201 (1985).

43. Research reports are generally "prospectuses" within the meaning of Section 2(10) of the 1933 Act, but they do not meet the requirements of Section 10(a) of the statute. It would therefore be illegal under Section 5(b)(1) to deliver a research report unless an exemption were available, and as we have seen the Section 4(3)(B) exemption is not available for the period during which the "official" prospectus must be delivered.

them in its own investment account for purposes of Regulation M (see Chapter 4) and resell them at a later date when market conditions have improved.

Unsold allotments do not lose their status as registered securities, however long they are retained by an underwriter and whether or not they are placed in an investment account. On the other hand, a current prospectus must be delivered when the securities are sold. The original prospectus may have to be updated because of Section 10(a)(3), which provides that if a prospectus is used more than nine months after the effective date of a registration statement, the information contained therein must be as of a date not more than 16 months prior to its use. This requirement applies in particular to the audited financial statements included in the prospectus. The original prospectus may also have to be updated because statements in the prospectus may no longer be true or may have become misleading because of the passage of time.

Underwriting agreements generally require the issuer to update the prospectus in order to protect the underwriter against liability for delivering an out-of-date prospectus or one that contains disclosure problems.[44] Typically, the issuer will bear the expense of updating for a period of nine months after the effective date of the registration statement. Thereafter, updating is at the underwriter's expense.

As discussed above, research material may ordinarily not be distributed during the prospectus delivery period because Section 4(3)(B) makes the dealer's exemption unavailable during this period. Section 4(3)(C) also makes the dealer's exemption unavailable, however, *at any time*—even after expiration of the prospectus delivery period—in respect of "[t]ransactions as to securities constituting the whole or a part of an unsold allotment." On its face, this means that a dealer with an unsold allotment may not distribute research on the registered securities, at least where the dealer

---

44. Delivery of a defective prospectus does not cause a violation of Section 5 (as opposed, for example, to a violation of Section 12(a)(2)). *But see SEC v. Manor Nursing Centers, Inc.*, 458 F.2d 1082 (2d Cir. 1972), *criticized in Jennings, Marsh & Coffee, Securities Regulation: Cases and Materials* 149-50 n.a (7th ed. 1992). The argument for a Section 5 violation may be barely credible where the delivered prospectus on its face does not conform to Section 10(a)(3)'s express updating requirement.

is actively trying to sell the unsold allotment. On the other hand, it should be permissible to distribute research if the dealer has placed the unsold securities into an investment account as discussed in Chapter 4. Also, such research may be entitled to the Rule 139 exemption discussed in Chapter 3.

• *Gun-jumping*

When the 1933 Act prohibits "offers" prior to the filing of a registration statement and limits the type of written offers that are permitted after filing, the prohibition is not limited to communications that constitute an offer in the common law contract sense or that on their face purport to offer to sell the security to be registered. The term "offer to sell" is broadly defined in Section 2(3) of the 1933 Act to include "every attempt or offer to dispose of, or solicitation of an offer to buy ... for value." The SEC has long cautioned that publicity efforts made in advance of a proposed offering "may in fact contribute to conditioning the public mind or arousing public interest in ... [an] issuer or in ... [its] securities ... in a manner which raises a serious question whether the publicity is not in fact part of the selling effort."[45]

Starting a selling effort prior to the filing of a registration statement is called "gun-jumping." Those who "jump the gun" on a forthcoming offering, whether by interviews with newspaper or magazine reporters, speeches, market letters or otherwise, violate the basic prohibitions of the 1933 Act.

In *Carl M. Loeb, Rhoades & Co.,*[46] the managing underwriters of an initial public offering were disciplined by the SEC for issuing a press release providing details of the proposed offering and holding a press conference at which the release was distributed and questions were answered. The SEC found that, in the two days following the release of this publicity, over 100 securities firms had contacted Loeb, Rhoades expressing interest in the offering. During the same period, the managing underwriters received numerous indications of interest from the public. In its opinion, the SEC stated its belief that it had a mandate from Congress to prevent issuers, underwriters and dealers from "initiating

---

45. *See* SEC Release No. 33-3844 (October 8, 1957).
46. *In re Carl M. Loeb, Rhoades & Co.,* 38 S.E.C. 843 (1959).

a public sales campaign prior to the filing of a registration statement by means of publicity efforts which, even though not couched in terms of an express offer, condition the public mind or arouse public interest in . . . particular securities."

At the same time, the SEC recognized that "difficult and close questions of fact" might arise in distinguishing between an "item of publicity" that is "part of a selling effort" or part of "legitimate disclosure to investors unrelated to such an effort." It identified as relevant circumstances in this regard "the nature, source, distribution, timing, and apparent purpose and effect of the published material."[47]

Gun-jumping can have severe business and legal consequences. If the SEC becomes aware of activity that it regards as improper, it can hold up effectiveness of the registration statement until such time as it believes the effects of the improper activity have dissipated. It can assess administrative penalties against any of the persons it believes to be responsible for the improper activity. Finally, even if the offering is successfully completed, any purchaser who has been the recipient of an illegal offer may be able for a period of one year to "put" his securities to the offending seller at the original purchase price.

• *Rule 135*

The SEC has long considered it appropriate to permit advance notice of certain offerings of securities. In 1955, it adopted Rule 135 to permit a brief notice to be sent to existing

---

47. The SEC also concluded in *Loeb Rhoades* that pre-filing publicity by prospective underwriters "must be *presumed* to set in motion or to be a part of the distribution process," and therefore involve prohibited offers to sell (emphasis added). This "presumption" was almost immediately qualified in *First Maine Corp.*, Release No. 34-5898 (March 2, 1959), where the SEC observed that "broker-dealers in the ordinary course of their business commonly furnish to customers and prospective customers a considerable volume of business and financial information," and that the *Loeb Rhoades* "presumption" would not necessarily apply to "incidental mention of an issuer or a security in financial information distributed by broker-dealers through the mails."

securityholders to inform them of the proposed issuance of rights to subscribe to additional securities.[48] Rule 135 was subsequently amended to permit a similar notice to be sent to the securityholders of the issuer or of another issuer advising them of a proposed exchange offer and to permit a notice of offerings to employees.[49] Finally, at the urging of the *Wheat Report* and certain securities exchanges, Rule 135 was amended in 1970 to permit the publication of a brief notice relating to any cash offering of securities to be registered under the 1933 Act.[50]

A proposed stock offering may be a material fact from the standpoint of existing shareholders. For example, an equity financing may result in the dilution of their holdings. Rule 135 seeks to accommodate the interests of existing shareholders and the interests of the SEC in prohibiting gun-jumping. It provides that for purposes of Section 5 a notice by an issuer that it proposes to make a public offering of securities to be registered under the 1933 Act will not be deemed an offer of the securities if the notice states that the offering will be made only by means of a prospectus and contains no more than the name of the issuer, the title, amount and basic terms of the securities to be offered, and a brief statement of the manner and purpose of the offering without naming the underwriters. The notice may take the form of a news release or a written communication directed to holders of the issuer's securities.

A major point to be stressed in the case of a Rule 135 notice is that it may not identify the managing underwriters. In the pre-filing period, not only are underwriters prohibited from offering the securities for sale, but also dealers are prohibited from offering to buy the securities. The SEC has said that the announcement of the underwriter's identity should be avoided during this period because "experience shows that such announcements are very likely to lead to illegal offers to buy."[51]

In 1969, Bangor Punta Corporation issued a press release announcing a proposed exchange offer of its securities for shares of

---

48. SEC Release No. 33-3568 (August 29, 1955).
49. SEC Release No. 33-4099 (June 16, 1959).
50. SEC Release No. 33-5101 (November 19, 1970).
51. SEC Release No. 33-4697 (May 28, 1964).

Piper Aircraft Corporation. The announcement was made prior to the filing of the registration statement and stated that there would be offered for the Piper shares "a package of Bangor Punta securities to be valued in the judgment of The First Boston Corporation at not less than $80 per Piper share." In a proceeding by Chris-Craft Industries, Inc. seeking to enjoin the exchange offer, Judge Waterman held that the categories of information permitted under Rule 135 are exclusive and that the statement that the package of securities would be valued at $80 made the press release an offer to sell that violated Section 5.[52]

• *Rule 135c*

The purpose of Rule 135 was to permit existing securityholders to be informed of an issuer's forthcoming registered offering in a manner that did not condition the market for that offering. Existing securityholders may also have an interest in an issuer's forthcoming *non-registered* offering, e.g., a private placement or an offshore offering. The SEC's interest in this situation is to prevent any news about the unregistered offering from arousing interest in the offering among the issuer's securityholders. As discussed in Chapter 9, a listed U.S. company that had completed in the early 1990s an offshore convertible debt offering in reliance on the SEC's new Regulation S filed a report of the transaction on Form 8-K. The SEC staff criticized the issuer in strong terms on the theory that the report amounted to an attempt to condition the U.S. market for the convertible securities. The staff position was untenable and eventually resulted in the adoption of Rule 135c,[53] which permits a reporting issuer (or a foreign issuer that files "home country" information with the SEC) to give a notice—which may consist of a news release, a written communication to securityholders or employees or "other published statements"—about an unregistered offering. The notice is limited to specified facts about the offering and may not be "used for the purpose of conditioning the market in the United States for any of the securities offered." It must be filed with the SEC as part of a report on Form 8-K or

---

52. *Chris-Craft Industries, Inc. v. Bangor Punta Corp.*, 426 F.2d 569, 574 (2d Cir. 1970).
53. SEC Release No. 33-7053 (April 19, 1994).

6-K or as part of a non-reporting foreign issuer's "home country" information.

• *Rule 134*

Once a registration statement is filed, certain limited written communications are permitted if they are deemed not to be a prospectus under the "safe harbor" of Rule 134. A communication will not be deemed a prospectus if it contains no more than the name of the issuer, the title of the securities, a brief indication of the general type of business of the issuer, the offering price or its method of determination, the yield or probable yield range in the case of a debt security, the name and address of the sender of the communication, the names of the managing underwriters, the approximate date of the proposed sale to the public, legal investment, tax and rating agency information, and certain other data in the case of a rights offering or a communication concerning the securities of a registered investment company.

If the registration statement is not effective, the communication must include a legend to the effect that a registration statement has been filed but has not yet become effective, that the securities may not be sold prior to effectiveness, and that the communication does not constitute an offer. The legend called for during the pre-effective period will not be required, however, if the communication is accompanied or preceded by a preliminary prospectus or does no more than state from whom a written prospectus meeting the requirements of Section 10 may be obtained, identify the security, state its price, and state by whom orders will be executed.

Pursuant to Rule 134, during the period between filing and effectiveness, a "tombstone" advertisement may be published to advertise the availability of the preliminary prospectus. In the usual case, however, the Rule 134 tombstone advertisement is published after the registration statement becomes effective, more for the purpose of recording the transaction and enhancing the status of the managing underwriter than for generating interest in the securities. A tombstone advertisement derives its name from its appearance.

It will undoubtedly soon become commonplace for tombstone advertisements to include the issuer's or underwriters' "Website" address. At this location, investors can obtain access to further Rule 134 information or even a preliminary or final prospectus, documents incorporated by reference or (assuming effectiveness of the registration statement and compliance with procedures discussed in Chapter 3) other information that goes beyond that permitted by Rule 134. One of the first examples of this practice was the September 30, 1996 tombstone advertisement relating to General Motors Acceptance Corporation's "SmartNotes" program.

The press release that customarily is issued after the filing of a registration statement must be kept within the confines of Rule 134, as must any pre-effective notices to shareholders to whom subscription rights are proposed to be issued. The press release must set forth the Rule 134 legend. Some public relations firms print the legend on the stationery on which pre-effective press releases are published.

As discussed above, there is interest among underwriters in permitting their sales personnel to use e-mail messages to inform customers of the availability of new offerings. Even if an e-mail message is assumed to be a "written" communication, it will still be permitted if its content is kept within the limits prescribed by Rule 134.

Rule 134(d) provides that a communication sent or delivered to any person pursuant to Rule 134 that is accompanied or preceded by a preliminary prospectus, may solicit from the recipient an offer to buy the security or request the recipient to indicate, upon an enclosed or attached coupon or card, or in some other manner (e.g., by e-mail), whether he might be interested in the security, provided that the communication contains substantially the following statement:

> No offer to buy the securities can be accepted and no part of the purchase price can be received until the registration statement has become effective, and any such offer may be withdrawn or revoked, without obligation or commitment of any kind, at any time prior to notice of its acceptance given after the effective date. An indi-

cation of interest in response to this advertisement will involve no obligation or commitment of any kind.

Rule 134(d) is not well known to the securities bar and is relied upon infrequently. It can prove useful, however, and should be kept in mind for that rare instance in which it can provide the answer to a difficult problem. Take the case of the 1964 initial public offering of common stock of Communications Satellite Corporation. Under the Communications Satellite System Act, communications common carriers were entitled to purchase half of the 10 million shares being offered. Any of the shares offered to the eligible communications common carriers and not purchased by them were to be underwritten and included in the shares sold to the public. It was essential, therefore, for the underwriters to know the number of shares for which they would be responsible prior to the effectiveness of the registration statement. The solution was to rely upon Rule 134(d). A document inviting orders was sent to the eligible common carriers along with a preliminary prospectus. This document was kept within the confines of Rule 134 and contained the statement required by Rule 134(d). It was stipulated that orders must be received by a specified date prior to the proposed effective date of the registration statement. The carrier offering was fully subscribed, and, as there was great demand for the shares, there was virtual certainty that no orders would be withdrawn. A notice of acceptance in accordance with Rule 134(d) was given to the carriers immediately after the registration statement became effective, and the underwriters proceeded with the public offering.

It should not be assumed that Rule 134(d)'s reference to "notice of . . . acceptance" is intended to make it possible for underwriters to set up "automatic acceptance" arrangements. Whatever the significance of this reference, the statute still prohibits "sales" prior to the effective date. Care must be taken to avoid an arrangement that amounts in effect to a contract of sale that is subject to conditions subsequent, i.e., the setting of the price (perhaps within a range) and the effectiveness of the registration statement. One can imagine the reaction of the SEC if an underwriter received "offers to buy" the registered securities from a large number of individual investors, each offer subject to a maximum price, and then proceeded to "accept" all of these offers—without further notice to the investors— once the price had been agreed to and the registration statement had become effective.

• *Research Reports*

Gun-jumping problems are particularly acute for a securities firm with an active research department and a retail sales system. The difficulty is that, depending on their timing and content and the audience to which they are addressed, research reports may be viewed by the SEC as illegal offers of the securities proposed to be sold under a registration statement. As research reports are written documents (or the equivalent thereof, as in the case of research that is distributed electronically), the problem exists both prior to the filing of the registration statement and after filing but prior to completion of the distribution of the registered securities.

Research problems in this context are discussed in detail in Chapter 3.

• *Offers and Sales*

The registration and prospectus delivery requirements of Section 5 come into play only when there is an "offer" or a "sale" of a security. Section 2(3) defines a "sale" to include any disposition of a security for value and an "offer" to include any offer or attempt to dispose of a security for value. For there to be a sale, the person to whom the security is issued or delivered must give some consideration or "value" in return. Thus, an ordinary stock dividend does not involve a sale.[54]

• • *Spin-offs.* The issue of whether a sale is involved arises in connection with a spin-off, where a corporation distributes to its shareholders shares of a subsidiary corporation. Logic would dictate that such a transaction does not involve a sale any more than does a stock dividend. But in the late 1960s the SEC became concerned with the whole spin-off phenomenon

---

54. This is true even though the shareholder has the right to choose between receiving stock or cash. SEC Release No. 33-929 (July 29, 1936).

and issued a release in which it referred to a pattern involving "the issuance by a company, with little, if any, business activity, of its shares to a publicly-owned company in exchange for what may or may not be nominal consideration" followed by a spin-off of these shares to shareholders of the public company "with the result that active trading in the shares begins with no information on the issuer being available to the investing public."[55] The SEC brushed aside the "theory" that no sale was involved in the spin-off on the basis that the distribution "does not cease at the point of receipt by the initial distributees of the shares but continues into the trading market involving sales to the investing public at large." The SEC simply did not wish to see trading markets spring up where there was no public information concerning the issuer.

The staff of the SEC will take no-action positions with respect to unregistered spin-off distributions of the stock of non-reporting subsidiaries if an information statement is furnished to the shareholders receiving the shares and a Form 10 registration statement is filed under the 1934 Act.[56] The letters requesting these no-action positions usually describe in more or less detail the "valid business purpose" of the spin-off, and it is sometimes said that this is a prerequisite for obtaining a no-action letter. Whether or not there is a valid business purpose to the spin-off should be irrelevant for SEC purposes, however, so long as adequate public information is available regarding the newly-public company. An explanation for the letters' preoccupation with "business purpose" may lie in the fact that such a purpose is sometimes important to the tax consequences of the spin-off.

• • *Rule 145.* The question of whether the issuance of securities in a merger or similar transaction involves a sale has had a long history culminating in the adoption of Rule 145. If a company seeks to acquire another company in a statutory consolidation or merger in which the stock of the company to be acquired

---

55. SEC Release No. 33-4982 (July 2, 1969).

56. *See,* e.g., SEC No-action Letters, *The Dun & Bradstreet Corporation* (available October 15, 1996), *Olin Corporation* (available October 15, 1996) and the letters cited therein.

will become or be exchanged for securities of the acquiring company, or if a company seeks to acquire all or substantially all of the assets of another company in exchange for its securities to be followed by a statutory liquidation, the transaction will require the affirmative vote or consent of the holders of a majority or more of the voting stock of the company to be acquired. A shareholder vote will also be required in the case of a reclassification which involves the substitution of one security for another security. The required vote is governed by state law.[57]

In transactions of this type, unlike a voluntary exchange of one security for another, a change in the shareholder's status occurs by operation of law and not because he makes an individual investment decision. Thus, during the first 40 years of the 1933 Act's operation, the SEC took the position that no "offer" or "sale" was involved where, pursuant to statutory provisions or provisions contained in the certificate of incorporation of the company to be acquired, there is submitted to a vote of shareholders a proposal for a transfer of assets or a merger or consolidation if the vote of a required favorable majority would bind all shareholders except for those asserting appraisal rights. This "no-sale theory" was codified in Rule 133, adopted by the SEC in 1951.[58] In 1972 the SEC did a complete about-face. It adopted Rule 145, which provides that such a transaction does indeed involve an offer and sale. Accordingly, when submitting such a transaction to a stockholder vote, a joint proxy statement and prospectus must be mailed to stockholders. Form S-4 has been adopted for the registration of securities to be issued in business combinations of this type.

With respect to resales of securities issued in a Rule 145 transaction, a person who is an affiliate of the company to be acquired at the time the transaction is submitted to a vote will be deemed an underwriter and must deliver a prospectus in connection with a resale of the registered securities, unless the securities are sold in accordance with the public information, limitation on the amount of securities sold, and manner of sale provisions of Rule 144. If the affiliate of the acquired corpora-

---

57. Under Delaware law, for example, a majority vote is required.
58. SEC Release No. 33-3420 (August 2, 1951).

tion does not become an affiliate of the acquiring corporation and holds his securities for two years, he may sell without limitation. If he holds the securities for one year, he may sell free of all but the current public information requirement.[59] The SEC has taken the position that the resale provisions of Rule 145 also apply to securities acquired in exchanges exempted under Section 3(a)(9) or Section 3(a)(10).[60]

• *Exempted Transactions*

In general, Section 4 exempts certain types of transactions from the registration and prospectus delivery requirements of Section 5, and Section 3 exempts certain types of securities. The transaction exemptions set forth in Section 4 appear on their face to be rather complicated. What they boil down to, however, is that Section 4(2) exempts private placements, which are the subject of Chapter 7. Subsections (1), (3) and (4) of Section 4 exempt trading transactions as opposed to distributions.

• • *Private Placements.* Corporate financing by means of private placements has been revolutionized in recent years by the SEC's adoption of Rule 144A. The history of the private placement exemption set forth in Section 4(2) of the 1933 Act and its culmination in Rule 144A are described in Chapter 7.

• • *Trading Transactions.* To understand the exemptions from the registration and prospectus delivery requirements of Section 5 available for trading transactions, it is necessary to analyze the separate subsections of Section 4, their relationship to certain definitions in Section 2, and the refinements to the Section 4 exemptions spelled out in Rule 144.

---

59. In early 1997, the SEC reduced the Rule 145 holding periods from three years and two years to two years and one year, respectively. SEC Release No. 33-7390 (February 20, 1997). It also proposed to eliminate the presumption that an affiliate of the acquired company is deemed to be an underwriter upon resale of the registered securities. SEC Release No. 33-7391 (February 20, 1997).

60. *See* J. William Hicks, *Resales of Restricted Securities* § 4.03[3][g] (1997 ed.).

Section 4(1) exempts from the provisions of Section 5 "transactions by any person other than an issuer, underwriter, or dealer." This is the exemption that allows an ordinary investor to sell 100 shares of common stock on an exchange or in the over-the-counter market without going through the futile exercise of asking the issuer to file a registration statement to cover the sale. Without the Section 4(1) exemption, the trading markets simply could not operate. The ordinary investor, of course, is not the "issuer" of the securities. As will be seen, if he bought the securities in the open market or in a registered offering, he will not be deemed an "underwriter." Nor is he a "dealer."[61] He will be selling through a dealer, however, and the securities firm through which he sells his 100 shares must find its own exemption under Section 4.

A dealer that is selling for a customer will usually rely on the "dealer's exemption" under Section 4(3). This section exempts transactions by a dealer (including an underwriter no longer acting as an underwriter in respect of the securities involved in the transaction), except under three circumstances. First, paragraph (A) removes the exemption for transactions taking place prior to the expiration of 40 days after the first date on which the security was bona fide first offered to the public by the issuer or by or though an underwriter. Second, as discussed above, paragraph (B) removes the exemption for transactions by a dealer taking place prior to the expiration of a specified number of days following a registered public offering. Finally, paragraph (C) removes the exemption for transactions in securities constituting a part of a dealer's unsold allotment as a participant in a distribution of the securities.

---

61. Section 2(12) of the 1933 Act defines the term "dealer" to mean

any person who engages either for all or part of his time, directly or indirectly, as agent, broker, or principal, in the business of offering, buying, selling, or otherwise dealing or trading in securities issued by another person.

An ordinary private investor should not be considered a "dealer," even though he may trade in securities on a regular basis.

The reasons for the exceptions are fairly obvious. Paragraph (A) permits the development of a market in securities that may have been the subject of an *illegal* unregistered distribution in the United States or a legal distribution outside the United States. It is the origin of the 40-day period following an offshore offering during which U.S. dealers will not make a market in the new security. Paragraph (B) was discussed above, and its prospectus delivery requirement was historically intended to encourage dissemination of the prospectus that was used to sell the new offering. Finally, paragraph (C) is intended to prevent reliance on the dealer's exemption *at any time* at which the dealer is trying to sell part of an unsold allotment from the offering.

A securities dealer unable to rely on Section 4(3) to execute a sell order for his customer—e.g., because prospectuses are unavailable to fulfill a delivery requirement or because the transaction takes place within the first 40 days following an offshore offering—may be able to execute the transaction in reliance on Section 4(4). This exemption applies to "brokers' transactions executed upon customers' orders on any exchange or in the over-the-counter market but not the solicitation of such orders." The SEC construes the exemption as being available only where the sell order is unsolicited and the dealer acts as agent and does not solicit the buy side of the transaction.

• • *Transactions by Underwriters.* Except under the limited circumstances of Section 4(4), an exemption under Section 4 is not available for transactions by an "underwriter." If an underwriter is involved in a transaction, registration is required unless the securities are exempted securities under Section 3. The term "underwriter" applies not only to a securities professional, whether acting as principal or agent, but also to any other person who comes within the statutory definition. Such a person is commonly known as a "statutory underwriter" to distinguish him from a professional.[62] Section 2(11) defines the term "underwriter" to mean

---

62. One of the authors was once required to explain the statutory underwriter concept to counsel for a person in this position who argued that his

any person who has purchased from an issuer with a
view to, or offers or sells for an issuer in connection
with, the distribution of any security, or participates or
has a direct or indirect participation in any such undertaking, or participates or has a participation in the direct
or indirect underwriting of any such undertaking.

For the purpose of this definition, and for no other purpose,
the term "issuer" includes, in addition to the actual issuer of
the securities, "any person directly or indirectly controlling or
controlled by the issuer, or any person under direct or indirect
common control with the issuer."[63]
Cutting through to the essence of this wordy definition, it
covers not only conventional underwriters, investment banking
firms underwriting a public offering of securities for an issuer
or a control person, but also individuals who buy securities
from an issuer in a private placement (called "restricted securities" under Rule 144) and redistribute them to the public under circumstances that lead to the conclusion that they
purchased the securities "with a view to distribution." A statutory underwriter problem often arises when a person sells a
privately-owned business to a larger publicly-owned company
in exchange for its stock and then decides to liquidate his holdings. The issue must also be addressed in connection with any
resale of privately placed securities.
Is an ordinary member of the public an underwriter if he
purchases securities from an issuer in a registered public offering with a view to their resale? If read literally, Section 2(11)
covers any purchase from an issuer with a view to distribution.
But Section 2(11) cannot be read literally in this context. Manuel F. Cohen, when Chief Counsel of the SEC's Division of

client obviously was not an underwriter because he operated a dry cleaning
business.
   63. This would include a controlling shareholder, a subsidiary of the
issuer, or a sister subsidiary in a holding company structure. Even though
an issuer may "control" a low-level employee, he is not considered a person "controlled by the issuer."

Corporation Finance, explained it this way in a speech delivered to the Association of the Bar of the City of New York:

> The Commission has not construed Section 2(11) to identify as underwriters public stockholders who intend to distribute shares acquired in a registered rights or other public offering, or in a transaction exempt under Sections 3(a)(9), 3(a)(10), or 3(b). In some of these situations, substantial blocks of securities, amounting to a "distribution" by any test, are in fact redistributed. It would be an inversion of the purposes and provisions of the Act, however, to subject members of the public, for whose protection the Act is designed, to the duties, responsibilities and liabilities of an underwriter.[64]

One may have a statutory underwriter problem if he purchases securities from a shareholder in a control relationship with the issuer, a person that Rule 144 calls an "affiliate." As noted above, a control person is an "issuer" solely for the purpose of the Section 2(11) definition. Thus, a Section 4(1) exemption would be available to a control person owning nonrestricted securities who stood on a street corner and hawked his securities to the public. It would not be available, however, if he sold his securities through an intermediary, such as a securities firm, in a transaction that constituted a distribution. Under these circumstances, the intermediary would be considered an underwriter.

The question of who is a control person is basically factual and takes into account the size of the person's holdings, his position with the issuer and other objective and subjective considerations. Rule 405 under the 1933 Act defines "control" as "the possession, direct or indirect, of the power to direct or cause the direction of the management and policies of a person, whether through the ownership of voting securities, by contract or otherwise." As far as the SEC is concerned, a hard look should be taken at a person's control status if he is a director or

---

64. M. F. Cohen, *Rule 133 of the Securities and Exchange Comm'n*, 14 *The Record of the Association of the Bar of the City of New York* 162, 178 (1959).

an executive officer of the issuer. The 1933 Act has been construed to recognize the concept of the "control group," such as a controlling family.[65]

• • *Rule 144.* A person who sells securities for the account of an "affiliate" or a person who sells "restricted securities" for his own account may claim a Section 4 exemption if the transaction does not constitute a "distribution." Rule 144 under the 1933 Act spells out those transactions that are not deemed to be distributions and that accordingly may be effected without registration. It provides that any "affiliate" (i.e., a control person) or any person who sells "restricted securities" of an issuer for his own account, or any person who sells restricted or any other securities of the issuer for the account of an "affiliate," will be deemed not to be engaged in a distribution of such securities and therefore not to be an underwriter thereof within the meaning of Section 2(11) if all of the conditions of the rule are met. Rule 144 defines "restricted securities" as including securities that are "acquired directly or indirectly from the issuer, or from an affiliate of the issuer, in a transaction or chain of transactions not involving any public offering."

In general, Rule 144 permits an affiliate or a holder of restricted securities to sell without registration in ordinary brokerage transactions, or to a market maker, an amount of securities that, together with his other sales during the preceding three months (other than pursuant to a registration statement or a private placement), does not exceed the greater of one percent of the amount of securities of that class outstanding or the average weekly volume of trading in those securities during the preceding four weeks.

To rely on Rule 144 for a sale of restricted securities, a minimum of one year must have elapsed between the acquisition of the securities from the issuer or an affiliate of the issuer and the date of their resale under the rule by the acquiror or any subsequent holder.

A holder of restricted securities who is not and has not been an affiliate of the issuer during the three months preceding the

---

65. *See,* e.g., *SEC v. Culpepper,* 270 F.2d 241 (2d Cir. 1959).

sale may sell free of any Rule 144 limitations if two years have elapsed from the time that the securities were acquired from the issuer or an affiliate of the issuer.[66]

In most cases, a Form 144 must be filed with the SEC before the sale is made. Also, there must be available adequate current public information with respect to the issuer of the securities, which means either that the issuer has been a reporting company for 90 days and has been current for 12 months in its reporting obligations or, in the case of a non-reporting issuer, that specified information about the issuer is otherwise publicly available.

• *Exempted Securities*

Whether or not a Section 4 exemption is available for a particular transaction, the securities involved in the transaction may be offered and sold without compliance with Section 5 if they are exempted securities under Section 3. For the most part, a Section 3 exemption is available because of the nature of the issuer.

• • *U.S. Government Obligations.* Section 3(a)(2) exempts securities issued or guaranteed by the United States or any person "controlled or supervised by and acting as an instrumentality" of the U.S. government pursuant to statutory authority. Securities exempted by Section 3(a)(2) include not only direct U.S. Treasury obligations, but also obligations issued or guaranteed by the various Federal agencies that finance in the public markets. Section 3(a)(2) is used most often to exempt debt

---

66. This brief summary of Rule 144 does not do justice to its many nuances. For further information, see the current edition of J. William Hicks, *Resales of Restricted Securities* (Clark Boardman Callaghan).

In early 1997, the SEC reduced the Rule 144 holding periods from three years and two years to two years and one year, respectively. SEC Release No. 33-7390 (February 20, 1997). It also proposed to eliminate the requirement that limited sales to ordinary brokerage transactions or to a market maker, to link the volume of sales exclusively to a percentage of shares outstanding and to increase the threshold requirements for filing Form 144. It also invited comment on proposals to address the application of the 1933 Act to the hedging of restricted securities. SEC Release No. 33-7391 (February 20, 1997).

securities, but it can also apply to equity securities of instrumentalities of the United States.[67]

The exemption is available for the great variety of obligations that are guaranteed by the Federal government. For example, the securities of The Chrysler Corporation that were guaranteed by the Federal government when that company was encountering financial difficulties were exempt from registration. Certificates representing interests in a pool of mortgages are exempted when guaranteed by the Government National Mortgage Association. Securities of foreign governments, however, are not exempt from registration.

The staff of the SEC has taken a no-action position with respect to debt securities issued by the Private Export Funding Corporation where the payment of interest is guaranteed by Eximbank and the payment of principal is secured by the pledge of securities guaranteed by Eximbank or by other instruments backed by the full faith and credit of the United States.[68]

In determining the availability of an exemption under Section 3(a)(2), the SEC will look to the substance of a transaction and not just its form. Thus, the staff has permitted reliance on this exemption where a limited partnership, organized for the sole purpose of renovating and redeveloping the City Post Office in Washington, D.C., proposed to issue non-recourse obligations to finance the project. These obligations were to be guaranteed by the U.S. Postal Service during the construction period and thereafter backed by a lease obligation of the United States acting through the Administrator of General Services (the "GSA"). The Postal Service is an instrumentality of the United States, and thus its guarantee provides an exemption for the bonds during the construction period. When the GSA lease obligation comes into effect, the holders of the bonds will be relying solely upon the credit of the GSA, and thus the bonds are the economic equivalent of U.S. government obligations. In taking a no-action position, the staff particularly noted that

---

67. *See,* e.g., SEC No-action Letter, *Federal Agricultural Mortgage Corporation* (available October 5, 1988).

68. SEC No-action Letter, *Private Export Funding Corporation* (available June 9, 1975).

both the guarantee and the lease obligation could be enforced directly by a bondholder.[69]

The securities of certain international organizations are exempted securities under the 1933 Act pursuant to federal enabling statutes. For example, a 1949 amendment to the Bretton Woods Agreements Act provides that securities issued or guaranteed by the International Bank for Reconstruction and Development (the World Bank) are deemed to be exempted securities within the meaning of Section 3(a)(2).[70] The statutes relating to the Inter-American Development Bank Act,[71] the African Development Bank[72] and the Asian Development Bank Act[73] contain similar exemptions for securities issued or guaranteed by these entities. The SEC has authority to suspend or impose conditions on these exemptions and, acting under this authority, has adopted regulations that require the filing of certain periodic and transaction-related reports.[74]

Securities issued by the Federal National Mortgage Association are exempted from the 1933 Act by the terms of the Charter Act that created that entity.[75]

• • *Municipal Obligations.* Section 3(a)(2) also exempts securities issued or guaranteed by the states and territories, their political subdivisions and public instrumentalities, or the District of Columbia. It also exempts certain industrial development bonds the interest on which is tax-exempt under Section 103(a) of the Internal Revenue Code. In the late 1960s, the SEC attempted to

---

69. SEC No-action Letter, *Postal Square Limited Partnership* (dated May 24, 1990). *See also* SEC No-action Letter, *Tennessee Valley Authority Office of Power Headquarters Building Project* (available February 18, 1983), where non-recourse obligations backed by a TVA lease were permitted to be issued in reliance upon Section 3(a)(2).

70. 22 U.S.C. § 286k-l(a) (1990).

71. 22 U.S.C. § 283h(a) (1990).

72. 22 U.S.C. § 290i-9(a) (1990).

73. 22 U.S.C. § 285h(a) (1990).

74. Regulations BW (World Bank), IA (Inter-American Development Bank), AFDB (African Development Bank) and AD (Asian Development Bank).

75. 12 U.S.C. § 1723c (Supp. 1996).

subject industrial development bonds to 1933 Act registration requirements by adopting Rule 131.[76] Rule 131 provided that any
part of an obligation evidenced by a bond issued by a governmental entity specified in Section 3(a)(2), "which is payable from payments to be made in respect of property or money which is or will
be used, under a lease, sale, or loan arrangement, by or for industrial or commercial enterprise," would be deemed a "separate security" issued by the industrial or commercial enterprise that is
the obligor under the lease, sale or loan arrangement. The separate
non-municipal security would, of course, not be entitled to the
Section 3(a)(2) exemption. Congress quickly responded by enact-
ing Section 401 of the Employment Security Amendments of 1970
to amend Section 3(a)(2) to override Rule 131 in the case of tax-
exempt industrial development bonds.[77] As changes in the tax law
have eliminated most industrial development bonds, the issue is
no longer of significant importance. The SEC continues to maintain, however, that private obligations underlying municipal "conduit" securities should be registered under the 1933 Act.

Tax law changes have led to the issuance of taxable bonds
by municipalities and their instrumentalities. The taxable or
tax-exempt status of interest on these securities does not affect
the availability of the Section 3(a)(2) exemption.[78]

Although municipal bonds are exempt from 1933 Act registration, many official statements used in connection with municipal offerings are as complete and as well prepared as any
1933 Act prospectus. Nonetheless, the SEC continues to express concern over the adequacy of disclosure in the area of
municipal finance. Its jurisdiction in this area is limited to some

---

76. SEC Release No. 33-4921 (August 28, 1968).

77. *See* SEC Release No. 33-5103 (November 6, 1970).

78. *See* SEC No-action Letter, *The East Central Missouri Water and
Sewer Authority* (available August 15, 1988); SEC No-action Letter, *Capital
Area Regional Solid Waste Authority, Harrisburg, Pennsylvania* (available No-
vember 25, 1987); SEC No-action Letter, *Redevelopment Authority of the
City of Harrisburg, Pennsylvania* (available November 25, 1987); SEC No-
action Letter, *Arkansas Development Finance Authority* (available Novem-
ber 25, 1987); and SEC No-Action Letter, *Helena-West Helena-Phillips
County Port Authority* (available November 25, 1987).

extent by Section 15B(d)(1) of the 1934 Act, which prohibits the SEC or the MSRB from requiring that any municipal issuer make any filing prior to the sale of municipal securities. In addition, Section 15B(d)(2) (the "Tower Amendment") prevents the MSRB from requiring any issuer to furnish any information either to the MSRB or to any prospective purchaser.

Notwithstanding Section 15B(d), the SEC has extensively regulated disclosure practices in the municipal securities field by means of its authority over broker-dealers and its power to define fraudulent conduct. Rule 15c2-12[79] thus makes it unlawful, as a means "reasonably designed" to prevent fraud, for a broker-dealer to act as underwriter of a primary offering of municipal securities in a principal amount of $1 million except in compliance with the rule's requirements. These requirements include the obtaining and review of an official statement that the issuer "deems final" (with certain authorized omissions) and the delivery to potential customers of preliminary and final official statements. The rule also requires an underwriter to "reasonably determine" that the issuer or any "obligated person" has agreed to provide annual financial information and notice of specified occurrences (if material) (e.g., delinquencies, defaults, unscheduled draws, substitution of credit enhancers or liquidity providers). Finally, the rule prohibits any broker-dealer from recommending the purchase or sale of a municipal security unless the broker-dealer has procedures in place that provide "reasonable assurance" that it will receive prompt notice of the specified occurrences.

The SEC has released three interpretive statements on the disclosure obligations of underwriters, broker-dealers and issuers in the municipal securities markets.[80] Insofar as underwriters are concerned, the SEC takes the position (without citing any authority) that "[b]y participating in an offering, an under-

---

79. SEC Release No. 34-26985 (June 28, 1989). The rule was originally proposed in SEC Release No. 34-26100 (September 22, 1988) at the same time as the SEC released to Congress the results of its investigation of the default of the Washington Public Power Supply System.

80. SEC Release No. 34-26100 (September 22, 1988), *modified in* Release No. 34-28985 (June 28, 1989); Release No. 34-33741 (March 9, 1994).

writer makes an implied recommendation about the securities."[81] Moreover, the SEC also believes that "most situations" in which a broker-dealer "brings a municipal security to the attention of a customer involve an implicit recommendation of the security to the customer."[82] From these premises, it is easy for the SEC to invoke prior precedents to the effect that a broker-dealer that recommends a security must have a reasonable basis for doing so. The broker-dealer can establish such a basis, in the SEC's view, by reviewing the issuer's disclosures in connection with a public offering and by taking into account available continuing disclosure in the case of securities traded in the secondary market.

When the SEC adopted Rule 15c2-12, it was by no means clear that it was correct in asserting that a broker-dealer "recommends" a security for purposes of triggering the "reasonable investigation" requirement merely because the broker-dealer acts as an underwriter. There is no visible historical support for this proposition. There is even less basis for the proposition that the requirement is triggered merely by "bringing a security to the attention of a customer." The SEC's position to this effect obliterates any distinction between a mere solicitation and a recommendation. Exactly what obligations a broker-dealer assumes in a given situation should depend, as they historically have, on all the facts and circumstances of the transaction. Nevertheless, the consequences under Rule 10b-5 of the SEC's position remain to be determined.

• • *Bank Securities.* An exemption is available under Section 3(a)(2) for securities issued or fully guaranteed by a national or state bank. Securities of foreign banks are not exempt, but the SEC interprets Section 3(a)(2) as exempting certificates of deposit and notes of U.S. branches or agencies of foreign banks to the same extent as domestic banks.[83] Securities of bank holding companies are not exempt under Section 3(a)(2). On the other hand, in 1994 Congress added a new Section

---

81. SEC Release No. 34-26100 (September 22, 1988).

82. SEC Release No. 34-34961 (November 10, 1994) at note 143.

83. SEC Release No. 33-6661 (September 23, 1986).

3(a)(12) to the 1933 Act that exempts the formation of a bank holding company where the stockholders of a bank receive stock of the holding company in accordance with specified criteria that seek to ensure a continuity of ownership, assets and liabilities.

The staff of the SEC has taken the position that a bank that is being newly organized may not offer its stock to the public without compliance with the registration requirements of the 1933 Act unless the invested funds are placed in escrow, or investors are otherwise fully protected against loss, until the bank is authorized to commence operations under applicable state law.[84] Escrows are not practical in underwritten transactions since underwriters will be reluctant to place their compensation in escrow and return it to investors in the event that the certificate of authority is not forthcoming.

For this reason, some banks in organization have registered their initial public offerings under the 1933 Act. To avoid this problem, in several instances involving new Connecticut banks, arrangements were made with the chartering authority in the State of Connecticut to issue the requisite final certificate of authority at the closing. The transaction was structured so that receipt of the funds and regulatory approval were conditions concurrent. Although no request was made to the SEC for approval of this procedure, investors clearly were not at risk prior to the issuance of the final certificate of authority, and the conditions of prior no-action letters were fully satisfied.

Section 3(a)(2) is not the end of the story for national banks or federally-licensed U.S. branches and agencies of foreign banks. Regulations adopted by the Office of the Comptroller of the Currency ("OCC")[85] require—unless an exemption is

---

84. *See* e.g., SEC No-action Letter, *County First Bank* (available March 31, 1989); SEC No-action Letter, *Commerce Bank Corporation* (available September 19, 1988); SEC No-action Letter, *The Springs Bank* (available June 15, 1987); SEC No-action Letter, *Constitution Bank* (available April 21, 1986); SEC No-action Letter, *First Allied Bank of Baton Rouge* (available July 24, 1985); SEC No-action Letter, *Bank of World* (available June 6, 1983).

85. 12 C.F.R. Part 16 (1996).

available—that these institutions not offer and sell their securities until a registration statement has been filed with and declared effective by the OCC. (The exemptions under the regulations incorporate, in general, the 1933 Act's non-bank exemptions.) The OCC regulations generally require the offering documents for non-exempt offerings to conform to the SEC form that would have applied if 1933 Act registration were required, although an abbreviated registration system is available for offers and sales of large denomination nonconvertible debt to accredited investors.[86]

The federal regulators for state banks and state-licensed branches and agencies of foreign banks have not imposed registration requirements.[87] Some states have adopted registration or filing requirements relating to securities of institutions subject to their jurisdiction.

• • *Thrift Institutions.* An exemption is provided under Section 3(a)(5) for securities issued by savings and loan associations and similar institutions. The exemption is not applicable to securities issued by these institutions' holding companies. As in the case of banks, however, Section 3(a)(12) exempts under certain circumstances the formation of a savings association holding company.

Again, however, the 1933 Act exemption is not the end of the story. Regulations adopted by the Office of Thrift Supervision ("OTS")[88] require OTS registration of securities offer-

---

86. 12 C.F.R. Section 16.6 (1996). *See* the letter dated May 31, 1995 from Ellen Broadman, Director, Securities and Corporate Practices Division, OCC, to Daniel M. Rossner of Brown & Wood, [1994–95 Transfer Binder] Fed. Banking L. Rep. (CCH) ¶ 83,610.

87. The FDIC has adopted a Statement of Policy on the Use of Offering Circulars that sets forth standards for the offer and sale of securities by insured state banks that are not members of the Federal Reserve System. 61 Fed. Reg. 46,807 (1996). The statement reminds banks of the applicability of the antifraud provisions of the federal securities laws and suggests the type of information that should be included in an offering circular of a state non-member bank.

88. 12 C.F.R. 563g (1996). For further guidance on these regulations, see a release of the Office of General Counsel of the Federal Home Loan

ings of OTS-regulated thrifts unless an exemption is available. Certain states have also adopted registration requirements for securities offerings by their state-chartered thrift institutions.

• • *Commercial Paper.* Section 3(a)(3) exempts notes with maturities of nine months or less where the proceeds are to be used for current transactions. This is the so-called "commercial paper" exemption. Commercial paper is discussed in more detail in Chapter 10.

• • *Equipment Trust Certificates.* Section 3(a)(6) exempts equipment trust certificates. The exemption originally applied to securities of railroads and motor carriers, the issuance of which was subject to the approval of the Interstate Commerce Commission. The exemption for railroad securities was removed in 1976 as a result of the Penn Central bankruptcy (see Chapter 5), and the motor carrier exemption was removed in 1982.

• • *Insurance Contracts.* Section 3(a)(8) exempts "any insurance or endowment policy or annuity contract or optional annuity contract" issued by a corporation subject to regulation by an insurance commissioner of a state, territory or the District of Columbia. The statement is made in the *House Committee Report* that insurance policies and similar contracts were not regarded in the commercial world as securities offered to the public for investment purposes.[89]

Insurance products are no longer so simple, and certain hybrid products will not qualify for the Section 3(a)(8) exemption. Thus, a "variable annuity," where the payout will depend on the performance of a portfolio of securities, may not be offered without registration.[90] The SEC has attempted to provide guidelines in its Rule 151, stressing that for the exemption to be available the insurer must assume the investment risk and the contract must not be marketed primarily as an investment.

Bank Board (the predecessor to the OTS) entitled "Questions and Answers on Part 563g: Securities Offering Regulations."
   89. H.R. Rep. No. 85, *supra* note 2, at 15.
   90. *SEC v. Variable Annuity Life Insurance Co.,* 359 U.S. 65 (1959).

• • *Exchanges with Existing Securityholders.* Section 3(a)(9) exempts any securities exchanged by an issuer exclusively with its existing securityholders where no commission or other remuneration is paid for soliciting the exchange. This is the exemption that permits a company to have convertible securities outstanding without maintaining a current prospectus (see Chapter 12). If not for this exemption, a prospectus would have to be delivered upon every conversion of a convertible security. This exemption is frequently relied upon in connection with recapitalizations where a company makes an offer to exchange new debt securities for existing debt securities (see Chapter 13).

The exemption provided by Section 3(a)(9) is in the nature of a transaction exemption in that it is not based upon the characteristics of the securities exchanged or of the issuer of the securities. This exemption originally was set forth in Section 4. It was moved to Section 3 when the 1933 Act was amended in 1934 in order to clarify that dealers could trade immediately in securities issued in an exempt exchange.[91]

• • *Court or Government Approved Exchanges.* Exchanges of securities are exempt under Section 3(a)(10) if the terms and conditions of the exchange are approved after a fairness hearing by any court—whether a U.S. or a non-U.S. court—or by any federal or state official, agency, commission or other authority having jurisdiction. For example, if the acquisition of a bank by a bank holding company requires approval as to fairness by a state banking commissioner and the governing statute provides for a public hearing, then the Section 3(a)(10) exemption may be relied upon when issuing securities in the acquisition transaction.[92] This exemption is also frequently relied upon in connection with insurance company acquisitions, as many state insurance laws require approval of the fairness of the terms of an acquisition by the state insurance regulatory body.

The staff of the SEC has taken a no-action position under Section 3(a)(10) where a Hong Kong company proposed to issue securities in exchange for the minority interest in an 80%

---

91. *See* SEC Release No. 33-646 (February 3, 1936).
92. *See,* e.g., SEC No-action Letter, *First NH Banks, Inc.* (June 27, 1988).

owned subsidiary where the transaction was required to be sanctioned by the Supreme Court of Hong Kong after a hearing and where, in making its determination, the court would consider "whether the proposal is such that an intelligent and honest man, a member of the class of minority shareholders and acting in respect of his interest, might reasonably approve."[93]

Like Section 3(a)(9), Section 3(a)(10) is in substance a transaction exemption and was originally contained in Section 4 and moved to Section 3 as part of the 1934 amendments to the 1933 Act.

• • *Bankruptcy.* Originally, Section 3(a)(10) exempted securities issued in exchange for claims in a bankruptcy proceeding. It now specifically excepts from the exemption securities exchanged for claims in a case under Title 11 of the United States Code. This is because the Bankruptcy Reform Act of 1978 sets forth in Section 1145 its own exemptions for securities issued in a bankruptcy proceeding.[94]

• • *Other Exemptions.* Certain other exemptions are contained in Section 3, including an exemption for securities issued by charitable organizations, intrastate offerings (elaborated upon in Rule 147), and certain small issues (Regulation A offerings and those made in compliance with Rule 504 of Regulation D).

The Future of the 1933 Act

After the first 25 years of experience with the 1933 Act, two observers could write that "[t]he controversies over fundamental concepts which were prevalent in the 30's are now almost forgotten, and such disagreements as now arise between the SEC and the industry are mostly over matters of detail and

---

93. SEC No-action Letter, *Hong Kong Telephone Company Limited and Hong Kong Telecommunications Limited* (February 12, 1988). *See also* SEC No-action Letter, *Pegasus Gold Ltd.* (available August 20, 1984).

94. *See* SEC No-action Letter, *Jet Florida Systems, Inc.* (available January 12, 1987).

technique."[95] It is rare to find such complacency as we approach the end of the century.

The last 20 years alone have seen developments that would have astounded the drafters of the 1933 and 1934 Acts. These developments, which have had a profound effect on the way securities are distributed, include the following:

–   a great expansion of publicly-held companies' periodic disclosure obligations under the 1934 Act;

–   progress in technology and communications that has revolutionized the dissemination and retrieval of information about reporting companies;

–   drastic changes in the SEC's administration of registration procedures under the 1933 Act, particularly in regard to the "integrated disclosure system" and shelf registration;

–   unprecedented institutionalization and globalization of the securities markets; and

–   radical changes in the techniques and economics of the distribution of securities.

In March 1996 the SEC published a report of the Task Force on Disclosure Simplification (the "Task Force Report"), and in July 1996 it published a report of the Advisory Committee on the Capital Formation and Regulatory Processes. These reports provided part of the basis for the SEC's publication in July 1996 of its concept release on Securities Act Concepts and Their Effects on Capital Formation.[96]

The concept release raised important questions for issuers, underwriters and investors that evidence an openness on the part of the SEC to reexamining fundamental securities law concepts that have been with us since 1933. Some of these questions were the following:

---

95. T.A. Halleran & J. N. Calderwood, *Effect of Federal Regulation on Distribution of and Trading in Securities,* 28 Geo. Wash. L. Rev. 86, 118 (1959).

96. SEC Release No. 33-7314 (July 25, 1996).

- Whether current SEC procedures permit issuers to have predictable and reliable access to the U.S. public markets in a way that enables them to take advantage of market opportunities.

- To the extent that this is not the case, should the current system be abandoned or is it capable of improvement?

- Whether technology and the "information explosion" have made obsolete any attempt to regulate "offers," and whether there is any longer a basis for a distinction between written and oral communications.

- Whether, assuming that improvements could be made in the current system, public companies would still need to retain the "safety valve" of being able to do private and/or offshore transactions.

- Whether investors are seriously disadvantaged by having to make investment decisions without the benefit of actual or constructive prior receipt of an offering document.

- Whether the role of underwriters as "gatekeepers" has so diminished that their liabilities for issuers' disclosure deficiencies need to be readdressed. For example, are issuers acting in effect as their own gatekeepers and, if so, should they be required or encouraged to adopt "disclosure enhancements" such as management certifications or disclosure committees of outside directors?

Each of the authors of this book has questioned the continuing need for 1933 Act registration for reporting companies.[97] As radical as such a proposal may have appeared at one time, it may no longer be radical enough. Elimination of 1933 Act registration for reporting companies—or even mandated 1933 Act registration for all their transactions, as contemplated by the Advisory Committee's proposal for "company registration"—

---

97. E.g., Joseph McLaughlin, *1933 Act's Registration Provisions: Is Time Ripe for Repealing Them?*, Nat'l L.J., August 18, 1986.

would still preserve too many restrictions for too many issuers and transactions.

The SEC should continue, of course, to require that mandated information be available to public investors. At the same time, it should step up its review of public companies' periodic filings. SEC administrative sanctions and the private antifraud remedies should also continue to apply to information on which investors rely in making investment decisions. But in the midst of what the current SEC chairman has called the "age of information," it is simply unrealistic for the SEC to continue to base its regulatory approach on a philosophy that regards information with fear and suspicion. It is time for the SEC to use its new exemptive authority under the Improvements Act to relax the 1933 Act's stranglehold on the timing and content of securities-related information and the means by which it is distributed.

Chapter 2

SYNDICATE PROCEDURES AND UNDERWRITING DOCUMENTS

Apart from the registration statement, the basic documents governing underwritten offerings of securities are the agreement among underwriters, which establishes the relationship among the managing underwriter, the co-managers (if any) and the other members of the underwriting syndicate, and governs the mechanics of the distribution; the underwriting agreement (or purchase agreement, as it is frequently called), in which the underwriters commit to purchase the securities from the issuing corporation or the selling securityholders; and the selected dealers agreement, in which dealers that are not members of the syndicate (the selling group) agree to certain provisions relating to the distribution.

Each of the major investment banking firms has its own form of underwriting documents, but basic similarities have developed over the years, reflecting the "street" practices that have evolved in the management of underwriting syndicates. In addition, most firms have a master agreement among underwriters that applies to all transactions that they lead-manage and that is pre-signed by other firms likely to participate in their deals.

If the securities are underwritten by a small group of managers, there may be no agreement among underwriters or only a short memorandum of understanding. In that case, the only underwriting documents will be the underwriting agreement and the selected dealers agreement (if any). If the offering is being made on an agency or "best efforts" basis, as is frequently the case with more speculative issues and with large limited partnership offerings, then an agency agreement, rather than a purchase agreement, will be entered into between the issuer and the securities firm handling the offering.[1] Continuous medium-term note programs may also be handled on an agency basis (see Chapter 8). If there are separate U.S. and international underwriting syndicates, the efforts of the two groups may be the subject of an Intersyndicate Agreement (see Chapter 9). For traditional syndicated fixed price offerings, however, the structural framework for the distribution is provided by the agreement among underwriters, the underwriting agreement and the selected dealers agreement.

Underwriting Syndicates

Traditionally, the standard method of distributing securities has been through a syndicate of investment banking firms that agree, on a firm commitment basis, to purchase the securities at a discount from the public offering price and resell them to investors. In the weeks preceding the adoption of Rule 415, the investment banking community became concerned as to the potential effect of shelf registrations on traditional syndicate practices. Morgan Stanley & Co. Incorporated stated in a letter to the SEC, dated February 2, 1982, that the proposed rule "could substantially impair the process by which most of the long-term private capital has been raised in this century—fixed price

---

1. If a best efforts underwriting is made on an "all-or-none" basis, or on any other basis that contemplates that payment is not to be made to the person on whose behalf the distribution is being made until some further event or contingency occurs, Rule 15c2-4 under the 1934 Act requires that the funds received by the broker-dealer from investors be placed in an escrow account with a bank. Rule 10b-9 under the 1934 Act prohibits the description of an offering as being on an "all-or-none" or similar basis unless the offering contemplates a prompt refund in the event that specified conditions are not met.

public offerings by syndicates of securities firms."[2] The financial press joined in the controversy. A February 12, 1982 article in *The Wall Street Journal* commented:

> Now it appears that the gentlemanly art of syndication may be supplanted by a sort of financial roller derby in which gutsy Wall Street risk-takers bid for big blocks of new securities on a moment's notice. In lieu of the old mystique will be a sharpshooter's sense of timing and a heightened readiness to commit huge amounts of capital quickly.[3]

The frequent use of shelf registration statements, principally those covering debt securities of major issuers that finance on a regular basis, has resulted in an increase in "bought deals" in which a small group of firms, in competition with other firms bidding for the securities, will take down an entire tranche for its own account without first attempting to market the securities to investors. But traditional underwriting syndicates continue to be used to distribute initial public offerings ("IPOs") and even many common stock offerings by "seasoned" issuers.

• *Pre-1933 Act Procedures*

According to Professor Louis Loss, Jay Cooke is credited with first using the syndicate method of distribution in an 1870 underwriting of Pennsylvania Railroad bonds.[4] The most common method of distribution during the latter part of the 19th century was for issuers to offer their securities directly to potential investors and for underwriters to stand by with a commitment to purchase any securities that were not subscribed for as a result of the issuer's efforts. Syndicate practices evolved

---

2. *See also* letter, dated January 7, 1982, from Goldman, Sachs & Co. to SEC.

3. T. Carrington, "Proposed SEC Rule on New Financings May Kill Gentlemanly Art of Syndication," at 8.

4. L. Loss & J. Seligman, *Securities Regulation* 325 (3d ed. 1989), citing Larson, *Jay Cooke* 314 (1936) [hereinafter *Loss & Seligman,* preceded by applicable volume number].

during the latter part of the 19th century and the early years of this century as corporations sought to raise the vast amounts of capital that were required to build the country's railroads and to finance the growth of American industry.[5] By the turn of the century, as the banking houses gained prestige, it became common for them to purchase issues and to be responsible for their sale, rather than merely agreeing to purchase the securities should the issuer not succeed in marketing them itself.[6] The increase in the size of financings strained the risk-bearing capacity of the individual investment banking firms. Thus, it became necessary for firms to join together in syndicates to share the underwriting risk.

Some of the early syndicate arrangements grew out of friendships and close business relationships, as charmingly described by Judge Medina in his opinion in the government's antitrust case against the major investment banking firms:

When the opportunity arose in the year 1906 for Goldman, Sachs & Co. to underwrite the financing of United Cigar Manufacturers, it was unable to undertake the entire commitment alone, and could not get the additional funds which it needed to underwrite from commercial banks or other underwriters, as they would not at that time underwrite this type of securities. Henry Goldman prevailed upon his friend Philip Lehman of Lehman Brothers to divert some of his capital from the commodity business and to take a share in the underwriting. The result was that the two firms, Goldman, Sachs & Co. and Lehman Brothers, became partners in the underwriting of the financing of United Cigar Manufacturers. When the opportunity arose in that same year for Goldman, Sachs & Co. to underwrite the financing of Sears, Roebuck & Co., it was perfectly natural for it again to turn to Lehman Brothers for assistance, and the two firms became partners in that enterprise. Thus it was

5. *See* V. P. Corosso, *Investment Banking in America* (Harv. U. Press 1970), Ch. 3 "The Development of the Syndicate to 1914."
6. *Id.* at 53.

through this oral arrangement between two friends, Henry Goldman and Philip Lehman, through this informal partnership, that Goldman, Sachs & Co. was able to obtain the capital which it needed to underwrite these two security issues in the year 1906. Without such capital, it would have been unable to enter the business of underwriting securities. The events which occurred in the year 1906 set the pattern for subsequent financings which Goldman, Sachs & Co. underwrote prior to the First World War. In the period from the year 1906 to the year 1917, although Goldman, Sachs & Co. occasionally underwrote financings with other partners, notably Kleinwort Sons & Co., merchant bankers of London, its principal partner was Lehman Brothers.[7]

Judge Medina went on to describe syndication practices during the period prior to the First World War.[8] During this period, it was common for an investment banking firm, the "originating banker" or "house of issue," to purchase an entire issue of securities directly from the issuer and to immediately resell them at a "step-up" in price to a relatively small number of firms comprising the so-called "purchase syndicate," which would in effect sub-underwrite the risk. The originating banker would be one of the members and the manager of the purchase syndicate. As American businesses grew in size and required greater amounts of capital, it became customary to form a second group, more numerous than the purchase syndicate, to further share the risk. The purchase syndicate would sell the securities at a further step-up in price to this larger group known as the "banking syndicate." The originating banker and the other firms that were members of the purchase syndicate

---

7. Corrected opinion of Harold R. Medina in *United States v. Morgan* at 19–20 (filed February 4, 1954) [hereinafter Medina Opinion]. The original opinion is reported at 118 F. Supp. 621 (S.D.N.Y. 1953).

8. *Id.* at 25. Much of Judge Medina's description is based on the historical account of investment banking practices set forth in *National Association of Securities Dealers, Inc.*, 19 S.E.C. 424 (1945).

usually became members of the banking syndicate, and the originating banker acted as its manager.

In the period following the First World War, it became customary to form an additional group called the "selling syndicate."[9] Initially, the members of a selling syndicate performed an underwriting function in that they assumed the obligation to purchase pro-rata any securities which the members of the selling syndicate were unable to sell. This was known as the "unlimited liability selling syndicate." Subsequently, a second type of syndicate developed, which was known as the "limited liability selling syndicate," in which the obligation of each member was limited to the amount of its commitment. When it distributed that amount, it was relieved of further liability. Out of the limited liability selling syndicate evolved the "selling group," in which the financial liability of each member was restricted to selling or taking up the amount of securities for which it subscribed. This arrangement is similar to the way that selected dealers operate today.

- *Post-1933 Act Procedures*

The Revenue Act of 1932 for the first time imposed a tax on the transfer of bonds. It also increased the amount of the stock transfer tax. The amendments to the 1933 Act adopted in 1934 limited an underwriter's liability to the offering price of the securities underwritten by it. Thus, the old purchase and banking syndicates with successive sales at increasing prices disappeared as a matter of economic necessity. Instead, it became the practice to have a single underwriting syndicate and for each underwriter to be in privity of contract with the issuer. Each would severally agree to purchase from the issuer a specified amount of securities.[10] This is the structure used today.

Where securities are distributed through a syndicate of investment banking firms, one or more firms will be designated by the issuer as the managing or lead underwriter or underwriters. If there are co-managers, one will be designated as the

---

9. Medina Opinion, *supra* note 7, at 30.

10. *Id.* at 41. *See also* P. P. Gourrich, *Investment Banking Methods Prior to and Since the Securities Act of 1933*, 4 Law & Contemp. Probs. 44 (1937).

"book-running" manager and its name will usually appear first on the left-hand side of the prospectus and in the same position on the tombstone advertisement. There generally is no written agreement between or among the managers as such other than the agreement among underwriters. The prospectus and other documents are printed in the distinctive type-style of the book-running manager, and that firm usually selects counsel for the underwriters. As shelf registration has evolved, underwriters' counsel may in effect be named by the issuer. However selected, underwriters' counsel's responsibility is to represent the entire syndicate.

The size of underwriting syndicates grew in the years following the Second World War. The 1956 initial public offering of 10.2 million shares of Ford Motor Company stock, valued at almost $660 million, was underwritten by a syndicate of 722 investment banking houses. This was the largest public stock offering up to that time, and the size of the syndicate set a record. Throughout the 1960s and 1970s, it was standard practice for an average size common stock offering to be underwritten by a syndicate of between 50 and 100 underwriters. Since the early 1980s, syndicates have become smaller, and it has become increasingly common for a single investment banking firm to underwrite an entire issue without forming a syndicate or for the underwriting group to be limited to two or three firms that will appear on the cover page of the prospectus as managing underwriters. These are referred to as "one-handed" or "two- or three-handed" deals.

The Agreement Among Underwriters

The agreement among underwriters (the "AAU") is essentially a power-of-attorney authorizing the managing underwriter to enter into an underwriting agreement with the issuer or the selling securityholders and to otherwise manage the distribution of the securities. The AAU will be addressed to the co-managers, if there is more than one, unless the book-running manager's master AAU is relied upon. The manager's authority is broad and sweeping, and it is considered bad form for a syndicate member to question the decisions of the firm running the deal.

Prior to the early 1970s, it was the practice for officers or partners of the various syndicate members to meet at the office of the book-running manager on the morning that the registration statement was scheduled to become effective for the purpose of reviewing and signing the AAU. Snowstorms and train delays could result in panic, for the price amendment to the registration statement could not be filed until all of the underwriters had signed the AAU. It had long been the practice for regional firms to provide the managing underwriter with powers-of-attorney authorizing it to sign the AAU on their behalf. The practice then evolved for all members of the syndicate, even those with a local office, to provide the book-running manager with written authority to sign the AAU on their behalf. Early morning meetings to sign the AAU were thus eliminated.

As underwriting procedures further evolved, many of the leading investment banking firms developed master AAUs, which were broadly structured to govern any and all future underwritten offerings managed by them. The firms distributed their master AAUs to the members of the underwriting community, and those that expected to participate in syndicates managed by them signed and returned to them their master AAUs. Thereafter, for a specific transaction, the managing underwriter would send by telex or otherwise to the prospective syndicate members an invitation containing information regarding the principal terms of the securities to be offered, the expected offering date and the amount of the underwriter's proposed underwriting participation. Acceptance of the invitation could be made orally or by telex, and the acceptance would remain in effect unless withdrawn in writing prior to a time specified in the invitation. In one or more subsequent communications, the underwriter would be informed of the amount of securities that would be allocated to it for purposes of resale, the initial public offering price, the interest or dividend rate in the case of fixed income securities, the conversion price of any convertible securities, the underwriting discount, the management fee, the selling concession and the reallowance. The master AAU would be deemed supplemented by these communications.

• *Underwriters' Questionnaire*

A number of disclosure and other aspects of an underwritten offering depend upon the accuracy of information concerning the underwriters. These include the existence of any material relationships between the issuer and any underwriter (Item 508(a) of Regulation S-K), any undisclosed arrangements to overallot or stabilize the securities being offered, any undisclosed discounts or commissions or other arrangements that might present NASD problems, and any relationships (in the case of debt offerings) that might present problems under the Trust Indenture Act of 1939. These items are the subject of an Underwriters' Questionnaire that is customarily made part of a master AAU and that may be supplemented by the invitation. An underwriter is obligated to note any exceptions in writing prior to the time specified in the invitation.

• *Manager's Authority*

Whether a separate AAU is used for a particular transaction or the transaction is governed by a master AAU as supplemented by the communications constituting the invitation, the basic terms of the AAU will be the same. First, and most fundamentally, the AAU authorizes the managing underwriter to execute on behalf of the participating underwriters an underwriting agreement with the issuer and any selling securityholders. Where a master AAU is used, it is specified that the underwriting agreement will be in such form as the managing underwriter shall determine. Otherwise, the underwriting agreement will be attached as an exhibit to the AAU. The AAU authorizes the manager to take such action as it deems necessary to carry out the underwriting agreement and the purchase, sale and distribution of the securities. The manager is authorized to exercise any overallotment option to the extent that it deems advisable. The manager should also be authorized to agree to any waiver or modification of any provision in the underwriting agreement (subject to limitations on the amount by which an underwriter's commitment may be increased). If, for example, a condition to the underwriters' obligations cannot be satisfied at the closing, then the managing underwriter should be in a position to waive the condition, whether or not it considers it to be material.

• *Price Maintenance*

The AAU will contain an agreement on the part of the underwriters that, when the securities are released for sale by the managing underwriter, they will offer to the public, in conformity with the terms of offering set forth in the prospectus, such of the securities as are not reserved for sale to selected dealers and others. Of the offering terms, the most important is the public offering price specified on the cover page of the prospectus. Most underwritten offerings are fixed price offerings in which the underwriters are obligated to offer the securities to the public at the specified public offering price. There is no legal requirement that offerings be conducted in this manner, but where there is a syndicate, it would be unwieldy to provide for other than a fixed price offering.

In the environment of Rule 415, there have been instances of public offerings at varying prices based on the market or on terms negotiated with individual purchasers. In some cases, the underwriter has provided a volume discount to purchasers of a large amount of the securities being offered. If the offering is structured as a fixed price offering, however, the manager will control the price and will have the sole authority to lower the price if it finds it necessary to do so. Where there is a fixed price offering, the rules of the NASD prohibit discounts or selling concessions to nonmembers (see Chapter 6).

• *Selling Allocations*

As permitted by the AAU, the syndicate manager will determine the amount of securities that will be available for sale by each of the underwriters. It has absolute discretion in this respect. It will reserve some of the securities for sale to selected dealers that are not members of the underwriting syndicate and to institutional investors that prefer to deal directly with the syndicate, rather than with individual underwriters or dealers. These securities are held in a syndicate account known as the "pot."

The amount of securities that will be allotted to any particular underwriter for sale to its customers will depend upon its distribution power. AAUs speak in terms of securities "retained" by an underwriter for direct sale and those "reserved" for sale to selected dealers and others. In the actual operation of a syndicate, a substantial portion of the underwritten securities will be allocated according to the expectations or tacit understandings of the participating firms, while the remainder will be allocated on the basis of customer orders. As discussed below, underwriters and dealers may receive selling credit for securities purchased by institutions out of the pot to the extent that the institution designates.

In the real world, the managers will sell most of the issue. Co-managers will compete with each other to demonstrate to the issuer that it was principally through their efforts that the offering was a success, always with a view to getting "the books" on the next deal.

• *Overallotment and Stabilization*

The AAU will authorize the managing underwriter to overallot for the account of the syndicate, i.e., to create a syndicate short position by accepting orders for more securities than are to be sold.[11] It will authorize the manager to effect stabilizing bids and purchases for the account of the syndicate (see Chapter 4). Overallotments and stabilizing purchases are made for the accounts of the underwriters as nearly as practicable in proportion to their respective underwriting commitments. The AAU will provide that at the close of business on any day an underwriter's net commitment, either for long or short account, resulting from overallotments and stabilizing purchases may not exceed a specified percentage, usually 15% or 20%, of its underwriting commitment.

---

11. The SEC at one time took the position that it was inappropriate to overallot in an offering made on a best efforts basis. There does not appear to be a current staff position on the matter.

Overallotments are made to provide for purchasers who renege on their commitments but, more importantly, to create buying power in the after-market. These short sales may be covered through stabilization while the distribution is still in process. After completion of the distribution, the syndicate short position may be covered through open market purchases or the exercise of the overallotment option, i.e., the option granted to the underwriters by the issuer or the selling securityholders allowing them to purchase during a specified period (usually 30 days) after the offering of additional securities solely for the purpose of covering overallotments.[12]

The SEC has long recognized the purpose of overallotments. In a release making public an opinion of the Director of the SEC's Trading and Exchange Division, discussing the ef-

---

12. The overallotment option is also called the "Green Shoe" option, or simply "the shoe," because it was first used in connection with a secondary offering of shares of common stock of The Green Shoe Manufacturing Company, the Boston-based manufacturer of Stride Rite shoes, not green shoes for leprechauns as some have supposed. The offering was made under a prospectus dated February 27, 1963, and the managing underwriter was Paine, Webber, Jackson & Curtis. The prospectus stated that of the 170,500 shares being offered, 155,000 shares were being purchased from certain shareholders of the company, and that the underwriters had a non-transferable option to purchase from such shareholders at the same price all or part of the remaining 15,500 shares covered by the prospectus. Contrary to current practice, the full 170,500 shares, including the option shares, were set forth at the top of the cover page of the prospectus. It was provided that the option would have to be exercised within 30 days of the date of the prospectus, but that it could be extended for an additional 30 days by the selling shareholders. In the original filing, no mention was made of the purpose of the option. In its letter of comments on the registration statement, the SEC said, "The discussion in the initial paragraph [of the cover page] of the 15,500 shares non-transferable option held by the underwriters should be followed by a reference to the section 'Underwriting' herein, which section should be expanded to include a statement of the conditions under which such option may be exercised." The "Underwriting" section in the final prospectus contained the statement, "It is the intention of the Underwriters to exercise this option only for the purpose of covering any short position which may be incurred in the initial distribution."

fect of the anti-manipulative provisions of the securities laws on the activities of a manager of an underwriting syndicate, the statement is made:

> In considering the question which you have raised, we may start with the premise that a syndicate overallotment is customarily made for the purpose of facilitating the orderly distribution of the offered securities by creating buying power which can be used for the purpose of supporting the market price.[13]

There is no legal requirement that an underwriter's net commitment be limited to a certain percentage of the offering. This is merely a contractual provision designed to limit the risks of the members of the syndicate. The size of the Green Shoe option, however, is limited by the rules of the NASD to 15% of the firm commitment securities.[14] The Green Shoe option is designed to protect the underwriters against loss if they overallot and the price of the securities rises in the after-market. Rather than purchasing securities in the open market to cover overallotments, the managing underwriter can exercise the Green Shoe option and cover overallotments by purchasing from the issuer or the selling securityholders additional securities at the original public offering price less the underwriting discount.

In recent years, the practice has been to overallot in an amount that substantially exceeds the Green Shoe option. The reason for this is to build a large short position that can be used to purchase securities sold into the syndicate bid by "flippers," i.e., hedge funds and other speculators who buy in underwritings not as investors but to turn a quick profit. This is an extremely serious problem that underwriters continually strive to deal with. To permit larger short positions, the contractual limitation on net commitments has tended to increase, and whatever limitation is imposed by the AAU has been construed by syndicate managers to be a percentage of the amount of securities offered plus the amount of the overallotment option.

---

13. SEC Release No. 34-3506 (November 16, 1943).
14. Rule 2710(c)(6)(B)(ix).

The securities covered by the Green Shoe option must, of course, be registered under the 1933 Act in order for the underwriters to be able to use them to cover their overallotments. It is therefore customary for the registration statement for the offering to include the full amount of the "shoe." If the option is not exercised in full, the remaining securities can be deregistered by a post-effective amendment, and nothing is lost except the SEC registration fee for those securities. When underwriters began to overallot in an amount substantially in excess of the Green Shoe option, they did so in the full expectation that they would have to repurchase the excess securities in the open market, with all of the risk that that entails. (One issuer, Borden Chemicals and Plastics Limited Partnership, did manage in connection with a 1987 offering to persuade the SEC staff that it should be permitted to register additional securities under a separate registration statement for the purpose of issuing additional securities to the underwriters to enable them to cover excess overallotments. It is not believed that other issuers have been permitted to do this.)

As discussed in Chapter 4, transactions for the purpose of reducing a syndicate short position are now the subject of disclosure and recordkeeping obligations.

• Control of the Syndicate

The manager will monitor closely the performance of the syndicate members in selling the securities allotted to them. In SEC Release No. 34-3506,[15] the point was made that the failure of a syndicate manager to inform himself with respect to the status of a distribution does not excuse his failure to assure compliance with the anti-manipulative provisions of the law. Indeed, the manager has an obligation to be in a position to know whether the individual underwriters or selling group members have securities remaining unsold and to require them to make available unsold securities to permit the extinguishment or reduction of the syndicate short position. The Release states:

---

15. *Supra* note 13.

In view of the foregoing, it would seem incumbent upon the manager to insure his ability to obtain all necessary information concerning the status of the distribution. In this connection, it would seem appropriate for the [AAU] to contain provisions stating, in effect, that the manager, upon request, shall be informed of the amount of the offered securities which the individual underwriters have remaining unsold. Moreover, it would also seem appropriate for the [AAU] to contain provisions requiring the individual underwriters, upon request of the manager, to deliver to him unsold securities, at or below the offering price, for the purpose of reducing the syndicate short position.

To this end, and for practical business reasons, the AAU will require each underwriter to advise the manager on its request of the amount of the underwriter's securities that remains unsold. The AAU will also require the underwriter to release to the manager upon its request all or any part of such unsold securities.

• *Trading Restrictions*

In 1943, prior to the adoption of Rule 10b-6 (since superseded by Regulation M, as discussed in Chapter 4), the Director of the SEC's Trading and Exchange Division expressed the opinion that an underwriter may not trade in securities of a class that are the subject of a distribution, through a trading department or otherwise, so long as the syndicate agreement remains in effect.[16] It then became the practice to include trading restrictions in AAUs. These restrictions are discussed in Chapter 4.

• *Penalty Bids*

A failure to place IPO securities with bona fide investors, with resulting resales into the syndicate bid, is not a new problem. AAUs have traditionally provided that, in recognition of the importance of distributing IPO securities to bona fide investors, if any securities sold by an underwriter are purchased by the syndicate in the open market or otherwise during the distri-

---

16. SEC Release No. 34-3505 (November 16, 1943).

bution period, that underwriter must repurchase the securities at the syndicate's cost, or its account will be charged with an amount not in excess of the concession to selected dealers. The theory is that under these circumstances the underwriter has not earned the selling concession.

This so-called "penalty" clause has been extremely difficult to police. The difficulty increased with the use of DTC to make deliveries and to settle syndicate accounts. Some underwriting firms resorted to physical delivery in order to enhance their ability to police the penalty clause. Since physical delivery is hardly consistent with the desire of the SEC and other regulators to promote the use of securities depositories, DTC has been working with the industry to develop an "Initial Public Offering Tracking System." The system would be activated upon request of a managing underwriter and would require DTC participants, for a specified period of time, to identify the seller of underwritten securities and permit DTC to report this information to the managing underwriter. After the availability of the system, new issues would be deemed to be "depository eligible" upon commencement of trading.

A syndicate bid pursuant to the penalty clause of an AAU is known as a "penalty bid." As discussed in Chapter 4, such bids are now the subject of disclosure and recordkeeping obligations.

• *Components of the Spread*

There are three components of the underwriting spread, i.e., the gross spread between the initial public offering price and the price paid by the underwriters for the securities being underwritten. These are the management component and the selling component, which are specified in the AAU, and the remainder which is called the underwriting component. Approximately 20% of the spread is paid by the syndicate members to the managing underwriter as compensation for its services in the management of the distribution. It is paid out of the spread, and not by the issuer or selling securityholders, to avoid a claim that the manager had received a benefit not shared by all other underwriters similarly situated, thus precluding it from having the benefit of the hold-down provision in Section 11(e) of the 1933 Act (see Chapter 5). The AAU does not specify how the management fee is to be split among the co-managers. The allocation of this fee is often a matter of intense dispute among the managing underwriters. The issuer sometimes will be called in as a mediator, a role that issuers universally resent.

The selling portion of the spread, known as the "selling concession," is the amount paid to dealers for actually selling the securities. As a rule of thumb, the selling concession will be 60% of the gross spread, although the amount may vary depending on how difficult it is to sell the securities. This amount is retained by an underwriter in respect of securities that it actually sells to its own customers. Institutions that purchase securities directly from the syndicate will designate the underwriters and other dealers that are to receive selling concession credit for the securities that they purchase. The term used in this context is "designated orders."

Money managers and institutions designate dealers to receive credit for securities purchased in underwritten offerings in order to compensate them for providing research services. The rules of the NASD governing this practice are discussed in Chapter 6. Some syndicate managers complain that institutions misuse designated orders. They will enter an order solely for the purpose of providing a selling concession to a dealer to whom they are obligated and will immediately resell the securities, thereby disrupting the distribution.

Dealers who purchase securities at the public offering price less the selling concession may resell them to other dealers at the public offering price less a so-called "reallowance," perhaps 25% of the selling concession (or as much as 50% on some debt transactions). Underwriters may do the same with respect to their retained securities. Some AAUs permit resales to reallowance dealers only with the specific consent of the manager, thus permitting the manager to retain tighter control of the distribution process.[17]

---

17. NASD Rule 2770 provides:

Selling syndicate agreements or selling group agreements shall set forth the price at which the securities are to be sold to the public or the formula by which such price can be ascertained, and shall state clearly to whom and under what circumstances concessions, if any, may be allowed.

The remaining portion of the spread, roughly 20% depending upon the size of the selling concession, theoretically is the compensation that the underwriters earn for committing their capital and taking an underwriting risk. Syndicate expenses, however, are paid out of this portion of the spread. Thus, the fee charged by underwriters' counsel, the cost of the tombstone advertisement, road show expenses, and the like must be paid before an underwriter will be compensated for its underwriting risk. In some cases, the lion's share of the underwriting portion of the spread will go to the payment of expenses. In some cases, expenses may exceed that portion of the spread.

- *Payment and Delivery*

The AAU will provide that payment for the securities must be made on such date as the manager specifies, usually the morning of the closing date. The closing usually is scheduled for the third or fourth business day after the date of the initial public offering to correspond to the normal settlement period between dealers and their customers. The amount that each underwriter agrees to pay to the manager is the public offering price less the selling concession, not the public offering price less the underwriting discount. The effect of this is that an underwriter will not receive its share of the underwriting portion of the spread until final settlement of its account. This makes it unnecessary, in most cases, for the manager to call upon the underwriters to pay their share of the syndicate expenses. These expenses will simply be deducted from the final payment.

The AAU will provide that delivery of securities retained by an underwriter for direct sale will be made to it as soon as practicable after receipt of the securities at the closing. Settlement and delivery will be effected through the facilities of DTC unless, as mentioned above, the manager opts for physical delivery to facilitate enforcement of the penalty clause.

- *Authority to Borrow*

The AAU authorizes the manager to advance its own funds for the accounts of the underwriters, charging current interest rates, or to arrange loans for their account, as the manager deems necessary or advisable for the purchase, carrying, sale and distribution of the securities. The manager is authorized to execute any notes or other instruments required in connection therewith and, in this connection, to hold or pledge the securities that the underwriters have agreed to purchase.

- *NASD Provisions*

To be a member of an underwriting syndicate, a securities firm must be a member in good standing of the NASD or a dealer with its principal place of business outside of the United States and not registered under the 1934 Act that agrees to make no sales within the United States (except that it may participate in syndicate sales to selected dealers and others) and to comply with certain NASD requirements (see Chapter 6). Each of the underwriters will make such a representation in the AAU. In the case of a fixed price offering, a selling concession may be allowed only to those dealers who are NASD members or foreign dealers who conform to the NASD requirements referred to above. The AAU will so limit the authority of the manager in making sales to selected dealers.

- *Claims Against Underwriters*

The AAU will contain a provision relating to the assertion of claims, litigation or governmental proceedings involving the syndicate arising out of alleged misstatements or omissions in the registration statement or prospectus. This provision will stipulate that any such claims may be settled by the manager, usually with the approval of a majority in interest of the underwriters, and that each underwriter will pay its proportionate share (based on its underwriting commitment) of all expenses, including legal fees, incurred in investigating and defending against the claim as well as its proportionate share of the aggregate liability incurred by all underwriters with respect to the claim. The manager is authorized to retain counsel for the underwriters, but any underwriter may retain separate counsel at its own expense.

One of the main reasons for this provision is that litigation based on alleged misstatements or omissions in a registration statement or prospectus will often be instituted against the manager without naming the entire underwriting syndicate. This provision in the AAU provides in effect that all of the underwriters will share in the expenses and liabilities even if they are not actually named in the complaint.[18]

• *Miscellaneous Provisions*

The AAU will contain a number of representations by members of the underwriting syndicate, such as their familiarity with the prospectus delivery requirements of the securities laws and their compliance with the net capital rule.[19] It will contain a provision to the effect that each underwriter will indemnify each other underwriter to the extent that and on the terms upon which the underwriters indemnify the issuer and other specified persons pursuant to the underwriting agreement. It will make reference to the obligations of the underwriters to increase their underwriting commitments to the limited extent provided in the underwriting agreement in the event of default by one or more of the underwriters. It will outline the mechanism for the settlement of syndicate accounts.

• *Termination*

The limitations in the AAU on the price at which the securities may be sold, the time that the penalty clause will remain in operation, authorization to stabilize and overallot, and trading restrictions will terminate by the terms of the AAU at a specified time (perhaps 45 days) after the commencement of the offering. Any or all of these provisions may be terminated at any time by the manager by notice to the underwriters, and in practice, price and trading restrictions often will be terminated within hours after the offering. It is unusual, except in a weak market, for these restrictions to continue in effect for more than a few days.

One of the principal reasons for specifying an automatic termination date is to avoid a charge that the price maintenance provisions of the AAU constitute a violation of the Sherman Act. This issue was considered by the SEC in reviewing an

---

18. For background on this type of clause, *see* J. C. Freund & H. S. Hacker, *Cutting Up the Humble Pie: A Practical Approach to Apportioning Litigation Risks Among Underwriters,* 48 St. John's L. Rev. 461 (1974).

19. Rule 15c3-1 under the 1934 Act.

NASD disciplinary proceeding decision which found that certain underwriters and dealers had violated the NASD's *Rules of Fair Practice* when they failed to comply with the price maintenance agreement in a 1939 underwriting of $38 million of first mortgage bonds of Public Service Company of Indiana managed by Halsey, Stuart & Co., Inc.[20] At the close of the hearing before the hearing examiner, the Antitrust Division of the Department of Justice intervened and filed a brief attacking the price maintenance, penalty, stabilization, uniform concession and reallowance and other clauses of the AAU as unlawful *per se* under the Sherman Act. The same position was taken by counsel for the Trading and Exchange Division of the SEC. In effect, this constituted an antitrust attack on the fixed price method of distributing securities.

The SEC found on technical grounds that the NASD did not have power to impose sanctions in this instance, but nevertheless went on to discuss the antitrust implications of fixed price offerings. The SEC observed that "because of the nature of the securities markets, price maintenance as to one security during a relatively short period of distribution may be distinguished from schemes affecting the long-term marketing of consumers' goods."[21] It concluded that agreements containing provisions for a fixed offering price, price maintenance, and stabilization are not *per se* unlawful, but, like many other contracts, may be entered into and performed under circumstances that amount to an unlawful suppression of competition. The SEC stated that among the factors to be taken into account in determining the lawfulness of this type of distribution are "the size of the group in relation to the size of the issue, the suppression of competition in bidding or negotiating for the business, and the duration of a syndicate dictated by the manager and major underwriters."[22] Judge Medina discussed this case at length in his opinion in the investment banking antitrust case, and in general agreed with the SEC's conclusions.[23]

------

20. *National Association of Securities Dealers, Inc.,* 19 S.E.C. 424 (1945).
21. *Id.* at 451.
22. *Id.* at 464.
23. Medina Opinion, *supra* note 7, at 149.

The Underwriting Agreement

The underwriting agreement, or purchase agreement, is the document pursuant to which the underwriters commit to purchase at a specified price, or at a price to be determined, the securities that are the subject of the underwriting. In addition to the basic purchase and sale commitment, the underwriting agreement will contain representations and warranties, covenants, conditions, indemnification provisions, and other terms governing the relationship between the issuer or the selling securityholders and the underwriters.

• *Several Commitments*

It is important to note that underwriting commitments are always several, and not joint and several, when they relate to securities other than municipal bonds. Where there is a syndicate, a schedule to the underwriting agreement will set forth the specific number of shares or other securities that each underwriter has committed to purchase. Each underwriter also will agree to purchase its proportionate share of any securities to be purchased pursuant to the exercise of the overallotment option. One reason why underwriting commitments are several is to limit the amount of the charge against the underwriters' net capital. The more important reason is to assure the availability of the hold-down provision in Section 11(e) of the 1933 Act, which limits an underwriter's liability to the total price at which the securities underwritten by it and distributed to the public are offered to the public. If all underwriters were jointly liable for the full underwritten amount, the hold-down provision would not be effective. To limit the liability of underwriters, joint and several commitments were abandoned after the hold-down provision was enacted in 1934.[24] Joint commitments are still used in underwriting municipal bonds, which are not subject to the 1933 Act.

• *Timing and Risk*

In a firm commitment underwriting, the underwriting agreement is not entered into until immediately before the final

---

24. *Id.* at 42.

amendment to the registration statement is filed (or after it is filed in the case of some Rule 430A filings). While some underwriters will enter into agreements in principle or letters of intent early in the registration process, they are not ordinarily intended to be binding agreements, except to the extent that they provide for the reimbursement of underwriters' expenses if the transaction does not go forward. Thus, the underwriters are not committed until the very last minute. By this time, except in the case of a bought deal taken off the shelf, they will have completed their marketing efforts and will have reasonable assurances that they will be able to sell the securities to be underwritten and to build an acceptable short position. If, at the time of pricing, the underwriters are not comfortable that all of the securities can be sold, the size of the transaction may be cut back or the underwriting may be postponed. Although underwriters do run risks and commit their capital, the risk is tempered by the timing of their final commitment and their knowledge of how well the deal has been accepted in the marketplace (the "size of the book") at the time that they do commit.

• *Rule 430A*

The form of the underwriting agreement will depend upon whether the issuer and the managing underwriter have elected to rely upon Rule 430A under the 1933 Act.[25] Rule 430A permits a registration statement that covers a cash securities offering to become effective without pricing information, provided that the omitted pricing information is included in a supplemented prospectus filed under Rule 424.[26]

Pursuant to Rule 424(b)(1), the prospectus containing the Rule 430A information must be filed no later than the second business day following the earlier of the date the public offering price is determined or the date the prospectus containing the Rule 430A information is first used. Under Rule

---

25. SEC Release No. 33-6714 (May 27, 1987). Rule 430A was originally proposed in SEC Release No. 33-6672 (October 27, 1986).

26. Rule 430A procedures provide the same benefits as so-called "formula pricing," which was used frequently prior to the adoption of the rule.

430A(a)(3), if the supplemented prospectus is not filed within 15 business days after the effectiveness of the registration statement, it must be filed as part of a post-effective amendment.[27] Rule 430A also requires the registration statement to contain an undertaking pursuant to Item 512(i) of Regulation S-K to the effect that, for purposes of determining 1933 Act liability, the omitted information contained in the Rule 424(b) prospectus "shall be deemed to be part of the registration statement as of the time it was declared effective." This is to ensure that such information is subject to liabilities under Section 11.

A decrease in the amount or price of securities offered may be reflected in the Rule 424(b) prospectus—rather than in a post-effective amendment—if the decrease does not materially change the disclosure contained in the registration statement at effectiveness. Under the SEC's Rule 462, adopted with the move to T+3 settlements, an increase in the amount or price of securities offered may also be reflected in the Rule 424(b) prospectus if it does not result in an increase of more than 20% in the maximum aggregate offering price set forth in the registration statement. If the increase requires the registration of additional securities within the 20% limit, this may be accomplished by means of an abbreviated registration statement consisting of a facing page, a statement incorporating by reference the contents of the earlier registration statement relating to the offering, all required consents and opinions, and the signature page. The abbreviated registration statement must be filed prior to the time sales are made and confirmations are sent or given. The abbreviated registration statement will be effective automatically upon filing with the SEC.[28]

---

27. The "pricing" period had been five business days until May 1995, when the SEC adopted various amendments designed to facilitate the new "T+3" standard settlement cycle. If the offering is not priced within 15 business days, a post-effective amendment is required. This may become effective automatically upon filing, however, unless it contains material changes from (or additions to) the prospectus previously filed as part of the effective registration statement.

28. The abbreviated registration statement may be filed with the SEC even when pricing occurs after the SEC's normal business hours. Electronic

• *Representations and Warranties*

Underwriting agreements traditionally contain representations and warranties running from the issuer (and in some cases the selling securityholders) to the several underwriters. Unlike representations and warranties contained in agreements relating to the sale of a business, those contained in underwriting agreements have never, to the knowledge of the authors, been the subject of litigation or otherwise enforced. They are nevertheless customary and in some cases become the subject of fierce negotiations. As discussed in Chapter 5, the real importance of representations and warranties is that they cause the issuer, the managing underwriter, and their counsel to focus upon potential problem areas. The negotiation of representations and warranties can be viewed as a part of the due diligence process.

A basic representation that is included in virtually all underwriting agreements is a representation by the issuer to the effect that, at the time it becomes effective, the registration statement will comply in all material respects with the requirements of the 1933 Act and the regulations thereunder and will not contain an untrue statement of a material fact or omit to state a material fact required to be stated therein or necessary to make the statements therein not misleading and that, at the time the registration statement becomes effective and at the time of closing, the prospectus will not include an untrue statement of a material fact or omit to state a material fact necessary in order to make the statements therein, in the light of the circumstances under which they were made, not misleading. This representation tracks the language of Section 11 of the 1933 Act with respect to the registration statement and the language of Section 12(a)(2) with respect to the prospectus. The representation traditionally will carve out misstatements or omissions made in reliance upon information furnished to the issuer

---

filers may file such registration statements from 5:30 p.m. to 10:00 p.m. by transmitting through EDGAR. Filings after the close of banking hours must be accompanied by a certification that the issuer has arranged for the payment of the additional filing fee.

by the underwriters. For the most part, this is a meaningless exception since the underwriters take responsibility for very little information included in the registration statement.[29] The issuer's representation with respect to the registration statement and prospectus in effect embraces all of the subsequent representations customarily found in underwriting agreements.

If the registration statement incorporates by reference documents filed with the SEC under the 1934 Act, the underwriting agreement will contain a representation with respect to the adequacy and accuracy of these documents. Other representations that frequently will be included in underwriting agreements are those that go to the independence of the accountants certifying the financial statements; the fair presentation in the financial statements of the issuer's financial position and results of operations; and the preparation of the financial statements in accordance with generally accepted accounting principles applied on a consistent basis. Another representation will relate to the absence of any material adverse change in the condition, financial or otherwise, or in the earnings, business affairs or business prospects of the issuer and its subsidiaries considered as one enterprise since the respective dates as of which information is given in the registration statement, as well as the absence since those dates of any material transactions entered into by the issuer other than in the ordinary course of business.

Other representations of a legal nature are frequently included in underwriting agreements, such as those that relate to the due incorporation and good standing of the issuer and its principal subsidiaries and their due qualification as foreign corporations in the states in which this is required; the due authorization of the securities; compliance with material contracts;

---

29. The underwriters will specify in a so-called "blood letter" delivered prior to the closing that they have provided only certain information relating to their intention to reoffer the securities, to stabilize the price of certain securities and to allocate the underwriting discount in a specified manner. All other information in the registration statement is the responsibility of the issuer, including information reflected in the underwriting agreement itself (for which the issuer can justifiably be expected to take responsibility, since it is a party to that agreement).

and the absence of material lawsuits or governmental proceedings, other than those disclosed in the registration statement.

Additional representations may be included depending on the nature of the issuer's business. For example, in the case of a high technology company, it may be appropriate to include a representation with respect to its patents. In the first major class action brought under Section 11, a claim was made that the issuer had failed to disclose that it had been placed on notice that it was allegedly infringing the patent of a competitor.[30] In preparing the registration statement, the issuer had simply forgotten that it had received a letter making this claim. If a representation had been included in the underwriting agreement to the effect that the issuer has not received any notices of patent infringement, then it might have focused upon the problem, and some reference to the claim might have been made in the prospectus.

• *Representations by Selling Securityholders*

Where there are selling securityholders, each of them makes special representations that are not joined in by the issuer. Principally, these representations relate to each seller's authority to enter into the underwriting agreement and its good title to the securities being sold. The most important of these representations is that each of the underwriters will receive good and marketable title to the securities purchased by it, free and clear of any pledge, lien, encumbrance, claim or equity.

Where there are a large number of selling securityholders, it is customary, for administrative purposes, for each of them to enter into a custody agreement and power-of-attorney with the principal selling securityholder or such other person or persons as may be designated. The attorney-in-fact signs the underwriting agreement on behalf of all the sellers. The custodian delivers the stock certificates at the closing. The underwriting agreement will contain representations by the sellers to the effect that these arrangements have been entered into.

These powers-of-attorney are drafted in a way so that it can be argued that they survive the death of the seller. They purport

---

30. *Cherner v. Transitron Electronic Corporation,* 201 F. Supp. 934 (D. Mass. 1962).

to be powers "coupled with an interest." Whether or not they will indeed survive has not been tested.

• *Purchase and Sale; Closing*

The underwriting agreement will specify a price that the underwriters will pay for the securities. This will be the public offering price less the agreed underwriting discount. One exception is where the securities are preferred stock with a fixed par value carrying a dividend calculated to have the public offering price be equal to par. An example would be preferred stock with a par value of $100 per share that will be offered to the public at that price. As a matter of corporate law in certain states, stock may not be issued for a consideration having a value less than its par value.[31] Accordingly, if shares of the preferred stock were issued to the underwriters at $100 per share less the underwriting discount, questions could be raised as to the validity of the issuance of the shares. To avoid this issue, the practice in these circumstances is to have the underwriters buy the preferred stock at par and to compensate them with a separate check covering what is then called their underwriting "commission."

Until the SEC's 1991 revision of its rules under the shortswing profit recapture provisions of Section 16(b) of the 1934 Act, the purchase and sale provisions of an underwriting agreement had to be written in an odd manner if an officer, director or 10% shareholder of a company proposed to sell shares issuable upon the exercise of warrants. Such persons are subject to the shortswing profit recapture provisions of Section 16(b) of the 1934 Act. Under Section 16(b), a person who is the beneficial owner of more than 10% of the equity securities of an issuer or who is a director or an officer of the issuer must repay to the issuer any profit realized by him from any purchase and sale, or any sale and purchase, of any equity security of the issuer within any period of less than six months. Thus, regardless of how long warrants were held, if shares were purchased at the exercise price and immediately resold to underwriters at the current market price less the underwriting discount, the difference between the purchase price and the sale price constituted a profit that was subject to recapture under Section 16(b). To avoid this absurd result, the underwriting agreement had to provide for the sale to the underwriters of the warrants,

---

31. E.g., Delaware General Corporation Law § 153(a).

rather than the underlying shares. The underwriters bought the
warrants at the price that they would otherwise have paid for
the shares, less the exercise price, and exercised the warrants at
the closing. Assuming, as can be expected, that the officer, director or 10% shareholder had held the warrants for more than
six months, the transaction did not come within Section 16(b).
All of this became unnecessary in 1991 when the SEC adopted
Rule 16b-6 to exempt the exercise of a warrant from the operation of Section 16(b).

The underwriting agreement will specify the date and place
of closing. Rule 15c6-1 sets "T+3" as the standard settlement
cycle for most transactions in non-exempted securities, but a
"T+4" cycle is permitted for firm commitment offerings that
are priced after 4:30 p.m. Eastern time. (See Chapter 3 for a
discussion of other exceptions to the T+3 requirement.)

Purchase agreements have traditionally provided for payment
in "next-day" clearing house funds rather than same-day funds.
In early 1996, however, DTC moved to same-day funds settlement, and many underwriters changed their policy accordingly.

• *Delayed Delivery Contracts*

Where non-convertible debt securities or preferred shares are
being underwritten, provision has sometimes been made for the
underwriters to satisfy their commitments by delivering to the issuer at the closing delayed delivery contracts entered into by institutional investors. Under a delayed delivery contract, the investor
will agree to purchase the securities at the public offering price on
a specified date subsequent to the closing. The reason for permitting a portion of the securities to be issued on a delayed basis is to
facilitate their marketing by accommodating institutions that wish
to invest but do not expect to have funds available for investment
until a time some months in the future (e.g., in the next calendar
or fiscal year). It may also be the case that the issuer does not
immediately need all of the proceeds of the offering.

Delayed delivery contracts have been used only rarely in the
recent past. Where they are used, however, the issuer will authorize the underwriters to solicit offers by institutions to enter into
delayed delivery contracts. There will be a contractual limit on the
amount of securities that can be covered by such contracts, and
each contract must be for a specified minimum amount. Each in-

stitution must be approved by the issuer. The issuer will pay the underwriters a commission, equal to the spread, with respect to delayed delivery contracts delivered at the closing.

The contracts will not be subject to any conditions, except that the purchase of the securities not be prohibited under the laws of the jurisdiction to which the purchaser is subject and that the sale of the securities to be purchased by the underwriters have been consummated. The principal amount of securities to be purchased by the underwriters is reduced by the principal amount of securities covered by the delayed delivery contracts. Once the contracts have been delivered, the underwriters will not have any responsibility in respect of their validity or performance.

In 1970, questions were raised by the SEC and the staff of the Federal Reserve Board as to whether the solicitation of delayed delivery contracts by underwriters constituted an arrangement of credit in violation of Regulation T. This came as a total surprise to the securities bar and caused great consternation in the investment banking community. A number of New York City law firms participated in the preparation of a written submission to the Federal Reserve Board to the effect that an issuer should not be viewed as extending credit to an institution when it enters into a delayed delivery contract. The Board responded in a *Federal Reserve Bulletin*[32] to the effect that, while in this type of transaction the issuer may be regarded as extending credit to the institutional purchaser at the time of closing when the obligations of both become fixed, Regulation T as then constituted provided that if a security when purchased is an unissued security, the time required for payment was seven days after the date on which the security is made available by the issuer for delivery to the purchaser. The Board concluded that non-convertible debt and preferred stock subject to delayed delivery contracts should not be regarded as having been issued until delivered to institutional purchasers pursuant to the contracts.[33]

---

32. 1971 Fed. Res. Bull. 127; 12 C.F.R. § 220.123 ¶ 5862.

33. This type of transaction is now governed by § 220.8(b)(1)(ii) of Regulation T.

Regulation T no longer prohibits most "arranging" of credit by a broker-dealer, but the Federal Reserve Board's position on delayed delivery contracts is instructive for purposes of Section 11(d)(1) of the 1934 Act. Section 11(d)(1) prohibits a broker-dealer from extending or arranging credit "on" a security that was part of a new issue in the distribution of which the broker-dealer participated within the past 30 days. Section 11(d)(1) has no application, however, unless the credit is secured by the new issue. If the security that is the subject of a delayed delivery contract is an "unissued" security, the broker-dealer can hardly be said to be extending or arranging credit that is secured by that security.[34]

• *Covenants*

The issuer customarily will covenant with the managing underwriter to notify it of any communications received from the SEC with respect to the registration statement. It will agree not to file any amendment to the registration statement or any supplement to the prospectus to which the managing underwriter or its counsel may reasonably object and that if any event occurs as a result of which it is necessary, in the opinion of counsel for the underwriters, to amend or supplement the prospectus, it will prepare and furnish to the underwriters the requisite amended or supplemented prospectus. Other customary covenants relate to the furnishing of sufficient copies of the prospectus to the underwriters and to filings under state blue sky laws.

---

34. Section 11(d)(1) expressly exempts bona fide delayed delivery contracts that settle within 35 days. The exemption applies, of course, to delayed delivery contracts between a broker-dealer and a customer involving *issued* securities that are executed within 30 days after the completion of the broker-dealer's participation in the distribution. The exemption does not imply that delayed delivery contracts involving *unissued* securities should be limited to 35 days.

Underwriting agreements will obligate the issuer to make generally available to its securityholders, as soon as practicable, an earnings statement (in form complying with the provisions of Rule 158 under the 1933 Act) covering a 12-month period beginning not later than the first day of the fiscal quarter next following the effective date of the registration statement. The purpose of this covenant is to call into play at the earliest possible date the provision of Section 11(a) of the 1933 Act that states that if a person acquires a security after the issuer has made generally available to its securityholders an earnings statement covering a period of at least 12 months beginning after the effective date of the registration statement, then the right of recovery is conditioned on proof that such person acquired the security relying upon the alleged untrue statement in the registration statement or relying upon the registration statement and not knowing of the alleged omission.

Rule 158 contains provisions relating to the adequacy of the earnings statement and provides that the earnings statement shall be deemed to be made generally available to the issuer's securityholders if it is required to file reports under the 1934 Act and has filed its reports on Form 10-K, Form 10-Q or Form 8-K or has supplied to the SEC copies of its annual report containing such information. Prior to the adoption of Rule 158, it was customary to make the earnings statement "generally available" by publishing a notice of its availability in *The Wall Street Journal.*

The underwriting agreement will obligate the issuer, even after the closing, to amend or supplement the prospectus as necessary to maintain it as a document that the underwriters may deliver in connection with the sale of the registered securities. This obligation applies for such period as the delivery of the prospectus is required for this purpose. For example, as discussed in Chapter 4, the underwriters may have placed a portion of the offered securities in an investment account. If the underwriters then decide to sell these securities four or five months after the original offering, it may be necessary to amend the prospectus to reflect material developments concerning the issuer or to include updated financial statements. The cost of amending the prospectus is usually borne by the issuer for the first nine months after the effective date of the registration statement (which is the period of time prescribed by Section 10(a)(3) of the 1933 Act after which the financial statements may become "stale"), while the underwriters bear the cost of any necessary amendments beyond the nine-month period.

The announcement by an issuer of a material business acquisition can sometimes complicate an underwriter's disposition of securities held in its investment account. For example, an issuer that announces an agreement to acquire a significant business may have no practical way of immediately filing the acquired company financial statements required by Rule 3-05 of Regulation S-X and the pro forma financial statements required by Article 11 of Regulation S-X. Item 11 of Form S-3 requires that the prospectus include this information. The instructions to Item 7 of Form 8-K also state that, with certain exceptions, "offerings should not be made pursuant to effective registration statements" until the filing of the required financial statements. Even though the SEC has recently relaxed the financial statement requirements for acquired businesses, a material acquisition can still prevent the issuer from updating the prospectus and an underwriter from selling securities from its investment account.

• *Lock-Up Agreements*

In the case of an offering of equity securities, the underwriters customarily will insist that the issuer, as well as certain of its officers, directors and principal securityholders, enter into agreements to the effect that they will not sell any additional securities of the same class, or any securities into which they may be convertible, for a specified period of time after the date of the prospectus. The time periods most frequently seen are 90 to 180 days. This "lock-up" agreement is designed to facilitate the distribution by preventing large blocks of securities from being dumped in the market while the distribution is in process. The managing underwriter has the right to consent to any sales or to terminate the agreement at any time. The manager normally will agree to any sales that will not disrupt the distribution or have an adverse effect on the after-market for the securities.

• *Closing Conditions*

The underwriting agreement will specify certain conditions precedent to the obligations of the underwriters to purchase the securities at the closing, including the receipt of an opinion of company counsel covering specified legal matters and a somewhat more general reference to an opinion of counsel for the underwriters. The issuer's inside counsel usually will have greater familiarity with its day-to-day legal affairs than the outside law firm that has been retained for the financing. Outside counsel may have been hired primarily for its expertise in the securities laws. In these cases, it is appropriate to provide for a split opinion. The inside counsel will opine on due incorporation, good standing, qualification as a foreign corporation, matters relating to subsidiaries, material contracts, and litigation. Special counsel will pass upon matters relating to the securities—the validity of their issuance and the accuracy of their description in the registration statement. Its opinion will also cover securities law matters, such as the effectiveness of the registration statement and its compliance as to form with the requirements of the 1933 Act and the regulations thereunder. Both counsel should be required to give negative assurance, with appropriate disclaimers of responsibility, that "nothing has come to their attention" that would lead them to believe that the registration statement is false or misleading in any material respect.

The opinions requested of company counsel can sometimes lead to controversy. It can be frustrating to counsel for the underwriters to be told by the law firm representing the issuer that only a particular form of opinion will do because this is the form decreed by the firm's opinion committee. A law firm does not serve its client well if the partner negotiating the terms of the underwriting agreement does not have the authority to agree to a form of opinion preferred by the managing underwriter that is not substantively different from that preferred by his firm. On the other hand, counsel for the underwriters should be reasonable in their requests for opinions from company counsel. No lawyer should ask another to render an opinion that he or she would not be comfortable giving if standing in the other lawyer's shoes.

A condition to closing customarily found in underwriting agreements is the delivery of an officer's certificate with respect to the absence of any material adverse change and to the effect that the representations and warranties in the underwriting agreement are true and correct with the same effect as though made at the time of closing.

• *Comfort Letters*

The underwriters will have received a comfort letter from the issuer's accountants at the time of execution of the underwriting agreement.[35] The underwriting agreement will also require a bring-down letter from the accountants as a condition to closing. Comfort letters are now governed by the accounting profession's Statement on Auditing Standards No. 72, which was adopted in 1993 and amended in September 1995 by Statement on Auditing Standards No. 76.

A typical comfort letter will confirm that the accountants are independent public accountants within the meaning of the 1933 Act and the SEC's rules. It will also express the accountants' opinion whether the audited financial statements included in the prospectus comply as to form in all material respects with the applicable accounting requirements of the 1933 Act and the SEC's rules. There is no need for the comfort letter to reiterate the accountants' report on the audited financial statements, since that report (which speaks as of its date) appears or is incorporated by reference in the prospectus.

If unaudited interim financial statements are included in the prospectus, the comfort letter may express "negative assurance" as to whether these statements comply as to form with SEC requirements and also as to whether any material modifications should be made to these statements for them to be in conformity with generally accepted accounting principles. The negative assurance may extend to financial information included or incorporated by reference in the prospectus because

---

35. *The Comfort Letter* (Little, Brown 1975), by Philadelphia lawyer-novelist, Arthur R.G. Solmssen, is a delightful fictional account of what happens when the conditions to the closing of an acquisition transaction are not satisfied.

of specific requirements of Regulation S-K (e.g., selected financial data, supplementary financial information, executive compensation and any presentation of the issuer's ratio of earnings to fixed charges). The letter may also express negative assurance as to changes in the issuer's capital stock, long-term debt or other specified financial statement or items during a specified period (the "change period") beginning immediately after the date of the latest audited financial statements in the prospectus and ending on a "cut-off" date that may be three business days before the date of delivery of the letter.

A comfort letter may also comment on tables, statistics and other financial information that appears in the registration statement and that is derived from the issuer's accounting records. Any comment on this information will be expressed not as "negative assurance" but rather as findings based on the application of limited procedures set forth in the letter. Counsel for the underwriters should assure that the accountants provide comfort with respect to all numbers and computations that can be checked without unreasonable effort. But counsel and its clients should not resort to overkill. An accountant cannot be expected to provide comfort with respect to any number that cannot be derived from the accounting records of the issuer.

Accountants have been frequent targets of litigation and are understandably reluctant to risk liability for activities that are outside the scope of their normal audit engagements. Strictly speaking, comfort letters are for the benefit of the underwriters as a means of helping to establish their "due diligence" defense under Section 11 or comparable provisions (see Chapter 5). The authors are not aware of any litigation against accountants arising out of any comfort letter delivered to underwriters, but the accounting profession has nevertheless been trying for some time to standardize the procedural and substantive aspects of comfort letters. In particular, there appears to be a concern that—at least on some transactions not registered with the SEC—"no one is doing any due diligence except the accountants." These concerns and their consequences for underwriters are discussed in Chapter 5.

• *Indemnification*

The issuer, and in appropriate cases the selling security-holders, will agree to indemnify each underwriter and each person, if any, who controls an underwriter, within the meaning of Section 15 of the 1933 Act, against liabilities and expenses arising out of alleged misstatements or omissions in the registration statement and prospectus. The indemnity agreement should make it clear that litigation expenses, including fees of counsel, will be reimbursed as incurred. The issuer should be liable only for the fees of one counsel for the underwriters in addition to any local counsel. The underwriting agreement will contain a cross indemnity from each underwriter with respect to information furnished by it. (As discussed above, such information is very limited.) Issuers often will insist that the indemnity agreement, insofar as it relates to any untrue statement or omission made in a preliminary prospectus but remedied in the final prospectus, will not be available to any underwriter from whom the person asserting the claim purchased the securities if a copy of the final prospectus was not given to such person and the receipt thereof would have constituted a defense to the asserted claim. This is not an unreasonable position for an issuer to take, but the fact is that there is very little litigation that arises out of the use of *preliminary* prospectuses.

The *Globus* case, decided in 1969,[36] raised questions as to the validity of indemnity agreements insofar as they relate to underwriters who have actual knowledge of a misstatement or omission in a registration statement. This led to concern as to the enforceability of indemnity agreements in general, and many courts have held indemnity agreements to be invalid as contrary to public policy even where the underwriter was not aware of the misstatement or omission.[37] For this reason, counsel often opine only that the underwriting agreement has been duly authorized, executed

---

36. *Globus v. Law Research Services, Inc.,* 418 F.2d 1276 (2d Cir. 1969), *aff'g* 287 F. Supp. 188 (S.D.N.Y. 1968), *cert. denied* 397 U.S. 913 (1970).

37. A recent case is *Eichenholtz v. Brennan,* 52 F.3d 478 (3d Cir. 1995).

and delivered and not that it is a valid and binding agreement enforceable in accordance with its terms.

In the case of a secondary offering by a selling securityholder, there is always an issue as to whether indemnification by the issuer is permitted as a matter of corporate law. The concern is that providing such a benefit to a securityholder without receiving any valuable consideration in return might be viewed as a waste of corporate assets. If the securities are being registered pursuant to an agreement that provides for registration rights, then indemnification by the issuer probably is enforceable. Indemnification may be deemed to be incidental to the obligation to register. To avoid any question on this issue, agreements providing for registration rights should contain a specific agreement on the part of the corporation that it will agree to indemnify underwriters through whom the securities are sold.

The argument has been made that there is justification for a corporate indemnity where shareholders are selling and the secondary offering enables the corporation to meet the listing requirements of an exchange or otherwise creates a more liquid market for its shares. In the case of an initial public offering, where there are a limited number of shareholders, the shareholders are sometimes requested to consent to the issuer's indemnification with respect to the selling shareholders' portion of the offering.

The sellers in the secondary offering should also be required to provide indemnity, but where the sellers are individuals, there is frequently concern as to whether they will have funds available to honor their indemnity if this should prove necessary. Perhaps the proceeds of the secondary offering will be frittered away. In the past, underwriters sometimes required individual selling securityholders to purchase an indemnity insurance policy, at least for a portion of the offering, naming the underwriters as beneficiaries. These policies are expensive, and they generally have not been required in recent years.

Even where there is a question as to the enforceability of the issuer's indemnification for the benefit of selling securityholders, underwriters will require it for what it is worth. So long as the underwriters understand that the indemnity may not be enforceable, this approach is not objectionable.[38]

There also is a legal question as to whether a trustee, executor, or other fiduciary should indemnify in the absence of specific authority in the governing instrument or a court order. Banks and other fiduciaries fear that if they do so they may be held liable in their individual capacities and not as fiduciaries. One way of handling this problem is to have an indemnitor, such as the principal beneficiary, indemnify on behalf of the trust or estate.[39]

The SEC considers it to be contrary to public policy for a registrant to indemnify any of its directors, officers or controlling persons against liabilities arising under the 1933 Act. Item 512(h) of Regulation S-K requires an undertaking to be included in the registration statement to the effect that if a claim for indemnification is made against the registrant by a director, officer or controlling person, the registrant will, unless in the opinion of its counsel the matter has been settled by controlling precedent, submit the question to a court and be governed by a final adjudication of the issue. If a person in a control relationship with an underwriter is also a director of the registrant, the underwriting agreement should state that, insofar as the indemnity agreement applies to such person, it is subject to the registrant's undertaking set forth under the applicable heading in the registration statement.

---

38. In the case of a combination offering by an issuer and selling securityholders, the lead-in clause to the indemnity provision would be:

The Company and each Seller (in the proportion that the number of Shares being sold by such Seller bears to the total number of Shares) agree to indemnify. . . .

39. An appropriate clause would be:

The Company, each Seller other than First Trust Company, as trustee for X and Y (the "Trustee"), and X, as indemnitor for the Trustee (the "Indemnitor"), agree to indemnify. . . . The Company, each Seller (other than the Trustee) and the Indemnitor shall be liable under this indemnity agreement only in the proportion that the number of Shares being sold by the Company, such Seller and the Trustee, as the case may be, bears to the total number of Shares.

The indemnity section of the underwriting agreement will specify the procedures to be followed if a claim is made. Each indemnified party must notify the indemnifying party of any action commenced against it. Many underwriting agreements provide that an indemnifying party may assume the defense of an action with counsel chosen by it and approved by the indemnified parties, unless the indemnified parties reasonably object on the grounds that they may have legal defenses that are different from or in addition to those available to the indemnifying party. In that case, the indemnified parties may be represented by their own counsel at the indemnifying parties' expense.

Over the years, it has become evident that underwriters must always have separate counsel in an action based on a registration statement because their interests and defenses always are different from those of the issuer. As the exception to the rule always applies, many modern underwriting agreements simply eliminate any reference to the assumption of the defense by the indemnifying party. They simply state that in no event shall the indemnifying party be responsible for the fees and expenses of more than one counsel for all indemnified parties in connection with any single action.

• *Contribution*

Section 11(f) of the 1933 Act provides that every person who becomes liable under Section 11 may "recover contribution as in cases of contract from any person who, if sued separately, would have been liable to make the same payment, unless the person who has become liable was, and the other was not, guilty of fraudulent misrepresentation." The provision is not a model of legislative draftsmanship. In order to resolve some of the ambiguities and open questions about how contribution would be applied in the event that the issuer's indemnity agreement were held to be unenforceable, underwriters customarily include contribution clauses in their forms of underwriting agreement.

These clauses state that if the indemnity agreement is for any reason held to be unavailable to the underwriters, then the issuer (and the selling securityholders, if any) and the underwriters will contribute to the aggregate losses of the nature contemplated by the indemnity agreement in such proportions that the underwriters will be responsible for that portion represented by the percentage that the underwriting discount bears to the initial public offering price and the issuer (and the selling securityholders, in the proportions that they have agreed to indemnify) will be responsible for the balance. Of course, it is also specified that no person guilty of fraudulent misrepresentation within the meaning of Section 11(f) of the 1933 Act will be entitled to contribution from any person who is not guilty of such fraudulent misrepresentation. Many underwriting agreements go on to provide that if this contribution formula is not enforceable, then contribution will be made on the basis of such factors as relative fault and relative benefit. The point of all of this is to provide an alternative to full indemnification based on the statutory underpinnings of Section 11(f), in the event that the indemnity agreement is not upheld.

Indemnity agreements sometimes provide that indemnity will not be available if the person seeking indemnity fails to give any required notice of a claim, at least where the failure to give notice is materially prejudicial to the person providing indemnity. Issuers sometimes seek to insert a similar condition into the contribution agreement. Since the underwriters are already entitled to contribution as a result of Section 11(f), the insertion of procedural conditions may have the effect of leaving them worse off for having an express agreement than if they had no agreement at all. This is clearly not a rational result, and procedural conditions to the issuer's contribution obligation should be avoided.

• *Termination*

Underwriting agreements routinely permit the managing underwriter to terminate the obligations of the syndicate if there has been any change in the issuer's general affairs, management, financial condition or results of operations. The language sometimes includes "any development involving a prospective change" or a reference to the issuer's "business prospects." In either case, the underwriters may terminate their obligation if the change is in their judgment so material and adverse as to make it inadvisable to proceed with the offering on the contemplated terms.

In years past, the material adverse change "out" was limited to matters relating to the actual condition of the issuer and did not cover its business prospects or developments involving a "prospective" change. The term "business prospects" was introduced into many underwriting agreements shortly after Fidel Castro came into power in Cuba. In connection with a convertible debenture offering by a company with substantial business interests in that country, there was an announcement between pricing and closing that Castro intended to impose a confiscatory tax that would have a material impact on the issuer's overall operations. Because there had not been any change in the issuer's actual condition or in its earnings, it was not clear whether the material adverse change clause could be invoked. If the words "business prospects" had been included, then the clause clearly would have been applicable.[40]

In the case of an offering of fixed-income securities, it is also common for the underwriters to reserve the option to terminate their obligations in the event of a downgrading in the company's ratings by a nationally recognized statistical rating organization (such as Moody's or Standard & Poor's). The option usually extends to the placement of the issuer's ratings on a "watch" or similar list for surveillance or review where this is announced as having "possible negative implications."

Underwriting agreements also often provide for a material adverse change "out" in the event of any loss or interference with the issuer's business from "fire, explosion, flood or other calamity." Labor disputes and adverse governmental action are sometimes also specified. The reference to "explosion" assumed actual importance on February 26, 1993 when a large bomb exploded beneath the World Trade Center in New York City. One of the authors was preparing on that Friday afternoon for the closing on the following Monday of the $900 million initial public offering of Dean Witter, Discover & Co.

---

40. The securities in question became known in the financial community as "Castro Convertibles."

("DWD") and the closing on the following Thursday of a $1.5 billion public offering of DWD's debt securities. (Half-way down the smoky staircase, the author considered asking an associate to return to the 58th floor to retrieve the closing documents. He thought better of it.) Reaching the street, the author proceeded to DWD's law department at 130 Liberty Street. It soon became clear that an explosion had caused the evacuation of both towers of the World Trade Center, including the headquarters not only of DWD but of the lead underwriter, issuer's counsel and the issuer's independent accountants. The author discussed the "explosion" clause of the underwriting agreements with DWD's internal counsel. After being forced to walk down another 29 flights of stairs because of Con Edison's turning off power to the building (at the request of the fire department), we proceeded north to DWD's "emergency command center" on Varick Street. We found there a large number of people hard at work establishing communications with DWD's numerous regional data centers and more than 300 broker-dealer branch offices. DWD's senior officers working on the transactions read the relevant language in the underwriting agreements and scheduled a telephone conference call with the underwriters for that weekend. During the call on Saturday afternoon, it became clear to the underwriters' satisfaction that DWD's decentralized operations made the explosion's consequences more of an inconvenience than a material adverse interruption of its business. (It was said that an employee in a branch office, on hearing about the explosion, had commented that "New York is only a cost center anyway.") The closing took place as scheduled, albeit at the offices of underwriters' counsel rather than issuer's counsel.

The author subsequently discovered that some of the other participants in the closing had repaired to the bar of the Millenium Hotel—a course of action he wished he had thought of.

It is also customary to permit the managing underwriter to terminate in the event of an external event that affects the marketing of the securities. Thus, the manager may be permitted to terminate the underwriting agreement "if there has occurred any new outbreak of hostilities [or, sometimes, any escalation of specified existing hostilities] or any calamity or crisis the effect of which on the financial markets of the United States [or, in the case of international offerings, any other relevant markets] is such as to make it, in the judgment of the managing underwriter, impracticable to market the securities or enforce contracts for the sale of the securities." From time to time, the typical calamity out has been modified in anticipation of specific events that could adversely affect the financial markets. For example, at one point during the 1960s, the financial markets anxiously anticipated a devaluation of the pound sterling. During this period, some underwriting agreements specified that devaluation would provide a basis for termination. In the spring of 1975, when The City of New York was facing a financial crisis, it became quite common to include a termination provision that would operate in the event of bankruptcy of a state or a major city or a default by it on its debt obligations. After the crisis passed in mid-June of that year, provisions of this type became less common.

The usual underwriting agreement also will provide an out in the event of trading suspensions on the exchanges or bank moratoriums. This particular termination provision has its roots in the disruptions of the early 1930s. The provision does not ordinarily extend, however, to mere market collapses such as the crash of October 19, 1987. Many underwritten public offerings that had been priced before that crash were routinely closed afterwards, notwithstanding a dramatic fall in the market price of the underwritten security.

It should be stressed that a calamity out is not a "market out." A market out would permit the managing underwriter to terminate if there is a substantial change in "market conditions" that renders it impracticable or inadvisable to market the securities. The revival of financing in 1935, following the worst part of the depression, was accompanied by a widespread use of market out clauses,[41] but by the 1950s their use was discontinued, at least by the major investment banking firms. Immediately following the October 1987 crash, some investment banking firms rushed to insert market out clauses in their un-

---

41. Gourrich, *supra* note 10, at 56.

derwriting agreements. After a time, however, cooler heads prevailed and their use has largely disappeared. Both the SEC and the NASD have taken the position that market outs are inappropriate for offerings that purport to be made on a firm commitment basis.

• *Default and Step-Up*

As stated above, the commitments of the underwriters are several. Thus, if one of the underwriters were to default, the issuer would receive less funds than it wished to raise unless some provision were made for a limited step-up by the remaining underwriters.

Underwriting agreements typically provide that if one or more of the underwriters fails at the closing to purchase the securities which it or they are obligated to purchase, then the manager has the right, within 24 hours thereafter, to make arrangements for one or more of the non-defaulting underwriters, or any other underwriters, to purchase all, but not less than all, of the defaulted securities. If such arrangements are not completed within that period, and if the amount of defaulted securities does not exceed 10% of the total, then the non-defaulting underwriters are obligated to purchase the full amount in the proportions that their respective underwriting commitments bear to the underwriting commitments of all non-defaulting underwriters. If the amount of defaulted securities exceeds 10% of the total, the underwriting agreement terminates without liability on the part of any non-defaulting underwriter.

The default provision almost never comes into play. Investment banking firms simply do not default on their obligations. It stands as backup insurance to the issuer while preserving the principle that underwriting commitments are several and not joint. One occasion on which it was necessary to operate under a default clause occurred in May 1973 when Weis Securities, Inc. was placed in liquidation under the Securities Investor Protection Act between the signing of the underwriting agreement and the closing of a public offering of 6.5 million shares of common stock of Consolidated Edison Company of New York, Inc. On the afternoon after the underwriting agreement was signed, the SEC applied to the court for the appointment of a temporary receiver of Weis Securities' assets, and the Securities Investor Protection Corporation applied for the appointment of a trustee for the firm's liquidation. Weis resisted, and it remained uncertain until shortly before the closing whether it would be able to honor its underwriting commitment. A trustee was appointed the day before the closing, and it became evident that it would be impossible for the trustee to honor Weis's commitment. Weis defaulted on the morning of the closing, and at the closing the non-defaulting underwriters purchased, pro rata, the shares that Weis had agreed to purchase. The book-running manager's form of underwriting agreement did not permit the managers to purchase the defaulted securities themselves or to substitute other underwriters, and thus it was necessary to apply the pro rata step-up provision. Most underwriting agreements have now been clarified to permit the substitution of underwriters and not merely an across-the-board step-up.

The SEC has sometimes taken the position that a step-up is necessary in order for the issuer and the underwriters to be able to represent that all of the offered securities will be sold if any are sold. The step-up may also be a source of comfort regarding the issuer's expectations that it will receive the full amount of the offering for the purposes described under "Use of Proceeds."

The Selected Dealers Agreement

The least important underwriting document is the selected dealers agreement. This document, which is also known as the "selling agreement," permits dealers who are not also members of the underwriting syndicate to purchase securities from the underwriters at the public offering price less a discount called the "concession." They will agree to maintain the public offering price in their resales, except that they may sell to other dealers at the public offering price less a discount called the "reallowance." Selected dealers will make the same representations as the underwriters with respect to their membership in, and good standing with, the NASD and will agree to comply with NASD regulations. They will confirm their familiarity with the prospectus delivery requirements of the securities laws.

In the case of an IPO, the selling agreement may contain a penalty clause requiring the repayment of the selling concession if securities sold by the dealer are purchased by the syndicate in the open market. The agreement contains other provisions of a routine nature relating to the distribution.

The practice of requiring dealers to enter into selling agreements in connection with specific transactions has all but disappeared, as the major investment banking firms have adopted master selling agreements that have been signed by the dealers that participate in their offerings and that govern all underwritings that they manage.

Some master agreements between underwriters and dealers cover a wide range of transactions that go far beyond public offerings of SEC-registered securities. The desire of underwriting firms to extend their distribution capabilities has led some of them to form alliances with "regional" broker-dealers who use their sales forces to sell products originated by the underwriting firm. These products can include commercial paper, private placements and various types of derivative products. The form of agreement generally calls for the dealer to agree that it will observe applicable selling restrictions, deliver required documents and assume responsibility for making suitability determinations.

Competitive Bidding

Competitive bidding is required by the public utility laws or utility commission regulations of many states. In some of these states exemptions will be granted quite readily, but in others the public utility commission will insist that bidding procedures be adhered to. In addition, until 1994, the SEC's Rule 50 under the Public Utility Holding Company Act of 1935 also required public utility holding companies and their operating subsidiaries to sell their securities through competitive bidding.

The SEC rescinded Rule 50 in 1994[42] because of the dwindling number of companies still subject to the Public Utility Holding Company Act, the many exceptions to which the competitive bid requirement was subject and, perhaps most important, the extensive disclosure requirements imposed by the other federal securities laws. The SEC anticipated that the rescission of the rule would permit companies in a registered public utility holding company system to choose the marketing method for their securities, including shelf registration, that offered the most advantageous terms.

Some public utilities have adopted streamlined bidding procedures. One public utility with an effective shelf registration statement covering its first mortgage bonds has been able to satisfy the requirements of its state public utilities commission without publishing a bidding notice. Instead it sends letters to those investment banking firms that have participated in its prior financings inviting them to submit bids. As set forth in these letters, provision is made for telephonic bids confirmed in writing within one hour after the close of bidding. Written confirmations are provided by facsimile, and the winning bid is accepted by the public utility's execution of the fax of the bid. Following Rule 415 procedures, rather than traditional competitive bidding procedures, a post-effective amendment is not required, but rather a prospectus supplement is filed with the SEC pursuant to Rule 424(b).

---

42. SEC Release No. 35-26031 (April 20, 1994).

Chapter 3

SELECTED ISSUES IN THE REGISTRATION AND DISTRIBUTION PROCESS

The process of bringing a securities offering to market may extend over several months in the case of an initial public offering. It may also be completed in as little as a few days if the issuer qualifies for Form S-3 and the securities being offered are investment-grade debt securities or common stock of a well-known issuer.[1] Some deals run like clockwork. Others are plagued by problems. In some cases, a stock offering will be a blowout. In others, it will be necessary for the underwriters to cut back on the size of the offering to get the deal done. Timing is crucial to many transactions. A favorable market climate may evaporate overnight; or the financing must be closed by the end of the year, and if the SEC does not produce its comments by the end of the day, the underwriters will be forced to come to market during the week before Christmas. This is what ulcers are made of.

---

1. For many years, the usual pattern was that the underwriters were ready to price and sell the securities but could not do so because the SEC had not completed its review. While this still happens, the usual pattern in the case of "high yield" debt securities or "story" common stocks (i.e., common stocks of issuers whose business situation is not well understood) registered "on the shelf" on Form S-3 is that the SEC formalities are (or can be) resolved well before the marketing effort is completed.

The working group must be prepared to deal with surprises. The deal may be rolling along smoothly and then "up jumps the devil." The SEC's accounting staff raises a major issue on income recognition. A co-manager informs counsel that its research department has just published a report on the issuer that may raise gun-jumping concerns. Most of these problems get solved, and the key to their solution is a cooperative working relationship among the representatives of the issuer, the lead underwriter, their respective counsel and the issuer's accounting firm.

Selecting the Investment Banker

If a privately held issuer decides to "go public," its first item of business will be to select the investment banking firm that will manage the transaction. If a reporting issuer decides to raise additional funds through the sale of securities, its first item of business will probably be to determine the type of security to be offered and whether the transaction should take the form of an SEC-registered public offering, a private placement or an offering in the offshore markets. The issuer's choice in this regard may influence its choice of investment banker to handle the transaction, since many investment bankers are perceived as having more expertise in one of these areas than in others.

It is often the case, of course, that various investment banking firms will have been soliciting the issuer's business for a considerable period of time.

In the days when relationship banking was far stronger than today, when most major corporations did business with only one investment bank, the issuer's president or chief financial officer would simply call upon the senior officer in the investment banking firm responsible for the relationship. Through a joint effort, a decision would be made as to the type of securities that would be most appropriate to meet the company's financial requirements. The choice might depend upon the issuer's capital structure, its debt to equity ratio, the market price of its common stock, prevailing interest rates, and the market's current appetite for specific types of securities. Frequently, the offering would be a part of a carefully devised financial plan worked out well in advance by the issuer and its traditional investment bank.

Today, investment banking relationships are less close than in the past. Few corporations that finance on a regular basis rely on the services of only one investment bank. Some corporations will have a strong relationship with an investment banking firm that will handle most of their business and a significant relationship with a number of other firms that they will call upon from time to time to manage one or more transactions. Other corporations will have an equally strong relationship with a core group of firms, with no one relationship reaching the level found in a single bank or dominant bank relationship.[2]

The result is a reduced flow of information from the corporation to the firms providing it with financial services.[3] The tendency now is for a corporation to rely more heavily than in the past on its own internal financial staff and for the chief financial officer to have a greater say in the selection of the type of transaction and of the investment bank that will manage the transaction. All but gone are the days when a firm was chosen because it was run by the chief executive's Princeton roommate.

When the time comes to choose a lead underwriter, the chief financial officer may have arrived at his own decision as to the nature of the financing, having relied upon the analysis of his own staff. He may then consult with a number of investment banking firms to discuss such issues as the probable price terms (including underwriting spread), whether the marketing focus should be primarily retail or institutional, and the firm's distri-

2. For ease of presentation, this chapter deals primarily with offerings by issuers, but the issues are essentially the same for registered secondary offerings.

3. For an extensive discussion of the different levels of investment banking relationships, *see* R. Eccles & D. Crane, *Doing Deals* (Harv. Bus. Sch. Press) (1988), particularly Ch. 4.

bution capacity in the relevant market. Based on these considerations and other factors, tangible and intangible, one or more managing underwriters will be chosen.[4] Sometimes a prospective issuer will hold a "beauty contest." A corporation that has no real tie with any investment bank may interview a number of firms and choose among competing underwriters on the basis of its officers' perception of their responsiveness to the corporation's needs, their knowledge of its business, and the chemistry that develops between the investment bankers and their counterparts at the corporation. This process frequently is used for initial public offerings, particularly by quality issuers being courted for their business. In the case of investment-grade shelf takedowns, however, the process more closely resembles competitive bidding on price terms alone.

Beauty contests sometimes begin with the mailing of questionnaires to a large number of firms. The responses provide the basis for deciding which firms will be invited to a face-to-face meeting. To a far greater extent than in the past, syndicate people (now known as "capital markets" specialists) play a major role in new business presentations. Veteran syndicate managers say that this has become a major part of their job.

The quality of a firm's research coverage is an important factor in getting new business, particularly in the case of initial public offerings. As one of the authors has previously written:

> Securities industry publications that track underwriters'
> success in being named to manage IPOs often refer to
> the winning underwriter's securities analyst as a key
> factor in the issuer's decision to choose a particular
> underwriter for this role. The primary reason for this

---

4. The firm that expects to be selected as book-running manager will usually argue against the need for co-managers. In some common stock offerings, however, the book-running manager may suggest that a regional firm be brought in as co-manager if it is expected that there will be interest for the securities in a particular area of the country. In other cases, a co-manager may be brought in to compensate for the book-running manager's relative weakness in covering institutional or retail customers, as the case may be.

emphasis is obvious: IPO candidates know their competition among publicly held companies in their industry, and they often know which analysts most capably cover these companies. They also know that newly public companies worry constantly about "getting lost in the crowd," and they understand that they will be dependent after their own IPO on analysts for disseminating news and developments about their company. It is logical that an analyst that has already successfully covered companies in the same industry, and who has a substantial institutional following, will be able to do the same thing for the IPO candidate. It also stands to reason that an analyst will be more willing to cover a newly-public company if his or her firm has played a significant role in bringing the IPO to market.[5]

Accordingly, a research analyst who has been named to the *Institutional Investor* "All American Research Team" for the issuer's industry can play a key role in his firm's selection as managing underwriter.

Some investment bankers believe that it is easier to obtain the mandate for an initial public offering than for the financing that follows it. The expectations that are created in the minds of the issuer's management through the investment banking firm's efforts to sell itself are so high that they can seldom be met. The issuer's disappointment may be fanned by the firms that were not selected. If the deal is not going well, these firms will not hesitate to call the chief financial officer to say, "We told you so."

Occasionally a firm having no prior relationship with an issuer will earn the job of managing an underwriting because it brought to the company a creative idea that met its financial needs. To compete effectively in an environment in which traditional relationships have declined in importance, investment bankers must be innovative. The major firms have formed product development departments to create new financial instru-

---

5. Joseph McLaughlin, *The Changing Role of the Analyst in Initial Public Offerings*, InSights, Aug. 1994, at 6.

ments, both debt and equity, that are marketed to potential issuers, whether or not they are traditional clients of the firm. The firm that convinces a chief financial officer to issue its own brand of tax-deductible preferred stock or variable coupon renewable notes or swap-driven foreign currency-denominated debt securities expects to be awarded the business of selling the issue.

Getting Organized and Other Preliminary Matters

Once the issuer has given an investment banker a mandate to proceed with an SEC-registered public offering (other than a shelf-registered takedown of investment-grade debt securities, as discussed in Chapter 8), it is time for the parties to get together to plan a course of action. The kickoff of a public offering is the organizational meeting, or "first meeting" as it is frequently called, at which all hands gather at the offices of the issuer or the book-running manager to set the underwriting process in motion. The managing underwriter and underwriters' counsel will meet with the issuer's principal officers and representatives of its accounting firm and the law firm that will act as issuer's counsel.[6] At this initial meeting, a timetable will be reviewed and the responsibility for the various documents will be assigned to the members of the working group.

The job of preparing a first draft of the registration statement usually is assigned to the issuer's lawyers and the company officers responsible for gathering the required factual data. The preparation of the financial statements to be included in the registration statement will be under the supervision of the issuer's chief financial officer, who will be assisted by the issuer's accounting staff and its independent public accountants. The underwriting documents will be prepared by underwriters' counsel. Preparation of the blue sky survey and the requisite state and NASD filings generally is the responsibility of un-

---

6. In many cases, particularly if the issuer is a major corporation, the issuer's legal work will be handled by its inside counsel. The underwriters, however, are always represented by an independent law firm whose client is the syndicate as a whole and not just the book-running manager.

derwriters' counsel. The fee of underwriters' counsel for performing this function and any blue sky or NASD filing fees customarily are paid by the issuer.

Numerous substantive issues will be considered at the first meeting, or reviewed with those present if already decided. Must the amount of authorized common stock be increased? Should the stock be split to facilitate the offering? Is it "probable" that the company will make a significant acquisition that might require additional financial statements? Are the financial statements about to become "stale"? Are there accounting or disclosure issues that should be the subject of a pre-filing conference with the SEC staff? Are there contracts or portions of contracts subject to the exhibit filing requirements that the issuer wishes to make the subject of an application for confidential treatment?

What, if any, "shark repellent" provisions should be adopted to ward off an unfriendly takeover attempt? If the transaction involves the sale of a minority interest in a subsidiary, what operating and tax-sharing agreements should be put into place? What plans does the company have for granting stock options to key employees? Will the filing of the registration statement trigger registration rights held by shareholders who acquired stock in a private placement? Other substantive issues to be considered at the organizational meeting are discussed below.

Housekeeping matters will be dealt with as well, such as the selection of a financial printer, an indenture trustee if debt securities are to be issued, and a transfer agent if the shares are not publicly traded. At this meeting or shortly thereafter, the issuer will be given a list of documents that the managing underwriter and counsel will need to review. Due diligence trips will be scheduled. (Due diligence is considered in more detail in Chapter 5.)

• *Form of Registration Statement*

By the time of the organizational meeting, counsel for the issuer will have made a determination as to whether the issuer is eligible to use Form S-2 or Form S-3 or whether the registration statement must be filed on Form S-1. The eligibility requirements for the principal registration forms have been discussed in Chapter 1, and a determination of eligibility should be relatively straightforward. One of the requirements for the use of Form S-2 and Form S-3, however, is that the registrant have "filed in a timely manner all [1934 Act] reports required to be filed during the 12 calendar months and any portion of a month immediately preceding the filing of the registration statement."[7] If the issuer files its documents electronically with the SEC, it must also have filed all required Financial Data Schedules in order to be able to use Form S-2, Form S-3 or Form S-8. These are matters that should not be assumed but should be the subject of inquiry by issuer's counsel.

The form of signature page for a registration statement on Form S-2 or Form S-3 requires a certification by the issuer that it has reasonable grounds to believe that it meets all of the requirements for filing on that form. The officer signing on behalf of the issuer must be in a position to make this certification, and the issuer's counsel should make sure that the certification properly can be made.

Underwriters' counsel should ask about the timeliness of the issuer's 1934 Act filings at the first meeting, or perhaps more discreetly in a side discussion with issuer's counsel. In an actual incident, the general counsel for a prospective issuer was asked at the organizational meeting whether the requisite filings had been made on a timely basis. He responded that he

---

7. Rule 12b-25 under the 1934 Act provides that an issuer that fails to file certain specified reports on time must file a Form 12b-25 by the day after the due date. The form must disclose the issuer's inability to file the report in a timely fashion and the reasons therefor in reasonable detail. The report will be deemed to have been filed on the prescribed due date if the Form 12b-25 represents that the delay could not have been prevented except by means of unreasonable effort or expense and that any late annual report will be filed within 15 calendar days or that any quarterly report will be filed within five calendar days; it is also necessary, of course, that the report actually be filed within such periods. By following this procedure, the registrant may retain its eligibility to use Form S-2 or Form S-3 once the filing is made; it may not use either form, however, until the filing is actually made.

personally had supervised the filing of the annual report on Form 10-K well in advance of the due date. Additionally, he had been advised by his company's accounting department, which was responsible for the filing of the quarterly reports on Form 10-Q, that each such report had been mailed to the SEC for filing precisely on the 45th day after the end of the quarter involved. When it was pointed out that "filed" does not mean mailed for filing, a hush fell over the room. The issuer had recently become otherwise eligible to use Form S-3, and it was quite clear that the chief executive officer would not be happy with a Form S-1 filing.

Company counsel was able to resolve the problem with the assistance of counsel for the underwriters. A joint telephone call was made to the branch chief at the SEC. The case was made that the responsible company officials had acted in good faith, that they were not lawyers, and that they had believed sincerely that they were complying with the filing requirements. While the SEC will use the eligibility requirements of the shorter form registration statements as a means of encouraging the timely filing of 1934 Act reports, the staff is not inclined to be punitive in this respect. If there has been an inadvertent error, as in this case, and the filing was only a few days late, then the staff may be persuaded to permit the use of the shorter form registration statement even where there has been a technical lack of compliance. In this case, the branch chief permitted the registration statement to be filed on Form S-3.

The question may be raised whether staff concurrence is sufficient. If an issuer does not strictly comply with the registrant requirements of Form S-2 or Form S-3, can a purchaser of the securities claim a 1933 Act violation on the basis that there was no effective registration statement in that it was filed on the wrong form? Rule 401(g) under the 1933 Act puts this issue to rest. It provides:

A registration statement or any amendment thereto shall be deemed to be filed on the proper form unless objection to the form is made by the Commission prior to the effective date.

Can counsel rely on Rule 401(g) to opine that the registration statement complies as to form in all material respects with the requirements of the 1933 Act? This may be a closer question.

- *Gun-jumping Questions*

It is appropriate at the organizational meeting to discuss the need for the issuer and the managing underwriters to avoid any conduct that would constitute an illegal offer of the registered securities. As discussed in Chapter 1, any offer of the securities prior to the filing of the registration statement constitutes "gun-jumping." Even after filing, it is illegal to make any written offer of the registered securities except by means of the preliminary prospectus. The common ingredient in these various types of illegal "offer" is a communication that attempts to "condition the market" for the new offering.

In particular, management should be warned to exercise caution in any discussions with the press or with analysts and above all to avoid references to the forthcoming issue. Indeed, unless there is to be a Rule 135 announcement of the proposed financing, knowledge of the prospective offering should be confined to those who "need to know." The fact that a financing is in the works should be assumed to be a material fact (although arguably a prospective debt financing may not be), and those in the know should not purchase or sell any of the issuer's securities until the financing is disclosed to the public.[8] If the company employs a financial public relations firm, its activities must be carefully monitored. If the company has an in-house

---

8. Whether or not prohibited by anti-manipulation rules (see Chapter 4) or insider trading restraints, it is usually not a good idea for individuals involved in the registration process to trade in the issuer's equity securities during this period of time. For example, if the president were to sell shares during the preparation of a common stock offering, the required Form 4 disclosure could have a chilling effect on the underwriter's marketing efforts. If an investment banker were to buy shares of an issuer while working on a financing for that issuer, it may be difficult for him to convince his superiors, or indeed the SEC, that he did not buy on the strength of favorable information uncovered in his due diligence investigation. In this context, it is best to be like Caesar's wife.

publication distributed to employees, this must also be monitored. (Such publications are often of value in connection with the due diligence investigation.)

• • *"Website" or Internet "Home Page"*. Many companies maintain a "Website" or Internet "home page" as a means of facilitating communication with stockholders. These pages may contain recent 1934 Act reports, annual and quarterly reports to stockholders, transcripts of officers' speeches, new product announcements, press releases or transcripts or summaries of stockholders' or analysts' meetings. Some issuers even include the text of broker-dealer research reports, although this practice—especially if only selected reports are included—involves some risk of the issuer becoming "entangled" with the report in a way that could result in liability for the report's contents.

So long as the Website has been maintained with reasonable regularity and does not contain any references to the offering (at least none that would not be permissible if made in written form), there should be no need for the issuer to "purge" its Website just because a securities offering is in the works. The SEC staff is believed to be addressing this issue.

• • *Product Advertisements*. When beginning work on a registration statement, it is advisable to review the issuer's advertising program. There is, of course, no reason why a company should stop advertising its products merely because it is about to go into registration. No one would suggest otherwise. But the type of advertisements that stress a company's strength and growth, which are sometimes seen in *The Wall Street Journal* in close proximity to the stock quotations, may well raise problems if the issuer has no track record of publishing such advertisements and they begin to appear at or about the time of an offering. As discussed in Chapter 9, it was this concern that motivated Deutsche Telekom AG, prior to its 1996 global IPO, to obtain no-action relief from the SEC staff regarding "image" advertising and certain other publicity.

• • *Annual Reports*. If the annual report to shareholders is scheduled to be released while the company is in registration, early drafts and final proofs should be reviewed by counsel to assure that no statements are made that could raise questions under the 1933 Act. The SEC has taken the position that annual reports should not present a problem if they are of the character and content normally published by a company and do not contain material designed to assist in a proposed offering.[9] Editing of the report to make sure that it does not contain statements that could be so construed is advisable under these circumstances. Particular attention should be paid to the president's letter, and any overly enthusiastic statements should be toned down in an appropriate fashion. An annual report should be judiciously worded in any event, but particular care should be taken to assure that this is the case if a company is to embark upon a financing.

• • *Presentations to Securities Analysts.* A chief executive officer frequently will ask at a first meeting whether there will be any problem with his or her scheduled appearance at a luncheon meeting of securities analysts. The question is usually a polite way of stating that there had better not be a problem. In fact, there is not likely to be much of a problem if the issuer is offering its debt securities. Even in the case of a common stock offering, the SEC's staff recognizes the importance of ongoing communications with analysts and will not object to them while an issuer is in registration so long as it has a consistent history of these activities.[10] It is not a good idea, however, to schedule such an appearance after work has begun on a common stock offering.

If the meeting is scheduled for a date prior to the filing of a registration statement for a common stock offering, then a press release meeting the requirements of Rule 135 should be issued several days in advance of the meeting. The chief executive officer cannot in good conscience make his or her presentation without advising the analysts that a financing is imminent. But if the analysts are informed of the proposed financing, then the public should be informed as well.

---

9. SEC Release No. 33-3844 (October 8, 1957).

10. *See* SEC No-action Letter, *William E. Chatlos; Georgeson & Co.* (available February 3, 1977).

Cancellation of a scheduled appearance is not without its risks. Analysts may speculate that the cancellation is a sign that the issuer is involved in preparations for a public offering or even an acquisition. Or, as America Online discovered when its stock dropped 10% after it canceled an appearance in October 1996, analysts may fear that the issuer had "nothing good to talk about."

Although a scheduled speech to analysts may be permitted, hard copies of the speech should not be distributed during the registration period. This created a serious problem for a transaction in the mid-1950s. Two weeks prior to the filing of a registration statement, the president of the issuer delivered a prepared address before the New York Society of Security Analysts. His talk had been scheduled several months earlier at a time when the registered offering had not been contemplated. In his speech, he discussed his company's operations and expansion program, its sales and its earnings. The speech included a forecast of sales and referred to the issuer's proposal to file with the SEC later in the month a registration statement with respect to a proposed offering of convertible debentures. Copies of the speech were distributed to approximately 4,000 analysts. The matter was discussed with the staff of the SEC. Because the speech had been booked months in advance, the staff agreed that the offering could proceed.

That was not the end of the story. At that time, acceleration of the effectiveness of a registration statement required action at a formal meeting of the SEC. The commissioners would meet every morning and declare registration statements effective. Despite the staff's affirmative recommendation, the commissioners decided at the last minute to deny acceleration until after the company had distributed copies of its preliminary prospectus to all persons who had been sent copies of the speech. In this case, the SEC was not concerned with the speech itself but rather with the widespread distribution of the hard copy. The result was a disaster. The market took a bad turn, and when the deal was later revived, it was on far less favorable terms.[11]

---

11. This incident was the subject of Example No. 7 in SEC Release No. 33-3844 (available October 8, 1957). *See also id.*, Example No. 6.

The analysts who attend a company presentation may be subject to their own restrictions about what they can report about the meeting. If their firms are prospective underwriters, they will be subject to the restrictions on research coverage discussed later in this chapter.

• • *Restricted Lists.* The managing underwriter that has a handshake agreement with an issuer to proceed with a financing must implement compliance procedures to avoid gun-jumping violations, Rule 10b-5 violations (based on trading the issuer's securities on the basis of material non-public information) and Regulation M violations. Members of the underwriting syndicate must do likewise when they decide to accept the manager's invitation to participate in the financing.

Before announcement of an offering, many underwriters will place the issuer's securities on a "gray" or "watch" list. This is a highly confidential list of securities whose market price could be affected by material unannounced transactions in which the underwriter is involved. The primary purpose of the list is to enable the underwriter's compliance department to monitor proprietary and employee trading to be on the alert for possible "leaks." In some firms, the list also serves as a means of prohibiting arbitrage activity and as a means of triggering special review procedures for research material.

Once a transaction has been announced (or, in some cases, when the firm's involvement in a previously announced transaction is publicly disclosed), the affected securities may be moved from the "gray" or "watch" list to a "restricted" list. While still a confidential document, the restricted list is much more widely distributed within a securities firm. It generally identifies securities in which a compliance officer's prior approval is required for any proprietary or employee transaction (and, in some cases, even customer transactions). Securities on the restricted list are also subject to special procedures that require that all related research be approved by a compliance officer (or, in some firms, a person designated by the director of research). See the discussion in Chapter 4 regarding Regulation M.

It is a good idea for underwriters' counsel to be familiar with the managing underwriters' "gray" or "watch" list or restricted list procedures and how (and by whom) they are implemented. Underwriters' counsel should also be familiar with the managing underwriters' "Chinese Wall" procedures (discussed later in this chapter).

• *Stock Exchange Listing; "Blue Sky" Considerations*

In the case of an initial public offering of common stock, an issue that will be raised at the first meeting is whether the stock should be listed on the NYSE or the American Stock Exchange (assuming the listing requirements can be met) or whether the over-the-counter NASDAQ market will best serve the interests of the company and its shareholders. Some investment bankers will advise that NASDAQ provides many issuers and their shareholders with as deep and as liquid a market as the auction market of the principal exchanges. Some issuers will opt for a stock exchange listing simply because they believe it provides a certain cachet that will help them in their business. This is not a matter of vanity; it is often a valid reason for listing on an exchange.

If the securities are to be listed on an exchange or quoted on NASDAQ, it will be necessary to "register" them under the 1934 Act as well as under the 1933 Act. In the case of an IPO, the relevant filings can incorporate the 1933 Act documents.

For many years, most state securities or "blue sky" laws provided an exemption from state registration requirements for public offerings of securities that were listed on the NYSE or American Stock Exchange (as well as certain securities of senior or equal rank). Most of these states extended the exemption to IPOs that were to be listed at the time of the offering. Some states also exempted securities that were quoted on the NASDAQ National Market. The exemption was extremely useful since the blue sky hurdles for a non-exempt offering could be formidable in terms of time, expense and possible inability to offer the shares in some states.

The blue sky situation has been considerably simplified by the National Securities Markets Improvement Acts of 1996 (the "Improvements Act"). That statute amended Section 18 of the 1934 Act to preempt state registration requirements for securities listed "or authorized to be listed" on the NYSE or the American Stock Exchange or "listed" on the NASDAQ National Market (or, in either case, securities of equal or senior ranking). It is presumably safe to rely on this preemption once a letter has been received from the NYSE or the American Stock Exchange confirming that the security will be listed, as is customary, "upon notice of issuance."[12] The preemption also extends, however, to a security that will be so listed "upon completion of the transaction." This is probably intended to permit underwriters to commence their marketing efforts before the issuer has received a listing "authorization" from the exchange. Reliance on the extended preemption to make offers in a given state may involve some risk in the event that the authorization is not forthcoming. Indeed, if an offering were abandoned, would a state seek administrative penalties against an underwriter for making illegal offers? This would presumably be contrary to the spirit of the Improvements Act.

• *Issuer-Directed Shares*

A topic of discussion that frequently arises in the early planning stages of an initial public offering is whether a portion of the offering should be reserved for sale to employees, customers, suppliers, and other "friends" of the company. The founder and chief executive officer is proud of the company that he has built and that he now plans to take public. He is convinced beyond question that his company's shares will be a terrific investment, that they surely will soar in value as the business continues to grow, strengthened by the new capital raised in the public offering. Shouldn't those employees who worked so hard through the difficult early years, those customers whose loyalty has been a key factor in the company's success, and those suppliers who were so generous with their credit terms in the days

---

12. It is not clear whether Congress intended the apparent distinction between listed and NASDAQ securities insofar as "authorization" is concerned. The NASD and at least one state securities regulator have been reported as having different views on this point. A further ambiguity arises because of the absence of a definition of the term "authorized." It is not clear, for example, whether a listing approval would be sufficient for purposes of the Improvements Act if it is conditioned not only upon issuance of the securities but also upon compliance with the market's distribution or governance requirements.

when cash was tight be assured that they will be able to buy shares in the public offering?

It can be persuasively argued that issuer-directed shares are not a good idea. Employees, in particular, can get in over their heads in an effort to demonstrate their loyalty to the company. Even for customers and suppliers, the goodwill that will prevail if the price of the stock does go up will never exceed the ill will resulting from a decline in the market price.

All of these arguments notwithstanding, underwriters will often defer to the wishes of the issuer and agree to reserve a specified portion of an initial public offering for sale to persons designated by the issuer. In almost all cases, the shares are reserved for sale to these persons at the public offering price. Any suggestion that they be sold at a discount should be resisted.[13] These shares are in fact being underwritten. The managing underwriter must find a home for any of the reserved shares that are not purchased and paid for by the issuer's designees. For the most part, the designees will not be established customers of the managing underwriter. Thus, the manager must incur the considerable expense of opening an account for what may well be a single trade. With no broker-customer relationship at stake, the issuer's designees may be the first to renege on their purchases if the price of the shares falls below the public offering price before the settlement date. The underwriters are entitled to be compensated for incurring these risks.

In some cases where issuer-directed shares have been offered at a discount, the offer was made directly by the issuer and not through the underwriters. This is not a very satisfactory procedure. Most issuers are simply not equipped to handle the bookkeeping details involved in the process of issuing shares and collecting payment from a substantial number of people. Moreover, it must run the risk of an unsuccessful offering. In some states a direct sale by an issuer may require registration as a dealer in securities.

---

13. The rules of the NASD do not prohibit two-tier pricing (*see* Chapter 6), so this is a business issue rather than a legal one.

The requirement that a registration statement describe the plan of distribution mandates that the arrangements for reserving shares for persons designated by the issuer be fully disclosed in the prospectus. The letter or other notice directed to the persons for whom shares are being reserved must satisfy the requirements of Rule 134.

Preparation of the Registration Statement

In the days following the organizational meeting, the company and its counsel will begin the preparation of the registration statement. If the registration statement is on Form S-3, a decision will have been made as to whether the prospectus is to be "bare bones" or "beefed up," i.e., whether it is to contain virtually no information as permitted by Form S-3 or whether for marketing reasons the underwriters would prefer to include a description of the issuer's business and at least summary financial data. Generally speaking, a more extensive description of the issuer will be found in prospectuses for large common stock offerings, for "high yield" bonds and for securities issued by companies that have been the subject of recent restructurings or involved in material acquisitions or divestitures.

The drafting of the registration statement requires far more than responding to the items of the applicable form and Regulation S-K. While the financial statements constitute the skeleton on which the registration statement is built, the business description and the management's discussion and analysis of financial condition and results of operations (the "MD&A") provide the muscle and flesh, whether they are set forth in the document itself or incorporated by reference to the annual report on Form 10-K.

• *"Plain English"*

The business description should be factual and nontechnical. The company's officers must be made to realize that the terms that they use in their daily business conversation may be incomprehensible to the average investor and thus may require clarification in the text of the registration statement.

Prospectuses are frequently criticized as being unreadable or, even worse, as being drafted "to obscure, rather than reveal, in plain English, the critical elements of a proposed business deal. . . ."[14] There are certainly horrible examples of badly written prospectuses, but good securities lawyers have always taken pains to avoid ambiguous or obscure statements in their disclosure documents. At the same time, it cannot be denied that many companies and transactions are complex or that disclosure documents are read primarily by professional investors or their advisers.

In early 1997 the SEC proposed amendments to its rules that would require the use of "plain English" writing principles when drafting the cover pages and the summary and risk factor sections of a prospectus.[15] It also released a draft text of *A Plain English Handbook: How to Create Clear SEC Disclosure Documents* as further assistance for lawyers and others responsible for preparing prospectuses.

The proposing release contains an explanation of the elements of plain English. It also describes various plain English techniques and identifies undesirable drafting conventions that should be avoided. An issuer's failure to meet specified plain English requirements for the cover pages and the summary and risk factor sections of the prospectus would be a factor that the staff could consider in deciding whether to accelerate the effective date of a registration statement.

The SEC proposals would also revise the format of the inside and outside cover pages of the prospectus, including the required legal warnings, so as to invite an investor to read the information that is provided. As discussed below, the format and content of the "risk factors" section would also be revised.

Investors can only profit from an increased use of plain English in offering documents. It is to be hoped, however, that the SEC's emphasis on plain English will not result in issuers having to reckon with adverse staff comments on the *style*, rather than the *substance*, of their disclosure. Since well-meaning attempts to simplify language often also change its meaning, se-

---

14. *Feit v. Leasco Data Processing Equip. Corp.*, 332 F. Supp. 544, 549 (E.D.N.Y. 1971) (Weinstein, D.J.).

15. SEC Release No. 33-7380 (January 14, 1997).

curities lawyers may be forgiven for harboring some anxiety about the anticipated new level of dialogue with the staff.

• *Risk Factors*

The draftsman must anticipate the problems that the company may face in the future and set them forth as possible risks for the investor. This is not to say that every prospectus must have a section containing a litany of "risk factors." This is required only where there are factors, as described in Item 503(c) of Regulation S-K, "that make the offering speculative or one of high risk." But every prospectus should point out where appropriate in the text those factors that could have a negative impact on the business.

Some issuers and underwriters tried in the past to straddle the question of whether or not an offering involved high risk by including a section with a heading such as "Certain Investment Considerations." The SEC amended Items 501(a) and 503(c) in 1995 to require that any discussion required by that item be captioned "Risk Factors," that it be included immediately following the summary section or cover page and that a specific reference to it (by page number) be included on the cover page of the prospectus and in the table of contents.[16]

It is unfortunate that issuers and underwriters, sometimes (but not always) at the urging of SEC examiners, have expanded the list of risk factors in many offerings to the point where the reader has difficulty distinguishing the real risks from the remote risks. Issuers and underwriters should exercise self-restraint in this regard and should not hesitate to argue to an SEC examiner checking off his or her list of favorite risk factors that the inclusion of boiler plate in the risk factor section will distract attention from the real risks that should be focused upon by potential investors and their financial advisers. All this being said, reasonable people can obviously disagree over which risks are real and which are remote or obvious. For example, the authors would regard "the lack of an established trading market" for an IPO as an obvious risk that does not need to be stated in the prospectus. On the other hand, Item 503(c) expressly refers to the absence of a previous trading market as a fac-

---

16. SEC Release No. 33-7168 (May 11, 1995).

tor to be disclosed *if* it makes the offering "speculative" or "high risk." This need not be the case, however, if the issuer's common stock is to be listed on the NYSE or the co-managers have a good track record of making a market in their IPO stocks.

Some of the problems associated with "risk factor" disclosure are addressed in the 1997 "plain English" release discussed above. One of the SEC's proposals was to revise Item 503(b) of Regulation S-K to require a prioritization of risk factors, i.e., that they be discussed in the order of their importance. In addition, "[g]eneric and boilerplate risk that could apply to any registrant or any offering should not be provided." The release also asked for comment on whether the number of risk factors should be limited (e.g., to eight risk factors or no more than two pages).

• *Prospectus Summary*

Item 503(a) of Regulation S-K advises issuers to include a summary of the information contained in the prospectus where the length or complexity of the prospectus makes it appropriate to include a summary. Some securities lawyers resisted for a time the inclusion of summaries in prospectuses because of their concern that something important might be omitted. It is a fact, however, that many investors and securities professionals will read only the summary section of the prospectus. For that reason, summaries are customary in initial public offerings and other offerings that require a sustained marketing effort.

As part of the 1997 "plain English" release discussed above, the SEC emphasized that a prospectus summary should "provide investors with a clear, concise and coherent 'snapshot' description of the most significant aspects of the offering." It also criticized "summaries" that ran 10 to 30 pages and asked for comment on whether prospectus summaries should be limited to a specific number of pages.

One of the most important parts of the summary—and sometimes the most difficult to write—is the capsule description of the issuer's business. This description should let the reader know in as few words as possible just what it is that the company does. It should also include those risks, if any, that are considered significant. These are simple goals, but they are often not easily achieved. For one thing, the underwriters and their counsel improve their understanding of the issuer's business as work on the transaction progresses. For another, the issuer's managers usually have strong (and sometimes conflicting) opinions about just what makes their company special. For these reasons, the business summary usually ends up being revised more often than any other part of the prospectus.

One example will suffice:

> Hard Rock Cafe plc (the "Company") operates and franchises restaurants serving high-quality, moderately priced American-style food and beverages, featuring the "rock scene" and rock and roll music as their basic theme. The highly charged and informal atmosphere of Hard Rock Cafes, enhanced by displays of rock memorabilia and a reputation for attracting musicians and other celebrities, attracts patrons of all ages, including family groups. The Company emphasizes the quality of its food, beverages and service to the same extent as it does its restaurants' unique rock and roll ambiance. At each of its restaurants, the Company sells merchandise such as t-shirts, jackets, hats and watches displaying the Hard Rock Cafe logo, which provides not only revenues but an effective form of advertising as well. Because of the success of its restaurants and merchandise sales, the Company is exploring other means of commercially developing the Hard Rock Cafe name and concept, particularly in the entertainment industry.

> The original Hard Rock Cafe was opened in London in 1971 and rapidly became a popular London "institution." The New York City Hard Rock Cafe was opened in March 1984 and was followed by the Dallas Hard Rock Cafe in November 1986. The Company currently plans to establish Hard Rock Cafes in Boston and Washington, D.C., and intends to open additional Hard Rock Cafes in other cities in the eastern United States, Europe and Asia. The Company has limited interests in several other Hard Rock Cafes. The Company intends to open a

separate retail store in the summer of 1987 adjacent to the New York Hard Rock Cafe.

Although the London Hard Rock Cafe has operated successfully since 1971 and the popularity of rock and roll music shows no signs of diminishing, the continued success of any restaurant that is based on a particular theme is subject to shifts in consumer tastes and interests, and there can be no assurance that the Hard Rock Cafe concept will continue to have the same appeal that it has in the past.

No book can provide adequate instructions on the preparation of a registration statement. This is an art that can be learned only by experience. A few additional points, however, may be worth mentioning: the changing role of the securities analyst in connection with IPOs, the preparation of the "MD&A" section of the prospectus, the role of projections and other forward-looking information, the significance of guarantees and other credit enhancement, the SEC's special disclosure and other requirements for IPOs, and the making of requests for confidential treatment.

• *Role of the Securities Analyst in IPOs*

We discussed above the important role of the securities analyst in soliciting a potential IPO issuer to use his or her firm as a managing underwriter. To a greater or lesser degree, analysts have been helping their firms solicit IPOs in this manner for many years. To be sure, there is currently more incentive for analysts to participate in investment banking transactions since declining commissions on securities transactions often do not cover the cost of providing research to investors. Another difference is that where the analyst would several years ago disappear from view after the winning of the IPO assignment until well after its completion, at which time he or she would resurface with a research report or recommendation, the analyst is today more likely to remain part of the investment banking team responsible for the IPO. There are several reasons for this, related both to due diligence and to the marketing of the transaction.

First, IPO candidates—particularly high-technology companies—often provide goods or services from an obscure niche of a complex sub-industry. A securities analyst familiar in general

terms with the issuer's products or services can often better analyze the subtle competitive, managerial and technological advantages that make the issuer's securities a good investment. Just as
important, the analyst can spot weaknesses in the issuer's strategy
or program that need to be investigated as a matter of due diligence and perhaps disclosed in the issuer's IPO prospectus.

It is also a fact of life that IPO investors insist upon receiving earnings estimates for the issuer's next several quarters or
fiscal year. Investment bankers regularly confirm that institutional customers, in particular, will not buy IPO shares without
such estimates. Issuers have available to them a "safe harbor"
under the SEC's Rule 175, but issuers' counsel also regularly
advise against including earnings estimates in the prospectus.
Estimates are therefore provided orally to investors, either at
road shows or by the sales force on the telephone. The issuer
will typically not take responsibility for these estimates, leaving it in many cases to the investment bankers working on the
IPO to supply estimates based on discussions with the issuer
and access to its internal projections. Investment bankers, however, are not always experienced in coming up with earnings
estimates, and salespersons and customers alike may regard
such estimates as "tainted" by the investment bankers' and the
issuer's stake in the success of the offering.

The analyst, on the other hand, is experienced in coming up
with earnings estimates and has a track record of credibility
with salespeople and customers. The analyst is also more likely
to identify unrealistic assumptions built into the issuer's internal projections. For this reason, analysts are increasingly permitted access to the issuer's internal projections for two related
purposes. First, the analyst wants to have a high degree of confidence in the estimates he or she will provide to salespersons
and customers. The issuer's own projections are obviously an
important part of this process, albeit less for the sake of specific numbers than for the reality of assumptions, the attainabil-
ity of production and sales goals and the taking into account of
such factors as regulation, obsolescence and competition. Second, the investment bankers will rely on the analyst's views in
assessing the degree of confidence that should be attached to
the issuer's business plan, both for the purpose of pricing the

new securities and for ensuring the adequacy of disclosure in the prospectus of the possibility of earnings disappointments.

Another contribution by the analyst is in advising on investors' concerns that should be addressed in the prospectus. Also, the analyst is able to advise on how information regarding the issuer should be presented in the prospectus so as to facilitate comparisons by investors of the issuer with other issuers in the same general business. Finally, the analyst is often involved in helping to price the new issue.

While the analyst is participating in the due diligence and marketing phases of the IPO, he or she is undoubtedly looking forward to the publication after the expiration of the post-offering "cooling-off" period (25 days in most cases) of a research report on the issuer. Most such reports are favorable. That this is the case is not necessarily (as is sometimes assumed) because of any lack of objectivity on the part of the analyst or because the analyst has a preconceived intent to give the newly offered securities a "shot in the arm." The fact is that analysts are more likely to favor issuers that they understand—as a result of having participated in the solicitation, due diligence and marketing efforts—and that the analyst's firm has already "sponsored" for purposes of the IPO.[17]

• *Management's Discussion and Analysis*

One of the most challenging assignments in the preparation of a registration statement, particularly in the case of an IPO, is the preparation of the "Management's Discussion and Analysis of Financial Condition and Results of Operations" that is required by Item 303 of Regulation S-K. The SEC has described the purpose of the MD&A requirements as being "to give investors an opportunity to look at the registrant through the eyes of management by providing a historical and prospective analysis of the registrant's financial condition and results of opera-

---

17. These paragraphs are based on Joseph McLaughlin, *The Changing Role of the Analyst in Initial Public Offerings*, InSights, Aug. 1994, at 6-7. The article also discusses the "selective disclosure" questions that might be raised by permitting the analyst to have access to the issuer's internal projections.

tions, with particular emphasis on the registrant's prospects for the future."[18]

The MD&A must cover the issuer's liquidity, capital resources and results of operations and such other information as may be necessary to an understanding of the issuer's financial condition, changes in financial condition and results of operations.

The discussions of the issuer's liquidity and capital are customarily combined. The discussion must identify "any known trends or any known demands, commitments, events or uncertainties that will result in or that are reasonably likely to result in the registrant's liquidity increasing or decreasing in any material way." It must also describe the issuer's material commitments for capital expenditures and the anticipated source of funds needed to fulfill these commitments. Any material changes in the mix and relative cost of capital resources must also be described.

The discussion of results of operations must focus on "unusual or infrequent events or transactions or any significant economic changes" that have materially affected income from continuing operations. In addition, the MD&A must describe "any known trends or uncertainties that have had or that the registrant reasonably believes will have a material favorable or unfavorable impact on net sales or revenues or income from continuing operations." If the issuer has experienced increases in sales or revenues, it must explain the degree to which the increases are attributable to price increases or increased volume of sales or the introduction of new products or services.

The MD&A is keyed in the first instance to the issuer's full-year and interim financial statements included in the prospectus, but other statistical data should be presented to the extent necessary for a full understanding. The causes of material changes from period to period in one or more line items of the financial statements must be described.

The first draft of the MD&A is usually prepared by the issuer's financial reporting staff. Particularly in the case of IPOs,

---

18. SEC Release No. 33-6835 (May 18, 1989) [hereinafter the *1989 Interpretive Release*]. *See also* the SEC's 1981 interpretive release on MD&A, SEC Release No. 33-6349 (September 29, 1981).

it is important that the underwriters and underwriters' counsel participate actively in the review and revision of the MD&A. The individuals involved in this assignment should obviously be familiar with the issuer's industry and have sufficient experience in financial and accounting matters to be able to carry out this responsibility.

The MD&A has an important forward-looking aspect. The instructions specifically call for a focus on material events and uncertainties that would cause reported financial information not to be necessarily indicative of future operating results or future financial condition. This type of forward-looking disclosure is *mandatory* in the SEC's eyes because it is based upon "presently known data" that may have an impact on future operating results. On the other hand, Item 303 provides that issuers are "encouraged, but not required, to supply forward-looking information."

The distinction between "mandatory" and "voluntary" disclosure of forward-looking information is sometimes elusive. The SEC advised issuers in the *1989 Interpretive Release* to "determine and carefully review what trends, demands, commitments, events or uncertainties are known to management." This is presumably a first step to be taken without regard to assessments of likelihood of occurrence or materiality of impact. The SEC then set forth a two-step procedure for management to follow in respect of "known" trends, etc. First, is the known trend, demand, commitment, event or uncertainty "likely to come to fruition"? If management determines that none of these is reasonably likely to occur, no disclosure is required. On the other hand, if management cannot make the determination that any of these is "not reasonably likely to occur," it must "evaluate objectively the consequences of the known trend, . . . [etc.], on the assumption that it will come to fruition. . . . Disclosure is then required unless management determines that a material effect on the registrant's financial condition or results of operations is not reasonably likely to occur."

In determining the materiality of a contingent event, the SEC considers the Supreme Court's "probability/magnitude" test[19] to be "inapposite to Item 303 disclosure." Rather, the

---

19. *Basic Inc. v. Levinson*, 485 U.S. 224, 238-41 (1988).

test in the SEC's view is whether, on the assumption that the event will "come to fruition," it is "reasonably likely to have a material effect."[20]

As we have seen, the SEC's view of the purpose of MD&A disclosure is to "give the investor an opportunity to look at the company through the eyes of management." As illustrated by the SEC's 1992 proceeding against Caterpillar, Inc.,[21] even management's vision may be blurred on critical issues relating to disclosure of prospective events.

In 1989, Caterpillar's subsidiary in Brazil contributed an exceptional 23% of the parent company's net earnings, greatly disproportionate to its contribution of 5% to the parent company's revenues. By mid-February 1990, Caterpillar management had recognized that there were substantial uncertainties as to whether the subsidiary would repeat its 1989 performance in 1990. By the end of the first quarter, management had recognized that the subsidiary's 1990 profit would be "substantially lower than in 1989." The MD&A in the company's 1989 10-K did not disclose the subsidiary's disproportionate contribution to net earnings in that year, and neither that document nor the 10-Q for the first quarter of 1990 disclosed the risk of lower earnings in 1990 or the possible magnitude of such a shortfall.

The SEC seized upon certain corporate events as indicating failure to comply with MD&A requirements: it noted that management had started to break out the subsidiary's results for purposes of presentations to the board of directors; also, the board received reports in February and April 1990 indicating the magnitude of the subsidiary's 1989 contribution and the unlikelihood that it would match this performance in 1990. The SEC brought cease and desist proceedings based on MD&A violations in both the 1989 10-K and the 10-Q filed for the first quarter of 1990.

Caterpillar consented to the entry against it of a cease and desist order barring it from future violations of Section 13(a) of

---

20. *1989 Interpretive Release* at note 27. In making this statement, the SEC was presumably stating its view as to the standard that should govern issuers' disclosure decisions and not the standard that a court would or should apply for civil liability purposes.

21. *In re Caterpillar, Inc.*, SEC Release No. 34-30532 (March 31, 1992).

the 1934 Act and Rules 13a-1 and 13a-13 thereunder and order-
ing it to "implement and maintain procedures designed to ensure compliance with Item 303 . . . ." The release stated that
Caterpillar had already voluntarily adopted such procedures but
did not state what they were.

The SEC made no findings as to Caterpillar's having violated
any antifraud statute or rule (such as Rule 10b-5), and it has generally limited its findings to 1934 Act reporting violations in the
many other MD&A proceedings that it has brought against issuers
that allegedly failed to meet the requirements of Item 303.[22] In the
case of a registered public offering, however, both the issuer and
the underwriters face the prospect of civil liability if the registered
securities decline in value after the offering because of unexpected negative news about the issuer's earnings or liquidity. The
intriguing question for underwriters and the issuer's outside directors is what level of inquiry into the issuer's procedures and underlying judgments would be "reasonable" for purposes of a
defense under Section 11 or Section 12(a)(2). It is difficult, after
all, for outsiders to second-guess management's determinations as
to what trends or other events are "known" or even as to the degree to which they are likely to occur.

• *Projections and Other Forward-Looking Information*

A company's stock price can be dramatically and adversely
affected by earnings disappointments. Such reverses are almost
invariably followed by a Section 11 lawsuit alleging that the issuer's prospectus or 1934 Act reports or public statements failed to
disclose the "likelihood" or "probability" of lower earnings.

In the case of IPOs, underwriters face a difficult choice. As
discussed above, investors in these offerings insist on being
supplied with earnings estimates. On the other hand, issuers
generally refuse to include projections in the prospectus (the
most common exceptions being certain high-yield securities,
restructurings and M&A transactions). The dilemma is gener-

---

22. *See,* e.g., *In re Bank of Boston Corp.*, Initial Decision Release No.
81, Admin. Proc. File No. 3-8270 (December 22, 1995), *In re Shared Medical Systems Corp.*, SEC Release No. 34-33632 (February 17, 1994), *In re
Gibson Greetings, Inc.*, SEC Release No. 34-36357 (October 11, 1995).

ally solved by the underwriters' orally providing projections to investors at road show presentations or, more commonly, by means of the underwriters' sales force. As discussed above, underwriters may enlist the help of their analysts in raising their comfort level with these projections.

"Forward-looking statements" that appear in a 1933 Act prospectus or 1934 Act report and certain other documents have been entitled for many years to the protection of a "safe harbor" under the SEC's Rule 175 (or its 1934 Act counterpart, Rule 3b-6). The safe harbor is not available, however, if the statement lacked a "reasonable basis" or was disclosed "other than in good faith." In the event of litigation, these conditions almost guarantee that the issuer and any other defendants will be unable to obtain the dismissal of a complaint without going to trial.

Issuers' dissatisfaction with the safe harbors as they applied to litigation arising out of "earnings surprises" was a principal factor in the enactment of the Private Securities Litigation Reform Act of 1995 (the "Reform Act"), which became effective over the President's veto on December 22, 1995. Among other things, the Reform Act creates in Section 27A of the 1933 Act and Section 21E of the 1934 Act a multi-channel safe harbor for forward-looking statements. The first channel of the safe harbor provides that a person will not be liable for a forward-looking statement, whether oral or written, if the statement is

> identified as a forward-looking statement and is accompanied by meaningful cautionary statements identifying important factors that could cause actual results to differ materially from those in the forward-looking statement.

As noted in the Conference Report,[23] this first channel of the safe harbor on its face does not require identification of "all" important factors that could cause results to differ materially. It remains to be seen, however, how the courts will deal

---

23. H. Conf. Rep. No. 104-369 (1995), reprinted in *Private Securities Litigation Reform Act of 1995: Law & Explanation*, Fed. Sec. L. Rep. (CCH) Extra Edition No. 1696 (January 10, 1996) at 68.

with the Conference Report's further statements that the safe harbor will not be lost by a "[f]ailure to include the particular factor that ultimately causes the forward-looking statement not to come true" or that plaintiffs should not have an opportunity to conduct discovery on what factors were known to the issuer at the time the statement was made or on the speaker's state of mind. It also remains to be seen how the courts will deal with the much-discussed situation where an issuer omits reference to a factor that may be the most likely factor to undermine the forward-looking statement.

Under the second channel of the safe harbor, a person is protected against liability if the forward-looking statement is immaterial. This preserves the ability of a defendant, for example, to argue that a statement was immaterial under the "bespeaks caution" doctrine even if the statement does not meet the new test referred to above.

Finally, even if a statement does not fit into either of the channels described above, the plaintiff loses unless it can prove that the forward-looking statement,

(1) if made by a natural person, was made with the actual knowledge by that person that the statement was false or misleading;
or
(2) if made by a business entity, was made by or with the approval of an executive officer of the entity with actual knowledge by that officer that the statement was false or misleading.

This last channel of the safe harbor flatly requires a plaintiff to demonstrate "actual knowledge" on the part of the speaker that the statement was false or misleading. Since the safe harbor applies to 1933 Act liability for prospectus disclosures, the Reform Act modifies to this extent the 1933 Act's private remedies by imposing liability based on actual intent to defraud rather than on a failure to act reasonably. The third channel of the safe harbor also enables a company to escape liability for a projection by a senior officer even though a more junior officer may have known facts tending to undermine the projection (the so-called "pipeline" problem).[24]

The Reform Act also provides a modified safe harbor for oral forward-looking statements by or on behalf of issuers that are subject to the reporting requirements of the 1934 Act. In these cases (for example, statements made at road shows), reference could be made to a "readily available written document" (e.g., a 1934 Act report) for information about the factors that could cause actual results to differ from the forward-looking statement.

The safe harbor can be relied upon by an issuer reporting under the 1934 Act, any person acting on its behalf, an "outside reviewer" or an underwriter (but only with respect to information provided by the issuer or information derived by the underwriter from such information). The safe harbor is not available for forward-looking statements that are included in financial statements prepared in accordance with generally accepted accounting principles (but it is available for statements included in MD&A), made in connection with IPOs or tender offers or 13D or similar ownership statements or that relate to issuers that have been sanctioned for securities violations during the past three years or that are blank check companies, partnerships or similar entities, investment companies, issuers of penny stock or issuers that are engaged in rollup or going-private transactions.

The Reform Act gives the SEC authority to expand the safe harbor, and the Conference Report recommends that the SEC do so "for established and reputable entities who are excluded from the safe harbor" under the Reform Act. The Conference Report refers to the Reform Act's safe harbor as a "starting point" and states its expectation that the SEC will continue its rulemaking proceedings in this area.[25]

---

24. *See*, e.g., *In re Kulicke & Soffa Industries Inc. Securities Litigation*, Fed. Sec. L. Rep. (CCH) [1990-91 Transfer Binder] ¶ 95,721 (E.D. Pa. Oct. 2, 1990) and *In re The Ultimate Corp. Securities Litigation*, Fed. Sec. L. Rep. (CCH) [1989 Transfer Binder] ¶ 94,522 and ¶ 94,523 (S.D.N.Y. Jun. 30, 1989).

25. Only a few days after the Reform Act became law, the SEC stated that in light of the Reform Act it would propose safe harbor relief for cer-

Unfortunately, the Reform Act's safe harbor does not cover projections in those cases where they are most needed, i.e., IPOs. For other transactions, however, the safe harbor offers significant protection to issuers and underwriters alike. For underwriters, a move by issuers to include projections in their prospectuses would be helpful in reducing underwriters' exposure, not only by diminishing their identification with the projections but also in ensuring an accurate dissemination of the projections together with the accompanying cautionary statements and assumptions.

The safe harbor will also be useful to underwriters, of course, to the extent that issuers in fact make more forward-looking information available to analysts and others. Such disclosure should increase market efficiency and avoid "earnings surprises"; however, this type of disclosure could still be inhibited by concerns about "selective disclosure." In those situations where issuers follow the practice of including their earnings projections in 1934 Act reports that are automatically incorporated into 1933 Act registration statements on Form S-3, both the issuer and the underwriter will enjoy the benefits of the safe harbor for the incorporated projections.

Finally, the SEC has it in its power to make the safe harbor available for initial public offerings. It should have every incentive to do so, given the concern often expressed by the staff about unequal disclosure of projections.

- *Guarantees and Credit Enhancement*

In many transactions, some form of guarantee or other credit enhancement is necessary in order for the securities to be sold at an acceptable price. A guarantee of a security is a separate security under Section 2(1) of the 1933 Act that must be registered—as a security issued by the guarantor—along with the security that it supports. Registration is not required, of course, if an exemption is available. As discussed in Chapter 10, a guarantee of commercial paper is subsumed into the com-

---

tain of the additional disclosures proposed to be required of issuers in its release on derivatives. SEC Release No. 33-7250 (December 28, 1995). It adopted such relief in SEC Release No. 33-7386 (January 31, 1997).

mercial paper and has the benefit of that instrument's exemption under the 1933 Act. Also as discussed in Chapter 10, a guarantee in the form of a letter of credit issued by a U.S. bank is not only exempt in its own right but bootstraps into exempt status the security that it supports.

There are many forms of credit enhancement that fall short of outright guarantees. The key difference is that credit enhancement generally takes the form of an agreement (often referred to as a "support agreement") between a third party and the issuer (or a trustee) where the agreement does not run directly to the securityholders. The SEC generally does not require a third party credit enhancer to register its obligations under the support agreement, but this does not mean that no disclosure need be provided about the third party. The staff takes the position that if an investor's return is materially dependent upon the third party credit enhancer, the issuer must provide sufficient information about the third party to enable an investor to assess the ability of the third party to meet the obligations undertaken in the support agreement.

The factors considered by the SEC staff as relevant in assessing the adequacy of disclosure in this area are discussed in Chapter 14.

The disclosure and related issues raised by third party credit enhancement must be addressed at an early stage of the preparation of the registration statement.

• *Initial Public Offerings*

Where common equity is being registered for which there is no established public trading market, the outside front cover page of the preliminary prospectus must set forth a bona fide estimate of the range of the maximum offering price of the shares to be offered.[26] The prospectus also must include a description of the various factors considered in determining the public offering price.[27] The following is an example of such a disclosure taken from the prospectus of a biotechnology company:

---

26. Regulation S-K, Item 501(b)(6).
27. Regulation S-K, Item 505.

Prior to this offering, there has been no public market for the Company's Common Stock. The initial public offering price has been determined by negotiations between the Company and the Representative of the Underwriters. Among the factors considered in determining such public offering price were the operating history of the Company, the quality of the Company's management and its approach to research and development, the prospects for the industry in which the Company operates, the prospects for the development of the Company's products and processes with an infusion of the additional capital to be raised in this offering, the general condition of the securities market at the time of the offering, and the demand for and market prices of stock of other companies engaged in biotechnology.

A question that is sometimes raised is the need to make a widespread distribution of an amended preliminary prospectus if the price that is ultimately fixed is below the range set forth on the cover page. Assume that the original preliminary prospectus sets forth a price range of $18 to $20 per share. An amended preliminary prospectus responding to SEC comments is distributed in accordance with the 48-hour requirement of Rule 15c2-8, and this preliminary prospectus contains the same price range. In the final few days before pricing, the managing underwriter reluctantly concludes that the only way to make the deal a success is to drop the offering price to $16. Can this be done at the last minute, or will it be necessary to first circulate a revised preliminary prospectus? Unless the proceeds of the offering are earmarked for a specific purpose and the price reduction materially affects the issuer's ability to achieve this purpose, it should be possible simply to insert the $16 offering price in the final prospectus without circulating a revised preliminary prospectus.

The prospectus for an initial public offering must identify any principal underwriter that intends to sell to any account over which it exercises discretionary authority and must include an estimate of the amount of securities so intended to be sold.[28] This information must be contained in a pre-effective amendment that is circulated if the information is not available when the registration statement is filed. To avoid this requirement, many managing underwriters simply include in the agreement among underwriters an undertaking not to sell to discretionary accounts, in which case the prospectus should state, "The underwriters do not intend to confirm sales to any accounts over which they exercise discretionary authority."

Where, as in the case in any IPO, there is no established public trading market in the United States, the prospectus must disclose the amount of common stock subject to outstanding options, warrants or convertible securities and the amount of common stock that could be sold pursuant to Rule 144 under the 1933 Act or that the issuer has agreed to register for sale by securityholders.[29] The purpose of this disclosure is to indicate the possibility that future sales of a substantial number of shares by existing shareholders could have an adverse impact on the market price of the stock being offered.

If equity securities are being registered for an IPO, the registration statement must include an undertaking by the registrant to provide to the underwriter at the closing certificates in such denominations and registered in such names as required by the underwriter to assure prompt delivery to each purchaser.[30] This requirement was designed to deal with abuses during the "hot issue" markets of 1959 to 1961 when certificates sometimes were withheld from investors to inhibit the resale of their shares.[31] This is less of a problem, of course, in an environment where DTC book-entry closings are the rule.

• *Requests for Confidential Treatment*

Item 601 of Regulation S-K sets forth the requirements for the filing of exhibits to the registration statement. One of the requirements that is often troublesome mandates the filing of every "con-

---

28. Regulation S-K, Item 508(j).

29. Regulation S-K, Item 201(a)(2).

30. Regulation S-K, Item 512(g).

31. *See Securities Exchange Commission, Special Study of Securities Markets* H. R. Doc. No. 95, pt. 1, at 527 (1963).

tract not made in the ordinary course of business which is material to the registrant and is to be performed in whole or in part at or after the filing of the registration statement . . . or was entered into not more than two years before such filing." Although the filing requirement is subject to numerous exceptions, issuers often object to the filing of particular contracts or portions of contracts because of competitive or related concerns.

Item 30 of Schedule A to the 1933 Act contemplates that the SEC may grant confidential treatment to contracts where disclosure "would impair the value of the contract and would not be necessary for the protection of investors." Rule 406 sets forth the substantive and procedural requirements for requesting confidential treatment for documents filed under the 1933 Act, and Rule 24b-2 does the same for 1934 Act documents. Guidance on these requirements is provided in the Division of Corporation Finance's "Staff Legal Bulletin No. 1 (CF)" dated February 28, 1997.

• *Posting an Internet Prospectus*

Up until the fall of 1996, relatively few prospectuses had been posted on the Internet as part of an underwritten public offering (as opposed to offerings by issuers directly to investors). Two notable examples were the prospectuses relating to the April 1996 IPO of Yahoo! Inc. and the May 1996 offering of Class B Common Stock of Berkshire Hathaway Inc. In the Yahoo situation, the issuer's identification with the Internet was so strong that it might have been surprising if the issuer had *not* posted its prospectus. In the Berkshire Hathaway situation, the posting of the prospectus was consistent with the issuer's desire to achieve the broadest possible distribution of the new securities.

Underwriters are probably not yet convinced that there are distribution or cost benefits in posting a prospectus on the Internet. In addition, some securities lawyers have expressed the following concerns about the practice.

• • *Federal Securities Law Concerns.* In an October 1995 release,[32] the SEC stated its view that "the use of electronic me-

---

32. SEC Release No. 33-7233 (October 6, 1995).

dia should be at least an equal alternative to the use of paper-based media." Insofar as the SEC is concerned, therefore, a preliminary or final prospectus may be posted on the Internet as a means of soliciting investors to purchase the registered securities. (In fact, the SEC's October 1995 release stated expressly that "offering may now be made exclusively through electronic means.")

It is difficult, however, to resist the temptation to expand an Internet posting that goes beyond the four corners of the preliminary or final prospectus.[33] It is easy to provide the investor with links that make possible a rapid switch to the issuer's own home page,[34] to the issuer's 1934 Act reports or even to a playback of the road show. (All of this can also be done by means of CD-ROM diskettes.) In the case of a preliminary prospectus, of course, none of this information can be provided to an investor unless it is part of the registration statement as filed with the SEC under the 1933 Act. Underwriters understandably have a reluctance to accept Section 11 liability for any of this information for which they would not otherwise have such liability.

---

33. The question also arises whether to include the Website address in the prospectus. If the Website contains only the prospectus, there is not much point in doing so. If it contains additional information (especially with links to other Websites), there has been some concern that merely supplying the Website address might expose the underwriters to liability for all information that could be accessed from the Website. (In theory, at least, this might be all the information on the Internet!) In late 1996 the SEC staff advised an issuer that the mere identification in a prospectus of its Website (together with a statement that the issuer's 1934 Act reports were available from that source) would not in and of itself "include or incorporate by reference any information into the registration statement which is included or hot linked to the Company's regular Website but is not otherwise incorporated by reference into the registration statement." SEC No-Action Letter *ITT Corporation* (available December 6, 1996). Of course, the staff position does not address an investor's ability to base a claim on alleged reliance upon information available from or through the Website.

34. According to a recent survey of the corporate membership of the National Investor Relations Institute, 55% of these companies currently had a Website and 29% were planning a Website within the next year. NIRI, *Utilizing Technology in the Practice of Investor Relations* (August 1996).

In the case of a final prospectus, on the other hand, the information can be provided without its being part of the registration statement since it is clearly "accompanied" by the final prospectus. The underwriters may still have Section 12(a)(2) or Rule 10b-5 liability for this information, however, and by this time the usefulness of the Internet posting as a selling tool has considerably diminished.

• • *Blue Sky and International Concerns.* Whether or not Internet prospectuses are "offers" or "advertising" under state "blue sky" laws was more of a concern before the Improvements Act, which preempts state securities laws insofar as they would otherwise apply to listed or NASDAQ National Market System securities or securities of equal or senior ranking. As to other securities, many states exempt prospectuses that are transmitted by radio or television or print media originating outside the state, but these exemptions do not expressly cover electronic formats such as the Internet.

Several states have already acted to exempt "Internet offers" from the registration and advertising provisions of their laws. For example, Pennsylvania issued an order in August 1995 that exempts Internet offers where (i) the offer states that it is not being made to persons in Pennsylvania, (ii) no offer is "otherwise specifically directed to any person in Pennsylvania by . . . or on behalf of the issuer" and (iii) where no sales of the securities are made in Pennsylvania as a result of the Internet offer. In addition, the North American Securities Administrators Association ("NASAA") adopted a resolution in early 1996 in which it urged states to take appropriate steps to adopt similar exemptions. By the fall of 1996, more than 20 states had adopted such an exemption.[35]

It goes without saying that state law presents no problem where the Internet offer is made only to exempt institutions (e.g., by means of a password available only to qualifying institutional customers). In the case of a non-exempt offering

---

35. For a comprehensive Internet site devoted to state securities regulation, administered by the Thurman Marshall Law Library of the University of Maryland Law School, see www.law.ab.umd.edu/marshall/bluesky.

where access is not restricted by means of a password, however, the trend is clearly in the direction of treating Internet-posted documents in the same manner as paper prospectuses. In this connection, paper prospectuses are frequently circulated in states where the related securities are neither exempt nor registered under state law. The prospectuses contain the customary legend, of course, to the effect that the prospectus is not intended as an offer or solicitation in any state or other jurisdiction where this would be unlawful. Given the adverse publicity that has accompanied most efforts to regulate use of the Internet for any purpose, it may be anticipated that there is little danger that state securities authorities will take action against an underwriter or issuer that posts a preliminary or final prospectus on the Internet and where access to the document is by means of a screen that contains the appropriate legend. It might be quite another thing, of course, if the document were used to make actual sales of non-exempt and non-qualified securities to non-exempt buyers in a particular state.

Concern is also expressed from time to time that a foreign securities regulator might regard the ability of its citizens to access an Internet prospectus as an illegal public offering of that security in that country, with possible regulatory or liability consequences. One can conceive of a Website being used to target investors in a given country, with predictable consequences. In other cases, given the international protest that was raised when German authorities recently sought to restrict the content of Websites accessible through Compuserve, adverse consequences would appear extremely unlikely. Again, however, it would be advisable to use an appropriate restrictive legend.

The SEC Review Process

Once a working draft of the registration statement has been prepared by the issuer and its counsel, it will be reviewed by the managing underwriters and counsel for the underwriters and a number of drafting sessions will be held to work on the disclosure. The managing underwriters, with the assistance of counsel, will complete their due diligence investigations (see

Chapter 5), and their insights will be reflected in the disclosure document.

During this period, the body of the prospectus may be on underwriters' counsel's word processing system, while the financial statements will be on the issuer's accountants' system. Both systems may be compatible with the printer's system, but this cannot always be assumed.

After the customary "all nighter" at the printer, when the final changes are made and proof pages are checked and rechecked, the registration statement will be filed at the SEC's Washington, D.C. office. Except in the case of offerings by foreign issuers, the filing will ordinarily be made in electronic form pursuant to the SEC's Regulation S-T by means of the Electronic Data Gathering, Analysis and Retrieval ("EDGAR") system.[36]

• *Selective Review*

The SEC's Division of Corporation Finance reviews registration statements on a selective basis. A registration statement on Form S-1 covering an IPO will almost always be selected for full review by the staff. Registration statements on Form S-2 or Form S-3 are less likely to be reviewed, particularly where the issuer's 1934 Act reports have recently been reviewed by the staff. If the registration statement covers a security that is "novel and unique," this will increase the chances for review (although the review may be less than a full review). The issuer's industry, whether or not it has been involved in a recent restructuring and whether or not its filing presents "hot button" issues (e.g., derivatives, environmental liabilities, regulatory problems) will also affect the chances for review.

It should be noted that all SEC examiners are soon to be armed with direct Internet access for the express purpose of enabling them to retrieve public information about the issuers

---

36. Instructions relating to the preparation of documents for electronic filing and the procedures to be followed in making such filings are set forth in the SEC's EDGAR Filing Manual. Registration fees in connection with electronic filings must be made to the SEC's "lockbox" depository. There are verification and timing advantages in paying these fees by wire transfer.

whose registration statements they are reviewing. Careful counsel will not allow themselves to be surprised by an SEC comment based on an Internet report of which they were unaware.

Oral advice that a registration statement will or will not be reviewed generally can be obtained from the SEC's staff within a few days after filing. If there is to be no review, the staff will confirm its telephonic advice by letter. If there is to be a full review, it is usually safe to assume under current staff policies that comments will be forthcoming within 30 days. In any event, the managing underwriter should plan its marketing efforts accordingly. If marketing begins too soon, investor interest may cool while the deal is hung up at the SEC.

• *SEC Comments*

Any questions that the Division of Corporation Finance may have with respect to the registration statement and any suggestions that it may have for improving disclosure will be set forth in a "letter of comments," a term that has come to replace the former pejorative term, "deficiency letter." Accounting comments sometimes will be made in a separate letter prepared by the SEC's accounting staff. If the comments are relatively brief, the examiner may be willing to read them over the telephone.

A lengthy comment letter is not necessarily an indication that a registration statement has been poorly prepared. While counsel is always pleased to receive a brief letter of comments, and even more pleased to receive no comments at all, he or she has no right to brag to the client if the SEC's comments are light. The length or complexity of a comment letter depends primarily upon the perceptions of the examiner. Experience proves that a skillfully drafted registration statement may draw heavy comments, particularly if the transaction is a highly visible one, while a registration statement that is no better prepared may receive few, if any, comments.

Some comments will take the form of questions designed to elicit assurance that certain disclosures have been adequately made. Some will seek supplemental information to support the disclosure or lack of disclosure of a particular matter. Others will simply indicate a lack of understanding on the examiner's part or a failure to read the document with sufficient care. Most comments, however, are well thought out, and some will lead to a substantial improvement in the registration statement. Counsel should welcome any suggestion made by the examiner to which he or she can respond, "That's a good comment."

• *Responding to Comments*

Some comments should be discussed with the examiner by telephone, if only to clarify their meaning and intent. But lengthy arguments should be avoided. The comment in dispute may have come from the examiner's superior, and the examiner will not have the authority to concede the point in question. The usual response will be, "Put it in your letter of transmittal, and we'll consider your argument." It is sometimes possible to resolve open items by the informal submission of draft language.

A face-to-face meeting in Washington is seldom called for and usually will be discouraged by the staff. An exception is a meeting to discuss significant accounting comments. SEC partners at the major accounting firms maintain a close working relationship with their counterparts at the SEC and frequently prefer to deal with accounting issues at a meeting at the SEC's offices.

Each and every comment should be addressed in the letter transmitting the amended registration statement to the SEC. A useful device is to attach a photocopy of the comment letter to the transmittal letter with each comment numbered. The comments can then be referred to by number as they are addressed in the transmittal letter. A comment should be referred to in the transmittal letter even if it has been responded to in full. This will speed up the review process by leading the examiner to the place in the registration statement where the particular comment has been dealt with. It takes little effort to state in the transmittal letter, "As requested by comment 12, the word 'excellent' has been changed to 'good' on page 34 of the prospectus." The change will have been black-lined, as will have been all changes made in the registration statement.[37]

---

37. Rule 472 requires the filing of at least five copies of each amendment to a registration statement marked to indicate, by underlining or in some other appropriate manner, the changes made. On the other hand, Rule

One of the most vexing problems that can arise during a financing is the 11th hour comment from the SEC. Even after the examiner has signed off and the offering has been priced, there is always the possibility of a phone call relating one last comment from the examiner's supervisor. This may result in an even later night at the printer. Even worse is the comment that is made after the price amendment has been filed or the registration statement has become effective pursuant to Rule 430A. Such a comment usually can be handled in the prospectus filed under Rule 424 without filing a further amendment to the registration statement.[38]

• *Recirculation*

After the SEC's comments have been dealt with and any necessary amendment to the registration statement filed, the managing underwriter may raise the question whether "recirculation" of the amended preliminary prospectus will be required. Recirculation is a somewhat misunderstood term. It should be used only to refer to a requirement imposed by the SEC that the amended preliminary prospectus be delivered to each person who received a copy of the preliminary prospectus as originally filed. The authors are not aware of any situation in recent years where the SEC has imposed such a requirement, although the staff will occasionally ask for assurances that investors will be orally informed of certain changes before they are asked to commit to a purchase. On the other hand, securities lawyers will often err on the side of caution where there have been extensive changes to the preliminary prospectus and advise the underwriters to recirculate the document. One reason for this advice in the case of IPOs may be that there will otherwise be doubt whether the distribution of the original

---

310 of Regulation S-T provides that for EDGAR filings all marking requirements "shall" be satisfied by electronic "tags." These tags are much less helpful than precise-blacklined hard copies of amended filings, but it is understood that SEC policy discourages its staff reviewers from requesting precise-blacklined hard copies. Accordingly, many practitioners volunteer these as a routine matter.

38. This procedure usually requires consultation with the SEC's staff.

preliminary prospectus satisfied the 48-hour distribution requirement of Rule 15c2-8 under the 1934 Act.

In some cases, the change may be so material, such as an accounting change that required a reduction in stated earnings per share, that the underwriters would be ill-advised to price the issue before the preliminary prospectus containing the change has received wide distribution in the marketplace. Here the issue is not whether the underwriters need to "recirculate," but to what extent must the revised information be disseminated to protect the underwriters from the possibility of complaints from purchasers who learn of the change only upon receipt of the final prospectus.

• *Price Information (Rule 430A)*

Traditionally, the final pricing of an offering would take place after the close of the market on the day before the registration statement was to become effective. The underwriting agreement would be signed and held in escrow until the following morning just prior to the filing of the price amendment, i.e., the amendment to the registration statement that reflected the pricing terms. The price information would be inserted in the registration statement and checked and rechecked at the printer.

Delays at the SEC in declaring the price amendment effective sometimes led to serious inconvenience on the part of the underwriters, who could not confirm sales until the registration statement became effective. As discussed in Chapter 2, the SEC addressed this problem in 1987 by adopting Rule 430A. This rule permits a registration statement to become effective without pricing information, provided that the omitted information is included in a supplemented prospectus filed under Rule 424.

Whether the price information is inserted into a price amendment or a prospectus supplement, the greatest care is required. This can be illustrated by an incident that occurred some years ago in connection with an offering of capital notes by a large New York City bank. The preliminary offering circular contained a statement on its cover to the effect that the initial optional redemption price of the notes was their "principal amount plus a premium of __%." The blank was to be filled in when the interest rate and the initial redemption premium were finally set. Negotiations resulted in a figure of, let us assume, 8%. When the final offering circular arrived on the chairman's desk the following morning, he noticed that the figure that appeared in the blank was "108%," the initial redemption *price* rather than the initial redemption *premium.* The notes were stated to be redeemable at their "principal amount plus a premium of 108%." None of the 20 people who had worked so carefully at the printer the previous evening had caught the error. Faces were red, and the circular was reprinted. The senior author obtained a copy of the erroneous circular and kept it in his desk for many years as a reminder that "there but for the grace of God go I."

Post-filing Issues

Once the registration statement has been filed and the underwriters are ready to market the issue, there are legal issues to be considered that are different from those that arise in the prefiling period. It is during this period that the difficult problems frequently arise. This is when counsel may be called upon to put out a fire that threatens the success of the deal.

• Road Shows (Electronic and Otherwise)

As part of its efforts to sell the securities, the managing underwriter will organize a "road show"—a series of meetings throughout the country, and frequently abroad, at which the company's management will make presentations to invited groups of institutional investors, money managers and securities salesmen. Where appropriate, the manager may arrange for the company's chief executive officer or another corporate official to have "one-on-one" meetings with important prospective investors. These marketing efforts may begin only after the registration statement has been filed.

The pitch to prospective investors at road show presentations clearly constitutes an offer of the subject securities. The purpose of the road show is to solicit interest from major potential investors. These offers are permissible because oral offers are permitted once the registration statement is filed. Just as registered representatives of the underwriters may solicit interest from their customers once the registration statement is filed, so too may company officers solicit interest from other prospective purchasers.

In preparing for a road show, corporate officers often will be told by their counsel that they cannot say anything that is not in the preliminary prospectus. This is overly conservative advice. There is nothing in the 1933 Act that states that statements made in an effort to market securities must be limited to statements contained in the registration statement. A road show presentation would be stilted indeed if the chief executive officer were not permitted to range beyond the factual statements in the prospectus and discuss with potential investors his or her own views as to his or her company's prospects, the prospects for the industry in which it operates, and the economic factors affecting its business.

The only written document that should be distributed at a road show presentation is the preliminary prospectus. The documents incorporated by reference into a Form S-3 prospectus may be distributed as well, although it is not customary to do so. Although annual reports may be distributed to shareholders during the registration period, they should not be used as part of a selling effort. By the same token, although slide presentations of charts are appropriate, hard copies of the charts should not be distributed to prospective investors. Whether a statement is an offer or a document is a prospectus will depend not only on its content but also on the context in which it is made or used. Admittedly, the practice may sometimes be otherwise, but from a legal standpoint, the distribution of annual reports and other written materials other than the preliminary prospectus has no legal justification where the object is to create interest in the securities being distributed.

Slide projections of charts and graphs customarily are used to punctuate the presentation. Are these written offers? No one has ever taken the position that they are. Presumably, the reason for distinguishing between oral offers and written offers during the pre-effective period is that oral offers are ephemeral while written offers are concrete and can have a greater impact on a prospective investor. The impact of a slide projection is not substantially greater than an oral statement.

From time to time, videocassettes have been prepared for use at road show presentations. It is questionable how effective they are, but they are not objectionable from a legal standpoint. It is true that Section 2(10) of the 1933 Act defines the term "prospectus" to include an offer that is "written or by radio or television." A radio or television advertisement broadcast to the public clearly is a prospectus for purposes of Section 5 of the 1933 Act, but it should be equally clear that this definition was not intended to extend to a videocassette presentation at a road show simply because it appears on a television or similar screen.

It would be a somewhat different question if a videotape of a road show presentation were made available to investors. There is a somewhat inconclusive no-action letter[39] to the effect that this might be permitted in small groups. The point is becoming more important as underwriters are increasingly

---

39. Under date of July 22, 1986, Exploration, Inc., a video production company, sought a no-action letter from the SEC with respect to its planned marketing of videocassette tapes to be used at road shows and to be sent to prospective underwriters and selling group members. The tapes would describe or highlight matters discussed in the preliminary prospectus, including the company's history, information concerning its products and services, its management's experience, and its objectives and strategy for growth. The videotapes usually would include short interviews with the issuer's management, as well as employees and customers. In each instance there would be a contemporaneous distribution of the preliminary prospectus. The request clearly stated, "The road show meetings are intended primarily to familiarize the professional investment community with the issuer and its management." Counsel made a convincing argument that videotape presentations at small gatherings are not prospectuses within the meaning of Section 2(10) of the 1933 Act.

The office of the chief counsel of the Division of Corporation Finance responded that, "[b]ased on the facts presented, but without necessarily agreeing with your legal analysis," no enforcement action would be recommended. The no-action letter went on to state, "We understand that the videotapes will be used at due diligence meetings attended by prospective members of underwriting syndicates and selling groups, as described in your letter, and will be sent to other prospective underwriters and selling group members."

making road show presentations available to investors by electronic means. Technology now permits an investor to use a CD-ROM diskette, an on-line computer link or a private communications system to access at the investor's convenience a video and audio playback of the road show. As in the case of e-mail messages (discussed in Chapter 1), the status of an "electronic road show" in one of these formats should depend on whether or not the presentation is being used as a substitute for an oral communication (e.g., in lieu of the investor's physical presence at the meeting). A closed-circuit transmission of a road show presentation would clearly be acceptable. If so, why not a simple playback of the same presentation? The line is admittedly hard to draw, and the task would become even more difficult if underwriters were to decide to dispense with the traditional road show in favor of providing investors with the equivalent of electronic selling literature. On the other hand, the SEC should have every reason to encourage the use of technology to expand road show access in view of its expressed concern over many years that individual investors were disadvantaged by their "exclusion" from the road show.

In early 1997, the SEC staff issued its first no-action letter on the subject of electronic road shows (*Private Financial Network* (available March 12, 1997)). A service proposed to provide to its subscribers—who were not limited to broker-dealers—video transmissions of road shows for registered securities offerings, either live as the shows occurred or on a delayed basis. The service undertook to limit the transmissions to subscribers who agreed not to videotape, copy or further disseminate the transmissions and who had received a copy of the current filed prospectus. Transmissions would include statements that would emphasize the importance of the written prospectus and the prohibition against copying or retransmission. Finally, issuers and underwriters would agree to take reason-

---

This, of course, is somewhat inconsistent with the request letter, which implied that prospective investors would be present at the road show meetings. SEC No-action Letter, *Exploration, Inc.* (available November 10, 1986).

able steps to ensure that the information disclosed in the road show was "not inconsistent" with the filed prospectus.

The staff stated that it would not recommend enforcement action if the service were to transmit road shows as described in its letter. The correspondence is significant as a first step by the Division of Corporation Finance in acknowledging the value of electronic road shows. In particular, there is no reason why underwriters should not be entitled to the same relief. On the civil liability front, however, a rule would be more helpful. In addition, there is some ambiguity in the requirement that the road show be "not inconsistent" with the filed prospectus, particularly inasmuch as information is often furnished at a road show that is simply not covered in the prospectus (e.g., projections).

• *Dealing With Gun-jumping Problems*

Counsel for the underwriters must be prepared to deal promptly with any gun-jumping problems[40] that arise during the course of a registered public offering. In some cases, a problem may be dealt with independently without involving the staff of the SEC, but in other cases, it can be handled only through consultation with the staff. It is a matter of judgment as to when and under what circumstances the staff should be consulted.

The problems that arise can be bizarre, but rarely as bizarre as the problem faced some years ago by a major investment banking firm that was acting as co-manager of a large offering of notes to be issued by one of New York City's principal bank holding companies. Late in the afternoon of the day before the registration statement was to become effective, the office manager of one of the firm's retail branch offices called frantically and said that he had a problem. He had discovered that one of his registered representatives had prepared a one-page flyer urging purchases of the notes, had taken a supply of them to the local Bloomingdale's parking lot, and had stuffed them under the windshield wipers of all of the cars on the lot.

---

40. After the filing of the registration statement, "gun-jumping" refers to the use of written offering material other than the preliminary prospectus.

The registration statement was to become effective on the following day. It was 4:00 in the afternoon. A meeting was held, and the co-manager's outside counsel was consulted. After developing the facts, counsel and an officer of the co-manager met with underwriters' counsel to review the alternatives. The initial reaction of underwriters' counsel was to phone the SEC. It was the view of the other law firm that at this late hour the SEC's involvement could be disruptive of a major financing. There was not sufficient time to explain the situation to the SEC without running the risk that the offering would be delayed. Both firms finally agreed that under the circumstances the matter could be handled internally. The problem was confined to one office, and the co-manager withdrew that office's allocation of notes. The office was instructed that it could not refer customers to any other office. Later, a compliance visit was made to the office, and a seminar was held on the restrictions imposed by the securities laws during a distribution. Also, the registered representative was fired. The action taken was documented in a memorandum to underwriters' counsel.

Here, the violation did not go to the integrity of the offering. Because the violation was confined to a particular locale, it was concluded that it would be sufficient to remove the offending office from the offering and that it would not be necessary to drop the entire firm from the deal. It was concluded that, if the SEC should raise a question in the future, the action taken could be justified.

The point has been made that whether a statement constitutes an offer and whether a document constitutes a prospectus depends as much on its context—i.e., timing and audience—as its content. An example of how this principle may be applied arose in the context of a registered common stock offering by a retailer of electronic equipment. The company had filed a registration statement but had delayed the offering pending the closing of an attractive acquisition opportunity that had been presented to it after filing. Once the deal was closed, it had every intention of amending the registration statement to reflect the acquisition and of proceeding with the sale of the common stock.

The company not only operated its own retail outlets but also had numerous franchisees. Its relationships with the manufacturers of the products that it sold were important to its business. Management decided that as soon as the acquisition was completed it would write to its franchisees and suppliers to assure them that the acquisition would strengthen the company and would make their business relationships with the company even more desirable. Counsel for the underwriters was asked whether the distribution of this written material in the manner proposed would raise problems under the 1933 Act in view of the pending public offering.

The material would contain strong positive statements that indeed would create problems if used in the context of a public offering. But, in this case, the statements were to be directed exclusively to franchisees and suppliers for the sole purpose of strengthening existing business relationships. Any of these persons might incidentally buy shares in the offering, but the communications were in no way designed to generate interest in the common stock. They were not intended to result in the sale of one additional share. Underwriters' counsel advised that, while he would like to review the documents before they were distributed, he did not expect that he would object to their use in this particular business context.

• • *Internet Publicity.* A more recent episode illustrates the dangers of electronic communication. The financial press reported in October 1996 the postponement because of "market conditions" of an "Internet-media" company's "long-awaited" IPO. There was also speculation, however, as reported in *The Wall Street Journal* on October 25, 1996, that the deal had been pulled because of an e-mail memorandum sent by the issuer's chief executive officer "to the company's 334 employees in the wake of news reports skeptical about the company's IPO prospects." The memo found its way onto an on-line service with 10,000 subscribers with the result that the sender's optimistic views were sent around the world just before the pricing of the planned IPO.

The company denied that the e-mail message had anything to do with the withdrawal of the offering. If it had been otherwise, one could have argued that the original communication was proper and that the issuer should not be penalized for a recipient's unauthorized public dissemination of the message. An analogy might have been made to an institutional investor who, despite warnings to the contrary, commented on a road show presentation to the press. On the other hand, the e-mail message was sent to a fairly large and possibly unsophisticated (at least when it comes to the securities laws) audience, and there is no indication that there were warnings to the employees that the message was to be treated confidentially. One might anticipate that the SEC staff's reaction would be that the issuer should not benefit from an employee's widespread dissemination of an upbeat message not in conformity with the securities laws, and that the staff might well require a reasonable postponement of the commencement of the offering.

• • *Press Coverage.* Unauthorized communications with the press can lead to difficult problems. Three weeks before the planned pricing of a 1990 common stock offering for a major company, the "Heard on the Street" column of *The Wall Street Journal* reported earnings projections on the issuer which had been confirmed to the author of the column by an analyst for one of the co-managers. Understandably, the SEC staff immediately demanded an explanation from the underwriters. It was eventually agreed that the projections would be included in the prospectus and identified as having been confirmed by the co-manager's analyst. The transaction proceeded on schedule, but the underwriters had to live with Section 11 liability for estimates that would ordinarily have been communicated only in verbal form.

As illustrated by the foregoing example, one of the realities of modern financial markets is the aggressive coverage of corporate securities transactions by the U.S. and international financial press. This coverage has directly conflicted on many occasions with the SEC's interpretation of the gun-jumping prohibitions of the 1933 Act as well as its more recent rules on "directed selling efforts" in the United States in connection with offshore offerings under Regulation S (discussed in Chapter 9). For a number of years, the conflict has been so pronounced that many issuers have excluded both the U.S. and foreign-based press from their offshore press conferences and similar activities whenever a current or proposed offshore securities offering (or tender offer) was being discussed. Congress required the SEC in the Improvements Act to adopt rules on the subject, but even before the Improvement Act became law the SEC acted to propose an exemptive rule (discussed in Chapter 9). It will be interesting to see whether the important purpose of the rule—to encourage more rather than less information—will not logically require the SEC to provide corresponding relief within the United States.

• • *Research Coverage.* Research material often presents problems under the 1933 Act because of the prohibition in Section 5(b)(l) against the dissemination of any prospectus unless it meets the requirements of Section 10 of the 1933 Act. Research material may constitute a prospectus as defined by Section 2(10) of the 1933 Act, but research material seldom meets the requirements of Section 10. Accordingly, the dissemination of research material must rely on an exemption from Section 5(b)(l).

The most common problems in this area arise as a result of the underwriters' research activity. It is understandable that analysts wish to maintain the continuity of their coverage, and it is certainly true that customers expect to receive continuous coverage. For this reason, the SEC in 1970 adopted a series of rules designed to minimize the number and scope of restrictions on research.[41] The rules were originally proposed in the *Wheat Report.*[42]

Rule 137 states in substance that a dealer is not an "underwriter" in respect of a registered offering of a reporting issuer if the dealer distributes research in the regular course of business and is not and does not propose to be a member of the underwriting syndicate or the dealer group. The rule also requires, as might be expected, that the dealer not receive any direct or indirect consideration from anyone participating in the

---

41. SEC Release No. 33-5101 (November 19, 1970).

42. "Disclosure to Investors—A Reappraisal of Administrative Policies Under the '33 and '34 Acts" (1969).

offering and that the dealer not be distributing the research pursuant to any arrangement with any such person. The effect of Rule 137 is to make a dealer eligible for the Section 4(3) exemption as a dealer who is not an underwriter. In the case of a reporting company, this means that the dealer may distribute research to its customers without limitation. Since the rule is not applicable to non-reporting companies, a dealer not participating in an IPO is unable to obtain any research advantage over an underwriter: Section 4(3) will not exempt research distributed prior to the offering date, and it exempts research distributed after the offering date on the same terms for participating and non-participating dealers alike.

Rule 138 provides that, if a qualified issuer has filed or proposes to file a registration statement relating to non-convertible debt securities or nonconvertible preferred stock, the publication in the regular course of business by a dealer of information, opinions or recommendations relating solely to the issuer's common stock or convertible securities will not be deemed to constitute an "offer" of the securities being registered, even though the dealer is a member of the underwriting syndicate. The reverse is also true, i.e., if the registration statement covers common stock or convertible securities, a dealer acting as an underwriter of those securities may continue to publish information and opinions solely with respect to the issuer's non-convertible debt securities or preferred stock.

A qualified issuer for purposes of Rule 138 is any issuer that meets both the registrant and transaction requirements of Form S-2 or the registrant requirements of Form S-3 or, in addition, any foreign private issuer that meets the registrant requirements of Form F-3 (except for the reporting history requirements) and meets the minimum float or investment grade conditions of the form and has had its securities traded for at least 12 months on a "designated offshore securities market" (see the discussion in Chapter 9 relating to Regulation S).

An instruction to Rule 138 makes clear that a dealer may rely on the rule to distribute research on the issuer's equity or debt securities notwithstanding its participation as an underwriter in discrete "takedowns" of debt or equity securities, respectively, from a "generic" or "universal" shelf registration statement (see Chapter 8).

Another rule in this series was Rule 139, which permitted an underwriter or prospective underwriter to publish in the regular course of business certain information, opinions or recommendations about registered securities issued by reporting companies under the 1934 Act. Conditions to Rule 139 required in effect, however, that references to the registered securities had to be accompanied by references to other securities, and that any opinion or recommendation could not be more favorable than a previous opinion or recommendation.

Notwithstanding the adoption of Rule 139 and its companion rules, the task of separating "normal" research from forbidden "gun-jumping" remained difficult. In addition, it became apparent in the early 1980s that the Commission's integrated disclosure system would not work without a broader involvement by securities analysts and the financial press.

Increasing conflicts between research and underwriting activity led many broker-dealers by the early 1980s to request more specific standards from the Commission on the bounds of permissible research. Some of these requests were supported by appeals to the First Amendment, which the Supreme Court had begun in the 1970s to apply to "commercial speech."[43]

The Commission accommodated these requests to some degree in 1984, when it adopted a major liberalization of Rule 139.[44] The principal liberalizing aspect of the amended rule was that it carved out, in Rule 139(a), those issuers that met the requirements for the use of Form S-3 or Form F-3 and that also met the minimum "float" or investment grade rating requirements of these forms. As to these issuers, the dissemination of information, opinions or recommendations does not constitute a violation of Section 5 if it is "contained in a publication

---

43. *Virginia State Bd. of Pharmacy v. Virginia Citizens Consumer Council, Inc.*, 425 U.S. 758 (1976). *See also* Petition for Rulemaking, Washington Legal Foundation, filed with the Securities Exchange Commission (December 20, 1995).

44. SEC Release No. 33-6550 (September 19, 1984).

which is distributed with reasonable regularity in the normal course of business."

Rule 139(a) permits considerable latitude for research relating to (1) those companies that meet the registrant requirements of Form S-3 or Form F-3 as well as the minimum float and investment grade securities provisions of that form or (2) foreign private issuers that meet the requirements specified above for Rule 138. For these companies and their securities, the only condition is that the research be "contained in a publication which is distributed with reasonable regularity in the normal course of business." An instruction to the rule states that a publication has not been distributed with "reasonable regularity" if it contains information, an opinion or a recommendation concerning a company with respect to which the dealer "currently is not publishing research." The significance of the instruction is not always clear. It obviously means that a dealer that hopes to be an underwriter in a forthcoming offering by a particular issuer cannot rely on the rule to initiate coverage of that issuer's securities. On the other hand, assume that a dealer proposes to initiate coverage of a new steel company by including it in a quarterly industry survey just prior to *another steel company's* registered offering. It would be unreasonable to read the instruction as requiring that the dealer exclude the new company from the survey and publish its views in a stand-alone report.

Securities research has come to be distributed more frequently in electronic form. It hardly deserves mention that screen-based research (which by its nature is made available to the investor rather than "distributed") is nonetheless eligible to qualify as a "publication" that is "distributed with reasonable regularity in the normal course of business."

When the issuer does not satisfy the requirements specified in Rule 139(a), the research material may still be permitted under Rule 139(b) if it is contained in a publication that meets the "reasonable regularity" test of Rule 139(a) and "includes similar information, opinions or recommendations with respect to a substantial number of companies in the registrant's industry or sub-industry, or contains a comprehensive list of securities currently recommended" by the dealer. In this case, the information, opinion or recommendation may be given no "materially greater space or prominence" in the publication than that given to other securities or issuers. Also, an opinion or recommendation "as favorable or more favorable" as to the company or its securities must have been published by the dealer in its last publication addressing the issuer or its securities prior to the commencement of the dealer's participation in the distribution. The "space or prominence" and "as favorable or more favorable" requirements are extremely difficult to apply in practice, particularly with respect to fixed-income securities.

An instruction to Rule 139(b) states that a publication that contains projections of an issuer's sales or earnings cannot meet the rule's conditions unless the projections (1) were previously published on a regular basis, (2) are included with respect to a substantial number of companies in the issuer's industry or sub-industry or all companies in a comprehensive list contained in the publication and (3) are not more favorable than previously published projections.

Rule 139 did not anticipate the degree to which fixed-income research has become an important market factor. Given the number of issuers of fixed-income securities, it is much more difficult for broker-dealers in these securities to meet the "reasonable regularity" test of Rule 139. On the other hand, the standard has to be a flexible one. "Reasonable regularity" of coverage for a common stock probably implies coverage over a period of at least several quarters. For a fixed-income security, however, it is probably fair to conclude that "reasonable regularity" can be established with a single report if it is published at a time when no underwriting is in sight and with the intention to maintain continuous coverage (as evidenced, perhaps, by continuous coverage of similar securities or products).

The provisions of Rule 139 can never be satisfied in the case of an IPO as there will have been no prior history of research coverage. Thus, the blackout period on research reports will extend through the 25-day or longer prospectus delivery period, and the initial research report may not be published until this period is over.

Despite these rules, questions with respect to research reports and similar material published by securities firms frequently arise in connection with underwritten offerings. Often the resolution of the question turns on timing. Research material should not be a problem if distributed by a managing underwriter prior to reaching an understanding with the issuer that it will manage a financing. In the case of a non-managing underwriter, the restriction on research reports will not apply until it decides to accept an invitation to participate in the underwriting.

Gun-jumping problems, whether of the press coverage or research variety, are among the types of problems that can arise in connection with any financing. Dealing with such issues is one of the most important tasks that must be performed by lawyers representing securities firms. The staff of the SEC makes every effort to be helpful when problems of this type arise as long as it is convinced that the problem arose through human error and with no intention of violating the securities laws.

All this being said, the SEC's rules on research are in need of a major overhaul. Investors require continuous in-depth research from broker-dealer firms in order to be able to cope with the volatility of securities markets, the complexity of financial instruments and the amount of information released by issuers. Increasingly, investors are receiving this research material by electronic means that cannot be easily interrupted when the issuer of the research finds itself participating in a distribution. The SEC concept release of mid-1996 cited "the deregulation of offers" as a possible means of resolving these conflicts.

- *Regulation M Problems*

In the case of equity offerings where the same securities are trading in the secondary market, it may occur that an underwriter will inadvertently enter a bid for or purchase the security during the restricted period contemplated by Rule 101 under Regulation M. The response of underwriters' counsel to this type of situation is discussed in Chapter 4.

- *"T+3" Settlement Date and Prospectus Delivery Problems*

As discussed in Chapter 1, a copy of the final prospectus must precede or accompany each confirmation of sale. For years, chronic delays in printing the final prospectus and in delivering it to underwriters in sufficient quantities have frequently caused delays in the mailing of confirmations. Historically, these delays especially affected underwriters located outside New York, thus giving rise to references to the "Texas problem" or the "California problem."

The problem threatened to become worse with the SEC's adoption in 1995 of its Rule 15c6-1 to require "T+3" settlements in lieu of the historical "T+5" settlement convention. In response to underwriters' concerns, the SEC simultaneously adopted amendments to its rules and registration forms to facilitate the delivery of prospectuses.[45] These amendments included (1) a package of changes to rules and registration forms designed to speed up the process of preparing full prospectuses for delivery to customers with confirmations, (2) a new Rule 434 designed to reduce the amount of paper involved in the confirmation process by permitting the use of "term sheets" as supplements to previously delivered preliminary or base prospectuses and (3) modifications to Rule 15c6-1 to permit, among other things, routine settlement on a T+4 basis of transactions in connection with firm commitment underwritings priced after the close of the market.

Rule 15c6-1 also permits a managing underwriter and an issuer to "expressly" agree to a longer settlement. The SEC has cautioned, however, that this "override provision" is intended to be used only in those circumstances where T+3 settlement is not "feasible." Underwriters' counsel should therefore be satisfied that there are important business reasons for a longer settlement.

Rule 15c6-1 also permits a longer settlement date if one is "expressly agreed to by the parties at the time of the transaction." The required agreement presumably includes not only the managing underwriter and the issuer but also the other underwriters, dealers and customers. It is simple enough to commit the parties in the underwriting agreement (including the non-managing underwriters and dealers) to a specific settlement date, but what about the customers? Nothing in the rule requires that the customers' agreement be in writing. The requirement that the agreement be obtained at the time of the transaction rules out the confirmation as a means of reaching such an agreement. A firm could rely on its sales people to obtain the customers' oral agreement. This would appear to be a satisfactory practice if the firm has a high degree of

---

45. SEC Release No. 33-7168 (May 11, 1995).

confidence in the ability of its sales people to follow prescribed procedures. It is certainly satisfactory in the case of offerings of fixed-income securities, where the settlement date is inevitably a part of the conversation between the salesperson and the customer.

Experience since the 1995 amendments suggests that underwriters are coping with T+3 principally by attempting to accelerate the prospectus production process at the printer. Underwriters' counsel and printers are therefore under greater pressure than ever to put prospectuses into the hands of the underwriters at the earliest possible time.

As noted in Chapter 1, the availability of the prospectus for delivery to the customer has a significance that goes beyond its linkage to the mailing of a confirmation. Unlike the confirmation requirement, which the underwriter can meet simply by enclosing a copy of the prospectus in the same envelope with the confirmation, Section 5(b)(2) of the 1933 Act requires that the prospectus "accompan[y] or precede[]" the *delivery* of the security to the customer.

An underwriter will normally debit a customer's account on the settlement date and deposit the security in the customer's account. Section 5(b)(2) says nothing about the underwriter's receiving payment from the customer. It appears to say, however, that the underwriter cannot deliver the security to the customer unless the customer has *received* the prospectus (not merely that it has been mailed or otherwise sent or given to the customer). The question therefore arises whether Section 5(b)(2) is violated if settlement occurs before the customer has actually received the prospectus.

It is hard to see how a customer is disadvantaged by the delivery to his account of a purchased security prior to the customer's actual receipt of the prospectus. Presumably, underwriters have been relying for many years on the assumption that confirmations were ordinarily sent out (with prospectuses) in time to provide reasonable assurance that they would be received by the customer on or before the T+5 settlement date. In a T+3 environment, of course, this is less certain.

Rule 434(a), discussed above as part of the SEC's T+3 initiative, provides that the "term sheet" procedure may be relied upon to permit not only the sending of the confirmation but also the delivery of the registered security. It would be desirable for the SEC, using its new exemptive powers under the Improvements Act, to clarify the Section 5(b)(2) situation as it applies to transactions in which the Rule 434 term sheet procedure is not followed.

In the meantime, it should be kept in mind that Section 5(b)(2) antedates the age of electronic settlements. It is therefore logical to interpret its requirements in the context of physical deliveries. A requirement that the security not be "carried through the mails or in interstate commerce . . . unless accompanied or preceded by a prospectus" could therefore be interpreted as requiring only that the prospectus has already been deposited in the mail or otherwise sent on its way.

• • *The Electronic Prospectus.* Printing efficiencies can go only so far, of course, and no efficiencies will be adequate to the task if the SEC eventually moves (as some expect) to a T+1 standard settlement cycle. Some securities lawyers have suggested that the prospectus delivery problem can best be solved, at least for offerings registered on Form S-3, by permitting an underwriter or dealer to incorporate the prospectus into the confirmation.[46] More recently, attention has been focused on the electronic delivery of the prospectus. In a February 1995 interpretive letter[47] and in an October 1995 interpretive release,[48] the SEC approved the use of an electronic prospectus as a means of satisfying the requirements of Section 5.[49] "Electronic" media for this purpose included audiotapes, videotapes, facsimiles, CD-ROM, electronic mail, bulletin boards, Internet Web sites and computer networks. The release states that the

---

46. Joseph McLaughlin, *'Ten Easy Pieces' for the SEC*, 18 Rev. Sec. & Commodities Reg. 200, 201 (1985).

47. SEC Interpretive Letter, *Brown & Wood* (available February 17, 1995).

48. SEC Release No. 33-7233 (October 6, 1995). *See also* SEC Release Nos. 33-7289 (May 9, 1996) and 34-37182 (May 9, 1996).

49. SEC Release No. 33-7233 expressly recognizes that "offerings may now be made exclusively through electronic means" (*id.* at note 16n and note 27).

SEC, as a general matter, would view "information distributed through electronic means as satisfying the delivery or transmission requirements of the federal securities laws if such distribution results in the delivery to the intended recipients of substantially equivalent information as these recipients would have had if the information were delivered to them in paper form." Whether an electronic communication is "delivered" or "transmitted" for purposes of this general statement will depend on (1) giving notice to the recipient that information is available in electronic form, (2) providing the recipient with access to the required disclosure and (3) following procedures that evidence delivery of the information.

The release elaborated on these three considerations as follows:

–   Notice of the availability of electronic information may be provided, e.g., by a supplemental communication (presumably a trailer on a confirmation would suffice).

–   Access to the electronic information must not be burdensome; in particular, it must not involve too many steps or require the downloading of a separate software program. The recipient must also have an opportunity to retain the information or to have ongoing access equivalent to personal retention. In addition, recipients must retain the right to receive a paper version of any required document.

–   Delivery may be evidenced by (a) an investor's "informed consent" to receive information through a particular electronic medium, (b) evidence of actual receipt (e.g., electronic mail return-receipt or confirmation of accessing, downloading or printing), (c) facsimile, (d) hyperlink or (e) inference from the investor's response in a particular format.

Consents may be revoked, in which case a provider of information would presumably need to find a different method of evidencing the delivery (or, alternatively, justifying the presumption of delivery) of the required information. On the other hand, since the SEC's October 1995 release expressly permits offerings that are made *exclusively* through electronic means, an investor who revokes his consent (or even one who simply requests a paper copy of the prospectus) may be summarily dropped from the offering.

Electronic prospectuses obviously pose novel challenges for securities lawyers. Both underwriters' and issuer's counsel will need to be alert to all electronic media being used in connection with the offering and to be in a position to verify that the content of all media is made a part of the registration statement filed with the SEC. The scope of disclosure opinions (or "disclosure letters") in connection with such media is not yet clear. Also, the role of underwriters' counsel is not yet clear when it comes to electronic selling material used by individual underwriters and dealers or to the procedures followed by individual underwriters and dealers in obtaining customer consent to electronic delivery.

The use of electronic prospectuses is not yet common for the purpose of permitting a confirmation to be sent to a customer. This will likely remain the case for as long as the SEC is unwilling to entertain the presumption that all investors have access to a computer or other terminal (as it does, for example, the presumption that each investor has a mailbox). The absence of such a presumption means that an underwriter will have to obtain the customer's "informed consent" in order to rely on electronic delivery. Even if a significant number of customers so consent, it is obviously less expensive and more reliable to send a paper prospectus to all purchasers.

Electronic prospectuses are much more popular for the purpose of posting electronic information about a security during a prospectus delivery period. As discussed in Chapter 1, it would violate Section 5 to send written offering material to investors during a prospectus delivery period unless the material were accompanied or preceded by a final prospectus. Posting the final prospectus on a Website or other electronic medium allows the simultaneous posting of research material or (in the case of asset-backed securities) performance information relating to the underlying collateral. It should also be possible, of course, to link the material in question to the EDGAR version of the prospectus, although this practice may have to await the implementation of promised improvements to the EDGAR system.

Chinese Walls

In the course of working on a registration statement, investment bankers may learn of material information, favorable or unfavorable, that is to be included in the disclosure document but has not yet been disclosed to the public. This is not a problem so long as the banker does not trade on the information personally and does not disclose it to anyone likely to trade on the information, especially the research, trading or sales arms of his or her firm. To assure compliance with this principle, an underwriting firm's written procedures will provide for an information barrier between investment banking and the other parts of the firm as impregnable as the Great Wall of China.[50]

The concept of the Chinese Wall grew out of the settlement of the administrative proceeding brought by the SEC against Merrill Lynch, Pierce, Fenner & Smith Incorporated and certain of its officers and employees in connection with a 1966 underwriting of convertible debentures of Douglas Aircraft Co., Inc.[51] The registration statement was filed on June 7, 1966. It contained an earnings statement for the first five months of the fiscal year ending November 30, 1966 that indicated that the company had earned 85 cents per share for that period. Two weeks after filing, Merrill Lynch, in its capacity as managing underwriter, received non-public information from Douglas to the effect that it would report earnings for the first six months of its 1966 fiscal year that were sharply lower than the 85 cents per share reported for the first five months. Merrill Lynch also learned that the company had reduced its 1966 earnings estimate and expected to show little or no profit for the fiscal year.

---

50. For a general discussion of Chinese Walls, *see* Report of SEC Division of Market Regulation, *Broker-Dealer Policies and Procedures Designed to Segment the Flow and Prevent the Misuse of Material Nonpublic Information* (March 1990).

51. SEC Release No. 34-8459 (November 25, 1968).

It also learned that Douglas had substantially reduced its projection of earnings for the following fiscal year. The SEC charged that Merrill Lynch had disclosed this information to certain of its institutional and other large customers prior to its dissemination to the public and that these customers had traded on the basis of this information.

Sanctions were imposed on the firm and certain of the individual respondents. As part of the settlement negotiated with the SEC, Merrill Lynch adopted a statement of policy that prohibited the disclosure of material non-public information obtained during the course of an investment banking transaction to any person other than persons involved in the transaction or senior executives of the firm and members of its Legal Department. All investment banking firms have now adopted similar policies, which are supplemented by restricted list and "gray" or "watch" list procedures (discussed earlier in this chapter). It should be noted that Section 15(f) of the 1934 Act imposes an affirmative duty on all broker-dealers to "establish, maintain and enforce written policies and procedures reasonably designed . . . to prevent the [illegal] misuse . . . of material, non-public information."

Inadvertent and Transient Investment Companies

The "inadvertent investment company" problem can be a trap for the unwary. Although not often encountered, it is always lurking in the bushes ready to spring out and create its mischief. Section 3(a)(1)(C) of the Investment Company Act of 1940 (the "1940 Act") defines the term "investment company" to include any issuer which

> [i]s engaged or proposes to engage in the business of investing, reinvesting, owning, holding, or trading in securities, and owns or proposes to acquire investment securities having a value exceeding 40 per centum of the value of such issuer's total assets (exclusive of Government securities and cash items) on an unconsolidated basis.

The key words are "owning" or "holding." No active investing, reinvesting or trading is required to fall within this definition, unlike the more conventional definition in Section 3(a)(1)(A). The term "investment securities" is defined to include all securities except (as here relevant) U.S. government securities and securities of subsidiaries, 50% or more of whose voting securities are owned by the issuer. Section 3(a)(1)(C) provides that, notwithstanding the Section 3(a)(3) definition, an issuer is not an investment company if it is "primarily engaged," directly or through wholly owned subsidiaries, in a business other than owning or holding securities. An issuer may also be excluded under Section 3(b)(2) if the SEC finds that it is primarily engaged in such a business directly or through majority-owned subsidiaries or controlled companies. If it does not exceed the limitations on securities ownership and income set forth in Rule 3a-1, it may be able to take advantage of the safe harbor provided by that rule.

There are statutory exclusions for domestic banks and insurance companies, as well as for broker-dealer firms and finance companies. Rules adopted by the SEC exempt certain foreign banks and foreign insurance companies (Rule 3a-6), certain finance subsidiaries of U.S. and foreign companies (Rule 3a-5) and certain issuers of asset-backed securities (Rule 3a-7). Some of these exemptions are discussed elsewhere in this book.

A company with no more than 100 securityholders (in addition to holders of its short-term paper) that does not propose to make a public offering of its securities is excluded under Section 3(c)(1). Also, the Improvements Act added a new Section 3(a)(7) that excludes a company whose securities are owned exclusively (but with certain exceptions) by "qualified purchasers" and that does not propose to make a public offering of its securities.

The difficulty is that a manufacturing company or one engaged in any other business may find that it is inadvertently an investment company. The solution is not registration under the 1940 Act, for such a company could not possibly operate within the strictures of that statute. But under Section 7 an unregistered investment company may not engage in any business in interstate commerce or sell its securities in interstate commerce, and under Section 47(b) its contracts may be unenforceable. It may seek an exemption from the SEC under Section 6(c), but this requires a lengthy application process.

Take the case of a company that, with funds raised in an intrastate offering, successfully develops a product, later transfers the business to a subsidiary, and then sells substantially all of the subsidiary's shares to a third party while retaining a small interest for itself. Time goes by, and the former subsidiary goes public. Its shares increase in value, and the company now holds a valuable asset, its sole asset other than cash items and a small amount of equipment. It uses its funds on research and development and reaches a point where it wishes to sell additional stock to the public to raise the funds required to begin manufacturing its new product and to build a sales force.

Out of the bush pops the inadvertent investment company problem. The shares representing a minority interest in the company's former subsidiary are "investment securities." In terms of their value, they constitute over 90% of its assets, far more than the 40% stipulated in Section 3(a)(1)(C) of the 1940 Act. The company proposes to make a public offering and thus cannot rely on Section 3(c)(1) or Section 3(c)(7), even if it had fewer than 100 securityholders or were owned exclusively by "qualified purchasers," neither of which happens to be the case. It is loathe to approach the SEC for a Section 6(c) exemption or even for a Section 3(b)(2) determination. It does not come close to meeting the threshholds permitted under Rule 3a-1. Perhaps its counsel can opine that it is primarily engaged in a business other than that of holding the shares, but it is just getting started on its new venture; not a single widget has been manufactured to date, and it has no operating earnings. Even if counsel is willing to render the opinion, will it be acceptable to underwriters' counsel when the problem goes to the very core of the underwriting, the validity of the issuance of the shares? This is an instance where the underwriters may be well advised to take no chances and to refuse to go forward with the financing in the absence of a Section 6(c) exemptive order.

An issue may arise under the 1940 Act as the result of an issuer's public offering, the making of substantial divestitures or the occurrence of other events that provide the issuer with a substantial amount of liquid assets. The issuer may well intend to invest the assets in majority-owned subsidiaries or other purposes that would not make it an investment company. To deal with these "transient investment companies," the SEC in 1981 adopted Rule 3a-2.[52] This rule provides that an issuer is deemed not to be engaged in the business of investing, reinvesting, owning, holding, or trading in securities during a period of time not to exceed one year, provided that the issuer has a bona fide intent to be engaged primarily in another business as soon as is reasonably possible (in any event by the termination of such period of time), such intent to be evidenced by its business activities and a board resolution or comparable documents. This rule is viewed by the SEC as a safe harbor, and in appropriate cases, the staff has been willing to provide no-action relief to transient investment companies after the expiration of the one-year period specified in Rule 3a-2.

Extension of Credit—Section 11(d)(1)

Counsel for the underwriters frequently will be asked by the managing underwriter whether the security being underwritten is "marginable." The answer to this question depends in the first instance, of course, on whether the security is marginable (or has "loan value") under Regulation T. Generally speaking, Regulation T assigns loan value only to exempted securities or "margin securities" (which include listed securities, "OTC margin securities," "OTC margin bonds" and certain other securities).

The answer to the question also depends, however, on an analysis of Section 11(d)(1) of the 1934 Act and Rule 11d1-1 thereunder. A securities firm that acts both as a broker and a dealer (and there are few, if any, firms that do not perform this dual function) may not sell to a customer on margin any security that is part of a "new issue" in which it is participating as an underwriter or a member of the selling group. Section 11(d)(1) provides that, subject to certain exceptions, such a broker-dealer may not effect

> any transaction in connection with which, directly or indirectly, he extends or maintains or arranges for the extension or maintenance of credit to or for a customer on any security (other than an exempted security) which

---

52. SEC Release No. IC-11552 (January 14, 1981).

was part of a new issue in the distribution of which he participated as a member of the selling syndicate or group within 30 days prior to such transaction.

One of the concerns of the Congress in 1934 was the apparent conflict of interest inherent in acting as a dealer trading for its own account and acting as a broker or agent for customers. There were those who called for the segregation of these functions, while others argued for the status quo. As a compromise, the 1934 Act directed the SEC to investigate the question of completely segregating the activities of brokers and dealers and to report to the Congress by a specified date. By prohibiting the extension of credit on new issues, the Congress believed that it was striking a blow at "one of the greatest potential evils inherent in the combination of the broker and dealer function in the same person, by assuring that he will not induce his customers to buy on credit securities which he has undertaken to distribute to the public."[53]

Although the segregation of broker and dealer activities is no longer a significant issue, Section 11(d)(1) continues to operate. The restrictions apply not only to transactions that are part of the initial distribution but also to certain transactions in the aftermarket during a 30-day period after the broker-dealer's completion of its participation in the distribution. As originally enacted in 1934, the restriction continued for six months. Rule 11d1-1(e) provides significant relief from the 30-day restriction insofar as it would otherwise be applicable to the shares of companies that are widely traded. When the new issue in which the broker-dealer has participated constitutes 50% or less of all securities of the same class to be outstanding after the completion of the distribution, the broker-dealer may extend credit on the security if it sells the security to the customer or buys it for the customer's account on a day when it is not participating in the distribution of the new issue. This exemption is almost always available for transactions in the shares of major corporations.

Rule 11d1-1(e) spells out when a broker-dealer will be deemed to be participating in a distribution of a new issue. It will be deemed

---

53. H.R. Rep. No. 1383, 73d Cong., 2d Sess. 22 (1934), 5 Leg. Hist., Item 18.

to be a participant if it "owns, directly or indirectly, any undistributed security of such issue" or if it is engaged in stabilizing activities or is a party to a syndicate agreement (an AAU) under which stabilizing activities are being or may be undertaken. Unlike Rule 101 (discussed in Chapter 4), Rule 11d1-1(e) does not adopt the concept that securities taken by an underwriter into an investment account are deemed to have been distributed. Thus, if new issue securities are placed by an underwriter in its own investment account, the underwriter presumably cannot take advantage of the Rule 11d1-1(e) exemption until it has sold those securities. A broker-dealer also will be considered a participant in the distribution of a new issue if it "is a party to an executory agreement to purchase or distribute such issue." An underwriting agreement remains executory until the closing, and accordingly credit may not be extended on purchases in the after-market in reliance on Rule 11d1-1(e) until (at the earliest) after the closing date.[54]

Rule 11d1-1 contains other exemptions. Although it has participated in the new issue, a broker-dealer may receive securities from a customer and place them in the customer's margin account if it has not sold the security to the customer or bought the security for the customer's account. It may take into a margin account securities that have been acquired by a customer in exchange with the issuer for an outstanding security of the same issuer on which credit was lawfully maintained for the customer at the time of the exchange. Also, the restrictions of Section 11(d)(1) do not apply to securities acquired by a customer upon the exercise of rights issued to that customer in a subscrip-

---

54. The "executory agreement" language presents problems in the context of continuous or delayed offerings. The SEC staff had at one point taken the position that an agency agreement relating to a medium-term note program was an executory agreement that would preclude the extension of credit to purchase outstanding notes. SEC No-action Letter, *Goldman, Sachs & Co.* (available December 4, 1986). It subsequently reversed this position and permitted an agent under a similar program to extend credit on notes of a particular series after the notes had been owned by the customer for at least 30 days. SEC No-action Letter, *Kidder, Peabody & Co. Incorporated* (available August 16, 1990). The staff appears to have accepted the theory for this purpose that the terms of each note issuance under the program were independently negotiated and unique.

tion offer to the issuer's shareholders where the subscription period does not exceed 90 days.

Section 11(d)(1) applies only to "new issues." It does not prohibit the extension of credit in the case of the normal secondary distribution of outstanding securities, no matter how large the distribution or how great the incentive to the underwriters to get the deal done.[55] The SEC has placed an administrative gloss on this concept, however. If the shares to be sold were acquired from the issuer shortly before the offering, for example in connection with an acquisition, then the offering may be viewed as a new issue. Thus, where the sellers exercised their registration rights four months after acquiring their shares, the staff of the SEC took the position that the acquisition was sufficiently close to the offering to make the secondary distribution a new issue.[56]

In another instance, however, shares acquired four months prior to an offering were considered to be marginal.[57] Where selling shareholders acquired their shares on December 31, 1975, upon the automatic conversion of convertible preferred stock, a secondary offering under a registration statement filed on October 6, 1976, some 10 months later, was not viewed as a new issue.[58]

But, where debentures proposed to be sold by a person in a control relationship with the issuer had been acquired in an exchange offer 15 months before a proposed sale, the staff refused to take a no-action position "particularly" because of the control relationship.[59] This emphasis on control is a misapplication of the statute, and the relationship between the seller and the issuer does not appear to have been a factor in any other instance where the

---

55. SEC No-action Letter, *Hewlett-Packard Co.* (available February 23, 1978); SEC No-action Letter, *Golden West Mobile Homes, Inc.* (available November 15, 1976).

56. SEC No-action Letter, *Geon Industries, Inc.* (available May 26, 1973).

57. SEC No-action Letter, *Flowers Industries, Inc.* (available December 4, 1976).

58. SEC No-action Letter, *Goldman, Sachs & Co.* (available December 27, 1976).

59. SEC No-action Letter, *Metro-Goldwyn-Mayer Inc.* (available November 29, 1975).

staff refused to take a no-action position. Also, the 15-month time span would appear to be sufficiently great to take the transaction out of the coverage of Section 11(d)(1).

Credit may not be extended on shares sold in a secondary offering if a stock split has been effected under circumstances that the staff views as intended to facilitate the distribution. In this case, the split shares would be considered a new issue. The staff refused to take a no-action position with respect to a secondary offering scheduled to take place on April 6, 1972, where on December 10, 1971, the issuer declared a 3% stock dividend payable January 14, 1972, to shareholders of record on December 23, 1971, and a three-for-two stock distribution payable February 1, 1972, to shareholders of record on January 6, 1972.[60] It mattered not that it was represented to the staff that the dividend and distribution were not intended to facilitate the offering. Nor did it matter that the shares to be sold were to be taken from shares owned prior to the corporate action. The time span of only four months may have been enough to lead to the staff's refusal, or it may have been influenced by the fact that the sellers were directors who voted in favor of the stock dividend and stock split.

Pursuant to a consent decree entered in September 1971, International Telephone & Telegraph Company was required within three years to divest its wholly owned subsidiary, Avis, Inc. In May 1972, Avis increased its 1,000 outstanding shares to six million by means of a stock split. In June 1972, ITT took the first step in the divestiture by selling 1.4 million shares to the public. In December 1972, a registration statement was filed covering a second secondary offering, this time a proposed sale of 1.5 million shares. The staff took the position that the June 1972 stock split created a new issue that was sufficiently close to the proposed sale to have the practical effect of facilitating the distribution. It refused to express a view as to any future sales made in connection with the divestiture.[61] Here it may be argued that the size of the split (6,000-for-1) and the circumstances under which it was made demonstrated that it could

---

60. SEC No-action Letter, *Leaseway Transportation Corp.* (available May 11, 1972).

61. SEC No-action Letter, *Avis, Inc.* (available February 7, 1973).

have had no purpose other than to facilitate the divestiture, no matter when the specific sales were made. Under these circumstances, proximity in time may not be a significant factor.

In another case, where a two-for-one stock split was approved by the board of directors of a company on March 31, 1977, prior to the seller's decision to make a secondary offering, the staff took the position that Section 11(d)(1) was not applicable, even though the registration statement covering the sale was filed on July 26, 1977, just four months later.[62] The staff also issued a no-action letter where a two and one-half-for-one split was authorized five months prior to a non-registered secondary offering, although it was not effected until two months prior to the offering.[63] Nor was Section 11(d)(1) found to be applicable where a two-for-one stock split was effected one year prior to a secondary offering where it was represented that the purpose of the split was to qualify the common stock for listing on the NYSE.[64] The same position was taken where the last of a series of stock splits, a two-for-one split, was effected one year and eight months prior to the offering.[65] Similarly, a three-for-one split of the common stock of Johnson & Johnson effected one year and 10 months prior to the filing of a registration statement did not raise Section 11(d)(1) problems, even though the sellers were J. Seward Johnson and the Robert Wood Johnson Foundation, shareholders in a control relationship with the issuer.[66]

In another case, an October 1972 recapitalization, in which the company's 15 million shares of common stock were reclassified into three million shares of preferred stock and six million shares of new common stock, did not make Section 11(d)(1) applicable to a June 1977 secondary offering where the shares to be sold had been purchased in the open market

---

62. SEC No-action Letter, *Tektronix, Inc.* (available September 9, 1977).

63. SEC No-action Letter, *Metro-Goldwyn-Mayer Inc.* (available June 22, 1975).

64. SEC No-action Letter, *Corroon & Black Corp.* (available May 22, 1978).

65. SEC No-action Letter, *Eli Lilly & Co.* (available May 23, 1973).

66. SEC No-action Letter, *Johnson & Johnson* (available April 14, 1972).

subsequent to the recapitalization.[67] In this instance, it is difficult to see why counsel felt it appropriate to approach the staff, for the stock clearly was marginable. The same can be said where the most recent split was four years before the offering[68] or even two and one-half years,[69] particularly, in the latter case, where the split was suggested by the NYSE.

Although stock dividends theoretically could raise new issue problems, a 5% or 10% stock dividend is far less likely to be viewed as facilitating a distribution than a split of substantially greater magnitude. The staff of the SEC has consistently taken no-action positions where asked to do so with respect to stock dividends. Thus, where a registration statement covering a secondary offering was filed on September 26, 1978, 10% stock dividends paid in each of the preceding three years, the most recent of which was three months prior to filing, did not create a problem under Section 11(d)(1).[70] The staff also was willing to take a no-action position where a 5% stock dividend was paid three and one-half months prior to the filing of a registration statement covering a secondary offering.[71]

In the case of a combination offering, where both secondary and newly issued shares are being sold in a single underwriting, none of the shares being offered should be considered marginable for purposes of Section 11(d)(1), for as a practical matter it is impossible to distinguish between the outstanding shares and the new shares.

Counsel should avoid the trap of concluding that shares are marginable after a careful Section 11(d)(1) analysis only to find that they are not listed or OTC margin securities and thus not marginable under Regulation T.

---

67. SEC No-action Letter, *Source Capital Inc.* (available June 15, 1977).

68. SEC No-action Letter, *S.S. Kresge Co.* (available May 8, 1976).

69. SEC No-action Letter, *The Lubrizol Corp.* (available March 29, 1971).

70. SEC No-action Letter, *Oakwood Homes Corp.* (available November 11, 1978).

71. SEC No-action Letter, *Applied Magnetics Corp.* (available August 2, 1982).

Chapter 4

MANIPULATIVE PRACTICES AND MARKET ACTIVITIES DURING DISTRIBUTIONS

A basic goal of the federal securities laws, rivaling in importance the principle of full and fair disclosure, is the prevention of manipulation. As the SEC recently observed, "[m]anipulation impedes the securities markets from functioning as independent pricing mechanisms, and undermines the integrity and fairness of those markets."[1]

In the 1934 Act, Congress prohibited certain conduct as manipulative. It also granted the SEC broad rulemaking authority to combat manipulative abuses. In exercising this authority, the SEC has especially focused on the market activities of persons participating in a securities offering. It has done so on the assumption that "securities offerings present special opportunities and incentives for manipulation that require specific regulatory attention."[2]

For more than 40 years, the SEC's principal antimanipulation rules in the area of securities offerings consisted of Rules 10b-6, 10b-7 and 10b-8 (known collectively as the "Trading Practice Rules"). The most important of these rules was Rule 10b-6, which prohibited underwriters, issuers and other per-

---

1. SEC Release No. 34-38067 (December 20, 1996) (adopting Regulation M) (the "Regulation M Release").

2. *Id.*

sons involved in a "distribution" from engaging in secondary market activity that might raise the price of the security to be distributed.[3] Rule 10b-7 regulated stabilizing activities in connection with a securities offering, and Rule 10b-8 regulated certain trading activities in connection with rights offerings.

From their adoption in 1955, the Trading Practice Rules gave rise to frequent interpretive questions. These questions even extended to the most basic question of all: when does a securities offering constitute a "distribution" that triggers the application of the rules? Many securities lawyers considered the rules to be among the most arcane administered by the SEC.

Rule 10b-6 received a major overhaul in 1983 and was further amended in 1987. Following a comprehensive review by the SEC in the 1990s of its antimanipulation regulations in the context of securities offerings,[4] the Trading Practice Rules were reborn in late 1996 in the form of a new Regulation M.[5]

Before discussing the application of Regulation M to securities offerings, it might be useful to review some of the history in this area.

Prohibition of Manipulative Practices

Long before the SEC's adoption of the Trading Practice Rules, Congress had taken action to prohibit specific manipulative practices, whether or not related to a distribution of securities. Section 17(b) of the 1933 Act prohibited "touting," i.e., the description of a security for an undisclosed "consideration" received directly or indirectly from an issuer, under-

---

3. The ultimate objective of Rule 10b-6 was to protect the integrity of the trading market as an independent pricing mechanism, thereby enhancing investor confidence in the marketplace. SEC Release No. 34-19565 (March 4, 1983).

4. The SEC's review included the publication in April 1994 of a concept release on the subject. SEC Release No. 34-33924 (April 19, 1994).

5. Regulation M became effective on March 4, 1997. Certain technical amendments were adopted on the same day in SEC Release No. 34-38363 (March 4, 1997). Related notice and recordkeeping changes were to become effective on April 1, 1997.

writer or dealer. More direct prohibitions were included in the 1934 Act, and the experience gained by the SEC over a 20-year period in enforcing these antimanipulative provisions played a major role in its adoption in 1955 of the Trading Practice Rules.

• *Fletcher Committee Investigation*

In 1934, the Congress was not concerned specifically with trading activities during distributions. It was interested rather in out-and-out fraud, blatant market manipulations that some believed were at the root of the 1929 crash.[6] The Fletcher-Rayburn bill, which became the 1934 Act, contained provisions outlawing manipulative practices on stock exchanges. These provisions were designed to prohibit in clear and specific terms the types of abuses exposed by the Senate Committee on Banking and Currency chaired by Senator Duncan U. Fletcher of Florida (the "Fletcher Committee").

In April 1932, a subcommittee of the Fletcher Committee began an exhaustive investigation into stock exchange practices in the context of the 1929 market crash. In January 1933, Ferdinand D. Pecora was retained as counsel to the subcommittee and began what has been called "one of the most extraordinary shows ever produced in a Washington committee room."[7] Under Pecora's direction, the subcommittee revealed to the public extensive manipulative practices that had been conducted on the exchanges and particularly on the NYSE.[8]

Of particular significance was the exposure of pool operations in which speculators, often stock exchange members or partners in member firms, would form a group to trade in a

---

6. Statement of Representative Adolph J. Sabath, *Stock Exchange Regulation: Hearings Before the House Interstate and Foreign Commerce Committee,* 73d Cong., 2d Sess. 826 (1934) [hereinafter *House Hearings*].

7. F.L. Allen, *Since Yesterday—The 1930s in America, September 3, 1929-September 3, 1939* 168 (Harper & Row 1940).

8. The subcommittee's findings are summarized in S. Rep. No. 1455, 73d Cong., 2d Sess., *Stock Exchange Practices, Report of the Senate Banking and Currency Committee Pursuant to S.Res. 84 (72d Cong.) and S.Res. 56 and S.Res. 97 (73d Cong.) (June 16, 1934)* [hereinafter S. Rep. No. 1455]. Pecora later recounted his experiences in *Wall Street Under Oath* (Simon & Schuster 1939).

stock and engage in fictitious transactions for the purpose of raising its price to enable them to unload their holdings at a profit. The Fletcher Committee found that pools would most frequently be organized in stocks that had attracted public attention, such as the "alcohol" or "repeal" stocks in which there was speculative interest during the summer of 1933 because of the expected repeal of the Eighteenth Amendment to the Constitution. Before beginning their operations, pool participants would often obtain options at fixed or graduated prices on substantial blocks of the stock. These options frequently were obtained from the corporation itself or from officers or large shareholders who might also participate in the pool. In some cases, the pool would drive down the price through short selling and the dissemination of false rumors and then accumulate blocks in the market at artificially reduced prices.

Trading activity on the exchange would then be instituted for the purpose of raising the price of the stock. These transactions included wash sales in which a person would simultaneously purchase and sell a like number of shares, a transaction in which, in effect, he would buy from and sell to himself, leading others to believe that a real trade had taken place. Another type of fictitious transaction was the matched order in which one manipulator would make an arrangement with another to buy and sell at the same time so that their orders would meet and be crossed on the floor of the exchange. As part of a pool operation, puts and calls frequently would be granted to other speculators to induce them to buy or sell a stock. In addition, the pool operators would cause market letters and tip sheets to be distributed to attract public attention to a security.

Officials of the NYSE played down or closed their eyes to the evils of pool operations. Following a sharp drop in stock prices in July 1933, led by the repeal stocks, Pecora requested the NYSE to institute an inquiry to determine whether pool operations had been conducted in repeal stocks during the preceding months.[9] The NYSE responded with a report that concluded

---

9. S. Rep. No. 1455 at 56.

that "there were no material deliberate improprieties in connection with transactions in these securities" and that there was no evidence of "activities which might have stimulated improperly the activity of these stocks."[10] Pecora caused an independent inquiry to be made by his staff. This resulted in the exposure of manipulative practices that the NYSE had failed to uncover.

• *Wall Street's Response*

The introduction of the Fletcher-Rayburn bill elicited a strong negative reaction from Wall Street. The opposition was led by NYSE President Richard Whitney, who in a letter dated February 14, 1934 to all members of the NYSE protested with patrician indignation that the bill "contains sweeping and drastic provisions which affect seriously the business of all members and which may have very disastrous consequences to the stock market resulting in great prejudice to the interests of investors throughout the country."[11] He went on to attack the section dealing with the manipulation of securities prices, although with less vigor than the other sections of the bill.

Senator Fletcher responded in a statement published in *The New York Times* on February 22, 1934:

The propaganda released by the exchange officials is intended to persuade the people that regulation of that exchange and the other exchanges by the Federal Government will hurt business. Whose business? Only that of brokers who have lined their pockets by disregarding the interest of their customers.[12]

Despite Whitney's initial objections, the NYSE did not launch a major attack on the antimanipulative provisions of the bill. At the hearings, there was vigorous debate as to whether

10. *Stock Exchange Practices: Hearings Before the Senate Committee on Banking and Currency,* 73d Cong., 1st Sess. 6613 (1934) [hereinafter *Senate Hearings*].
11. 4 Ellenberger & Mahar, Leg. Hist., Item 6.
12. 4 Ellenberger & Mahar, Leg. Hist., Item 7.

stabilization was a legitimate practice, but when it came to hard-core pool manipulations, the NYSE's objections were limited to the argument that the rules of the NYSE and existing law were adequate to deal with the problem and some minor drafting issues.[13] In general, the events bore out the observation of Thomas G. Corcoran at the House Hearings that the control of manipulation was not one of the "real battlegrounds of this act."[14]

Except for the provision on stabilization, which was left entirely to SEC rule making, the provisions of the bill designed to control manipulation passed virtually unchanged from the original draft.

• *Prohibition of Manipulation—Section 9*

As ultimately enacted, Section 9 of the 1934 Act bore the title "Prohibition of Manipulation of Securities Prices." Section 9(a)(1) prohibited wash sales, where there is no change in beneficial ownership, and matched purchase or sell orders, where one confederate places a buy or sell order intended to meet on the exchange floor a sell or buy order placed by the other confederate.

In the House report on the Fletcher-Rayburn bill, it was noted that "the most subtle manipulating device employed in the security markets is not simply the crude form of a wash sale or a matched order" but rather "the conscious marking up of prices to make investors believe that there is a constantly increasing demand for stock at higher prices, or a conscious marking down of stocks to make investors believe that an increasing number of investors are selling as prices recede."[15] To this end, Section 9(a)(2) provided that it was unlawful

[t]o effect, alone or with one or more other persons, a series of transactions in any security registered on a na-

---

13. *See* Statement of Richard Whitney, *Senate Hearings* at 6624. *See also* discussion between Roland L. Redmond, counsel to the NYSE, and Thomas G. Corcoran, one of the draftsmen of the bill, *Senate Hearings* at 6506.

14. *House Hearings* at 85.

15. H.R. Rep. No. 1383, 73d Cong., 2d Sess. (1934) at 10.

tional securities exchange creating actual or apparent active trading in such security, or raising or depressing the price of such security, for the purpose of inducing the purchase or sale of such security by others.

The House report recognized that "any extensive purchases or sales are bound to cause changes in the market price of the security" and stressed that such transactions are unlawful "only when they are made for the purpose of raising or depressing the market price."[16]

Section 9(a)(3) made it unlawful for sellers or buyers of securities to circulate information to the effect that the price of a security registered on a national securities exchange is likely to rise or fall because of market operations conducted for the purpose of raising or depressing the price of such security.

Section 9(a)(4) made it unlawful for persons selling or offering for sale or purchasing or offering to purchase a security registered on a national securities exchange, for the purpose of inducing the purchase or sale of the security, to make any false or misleading statement of a material fact.

Section 9(a)(5) made it unlawful, for a consideration received from a person purchasing or selling a security, to circulate predictions of price changes of securities registered on a national securities exchange for the purpose of raising or depressing the price.

Sections 9(a)(3) and 9(a)(5) were aimed at tip sheets and the spreading of rumors with respect to pool operations.[17]

Section 9(a)(6) made unlawful stabilizing transactions in contravention of such rules as the SEC might adopt. In this way, Congress delegated to the SEC the task of prescribing such rules "as may be necessary or appropriate to protect investors and the public from the vicious and unsocial aspects of these practices."[18]

Sections 9(b) and 9(c) gave to the SEC the power to regulate transactions in puts, calls, straddles or other options.

---

16. *Id.* at 20.
17. *Id.* at 21.
18. S. Rep. No. 1455 at 55.

It should be noted that Section 9(a) was made applicable only to securities registered on a national securities exchange. It did not specifically address manipulation in the over-the-counter market. The reason for this was concern by the draftsmen of the bill as to its constitutionality if it had a broader scope.[19]

• *Effects of Section 9*

Although it was essential as a political matter for the Congress to have adopted Section 9 in response to the manipulations exposed by the Fletcher Committee, it has been suggested that the provisions of that section did little more than codify the substantive law existing at that time.[20] The decision of Judge Woolsey in *U.S. v. Brown*,[21] denying a motion to quash a mail fraud and conspiracy indictment of the operators of a pool in the NYSE listed stock of Manhattan Electric Supply Company, had demonstrated that the existing criminal law could be applied to stock manipulation.[22]

Judge Woolsey based his decision on 19th-century English cases,[23] including *Rex v. Berenger*[24] (which involved a conspiracy to raise the price of British government funds and other government securities by circulating a false report of the death of Napoleon Bonaparte and predicting that peace would soon be concluded between England and France) and *Scott v. Brown*[25] (which related to a conspiracy to purchase shares in a company in order to induce persons who might subsequently purchase shares to believe, contrary to fact, that there was a

19. *Senate Hearings* at 6507.

20. This point is made in A.A. Berle, Jr., *Stock Market Manipulation*, 38 Colum. L. Rev. 393 (1938).

21. 5 F. Supp. 81 (S.D.N.Y. 1933).

22. *See also Harris v. U.S.*, 48 F.2d 771 (9th Cir. 1931).

23. The opinion should be read, if for no other reason, for its in-depth review of the English cases. Professor Loss also discusses these decisions. 8 Loss & Seligman, *Securities Regulation* 3942-47 (3d ed. 1991). *See also* Moore & Wiseman, *Market Manipulation and the Exchange Act*, 2 U. Chi. L. Rev. 46, 57 (1934).

24. 3 Maule & Selwyne's Reports 67 (1814).

25. 2 Q.B. 724 (1892).

bona fide market for the shares and that the shares were trading at a real premium). In upholding the indictment, Judge Woolsey stated:

> It is obvious that, when two or more persons, by a joint effort, raise the price of a listed stock artificially, they are creating a kind of price mirage which may lure an outsider into the market to his damage.
>
> In my opinion, such a procedure would of itself constitute a fraud on the public—just as was held in *Scott v. Brown* [citation omitted]. *A fortiori,* when such a procedure is accompanied by active propaganda seeking to interest the public in the shares thus artificially raised in price, it becomes the grossest kind of fraud. That is what I find set forth in the indictment before me.

A.A. Berle, Jr., has made the point that it was Section 17(a) of the 1933 Act, the general antifraud provision of that statute, rather than the 1934 Act, that brought the SEC (or more precisely its predecessor, the Federal Trade Commission) into the enforcement arena "as investigator, plaintiff in an injunction suit, or stimulator of a criminal action," and that in the early years, even after passage of the 1934 Act, the SEC's chief enforcement vehicle had been Section 17(a) of the 1933 Act.[26] Nonetheless, as will be seen, during the 20-year period prior to the adoption of the Trading Practice Rules, Section 9(a)(2) provided a major statutory underpinning for the SEC's attacks on manipulation and for the development of its views on the restrictions that should be imposed on market activities during distributions.

• *The Next Twenty Years*

The 20-year period between the enactment of the 1934 Act and the adoption of the original Trading Practice Rules was marked by extensive enforcement activity aimed at market ma-

---

26. Berle, *supra* note 20, at 399.

nipulation[27] as well as efforts by the SEC to develop and refine the principles that would be embodied in the rules ultimately adopted in 1955.

• • *Over-the-Counter Manipulations.* In an administrative proceeding against Barrett & Company and two other broker-dealers to determine whether they should be suspended or expelled from the NASD for manipulating the price of a security in the over-the-counter market, the SEC held, citing *U.S. v. Brown* and several law review articles, that practices that would be illegal under Section 9(a)(2), if effected on a securities exchange, would likewise be fraudulent under the 1934 Act if conducted in the over-the-counter market.[28] The SEC said that there is no reasonable distinction between the manipulation of over-the-counter prices and the manipulation of prices on a national securities exchange and that both are condemned as fraudulent by the 1934 Act and, in fact, were fraudulent at common law. The SEC went on to state that the 1934 Act contemplates that Section 15(c)(1), which was adopted as an amendment to the 1934 Act in 1936, affords to the over-the-counter market at least as great a degree of protection as is afforded to the exchange market by Section 9(a).

Section 15(c)(1), as then in effect, made it unlawful to effect a transaction in a security otherwise than on a national securities exchange "by means of any manipulative, deceptive, or other fraudulent device or contrivance." In 1937, the SEC adopted Rule X-15C1-2, which in paragraph (a) defined the term "manipulative, deceptive, or other fraudulent device or

---

27. For example, in its *Fourth Annual Report,* covering the fiscal year ended June 30, 1938, the SEC reported on thirteen Section 9 cases resulting in injunctions, stock exchange expulsions or suspensions from membership or criminal convictions.

In its *Seventeenth Annual Report,* covering its fiscal year ended June 30, 1951, the SEC believed itself able to state (at page 38) that as a result of its administration of the 1934 Act "manipulation has been reduced to a point where it is no longer an appreciable factor in our markets." As Professor Loss aptly points out, "[t]his sanguine belief was not retained for long." 8 Loss & Seligman, *Securities Regulation* 3984 (3d ed. 1991).

28. *Barrett & Company,* 9 S.E.C. 319 (1941).

contrivance" to include "any act, practice, or course of business which operates or would operate as a fraud or deceit upon any person." In *Barrett,* the SEC found that the activities in question constituted an "act, practice or course of business" which operated as a "fraud or deceit" and that Barrett & Company and the other respondents had violated Section 15(c)(1) and paragraph (a) of Rule X-15C1-2 thereunder.

• • *Meaning of Term "Transactions."* In *Kidder Peabody & Co.,*[29] counsel for the respondents argued that the term "transactions" as used in Section 9(a)(2) meant "completed purchases or sales." The SEC disagreed, pointing to the legislative history which demonstrated that the original bill sought to prohibit "transactions for the purchase and sale" for manipulative purposes while Section 9(a)(2) as finally enacted contained broader phrasing. The SEC stated that Section 9(a)(2) prohibits the manipulation of prices on a securities exchange by means of the placing of bids on the exchange and that in an auction market the placing of bids, although not met by sellers, may be as effective an influence on price as a completed sale.

• • *Inference of Motive.* To be in violation of Section 9(a)(2), the transactions in question must be "for the purpose of inducing the purchase or sale" of the security by others. Thus, motive is an ingredient of the offense. But the required statutory motive may be inferred from the facts of the case.[30]

The issue of intent in the context of an underwritten offering of securities was addressed in an opinion of James A. Treanor, Jr., Director of the SEC's Trading and Exchange Division,[31] rendered in response to an inquiry whether prior to the completion of sales of debentures at the fixed public offering price, an underwriter,

---

29. 18 S.E.C. 559 (1945).

30. *Michael J. Meehan,* 2 S.E.C. 588 (1937). In this case, the SEC stated, "As to the respondent's motive, there is no direct testimony. The existence or nonexistence of the required statutory motive must thus be a matter of inference from the voluminous testimony introduced in the case." *See also Russell Maguire & Company,* 10 S.E.C. 332 (1941); *Halsey, Stuart & Co.,* 30 S.E.C. 106, 112 (1949).

31. SEC Release No. 34-3505 (November 16, 1943).

through its trading department, could buy and sell debentures at prices which might exceed the price at which debentures were being offered at retail. The opinion stated, "[w]hen an underwriter is engaged in the distribution of a security, he obviously has the purpose of inducing the purchase of that security by others." It went on to state, in effect, that even though an underwriter may have sold all of the securities retained by or allotted to it in the distribution, it may not trade in the securities, through a trading department or otherwise, so long as the syndicate agreement remains in effect. As a result of this opinion, it became the practice to include in agreements among underwriters absolute prohibitions against trading during distributions.[32]

• • *Stabilization Before Rule 10b-7.* In 1936, in response to an inquiry on the question of stabilization during an underwritten public offering of securities, the general counsel of the SEC rendered an opinion to the effect that Section 9(a)(6) of the 1934 Act, in making unlawful stabilizing in contravention of SEC regulations, "seems conclusively to indicate that stabilization not in contravention of such rules, or in the absence of [SEC] rules, as in the present case, is not illegal."[33] He went on to state:

> Turning to your second question, I may further state that, in my opinion, the accepted concept of stabilization does not require that the price of the security be held to one particular quotation. Of course, activities designed substantially to raise or lower stock exchange prices are clearly manipulative, and therefore within the prohibition of Section 9(a)(2).

The SEC adopted no rules on stabilization until 1939, when it adopted Rule 17a-2 under the 1934 Act (requiring reports of stabilizing activity) and a rule under the 1933 Act requiring a notice in the prospectus of any intention to overallot or stabi-

---

32. Foshay, *Market Activities of Participants in Securities Distributions*, 45 U. Va. L. Rev. 907, 911 (1959).
33. SEC Release No. 34-605 (April 17, 1936).

lize.[34] In 1940, however, the SEC adopted Rule X-9A6-1, which regulated stabilization in connection with "at the market" offerings of listed securities.[35] As offerings of this type soon became virtually extinct, the rule had no effect.

Shortly after the adoption of Rule X-9A6-1, the SEC issued a statement on the question of regulating stabilization.[36] In this statement, the SEC said that it was faced with three choices. It could permit stabilization to continue unregulated, or it could adopt a program for the regulation of stabilization in an effort to eliminate particular abuses, or, finally, it could decide that stabilization is inherently so detrimental to the interest of investors that the SEC should recommend to Congress that all stabilization be prohibited. After reviewing the pros and cons of stabilization, the SEC stated that one of the major deterrents to earlier action on the adoption of rules regulating stabilization had been its reluctance to adopt any program of comprehensive regulation upon which competent representatives of the securities industry could not reach substantial agreement. The release ended inconclusively with a discussion of new Rule X-9A6-1. Commissioner Healy entered a sharp dissent arguing that stabilization should be outlawed.

Following the issuance of its statement of policy in 1940, rather than promulgating specific rules in connection with stabilizing practices, the SEC depended upon informal interpretations, some of which were issued in the form of releases, but most of which were rendered individually by letter or telephone in answer to specific requests.[37]

In a 1948 report on an investigation of an offering of common stock of Kaiser-Frazer Corporation, the statement was made that stabilization for the sole purpose of preventing or retarding a decline in the price of a security does not violate Section 9(a)(2) or any other provision of the 1934 Act so long

---

34. SEC Release No. 34-2008 (February 9, 1939). The 1933 Act disclosure requirements are now set forth in Items 502(d), 508(k) and 508(l) of Regulation S-K.

35. SEC Release No. 34-2363 (January 3, 1940).

36. SEC Release No. 34-2446 (March 18, 1940).

37. For examples of these informal interpretations, see Foshay, *supra* note 32, at 911-13.

as the purchases are effected at the lower of "a *bona fide* independent market price for the security being stabilized" or the public offering price and that "within these restrictions there is no limit under existing statute and rules on the amount of securities which may be purchased in the stabilizing process."[38]

In 1949, two members of the SEC's staff published a law review article of major significance bringing together in one place the principles and interpretations governing stabilization in connection with fixed price offerings.[39] This article became the principal reference for securities lawyers advising clients as to permitted stabilization practices and continued to be a useful interpretative guide even after the adoption of the Trading Practice Rules.

• Adoption of the Original Trading Practice Rules

Despite its earlier reluctance to act, in 1954 the SEC finally took steps to formalize its positions with respect to market activities during distributions and stabilization practices. This required some Congressional prodding. As reported in the SEC's *Twentieth Annual Report,* the Committee on Interstate and Foreign Commerce of the House of Representatives recommended in a report dated December 30, 1952 that "the Commission should earnestly and expeditiously grapple with the problem of stabilization with the view either of the early promulgation of rules publicly covering these operations or of recommending to the Congress such changes in legislation as its experience and study show now to be desirable."[40]

After intensive study by the staff and review by the SEC, the proposed rules, designated Rules X-10B-6, X-10B-7 and X-10B-8, were circulated for public comment in May 1954.[41] A revised proposal was published for comment in April 1955,[42] and the SEC adopted the final rules in July 1955.[43]

---

38. SEC Release No. 34-4163 (September 16, 1948).
39. Parlin & Everett, *The Stabilization of Security Prices,* 49 Colum. L. Rev. 606 (1949).
40. H.R. Rep. No. 2508, 82d Cong., 2d Sess. 3 (1952).
41. SEC Release No. 34-5040 (May 18, 1954).
42. SEC Release No. 34-5159 (April 19, 1955).
43. SEC Release No. 34-5194 (July 5, 1955).

• *Subsequent Revisions of the Trading Practice Rules*

By 1983, the securities markets had changed considerably. The SEC and its staff had attempted for many years to accommodate Rule 10b-6 to changing markets and underwriting practices through the granting of exemptive relief and the issuance of no-action and interpretive letters. In many cases, underwriters and issuers were required to make time-consuming identical applications for substantially the same relief. It was probably no coincidence that Rule 10b-6's first major overhaul occurred in 1983[44] on the occasion of the introduction of shelf registration. The 1983 amendments introduced a definition of the term "distribution." They also exempted nonconvertible investment-grade debt and preferred securities, relaxed prohibitions on research, dealt with the relatively new phenomenon of exchange-traded options and reduced the rule's applicability to "affiliated purchasers."

Just as important, the 1983 amendments relaxed various trading prohibitions, including delaying certain prohibitions of the rule until the start of a "cooling-off" period of two business days prior to the commencement of a distribution in the case of stock with a minimum price of $5 per share and a minimum float of 400,000 shares or nine business days in the case of other securities. (Previously, the trading restrictions began for a prospective underwriter when it reached an understanding with the issuer or selling securityholder that it would participate in the distribution, except that over-the-counter trading was permitted through the tenth business day prior to the offering.)

In 1987 the SEC further amended the rule[45] to permit underwriters to engage in solicited brokerage transactions prior to the "cooling-off" period, to adjust further the concept of "affiliated purchaser" and to permit the exercise at any time throughout a distribution of previously-established standardized call option positions.

Until 1987, the preamble to Rule 10b-6 had stated that violations of the rule were violations of Section 10(b) of the 1934

---

44. SEC Release No. 34-19565 (March 4, 1983).
45. SEC Release No. 34-24003 (January 16, 1987).

Act, which prohibits the use of any "manipulative or deceptive device or contrivance" in violation of SEC rules. As part of the 1987 amendments, the SEC modified the preamble to state that violations of the rule were "unlawful." In so doing, the SEC intended "more completely [to] reflect the prophylactic scope of the Rule, the authority for the Rule's provisions, and the Commission's intention to use its full statutory authority, including the authority to adopt rules that are reasonably designed to prevent fraudulent, deceptive, or manipulative acts and practices."[46] The SEC's action was undoubtedly based on Division of Enforcement concerns that action in compliance with the various exceptions to the rule might be impervious to attack even if there was clear evidence of manipulative intent; it was probably also based on concern that the SEC might have to prove *scienter* or other elements of a Rule 10b-5 proceeding.[47] In any event, the SEC position was that Rule 10b-6 was based on its authority under at least Sections 2, 3, 9(a)(6), 13(e), 15(c) and 23(a) of the 1934 Act.

The 1987 amendments also made explicit the SEC's position that the exceptions to Rule 10b-6's prohibitions could not be relied upon as "safe harbors" from charges of manipulation. They did so by providing that transactions in reliance on the exceptions could not be "for the purpose of creating actual, or apparent, active trading in or raising the price of any such security."

In 1993 the SEC adopted Rule 10b-6A[48] to permit "passive market making" during a distribution and also amended Rule 10b-6[49] to exempt transactions in certain Rule 144A-eligible securities of foreign issuers offered and sold in the United States exclusively to QIBs. The SEC also continued its efforts

---

46. In support of this contention, the SEC cited Section 13(e)(1) of the 1934 Act (applicable to issuer repurchases) and Section 15(c)(2) of the 1934 Act (applicable to OTC transactions). *Id.* at note 51.

47. It is true that some courts held that *scienter* had to be alleged and proved as one element of a Rule 10b-6 violation, but this is of more relevance to a litigator than to an advisor to issuers and underwriters.

48. SEC Release No. 34-32117 (April 8, 1993).

49. SEC Release No. 34-33138 (November 3, 1993).

to accommodate the Trading Practice Rules to innovative securities market products such as "baskets" of securities, as well as to international securities offerings. In connection with international offerings, it granted exemptions in 1993 to facilitate global equity distributions by large German issuers.

• *Adoption of Regulation M*

In April 1994 the SEC published a Concept Release on its anti-manipulation regulation of securities offerings. In the release, it invited comment on whether certain classes of securities, transactions or investors needed the protection of the Trading Practice Rules. It noted changes in the securities markets that it believed might make manipulation less likely to occur in many situations. These included the role of institutions, whose sophistication and "bargaining power" could be expected to provide protection against abusive conduct on the "sell-side" of an offering, the increased transparency and liquidity of secondary markets and the more sophisticated surveillance techniques employed by SROs.

Based on responses to the Concept Release, the SEC proposed in April 1996 to adopt a new Regulation M that would supersede the old Trading Practice Rules. After a relatively short comment period, made possible in part by the significant response solicited by the Concept Release, the SEC adopted Regulation M in late December 1996. The new rules became effective on March 4, 1997.

Regulation M

Regulation M represents the most significant overhaul of the Trading Practice Rules since the adoption of Rules 10b-6, 10b-7 and 10b-8 in 1955. Its format differs significantly from that of the old Trading Practice Rules:

Rule 100 of the new regulation defines terms used in the rules.

Rules 101 and 102 replace Rule 10b-6 for (a) distribution participants such as underwriters and (b) issuers or selling securityholders, respectively.

Rule 103 replaces Rule 10b-6A and permits "passive market-making" in NASDAQ securities during all distributions (except best efforts or at-the-market offerings or at any time when a stabilizing bid is in effect).

Rule 104 replaces Rule 10b-7 and governs stabilization.

Rule 105 replaces Rule 10b-21 and governs the covering of short sales with securities purchased in a public offering.

• *Rule 101—Basic Prohibitions*

Like old Rule 10b-6, new Rule 101 prohibits distribution participants (such as underwriters) and their affiliated purchasers from bidding for, purchasing or attempting to induce any person to bid for or purchase specified securities at specified times during a "distribution." The definition of "distribution" is a function of whether a transaction is distinguished from ordinary trading transactions by the "magnitude of the offering" *and* the presence of "special selling efforts and selling methods."

Rule 101 applies, however, only to "covered securities," which are defined as the security being distributed and any "reference security." In turn, "reference security" means any security into which the security being distributed may be converted, exchanged or exercised or that may significantly determine the value of the security being distributed.

Rule 101 does not apply at all to certain actively-traded or investment-grade or exempted securities, and it applies to other securities only during certain "restricted periods" of one or five business days. Even during such restricted periods, the rule permits ten specified categories of activity.

• *Distributions*

Regulation M did not change the definition of "distribution," which remains a key term under Regulation M as it was under the old Trading Practice Rules.

As originally adopted, Rule 10b-6 did not contain a definition of the key term "distribution." It had been recognized from the outset, however, that the rule applied to all "distributions" whether or not registered under the 1933 Act and whether or not underwritten.

The *Bruns, Nordeman* case established, although in broad terms, the standard for determining whether or not there was a distribution for Rule 10b-6 purposes.[50] The SEC there stated that the determination should be made "upon the basis of the magnitude of the offering and particularly upon the basis of the selling efforts and selling methods utilized."[51]

• • *Block Trades.* During the late 1960s, as the markets became increasingly institutional, securities firms established block trading departments to facilitate transactions in large blocks of listed stocks. Securities practitioners were faced with the question of whether, by virtue of their sheer size, these trades would be viewed as distributions for Rule 10b-6 purposes.[52]

The execution of a block trade is fairly straightforward. If an institution wishes to sell a large block of a listed security on a "net" basis, and the exchange's auction market cannot readily absorb the block, a securities firm's "block desk" will quickly communicate with institutions, including those it may know to have an interest in the security. A commitment will be made to the seller, and the buy and sell orders will be crossed on the exchange. If the block trader cannot readily obtain orders for the entire block, it may position a portion itself in order to facilitate the transaction.[53]

If a block trade were considered a distribution subject to Rule 10b-6, the feasibility of this type of transaction would have been in jeopardy.[54] The block trader would be prohibited from bidding for or purchasing the same security while it was trying to put together the block transaction. This would have made it unable to carry on normal trading activity. In addition, its abrupt withdrawal from the market would "signal" other market participants that a trade was in the works.

A 1972 report delivered to the SEC by its Advisory Committee on Block Transactions addressed the issue in a constructive fashion:

---

50. *Bruns, Nordeman & Company,* 40 S.E.C. 652 (1961).

51. *Id.* at 660.

52. *See* Bialkin, *Block Distributions,* 4 Rev. Sec. Reg. 985 (1971).

53. *See* NYSE Rules 97 and 127.

54. As discussed below, Regulation M now exempts actively-traded securities with a large public float; these are the securities most often involved in block transactions.

The Committee believes that the normal handling of block transactions does not involve a "distribution" as that term is utilized in Rule 10b-6; such application was not within the purview of that Rule as originally conceived and constructed or as subsequently administered. We believe that the Commission should confirm this by exemption or otherwise, and that concurrently there should be promulgated by the Commission areas of permissible market activity appropriate for and specifically adapted to the normal techniques employed in block positioning. In addition to Rule 10b-6, Rule 10b-7 as well as recently adopted Rule 97 of the New York Stock Exchange would be involved in the process.[55]

Unfortunately, the SEC did not follow up on the Advisory Committee's suggestion.

• • *The Jaffee Case.* In 1970, the SEC held that any offering under a 1933 Act registration statement constitutes a "distribution" regardless of the size of the offering or the manner in which the sale is made.[56] A market maker purchasing securities under a shelf registration was therefore deemed to be participating in the distribution of such securities and to have violated Rule 10b-6 because it continued to make a market while purchasing and reselling securities under the shelf registration. The case distinguished similar activity by a specialist on an exchange.

Jaffee created a great deal of uncertainty as to the status of market makers in the context of a shelf registration where stockholders are selling from time to time into the over-the-counter market. The fear was that market makers would refuse to purchase distribution securities in a shelf registration or a new issue for fear of violating Rule 10-6.[57] After *Jaffee,* market makers were extremely reluctant to purchase securities covered by shelf registration statements relating to secondary offerings. Indeed, it was rumored at the time that two-tiered markets had developed in cer-

---

55. [1972-1973 Transfer Binder] Fed. Sec. L. Rep. (CCH) ¶ 78,967.

56. *Jaffee & Co.*, SEC Release No. 34-8866 (April 20, 1970), aff'd in relevant part sub nom. *Jaffee & Co. v. SEC,* 446 F. 2d 387 (2d Cir. 1971).

57. *See* Solomon, *The Jaffee Case,* 4 Rev. Sec. Reg. 829 (1971).

tain stocks where a shelf registration statement was in the picture, with dealers being willing to purchase the registered securities only at a discount from the actual market price.[58]

In 1975, the SEC came to its senses and abandoned its position that a sale under a registration statement is necessarily a distribution.[59] In doing so, it returned to the *Bruns, Nordeman* formulation as the sole standard.[60]

• • *The 1983 Definition.* In March 1982, the SEC proposed a number of amendments to Rule 10b-6, including the adoption of a definition of the term "distribution."[61] The proposed definition, which purported to codify existing case law, provided that the term "distribution" means

> an offering of securities, whether or not subject to registration under the Securities Act of 1933, which is distinguished from ordinary trading transactions by the magnitude of the offering or the presence of either special selling efforts and selling methods or the payment of compensation greater than that normally paid in connection with ordinary trading transactions.

The proposed definition went on to set forth, with unfortunate negative implications, the proviso that

> the sale of securities will not constitute a distribution for purposes of this section if the sale has been made in

---

58. In 1971, when Faulkner, Dawkins & Sullivan, a market maker in the stock of White Shield Corporation, learned that White Shield shares it had agreed to purchase were covered by a shelf registration statement, it refused to accept delivery. In subsequent litigation, the court said that failure to disclose the fact that stock was, in fact, registered stock was a material omission, particularly in light of the *Jaffee* decision. *Byrnes v. Faulkner, Dawkins & Sullivan*, 413 F. Supp. 453, 458 (S.D.N.Y. 1976).

59. *Collins Securities Corp.*, SEC Release No. 34-11766 (October 23, 1975), *remanded on other grounds sub nom. Collins Securities Corp. v. SEC*, 562 F.2d 820 (D.C. Cir. 1977).

60. *Oppenheimer & Co., Inc.*, SEC Release No. 34-16817 (May 19, 1980).

61. SEC Release No. 34-18528 (March 3, 1982).

compliance with both the volume limitations and the manner of sale provisions contained in paragraphs (e) and (f) of Rule 144 under the Securities Act of 1933.

A year later, the SEC adopted the Rule 10b-6 amendments in somewhat altered form after receiving comments from members of the securities industry and others.[62] The definition of "distribution," as finally adopted, came closer to the *Bruns, Nordeman* test than the definition originally proposed. Instead of applying a three-pronged test, expressed disjunctively through the use of "or," the revised definition simply stated that the term means

> an offering of securities, whether or not subject to registration under the Securities Act of 1933, that is distinguished from ordinary trading transactions by the magnitude of the offering and the presence of special selling efforts and selling methods.

The SEC stated in a footnote to the adopting release:

> The presence of special selling efforts and selling methods may be indicated in a number of ways, including the payment of compensation greater than that normally paid in connection with ordinary trading transactions.

The proposed Rule 144 proviso, referred to for the first time in the adopting release as a "safe harbor," was not adopted in deference to objections from commentators that it was unnecessary and might become a prescriptive standard.

The adoption of a definition served the useful function of codifying the *Bruns, Nordeman* test in the rule itself, thus making it readily apparent to lawyers who might not be familiar with the prior case law. The definition, through the use of the conjunctive "and," made it clear that size alone is not the determining factor.

In the 1994 Concept Release, the SEC referred to the 1983 definition as a "functional" one that was intended "to provide

---

62. SEC Release No. 34-19565 (March 4, 1983).

a greater degree of guidance on, and certainty to, the types of offerings that would give rise to an incentive to artificially condition the market for the offered security." The reference to an "incentive" to manipulate is unfortunate, of course, because it harks back to a time when the Division of Enforcement saw a "distribution" whenever *it* perceived a "temptation to manipulate" on the part of a broker-dealer. The object of a definition, of course, should be to minimize the subjective element.

In the Concept Release, the SEC noted that a "distribution" must have both elements, i.e., "magnitude" and "special selling efforts and selling methods." It went on to explain (footnotes omitted):

> Factors relevant to the magnitude element are: the number of shares to be registered for sale by the issuer, and the percentage of the outstanding shares, public float, and trading volume that those shares represent. The Commission has indicated that providing greater than normal sales compensation arrangements pertaining to the distribution of a security, delivering a sales document, such as a prospectus or market letters, and conducting "road shows" are generally indicative of "special selling efforts and selling methods." Based upon an analysis of their individual characteristics, the following transactions, among others, have been viewed as involving distributions under this definition: registered public offerings, private placements, Rule 144A transactions, rights offerings, warrant exercise solicitations, dividend reinvestment and stock purchase plans, the issuance of securities in connection with a merger or exchange offer, "major sales campaigns" by a broker-dealer, and sales made pursuant to a shelf registration statement.

While the foregoing is a useful compendium of factors that the SEC deems relevant, it is hardly conclusive. It overlooks the fact that the rule's definition of "distribution" really has *three* elements: (1) magnitude, (2) special selling efforts and selling methods *and* (3) whether or not the transaction because of the presence or absence of the first two elements resembles or does not resemble an "ordinary trading transaction." For example, two different firms might execute the same transaction in entirely different ways depending on the depth and efficiency of their block trading desks. This is not to suggest that there is a special definition of "distribution" for certain large block trading firms, but it is surely relevant that a given trade— e.g., a block equal to five days' trading volume—would be executed by a particular broker-dealer in a routine fashion similar to its other "ordinary trading transactions."

• • *Shelf Registrations.* Under early SEC staff interpretations of Rule 10b-6, any shelf registration that constituted a "distribution" was considered a "single distribution" for purposes of the rule, i.e., each takedown was subject to Rule 10b-6 regardless of its magnitude or other circumstances. Under the SEC's interpretation of Regulation M, on the other hand, "each takedown off a shelf is to be individually examined to determine whether such offering constitutes a distribution," i.e., based on its size or "magnitude" and whether or not "special selling efforts and selling methods" will be used.[63] Contrary to another early interpretation, the Regulation M Release states that the mere description in a shelf registration statement of various potential selling methods (some of which might constitute "special selling methods") would not require a broker-dealer to consider itself involved in a distribution unless it in fact used special selling efforts or methods in connection with particular sales off the shelf and the sales met the magnitude test.

The Regulation M Release states that a broker-dealer would "likely" be subject to Rule 101 if it entered into a "sales agency agreement that provides for unusual transaction-based compensation for the sales, even if the securities are sold in ordinary trading transactions." Unless one is willing to assume that "unusual compensation" always means "special selling efforts and selling methods" (a proposition that is not self-

---

63. Regulation M Release (text at note 46).

evident), this statement would appear to be contrary to the plain language of the rule.

* *"Distribution Participant"*

Assuming that an offering involves a "distribution," Rule 101's prohibitions apply to any person who is a "distribution participant." Under the definition in Rule 100, the term "distribution participant" means an underwriter, a "prospective underwriter" or a broker, dealer "or other person who has agreed to participate or is participating in a distribution."

A "prospective underwriter" means a person who has either (1) "submitted a bid to the issuer or selling securityholder, and who knows or is reasonably certain that such bid will be accepted" or (2) "reached, or is reasonably certain to reach, an understanding with the issuer or selling securityholder . . . or managing underwriter that such person will become an underwriter," in either case "whether or not the terms and conditions of the underwriting have been agreed upon."

A person who is participating in a distribution remains subject to Rule 101's prohibitions until he has completed his participation. This is discussed below.

Identifying the commencement of a person's participation in a distribution is less often an important task under Rule 101 than used to be the case under Rule 10b-6. This is because the prohibitions of Rule 101 apply only during specified "restricted periods," while the prohibitions of Rule 10b-6 applied from the moment of commencement of a person's participation in the distribution (subject, to be sure, to a number of exceptions). Even under Rule 101, however, it can be important to identify the commencement of a person's participation in a distribution. For example, it is possible that such participation may commence *during* the applicable restricted period where a securities firm receives an invitation to bid from an issuer or an invitation to join a syndicate from a managing underwriter.

The SEC's traditional view in this situation has been that "there is frequently some point prior to when a bid actually has been accepted, or a broker-dealer has been told that it will be an underwriter, when it is reasonably certain that such person will be an underwriter, and that the incentive to facilitate the distribution is present at that point."[64] Rule 10b-6 therefore measured the commencement of a broker-dealer's participation from the time it decided to submit a bid to a person who had requested bids or from the time it reached an understanding that it would become an underwriter. This was replaced in the proposed Regulation M by reference to the broker-dealer's "reasonab[e] expect[ation]" and, in turn, in the final Regulation M by reference to the broker-dealer's "reasonabl[e] certain[ty]."[65] The Regulation M Release admitted that the final definition did not provide "a bright line test" but anticipated that its "practical effect should be to reduce the circumstances in which a broker-dealer will be a prospective underwriter."

Under Rule 10b-6, broker-dealers maintained "restricted lists" for the purpose, among other things,[66] of preventing bids for or purchases of securities as to which a broker-dealer had become a "prospective underwriter" or the publication of certain research relating to such securities. In addition, many firms programmed their quotation machines to generate a flashing "R" or similar symbol whenever a quote was requested on a stock on the restricted list. The disadvantage of these procedures was that they made it difficult to preserve the confidentiality of a proposed offering. Prior to an offering's public announcement, therefore, managing underwriters would often put a security on a "gray" or "watch" list at the time a tacit understanding was reached that an offering should go forward, as evidenced by the preparation of a timetable or directions to counsel to begin work on the registration statement. The effect of the "gray" or "watch" list was to limit certain types of proprietary trading while enabling the firm to monitor all other transactions as well as research.

---

64. Regulation M Release (text following note 16).

65. One way in which a broker-dealer may be "reasonably certain" that it would participate in a shelf distribution would be on the basis of a "continuing agreement" regarding its participation in takedowns off the shelf. Regulation M Release at note 116.

66. E.g., to prevent any actual or perceived misuse of material nonpublic information received in a capacity of trust or confidence. See the discussion in Chapter 3.

Practice was not uniform in this regard, however, or as to the treatment of such situations as the receipt of an invitation from a managing underwriter. Some firms regarded their participation as commencing from the time of receipt of such an invitation, while others focused on the time of their acceptance. Still others engaged in considerable hairsplitting on the basis of whether it was likely that they would accept the invitation (e.g., because they had participated in prior deals of the same issuer).

Regulation M may affect traditional practice in two ways. First, because restrictions do not commence until the start of the restricted period (if any), it will no longer be necessary to carry a security on the restricted list for the full period of time a broker-dealer is a prospective underwriter. Some firms may, of course, choose to continue the prior practice for the purpose of monitoring transactions and research. Second, the "reasonably certain" standard will probably postpone the time in many cases when a firm must regard itself as a prospective underwriter. Again, however, some firms may choose to continue their prior practice.

Rule 101 also applies to dealers who are not acting as underwriters, i.e., members of the selling group, but only to the extent that they have agreed to participate or are participating in the distribution. Like Rule 10b-6, the new rule does not speak of a "prospective" participating dealer as it does of a "prospective underwriter," only of a dealer who has agreed to participate or is participating in the distribution.

• *Affiliated Purchasers*

The 1983 amendments to Rule 10b-6 added to the categories of restricted persons "affiliated purchasers," i.e., persons having certain defined relationships with issuers, selling securityholders, underwriters and other participants in a distribution. This amendment formalized, and in some ways limited (especially as a result of a further amendment in 1987), the SEC's traditional position that the restrictions of Rule 10b-6 extended to affiliates of distribution participants, persons whose relationship with a distribution participant would provide an incentive to condition the market to facilitate the distribution of the offered security.[67]

Regulation M defines an "affiliated purchaser" as any person who acts "in concert" with a distribution participant, issuer or selling securityholder in connection with the acquisition or distribution of a covered security. The term also includes any affiliate (including a separately identifiable department or division) whose purchases are under the control of (or whose purchases are controlled by or under common control with) a distribution participation, issuer or selling securityholder.

In addition, an affiliated purchaser includes any other affiliated person "that regularly purchases securities for its own account or for the account of others, or that recommends or exercises investment discretion with respect to the purchase or sale of securities." In order to accommodate underwriters that are part of organizational complexes that provide diversified financial services, the definition then excludes affiliates (including a separately identifiable department or division) where the underwriter establishes, maintains and enforces written information barriers between itself and the affiliate and obtains an annual independent assessment of the operation of such information barriers. The affiliate must not, however, act during the applicable restricted period as a market-maker (other than as a specialist) or as a broker-dealer in solicited transactions or proprietary trading activities in covered securities.[68]

Distribution participants are ordinarily subject to Rule 101, but a distribution participant that is also an affiliated purchaser of an issuer or selling securityholder can also be subject to Rule 102. Regulation M resolves the possible overlap by providing that a distribution participant is subject to Rule 101 under these

---

67. *See SEC v. Burns*, 816 F.2d 471, 474-75 (9th Cir. 1987).

68. Regulation M does not perpetuate the additional requirements of Rule 10b-6 that, in order to be excluded from the definition, distribution participants and their affiliates would have to have separate compensation arrangements, separate and distinct organizational structures and no common officers or non-ministerial employees (except that Regulation M does not permit common officers or employees who direct, effect or recommend transactions in securities).

circumstances, unless the distribution participant is itself acting as the issuer or selling securityholder.[69]

• *Duration of Restricted Period*

Rule 10b-6 imposed restrictions during the entire distribution
with exceptions that permitted certain activities during "cooling-
off" periods of two and nine business days prior to the commencement of offers and sales. Regulation M imposes restrictions only
during a "restricted period," the length of which depends on the
trading volume and "public float" of the security being distributed.

First, as discussed below, Rule 101 does not apply at all to
securities with an "average daily trading volume" ("ADTV")
of at least $1,000,000 *and* whose issuer—unaffiliated with the
underwriter—has common equity securities with a public float
value of at least $150 million. (The computation of ADTV and
public float are discussed below.)

Second, where the securities meet an ADTV standard of
$100,000 and the issuer meets a float test of $25 million, Rule
101 imposes restrictions during a "restricted period" that begins one business day[70] prior to the determination of the price
of the security to be distributed.

Third, in the case of all other securities, the restricted period begins five business days prior to such determination.

As discussed below, the restricted period terminates when
an underwriter completes its participation in a distribution.

The new restricted periods replace the Rule 10b-6 concept
of a lengthy period during which restrictions apply across the
board except as relieved by certain exceptions that are available prior to the start of specified "cooling-off" periods. To the
extent that the new restricted periods resemble the old cooling-
off periods, the ADTV and public float criteria are very differ-

---

69. Rules 101(a) and 102(a). The Regulation M Release notes that the
variety and complexity of organizational structures in the financial services
industry may cause Regulation M to apply to some affiliates that it may be
appropriate to exclude. In those cases, the SEC's Division of Market Regulation will entertain exemption requests.

70. Rule 100, as amended in SEC Release No. 34-38363 (March 4,
1997), defines "business day" as a 24 hour period that includes an entire
trading session in the principal market for the security to be distributed.

ent from those that applied under Rule 10b-6, which required a nine business day cooling-off period except for securities that met a $5 share price and 400,000 share float test (in which case the cooling-off period was two business days).

As noted in the Regulation M Release, however, the new rules do not automatically mean a shorter restricted period for all securities. According to the release, about 31% of listed and NASDAQ securities that were formerly subject to a two-day cooling-off period are now excluded entirely from the rule, while approximately 44% are subject to a one-day restricted period. About 25% of such securities, however, are now subject to a five-day restricted period.

The definition of "restricted period" in Rule 100 specifies that a restricted period does not start for a distribution participant until that person actually becomes a distribution participant.

The SEC continues to believe that mergers, acquisitions and exchange offers involve distributions in which interested persons may have incentives to manipulate. Regulation M clarifies the restricted period for such transactions, however, as follows:

- – Rule 100 states that the restrictions begin on the day when proxy solicitation or offering materials first are disseminated to securityholders and end with the completion of the distribution, i.e., the time of the shareholder vote or the expiration of the exchange offer; and

- – By SEC interpretation, a new restricted period will also apply during any period where the market price of the offered security will be a factor in determining the consideration to be paid (i.e., a valuation period).[71]

• *Termination of Restricted Period*

The restricted period ends when an underwriter completes its participation in a distribution. This is determined under Regulation

---

71. Rule 10b-13 will continue to prohibit any purchases of securities that are the subject of an exchange offer (or securities immediately convertible into or exchangeable for such securities) from the time of public announcement until the expiration of the exchange offer.

M in the same manner as under Rule 10b-6, i.e., when the under-writer has sold its participation (including other securities of the same class acquired in connection with the distribution, e.g., those acquired in stabilization) and when stabilization arrangements and trading restrictions in connection with the distribution have been terminated.[72] Other persons, including dealers, are no longer sub-ject to Rule 101 when they have distributed their participations.

A person, including an underwriter or dealer, is deemed for this purpose to have distributed securities acquired "for invest-ment" as discussed below.

Although not stated in the rule, an affiliated purchaser should be viewed as standing in the shoes of the underwriter or other person with whom it has the affiliation that gave rise to its affiliated purchaser status.

• • *Successful Offering.* How do these principles apply in the context of a successful underwritten offering? Assume that the syndicate manager is satisfied shortly after the pricing and release of the securities that the offering has gone extremely well. There may be a syndicate short position created through overallotments in an amount that the manager considers adequate and prudent.[73] There may be a stabilizing bid maintained at the public offering price, and stabilizing purchases may have been made in moderate amounts, thus reducing somewhat the original syndicate short po-sition. The syndicate members have assured the manager that they have sold all securities retained by them for direct sale.[74]

---

72. These provisions are contained in the AAU as discussed in Chapter 2. A "lockup" agreement, under which an issuer, selling securityholders and other securityholders agree to refrain from making additional sales for a specified period following the effectiveness of a registration statement, is not a trading restriction for this purpose.

73. See Chapter 2 for a discussion of the purpose and effect of overal-lotments and the use of overallotment, or Green Shoe, options.

74. The manager should be entitled to accept at face value "all sold" assurances received from members of the syndicate. Of course, syndicate members may be reluctant to admit that they have unsold shares even if in fact they do. Under these circumstances, the syndicate member with an un-sold allotment remains subject to Rule 101.

At this point, the manager may pull the stabilizing bid and inform the syndicate members of the termination of trading restrictions.[75] The distribution has at this point been completed for purposes of Rule 101, and the underwriters are no longer subject to the rule's prohibitions (assuming that they have in fact sold all of their participation or, as discussed below, acquired the unsold portion "for investment"). They may now participate in a two-way trading market for the securities.

The syndicate manager may now go into the market and cover the syndicate short position free of the restrictions of Rule 101.[76] Prior to this time, the short position could have been reduced only through stabilizing purchases or through otherwise "excepted" purchases (discussed below).

It used to be suggested that it might be prudent for the manager to wait for the mailing of confirmations, for the receipt of payment from customers or for the closing with the issuer or selling securityholder (now usually three business days after the offering) before considering the distribution completed. The delay was presumably to guard against the possibility of reneging customers. Nothing in the rule requires any such delay, provided that the underwriter or dealer is relying in good faith on the customer's agreement to purchase.

At one time, the SEC took the position that the overallotment option must either be exercised or irrevocably terminated before the managing underwriter would be permitted to go into the market to cover the syndicate short position. Rule 10b-6 was amended in 1983 to provide, as does Regulation M, that market making is now permitted even while the overallotment option remains unexercised, provided that the option is not exercised for an amount in excess of the *net* syndicate short posi-

---

If a syndicate member does have unsold shares, the manager should take these back and apply them against the syndicate short position before covering purchases are made in the market.

75. Pursuant to the AAU, these restrictions may be terminated by the managing underwriter at any time (see Chapter 2).

76. SEC Release No. 34-3506 (November 16, 1943) contains certain pre-Rule 10b-6 guidelines to be followed in covering overallotments. These no longer need to be taken into consideration.

tion at the time of exercise (i.e., the short position at the time the distribution is terminated as reduced by subsequent purchases for the account of the syndicate). If the overallotment option is exercised for securities in excess of the amount necessary to cover the short position, the distribution will not be deemed to have been completed, and any open market purchases made prior to the exercise of the option could in theory constitute a retroactive violation of Rule 101.

In the course of an underwriting, the syndicate manager and other underwriters may have created a short position in their customer accounts, i.e., the accounts out of which they have sold securities retained or allotted to them for direct sale to customers. Like the syndicate short position, these short positions may not be covered until trading restrictions and stabilization authority have been terminated. In addition, of course, the underwriter must have sold its participation or applied it against its short position. If these conditions have been met, there is no reason why a non-managing underwriter may not cover a short position in its customer accounts or make a two-way market in the covered securities without limitation other than those imposed by general antimanipulative principles.

In the case of the syndicate manager, however, it can be argued that it should not trade in the securities for its own account or cover its own short position until the syndicate short position has been covered. The manager is an agent for the rest of the underwriting group, and, under general agency principles, it should not take any action for its own benefit that might conflict with the interests of the members of the syndicate. Securities professionals have taken the position, however, that in many if not all cases, it actually may be to the benefit of the syndicate for the manager to make a two-way market while the syndicate still has a short position. It is correct that this would not be prohibited by Rule 101. As a matter of prudence, however, if the manager does make a market under these circumstances, it should consider applying any long position existing at the end of any business day against any remaining short position in the syndicate account and not covering the short position in its customer accounts until the syndicate short position has been covered.

• • *Unsuccessful Offering.* Assume next a sticky deal, an unsuccessful underwriting. The securities are not all sold. The market is in a state of flux. The stabilizing bid may be hit in force, and the syndicate manager may be buying more securities for the syndicate than it would like. Several members of the syndicate may be having trouble disposing of their securities. If the securities are traded over-the-counter rather than on an exchange, there may be great pressure from the issuer and from customers for the underwriters to commence participation in a regular two-way market. What are the options in the context of Rule 101?

The manager could try to hold the syndicate together and perhaps raise the selling concession. He could maintain price restrictions and lower the public offering price, as authorized under the AAU and under the language of the typical prospectus.[77] He could maintain the original terms of the offering and engage in purchase and sale transactions in reliance on exceptions 5 and 9 to Rule 101 as discussed below under "Unsolicited Purchases."

Another option is to terminate the syndicate and turn over to the underwriters the unsold securities that they are committed to purchase. In this case, the manager would terminate price and trading restrictions, pull the stabilizing bid, and let each of the underwriters sell its securities as best it can into an unsettled market. After each underwriter disposes of its participation, probably at a loss, it may commence regular trading activity. (Of course, if an individual underwriter with an unsold allotment does not wish to sell at a loss, it may place the unsold allotment in an investment account (as discussed below) and immediately commence regular trading activity.)

When stabilization and trading restrictions are terminated prior to the completion of the distribution, the Rule 101 restrictions apply on an underwriter-by-underwriter basis, so that if a particular underwriter has distributed its participation, it may

---

77. The prospectus should state, "After the initial public offering, the public offering price, concession and discount may be changed." If it does, the price may be reduced or the concession increased without stickering the prospectus.

make a market even though other members of the now-disbanded syndicate are still distributing securities. That is not the case if the syndicate is being held together and trading restrictions have not been terminated. However, breaking the syndicate and leaving the underwriters to distribute the securities as best they can is not a very satisfactory way to handle an unsuccessful offering.

Occasionally, in a sticky deal, if there is not too much unsold stock, the managing underwriter will take back securities from members of the syndicate and sell them to an institution that has made a so-called "clean-up bid." This approach may work if the manager is able to find an institution that is willing to buy all of the remaining unsold securities at a price somewhat below the public offering price.

• • • *Investment Account.* A more common approach in recent years is for the manager to stand behind the deal and purchase "for investment" for its own account the securities taken back from the syndicate. As previously noted, Rule 101 specifically states that a distribution is deemed to have been completed as to any securities that are acquired by an underwriter for investment.

Large, well-capitalized investment banking firms can afford to take this risk in expectation of a stronger market. As the distribution is deemed to have been completed at this point, the manager and all other members of the syndicate may trade in the securities free of Rule 101 restrictions.

Of course, even if the syndicate manager does not take securities back from the syndicate, any syndicate member with an unsold participation may place the securities into its own investment account and commence trading.

Under what circumstances and subject to what restrictions may an underwriter later sell securities acquired for investment? The SEC does not apply the same tests under the 1934 Act as it does under the 1933 Act in determining when a person may sell securities acquired for investment. The best advice that one can give is that there is no magic holding period, but securities should be ordinarily be held for several months, rather than several weeks, to demonstrate that they were actually acquired for investment. An earlier rather than a later sale might be justified by an unexpected and significant change of circumstances affecting the underwriter, the issuer or the market for the securities. The theory in that situation would be that the early sale was not inconsistent with an investment intent because of the intervention of the change of circumstances.

At such time as an underwriter decides to sell securities out of its investment account, the provisions of Rule 101 may again apply, depending on whether the sale involves a "distribution" at the time. This will again depend on the magnitude of the unsold allotment and the selling efforts and selling methods that will be employed in connection with its sale. Of course, the security may in the meantime have qualified for the $1,000,000 ADTV/$150 million public float test so that Rule 101 will not apply to the distribution of the unsold allotment. If this is not the case, the underwriter will be required to stop making a market during the applicable period of one or five business days before the determination of the offering price.

The Rule 101 principle that a distribution has been completed when an underwriter acquires securities for investment is not relevant to a 1933 Act analysis. For purposes of the 1933 Act, the distribution will be viewed as continuing, and the prospectus delivery requirements must be met at such time as the underwriter sells its securities. A sale of securities from an investment account must therefore be made in accordance with the prospectus delivery requirements of the 1933 Act, and the prospectus, when delivered to a purchaser, must meet the updating requirements of Section 10(a) of the 1933 Act as well as not violate the disclosure requirements of Section 12(a)(2) of the 1933 Act or Rule 10b-5 under the 1934 Act.

Before the underwriter sells the securities out of its investment account, it must therefore satisfy itself that the prospectus does not need to be amended to replace "stale" financial statements or to reflect changes in the issuer's business. Of course, the underwriting agreement should provide (as discussed in Chapter 2) that the issuer will amend the prospectus as necessary for this purpose. This obligation applies, however, only during any period when a prospectus is required to be delivered. For this reason, it will usually be necessary for the underwriter to take the initiative and check with the issuer about any need for amendments to the prospectus. It may come as a surprise to the issuer, of course, that the underwriter did not sell all of its securities prior to the closing!

It is generally not necessary to amend the prospectus merely to reflect the fact that the underwriter is selling securities from the investment account.

• *Disclosure, SRO Notification and Recordkeeping*

As part of the adoption of Regulation M, the SEC increased the prospectus disclosure, SRO notification and recordkeeping obligations associated with stabilizing activity, "syndicate covering transactions"[78] and "penalty bids."[79] These obligations are discussed below under "Disclosure, SRO Notification and Recordkeeping."

• *Covered Securities*

Rule 10b-6 applied to (a) the security being distributed, (b) any "right to purchase" that security and (c) any security that was of the "same class and series" as the distributed security.

Rule 101 eliminates (b) and (c). It applies only to the security being distributed and to any "reference security," which is defined as a security into which the security that is the subject of the distribution may be converted, exchanged or exercised or which, under the terms of the distribution security, may in whole or significant part determine the value of the security being distributed.

Derivative securities (i.e., those that derive all or part of their value from a security being distributed) are therefore not subject to the prohibitions of Rule 101. Thus, bids for or purchases of options, warrants, rights, convertible securities or equity-linked securities are not restricted during a distribution of the related common stock because, according to the Regula-

---

78. Rule 100 defines a syndicate covering transaction as the placing of any bid or the effecting of any purchase to reduce a syndicate short position.

79. Rule 100 defines a penalty bid as an arrangement that permits a managing underwriter to reclaim a selling concession from a syndicate member when the securities originally sold by the member are purchased in syndicate covering transactions. See the discussion in Chapter 2.

tion M Release, "while they derive their value from the security being distributed, they do not by their terms affect the value of the security in distribution." The SEC specifically rejected an NASD suggestion that it limit the exclusion to derivative securities "not likely to present manipulative risk, such as 'out-of-the-money' options."

Consistent with its new approach to derivative securities, the SEC as part of its adoption of Regulation M rescinded old Rule 10b-8, which had regulated distribution participants' bids for rights in connection with a rights offering.

On the other hand, Rule 101 does apply to the underlying security in the case of a distribution of a derivative security the return on which is a function of the value of the underlying security. This could include an issuer's common stock underlying the same issuer's convertible debt offering or the common stock underlying a different issuer's cash-settled equity-linked security offering. In many cases, of course, the underlying security will be eligible for the $1,000,000 ADTV/$150 million float exception.

The new rules mean the end of having to make judgments about whether an outstanding debt security is of the same "class and series" as a new debt security. According to the Regulation M Release, an issuer's outstanding securities would be restricted only where they are "identical in all of [their] terms" to the securities being distributed. This means, according to the release, that identity is destroyed by "a single basis point" difference in coupon rates or "a single day's difference" in maturity dates. This change has particular importance to transactions in which an underwriter and a customer "swap" newly-distributed securities for outstanding securities of the same issuer.[80] While this is good news for underwriters, they need to keep in mind the NASD's "Papilsky" requirements (discussed in Chapter 6) that are applicable to "securities taken in trade" in connection with a fixed price public offering.

The new rules also mean the end of SEC interpretations that had treated standardized call options as "rights to purchase"

---

80. On the other hand, the Release states that voting and non-voting equity securities will be treated as the *same* security for Rule 101 purposes.

the underlying security and standardized put options as continuing "bids" for the underlying security.[81]

• *Excluded Securities*

Three types of securities are excluded entirely from Rule 101. The first is "exempted securities" under the 1934 Act (e.g., municipal bonds). The second is nonconvertible debt or preferred securities rated investment-grade by at least one nationally recognized statistical rating organization.

The status of asset-backed securities under the comparable "investment-grade" exception of Rule 10b-6 was sometimes thought to be doubtful since such securities as a technical matter often represent equity interests in a pool of collateral. Rule 101 now expressly excludes asset-backed securities on the same basis as other investment-grade nonconvertible securities; it defines "asset-backed securities" for this purpose as that term is defined for purposes of Form S-3.

Shortly after Rule 10b-6 was amended in 1983 to exclude investment-grade debt and preferred securities, the staff took the position that the exclusion did not apply to preferred stock that was offered by means of an auction process. The staff position has been much criticized as inconsistent with the plain meaning of the exclusion, and it is not referred to in the Regulation M Release. It is hard to see how the staff position can be regarded under the circumstances as anything other than a dead letter.

The third type of security that is excluded from Rule 101 is any security that has an "average daily trading volume" ("ADTV") of at least $1,000,000 *and* whose issuer—unaffiliated with the underwriter—has common equity securities with a public float value of at least $150 million. ADTV means "the worldwide average daily trading volume during the two full calendar months immediately preceding, *or* any 60 consecutive calendar days ending within the 10 calendar days preceding, the *filing* of the registration statement" (emphasis added). (In the case of shelf offerings or unregistered distributions, the relevant periods are measured from the time of determination of the offering price.) According to the Regulation M Release, the SEC decided against designating "ac-

---

81. SEC Release No. 34-17609 (March 6, 1981).

ceptable information sources" for determining ADTV; rather, distribution participants will have flexibility in determining ADTV from information that is publicly available (if the participant "has a reasonable basis for believing that the information is reliable"). Also, "any reasonable and verifiable method" may be used to calculate ADTV (e.g., by multiplying the number of shares by the price in each trade, or by multiplying each day's total volume of shares by the closing price on that day).[82] Public float is determined in the same manner as provided in Form 10-K (even if the issuer is not required to file Form 10-K).[83]

The SEC stated in the release that the $1,000,000 ADTV/ $150 million float exception "removes from Rule 101 the equity securities of approximately 1,900 domestic issuers, as well as those of a substantial number of foreign issuers."[84]

It should be noted that ADTV is calculated on a worldwide basis. In the case of a publicly-held foreign issuer that is making its first distribution of securities into the U.S. market, the trading volume in the home country may be taken into account for purposes of the ADTV test.

As noted above, the SEC did not adopt in Regulation M the suggestions of commenters that Rule 101 and its companion rules provide for a "safe harbor," i.e., that they define conduct

---

82. In its Notice to Members 97-10 (March 1997), the NASD announced an expansion of the Underwriting Activity Report issued by the NASD's Corporate Financing Department to the managing underwriter. The expanded report would include ADTV and public float value for each subject and reference security that is publicly traded before the offering and would also indicate whether the security qualifies under Rule 101 as an actively-traded security or for the one-day or five-day restricted periods.

83. Form 10-K requires an issuer to disclose the aggregate market value of voting stock held by non-affiliates. If a determination as to whether a particular person or entity is an affiliate cannot be made without involving unreasonable effort and expense, an instructional note to Form 10-K permits information to be disclosed on the basis of "assumptions reasonable under the circumstances."

84. According to the Regulation M Release, this would include (on the basis of 1995 transaction information) approximately 1100 securities listed on the NYSE, 36 securities listed on the American Stock Exchange and 770 securities quoted on NASDAQ.

that would not only be deemed to be in compliance with the rules but also in compliance with the antifraud and antimanipulation prohibitions of Sections 9(a) and 15(c)(1) of the 1934 Act and Rule 10b-5. Nothing in the comments changed the SEC's view expressed in the proposing release that "[a] safe harbor from manipulation charges is inappropriate in contexts where it is reasonable to infer that manipulative incentives are present, such as during securities distributions." See the discussion below of "Manipulation Outside the Trading Practice Rules."

• *Excepted Activities*

Rule 101 excepts ten specified activities from its prohibitions. These are designed to facilitate an orderly distribution of securities or to limit disruptions of the trading market for the securities being distributed.

• • *Research.* Exception 1 to Rule 101 permits the publication or dissemination of any information, opinion or recommendation relating to a covered security if the conditions of either Rule 138 or Rule 139 under the 1933 Act are satisfied. A proposed requirement that the material be published or distributed "in the ordinary course of business" was deleted as redundant. The Regulation M Release also clarifies that if a distribution participant in the normal course of its business provides research to independent research services that make such reports available to their subscribers electronically, whether or not the subscribers are customers of or have previously received research from the distribution participant, such research is still excepted from Rule 101. (This clarification presumably applies also to hard-copy research that is distributed by third parties.) "Similarly, a distribution participant may update its mailing list (i.e., new persons may be added) where it is intended that they receive all future research sent to others on the list, and not just the research related to the security in distribution."

Rules 138 and 139 apply by their terms to the dissemination of research during registered offerings. The release states, however, that the exception from Rule 101 will be available during distributions that are not registered under the 1933 Act so long as all of the other conditions of either rule are met. The release also states that Rules 138 and 139 "define the appropriate parameters" even for research disseminated outside the United States during a global offering, whether or not in conformity with local rule or custom, if securities are to be distributed in the United States. The implications of this position for global equity offerings remain to be seen.

• • *Passive Market-Making and Stabilization Transactions.* Passive market-making transactions in compliance with Rule 103 and stabilization transactions in compliance with Rule 104 are excepted (exception 2) from the prohibitions of Rule 101, as they were from the prohibitions of Rule 10b-6. Passive market-making and stabilization are discussed below.

• • *Odd-Lot Transactions.* Exception 3 to Rule 101 permits a distribution participant to purchase odd-lots during a restricted period. Among other things, this exception permits a distribution participant to engage in activities in connection with issuer odd-lot tender offers conducted pursuant to Rule 13e-4(h)(5) under the 1934 Act, including effecting purchases necessary to permit odd-lot holders to "round up" their holdings to 100 shares.

• • *Exercises of Securities.* Exception 4 to Rule 101 permits distribution participants to exercise any option, warrant, right or any conversion privilege set forth in the instrument governing a security. Unlike the corresponding exception in Rule 10b-6, this exception does not distinguish call options acquired prior to becoming a distribution participant from those acquired afterwards. In addition, the exception covers the exercise of nonstandardized call options. The broadened exception is based on the SEC's belief that exercises or conversions of derivative securities generally have an uncertain and attenuated manipulative potential and, for that reason, do not need to be subject to the prohibitions of Regulation M.

• • *Unsolicited Transactions.*

• • • *Unsolicited Brokerage Transactions.* The first part of exception 5 to Rule 101 permits brokerage transactions not involving solicitation of the customer's order. In the case of a customer's unsolicited buy order, it could be argued that this exception is not necessary because such a transaction would not involve a bid or purchase by the broker for an account in which it has a beneficial interest. It would also not constitute an inducement to purchase.

The exception makes it clear, however, that although it is participating in a distribution, a broker may continue to execute on an agency basis unsolicited buy orders received from customers. It may also execute unsolicited sell orders for a customer even though this requires the solicitation of buy orders on the other side of the transaction.

Suppose that a registered representative of an underwriter participating in an offering of common stock listed on the NYSE solicits a customer to purchase stock in the offering. After discussing with the customer the merits of the stock and the timing of the offering, the broker sends the customer a preliminary prospectus. Two days later—during the restricted period—the customer calls and says that he has read the document, that he likes the stock and wishes to buy 5,000 shares immediately. Without any suggestion from the broker, the customer places an order to buy 5,000 shares on the NYSE. Can the broker fill the order in reliance upon the unsolicited brokerage exception?

Under one school of thought, the exception should be available because the broker intended to solicit the customer to buy on the offering and not in the secondary market. This approach involves difficult compliance problems, however, and it is probably more common for underwriters to consider the exception as not being available where the customer has been solicited to participate in the offering.

Rule 10b-6 used to permit *solicited* brokerage transactions that were executed prior to the start of the applicable cooling-off period. Rule 101 does not contain such an exception for the simple reason that its prohibitions (unlike those of Rule 10b-6) do not commence until the start of the applicable restricted period. What is not prohibited does not require an exception.

• • • *Unsolicited Purchases.* The second part of exception 5 permits "unsolicited purchases" of a security that are not effected from or through a broker or dealer, on a securities exchange, or through an inter-dealer quotation system or electronic communications network (ECN). Rule 101 deletes the conditions in the corresponding exception in Rule 10b-6 that required the purchase to be in "block" size and to be "privately negotiated."

This part of exception 5, when used in conjunction with exception 9, can be extremely useful to a syndicate manager. Assume that a substantial block of common stock is shown to a managing underwriter during a restricted period and just before the pricing of a common stock offering. The existence of this block overhanging the market could have a depressing effect on the price of the stock. The manager can purchase the block as principal at a negotiated price relying on exception 5 and resell it as part of the distribution, or otherwise, relying on exception 9.

The exception is also useful during the period following a less-than-successful offering, particularly of high-yield securities, where the syndicate manager is maintaining trading restrictions and trying to sell the rest of the offering. Customers who have already bought the securities may be insisting on a bid or even that they be taken out of their position. Exception 5 permits the syndicate manager to purchase the customer's securities in this situation, while exception 9 permits the manager to seek buyers for the securities (and the unsold remainder of the offering) in as aggressive a fashion as the manager chooses. This is not quite the same as making a regular two-way market, but it relieves the pressure while the manager is trying to complete the distribution.

Questions can arise because of the restrictions in exception 5 on the manner in which purchases may be made. Purchases in reliance on the exception may not take place on an exchange (thus reinstating a condition that the SEC dropped in 1983). They may also not be effected from or through a broker or dealer, thus excluding such systems as Instinet. The condition that purchases not be effected "through an inter-dealer quotation system" is stated in the Regulation M Release to apply only to NASDAQ.

Purchases in reliance on exception 5 may also not be effected "through" an ECN. It therefore becomes important to determine whether a particular trading system constitutes an ECN for purposes of exception 5. Rule 100 defines an ECN by means of a cross-reference to Rule 11Ac1-1(a)(8). As there defined, an ECN is "any electronic system that widely disseminates to third parties orders entered therein by an exchange market maker or OTC market maker, *and* [that] permits such orders to be executed against in whole or in part" (emphasis added). The definition excludes systems that permit the "crossing" of orders at specified times as well as systems operated by broker-dealers for the purpose of facilitating their own executions as principal.

An ECN must therefore offer execution capability, but exception 5 would appear to require only that the purchase not be effected "through" the ECN. Also, one of the ingredients of the definition of "OTC market maker" for purposes of the definition of an ECN is that a dealer must hold itself out as being willing to buy and sell a security "in amounts of less than block size." It would therefore appear that a transaction in fixed-income securities could be effected in reliance on exception 5 through an inter-dealer broker since such brokers typically receive and disseminate quotes only in block size.

The Regulation M Release also states (in note 69) that "[a] purchase in response to an order or quote displayed on an ECN would not constitute an unsolicited transaction." The meaning of this statement is unclear. If an institution displays an order or quote without being solicited to do so, the unsolicited nature of the order or quote is not changed by the fact that it is displayed through an ECN. If the statement means that the exception is not available where an order or quote displayed on an ECN results in a purchase executed away from the ECN, it would appear to be inconsistent with the rule.

• • *Basket Transactions.* Distribution participants often wish to purchase a large number of stocks at the same time, usually where the stocks are part of either a standardized or customized index (a "basket transaction"). For example, an underwriter may have sold a futures contract on a standardized index and wish to purchase the stocks in the index in order to lock in an arbitrage profit. If the index includes a covered security, i.e., a stock involved in a distribution, then purchases of the stock during a restricted period would violate Rule 101 unless an exception were available.

Exception 6 to Rule 101 permits bids for or purchases of a covered security in the ordinary course of business, in connection with the purchase of a basket of securities consisting of at least 20 stocks, where the covered security constitutes 5% or less of the value of the basket. The basket may be index-related or "customized," but the Regulation M Release cautions that the requirement that the purchase be "in the ordinary course of business" means that the decision to include the covered security in the basket must be "independent of the existence of the distribution" of the covered security.

Bids and purchases are also permitted in order to adjust a basket position to reflect changes in the composition of *any* standardized index; in the case of a customized basket, however, similar adjustments would be permitted only if the basket met the 20 security/5% test.

• • *De Minimis Transactions.* Exception 7 to Rule 101 permits purchases during a restricted period that total less than 2% of the ADTV of the security being purchased. It also permits unaccepted bids. In either case, however, the person making the purchase or bid must be maintaining and enforcing written policies and procedures reasonably designed to achieve compliance with the rule. The Release explains the requirement of policies and procedures as arising out of the SEC's intention that the exception cover only "inadvertent" violations. The Release states that "[o]nce inadvertent transaction(s) are discovered, subsequent transaction(s) would not be covered by this exception." Moreover, "repeated reliance on the exception would raise questions about the adequacy and effectiveness of a firm's procedures." The Release states that "upon the occurrence of *any* violation, a broker-dealer is expected to review its policies and procedures and modify them as appropriate" (emphasis added). Also, *any* purchase—even if the trade is "broken"—must be considered a purchase (and a violation) for purposes of the exemption.

The *de minimis* exception is not available in the case of NASDAQ passive market making transactions.

• • *Transactions in Connection with a Distribution.* Exception 8 to Rule 101 excepts transactions among distribution participants in connection with a distribution and purchases of securities from an issuer or selling securityholder in connection with a distribution that are not effected on a securities exchange or through an inter-dealer quotation system or ECN.

Without this exception, the underwriters technically would be prohibited from purchasing the securities from the issuer or selling securityholders pursuant to the underwriting agreement prior to the completion of the distribution and dealers would be prohibited from purchasing from the underwriters. This exception also permits the syndicate manager to allocate and reallocate securities among underwriters and dealers.

One of the few *more* restrictive results under Regulation M is the condition in this exception that bars transactions from taking place through an inter-dealer quotation system or ECN. The April 1996 proposing release explained that this exception had been included in Rule 10b-6 to permit transactions that are not publicly reported and that many over-the-counter transactions are today as transparent as transactions on an exchange.

• • *Transactions in the Securities Being Distributed or Securities Offered As Principal.* The first part of exception 9 to Rule 101 permits "offers to sell or the solicitation of offers to buy the securities being distributed (including securities or rights acquired in stabilizing). . . ." Without this exception, the inducement of customers to purchase the securities being distributed would violate the rule, an absurd result that the exception remedies. Because of this exception, the restrictions apply to open market purchases and not to the very act of distribution.

The second part of exception 9 permits offers to sell or the solicitation of offers to buy "securities or rights offered as principal by the person making such offer to sell or solicitation." Thus, if a prospective underwriter has a long position in a security when the Rule 101 restrictions become applicable, it may close out its long position, even though this may involve the solicitation of buy orders. Also, as discussed above, an underwriter can rely on exception 9 to offer and sell securities that it has purchased during a restricted period in reliance on the second part of exception 5.

It is sometimes overlooked that exception 9 permits short sales. To be sure, a distribution participant might be prevented from covering the short sale by a purchase during a restricted period. The fact that a transaction is permitted under exception 9 does not, of course, mean that it is immune from attack by the SEC under general antimanipulation or antifraud principles. See the discussion below of "Manipulation Outside the Trading Practice Rules."

• • *Transactions in Rule 144A Securities.* Exception 10 permits transactions in Rule 144A-eligible securities offered and sold in the United States solely to "qualified institutional buyers" ("QIBs") in transactions exempt from 1933 Act registration pursuant to Rule 144A, Section 4(2) or Regulation D or to persons not deemed to be "U.S. persons" for purposes of Regulation S. The SEC did not accept comments urging it to expand the exception to transactions that involve offerings to institutional accredited investors as well as QIBs.

Unlike the corresponding exception in Rule 10b-6, exception 10 of Rule 101 applies to Rule 144A-eligible securities of U.S. issuers as well as non-U.S. issuers.

Passive Market-Making

Rule 103 replaces Rule 10b-6A and permits "passive market-making" during a distribution of a NASDAQ security. The former "eligibility criteria" of Rule 10-6A have been eliminated in the new rule, so that the exemption now permits passive market-making in *all* NASDAQ securities throughout the applicable restricted period and extends to all distributions (except best efforts or at-the-market offerings or at any time when a stabilizing bid is in effect).

Like its predecessor, Rule 103 generally limits a passive market marker's bids and purchases to the highest current independent bid (i.e., a bid of a NASDAQ market maker who is not participating in the distribution). It also limits the amount of net purchases that a passive market maker can make on any day to the greater of (a) 30% of the market maker's ADTV in that security during a "reference period" of two full calendar months or (b) 200 shares, except that a market maker may purchase all of the securities that are part of a single order even if this would equal or exceed its purchase limitation.

The Regulation M Release preserves certain earlier interpretations relating to contemporaneous transactions,[85] including one to the effect that if a passive market maker is involved in a contemporaneous purchase and sale of a security, the market maker can "net" the transactions for purposes of the ADTV calculation so long as the two transactions are reported within 30 seconds of each other. Another such interpretation permits offsetting two customer orders received within 15 minutes of each other without affecting net purchasing capacity.

Rule 103 limits the bid size a passive market maker may display and contains requirements relating to notification, identification and disclosure of passive market-making.

Rule 103 allows passive market makers to make bids or purchases at a price higher than the highest independent bid where necessary to comply with any SEC or NASD rule relating to the execution of customer orders. It is important to note that the SEC did *not* adopt an exception comparable to the *de minimis* exception in Rule 101.

Stabilization and Related Activities

As discussed above, the SEC adopted Rule 10b-7 in 1955 to implement Section 9(a)(6) of the 1934 Act. The rule for many years had two independent functions. First, stabilizing transactions effected in compliance with Rule 10b-7 were exempted from Rule 10b-6. Second, the rule declared it to be a "manipulative or deceptive device or contrivance" as used in Section 10(b) of the 1934 Act to effect any transaction in violation of Rule 10b-7.

As noted above, Rule 101 continues to exclude transactions effected in compliance with Rule 104. It also continues to be self-operative, except that it now provides that any transaction in violation of the rule is "unlawful." This is consistent with

---

85. Regulation M Release (text at note 115).

the SEC's view that the Trading Practice Rules are based on a broader SEC authority than that available to it under Section 10(b).

Unlike Rules 101 and 102, the conduct governed by Rule 104 relates to "offerings" of securities. This is a term that, according to the Regulation M Release, has broader application than "distributions."

Stabilization is defined in Rule 100 as "the placing of any bid, or the effecting of any purchase, for the purpose of pegging, fixing or maintaining the price of a security."[86] Rule 104 applies to the stabilization of the price of a security "in connection with an offering," not as in the case of Rule 10b-7 to stabilization "to facilitate an offering." The only subjective element relevant to the application of Rule 104 is therefore the intent to affect the price of a security, rather than to do so for the purpose of facilitating the offering. The significance of the change remains to be seen.

• *Mechanics*

As a practical matter, stabilization generally takes place only in connection with an offering of common stock. Although underwriters reserve the right to stabilize in connection with distributions of many debt securities or preferred stock, it would be highly unusual for the manager to stabilize in this type of transaction. It would also be unusual (although not unheard of) for an underwriter to stabilize outstanding common stock to facilitate an offering of convertible securities.

In practice, stabilizing transactions are effected exclusively by the managing underwriter. In the usual AAU, the manager reserves the right to stabilize on behalf of the syndicate.[87] Cen-

---

86. The reference to "maintaining" the price of a security is new and replaces Rule 10b-7's former somewhat circular definition that included a bid or purchase for the purpose of "stabilizing" a security.

87. Rule 104 eliminated a provision of Rule 10b-7 that in effect protected a syndicate manager from liability for a syndicate member's stabilizing violations if the manager had no knowledge of such violations. The elimination of the provision is probably harmless since it is hard to imagine how the manager could violate the rule under those circumstances.

tralized control of stabilizing is required by Rule 104, which prohibits a syndicate from maintaining more than one stabilizing bid in any one market at the same price at the same time.

The AAU limits the net commitments of the underwriters resulting from overallotments and stabilization to a fixed percentage, usually 15% or 20% of the amount of securities being offered. This limitation is for the purpose of limiting the underwriters' risk and is not required by SEC rules. The issuer or a selling securityholder normally does not effect stabilization transactions in connection with an underwritten offering.

A managing underwriter may have its representative on the exchange floor hold a stabilizing bid in reserve to be placed when certain market conditions occur. A managing underwriter who is not an exchange member could have the stabilization bid held in reserve for its account by an exchange member. On an exchange, a stabilizing bid is placed with the specialist. In the over-the-counter market, stabilization bids are placed with dealers.

• *General Requirements*

Rule 104 contains a number of general requirements applicable to all stabilization transactions. No stabilizing bid or purchase may be made except for the purpose of preventing or retarding a decline in the market price of a security. In addition, stabilization may not be effected at a price which the stabilizer knows or has reason to know is the result of activity that is fraudulent, manipulative or deceptive under the securities laws "or any rule or regulation." The effect of this provision is that if the market for a security has been manipulated at any time during the course of stabilization, it is improper for the underwriters (if they know or have reason to know of such activity) to initiate or continue stabilization transactions even if they had nothing to do with the manipulation.[88] Of course, if an underwriter has reason to believe that the market has been manipulated for a security that it plans to distribute, it has more serious problems than whether it may enter a stabilizing bid. There is no way that such an offering can go forward.

---

88. Rule 10b-7 literally applied this prohibition only to the "initiation" of stabilizing activity, not to its continuation.

When a stabilization bid is placed, it must be disclosed as such. In other words, the specialist or the over-the-counter dealers with whom the bid is placed must be told that the bid is a stabilizing bid. In addition, Rule 104 now requires that notice be given to the market on which stabilizing will be effected.[89]

Priority must be given to non-stabilizing bids "to the extent permitted or required by the market where stabilizing occurs." The stabilizer is a reluctant buyer, and independent bids at the same price must be filled before the stabilizer's bid. The size of the independent bid is irrelevant.

A person may not effect any stabilizing transaction to facilitate an offering "at the market," i.e., an offering at other than a fixed price.[90] For example, there may be no stabilization in connection with the type of shelf registration where securities are offered from time to time at prices current at the time of sale.

• *Excepted Securities*

It is important to note that there is no exception in Rule 104 comparable to Rule 101's exceptions for actively-traded or investment-grade securities. This means that stabilization of actively-traded or investment-grade securities must comply with Rule 104. The rule does not, however, apply to exempted securities (e.g., municipal bonds). Like Rule 101, it also does not apply to transactions in Rule 144A-eligible securities of a foreign or domestic issuer, where the distribution is made only to QIBs or to persons deemed not to be U.S. persons for Regulation S purposes.

• *Prices at Which Stabilization May Take Place*

Rule 104 regulates the prices at which stabilizing bids may be initiated and continued. In general, the rule permits a stabilizing bid to be initiated in any market based on independent

---

89. NASD Rule 4614, as amended in NASD Notice to Members 97-10 (March 1997), requires market makers who intend to initiate stabilization to request permission to do so. Stabilizing bids are then identified by a symbol on the NASDAQ quotation display.

90. Rule 10b-7 defined an at-the-market offering as one in which it was contemplated that any offering price set in any calendar day would be increased more than once during such day.

prices in the "principal market" for the security (whether the principal market is located in the United States or abroad). Such a bid may then be maintained, reduced or raised to follow the independent market, so long as the bid does not exceed *either* the offering price of the security or the stabilizing bid in the principal market. The "principal market" is defined as the "single securities market with the largest aggregate reported trading volume for the class of securities during the 12 full calendar months immediately preceding the filing of the registration statement. . . ."[91]

According to the Regulation M Release, "Rule 104 incorporates a knowledge-based standard to avoid imposition of an undue burden on underwriters to discover the prices of obscure transactions, whether reported or not."[92]

• • *Initiating Stabilization When There Is No Market for the Security.* If there is no market for the security being distributed (as would be the case in an IPO), stabilizing may be initiated at a price not in excess of the offering price.

> *Example:* Offering price is 20. Stabilizing bid may be entered at 20 or less.

• • *Initiating Stabilization When the Principal Market Is Open.* Assume that the NYSE is the principal market for a security. The underwriters may initiate stabilization after the NYSE opening at a price no higher than the last independent transaction price for that security on the NYSE. This price level applies, however, only if the security traded on the NYSE on the day stabilizing was initiated (or on the preceding business day) (i.e., the last sale price must not be "stale") *and* the current asked price on the NYSE is equal to or greater than the last independent transaction price (i.e., the last sale price must not be "obsolete").

---

91. If there is no registration statement or if the securities are registered on a shelf basis, the relevant period is 12 full calendar months immediately preceding the determination of the offering price.

92. Regulation M Release at note 122.

Example: Offering price is 20. Security has not yet opened on NYSE. Previous day's close was 20, and current asked price is 20-1/4. Stabilizing bid may be entered on NYSE at 20 (i.e., not higher than the offering price).

Example: Same as above, except that offering price is 20-1/4. Stabilizing bid may not exceed 20 (i.e., last independent transaction price). This is a good reason not to price offerings at a price higher than the last sale.

It would be unusual for the last sale price on the NYSE to ever be "stale"; however, that price could become "obsolete" if the market moves down. In that case, stabilizing may be initiated after the NYSE opening at a price no higher the highest current independent bid for the security.

Example: Offering price is 20. Security has not yet opened on NYSE. Previous day's close was 20, but current independent asked price is now 19-3/4 (which makes the last sale "obsolete"). If current independent bid price is 19-1/2, stabilizing bid may be entered on NYSE at no more than 19-1/2. (This would be an unusual situation, since the underwriters should have entered a stabilizing bid at 20 *before* the market moved down.)

Assume now that another market is the principal market for the security and that that market is open at the time the underwriters wish to initiate stabilization. The rule permits stabilization on the NYSE at a price no higher than the last independent transaction price for that security on the principal market (assuming that the price is neither "stale" nor "obsolete"). If the last independent transaction price is either stale or obsolete, stabilization may be initiated on the NYSE at a price no higher than the highest current independent bid in the principal market.

Example: Offering price is 20. Principal market is Frankfurt Stock Exchange, where security recently traded at equivalent of 20. Current asked price in Frankfurt is above 20. Stabilizing bid may be entered on NYSE at 20.

Example: Same as above, except that current bid in Frankfurt is 19-7/8. Stabilizing bid in New York may not exceed 19-7/8.

• • *Initiating Stabilization When the Principal Market Is Closed.* Assume that the NYSE is the principal market for a security and that the offering price is established just after the close of trading. Stabilizing may be initiated in the over-the-counter market at a price no higher than the *lower* of:

– the price at which stabilizing could have been initiated at the close of trading on the NYSE (see above), or

– the last independent transaction price for the security in the over-the-counter market before stabilizing began, but only if the security has traded on that day or the previous day (the price must not be "stale") and if the current asked price in the over-the-counter market is not less than the last independent transaction price (the price must not be "obsolete"). If either condition is not met, stabilizing may be initiated at a price no higher than the highest current independent bid for the security in the over-the-counter market.

Example: Closing price on NYSE is 20, and offering price is 20. Stabilizing may be initiated in over-the-counter market at 20 (assuming that asked price at close was not less than 20 and that managing underwriter does not know of any intervening transactions at a lower price).

If the underwriters wait until the next day to stabilize, they may enter a bid on the NYSE just before the opening of trading at a price no higher than the *lower* of

– the price at which stabilizing could have been initiated at the close of trading on the NYSE, or

– the most recent price at which an independent transaction in the security has been effected in any market since the close of trading on the NYSE (assuming that the person stabilizing knows or has reason to know of such transaction).

Example: Offering price is 20. Stabilizing could have been initiated at previous day's NYSE close at 20, and managing underwriter has no reason to know of any intervening independent transaction in the security at a lower price. Stabilizing bid may be entered at 20.

Example: Same as previous example, but underwriter knows of an intervening transaction at 19-7/8. Stabilizing bid may be entered at no more than 19-7/8.

Assume that the Frankfurt Stock Exchange is the principal market for the security and that stabilizing is initiated on the NYSE after the close in Frankfurt. Under these circumstances, stabilization may be initiated at or after the NYSE opening at a price no higher than the *lower* of:

– the price at which stabilizing could have been initiated in Frankfurt at its previous close, or

– the last independent transaction price for the security on the NYSE if the security has traded in that market on the day stabilizing is initiated (or on the last preceding business day) *and* the current asked price in that market is equal to or greater than the last independent transaction price. If either condition is not satisfied, then stabilizing may be initiated at a price no higher than the highest current independent bid on the NYSE.

Example: German stock is priced at 20 after close of Frankfurt Stock Exchange. Last trade in Frankfurt was at 20, and stabilization could have been initiated at this price. Underwriters are aware, however, that last trade in German over-the-counter market was at 19-7/8. Stabilizing bid may be entered on NYSE before the opening at the equivalent of 19-7/8. (Of course, the underwriters could have prevented the trade at 19-7/8 by entering a stabilizing bid in the German over-the-counter market at the equivalent of $20.)

• • *Initiating Stabilization Before the Offering Price Is Determined.* Stabilizing may be initiated on rare occasions before the offering price is determined. In these cases, stabilization may be continued after the determination of the offering price at the price at which stabilizing then could be initiated.

Example: Underwriters stabilize stock at 20 on the NYSE prior to pricing of offering. Stock then trades up and closes on NYSE at 20-1/4. Offering is priced at 20-1/4. Stabilization may be resumed in over-the-counter market at 20-1/4, assuming that current asked price is not less than 20-1/4.

• • *Maintaining or Carrying Over a Stabilizing Bid.* A stabilizing bid initiated at a permissible price level and that has not been discontinued may be maintained, or carried over into another market, without regard to changes in the independent bids or transaction prices for that security. The Regulation M Release states that the end of a trading session will not be deemed to discontinue a stabilizing bid in effect at the close. Rather, a stabilizing bid in effect at the market's close may be maintained between trading sessions and used to establish a stabilizing bid just prior to the market's opening on the next trading day.

Example: German stock is priced at 20 after close of Frankfurt Stock Exchange. Last trade in Frankfurt was at 20, and stabilization could have been initiated at this price. Stabilizing bid may be entered on NYSE before the opening at the equivalent of 20. Bid may be carried over on the next day onto Frankfurt Stock Exchange and maintained at 20 notwithstanding any decline in the price of the stock.

• • *Increasing or Reducing a Stabilizing Bid.* In what the SEC believes to be perhaps the most significant change from

Rule 10b-7, the new rule permits a stabilizing bid to be increased to a price no higher than the highest current independent bid for the security in the principal market if the principal market is open. If the principal market is closed, then the bid may be increased to a price no higher than the highest independent bid in the principal market at its previous close.

It is still the case, however, that the stabilization bid may never exceed the offering price.

A stabilizing bid may be reduced, or carried over into another market at a reduced price, without regard to changes in the independent bids or transaction prices for the security.

If stabilizing is discontinued, it may not be resumed at a price higher than the price at which stabilizing could then be initiated.

• • *Effects of Exchange Rates.* If a stabilizing bid is expressed in a currency other than the currency of the principal market for the security, it may be initiated, maintained or adjusted to reflect the current exchange rate. If it is necessary for this purpose to round up or down to a trading differential (e.g., one-eighth), the bid must be rounded down.

• • *Adjustments to Stabilizing Bid.* If a security goes ex-dividend, ex-rights or ex-distribution, the stabilizing bid must be reduced by an amount equal to the value of the dividend, right or distribution. If it is necessary for this purpose to round up or down to a trading differential (e.g., one-eighth), the bid must be rounded down.

• *Stabilization Outside the United States*

To accommodate cross-border transactions, Rule 104 does not apply to stabilization outside the United States during an offering in the United States if there is no stabilization in the United States, the foreign stabilization is not conducted above the U.S. offering price, and the foreign stabilization is conducted in a jurisdiction with comparable regulation of stabilization activities. The Regulation M Release states that the SEC recognizes as comparable the stabilization regulations of the U.K. Securities and Investments Board and invites appropriate requests to recognize other markets as having comparable regulations for purposes of this provision.

• *Prospectus Disclosure, SRO Notification and Recordkeeping*

As noted above, Rule 104 requires disclosure of the purpose of a stabilizing bid to the person with whom that bid is entered. As discussed in the next section, persons who engage in stabilization, syndicate covering transactions or the imposition of penalty bids are also subject to prospectus disclosure requirements, SRO notification requirements and recordkeeping obligations.

Disclosure, SRO Notification and Recordkeeping

As amended with the adoption of Regulation M, Item 502(d)(1)(i) of Regulation S-K now calls for a statement on the inside front cover of the prospectus—to the extent applicable—that persons participating in the offering may engage in transactions that stabilize, maintain or "otherwise affect" the price of the offered securities. The statement must also identify the types of such transactions that may be engaged in and direct the reader to a discussion in the "Plan of Distribution" section of the prospectus or other offering document.

In turn, Item 508(l) of Regulation S-K ("Plan of Distribution"), as amended as part of the adoption of Regulation M, now requires a statement of intent to engage in (and a brief description of) stabilizing transactions, syndicate short covering transactions, penalty bids "or any other transaction in connection with the offering that may stabilize, maintain, or otherwise affect the offered security's price." In the case of an unregistered offering where there is no offering circular (or in the case of a registered offering where the prospectus delivery period has expired), the statement should be made on the confirmation.[93]

---

93. The SEC considered in connection with the adoption of Regulation M a requirement of similar disclosure to purchasers of securities that are the subject of syndicate short covering activities or penalty bids. It decided against such disclosure for the time being but stated that it intended to re-

The following statement should constitute a satisfactory response to the new "Plan of Distribution" disclosure requirements regarding aftermarket activities in connection with a common stock offering. Revisions would be necessary for a NASDAQ issuer where the underwriters intend to take advantage of Rule 103 to engage in passive market-making. Also, the first sentence assumes that Rule 101's "$1,000,000 ADTV/ $150 million public float" exemption does not apply. And, of course, it would not be appropriate to refer to a penalty bid where none was contemplated by the AAU.

> Until the distribution of the Common Stock is completed, rules of the Securities and Exchange Commission may limit the ability of the Underwriters and certain selling group members to bid for and purchase the Common Stock. As an exception to these rules, the Representatives are permitted to engage in certain transactions that stabilize the price of the Common Stock. Such transactions consist of bids or purchases for the purpose of pegging, fixing or maintaining the price of the Common Stock.
>
> If the Underwriters create a short position in the Common Stock in connection with the offering, i.e., if they sell more shares of Common Stock than are set forth on the cover page of this Prospectus, the Representatives may reduce that short position by purchasing Common Stock in the open market. The Representatives may also elect to reduce any short position by exercising all or part of the overallotment option described above [i.e., the "Green Shoe" option].
>
> The Representatives may also impose a penalty bid on certain Underwriters and selling group members. This means that if the Representatives purchase shares of Common Stock in the open market to reduce the Underwriters' short position or to stabilize the price of the Common Stock, they may reclaim the amount of the selling conces-

---

consider the need for such disclosure as it reviewed developments relating to aftermarket activity.

sion from the Underwriters and selling group members who sold those shares as part of the offering.

In general, purchases of a security for the purpose of stabilization or to reduce a short position could cause the price of the security to be higher than it might be in the absence of such purchases. The imposition of a penalty bid might also have an effect on the price of a security to the extent that it were to discourage resales of the security.

Neither the Company nor any of the Underwriters makes any representation or prediction as to the direction or magnitude of any effect that the transactions described above might have on the price of the Common Stock. In addition, neither the Company nor any of the Underwriters makes any representation that the Representatives will engage in such transactions or that such transactions, once commenced, will not be discontinued without notice.

Item 502(d)(1)(ii) of Regulation S-K provides that if stabilization began prior to the effective date of the registration statement (or the determination of the public offering price in the event of a Rule 430A offering), the amount of securities bought, the price at which bought, and the periods within which they were bought must be disclosed in the prospectus. This information may be set forth immediately following the stabilization legend or, perhaps more appropriately, as a final paragraph under the heading "Price Range of Common Stock." If necessary, it may be set forth in a sticker.

There is no reason to make excuses for pre-effective or pre-pricing stabilizing purchases, as was done, to the amusement of Wall Street, in a supplement to a March 11, 1982 prospectus covering an offering of common stock by The Washington Water Power Company:

Because of fog problems in the Washington, D.C., area on March 11, 1982, the filing of the price amendment to, and the effectiveness of, the Registration Statement, were delayed. Kidder, Peabody & Co. Incorporated and

Dean Witter Reynolds Inc., as Representatives of the Underwriters, have advised the Company that on March 11, 1982, prior to the effectiveness of the Registration Statement, they made stabilizing purchases of 11,700 shares of the Company's Common Stock at 18-1/4.

Rule 104 requires prior notice to the relevant SRO by any person who displays or transmits a stabilizing bid or who purchases securities for the purpose of reducing a syndicate short position or with the purpose of reclaiming a selling concession otherwise payable to an underwriter or dealer. Both the NYSE (new Rule 392, approved in SEC Release No. 34-38478 (April 4, 1997)) and the NASD (Notice to Members 97-10 (March 1997) and SEC Release No. 34-38399 (March 14, 1997)) have prescribed procedures for this purpose. Rule 104 does not require that the notice to the SRO be a public notice, but the SEC stated in the Regulation M Release that it might revisit this issue if circumstances were to indicate that a public notice was warranted.

Rule 17a-2 under the 1934 Act has long required that the manager who effected the stabilization transactions maintain records of stabilizing activities. As amended with the adoption of Regulation M, it also applies to syndicate short covering transactions and the imposition of penalty bids. It applies to registered and Regulation A transactions and to other transactions where the aggregate offering price exceeds $5,000,000.

Trading Restrictions for Issuers and Selling Securityholders (Rule 102)

Rule 102 covers bids, purchases and related activity by issuers and selling securityholders during a distribution of securities by or on their respective behalf. The rule's prohibitions also apply to the "affiliated purchasers" of issuers and selling securityholders, but this term is significantly narrowed as in the case of affiliated purchasers of underwriters (discussed above). In addition, any affiliated purchaser that is a distribution participant may comply with Rule 101 rather than with

Rule 102 (unless the distribution participant is itself the issuer or the selling securityholder).[94]

Rule 102 is similar in format to Rule 101, but it contains fewer exceptions than Rule 101 because of the SEC's belief that issuers and selling securityholders "have the greatest interest in an offering's outcome and generally do not have the same market access needs as underwriters."

Exceptions to Rule 102 permit transactions in nonconvertible investment-grade securities, transactions during Rule 144A distributions, unsolicited purchases, and exercises of options and other securities (including rights). Closed-end investment companies that engage in continuous offerings of securities may conduct certain tender offers for those securities during such distributions.

Rule 102 applies during a restricted period of one or five business days, depending on the ADTV and public float of the security in distribution, as in the case of Rule 101. There is, however, no general exception under Rule 102 for securities meeting the $1 million ADTV/$150 million public float test; even these are subject to a restricted period of one business day. There is a limited exception for certain actively-traded reference securities, e.g., in the case of equity-linked notes.

Rule 102 divides stock-issuance plans[95] into three categories: (a) employee-shareholder plans, (b) plans not limited to employees and shareholders where securities are purchased in the open market or in privately negotiated transactions by an agent independent from the issuer ("open market plans") and (c) plans not so limited where securities are purchased from the

---

94. Directors, officers and controlling persons of an issuer may be "affiliates" of the issuer, but they are less likely to be "affiliated purchasers" under Regulation M's more narrow definition of the term. They are therefore usually free to purchase the underwritten securities. The Regulation M Release refers approvingly to a no-action letter in which the staff stated that "purchases [by directors of an issuer] in a distribution of the securities being distributed . . . are not the type of purchases prohibited by Rule 10b-6." SEC No-Action Letter *VLI Corp.* (available November 16, 1983), cited in Regulation M Release at note 20.

95. The new rule clarifies that plans offered by bank transfer agents and registered broker-dealers qualify for the plan exception.

issuer ("direct issuance plans"). An exception from Rule 102 is available for the first two categories.[96] Rule 102 applies fully, however, to direct issuance plans. Of course, it is still necessary that a plan involve a "distribution" in order for Rule 102 to apply. In this connection, the Release describes the factors that should be considered in determining the "magnitude" of a direct issuance plan and whether or not it involves special selling efforts or selling methods.

As noted in the Regulation M Release, Regulation M supersedes prior SEC releases and staff no-action letters insofar as these related to issuer stock plans and Rule 10b-6, but the prior advice remains in effect insofar as it addressed other securities law issues such as Section 5 under the 1933 Act.

In connection with the adoption of Rule 102, the SEC also amended Rule 10b-18. That rule provides a safe harbor for issuers or affiliated purchasers who repurchase the issuer's common stock. The amendment precludes reliance on the rule when the issuer or an affiliated purchaser is in a Rule 102 restricted period for a distribution of the issuer's common stock or any security for which the common stock is a reference security.

Dealing with Problems under the Trading Practice Rules

In the Rule 10b-6 era, the timing of a securities offering or even the membership of the underwriting syndicate could occasionally be threatened by the discovery of an inadvertent violation. Securities lawyers were called upon to deal with the crisis. These problems will be less frequent under Rule 101, given that rule's shorter restricted periods, the *de minimis* exception and the many securities to which the rule will have no application.

---

96. The Regulation M Release describes the limits of the issuer's permissible involvement in the agent's activities. Such involvement does not extend to specification of the broker-dealer who makes purchases for the plan or changing the source of the securities more often than once in any three-month period. The SEC plans to examine these issues in connection with a planned review of Rule 10b-18.

In one instance, late in the afternoon on the day before a registration statement covering a common stock offering was to become effective, it was discovered that a member of the underwriting syndicate that was the specialist for the common stock of the issuer had failed to give up its book to another firm (as would have been expected under the circumstances) and had continued to make purchases up to the time of the closing bell. These purchases violated Rule 10b-6. The managing underwriter had no alternative but to advise the firm that it would be dropped from the underwriting syndicate unless it could persuade the SEC that this would not be necessary in view of the inadvertent nature of the violation. The firm contacted the SEC's staff, and as the question rose higher through the SEC's hierarchy, the news came back that not only must the offending firm withdraw from the syndicate but, because there had been a violation that could have affected the price of the stock, the offering must be delayed.

This was a totally unanticipated response. Previously, it had been the accepted wisdom that a Rule 10b-6 violation such as this could be remedied by dropping from the syndicate the firm that was responsible for the violation. Before he could be contacted, the senior SEC official who had made the decision left on an evening flight to Chicago. His subordinates were in no position to overrule him. Finally, at 11:00 p.m., he was reached at his Chicago hotel and the matter was resolved through the expedient of disclosure. The registration statement was declared effective, but the final prospectus was required to carry a sticker setting forth the total number of shares purchased by the firm "through inadvertence" over a specified period of time. The firm was not named but was identified only as "a securities firm which had intended to act as an underwriter." The sticker concluded with the statement that, as a result, the firm had decided not to participate in the offering.

In another instance, disclosure provided the solution when a managing underwriter inadvertently entered a stabilizing bid in connection with a common stock offering at a level above that permitted by Rule 10b-7. Corrective measures were taken and the registration statement became effective. Each prospectus delivered to investors bore the following sticker:

The Company has been advised by [Name of Manager], as Representative of the several Underwriters, as follows:

[Name of Manager], as Representative of the several Underwriters, purchased in stabilizing transactions on the New York Stock Exchange, Inc. an aggregate of 771,000 shares of Common Stock on January 12, 1977, of which 621,300 were purchased at 16-3/4 and 149,700 at 16-5/8 and an aggregate of 7,700 shares of Common Stock on January 13, 1977, at a price of 16-5/8. On January 13, 1977, the high and low sales prices of these shares on the New York Stock Exchange, Inc. were 16-7/8 (high) and 16-5/8 (low) and the last sale on that Exchange was at 16-7/8. On January 14, 1977, the high and low sales prices of these shares on the New York Stock Exchange, Inc. were 16-7/8 (high) and 16-3/4 (low) and the last sale on that Exchange was at 16-7/8.

The initial stabilizing bid of 16-3/4 on January 12, 1977, was higher than the last independent sale price on that Exchange, which on January 11, 1977, was 16-1/2, and accordingly was higher than that permitted under the applicable rules of the Securities and Exchange Commission.

In some cases, a transaction by a co-manager or other member of the underwriting syndicate may be entirely permissible, but the firm will be required by the book-running manager to clear the transaction with the staff of the SEC. This will usually be the result of genuine concern on the part of the firm running the books. In one case, a co-manager's purchase of a large block of stock, as permitted by exception (ii) of Rule 10b-6, was questioned by the book-running manager. It insisted upon SEC approval if the co-manager was to continue as such. Fortunately, it agreed that oral clearance with a confirmatory letter to the SEC from the co-manager's counsel would be sufficient and that a no-action letter from the staff would not be necessary. The Division of Market Regulation had no problem with the purchase, and the confirmatory letter from counsel, which spelled out in great detail the transaction and its legal justification, was viewed as sufficient by the manager and underwriters' counsel. The time required to obtain a no-action letter could have effectively forced the co-manager out of the financing.

As these examples illustrate, the staff of the Division of Market Regulation has been helpful to underwriters and their counsel on many occasions in resolving problems under Rule 10b-6. Based on this experience, it would appear advisable to have two items of information available when calling the staff regarding possible violations of Regulation M. The first would consist of detailed factual information on the bids or purchases or other conduct that appears to have violated the rule, e.g., the number of shares traded, the trade price and the time of the trade, together with contemporaneous volume and price information for the security. This information enables the staff to form a view as to whether the violations may have affected the market for the security. The second category of information is simply an explanation of how the violation occurred and what steps are being taken to prevent a repetition.

Covering Short Sales with Registered Securities (Rule 105)

Syndicate managers face many problems in bringing a stock offering to market. For many years, one of the principal reasons for their sleepless nights was the practice engaged in by hedge funds and other institutions of entering indications of interest for shares to be distributed in an underwriting, selling short aggressively prior to the effective date of the registration statement in an effort to drive down the market price of the shares, and covering their short position with shares purchased in the underwriting. Persons selling short in anticipation of a public offering are not subject to the usual market risk accompanying the covering transaction, but are assured of covering with offered securities purchased in the public offering at a fixed, and generally lower, price.

In 1972, the SEC published a staff opinion that addressed short selling prior to a public offering.[97] The release observed that this short selling may be "disruptive of fair and orderly markets in [the] securities" and, where the short sales are intended to depress the market price of the security so that the

---

97. SEC Release No. 34-9824 (October 16, 1972).

short position can be covered at a lower price, the activity violates the antimanipulative provisions of the 1934 Act.

Then, in 1974, the SEC proposed for adoption Rule 10b-21,[98] and the following year reproposed the rule in revised form.[99] A third version of the rule was published for comment at the end of 1976.[100]

On the same date that the SEC first proposed Rule 10b-21, it commenced a proceeding against the brokerage firm of A.P. Montgomery & Co., Inc., charging that, for its own account or for the accounts of customers, it made short sales of securities prior to the effective dates of several registration statements which caused, or contributed to, a decline in the market price for the securities and affected the pricing of the offering. This was alleged by the SEC to be a manipulative practice. Montgomery subsequently consented to SEC sanctions.[101] A few years later, the SEC brought a similar proceeding against another broker-dealer.[102]

The underwriting community was delighted at the prospect that Rule 10b-21 would be adopted, but years passed and nothing happened. The sharks continued to circle the boat, darting in with their short sales at the most inopportune times. Syndicate managers continued to have sleepless nights. The problems of Wall Street were not high on the SEC's agenda in the post-Watergate era.

In 1987, the SEC once again proposed Rule 10b-21, this time in response to a petition for rulemaking filed by the NASD.[103] A number of commentators responded to the SEC's request for comment regarding the extent of pre-offering short selling and its impact on the costs to issuers of completing an offering. Most of these commentators described firsthand experiences with the adverse effects of short selling activity, which caused them to cancel proposed offerings or to complete offer-

---

98. SEC Release No. 34-10636 (February 11, 1974).

99. SEC Release No. 34-11328 (April 2, 1975).

100. SEC Release No. 34-13092 (December 21, 1976).

101. SEC Release No. 34-10909 (July 9, 1974).

102. *J.A.B. Securities Co., Inc.,* SEC Release No. 34-15948 (June 25, 1979).

103. SEC Release No. 34-24485 (May 20, 1987).

ings even though the issuer was deprived of proceeds that would have been realized had the market not been adversely affected by this activity.

The NASD submitted information relating to investigations of three separate public offerings, and stated that, based on these investigations and others involving similar circumstances, it believed that the practice of short selling before a public offering with the intention of covering with shares purchased in the public offering was not uncommon. The investigations revealed substantial short selling activity by certain firms after the filing of the registration statement and a decline in the price of the stock prior to the effective date. In each instance, the short sellers covered their positions at a profit immediately after the offering with shares purchased from entities that had obtained them in the public offering.

In August 1988, Rule 10b-21(T) finally was adopted, although on a temporary basis.[104] The rule was made permanent as of March 1994.[105]

The rule quite simply states that it shall be unlawful for any person who effects one or more short sales of equity securities of the same class as securities offered for cash pursuant to a registration statement filed under the 1933 Act to cover such short sale or sales with offered securities purchased from an underwriter or broker or dealer participating in the offering, if such short sale or sales took place during the period beginning at the time that the registration statement is filed and ending at the time that sales may be made pursuant to the registration statement. The SEC stated in the adopting release that covering purchases effected by prearrangement with other purchasers in the offering were proscribed through the operation of Section 20(b) of the 1934 Act, which prohibits a person from doing indirectly any act that he is prohibited from doing directly by the 1934 Act or any rule thereunder. Rule 10b-21 specifically did not apply to shelf offerings filed under Rule 415 or to offerings that are not made on a firm commitment basis.

---

104. SEC Release No. 34-26028 (August 25, 1988).
105. SEC Release No. 34-33702 (March 2, 1994).

Rule 10b-21 was replaced in late 1996 by Rule 105. The new rule applies only to short sales effected during the shorter of (a) the period commencing five business days prior to the pricing of the offering and ending with such pricing or (b) the period beginning with the initial filing of a registration statement (or Form 1-A) and ending with the pricing. The Regulation M Release stated that the SEC considered suggestions (particularly from the NASD) to preserve and even extend the prohibitions of Rule 10b-21. The SEC rejected these suggestions on the basis of its belief that the shorter period of applicability was more consistent with the structure of Rules 101 and 102.

Manipulation Outside the Trading Practice Rules

As discussed above, the SEC rejected suggestions that Regulation M should be regarded as establishing "safe harbors" against violations of the general antifraud and antimanipulation provisions of the 1934 Act. The preliminary note to Rule 100 makes this explicit. This means that a transaction that is not in violation of Regulation M may still be held to have violated the 1934 Act or, more generally, an SRO's rules regarding "just and equitable principles of trade."

For example, it has been noted that Rule 101—like Rule 10b-6 before it—does not prohibit an underwriter from engaging in short sales during the restricted period. Some traders had to learn this the hard way. In November 1990, for example, Shearson Lehman Brothers Inc. was the sole underwriter of a 4.4 million share offering of common stock of ConAgra Inc., a major food company.[106] By November 20, it had obtained indications of interest to purchase the entire block at prices up to $33.25. ConAgra's stock traded at that price during most of the afternoon, but 5900 shares traded during the last minute of trading on the NYSE at $33.375. Following the NYSE close, several prospective purchasers informed Shearson Lehman that they were not willing to buy at $33.375. Shearson Lehman suggested to ConAgra that the offer-

---

106. The facts regarding this matter are taken from NYSE, *Hearing Panel Decision 92-84* (May 21, 1992), NYSE, *Hearing Panel Decision 92-85* (May 22, 1992) and press reports.

ing price of the 4.4 million shares be lowered to $33.25, but Con-
Agra took the position that it did not want the offering to appear to
have been priced at a discount. A decision was postponed until the
close of trading on the Pacific Stock Exchange.

A senior trader for Shearson Lehman issued instructions to
a specialist and a floor broker on the Pacific Stock Exchange
(both employees of Shearson Lehman) that resulted in the short
sale by a "$2 broker" of 100 shares of ConAgra at $33.25.
This was the closing transaction in the stock on that day. Shearson Lehman and ConAgra then agreed to price the 4.4 million
share offering at $33.25.

Upon discovering the facts, Shearson Lehman conducted an
internal investigation and reported its results to the NYSE. It
also suspended certain of the employees involved in the Pacific
Stock Exchange transaction and paid $550,000 to ConAgra, this
being the additional amount that ConAgra would have received
if the offering had been priced at $33.375. Without referring to
the word "manipulation," an NYSE hearing panel found Shearson Lehman and its co-head equities trader to have violated
just and equitable principles of trade. It censured both the firm
and the trader, fined Shearson Lehman the sum of $500,000
and the trader $100,000, suspended the trader for four months
and accepted an undertaking from Shearson Lehman regarding
improvements in its internal procedures.

In a similar incident that occurred earlier but that required
more time to be resolved, an trader/salesman for Drexel Burnham Lambert Inc. and a trader for one of its hedge fund clients
ended up suffering more serious consequences than the Shearson Lehman trader. According to SEC proceedings,[107] Drexel
Burnham was to price an underwritten offering of $25 million
offering of convertible debentures of C.O.M.B. Co. on April
11, 1985. Michael Milken of Drexel Burnham was upset about
the strong performance of the C.O.M.B. common stock and

---

107. In the Matter of *Charles M. Zarzecki*, SEC Release No. 34-31764
(January 26, 1993), In the Matter of *Bruce L. Newberg* (Admin. Proc. File
No. 3-7651) (September 1, 1993). *See also* Steve Thel, *$850,000 in Six
Minutes—The Mechanics of Securities Manipulation*, 79 Cornell L. Rev. 219,
273-274 (1994).

may even have believed that it was being manipulated upwards. A higher price for the C.O.M.B. common stock would, of course, make it harder to sell the convertible securities. A trader/salesman for Drexel Burnham called one of his accounts, a trader at a hedge fund, and expressed his desire that the C.O.M.B. stock not be at "16 bid" but rather that it be "down to at least 15-3/4, and hopefully lower." He added that the hedge fund would be "indemnified." The hedge fund trader then sold short two blocks of C.O.M.B.

Unfortunately for the two individuals, their conversations were taped and eventually made public as part of the notorious "sleaze bag" tapes. The government used the tapes to support its *criminal* prosecution of the two individuals on a variety of charges, including securities fraud. Both individuals were convicted and eventually sentenced to three months imprisonment, two years probation on release and fines of $155,000. The convictions on securities fraud and certain other counts were upheld on appeal, while certain other convictions were vacated and remanded.[108] On remand, Judge Carter of the Southern District of New York expressed displeasure that other persons he regarded as "major actors" in the case were getting off "scott free." He accordingly vacated the two individuals' sentences, not least because of the relatively mild non-criminal punishment handed out in the Shearson Lehman case by the NYSE (and presumably acquiesced in by the SEC). Judge Carter's views did not stop the SEC, however, from obtaining permanent bars of the two individuals from the securities industry.

At the time of the ConAgra and C.O.M.B. offerings, of course, Rule 10b-6 would have prevented Shearson Lehman and Drexel Burnham, respectively, from purchasing shares of the two issuers in the open market or from inducing others to do so. As noted above, however, it would not have prohibited either prospective underwriter from engaging in short sales of the shares. These sales would have been expressly permitted by exception (vi) of Rule 10b-6 as "securities . . . offered as

---

108. *U.S. v. Regan*, 937 F.2d 823 (2d Cir.), *modified* 946 F.2d 188 (2d Cir. 1991), *cert. denied* 504 U.S. 940 (1992).

principal," an exception that is carried forward into exception 9 of Rule 101.

At the time of the two proceedings, however, the SEC's and the U.S. government's theory was that all investors are under a "general duty" not to manipulate. Moreover, manipulation could be found whenever an investor—who did not need to be a fiduciary or an insider of an issuer—engaged in securities transactions in the open market "with the sole intent to affect the price of the security" (i.e., without an "investment purpose").[109] In decisions rendered only two weeks apart, one panel of the Second Circuit expressed "doubt" and "misgivings" about the government's view of the law,[110] while another—the panel reviewing the convictions of the Drexel Burnham and hedge fund traders—accepted it without serious reservation.

The hedge fund trader asked the Supreme Court to review the Second Circuit's affirmance of his convictions. The U.S. government (with the SEC's participation) declined to submit its broad theory to the Court and argued instead that the trader's convictions should be affirmed because he had sold the C.O.M.B. stock on Drexel Burnham's behalf. Since an underwriter such as Drexel Burnham "has a duty to both 'the issuer and the investing public,' " the trader's conduct would be criminal even under a narrower theory than the government's.[111]

Under the government's modified theory, therefore, the underwriter has a duty to the issuer as well as to the "investing public." Under the circumstances of the ConAgra and C.O.M.B. offerings, however, it is hard to see how any duty to the "investing public" is violated by action that results in the public's paying less for a security. It is much easier, of course, to see how an underwriter might violate a duty to an issuer under these circumstances. Even here, however, much depends on the particular facts. ConAgra, for example, might have been

---

109. *U.S. v. Mulheren*, 938 F.2d 364, 368 (2d Cir. 1991).
110. *Id.*
111. Brief for the United States in Opposition, *Zarzecki v. U.S.*, No. 91-1223 (S.Ct.) at 12-13.

perfectly happy to have the offering priced at $33.25 so long as it did not appear that the stock was being sold at a discount. There is no suggestion in the record, of course, that ConAgra knew what Shearson Lehman's trader was doing. But would there have been a violation if it had been informed of the facts and agreed to the short sale?

Persuasive arguments have been made that "real" (i.e., not sham) trades should not be prohibited as manipulative regardless of the intent of the trader,[112] and it remains to be seen how the SEC's aggressive theory of manipulation would be treated in the Supreme Court.

In the meantime, the advent of Regulation M means that underwriters will have to become accustomed to an environment in which more transactions can be questioned as "manipulative" for the simple reason that Rule 10b-6 no longer prevents the transaction from being effected in the first place. Just prior to the effective date of Regulation M in early 1997, there was discussion among some underwriting firms of a "voluntary" (i.e., contractual) prohibition on bids and purchases for some period of time—perhaps a few hours—prior to the pricing of a distribution of a security for which Rule 101 imposed no restricted period. Some of these firms may have been concerned that their own proprietary trading during this period might raise questions under general antimanipulation principles. Another possible explanation is that the firms feared that issuers might put pressure on a managing underwriter to go into the market to purchase stock in order to raise its price—the exact opposite of the ConAgra and C.O.M.B. situations described above but one just as likely to be construed as manipulative.

"Voluntary" prohibitions on purchases prior to the pricing of a distribution should be entirely unnecessary. An underwriter acting on its own prior to pricing is not likely to be accused of manipulation in connection with a given trade, particularly since no underwriter has an interest in raising the

---

112. Fischel & Ross, *Should the Law Prohibit "Manipulation" in Financial Markets?*, 105 Harv. L. Rev. 503 (1991).

price of the security that it is about to underwrite, i.e., in making the security more difficult to sell to its customers. And any issuer trying to persuade the underwriter to engage in such conduct during the applicable restricted period would likely itself be violating Rule 102.

Chapter 5

LIABILITIES AND DUE DILIGENCE

The term "due diligence" does not appear in the federal securities laws. It is generally understood, however, to refer to the "reasonable investigation" defense against civil liability that is contemplated by Section 11(b)(3)(A) of the 1933 Act or to the "reasonable care" defense contemplated by Section 12(a)(2)[1] of the 1933 Act. More broadly, it is understood to include the entire process by which an underwriter or other marketer of securities reaches the conclusion that its comfort level with the issuer is sufficiently high to justify proceeding with a securities offering. Litigation risk is obviously one of the factors considered in reaching this conclusion, but so is the underwriter's concern for its reputation and the good will of its customers.

Traditionally, a managing underwriter of an SEC-registered securities offering was thought of as a "gatekeeper" or "reputational intermediary" on whom investors relied to reduce their information costs. Members of the underwriting syndicate, who could not as a practical matter conduct their own due diligence, also relied on the managing underwriter for similar purposes.

---

1. Section 12(2) of the 1933 Act was redesignated as Section 12(a)(2) by the Private Securities Litigation Reform Act of 1995.

Under the traditional arrangement, therefore, an investment banking firm that placed its name on a prospectus had a vital reputational interest in a complete and accurate disclosure document. Moreover, generally uniform high standards of due diligence among other underwriters—and the likelihood of detailed SEC comments on the registration statement—meant that even the most recalcitrant issuer was likely to cooperate with the underwriter in this exercise.

To some degree, the traditional model is still alive and well. Initial public offerings and certain "high-yield" financings call for the application of traditional due diligence techniques. At the same time, securities offerings have been revolutionized during the last two decades by developments that include:

   –   a great expansion of publicly held companies' periodic disclosure obligations under the 1934 Act,

   –   progress in technology and communications that has revolutionized the dissemination and retrieval of information about reporting companies,

   –   drastic changes in the SEC's administration of registration procedures under the 1933 Act, particularly in regard to the "integrated disclosure system," shelf registration, and review of filed documents,

   –   unprecedented institutionalization and globalization of the securities markets, and

   –   radical changes in the techniques and economics of the distribution of securities.

Many of these changes were described in detail in a 1993 report prepared by a Task Force of the Federal Regulation of Securities Committee of the Section on Business Law of the American Bar Association.[2] The report described the effect of the changes on underwriters' ability to carry out traditional due diligence and concluded that as to "the great bulk of non-

---

2. Report of the Task Force on Sellers' Due Diligence and Similar Defenses Under the Federal Securities Laws, 48 Bus. Law. 1185 (1993) (the "ABA Task Force Report"). One of the authors of this book served as co-chair of the Task Force.

exempt securities underwritten by or placed through securities firms" there existed "a wide discrepancy between underwriters' theoretical liabilities and their practical ability to escape them, as well as a growing deviation from the premises that led the Congress in 1933 to impose liabilities on underwriters."[3]

The Task Force Report focused in detail on three types of transactions that impose particular strains on underwriters' ability to perform traditional due diligence. These transactions— the shelf takedown of investment-grade debt, the medium-term note offering, and the non-underwritten registered equity secondary offering—are treated elsewhere in this book. Certain other types of transactions—commercial paper offerings, private placements (including Rule 144A offerings), securitization transactions and international offerings—present their own due diligence problems and are also treated elsewhere in this book.

The remainder of this chapter deals with "general principles" of due diligence as they apply to "traditional" transactions—especially initial public offerings—and as they apply to important aspects of the non-traditional offerings discussed elsewhere.[4]

Statutory Bases for Liability

Section 11 of the 1933 Act provides the principal basis for imposing civil liability upon underwriters of securities. Section 12(a)(2) creates potential liability for any seller of a security in the public markets, whether or not the security is registered under the 1933 Act, unless the security is exempted by Section 3(a)(2). Rule 10b-5 under Section 10(b) of the 1934 Act lurks in the background, but for reasons to be discussed it is not as

---

3. *Id.* at 1215.

4. Potential defendants such as directors and officers of issuers of securities, experts such as accounting firms and certain "control persons" may also have due diligence defenses. This book's discussion of due diligence defenses, however, is largely limited to those available to underwriters and sellers of securities.

effective a remedy for a purchaser of securities in a public offering.

• *Section 11*

Section 11(a) of the 1933 Act provides that a person acquiring a security covered by a registration statement may recover damages from the issuer, its directors, its officers who sign the registration statement,[5] accountants and other experts named in the registration statement with their consent, and every underwriter with respect to such security if "any part of the registration statement, when such part became effective, contained an untrue statement of a material fact or omitted to state a material fact required to be stated therein or necessary to make the statements therein not misleading."[6]

A defense to a Section 11 claim is available if it can be proved that, at that time he or she acquired the securities, the person asserting the claim knew of the alleged untruth or omission. This is a difficult defense to sustain, particularly in the context of a class action—and virtually all Section 11 claims are asserted as class actions. Also, if the defendants can prove that any portion or all of the "depreciation in value" of the registered security did not result from the registration statement's being false or misleading—the so-called "negative causation" defense—then Section 11(e) provides that such portion or all of plaintiff's damages are not recoverable. Thus, if the market price of the securities declined solely because of gen-

---

5. Section 6(a) provides that a registration statement must be signed by the issuer's principal executive officer, its principal financial officer, and its comptroller or principal accounting officer. A majority of the directors must sign the registration statement, but each director has potential Section 11 liability, whether or not he or she actually signs the document.

6. Rule 405 under the 1933 Act provides:

The term "material," when used to qualify a requirement for the furnishing of information as to any subject, limits the information required to those matters to which there is a substantial likelihood that a reasonable investor would attach importance in determining whether to purchase the security registered.

eral market conditions, then the plaintiffs could not recover damages.[7]

Section 11(e) also contains a so-called "hold-down" provision, adopted as part of the 1934 amendments to the 1933 Act, which provides that in no event shall any underwriter (unless such underwriter shall have knowingly received from the issuer for acting as an underwriter some benefit, directly or indirectly, in which all other underwriters similarly situated did not share in proportion to their respective interests in the underwriting) be liable for damages in excess of the total price at which the securities underwritten by it and distributed to the public were offered to the public. Thus, an underwriter's damages are limited to the aggregate public offering price of the securities that constituted its underwriting commitment. This is the principal reason why the commitments of members of an underwriting syndicate are several and not joint and several.[8]

In the usual case, the managing underwriter does not receive any special benefits from the issuer. The management fee is not paid by the issuer, but rather by the syndicate out of the underwriting spread. If the managing underwriter were to receive warrants or cheap stock from the issuer—to the exclusion of the other underwriters—then it is at least arguable that the managing underwriter will not be entitled to the benefits of the hold-down provision. Under these circumstances, the managing underwriter would presumably argue that it had received the additional benefit in consideration of advisory or other ser-

---

7. See *Akerman v. Oryx Communications, Inc.*, 810 F.2d 336 (2d Cir. 1987) (decline in price found to have occurred prior to corrective disclosure); *In re Fortune Systems Securities Litigation*, [1988-1989 Transfer Binder] Fed. Sec. L. Rep. (CCH) ¶ 93,390 (N.D. Cal. July 30, 1987) (defendants argued that price decline of registered shares was due to "poor management of the IPO" and resulting cancellation of orders); *Beecher v. Able*, 435 F. Supp. 397 (S.D.N.Y. 1977) ("value" of registered shares held not necessarily to be same amount as market price where latter was influenced by "panic selling").

8. Rule 2720 of the NASD requires in the case of public offerings by NASD members or their affiliates that due diligence be performed by a "qualified independent underwriter." See Chapter 6.

vices that it had provided to the issuer, i.e., that it was not "similarly situated" with the other underwriters in respect of the additional benefit.

An action under Section 11 can be brought only by persons who acquired securities covered by the registration statement.[9] Theoretically, if other securities of the same class are outstanding, the person bringing the action must demonstrate that he or she purchased registered securities and not outstanding securities. Securities trading in the after-market are fungible, and accordingly this is a difficult burden. The issue is more theoretical than real, however, because the class action complaint will state that the suit is brought on behalf of all persons who purchased securities covered by the registration statement, and the actual members of the class will not be determined until after the case is decided or settled.

Section 11's remedy is not limited to those persons who purchased directly in the offering. After-market purchasers are also entitled to sue under Section 11, so long as they purchased securities covered by the registration statement. There is no requirement of privity.

If the securities are acquired after the issuer has made generally available to its securityholders an earnings statement covering a period of at least 12 months beginning after the effective date of the registration statement, then the right of recovery is conditioned upon proof that the person asserting the claim acquired the security relying upon the untrue statement in the registration statement or relying upon the registration statement and not knowing of the omission.[10] It is for this reason that underwriting agreements contain a covenant requiring the issuer to make such an earnings statement available at the earliest practicable date. Rule 158 under the 1933 Act permits

---

9. *Barnes v. Osofsky*, 373 F.2d 269 (2d Cir. 1967); *Colonial Realty Corp. v. Brunswick Corp.*, 257 F. Supp. 875 (S.D.N.Y. 1966); *Rudnick v. Franchard Corp.*, 237 F. Supp. 871 (S.D.N.Y. 1965).

10. *See In re Gap Stores Securities Litigation*, 79 F.R.D. 283, 297 note 14 (N.D. Cal. 1978); *Emmi v. First-Manufacturers National Bank*, 336 F. Supp. 629, 634 note 5 (S.D. Me. 1971).

an issuer's 1934 Act reports to serve as the earnings statement contemplated by Section 11.

Section 13 of the 1933 Act provides that the statute of limitations for an action under Section 11 is one year after the untrue statement or omission was discovered or should have been discovered by the person asserting the action or, at the outside, three years after the public offering.

The principal defense under Section 11 is the so-called "due diligence" defense, which is available to all defendants other than the issuer. In specifying when this defense is available, Section 11 distinguishes between that portion of a registration statement that is covered by the opinion of an expert, such as the certified financial statements or information covered by an opinion of a petroleum engineer, and that portion that is not expertized.

As to *non-expertized* portions of the registration statement, Section 11(b)(3)(A) permits the underwriter to avoid liability if he can sustain the burden of proof that "he had, *after reasonable investigation,* reasonable ground to believe and did believe, at the time such part of the registration statement became effective, that the statements therein were true and that there was no omission to state a material fact required to be stated therein or necessary to make the statements therein not misleading" (emphasis added). The concept of "due diligence" derives from the words "reasonable investigation." Section 11(c) provides that, in determining what constitutes reasonable investigation and reasonable grounds for belief, "the standard of reasonableness shall be that required of a prudent man in the management of his own property."

By contrast, Section 11(b)(3)(C) does not by its terms require an underwriter to show that he has made a reasonable investigation concerning those portions of the registration statement made on the authority of experts.[11] In order to sustain

---

11. It should be noted that the interim unaudited financial statements in a registration statement are not expertized. Nor are numbers in a registration statement expertized merely because they are covered by an accountant's comfort letter (see Chapter 2). An effort should be made to have the auditors *expertize,* in accordance with SAS No. 42, the previously audited numbers in the selected financial data that are not included in the certified

their defense in this situation, they merely must prove that they had no reasonable ground to believe, and did not believe, that the expertized portions of the registration statement were materially untrue or omitted material facts.

Although under the statute the requirement of reasonable investigation or due diligence does not extend to the certified financial statements or other expertized portions of the registration statement, an underwriter should take great care to avoid a charge that it had a reasonable ground to believe that these portions of the registration statement were false or misleading. The financial state-

---

and expertized financial statements included or incorporated by reference in the prospectus. This requires an additional paragraph in the auditors' opinion, which SAS 42 suggests might read as follows:

> We have also previously examined, in accordance with generally accepted auditing standards, the consolidated balance sheets as of December 31, 19X3, 19X2, and 19X1, and the related consolidated statements of income, retained earnings, and changes in financial position for the years ended December 31, 19X2 and 19X1 (none of which are presented herein); and we expressed unqualified opinions on those consolidated financial statements. In our opinion, the information set forth in the selected financial data for each of the five years in the period ended December 31, 19X5, appearing on page XX, is fairly stated in all material respects in relation to the consolidated financial statements from which it has been derived.

The "Experts" section of the prospectus should provide as follows:

> The financial statements included in this Prospectus, the financial statements from which the selected financial data included in this Prospectus have been derived and the related supplemental schedule included elsewhere in the Registration Statement, to the extent and for the periods indicated in their opinions, have been examined by [   ], independent auditors, as stated in their opinions appearing herein and elsewhere in the Registration Statement, and such financial statements, related supplemental schedule and selected financial data included herein and elsewhere in the Registration Statement have been so included in reliance upon such opinions given upon the authority of that firm as experts in accounting and auditing.

If this procedure is followed, it is not necessary to cover the selected financial data in the comfort letter.

ments go to the very heart of a registration statement, and the underwriter must be sure that he understands the accounting principles applied and has no reason to believe that the financial statements do not fairly present the issuer's financial position and the results of its operations. The subject of due diligence in relation to financial statements is discussed below in greater detail.

• *Section 12(a)(2)*

Section 12(a)(2) imposes liability on any person who offers or sells a security by means of a prospectus or oral communication "which includes an untrue statement of a material fact or omits to state a material fact necessary in order to make the statements in the light of the circumstances under which they were made, not misleading." Liability, which may be for rescission, or for damages if the security is no longer owned, extends to any person who sells a security—whether or not that person is an underwriter. Liability under Section 12(a)(2) may be incurred whether or not the securities are exempt from registration, except in the case of United States government, municipal, and bank securities exempted under Section 3(a)(2), as to which there is no Section 12(a)(2) liability.

Under a recent decision of the U.S. Supreme Court, *Gustafson v. Alloyd Co.*,[12] Section 12(a)(2) applies only in the case of public offerings by an issuer or a controlling securityholder. This decision came as a surprise to many securities lawyers, who had long assumed that an investment banker had Section 12(a)(2) liability in connection with private placements and even in connection with certain secondary market transactions. The most important category of non-registered securities offering remaining subject to Section 12(a)(2) liability after *Gustafson* would appear to be commercial paper programs, which are neither registered nor exempt under Section 3(a)(2). On the other hand, it is possible that purchasers of securities in an overseas offering (including an offering pursuant to Regulation S) might claim rights under Section 12(a)(2) if they could show that their purchase involved the use of the U.S. mails or other "jurisdictional means."[13]

---

12. *Gustafson v. Alloyd Co.*, 115 S.Ct. 1061 (1995).
13. Any purchaser located abroad would undoubtedly have to persuade a U.S. court to exercise its subject matter jurisdiction over such a claim.

In the case of a registered public offering, a securities firm that acts as a dealer, but not as an underwriter, may have liability under Section 12(a)(2), even though it will not have liability under Section 11. Section 2(11) excludes a member of the dealer group from the definition of the term "underwriter" by stating that the term "shall not include a person whose interest is limited to a commission from an underwriter or dealer not in excess of the usual and customary distributors' or sellers' commission." Rule 141 provides that the term "commission" as used in Section 2(11) includes "such remuneration, commonly known as a spread, as may be received by a distributor or dealer as a consequence of reselling securities bought from an underwriter or dealer at a price below the offering price of such securities" as long as the spread is not in excess of what is usual and customary in the distribution and sale of issues of similar type and size. Thus, a dealer, even though it does not have underwriters' liability under Section 11, does have potential liability under Section 12(a)(2) if the prospectus used by it in selling the securities is materially false or misleading.

A dealer that sells an unusually large portion of an offering runs the risk of incurring Section 11 liability as well as liability under Section 12(a)(2). Rule 141 excludes from the term "usual and customary distributors' or sellers' commissions" amounts paid to "any person whose function is the management of the distribution of all or a substantial part of the particular issue, or who performs the functions normally performed by an underwriter or underwriting syndicate." Although Rule 141 has not been interpreted by the SEC, except with respect to a dealer who received a larger selling concession than that afforded to other dealers,[14] if a dealer plays a dominant role in a transaction and sells such a large portion of the offering that he can be viewed as performing "the functions normally performed by an underwriter," underwriter's liability could result.

Under Section 12(a)(2), unlike Section 11, the seller of the security is liable only to "the person purchasing such security from him." (As previously noted, a person who purchases se-

---

14. *In re Diotron, Inc.,* 42 S.E.C. 236 (1964).

curities in the after-market from a dealer unrelated to an under-writer may bring an action under Section 11 against *any* underwriter of the securities.) Section 12(a)(2) does not limit liability to the person who transfers title to the security. An agent who solicits the purchase will be considered to be among those "from" whom the buyer "purchased" the security if the agent did so for his or her own financial benefit or that of the seller.[15]

A defense may be sustained under Section 12(a)(2) if the person selling the security can demonstrate "that he did not know, and in the exercise of reasonable care could not have known," of the untruth or omission. The language of the statute suggests that the defendant need not prove that he in fact exercised due diligence but only that if he had exercised due diligence, he could not have discovered the untruth or omission in the prospectus. The Court of Appeals for the Seventh Circuit, however, has read this language as requiring affirmative due diligence in order to sustain the defense.[16] The ABA Task Force Report criticized the Seventh Circuit decision and concluded that it should be confined to its facts.[17]

Section 12(a)(2) does not refer to expertization (for example, of financial statements) as a part of a seller's defense. Until recently, it was also unclear under Section 12(a)(2) whether a defendant could benefit from "negative causation" as in the case of a Section 11 claim, i.e., be able to reduce the amount of damages by showing that the reduction in value of the purchased security resulted from factors not relating to a misstatement or omission. As amended by the Private Securities Litigation Reform Act of 1995, Section 12(a)(2) claims are now subject to such a "negative causation" defense.

Section 13 of the 1933 Act provides that an action under Section 12(a)(2) must be brought within the same time frame as required for actions brought under Section 11.

---

15. *Pinter v. Dahl*, 486 U.S. 622 (1988).

16. *Sanders v. John Nuveen & Co.*, 619 F.2d 1222 (7th Cir. 1980), *cert. denied*, 450 U.S. 1005 (1981).

17. ABA Task Force Report at 1238.

• *Rule 10b-5*

Section 12(a)(2) by its terms does not apply to securities exempt from 1933 Act registration pursuant to Section 3(a)(2). Also, according to the Supreme Court's *Gustafson* decision, Section 12(a)(2) does not apply to private placements. For many years, however, the federal courts have implied a private remedy from the SEC's Rule 10b-5 that is applicable to all transactions in securities. Persons who sue under Rule 10b-5 enjoy some advantages and face a number of disadvantages. The major advantage of Rule 10b-5 is that it reaches all persons who commit a disclosure violation in connection with the purchase or sale of securities. It is not limited, like Section 11 or Section 12(a)(2), to specific categories of defendants. The reach of the rule has been somewhat curtailed, to be sure, by a U.S. Supreme Court decision that rejected the ability of plaintiffs to use Rule 10b-5 to reach persons who merely "aided and abetted" another person's violation of Rule 10b-5.[18]

As an implied remedy based on common law deceit, Rule 10b-5 has been held to require proof that the defendant acted with scienter, i.e., that he intentionally or at least recklessly acted to cause a disclosure violation. Also, the Private Securities Litigation Reform Act of 1995 requires a plaintiff to state facts in the complaint that "giv[e] rise to a strong inference that the defendant acted with the required state of mind." It remains to be seen how the new statutory pleading requirement will work out in practice.

Rule 10b-5 claims are typically thrown into complaints arising out of securities offerings along with claims based on Section 11, Section 12(a)(2), state securities law remedies and common law remedies. Because of the scienter requirement, Rule 10b-5 is generally thought to represent a "fraud-based" remedy, unlike Section 11 or Section 12(a)(2), which are generally regarded as "negligence-based" remedies. It is difficult to see how an underwriter or other defendant who has performed sufficient due diligence to prevail under Section 11 or

---

18. *Central Bank of Denver v. First Interstate Bank of Denver*, 114 S.Ct. 1439 (1994).

Section 12(a)(2) could possibly be found to have acted with scienter so as to be exposed on a Rule 10b-5 claim.

As noted above, the remedy provided by Rule 10b-5 has been implied by the courts. Understandably, there is therefore no specific federal statute of limitations (such as Section 13 of the 1933 Act) applicable to claims brought under Rule 10b-5. At one time, plaintiffs were able to rely on state statutes of limitations—which are frequently longer than those set forth in Section 13 of the 1933 Act—to provide the period within which a claim had to be brought. This advantage disappeared in 1991 when the U.S. Supreme Court decided that the appropriate statute of limitations for a Rule 10b-5 claim was that found in Section 9(e) of the 1934 Act, i.e., "one year after the discovery of the facts constituting the violation and within three years after such violation."[19]

Most recent court decisions have refused to imply a private right of action from Section 17(a) of the 1933 Act.[20] Section 17(a) remains available to the SEC, however, as a basis for enforcement proceedings.

• *Controlling Persons*

Section 15 under the 1933 Act provides that every person who controls any person liable under Section 11 or Section 12 shall also be liable jointly and severally with and to the same extent as such controlled person unless the controlling person "had no knowledge of or reasonable ground to believe in the existence of the facts by reason of which the liability of the controlled person is alleged to exist." Section 20(a) of the 1934 Act contains a similar provision that could render a controlling person liable for a Rule 10b-5 violation by a person it controls "unless the controlling person acted in good faith and did not directly or indirectly induce the act or acts constituting the violation or cause of action." Both of these provisions are

---

19. *Lampf, Pleva, Lipkind, Prupis & Petigrow v. Gilbertson*, 501 U.S. 350, 364 (1991).

20. *See* Richard W. Jennings, Harold Marsh, Jr. and John C. Coffee, Jr., *Securities Regulation: Cases and Materials* 836-39 (7th ed. 1992) (collecting cases).

sometimes used to expand the scope of a lawsuit to include persons such as parent companies and major holders of voting securities.

SEC and Judicial Interpretations Concerning Due Diligence

There have been relatively few interpretations by the SEC or the courts as to the type of investigation that will satisfy the due diligence standard applicable to a particular offering.[21]

The SEC has no formal role in Section 11 or Section 12(a)(2) proceedings. Of course, it prescribes the contents of registration statements under the 1933 Act by its adoption of rules and registration forms. Its views are, therefore, important on whether participants in public offerings have complied with these requirements. The SEC has also exercised its rulemaking authority to enumerate "relevant circumstances" for purposes of assessing the reasonableness of conduct for Section 11 purposes and to provide a "safe harbor" for certain forward-looking information.

The SEC's influence in the area of due diligence is primarily exercised through its power to bring enforcement proceedings against issuers, underwriters and other persons who participate in securities offerings. These proceedings may be brought under Section 17(a) of the 1933 Act or Rule 10b-5, or they may allege violations of an issuer's reporting obligations under Section 13(a) of the 1934 Act.

• *The Richmond Case*

As early as 1953, the SEC found that an underwriter "owe[d] a duty to the investing public to exercise a degree of care reasonable under the circumstances of th[e] offering to assure the substantial accuracy of representations made in the prospectus . . . ."[22] In a 1963 stop order proceeding, *In re The*

---

21. *See generally*, on the subject of underwriters' due diligence, the ABA Task Force Report.

22. *In re Charles E. Bailey & Co.*, 35 S.E.C. 33, 41 (1953).

Richmond Corp.,[23] the SEC criticized an underwriter for failing to perform a reasonable investigation. The SEC stressed that reliance on the representations of management does not satisfy the obligations imposed on an underwriter. It noted critically that the underwriter's investigation of the issuer's business consisted of visits to two of its three tracts of land, an examination of a list of its shareholders, and the obtaining of a credit report, and that, as to all other matters in connection with the registration statement, the underwriter relied only on representations of management. The SEC concluded that this did not constitute the "investigation in accordance with professional standards" that an underwriter impliedly represents that it has made when it associates itself with an offering. "The underwriter who does not make a reasonable investigation is derelict in his responsibilities to deal fairly with the investing public."

The SEC has often embraced the idea expressed in *Richmond* that an underwriter has an *affirmative obligation* to perform a reasonable investigation, i.e., that an underwriter is not free simply to "take its chances" on whether or not it will need to invoke a due diligence defense. Apart from the "shingle theory" approach in *Richmond*, it has also based this idea on the theory that by participating in an offering an underwriter makes an implied recommendation of the securities being offered, and that under general antifraud principles it must have an "adequate basis" for such a recommendation.[24]

In connection with the 1992 settlement of an administrative proceeding involving municipal securities, the SEC issued a report in which it summarized its views about an underwriter's affirmative obligation to make a reasonable investigation.[25] It found the underwriter to have violated Section 17(a) of the 1933 Act and Rule 10b-5 in not following up on information known to the underwriter that called into question the legitimacy of certain key transactions. Significantly, it found that the

---

23. *In re The Richmond Corp.*, 41 S.E.C. 398 (1963).

24. *See*, e.g., Municipal Securities Disclosure, SEC Release No. 34-26100 at 89,441-43 (1988).

25. *In re Donaldson, Lufkin & Jenrette Securities Corporation*, SEC Release No. 34-31207 (September 22, 1992).

presence of underwriter's counsel at some of the key meetings did not excuse the underwriter from its obligation "to adequately explore questions concerning the business and financial aspects of the offering which were raised during the due diligence process."

• *The BarChris Case*

The first extended discussion by a court of the due diligence defense was Judge McLean's opinion in *BarChris*.[26] BarChris was engaged in the construction and installation of bowling alleys, an industry that had experienced dramatic growth after automatic pinsetters were first introduced in 1952. The company's sales had increased over the years and, to meet its need for working capital, it sold subordinated debentures under a registration statement that became effective in 1961. Drexel & Co. was the managing underwriter.

In 1961 and 1962, it became apparent that the industry was overbuilt, and in 1962, BarChris entered bankruptcy. Judge McLean found that the registration statement covering the debentures was false and misleading and that Drexel & Co. had not satisfied the due diligence standard.

In the course of their investigation, the managing underwriter and its counsel reviewed only a limited range of materials. They read the annual reports and prospectuses of other bowling alley builders, a prior prospectus and earlier reports of the company, minutes of the company's board of directors and executive committee, and minutes of certain subsidiaries. They contacted BarChris's banks and James Talcott Inc., its factor, inquired about the company, and received favorable replies. They also obtained a Dun & Bradstreet report. A series of meetings was held with several BarChris officers at which the registration statement was considered and reviewed. Several of the points that later became the subject of the lawsuit were discussed at these meetings. As to these matters, representatives of the company assured the managing underwriter and its counsel that there were no problems.

---

26. *Escott v. BarChris Construction Corp.*, 283 F. Supp. 643 (S.D.N.Y. 1968).

The managing underwriter and its counsel, however, did not make an adequate review of documents. They did not insist upon the preparation of missing minutes, nor did they inspect the notes of meetings for which no minutes were available. They failed to ask for a schedule of customer delinquencies or for copies of such delinquencies and correspondence from Talcott. They did not review contracts with Talcott or the company's customers. Many of these documents contained information that would have alerted them to the problems facing the company.

Judge McLean expressed his views on the proper relationship between underwriters and management as follows:

> In a sense, the positions of the underwriter and the company's officers are adverse. It is not unlikely that statements made by company officers to an underwriter to induce him to underwrite may be self-serving. They may be unduly enthusiastic. As in this case, they may, on occasion, be deliberately false.[27]

For the underwriters' participation in an offering to be of any value to investors, it was therefore necessary for the underwriters to "make some reasonable attempt to verify the data submitted to them. They may not rely solely on the company's officers or on the company's counsel. A prudent man in the management of his own property would not rely on them."[28]

Not surprisingly, Judge McLean refused to be specific as to the degree of effort required in order to perform a "reasonable investigation." It was impossible to lay down a rigid rule. Rather, "[i]t is a question of degree, a matter of judgment in each case."[29]

• *The Leasco Data Processing Case*

Due diligence was discussed at length in *Leasco Data Processing*.[30] In *Leasco*, the court found that the dealer managers

---

27. 283 F. Supp. at 696-97.

28. *Id.* at 697.

29. *Id.*

30. *Feit v. Leasco Data Processing Equip. Corp.*, 332 F. Supp. 544 (E.D.N.Y. 1971).

for a registered exchange offer had "just barely" satisfied the due diligence standard and were accordingly not liable under Section 11. The case involved an exchange offer by Leasco for the outstanding shares of Reliance Insurance Company. A major factor in Leasco's decision to seek to acquire Reliance was the latter's "surplus surplus," that portion of its surplus not required to support its insurance operations. The exchange offer prospectus did not quantify the amount of surplus surplus.

Prior to acting as dealer-managers in this transaction, White Weld & Co. and Lehman Brothers examined the report of an actuary and several other reports that specifically dealt with surplus surplus. Meetings were held with Leasco officers, at which time the surplus surplus issue was explored. Uncertainty existed as to the exact amount of Reliance's surplus surplus in that there were several methods of calculation and the basic data for the calculation were in the possession of Reliance and the Pennsylvania Insurance Commission.

A key element in the underwriters' due diligence defense was their lack of access to the information necessary to calculate surplus surplus. The underwriters were unable to review the data primarily because of the hostility of the members of Reliance's management and their refusal to cooperate in the preparation of the registration statement. Several weeks prior to the effectiveness of the registration statement, however, Reliance and Leasco entered into an agreement of which the dealer-managers were aware. This agreement provided for the cooperation of Reliance's management. Even after this agreement was signed, however, counsel for the dealer-managers received a copy of a letter from Leasco's counsel to the SEC stating that the Reliance management still declined to furnish any information.

The weakness in the due diligence of the dealer-managers was, first, that they did not attempt to contact directly third parties having the necessary information and, second, that they failed after the agreement was signed to insist that Leasco press its new advantage in order to obtain the surplus surplus data from Reliance. The court described the dealer-managers' role as being "to exercise a high degree of care in investigation and independent verification of the company's representations"; in this connection, they must play "devil's advocate." The court concluded, however, that "on balance" the dealer-managers had "just barely" managed to establish the reasonableness of their investigation, including the verification of Leasco's representations that access to Reliance's management was not available.[31]

• *The Chris-Craft Case*

The Second Circuit's decision in *Chris-Craft*[32] also discussed the due diligence obligation of underwriters, albeit in the somewhat unusual context of Section 14(e) of the 1934 Act. The following excerpt from Judge Timbers's opinion relates to the liability of First Boston, as dealer-manager of a registered exchange offer, for the lack of disclosure in the registration statement of a proposed disposition by Bangor-Punta Corp. to Amoskeag Corp. of its interest in the Bangor & Aroostook Railroad:

> Since we already have concluded that the BPC [Bangor-Punta Corp.] registration statement and prospectus were materially deficient, the remaining issue to be determined is First Boston's culpability. First Boston is a skilled, experienced and well respected dealer-manager and underwriter. It had an obligation with respect to the BPC exchange offer to reach a careful, independent judgment based on facts known to it as to the accuracy of the registration statement. Moreover, if it was aware of facts that strongly suggested, even though they did not conclusively show, that the registration materials were deceptive, it was duty-bound to make a reasonable further investigation.
>
> We hold that First Boston did not adequately perform its duty in these respects. . . . First Boston did not seek verification of the officials' answer that a sale [of the Bangor & Aroostook Railroad to Amoskeag] was not anticipated at that time. . . . It did not make a more care-

---

31. *Id.* at 583.

32. *Chris-Craft Industries, Inc. v. Piper Aircraft Corp.*, 480 F.2d 341 (2d Cir.), *cert. denied*, 414 U.S. 910 (1973).

ful search of BPC's records, nor did it talk to officials at Amoskeag after it discovered from the minutes that Amoskeag was the likely buyer. Under these circumstances, First Boston's certification of the BPC registration statement carrying the BAR [Bangor & Aroostook Railroad] at $18.4 million amounted to an almost complete abdication of its responsibility to potential investors, to CCI [Chris-Craft Industries], and to others who relied upon it to detect misrepresentations.[33]

* *Summary Judgment*

Because the adequacy of due diligence is so oriented to the facts and circumstances of a particular offering, underwriters have seldom been able to prevail on motions for summary judgment. In recent years, however, courts appear to be more willing to dispose of cases at an early stage. In a recent decision,[34] the Ninth Circuit affirmed most of the trial court's grant of a summary judgment motion in favor of underwriters. On one issue, however, it deemed summary judgment to be inappropriate. This issue involved the issuer's booking of large consignment sales at the end of the most recent quarter. The Ninth Circuit found that the underwriters, despite the presence of "red flags" as to these sales, had done little more for their due diligence investigation than to rely on the issuer's assurances that these sales were legitimate. It was, therefore, inappropriate to grant summary judgment on the adequacy of due diligence on this issue.

* *Few Judicial Decisions*

As noted in the ABA Task Force Report, one of the major reasons that cases such as *Bar Chris* still loom large in any discussion of underwriters' due diligence is that there have been so few judicial opinions on the subject. The fact is that defendants in Section 11 litigation tend to settle cases without proceeding to trial for a full development of relevant facts that can

---

33. 480 F.2d at 371-73. Of course, there is no such concept as "certification" of a registration statement.

34. *In re Software Toolworks Inc. Securities Litigation*, 50 F.3d 615 (9th Cir. 1994).

then be analyzed in a judicial opinion.[35] It has even been asserted on the basis of an admittedly incomplete collection of data that the pressures to settle are so great that the merits of a Section 11 claim appear to have little to do with the amount for which a case is settled.[36]

Due Diligence Standards

As stated above, reasonable investigation or due diligence is defined in terms of the prudent man test. It is difficult to define in advance with respect to any particular issuer the scope and depth of the investigation that will satisfy the statutory standard.

One difficulty in sustaining a due diligence defense is that the trier of fact will have the benefit of hindsight in determining whether the requisite standard has been met. It is, of course, improper to apply hindsight in making such a determination, but there may well be a subconscious tendency to do so. An issuer encounters difficulty after its registration statement has become effective, the market price of its stock declines, and the prospectus is scrutinized by disgruntled stockholders and members of the plaintiffs' bar to determine whether a charge can be made that it was false or misleading in some material respect. Thus, in performing due diligence, the investment banker and its counsel must be alert to determine what could go wrong with the issuer and to anticipate in the prospectus those problems that it might face in the future.

The time and effort required to perform due diligence will depend on the nature of the issuer and the investment banker's relationship with the issuer. For example, the level of due diligence required in connection with new high-risk ventures is particularly high. The SEC has stated that a "thorough and intensive underwriters' investigation is especially important in an initial public offering by companies in the developmental stage or those dealing with 'high technology' products or processes.[37]

---

35. ABA Task Force Report at 1210-12, 1229-30.

36. Janet C. Alexander, *Do the Merits Matter? A Study of Settlements in Securities Class Actions*, 43 Stan. L. Rev. 497 (1991).

37. SEC Release No. 33-5275 (July 26, 1972).

When an investment banker is dealing with an established client, the amount of due diligence required in connection with a particular offering may be substantially less than in the case of a new client. In some cases, the investment banker may be engaged in a continuous due diligence process through its day-to-day work with its client. Its knowledge of the client may be so extensive that an update is all that is required. In most cases, however, the amount of due diligence that must be exercised will fall somewhere between the two extremes.

One problem that investment bankers face is the standard of due diligence required in connection with an offering of securities registered on a "shelf" basis, usually by means of a registration statement on Form S-3, which incorporates by reference the issuer's Form 10-K and subsequent filings under the 1934 Act. Investment bankers and their counsel have been concerned that underwriters may be held liable for inadequate disclosure in the Form 10-K and other documents incorporated by reference in the Form S-3 prospectus, documents that the underwriters and their counsel had no role in preparing. These concerns are magnified when securities are "taken down" on short notice from the shelf registration statement. It is essential, of course, for the underwriter to review the documents incorporated by reference and to ask questions of management designed to ascertain the accuracy of those documents. Issuers, however, may be reluctant to amend filed documents to conform to the views of underwriters and their counsel as to improved disclosure. Due diligence concerns in the context of shelf registration statements and Form S-3 are discussed in Chapter 8.

As indicated above, underwriters have been criticized for relying on representations by an issuer's management without independent verification. This is a matter that calls for discretion and tact. The extent to which factual statements must be verified independently depends in large part upon the nature of the information being disclosed. For example, if a corporation's personnel manager, after checking corporate records, states that the corporation has approximately 3,750 employees, 2,500 of whom are covered by a collective bargaining agreement expiring on a specified date, it would not be reasonable to require the underwriter to recheck the records to determine the accuracy of the count. This is a fact that management would have no incentive to misstate, and it is entirely reasonable for the underwriter to rely upon the count made by the corporation's personnel manager. On the other hand, counsel for the underwriters should review the collective bargaining agreement to determine whether it has any unusual features and to ascertain the accuracy of the stated expiration date.

In other words, a rule of reason must be applied in deciding which facts provided by management should be made the subject of independent verification. The process of verifying facts, however, should not obscure the real thrust of due diligence, which is getting to the core of the issuer's business and financial position and uncovering the problem areas.

Although it is difficult to establish disclosure guidelines that are applicable to all issuers, the SEC has experimented with guidelines for particular industries. The most significant of these is *Guide 3* relating to statistical disclosure by bank holding companies.

Due Diligence Procedures

There are certain basic procedures that should be followed in connection with a registered offering of securities if time permits. It is true that no more than limited diligence is possible in the case of a Form S-3 filing with an accelerated time schedule. But in the case of an initial public offering or a financing for a new client where a reasonable timetable has been established, real due diligence can and should be performed. These due diligence procedures can best be appreciated if reviewed chronologically in the context of the underwriting process.

• *Integrity of Management*

Before a commitment is made to establish an investment banking relationship with a prospective client, a securities firm should be satisfied as to the integrity of the client's management. Many financial scandals involving inadequate disclosure in registration statements or other SEC filings have involved outright fraud on the part of management. No amount of due diligence can assure an accurate registration statement if the issuer's management is consciously prepared to withhold information.

In the case of a long-standing investment banking client, the relationships that have developed over the years provide the best assurance of management integrity. In the case of a new client, however, inquiry should be made of appropriate sources to determine whether the corporation is being run by the type of persons with whom the investment banker would wish to be associated. This may be difficult at times, particularly if it is important to maintain the confidentiality of a proposed financing. Also, there may be legitimate concern that the very fact that inquiries are being made would, in the eyes of management, imply a lack of trust.

In some instances, it may be appropriate to go no further than to rely on the judgment of persons within the securities firm such as a branch office manager in the city where the corporation's headquarters are located or a knowledgeable research analyst. If there is any hint of sharp practices, questionable accounting, previous difficulties with the SEC, or litigation that reflects on the integrity of management, more probing inquiries will be necessary. In some cases, it may be appropriate, with the consent of management, to speak with the corporation's commercial bankers and its principal suppliers and customers.

Many underwriters have a formal procedure for approving their participation in securities offerings, particularly as managing underwriter. The procedure ordinarily involves written reports to a commitment committee by those of the underwriter's personnel who are supporting the establishment of a relationship with the issuer. These reports are part of the underwriter's due diligence just as much as the comfort letter and legal opinions. They should be prepared with a commensurate degree of care.

• *Checklists*

The SEC has suggested the adoption by underwriters of comprehensive checklists to be used in performing due diligence for all registration statements. But a checklist cannot be devised that will cover all situations. Moreover, checklists can be dangerous in that they may lead the person performing due diligence to believe that the job has been completed if all items on the list are covered. As one of the authors has put it, most checklists are worth no more than one's neighbor's shopping list: they may be interesting, and there may be some overlap, but they cannot be relied upon as a guide for prudent behavior. Also, checklists can distract the participants in an offering from the essential due diligence function, which is to understand fully the business of the issuer, to identify the problems it faces and may face in the future, and to assure that the registration statement is complete and accurate.

• *Staffing*

It is important for the investment bankers and their counsel to assign people to the transaction who are sufficiently prepared to carry out their responsibilities. All securities lawyers should remember the adverse inference drawn by Judge McLean in *BarChris* from the fact that a junior associate[38] had failed to identify important information during the course of reading minutes. It is vital that each member of the team understand his or her responsibilities and how these relate to the underwriters' overall objective of conducting a reasonable investigation.

In particular, team members (especially junior ones) should understand why due diligence is important to the achievement of their clients' objectives of completing a transaction with an intact reputation, happy customers and no prospect of litigation in the future. They should also understand the SEC's views on due diligence. Each member of the team should understand the role of other members of the team in order to minimize the likelihood of erroneous assumptions that someone else is handling an important task. In the view of the authors, junior lawyers who read minutes and review corporate documents should also participate in drafting sessions. Such participation provides a context for their other work, and they may be better prepared than anyone else in the room to spot an issue that relates to their work.

---

38. "Stanton was a very junior associate. He had been admitted to the bar . . . some three months before. This was the first registration statement he had ever worked on." 283 F. Supp. at 694 note 23.

Team members should understand the documentation policies that will govern the transaction. They should be encouraged to memorialize their work on a contemporaneous basis. Records are more convincing when written close to the fact, and prompt preparation of written memoranda facilitates their circulation to other persons involved in the transaction.

It goes without saying that junior team members should be encouraged to ask questions and raise problems. One of the authors is fond of observing that "there are no dumb questions, only dumb assumptions." Team members should also be warned of the dangers of complacency, of "tunnel vision" and of losing objectivity. They should be encouraged to stay informed, budget their time and regard their efforts as an indispensable learning experience.

• *Review of Industry*

A company is much more easily understood against the background of the industry in which it operates. Both the investment bankers and their counsel should therefore become familiar with the industry by means of a study of prospectuses, Form 10-Ks and annual reports prepared by other companies in the industry. Research reports on the industry and major companies in the industry should be reviewed, including those prepared by other securities firms.

If the industry is subject to a particular system of regulation, as, for example, transportation, banking, insurance or communications, the investment bankers should verify that they are current on any new developments. Counsel for the underwriters can provide assistance in this respect.

The investment bankers should become acquainted with relevant trade publications, which may identify environmental problems, litigation exposures or labor difficulties that are of concern to the industry. In many cases, one of the firm's research analysts will be asked to provide current information and an evaluation of the overall prospects for the industry.

• *Role of Analysts in Due Diligence*

In recent years, research analysts have been making an increasing and perhaps indispensable contribution to the success of investment banking transactions, particularly initial public offerings ("IPOs"). Analysts play a major role in helping their firms solicit IPO issuers for the purpose of being named as the managing underwriter of the offering. They also play a major role in the underwriter's due diligence investigation, particularly in the case of high-technology companies where an analyst familiar in general terms with the issuer's products or services can often better analyze the subtle competitive, managerial and technological advantages that make the issuer's securities a good investment. Just as important, the analyst can spot weaknesses in the issuer's strategy or program that need to be investigated as a matter of due diligence and perhaps disclosed in the issuer's IPO prospectus.

IPOs usually cannot be marketed without an earnings estimate. Analysts are often called upon to produce such an estimate for use by persons engaged in selling the registered securities. Many underwriters are prepared for this purpose—and with the issuer's consent—to take the analyst "over the [Chinese] Wall," i.e., made privy to information that will not be disclosed in the prospectus.[39]

• *Preliminary Review of Basic Documents*

Immediately after the investment banking firm decides to proceed with a financing, its counsel will usually send the issuer a letter requesting basic documents regarding the issuer. These would include corporate documents such as the articles of incorporation, by-laws and loan agreements. They will also include all documents filed with the SEC since the issuer became a reporting company under the 1934 Act or during its past five fiscal years, whichever is less, and all reports and other communications sent to shareholders during this period. Documents filed with the SEC would include reports on Form 10-K, Form 8-K and Form 10-Q; registration statements relating to the sale of other securities; and any proxy statements for annual meetings, acquisitions, or other transactions requiring a shareholder vote. Documents sent to shareholders would in-

---

39. *See* Joseph McLaughlin, *The Changing Role of the Securities Analyst in Initial Public Offerings*, 8 Insights 6 (August 1994).

clude the corporation's annual reports, its quarterly reports, any follow-up reports on its annual meeting, and shareholder letters and press releases.

Care should be taken to tailor the document request to the specific circumstances of the offering. Nothing can get an offering off to a worse start than sending the issuer a lengthy request for documents that has clearly been generated by a word processor without the application of common sense or an appreciation of the difficulties and cost that the issuer might experience in attempting to comply with the request.

The investment bankers—or, in some cases, their counsel—should review the basic documents furnished by the issuer in response to the document request. In reviewing annual and quarterly reports, particular attention should be directed to the president's letter. If there is a recent private placement memorandum or a written rating agency presentation, this too should be reviewed.

In appropriate cases, a NEXIS or other electronic data base search should be performed to verify product announcements, litigation developments, regulatory proceedings or even personnel changes.

Underwriters' counsel should review all indentures and loan agreements to which the issuer or any subsidiary is a party, primarily for the purpose of evaluating any restrictive covenants and analyzing the impact that they may have upon the corporation's operations and the prospective financing.

- *Preliminary Analysis and List of Questions*

After completing a study of the industry and a review of the corporation's basic documents, the investment bankers should prepare an analysis of the corporation in relation to others in its industry. They should determine how the issuer compares with similar corporations in terms of basic financial ratios, such as debt to equity, current liabilities to current assets, earnings to fixed charges, return on equity, and common stock price to earnings per share.

At this point, it may be helpful to prepare a written memorandum setting forth questions to be asked of management and areas to be explored in greater depth. Although a formal check-list to be used for all registered offerings may create more problems than benefits, a list of questions tailored to a specific issuer prepared following an initial review of documents and prior to in-depth discussions with management can be helpful in the due diligence process.

• *Review of Registration Statement*

After receiving the first draft of the registration statement, the investment bankers and underwriters' counsel should read it carefully for content, should read it a second time against the items of the applicable form and Regulation S-K (to the extent covered by the applicable form), and should note any questions or suggestions for improved disclosure. They should then meet with those officers of the corporation responsible for the registration statement, the corporation's counsel, and a representative of the certified public accountants for the purpose of reviewing the registration statement on a line-by-line basis. As the issuer's accounting firm will have general knowledge of all aspects of the issuer's business, not only its financial reporting, it can be helpful for a representative of the accountants to be present at all review sessions, not just those relating to the financial statements.

In the review process, the disclosure in the registration statement will be discussed in depth, and invariably the registration statement will be revised in an effort to improve upon the disclosure. The give-and-take over a period of days or weeks in working on a registration statement often is the most effective means for performing due diligence and assuring full and accurate disclosure. Probing inquiry by the investment bankers will often lead management to take a fresh look at the corporation's business, to recall items of disclosure that may have been overlooked, to focus on problem areas, and to revise those portions of the registration statement that can be improved upon. The time spent in perfecting a rider on a key point often can be the most important time spent in the entire registration process. During the course of the review, officers who were previously interviewed may be called upon again to concentrate on particular points discussed in the registration statement.

In preparing a registration statement, it is not sufficient to follow to the letter the requirements of the applicable form. Rather, Rule 408 under the 1933 Act states:

> In addition to the information expressly required to be included in a registration statement, there shall be added such further material information, if any, as may be necessary to make the required statements, in the light of the circumstances under which they are made, not misleading.

The most difficult part of the disclosure process is eliciting and presenting that additional information.

The prospectus should be written so as to be comprehensible to the average investor. The information should be presented in clear, understandable prose. The investment banker should take to heart the following criticism leveled by Judge Weinstein against prospectuses in general:

> In at least some instances, what has developed in lieu of the open disclosure envisioned by the Congress is a literary art form calculated to communicate as little of the essential information as possible while exuding an air of total candor. Masters of this medium utilize turgid prose to enshroud the occasional critical revelation in a morass of dull, and—to all but the sophisticates—useless financial and historical data. In the face of such obfuscatory tactics the common or even the moderately well informed investor is almost as much at the mercy of the issuer as was his pre-SEC parent. He cannot by reading the prospectus discern the merit of the offering.[40]

Care should be taken that the due diligence record not leave any questions unresolved. One of the authors vividly recalls receiving, as a young lawyer, a kick in the foot from a senior partner at a review and revision session for a registration state-

---

40. 332 F. Supp. at 565. See the discussion in Chapter 3 of "plain English."

ment. The author had prepared diligently for the session, including inserting handwritten comments and questions in the margin of the draft of the document. The session went well, with the issuer's management responding candidly to the comments and questions, until the young lawyer failed to record a response. The senior partner's action was well-taken: if a question is important enough to be written down, the record should show that the question was answered. Anything else might be interpreted, years later and with the benefit of hindsight, as casual or reckless indifference to the completion or accuracy of the document.[41]

When the participants in the offering are relatively satisfied with a draft of the registration statement, it should be distributed to all directors and key officers. The investment bankers should satisfy themselves that the corporation has established adequate procedures for collecting and evaluating comments on the document from those persons to whom it has been furnished. This is particularly important for "soft" portions of the document, such as Management's Discussion and Analysis (MD&A) and any forward-looking statements that are included in the registration statement. See Chapter 3.

• *Accounting Matters*

To paraphrase Clemenceau, accounting matters are too important to be left to the accountants. As noted above, Section 11 does not expressly require a "reasonable investigation" as to "expertized" material such as certified financial statements. This does not mean, however, that an underwriter should not understand the issuer's financial statements and the choices that were made in preparing them.

> – First of all, even as to expertized material, Section 11(b)(3)(C) still requires an underwriter to show that it had "no reasonable ground to believe" that the ma-

---

41. *See, e.g., Kronfeld v. Trans World Airlines, Inc.*, 832 F.2d 726, 736 (2d Cir. 1987) (investment banking associate's notes held to evidence that reorganization was a "live" option and to raise issues of fact sufficient to reverse grant of summary judgment).

terial was false or misleading. Moreover, as noted above, Section 12(a)(2) contains no express expertization defense.

– Second, interim financial statements and other unaudited financial information are not expertized. It is difficult to understand interim financial statements without close examination of the audited financial statements. Any deficiencies in the audited financial statements are likely to render misleading at least some of the disclosure in the prospectus outside the financial statements.

– Third, financial statement analysis plays a major role in an underwriter's decision to underwrite an issuer's securities in the first place, in marketing the securities to customers and in comparing the issuer's performance to the performance of other companies for pricing purposes. An underwriter will not want to risk embarrassment in these areas because of a failure to have understood the issuer's accounting.

Due diligence in regard to the issuer's financial statements should therefore be planned as carefully as due diligence in regard to any other part of an offering document. For example, the following matters might be considered as part of the planning process:

– How does the issuer's choice of accounting principles compare to that of other companies in the same industry? Have there been accounting failures in the industry? Has the industry's accounting come under criticism from the SEC, regulators or others?

– Has the issuer made a recent significant change in accounting policy or principles? Is the change in the direction of greater or lesser clarity?

– Does the issuer's explanation of its accounting principles explain adequately the nature of the choices that should be highlighted?

- Are there new FASB standards now or soon to be applicable to the issuer? What is the issuer's plan for implementing the new standards? What effect will implementation have on financial condition and results? Does the issuer's industry present issues that are the subject of study by the Emerging Issues Task Force of the FASB?

- Even if the issuer's financial statements meet the requirements of U.S. gaap, are there additional SEC requirements that need to be considered?

The audited financial statements should be carefully reviewed in advance for inconsistencies, obscurities, unexplained fluctuations from period to period, and whether or not additional matters should be discussed in the MD&A. This review should be followed by a meeting among the issuer's accounting personnel, the outside auditors, counsel and the underwriters in which the financial statements are reviewed on a line-by-line basis with particular attention to the explanations given in the MD&A for period-to-period variations and the existence of undisclosed "trends, demands, commitments, events or uncertainties."

• *Forward-Looking Statements*

Provisions of the Private Securities Litigation Reform Act of 1995 (the "Reform Act") protect certain forward-looking statements by public companies, so long as the statements are accompanied by "meaningful cautionary statements identifying important factors that could cause actual results to differ materially from those in the forward-looking statement."

It remains to be seen whether issuers will be more willing under the Reform Act than under the SEC's limited safe harbor rules to make forward-looking statements in a 1933 Act registration statement or prospectus. Issuers' traditional reluctance to do so creates a problem for underwriters, since investors (particularly in the case of initial public offerings) generally insist on knowing what the issuer will be likely to earn in the next succeeding fiscal quarters and fiscal year.

By default, earnings projections are generally provided to investors by a lead underwriter. These projections are often made by the lead underwriter's analyst on the basis of discussions with management and sometimes access to management's internal projections. To avoid violations of Section 5 of the 1933 Act, the projections are provided to investors in non-written form at "road show" meetings or in telephone discussions with salespersons.

Apart from selling considerations, underwriters are trying to accomplish two objectives in coming up with an earnings projection to be orally disclosed to investors in connection with the sales effort for an initial public offering:

–   They are trying, of course, to be sure that their own projection is one in which they have a high degree of confidence, and much will depend in this connection on the assumptions that are used in coming up with the projection.

–   They are also trying to increase their comfort level that the issuer's earnings history as disclosed in the prospectus is not misleading because it omits to disclose material facts about earnings reverses in the near future.

To accomplish both objectives, underwriters will make extensive inquiry of management about its earnings projections for succeeding quarters, the next fiscal year and farther out into the future. They will closely examine management's assumptions, particularly with regard to such variables as competition. In this connection, they will ordinarily make use of their analyst's expertise in the issuer's industry to test management's assumptions in the light of problems to which the industry is subject. At least in the case of initial public offerings, the analyst may be permitted access to the issuer's internal projections.

• *Derivatives*

Widely publicized losses on "derivatives" by certain publicly held companies during the mid-1990s led the SEC and the

FASB to review more closely issuers' accounting and disclosure practices in this area.

In October 1995 the SEC announced the commencement and settlement of administrative proceedings against Gibson Greetings and two of its officers for alleged violations of the reporting and books and records requirements of the federal securities laws.[42] In addition, the SEC adopted in early 1997 (Release No. 33-7386 (Jan. 31, 1997)) amendments to Regulation S-X and Regulation S-K that require increased quantitative and qualitative disclosure regarding public companies' use of derivatives.

There should no longer be any doubt that due diligence procedures should be applied to an issuer's activity in derivatives. As in other areas, however, due diligence in respect of derivative activity has two objectives. The first is the immediate objective of verifying that the issuer's disclosure and accounting presentation are in conformity with applicable rules. The second is the more general objective of understanding how the issuer's derivative activity relates to its business. In this connection, the following areas of inquiry should be considered:

- What is the issuer doing and why? Is the activity authorized by board action? (It should not be assumed that there is no risk associated even with "plain vanilla" derivatives.)

- What are the issuer's controls? (Is there someone who is competent and independent to oversee what is being done, including pricing of positions?)

- Who is conducting the activity? (I.e., who are the highly compensated traders responsible for derivative activity? Who supervises them? Do the supervisors understand what the traders are doing?)

- Are compensation schemes geared to reward "bet-the-company" activity? (It should be noted that some regulators may be considering guidelines that will focus on

---

42. *In re Gibson Greetings, Inc.*, SEC Release No. 34-36357 (October 11, 1995).

whether banks have compensation policies that encourage hazardous trading practices.)

- Are credit criteria established to control counterparty risk? Who monitors limits? Who tracks authorization and suitability issues?

- What are the cash requirements under various stress scenarios? Have actual cash movements been consistent with what would be expected to result if the issuer's stated risk tolerance was being observed?

• *Visits to Principal Facilities*

In the case of a manufacturing enterprise, it is advisable to visit one or more of the corporation's principal plants, if for no other reason than to obtain a feel for the corporation's products and the manner in which they are produced. For example, if a corporation manufactures medical and surgical devices, it would be virtually impossible to understand its business without visiting a plant to see how the devices are manufactured and distributed. The extent to which an issuer's facilities should be inspected will depend on the particular circumstances. In all cases, a rule of reason must be applied.

• *Meetings With Principal Officers*

After reviewing the first draft of the registration statement, but prior to engaging in a line-by-line discussion of the document, individual meetings should be held with executive officers responsible for significant aspects of the corporation's business. For example, if the issuer is an electric public utility, it would be appropriate to hold separate meetings with officers responsible for engineering and plant construction, rate matters, finance, fuel purchasing, regulation and governmental relations, environmental matters, employee relations, and other areas. The thrust of these interviews should be to obtain a deeper understanding of the corporation's business and prospects and particularly any problems that it may face in the future. Here a list of questions prepared in advance can be helpful in focusing the discussions. It is appropriate to ask the same questions of different corporate officials in order to evaluate the answers received and to obtain different perspectives on potential problems.

It is essential to have at least one meeting with the corporation's chief executive officer to review the broad aspects of the business and to obtain his personal assessment of the corporation's strengths and weaknesses. This interview should be as far-reaching as the chief executive wishes. The key is to let him talk, not to intrude on his presentation, and to listen very carefully and critically.

• *Legal Review*

Counsel for the underwriters must conduct a legal review of the corporation to enable them to render the opinions required by the underwriting agreement, such as due incorporation and the validity of the issuance of the corporation's stock. The legal review will include a study of the certificate of incorporation and by-laws, indentures, loan agreements and other debt instruments.

Pursuant to the document request, counsel for the underwriters will have received a copy of all litigation letters from company counsel furnished in response to the auditors' request in connection with the most recent audit of the financial statements. Counsel should determine whether any material lawsuits or administrative proceedings have been filed subsequent to the dates of these responses. Counsel should review relevant pleadings in connection with any material litigation of which it is made aware. In some instances, it may be appropriate for counsel to meet with the issuer's outside counsel handling material litigation. Counsel should evaluate the determination of the issuer and its counsel as to which litigation is sufficiently material to be described in the registration statement and should check on the accuracy of any such description.

Counsel should review stock option plans and pension and profit sharing plans, employment contracts, leases, license agreements, and supply and sales agreements, to the extent material, as well as other documents described in or filed as exhibits to the registration statement. Counsel should compare the actual documents with their descriptions in the registration statement. This comparison should extend to documents described in the notes to the financial statements.

• *Minutes*

It is interesting to speculate whether lawyers would still be reviewing minutes in connection with securities transactions if the minutes of BarChris Construction Corp. and its subsidiaries had not played such a large role in the litigation that bears that company's name.[43] Clearly, many companies have streamlined their corporate minutes so that they are limited to the "bare bones" of corporate housekeeping. There are enough exceptions to this rule, however, particularly at the operating division or subsidiary level, to justify continued efforts in this area. In 1992, for example, the SEC brought administrative proceedings against Caterpillar, Inc. for deficiencies in its MD&A reporting; the SEC cited references in Caterpillar's minutes to the earnings of its Brazilian subsidiary as evidence that the MD&A should have been expanded.[44]

A reading of minutes is indispensable to a lawyer's opinion on the corporate aspects of a securities offering. Typically, the minutes read will include those of meetings of the corporation's stockholders, board of directors and executive committee for the past five years, as well as such minutes for each of the corporation's major subsidiaries. Again, the lawyer assigned to read minutes should know what he or she is looking for. An opinion on due incorporation may require a review of the corporate law in effect at the time the corporation was organized. An opinion on validity of stock will require one level of review if all outstanding stock is to be covered and another level if only the securities being offered are to be covered.

---

43. In *BarChris,* counsel was criticized for failing to review the minutes of certain subsidiaries and for failing to insist that the minutes of certain recent meetings be prepared. *See* Riordan and Wragg, *Examination of Corporate Books in Connection with Stock Offerings and Acquisitions,* 18 Bus. Law. 677 (1963).
44. *In re Caterpillar, Inc.,* SEC Release No. 34-30532 (March 31, 1992).

The review of minutes by counsel should be directed not only to matters of a purely legal nature but also to uncovering problems faced by the issuer and an evaluation of the adequacy of the disclosure made in the draft of the registration statement. For example, mention of loans to corporate officers or other related-party transactions may trigger the need for additional disclosure.

• *Officers' and Directors' Questionnaire*

A registration statement on Form S-1 must include information on the corporation's officers and directors, their remuneration and employee benefits, and material transactions that they have had with the corporation. This information need not be included in a registration statement on Form S-2 or Form S-3. It is standard procedure for corporate counsel to prepare an "officers' and directors' questionnaire" addressed to these disclosure requirements, which the corporation's officers and directors are required to complete in connection with the preparation of a Form S-1 registration statement. Counsel for the underwriters should review the completed questionnaires and compare them with the disclosure in the registration statement.

• *Review of Other Documents*

In the course of working on the registration statement at the corporation's headquarters, time should be allocated for the study of documents not previously furnished to the managing underwriters, including those of a confidential nature that the corporation would prefer not to be taken from its offices. These would include such documents as five-year plans, financial forecasts, budgets, periodic reports by operating units to senior management or the board of directors, and at least the most recent management letter prepared by the accountants in connection with their audit. The visit to corporate headquarters to review the registration statement is a convenient occasion to review such bulky documents as product catalogs and operating manuals.

• *Negotiation of Underwriting Agreement and Comfort Letter*

As discussed in Chapter 2, the process of negotiating the representations, warranties and legal opinions required by the underwriting agreement is a further opportunity for performing due diligence. As management focuses upon the representations and opinions requested by the underwriters, problems may be called to mind that should be discussed in detail and possibly disclosed in the registration statement.

In the same way, the negotiation of the accountants' comfort letter often can bring out matters for possible disclosure. The process is somewhat less effective than in the past, however, because of the accounting profession's adoption of standards that have steadily reduced accountants' freedom of action in this area. This is especially regrettable since comfort letters, which are usually thought of as exclusively the underwriters' concern (apart from questions of cost to the issuer), are also commonly addressed to the issuer and often to the issuer's directors. They therefore serve an important verification function that can be valuable to the issuer's directors and officers who have potential Section 11 liability in a registered offering. They can also provide "comfort" to the issuer and its directors and officers in the case of an unregistered offering such as a private placement or Regulation S transaction.

Nevertheless, accountants have been concerned for some time that on certain transactions "no one is doing any due diligence but the accountants." Effective June 30, 1993, therefore, the accounting profession adopted a new Statement on Auditing Standards No. 72 on the subject of comfort letters to underwriters and certain other financial intermediaries. SAS 72 was amended in September 1995 by SAS 76, which was effective on April 30, 1996.

In connection with transactions registered under the 1933 Act, the new standards permit the giving of negative assurance on interim financial information only if the accountants have performed an interim review in accordance with SAS 71, *Interim Financial Information.* Moreover, negative assurance on subsequent changes in specific financial statement items is available under SAS 72 only within 135 days from the end of the most recent period for which the accountants performed an SAS 71 review. (The 135-day cutoff can create problems for foreign issuers who do not normally report on a quarterly basis.)

In addition, a traditional negative assurance comfort letter will be available to a person other than a "named underwriter" in a registered transaction only if a legal opinion is delivered to the effect that the person has a due diligence defense under Section 11 of the Act. This requirement will apply, for example, to agents in medium-term note offerings. If the opinion is not or cannot be delivered, the agent must be content with a "procedures letter" (discussed below) as in the case of unregistered offerings.

In connection with unregistered offerings, the new standards make it more difficult for financial intermediaries to obtain a traditional "negative assurance" comfort letter. In the case of such transactions, underwriters or agents will have to make a choice as to the kind of "comfort" they wish to receive on the transaction.

The first alternative for unregistered transactions, which results in a traditional "negative assurance" comfort letter, requires compliance with the SAS 71 conditions described above. In addition, the recipient must represent in writing that it has conducted a "review process . . . substantially consistent" with the due diligence process that would be performed if the transaction were registered under the Act.[45] It also requires a representation that the requesting person is "knowledgeable with respect to the due diligence review process that would be performed if this placement of securities were being registered pursuant to the Act."

If, for whatever reason, the foregoing representation letter cannot be given, the underwriter or agent in an unregistered transaction is limited to requesting that the accountants follow agreed-upon procedures as to specified elements of financial

---

45. SAS 72 purports to recognize that "what is 'substantially consistent' may vary from situation to situation and may not be the same as that done in a registered offering of the same securities for the same issuer; whether the procedures being, or to be, followed will be 'substantially consistent' will be determined by the requesting party on a case-by-case basis." SAS 72 at 7 note 4.

statement information contained in the offering document and that the accountants report on these procedures in a "procedures letter" issued under SAS 72 (as amended by SAS 76). (An example of such a letter is included in SAS 76 as Example Q.) Such a letter may "not provide negative assurance on the financial statements as a whole, or on any of the specified elements, accounts, or items thereof."

Neither option is completely satisfactory. The SAS 72 representation letter calls for a characterization of due diligence performed on an unregistered transaction for which there may not be a registered analogue (e.g., there are not many SEC-registered offerings of municipal securities or bank securities). Also, the standard of care required under Section 11 is generally thought to be more severe than under Section 12(a)(2) (which applies to public unregistered offerings of non-exempt securities).

The alternative of the "procedures letter" is thought by some investment bankers to provide less in the way of comfort than a negative assurance letter. It also requires a detailed discussion among investment banking personnel, counsel and the issuer's accountants as to which items of information should be the subject of investigation by the accountants and the procedures that the accountants should follow. (The accountants will insist that the underwriters take responsibility for the interpretation of the findings and the adequacy of the procedures, but they are usually prepared to assist in suggesting appropriate procedures.) There is a school of thought to the effect that a procedures letter can be as valuable as a negative assurance letter, particularly because it encourages the kind of inquiry and discussion that is the foundation of the traditional due diligence process.

All this being said, public offerings under modern conditions often leave little time for inquiry and discussion. This is where the new comfort letter standards are particularly useful insofar as they encourage or even mandate SAS 71 reviews. Despite the cost factor, many issuers and their outside directors should and do take comfort from having their independent accountants perform these reviews. Moreover, there is no question but that routine performance of SAS 71 reviews will facilitate the due diligence process when the time comes to offer securities.

SAS 72 makes useful suggestions relating to the timely issuance of the comfort letter. It properly notes the limitations on what accountants can do in respect of interim financial statements and other information that has not been the subject of an audit in accordance with generally accepted auditing standards. It emphasizes the value of an early meeting regarding the subject matter of the letter and the procedures to be followed, as well as the desirability of the accountants' producing a draft letter on which the underwriters may comment.

• *Documentation*

An underwriter has the burden of proving its due diligence defense under Section 11. Reasonable care may have been exercised by the managing underwriter in accordance with the statutory standard, but if a lawsuit is brought on the registration statement and the managing underwriter is unable to prove in court that it did in fact exercise due diligence, its efforts will be wasted.

It is difficult to prove due diligence unless the investigation is adequately documented. Some underwriters take the position that "the best evidence of our due diligence is the prospectus" or other offering document. It is undoubtedly true that a carefully prepared prospectus and the usual closing documents such as officers' certificates, legal opinions and comfort letter constitute persuasive evidence of due diligence. It would be preferable in most situations, however, to have a more complete record of the numerous verification issues that arose during the course of the transaction and the manner in which they were resolved.

There is no single right answer on the documentation that should be retained by the underwriters or their counsel following the closing of a securities transaction. At one time, it was customary for one of the investment bankers working on the financing to be responsible for maintaining a due diligence file. This file would contain a list of documents reviewed and notes taken at visits to corporate facilities, at interviews of corporate officers, and at meetings held to review the registration statement. It might also contain drafts of the prospectus and other

disclosure documents. Above all, however, the person responsible for the file would try to prune it of material that reflected
careless speculation, the presence of unresolved disclosure issues, or comments that contained gratuitous and unflattering
characterizations of the issuer or its management. Such material is sure to be disclosed in the event of litigation, and it can
and has prejudiced the underwriters' legal defense even where
the highest due diligence standards were applied.

For some investment bankers, the "complete file" approach
is still feasible. Given the faster pace of modern securities
transactions, however, the complete file approach requires intense effort and places a severe burden on the person or persons
charged with responsibility for the task. If the file is carelessly
put together, without review of its contents and without verification that all necessary documents (including computer diskettes and e-mail records) are included, the file will work
against the underwriter in the event of litigation.

Some underwriters follow the practice of retaining a complete file only on IPOs and not on other transactions. This is a
defensible practice and is preferable to making *ad hoc* decisions about which transactions should receive the complete file
treatment.

A modified approach to document retention is to rely more
on underwriters' counsel for this purpose. Counsel will already
have prepared and retained summaries of key corporate documents, including minutes. It is usually feasible also to request
counsel to memorialize important aspects of the transaction.
These may include notes of any visits to principal facilities,
meetings with management, and registration statement review
sessions, as well as summaries of discussions at which disclosure or accounting issues were resolved or earnings estimates
were developed.

The Penn Central Affair

One of the most celebrated examples of effective due diligence is the job performed by William J. Williams, Jr., of Sullivan & Cromwell in representing the underwriters of a

proposed $20 million debenture offering in the Euromarket by a subsidiary of the Penn Central Company.

The Penn Central Transportation Co. was formed on February 1, 1968 by the merger of the Pennsylvania and the New York Central railroads. At the time, there were fanfares of optimism. The merged railroad was expected to be more efficient and to produce substantial earnings for its shareholders. Moreover, diversification into real estate development and other areas was seen as the beginning of a major conglomerate enterprise. The price of the stock soared following the merger. Two and one-half years later the railroad was bankrupt, at the time the largest bankruptcy in the nation's history. In September 1970, the SEC commenced an investigation of the Penn Central collapse, and almost two years later it published a report on its findings.[46]

The SEC's report includes the story of how the scrutiny applied and disclosure required by investment bankers and their counsel thwarted the efforts of a failing company to stay afloat by selling its securities to the investing public. Pennsylvania Co. ("Pennco"), a wholly owned subsidiary of the transportation company, had as its principal assets large holdings of the stock of the Norfolk & Western and Wabash railroads and the stock of its "diversification" subsidiaries, Buckeye Pipeline Corporation and two real estate development corporations, Great Southwest Corporation and Arvida Corporation. In December 1969, Pennco had a successful $50 million offering of debentures exchangeable for common stock of Norfolk & Western, its most valuable asset from the standpoint of underlying value and income production. This offering was underwritten by First Boston Corporation and Glore Forgan, Wm. R. Staats, Inc. It was not registered with the SEC because the issuance of Pennco's securities was subject to the jurisdiction of the Interstate Commerce Commission and at the time Section 3(a)(6) of the 1933 Act provided an exemption for such securities.

---

46. *Staff Report of the Securities and Exchange Commission to the Special Subcommittee on Investigations of the House of Representatives Committee on Interstate and Foreign Commerce on the Financial Collapse of the Penn Central Company,* Subcommittee Print (1972).

In February 1970, Jonathan O'Herron, who in November 1969 had become the principal assistant to David Bevan, Penn Central's chief financial officer, contacted N. Gregory Doescher of First Boston to explore the possibility of another debenture offering for Pennco, a $100 million offering that would include warrants to purchase the stock of the Penn Central Company (the holding company for the enterprise that had been organized in October 1969) and Great Southwest Corporation. The SEC observed in its report that the fact that this proposal was made less than two months after Pennco had completed a similar offering "was a clear indication of the serious cash drain and the limited financing possibilities."[47] One complication was encountered immediately. Penn Central had proposed the use of Great Southwest warrants despite the fact that Great Southwest had been forced to abandon a proposed public offering in late 1969 because of the adverse disclosure that would have been required in a registration statement. Penn Central had hoped to avoid the disclosure problem by delaying the registration of the warrants until their proposed exercise date on July 1, 1971. Great Southwest and its outside counsel were not happy with this approach. Even if registration could be delayed, Great Southwest would have a registration commitment hanging over its head, and its affairs were deteriorating. Sullivan & Cromwell had serious legal reservations as to whether registration could be delayed, and ultimately the plan to issue warrants was abandoned.

At the same time as it was pursuing the Pennco debenture offering, the Penn Central management was gearing up for a simultaneous offering in Europe of $20 million of debentures of a newly formed subsidiary, Penn Central International Corp. First Boston and Pierson, Heldring & Pierson of Amsterdam were to be the underwriters. In the course of preparing the offering circular, concerns arose as to the company's cash flow. As described in the SEC's report:

> The preparation of the circulars proceeded routinely, except for the warrant question, until mid-March. At that

---

47. *Id.* at 110.

time, the underwriters began receiving materials, including financial statements, from Penn Central. The underwriters' counsel had indicated that the preparation of financial information should take the SEC standards into consideration even though the circulars would not be filed with the SEC. Counsel had also asked for cash flow information. The information began to alarm the underwriters and counsel for the underwriters. They were also concerned about whether the company was making full disclosure to them. On March 18 Bevan and O'Herron met with the underwriting group working on the domestic issue. Bevan stated that budget projections showed break-even results in third quarter of 1970 and a profit in fourth quarter. The statement was not based on fact. The railroad had already lost as much as was projected for all of 1970 and there was no indication of a reversal. The underwriters knew or should have known that these projections were not founded on fact because Penn Central did not have established forecasts or budgets.[48]

Doescher testified to the SEC that he was surprised that the transportation company had not prepared budgets. The reason given to him was the size of the railroad and the lack of financial controls. Bevan, however, gave the underwriters his own forecast of the railroad's results for 1970. The investment bankers at First Boston were "uncomfortable" about the international offering but decided that they would go along because of its small size. Williams, however, was not satisfied:

At the same time that the underwriters were being appeased by Bevan, William Williams, counsel to the underwriters on the international issue, was becoming increasingly concerned about what he was seeing. He was particularly concerned about the cash situation at Penn Central. In light of the excess of current liabilities, debt due within 5 years and the growing losses, Williams concluded that "there was a risk, perhaps a signifi-

---

48. *Id.* at 112.

cant risk, that some time within the next 1 or 2 years that the railroad could end up in bankruptcy whether they obtained $120 million or not." On March 19 Williams spoke with John Arning, counsel to the underwriters on the domestic offering, and then with the working group members representing the underwriters on the international offering. He told the working group members to bring to the attention of the senior underwriting representatives the adverse information that was being uncovered.

The following day, Williams and other members of the International offering working group were in Philadelphia for a regular session on the circular. As a routine question in light of large writeoffs in 1969 the underwriters asked the Penn Central representatives whether any additional writeoffs were contemplated for 1970. The comptroller, [Charles] Hill, stated that a major writeoff of track was being contemplated. Hill produced a book describing the writeoff plans. He also submitted a draft of the 1969 annual report to shareholders which was to be issued shortly and which contained the following statement:

> *Redesign of System Trackage.*—We have launched a project to streamline our railroad by eliminating 5,800 miles of surplus track from our total of 40,000 miles. This could bring benefits of $90 million of equivalent capital and save $9 million annually in operating expenses.
>
> Efficiency of our remaining plant will be enhanced through disposition of these unneeded freight facilities, seldom-used branch lines, excess yard trackage, and duplicate lines.

Williams indicated that the writeoff against earnings that would result should be disclosed in the circulars and that a press release should be issued no later than the issuance of the circular if such a writeoff was imminent. E.K. Taylor, Penn Central's house counsel who was working on the offering, then suggested that this be taken up with Bevan. After Hill had briefed Bevan, the working group was called to Bevan's office. Bevan was annoyed about this question of disclosure. He stated that much of any writeoff would be covered by the merger reserve and would not have to be reflected in earnings. He said the abandonment plan was subject to constant change. When asked why the abandonment was mentioned in the annual report he said he did not know of it and considered such reference to be stupid. He left the room to consult with Saunders and returned to assure the working group that there were no plans for abandonment "in the foreseeable future." Williams pressed Bevan on the meaning of "foreseeable future." Bevan finally indicated that it would not take place in 1970. Hill agreed with Bevan. [Footnotes omitted.][49]

Williams was troubled by the inconsistency between Bevan's position and the earlier statements made by Hill. With some reluctance, Williams testified to the SEC that it was his impression that Bevan was being evasive. He also testified that he considered the possibility that a writeoff had been contemplated, but that Bevan was denying it to avoid a damaging disclosure in the offering circular. Denial of a proposed course of action is not an unusual reaction by a corporate officer who is seeking to avoid disclosure. Where, as in this case, the contemplated action had gelled sufficiently as to be the subject of a paragraph in a draft annual report, denial can be given little credence. A strong reaction to a problem and the use of terms such as "stupid" in an effort to intimidate are indications of the seriousness of a problem.

The only response to intimidation is increased diligence. Williams, of course, continued to pursue the matter:

Arning was out of the country from March 21 to April 4 during which time Williams covered the work on both the Pennco and the International offering. On March 23, Williams informed Arthur Dean, senior partner of Sullivan & Cromwell, about what he had told the junior members working on the International offering, includ-

---

49. *Id.* at 112-13.

ing the possibility of bankruptcy of the railroad. Dean advised him to be sure the senior underwriting officers were aware of the problem. Williams then contacted the senior members to say that Sullivan & Cromwell would not go along with the International offering unless the underwriters were fully aware of the facts.

Doescher of First Boston then reviewed the International circular and, after speaking with a representative of Pierson, Heldring & Pierson, decided to recommend postponing the International offering because the "disclosures are very severe and [the underwriters] did not want to be in a position of appearing to sell something abroad which could not be sold at home" according to a note made by Doescher. On the 24th and 26th, further conferences involving the underwriters, counsel, accountants, and officers of Penn Central took place. At about this time, Dean decided to call a meeting of the top officers of each of the underwriters to make certain that they understood the facts. The meeting was set for March 31. This was acknowledged to be an extraordinary meeting which resulted in part from Williams' growing concern that "someday this whole thing would blow up, and I wanted to make sure that the firm was focusing on it at the stage where we could do something about it, focusing on it at the highest levels. . . ."

Bevan was growing increasing [*sic*] concerned for his own reasons. Every probe was uncovering embarrassing information that was contradicting his representations, which he knew were false. On March 27 Dean met with Bevan at Bevan's request. Bevan criticized Williams and asked that Williams be removed. In response, Dean noted that Williams belonged to a younger generation and that certain duties were imposed by a case known as *BarChris*. [Footnotes omitted.]⁵⁰

An attempt by a corporate officer to have underwriters' counsel removed from a deal is the ultimate sign of weakness and des-

---

50. *Id.* 114-15.

peration. In this case, Bevan's attempt to remove Williams was a strong indication that Penn Central's financing efforts would ultimately fail. Williams continued to question Bevan and elicited an admission that losses for the first quarter of 1970 would be greater than those for the comparable period in 1969. Bevan also stated that there were assets that could be sold. When Williams referred to the negative pledge clause in the revolving credit agreement, Bevan said that he was negotiating with First National City Bank to get a release of the assets.

On March 28, 1970, Williams wrote a memorandum to Arthur Dean outlining some of his concerns, including the fact that substantially all of the railroad's system lines were mortgaged or otherwise encumbered, the pledge of a substantial portion of Pennco's investments, the extremely large losses from railroad operations, the uncertainty of Penn Central's earnings prospects, the company's accelerated efforts to exchange stock of the Wabash railroad for stock of Norfolk & Western, which would result in a large paper profit in the first quarter, and the fact that Penn Central had arranged financings through a convicted defrauder of the U.S. government. At Williams's request, First Boston contacted First National City Bank to review the credit position of the company. They were informed that the railroad could be in trouble if there was not a turnaround, that the bank had turned down Bevan's request for a bridge loan, which later was made by a group of banks led by Chemical Bank, and that one of the Penn Central subsidiaries, Executive Jet Aviation, was in default on certain of its obligations to the bank.

A meeting of the underwriters and their counsel was held at the offices of Sullivan & Cromwell on March 31, 1970. The leaders of the investment banking firms were there along with Dean and Williams. Williams's March 28 memorandum was distributed to those in attendance. There was a discussion of the possible bankruptcy of the railroad, and, in response to a question from the underwriters, counsel expressed the view that, as a legal matter, Pennco would withstand the bankruptcy of the railroad. This danger most directly affected the international offering, and it was decided that it would be "postponed." It was also decided that work on the Pennco offering would continue on the understanding that Sullivan & Cromwell would include any disclosures needed to protect the underwriters from liability. The underwriters knew that they were running a risk, but they were unwilling to be known in the financial community as the cause of the collapse of the Penn Central.

A major hurdle to the Pennco offering was encountered on April 22, 1970, when Penn Central released its results for the first quarter. The reported loss was greater than Bevan had previously indicated to the underwriters. In the accompanying press release, management attempted to play down the losses, which were lessened on a consolidated level by a $51 million profit on the acceleration of the Wabash exchange and on the transportation company level by the sale of a coal company to Pennco. The significance of the railroad losses was a cause of their being set forth in the offering circular for the first time. On April 27, 1970, the application for the Pennco offering was filed with the Interstate Commerce Commission, and the next day copies of the offering circular were mailed to prospective selling group members, selected institutions and certain publications. The reaction to the offering was poor. On May 15, 1970, Pennco's rating was downgraded from BBB to BB, thereby effectively eliminating the institutional market. Following the announcement of the first quarter loss, there was a run-off of the company's commercial paper. The price ideas floated by the underwriters on May 15, 1970 failed to generate any interest in the issue. On May 21, 1970, the underwriters were told that the company did not intend to go forward with the offering. They were relieved that at last they were off the hook.

A month later, the transportation company filed for bankruptcy. Through the diligence of the lawyers, supported by their investment banking clients, the investing public was spared the losses that would have been sustained if the proposed deals had gone forward. As a result of the Penn Central collapse, Section 3(a)(6) of the 1933 Act was amended to bring railroad securities under the jurisdiction of the SEC.

The Hughes Tool Company Initial Public Offering

There are times when a managing underwriter and its counsel must go to extraordinary lengths to perform the diligence required for a public offering of securities. This was true in the case of the December 7, 1972 initial public offering of common stock of Hughes Tool Company managed by Merrill Lynch, Pierce, Fenner & Smith Incorporated.

The company was formed to acquire the business and assets of the oil tool division of Summa Corporation, which prior to the offering was known as Hughes Tool Company. The company's business had been founded in 1908 to develop, manufacture and distribute a rock drilling bit that had been patented by Howard R. Hughes, Sr. The bit was a significant factor in the development of the oil and gas well drilling industry, and its success had been the foundation of the Hughes family fortune. All of the stock of Summa Corporation was owned by Howard R. Hughes, the billionaire recluse and the son of the founder of the business.

At the time that the offering was conceived, Hughes was ensconced on the seventh floor of the Intercontinental Hotel in Managua, Nicaragua, a country ruled at the time by the dictator Anastasio Somoza. The only persons who had seen Hughes in many years were his Mormon attendants, who maintained a 24-hour-a-day vigil. There were rumors as to Hughes's mental state and appearance. He was said to have an obsessive fear of germs and to have foot-long finger- and toenails.

Merrill Lynch and its counsel had been presented with a document bearing the signature "Howard R. Hughes," acknowledged by two witnesses, Howard Eckersley and James H. Rickard. The document constituted a consent to the transfer of the assets of the oil tool division to the new company and the sale of the shares of the new company to underwriters managed by Merrill Lynch. It contained certain indemnities and appointed Raymond M. Holliday as proxy and attorney-in-fact to carry out all matters relating to the conveyance of the assets and the sale of the securities. Holliday was to be the chairman of the board and chief executive officer of Hughes Tool Company.

Was the document real? No one had any reason to doubt Holliday's integrity, but he had an interest in the transaction and millions of dollars were at stake. No one was absolutely sure that Hughes was alive (there had been rumors of his death). If he was alive, was he competent to act? A few months before, a purported autobiography of Howard Hughes, which actually turned out to be authored by one Clifford Irving, had been exposed as a fraud to the great embarrassment of the distinguished publishing house that had accepted it for publication. Merrill Lynch and its counsel would face even worse embarrassment, to say nothing of monetary exposure, if they participated in an initial public offering of shares worth close to $150 million and it turned out that the transaction had not been authorized by the sole owner of the business.

J. Courtney Ivey, the senior partner of Brown, Wood, Fuller, Caldwell & Ivey, the firm acting as underwriters' counsel, had met Howard Hughes on two previous occasions. He felt certain that he would know Hughes if he saw him again. Julius H. ("Dooley") Sedlmayr, the head of investment banking at Merrill Lynch, had spoken by telephone with Hughes on at least one occasion. The two men determined that the only way that the deal would be done was for them to fly to Nicaragua, meet with Hughes, and actually see him sign a certificate confirming the instrument authorizing the transaction. This, of course, was strongly resisted by Hughes's people. Mr. Hughes simply did not see outsiders. There was no way that he would consent to such a meeting. Ivey and Sedlmayr persisted. There was too much at stake. This was a matter that went to the very heart of the deal. If they did not meet with Howard Hughes, there would be no public offering managed by Merrill Lynch.

Time passed, and there was no affirmative response. The deal was in danger of cratering. Finally, Ivey and Sedlmayr received word that Hughes would see them. They were to go to Nicaragua on September 22, 1972. Ivey related the story of the trip in a sworn statement prepared shortly after his return:

> Re: Discussion with Howard R. Hughes on Monday morning, September 25, 1972 at the Intercontinental Hotel, Managua, Nicaragua
>
> On Friday, September 22, Mr. Julius H. Sedlmayr, Group Vice President of Merrill Lynch, and I flew to Managua, Nicaragua, for the purpose of seeing Mr. Howard R. Hughes and obtaining from him a signed certificate regarding the power of attorney which he had

executed on Saturday, September 16. We arrived at the Intercontinental Hotel in Managua around 6:30 P.M. The next day, Saturday, September 23, Mr. Raymond Holliday, Executive Vice President of Hughes Tool Company, and Mr. Milton H. West, Jr., a partner in the firm of Andrews, Kurth, Campbell & Jones, of Houston, Texas, counsel for Hughes Tool Company, arrived in Managua. We talked to them Saturday morning and Raymond Holliday thought our appointment with Mr. Hughes would be around 8:00 P.M. Sunday evening, September 24. Around lunch time on Sunday, Mr. Holliday advised that the meeting had been postponed until around 11:00 P.M.

After dinner on Sunday, the four of us went to Mr. Holliday's room on the third floor of the hotel and we waited there. During the evening Mr. Holliday called Mr. Hughes' quarters for a progress report and we got little encouragement until around 3:30 A.M., when Mr. Holliday was advised that the meeting would take place in an hour or an hour and a half. At this point, Mr. Sedlmayr and I returned to our respective rooms and made preparations for leaving on the 6:45 A.M. plane for New York.

A little after 5:00 A.M., Mr. Holliday called Mr. Sedlmayr's room and advised us to meet on the seventh floor at the elevator doors. We then proceeded to the seventh floor, met Messrs. Holliday and West and then the four of us went into the living room of Mr. Hughes' quarters. We sat there for five or ten minutes. Mr. Clarence A. Waldron and Mr. George A. Francom were in and out of the room, and around 5:40 A.M., Mr. Waldron advised us Mr. Hughes was ready to see Mr. Sedlmayr and myself. We went into another room and there we were introduced to Mr. Hughes. Mr. Hughes was seated in a chair with a footrest. He wore a beard from ear to ear and a mustache. He had a blanket spread over him up to his waist and was bare from waist up except a light jacket was draped around his shoulders. Mr. Waldron sat on Mr. Hughes' right and Mr. Francom on his left. Mr. Sedlmayr and I sat in two straight armchairs directly in front of Mr. Hughes and only about two or three feet away from him.

Mr. Hughes stated that he thought he had talked to Mr. Sedlmayr before on the telephone, which Mr. Sedlmayr confirmed, and Mr. Sedlmayr also stated that I had seen Mr. Hughes some years ago with Mr. Maury Bent. I proceeded to tell Mr. Hughes the occasion of our previous visit, but was not able to finish because he was not able to hear me. He was then handed his hearing aid and proceeded to manipulate the batteries, and finally was given a new set of batteries by Mr. Waldron and inserted them in the hearing aid.

Mr. Hughes recalled the TWA stock financing in 1966 and stated he was very pleased with it; that he was glad that the stock went up after the offering, and, in accordance with the advice given him many years before by Mr. Randolph Hearst, Sr., a very good friend of his, he did not wish to get the last dollar but would let someone else make that. Mr. Sedlmayr reminded Mr. Hughes that Merrill Lynch had had two deals with him—referring to the approximately $100,000,000 debenture issue with warrants of TWA which were publicly offered in 1963. Mr. Hughes told Mr. Sedlmayr that he hoped Merrill Lynch would be able to get him a good price, but that he was not satisfied with any of the figures which had been given him to date. In the course of this discussion, Mr. Hughes stated that of course this was not the purpose of the meeting, that is, the fixing of the price for the stock of the Tool Company. Mr. Sedlmayr advised Mr. Hughes that Merrill Lynch would get the best price it possibly could. Mr. Hughes further stated that if he were Merrill Lynch, he would sell the stock to customers at the most favorable price he could get for the customers because Mr. Hughes was getting along and very probably there would be no more deals to go to Merrill Lynch from Mr. Hughes. Mr. Sedlmayr advised him that was not the way Merrill Lynch operated, that Merrill Lynch would get the best price it could that would be fair to both Mr. Hughes and Merrill

Lynch's customers. Mr. Hughes also told Mr. Sedlmayr that he wanted him to go back and tell Mr. [Winthrop R.] Smith and others that he wanted a good price.

In the course of our discussion, Mr. Hughes wanted to know if Mr. Sedlmayr and I had missed our plane and stated that if we had, he would have one sent down from Miami to take us back.

He reminisced about his acquisition of the Tool Company through inheritance and purchase of parts of the stock from other relatives who had also inherited from Mr. Hughes' father. He further reminisced about his father's participation in World War I and described a tool that his father had invented to bore a hole under the ground parallel to the surface that could be used to place bombs near the enemy's trenches and then detonated. There was also some discussion about an Army colonel who came to work for Hughes Tool during his father's life and later took over the operations on his father's death. Mr. Hughes stated that the Army colonel was let go as a result of claims of fraud made by Mr. Noah Dietrich. I gather that Mr. Dietrich made a federal case of the incident but Mr. Hughes stated that it was nothing more than taking a company truck to haul manure to his farm. He stated that it was a trivial matter—like a man using the company car to go to the movies instead of his own car. There was also some by-play about the handwriting experts in the recent Irving debacle.

During the discussions Mr. Hughes told us of a new hearing aid that a doctor had given him and he described it in some detail. He stated that the entire instrument, including the batteries, was inserted in the ear and it was really a good instrument but he continued to use his old one. He further stated that he thought the scientists at Hughes Aircraft would be able to design a hearing aid that would be the best ever. I am not sure that he stated that Hughes Aircraft was at the present time working on such a device, but I received the impression that they were or would be.

During the many discussions with Mr. Raymond Holliday, we were told a good deal about the eight or nine people that customarily worked in Mr. Hughes' quarters. I think all are Mormons and are married. They shuttle back and forth from their homes in Salt Lake or Los Angeles on a fixed schedule basis—so many days off and so many days on. At least one and possibly two men are present on a 24 hour day, three eight hour shifts. At one point Mr. Holliday stated that Clarence Waldron had been with Mr. Hughes for approximately fifteen years and I gather that all of them had been with him for several years.

After testing two pens, Mr. Hughes picked one and in our presence and in the presence of Mr. Waldron and Mr. Francom, signed the certificate we had brought with us to Managua, and Mr. Waldron and Mr. Francom witnessed the signature. A xerox copy of the signed certificate is attached hereto.

The foregoing is my best present recollection of the conference with Mr. Hughes, although the items mentioned above probably did not occur in the order given.

In 1954 in connection with the possible sale of approximately 25% of the stock of the Hughes Tool Company, Mr. Winthrop Smith, Mr. George Leness and Mr. Maury Bent and I had about a two hour conference with Mr. Hughes and Mr. Tom Slack, his attorney at the time and a former partner of Andrews, Kurth, Campbell & Jones, at the Beverly Hills Hotel. I also saw Mr. Hughes for about fifteen minutes with Messrs. Smith, Leness and Bent outside the Beverly Wilshire Hotel before we departed for the airport for our return trip to New York. The conference in 1954 with Mr. Hughes was unusual even at that time in that few people, other than his personal staff, ever saw him. Because of the unusual nature of the conference, the events that occurred before, during and after the conference were inscribed on my memory much more than a run of the mill business conference would be. Also, I have described many times since 1954 the things that occurred and this has helped in my recollections of Mr. Hughes.

Prior to going to Los Angeles, Mr. Ralph L. Jones, one of my partners, and I spent at least a week in Houston working on a registration statement. Off and on during the 1960s I spent considerable time in California regarding a possible underwriting of stock of Hughes Aircraft and later in New York on the two underwritings of TWA securities. This involved a great deal of contact with trusted representatives of Mr. Hughes and as a result I learned a good deal about Mr. Hughes and his financial operations.

Although the previous conference with Mr. Hughes took place approximately eighteen years ago, because of the unusual nature of the conference as mentioned above, and reinforced by numerous pictures that I have seen over a considerable period of time, particularly in the recent past, and, notwithstanding the addition of a beard, the man we had our discussions with on September 25 did resemble the Mr. Hughes I saw in 1954.

From these recollections and our discussions summarized above, together with knowledge gained over the years, I am convinced that the man with whom we talked and who signed the certificate was the real Howard R. Hughes. I was also convinced that Mr. Hughes was capable of making decisions and mentally competent.

It was difficult to get away from Mr. Hughes after he had signed the certificate and I believe if time had permitted he would have talked to us for two or three hours—he was in a talking mood. As we left, Mr. Hughes shook hands with each of us with a firm hand grip.

We left Mr. Hughes' rooms around 6:15 A.M. and after picking up our baggage on the eighth floor left for the airport. We caught the 6:45 A.M. plane back to New York.

Mr. Ivey's statement failed to relate the fact that he and Mr. Sedlmayr each ordered a double martini before breakfast on the return flight to New York.

Chapter 6

NASD REGULATIONS

Several important aspects of the underwriting process are regulated by the National Association of Securities Dealers, Inc. ("NASD"). The NASD is a "national securities association" registered as such with the SEC pursuant to Section 15A of the 1934 Act. It is the only association so registered. Section 15A(a)(6) requires its rules to be designed, among other things, "to promote just and equitable principles of trade."

The NASD is a "self-regulatory organization" or "SRO" within the meaning of Section 3(a)(26) of the 1934 Act, as are the national securities exchanges. As such, it is subject to supervision by the SEC pursuant to Section 19 of the 1934 Act. Pursuant to Section 19(b)(1) and Rule 19b-4 thereunder, the NASD and other SROs must file with the SEC for approval any proposed rule or any proposed amendment to an existing rule.

More than 5,400 securities firms were members of the NASD as of the end of 1995.[1] Indeed, Section 15(b)(8) of the 1934 Act requires every broker or dealer registered with the SEC under Section 15 (other than one that deals exclusively in commercial paper, bankers' acceptances or commercial bills)

---

1. *NASD 1995 Annual Report* at 3.

to be a member of the NASD unless it effects transactions in securities solely on a national securities exchange of which it is a member. Because of this requirement and the limitation imposed by the NASD on dealings between members and non-members—a limitation that is expressly authorized by Section 15A(e)(1) of the 1934 Act—virtually every investment banking firm in the United States is a member of the NASD and as such is subject to its regulation.

In addition to regulating its member firms, the NASD also operates "The Nasdaq Stock Market"—the largest electronic, screen-based equity market in the world ("Nasdaq" or "NASDAQ"). In 1994, a Department of Justice investigation of NASD market makers and an SEC investigation of the NASD's enforcement of Nasdaq trading rules led to the appointment of a seven-member committee under the leadership of former U.S. Senator Warren Rudman to review NASD governance and oversight. The committee recommended that the NASD's relationship with Nasdaq be restructured so as to put substantial "daylight" between the membership association and the market.

Accordingly, the NASD was reorganized in early 1996 as a parent company with two operating subsidiaries.[2] One of the subsidiaries operates Nasdaq. The other—NASD Regulation, Inc. ("NASDR")—has the primary authority to regulate NASD member firms. This authority includes the development and administration of the NASD Rules of Fair Practice (subsequently redesignated as "Conduct Rules"), membership rules and operational requirements for member firms. NASDR also has examination and investigation responsibility for member firms and their "associated persons" as well as enforcement and disciplinary authority.

Provision is made in the NASD by-laws to assure representation of the 13 districts into which the NASD is divided for administrative purposes. The NASD functions through district committees and various standing committees, including district and national Business Conduct Committees. Another standing committee, the Committee on Corporate Financing, has primary responsibility for regulating underwriting practices.

---

2. *See* NASD *Notice to Members* 95–101 (December 11, 1995).

The rules of the NASD have their roots in the Investment Bankers Code adopted in 1932 by the investment banking industry pursuant to the National Industrial Recovery Act ("NIRA"). The code was amended in 1934 to incorporate certain rules of fair practice. When NIRA was declared unconstitutional in 1935,[3] the securities industry continued on a voluntary basis to meet the standards of the code under the direction of the Investment Bankers Conference Committee, which later became the Investment Bankers Conference, Inc. (the "IBCI"). Without legislative authority, however, the enforcement of self-regulation proved to be difficult. Accordingly, in 1938, Congress adopted the Maloney Act, named for its sponsor, Senator Francis T. Maloney of Connecticut, which amended the 1934 Act by adding Section 15A to provide for regulation of the over-the-counter market by national securities associations registered with the SEC.[4] The statutory objective was to establish a mechanism to regulate brokers and dealers operating in the over-the-counter market comparable to that provided by the national securities exchanges.[5] The Congressional reports on the bill pointed out that "the primary operations of the great underwriting houses take place over the counter" and that, accordingly, the over-the-counter market provided the principal channel by which savings flowed into new financing.

The Maloney Act was designed, among other things, "to cope with those methods of doing business which, while technically outside the area of definite illegality, are nevertheless unfair both to customer and to decent competitor, and are seriously damaging to the mechanism of the free and open market."[6] The underlying principle was "cooperative regulation" performed by representative organizations of investment bankers, dealers and brokers, with the Federal government, acting through the SEC, exercising appropriate supervision and exercising supplementary powers of direct regulation.[7]

---

3. *A.L.A. Schecter Poultry Corp. v. U.S.*, 295 U.S. 495 (1935).

4. Pub. L. No. 719, 75th Cong., 3d Sess. (June 25, 1938). *See* Comment, *Over-the-Counter Trading and The Maloney Act,* 48 Yale L.J. 633 (1939).

5. S. Rep. No. 1455, 75th Cong., 3d Sess. 1 (1938).

6. *Id.* at 3.

7. *Id.* at 4–5.

After the adoption of the Maloney Act, the IBCI appointed a drafting committee to draw up the necessary certificate of incorporation and to prepare by-laws, rules of fair practice and a code of procedures. After approval by the IBCI membership, the initial registration statement of the NASD, as successor to the IBCI, was filed with the SEC in July 1939 and approved the following month.[8]

As noted above, underwriting activities in the United States are not conducted through the facilities of the stock exchanges. Nor, for that matter, are they conducted through Nasdaq. Rather, securities that are the subject of registered underwritten public offerings are sold directly to customers of the underwriters and the dealers participating in the distribution. Thus, to the extent that underwriting practices are subject to industry self-regulation, that regulation is imposed and administered by the NASD as a regulator of its member firms rather than by the exchanges or by the NASD in its capacity as the operator of the Nasdaq market.

Stock exchange rules have little impact on investment banking as such. In the case of a secondary offering of a listed security, however, the exchange's restrictions on "off-board trading" may be applicable. The principal exchanges have rules (e.g., NYSE Rule 393) that permit the managing underwriter to apply for permission to conduct an off-board secondary distribution on the basis, among other things, that the distribution is too large to be absorbed by the regular auction process. As a practical matter, the exchanges are seldom in a position to quarrel with the managing underwriter's judgment in this regard.

Another exchange requirement applicable to public offerings is that a company with stock listed on an exchange must list any additional shares that it issues that are of the same class.

---

8. *Report of National Association of Securities Dealers, Inc.* to the *Special Subcommittee on Legislative Oversight of the Interstate and Foreign Commerce Committee of the House of Representatives: History of National Association of Securities Dealers, Inc., Its Activities, Membership Data, Sanctions Imposed, Members Expelled, Financial Statements, Liaison and Supervision by SEC From 1936 to November 30, 1958,* Subcommittee Reprint, 85th Cong., 2d Sess. (1959).

In addition, there are exchange requirements of a technical nature applicable to rights offerings (see Chapter 13).

The fact that the NASD is a self-regulatory organization does not mean that it is inclined to go easy on its members. Support for this proposition can easily by obtained by a casual glance at the NASD's monthly published list of disciplinary proceedings or at the annual surveys of SRO disciplinary practices and proceedings published by the ABA's Section of Litigation. Moreover, a majority of the new NASD parent company's board and of the new NASDR subsidiary's board is from outside the industry. NASDR has announced plans to create a national enforcement unit and an Office of Professional Hearings Officers that will provide professional hearing officers in all disciplinary cases. In late 1996, NASDR increased its budget by $43 million and approved the hiring of 130 new enforcement and examination officials. It would be surprising, to put it mildly, if NASDR's staff proves to be any less independent or aggressive than the NASD's former regulatory and surveillance staff.

The NASD has the statutory authority to enforce its regulations through disciplinary proceedings against its members, and it does not hesitate to use its enforcement powers in appropriate cases.[9] In 1988, the SEC approved the elimination of the previous $15,000 ceiling on disciplinary fines,[10] and the NASD has since aggressively pursued monetary fines as a means of tailoring sanctions to fit the facts and circumstances of individual cases. The NASD has published its *NASD Sanction Guidelines* since 1993 in order to "achieve greater consistency, uniformity and fairness when imposing sanctions." The most recent edition, published in April 1996, emphasizes disgorgement, restitution and (in some cases) rescission of transactions.[11] Sanctions can also include suspensions of member

---

9. *See* T. Grant Callery & Anne H. Wright, *NASD Disciplinary Proceedings—Recent Developments*, 48 Bus. Law. 791 (1993).

10. SEC Rel. No. 34-25999 (August 6, 1988).

11. The authors have some doubt whether the SEC or the SROs have the authority to obtain disgorgement, restitution or rescission in all cases where they claim the ability to do so. For example, Congress provided an

firms or their employees for shorter or longer periods as well as, in extreme cases, expulsion from the NASD. Disciplinary actions by the NASD are subject to review by the SEC.[12]

The NASD's Rules of Fair Practice were reorganized in 1996 as part of an overall reorganization of the NASD *Manual*. The Rules of Fair Practice now form part of the NASD's "Conduct Rules." Rule 2110 (formerly Article III, Section 1) still establishes the basic overriding principle: "A member, in the conduct of his business, shall observe high standards of commercial honor and just and equitable principles of trade."[13] This broad and sweeping statement is implemented by a number of rules and interpretations adopted by the Board of Governors.

Rule 2710 provides for NASD review of underwriting terms and arrangements and is concerned primarily with the fairness of such terms and arrangements. It requires that a filing be made in connection with most public offerings of securities to enable the Corporate Financing Department of the NASD to determine that the proposed underwriting compensation and other arrangements are not unfair or unreasonable.

An interpretation of Rule 2110—"IM-2110-1"—relates to "free-riding and withholding." It is based on the premise that NASD members have an obligation to make a bona fide public distribution at the public offering price of securities that are part of a "hot issue."

Rules 2730, 2740 and 2750—the so-called *Papilsky* rules— are designed to prevent rebates of selling concessions in fixed-price offerings. Rule 2420 prohibits transactions with non-

---

express remedy for the purchaser of unregistered securities and conditioned the remedy on compliance with a short statute of limitations. This suggests that neither the SEC nor an SRO should be able to obtain disgorgement, restitution or rescission where the purchaser has failed to take action under the available express remedy.

12. *See* Barnes, *NASD Disciplinary Proceedings,* 21 Rev. Sec. & Com. Reg. 161 (1988).

13. The NASD construes this "fundamental rule of ethical practice" in broad fashion. For example, it interprets the rule to prohibit "abusive communications" with customers or with employees of other broker-dealers. *See* Notice to Members 96-44 (July 1996).

member broker-dealers (other than certain foreign dealers) except on the same terms accorded to the general public.

Finally, Rule 2720 (formerly Schedule E to the NASD's by-laws) regulates the participation by a member in a public offering of securities issued by that member or its affiliates *or* where the member has a "conflict of interest" with respect to the offering (defined as beneficial ownership by the member and certain related persons of more than 10% of specified securities of the issuer). Certain procedures under this rule are also applicable (a) where a member or related person is to receive more than 10% of the proceeds of an offering and (b) where a member participates in an IPO and where it or related persons own securities of the issuer at the time of the IPO and wish to dispose of any of them as part of the IPO or within 90 days thereafter.

These are the principal NASD regulations that must be contended with in connection with public offerings of securities, other than "exempted securities" (as defined in Section 3(a)(12) of the 1934 Act).[14] As they are rules that govern the conduct of the underwriters and selected dealers, rather than provisions relating to the overall transaction, the responsibility for assuring compliance rests with the managing underwriter assisted by underwriters' counsel (and, increasingly, by the underwriter's in-house legal or "special execution" staff). It is the job of underwriters' counsel to assure that the requisite filings are made, that the underwriting documents contain the necessary provisions to assure compliance, and that the underwriters are aware of their responsibilities as members of the NASD.

Review of Corporate Financing

Rule 2710, the "Corporate Financing Rule," is based on the premise that it would be contrary to high standards of commercial honor and just and equitable principles of trade for an NASD member to participate in the distribution of securities if the underwriting or other arrangements are unfair or unreason-

---

14. Rule 2810 regulates public offerings of direct participation programs, i.e., limited partnerships and similar entities that provide for flow-through tax consequences.

able.[15] Full disclosure of all underwriting compensation must be made in the section of the offering document dealing with underwriting arrangements.[16]

The NASD first became concerned with unfair underwriting arrangements in the wake of the hot issue market that existed from 1959 through 1961. In late 1961, it established a standing committee on underwriting arrangements to review offerings of securities of unseasoned companies to determine whether the underwriting arrangements were fair and consistent with just and equitable principles of trade.[17] This committee is now known as the Committee on Corporate Financing. In January 1962, the NASD requested that members file offering documents with it at the same time as they were filed with the SEC.[18] The corporate financing interpretation was adopted in 1970[19] and became a rule in 1992.[20]

- *Filing Requirements*

Unless a public offering is specifically exempted from the provisions of the interpretation, specified documents and information must be filed with the NASD to enable the staff of the Corporate Financing Department to pass upon the fairness and reasonableness of the underwriting arrangements. An NASD filing may be required even where there is an exemption from registration under the 1933 Act. Public offerings by banks and intrastate offerings are examples.

In the case of an underwritten issue, the managing underwriter has the responsibility to assure that the filing is made. The filing will take the form of a letter prepared by counsel for the underwriters to the NASD's Corporate Financing Department in Rockville, Maryland, enclosing five copies of the reg-

---

15. Underwriting compensation also is regulated by certain state securities laws, although the significance of such laws in this respect has diminished since the passage of the Improvements Act. *See* Chapter 3.

16. This disclosure also is required by Item 508(e) of Regulation S-K.

17. NASD Notice to Members (December 26, 1961).

18. NASD Notice to Members (January 11, 1962).

19. NASD Notice to Members (March 10, 1970).

20. NASD Notice to Members 92-28 (May 1992).

istration statement (or other offering document) and three copies of the underwriting documents and any other documents describing the underwriting or other arrangements relating to the distribution. Amended and final copies of the registration statement and underwriting documents must also be filed. All documents must be filed with the NASD not later than one business day after they are filed with the SEC or any other regulatory authority or, if there is no filing with the SEC or any other regulatory body, at least 15 business days prior to the anticipated offering date. The filing fee is $500 plus .01% of the gross dollar amount of the offering, not to exceed a fee of $30,500.[21]

The letter constituting the original filing with the NASD must set forth an estimate of the maximum public offering price and the maximum underwriting discount or commission, information as to any arrangement for the reimbursement of underwriters' expenses, including the fees and disbursements of underwriters' counsel, the maximum financial consulting and/or advisory fees to the underwriter and related persons, maximum finder's fees, and a statement of any other type and amount of compensation that may accrue to the underwriters and related persons. For purposes of the rule, the term "underwriter and related person" is deemed to include "underwriters, underwriter's counsel, financial consultants and advisors, finders, members of the selling or distribution group, any member participating in the public offering, and any and all other persons associated with or related to *and members of the immediate family of* any of the aforementioned persons" (emphasis added).[22] The term "financial consultants and advisors"

---

21. Rule 2710(b)(10).

22. A "person associated with a member" or an "associated person of a member" means

> every sole proprietor, partner, officer, director, or branch manager of any member, or any natural person occupying a similar status or performing similar functions, or any natural person engaged in the investment banking or securities business who is directly or indirectly controlling or controlled by such member. . . .

NASD By-laws, Article I(q).

should be read to mean financial consultants and advisors to the underwriters, rather than to the issuer.

The letter must identify and provide information regarding any association or affiliation between any NASD member and any officer, director or 5% securityholder of the issuer (*any* securityholder in the case of IPOs). In the case of securities ownership, the letter should identify the amount of securities owned and the acquisition date and price. The letter must also set forth a "detailed explanation" of any arrangements during the preceding 12 months involving the issuer's transfer to the underwriter and related persons of any "items of value" or warrants, options or other securities. The rule sets forth factors to be considered in establishing whether items of value or securities were acquired in connection with the distribution. The letter should address these factors as well as other potential problems relating to the fairness of the underwriting arrangements. Frank discussion of problem areas can expedite their resolution.

Information necessary for the filing under the Corporate Financing Rule will be obtained by underwriters' counsel from questionnaires completed by the underwriters and by the issuer's officers, directors and substantial securityholders. These questionnaires will usually be based on standard forms used by major law firms, but it is necessary, as in the case of any standard form, to consider what revisions are required for the particular transaction. Persons who receive questionnaires should be encouraged to complete them in time to permit a timely NASD filing.

The SEC will not declare a registration statement effective unless the NASD has signed off on the fairness of the underwriting arrangements.[23] Approval will be set forth in a written opinion from the Corporate Financing Department. If there is a time bind, the NASD examiner is often willing to place a telephone call to his or her counterpart at the SEC, and the registration statement may be declared effective based on this oral assurance.

---

23. Rule 461(b)(6) under the 1933 Act provides that the SEC may refuse to accelerate the effectiveness of a registration statement where the underwriting compensation and arrangements are required to be reviewed by the NASD and the NASD has not issued a statement expressing no objections.

• *Exemptions*

Certain offerings are exempt from the filing requirements of the rule, unless subject to Rule 2720 (formerly Schedule E) (discussed below). One of the most important exemptions is that which relates to securities (debt or equity, but *not* an IPO of equity securities) offered by a corporate, foreign government, or foreign government agency issuer which has unsecured non-convertible debt with a term of at least four years, or unsecured non-convertible preferred stock, rated by a nationally recognized statistical rating agency in one of its four highest generic rating categories. An offering of investment grade non-convertible debt securities or preferred stock is exempt from the filing requirement even though the issuer has no outstanding securities that have an investment grade rating.

Because of the exemption for issuers with outstanding investment grade securities, many major corporations are not required to file with the NASD when going to market. Corporations of this caliber have the economic clout to assure that the underwriting spread will be reasonable. Their managing underwriters will be the major investment banking houses that do not request or accept warrants or cheap stock in connection with public offerings. Thus, review by the Corporate Financing Department is a matter of concern principally for first-time issuers and companies whose circumstances compel them to deal with the more flamboyant underwriters.

There is an exemption from filing for securities registered with the SEC on Form S-3 or Form F-3 and offered pursuant to the shelf registration provisions of Rule 415.[24] Shelf takedowns under Rule 415 could not be effected on an expeditious basis if it were necessary to seek NASD approval each time an issue is taken off the shelf.

No filing is required in connection with offerings of asset-backed securities that are rated in one of the four highest generic rating categories or for certain redemption standby arrangements.

---

24. Somewhat stubbornly, the NASD for this purpose applies the standards for Form S-3 and Form F-3 that applied prior to October 21, 1992. An issuer must therefore have a 1934 Act reporting history of 36 months rather than the 12 months that the SEC requires.

Although the foregoing offerings are exempt from the filing requirements, the rule's substantive fairness requirements for underwriting arrangements are still applicable. On the other hand, offerings of certain securities are exempt from the rule itself and not just the filing requirement. These include securities sold in private placements (including Rule 144A offerings), U.S. government and municipal and other "exempted" securities, open-end investment company securities, mutual fund shares, and securities issued pursuant to competitive bidding arrangements that meet the requirements of the Public Utility Holding Company Act of 1935. Commercial paper is not a "security" within the meaning of the 1934 Act (unlike the 1933 Act), and NASD filings are not made for commercial paper programs. Tender offers made pursuant to Regulation 14D under the 1934 Act are also exempt from the rule.

• *Request for Underwriting Activity Report*

Even where an exemption is available from the rule's filing requirements, the managing underwriter of an offering that is subject to Rule 101 (the SEC's anti-manipulation rule discussed in Chapter 4) must submit a request to the NASD's Corporate Financing Department for an Underwriting Activity Report with respect to the securities that may be subject to Rule 101 or related rules. The purpose of the requirement, which was added to the rule by NASD Notice to Members 97-10 (March 1997) and amended in SEC Release No. 34-38399 (March 14, 1997), is to enable the NASD to provide information to the managing underwriter regarding the trading volume and public float of the relevant securities, thus facilitating compliance with Rule 101 and related rules. At its option, a managing underwriter may also use the Underwriting Activity Report to submit a request to stabilize a NASDAQ security and to provide notification of the intent to impose a penalty bid or conduct syndicate covering transactions.

In April 1997, the NYSE adopted a new Rule 392 that requires notice to it of any offering in a listed security.

• *Items of Compensation*

The items to be included in determining the total amount of underwriters' compensation for purposes of the rule are all items of value received "in connection with or related to the distribution of the offering,"[25] including: the discount or commission, reimbursed underwriters' expenses, the fees and expenses of underwriters' counsel, finder's fees, financial consulting and advisory fees, stock, options, warrants and other securities, rights of first refusal, compensation received during the 12 months following the offering as the result of exercise of warrants, options or similar securities and any "busted deal" expense reimbursement received during the preceding six months. Securities deemed to be underwriting compensation may not be sold, transferred, assigned, pledged or hypothecated for a period of one year after the offering, except to officers or partners of the firm receiving the compensation or to another firm participating in the offering or its officers or partners.

The rule provides that stock received as underwriting compensation is to be valued by taking into consideration the difference between its cost to the underwriter and the proposed public offering price, or if there is a market for the stock, the market price on the date of acquisition. The rule also sets forth a formula for valuing options, warrants, or convertible securities received as underwriting compensation. A lower value may be assigned to securities that are subject to restrictions on resale for longer than the normal one-year period.

A right of first refusal to underwrite future offerings is an item of compensation that will be valued at 1% of the offering proceeds or that dollar amount, if any, contractually agreed to by the issuer and the underwriter as the price for a waiver of the right of first refusal. The rule also imposes certain substantive restrictions on rights of first refusal (see below).

All items of compensation will be totaled by the NASD's Corporate Financing Department, and a calculation will be made to determine their percentage of the total offering price.

---

25. In *May & Co., Inc.,* SEC Release No. 34-8975 (September 8, 1970), a vice president of the underwriter of a small Regulation A offering made at $2 per share purchased 40,000 shares from the issuer two months before the offering at a price of 50 cents per share. The vice president knew when he made his purchase that a public offering was contemplated and that his firm would be the managing underwriter. The difference between his cost and the public offering price, less a 20% discount, was deemed to be underwriting compensation.

• *Standards of Fairness*

The NASD has not published standards as to the amount of underwriting compensation that will be considered unfair or unreasonable. It does have internal guidelines, however, and the maximum permissible percentage compensation will vary inversely with the overall size of the deal and directly with the amount of risk borne by the underwriters. The NASD's staff has not formally disclosed these guidelines.

The rule states that, in reaching a determination of fairness, the factors to be taken into consideration include the size of the offering (the smaller the offering, the more the amount of compensation that may be reasonable), "the amount of risk being assumed by the underwriter and related persons" (which is deemed to be a function of whether the underwriting is a firm commitment or "best efforts" arrangement and whether it is a primary or secondary offering) (the greater the risk, the more the amount of compensation that may be reasonable) and the type of securities being offered. In addition, "any other relevant factors and circumstances shall be taken into consideration."

The net result is that filing and NASD clearance under the Corporate Financing Rule is a routine procedure for most offerings underwritten by major investment banking firms, assuming that filing is required at all. The only time that a major firm will encounter difficulties is where it has received compensation in connection with a separate transaction and is called upon to persuade the NASD that this compensation was not received "in connection with or in relation to the offering."

An NASD member "aggrieved" by an adverse determination by the Corporate Financing Department may request review by a hearing committee of a national standing committee of the Board of Governors pursuant to Rule 9800 of the NASD's Code of Procedure.[26]

---

26. Rule 9800 of the Code of Procedure was adopted in 1992 at the same time as the predecessor to Rule 2710. *See* NASD Notice to Members 92-28 (May 1992).

• *Unfair Underwriting Arrangements*

The rule sets forth certain arrangements that it deems to be unfair on their face. These include:

–   excessive expense reimbursement arrangements, including non-accountable expense reimbursement allowances in excess of 3% and accountable expense allowances that cover the underwriter's general overhead or similar expenses,

–   excessive rights of first refusal, including rights that have a duration of more than three years, that provide more than one opportunity to waive or terminate the right in consideration of any payment or fee, or that provide for waiver or termination fees that are either non-cash or that exceed specified guidelines,

–   the receipt of options, warrants or convertible securities as underwriting compensation where they are exercisable or convertible for a period of more than five years, where the exercise or conversion price is less than the public offering price or independent market price at the time of receipt, or where the option, warrant or convertible security does not meet the specific standards relating to registration rights, anti-dilution provisions and other matters set forth in the rule,

–   the receipt of items for which a value cannot be determined at the time of the offering,

–   the receipt of an overallotment option in connection with a firm commitment underwriting if the option is in excess of 15% of the amount of securities being offered (such an option calls into question, in the view of the NASD, whether the underwriting is really on a firm commitment basis),

–   receipt of securities that constitute underwriting compensation in an amount greater than 10% of the offering (excluding securities deemed to be underwriting compensation, securities issued pursuant to an overallotment option, securities not sold in the case of a best efforts arrangement and any securities underlying warrants, options or convertible securities that are part of the proposed offering (except where acquired as part of a unit)),

− receipt from an issuer of non-cash sales incentives, including travel bonuses, prizes and awards, in excess of $100 per person per issuer annually.

A prohibition not related to the rule's general purpose of promoting fair and reasonable underwriting arrangements states that a member may not participate with an issuer in a public non-underwritten distribution if the issuer has hired persons primarily for the purpose of distributing or assisting in the distribution of the securities. An exception to the prohibition suggests that its purpose is to prevent NASD members from collaborating with issuer employees that may be acting as unregistered broker-dealers. The exception states that the prohibition does not apply if the issuer's personnel are in compliance with "applicable state law" (presumably broker-dealer registration requirements) and with the SEC "safe harbor" rule (Rule 3a4-1 under the 1934 Act) relating to issuer's employees.

• *Securities Acquired in Connection with the Offering*

The rule states that the NASD will examine all items of value received during the preceding twelve months and at the time of—and subsequent to—the public offering to determine whether they are underwriting compensation in connection with the offering. Any items of value received during the preceding six months will be presumed to be underwriting compensation, but the presumption may be rebutted. Items of value received more than twelve months prior to the offering are presumed not to be underwriting compensation, but this presumption may also be rebutted.

The rule contains a list of factors to be considered, together with "any other relevant factors and circumstances," in determining whether an item of value is in connection with or related to the distribution of a public offering. In the case of "items of value" (which often consist of fees for services), the rule focuses on the date of performance of any service, the date of receipt and the date of any agreement relating to the service (the shorter the time, the more likely the item will be deemed to be in connection with the offering). The rule also focuses on the relationship between the services and the public offering, whether or not there is an affiliation between the issuer and the recipient of the item of value and whether or not the item of value was the subject of arm's-length bargaining (the existence of an affiliation and the absence of arm's-length bargaining will tend to indicate that the item of value was received in connection with the offering).

In the case of securities received by the underwriter or related persons, the above factors are considered *together with* the following additional factors: any disparity between the price paid for the securities and the offering price or market price (a greater disparity will tend to indicate that the securities constitute compensation), the amount of risk assumed by the recipient (e.g., restrictions on exercise and resale, and whether the securities are warrants or stock or debt) and the amount of securities (a larger amount of saleable securities or warrants tends to indicate compensation) and the relationship of the receipt of securities to purchases by unrelated persons on similar terms at approximately the same time (an absence of such purchases will tend to indicate compensation).

Financial consulting and advisory fees may be excluded from underwriting compensation if the NASD determines that an "ongoing relationship" between the issuer and the underwriter and related persons had been established at least 12 months prior to the offering or that, if established later, was not entered into in connection with the offering and that "actual services have been or will be rendered which were not or will not be in connection with or related to the offering."

The increasing involvement by investment banking firms in merchant banking and venture capital activities has made it important to determine whether securities or other "items of value" received prior to an offering should be considered as compensation in connection with the offering. Under the interpretation that was the predecessor of the current Corporate Financing Rule, this was often the most troublesome problem arising under the rules administered by the NASD in connection with public offerings.

In the view of the authors, no public purpose is served by artificially attributing to one transaction compensation that is directly related to another. If an investment banker performs a service or provides funds and receives compensation therefor that is not out of line with the fee that would be charged by others, no one is benefitted by relating that compensation to a subsequent public offering, even if that offering was contemplated at the time that the compensation was paid. Close proximity in time should be a minor factor in the analysis. Compensation paid in connection with a transaction should be attributed to a subsequent transaction only if it is clearly excessive in relation to the services rendered or the risks incurred, and then only to the extent of the amount by which the compensation is found to be excessive.

• *Venture Capital Restrictions*

As noted above, an underwriter or related person may be required under the Corporate Financing Rule to "lock up" for at least one year securities that are deemed to be underwriting compensation. The rule also requires NASD members who own an issuer's securities at the time of its initial public offering—and who wish to participate in the offering—to refrain from selling such securities during the offering and to "lock up" the securities for a period of 90 days following the offering unless the securities owned are 1% or less of the securities being offered *or* the securities offered to the public are priced on the basis of a recommendation of a "qualified independent underwriter" (see below).

• *Proceeds Directed to a Member*

During the late 1980s, the NASD became concerned that NASD members were underwriting securities the proceeds of which would be used in whole or in part to pay off "bridge loans" extended to the issuer by the NASD member or an affiliate. In order to reduce the NASD member's perceived conflict of interest and possible disincentive to conduct adequate due diligence, the NASD amended the predecessor of the Corporate Financing Rule to address those underwritings where more than 10% of the proceeds are intended to be paid to members participating in the distribution (or their related persons).

In these cases, the securities offered to the public must be priced on the basis of a recommendation of a "qualified independent underwriter" (see below). Certain offerings are exempted from this requirement, including real estate investment trusts and certain direct participation programs (unless the proceeds are to be used to repay loans used to acquire an interest in a preexisting company).

Hot Issue Markets—Free-Riding and Withholding

Free-riding and withholding has been a recurring problem in hot issue markets. If there is strong demand for a new issue, unscrupulous underwriters and dealers have been known to withhold shares for their own account or for the accounts of their officers, partners and other insiders, thus creating a further imbalance between the demand for the shares and the supply available for members of the public. Often the shares have been subsequently sold at a substantial profit, thereby giving the insiders a "free ride." An interpretation by the Board of Governors—"IM-2110-1"—states that free-riding and withholding is inconsistent with the requirement of Rule 2110 that NASD members observe high standards of commercial honor and just and equitable principles of trade.

• *The 1959–1962 Hot Issue Market*

To place the free-riding problem in context, it is instructive to examine the hot issue market of the early 1960s as described in the SEC's 1963 *Special Study of Securities Markets.* From 1959 until the market decline of early 1962, the number of first-time public offerings reached a higher level than ever before in history. This activity took place in a climate of intense speculation that reached a climax in 1961. The public eagerly sought out new issues of companies in glamour industries, especially electronics, in the expectation that they would quickly rise to a substantial premium. This expectation was often realized. Within a few days, or even hours, after the initial distribution, these so-called hot issues would trade at premiums of as much as 300% above the initial public offering price. After the

1962 market break, many of these hot issues fell to a fraction of their offering price.

Certain statistics reported by the *Special Study* are revealing.[27] The Special Study found that of 1,671 unseasoned common stock issues publicly offered during the years 1959 through 1961 for which later prices were available, 79% sold at a premium immediately after the offering and 66% sold at a premium one month later. The proportion of issues selling at a premium reached a peak in 1961, with 85% of the unseasoned common stock issues selling at a premium immediately after the offering and 68% one month later. In 1961, 75 unseasoned issues more than doubled in price immediately after the offering. In 1959 and 1961, 89%, and in 1960, 83%, of the new issues of electronic and electrical equipment manufacturing companies went to immediate premiums.

The booming hot issue market of 1961 came to a grinding halt in the spring of 1962 when stock prices dropped dramatically. The paper profits made on companies with little or no real substance disappeared with the collapse of the market. Here the statistics tell a sadder tale. Of 1,121 unseasoned common stock issues offered in 1961, the *Special Study* reported that price quotations were not available in September 1962 for 12% of the issues registered under the 1933 Act and 48% of the Regulation A issues. At the end of September 1962, only 22% of the issues for which prices were available were selling above their 1961 offering prices. By contrast, 85% had sold at a premium immediately after offering.

• *Special Study Observations on Free-Riding*

The *Special Study* found some degree of free-riding by underwriters or selling group members in each of the new issues that it examined. It set forth numerous examples of the extent to which this practice infected the markets. For example, Hill, Thompson & Co., co-underwriter of a public offering by Cove Vitamin and Pharmaceutical, Inc., allotted 10,150 units to 27 relatives of principals in the firm, out of a total allocation to the

---

27. *Special Study* Pt. 1 at 516–18.

firm of 54,000 units.[28] In the case of an offering of 165,000 shares of common stock of Custom Components, Inc., at least 32,905 shares were sold to accounts of participants in the distribution and their officers, partners and employees (or to accounts in which such persons had a beneficial interest), other broker-dealers and their officers, partners and employees, and individuals closely associated with participants who, in certain instances, bought their shares in nominee names.[29]

The *Special Study* stated that free-riding had been a problem of major concern to the SEC during every period of recent history in which speculative new issues had proliferated. It noted that in April 1946, the SEC issued a release which concluded that free-riding practices were a major factor in driving the price of new stock issues above the public offering price.[30] In this release, the SEC proposed a rule that would have made it a fraudulent practice for any broker-dealer participating in a distribution to offer any of the securities at a price above the initial public offering price unless a bona fide offering had been made for a reasonable time to distribute the shares at no more than the price set forth in the prospectus. Under the proposed SEC rule, a bona fide offer would not include a sale or offer to a partner, officer, director or employee of a broker-dealer or to any account with which such person had a control relationship or in which he had a beneficial interest. Shares taken for investment were exempted after the allocation was disclosed in the prospectus.

The *Special Study* stated that the proposed rule met a "barrage of criticism" from the securities industry, based largely upon the argument that it would have the effect of depriving persons connected with underwriters and selling group members of the opportunity to invest in new issues of securities. According to this reasoning, such persons "were members of the public and should not be treated as second-class citizens." In addition, the NASD claimed that, as a self-regulatory organization, it and not the SEC should undertake the regulation of

---

28. *Id.* at 529.
29. *Id.* at 531.
30. SEC Release No. 34-3807 (April 16, 1946).

free-riding practices.[31] With the market decline of September 1946, the problem became less urgent, and the proposed rule was never adopted.

• *History of Response to Free-Riding by NASD and SEC*

In 1950, the NASD adopted its initial free-riding and withholding interpretation. This interpretation stated that it was a violation of what was then Article III, Section 1 of the *Rules of Fair Practice* for any member, directly or indirectly, to withhold a portion of any public offering for its own account or to sell any such portion to persons connected with it, members of their immediate families, or accounts in which such member or such persons had a beneficial interest. Securities taken for investment were exempted from the interpretation if the allotment was in accordance with the purchaser's normal investment practice. In May 1959, the interpretation was amended to include the additional requirement that any stock taken by insiders not be disproportionate in amount to allotments made to the public.

As the market for new issues heated up in 1959, the SEC published a preliminary report submitted to it by the director of its Division of Trading and Exchanges discussing the results of an inquiry into the circumstances surrounding the distribution of hot issues.[32] One practice that the report described was that in which an underwriter would allot securities, not only to its own customers and to selling group members, but also to trading firms at the public offering price. These firms were expected to immediately make a market in the securities.

The report observed that this practice might involve violations of several requirements of the Federal securities laws. First, the registration statement might be misleading because of the failure to disclose the actual plan of distribution and the marketing arrangements for the issue. The SEC's staff considered the trading firms receiving allotments to be underwriters who should be identified as such. The antifraud provisions of the securities laws might be violated in that the public would be led to believe that a stated number of shares were being pub-

---

31. *Special Study* Pt. 1 at 532.
32. SEC Release No. 34-6097 (October 23, 1959).

licly offered at the initial public offering price when, in fact, they were not being so offered and the initial supply on the market was therefore less than anticipated. Also, the activities of the trading firms might constitute a violation of what was then Rule 10b-6.

The SEC's staff turned over to the NASD for such disciplinary action as it considered to be appropriate the evidence obtained with respect to free-riding by certain of its members. The report stated that the staff had been informed by the NASD that it "is reviewing its policy with respect to 'free riding' and the enforcement of such policy to determine what further steps, if any, it should take in the matter." In April 1960, the NASD's free-riding interpretation was further amended by the addition of the requirement that aggregate sales made by participants in public offerings to insiders be "insubstantial."

The *Special Study* found that, despite the tightening of the free-riding interpretation and attempts by the NASD to enforce it, "free-riding practices seem to have continued without abatement."[33] The *Special Study* went on to observe that until the introduction of the "disproportionate" and "insubstantial" tests, it was possible for participants in public offerings to allot large portions of new issues to insiders and defend the practice on the ground that the stock was taken for investment. If this were done frequently enough, it could also be claimed that this was a "normal investment practice." The *Special Study* concluded that it did not appear that the 1959 and 1960 amendments to the interpretation had significantly altered the practices of many broker-dealer firms. It questioned the effectiveness of the NASD's enforcement practices.

The *Special Study* recommended that the NASD strengthen its enforcement of the prohibitions against free-riding and withholding by requiring, in the case of any initial public offering of common stock which traded at a specified premium (say 20%) within a specified number of days after the offering (say 40), reports of all allocations of stock to participants in the distribution (other than stock resold at or below the public offering price) or to their principals or members of their immediate

_____

33. *Special Study Pt.* 1 at 532.

families or to any broker-dealer that is not a participant in the distribution. The *Special Study* also recommended that the NASD impose substantially more severe penalties in flagrant cases.[34]

In addition to free-riding, the *Special Study* pointed to other practices designed to drive up the price of stock by artificially restricting the supply in the after-market while at the same time fanning the demand.[35] It found that many distributors of new issues adopted a policy of allotting stock only to customers who would not immediately resell in the after-market. They implemented this policy by such measures as making allotments only to customers with a record of not reselling new issues, allotting to discretionary accounts or to a relatively small number of customers who customarily relied upon their advice, or penalizing salesmen whose customers sold their allotments in the immediate after-market. Sometimes customers would be advised of a "requirement" or "expectation" that they would not immediately resell or that immediate resale would reduce their chances of being considered for future new issues. Some underwriters would simply refuse to execute customers' sell orders in the after-market. Some would delay in delivering stock certificates so that the customer would find it difficult to sell through another broker.

Attempts to restrict artificially the after-market supply of a security by refusing to execute customers' sell orders or to deliver stock certificates are clearly indefensible. A clear distinction must be observed, however, between these activities and longstanding standard underwriting practices that are designed to encourage underwriters to sell to investors who are purchasing for more than a quick profit. The penalty clause found in many AAUs, for example, which imposes a monetary penalty on an underwriter if any shares sold by it are repurchased by the syndicate, is an accepted device used to achieve the objective that underwriters should find a "good home" for the securities being distributed.

---

34. *Id.* at 558–59.
35. *Id.* at 555.

• *Response to the 1968–1969 Hot Issue Market*

By the time that the *Special Study* was published, the hot issue market had been chilled by a general market decline. Many believed that the public had learned its lesson and that investors who had lost their shirts by speculation in worthless companies could not be fooled again. This did not prove to be the case.

In 1968 and 1969, the hot issue phenomenon reoccurred. The fast food business replaced electronics as the glamour leader, and new faces appeared among the underwriters of hot issues. But the pattern was much the same, and after the market decline of early 1970, the hot issue purchaser had more worthless stock certificates to add to his collection.

In late 1971, with memories of the 1968–1969 hot issue market freshly in mind, the SEC ordered an investigation of hot issues.[36] Public hearings were held from February to early June of 1972. Although the market had cooled, the SEC wanted to find some answers before another hot issue craze reoccurred.

In July 1972, the SEC issued a series of proposals.[37] These fell into two principal categories. The first group of proposals was characterized by the SEC as "initial steps to help curtail excesses of hot issues." They were directed towards the character of the after-market, the quality of underwriters' due diligence, suitability standards for hot issues sold in the after-market, sales of hot issues to discretionary accounts, and prompt delivery of certificates. The second group of proposals related to improved prospectus disclosure.

The two areas most directly related to hot issue abuses, namely the quality of the after-market and suitability standards, were left to the NASD for further study. The question of due diligence standards, which related only tangentially to the problem of hot issues, likewise was referred to the NASD for further consideration. Apart from these matters, the SEC made only two specific proposals in the July 1972 releases, one relating to disclosure of expected sales to discretionary accounts

---

36. SEC Release No. 33-5204 (October 21, 1971).

37. SEC Release No. 33-5274 (July 26, 1972); SEC Release No. 33-5275 (July 26, 1972); SEC Release No. 33-5276 (July 26, 1972).

and one relating to a registration statement undertaking with respect to certificate delivery. These two proposals subsequently were adopted by the SEC (see Chapter 3).

To deal with the matters referred to it in the hot issue releases, the NASD established an ad hoc committee to recommend appropriate rule changes. This committee submitted its recommendations to the NASD's Board of Governors, which in March 1973 submitted to the NASD membership proposed new rules relating to due diligence, the qualifications of members engaged in underwriting, and suitability standards.[38] The proposed rules relating to due diligence standards and rules relating to the qualification of members engaged in underwriting were hotly debated, and the NASD finally was convinced that provisions of this type were inappropriate.

Although the NASD has since adopted suitability provisions relating specifically to speculative low-priced issues,[39] its enforcement of the interpretation with respect to free-riding and withholding continues to be an important means by which it seeks to protect the integrity of the public offering system.[40]

---

38. NASD Notice to Members 73–17 (March 14, 1973).

39. The principal relevant provision is now designated as Rule IM-2310-2(b)(1) ("Fair Dealing With Customers—Recommending Speculative Low-Priced Securities"), which condemns the recommendation of speculative low-priced securities to customers without having or attempting to obtain relevant information regarding the suitability of such securities for the customers to whom the recommendations were made. More recently, the NASD has "clarified" that the interpretation applies to situations in which an NASD member "brings a specific security to the attention of the customer through any means," even where the transaction might be viewed for other purposes as "unsolicited." NASD Notice to Members 96-60 (September 1996). The authors do not consider this to be a reasonable interpretation of the term "recommendation."

40. E.g., *G.K. Scott & Co., Inc.*, SEC Release No. 34-33485 (January 14, 1994); *First Philadelphia Corp.*, SEC Release No. 34-28466 (September 25, 1990); *Robert S.C. Peterson*, Inc., SEC Release No. 34-24688 (July 9, 1987); *Edward D. Jones & Co.*, SEC Release No. 34-22449 (September 24, 1985); *Donald L. Walford*, SEC Release No. 34-18025 (August 10, 1981); *P. Lynn Dixon*, SEC Release No. 34-17192 (October 3, 1980); *Carolina Securities Corp.*, 45 S.E.C. 777 (1975); *Albert H. Harris*, 45 S.E.C. 971 (1975);

• *Free-Riding and Withholding Interpretation*

With this background, it is appropriate to look more closely at the interpretation of the Board of Governors with respect to free-riding and withholding. As previously noted, the interpretation is now part of the NASD's "Interpretive Material" to Rule 2110 and is designated as "IM-2110-1."

The interpretation states that it is

> based upon the premise that members have an obligation to make a bona fide public distribution at the public offering price of securities of a public offering which trade at a premium in the secondary market whenever such secondary market begins (a "hot issue") regardless of whether such securities are acquired by the member as an underwriter, as a selling group member, or from a member participating in the distribution as an underwriter or a selling group member, or otherwise.

The interpretation notes that the failure to make a bona fide public distribution where there is demand for an issue can be a factor in artificially raising the price.

• • *Definition of Hot Issue.* An issue is hot if, in fact, the securities trade at a premium over the public offering price at the time that the secondary market begins.[41] But how can the underwriters and selling group members know whether or not they are marketing a hot issue at the time that they are engaged in their selling efforts? Until recently, the simple answer was that they could not.

Robert E. Meyers & Company, 45 S.E.C. 211 (1973); *Safeco Securities, Inc.,* 45 S.E.C. 303 (1973).

41. The interpretation formerly defined a hot issue as one which trades at a premium "immediately after the distribution process is commenced." It was amended as a result of the SEC's decision in *Lowell H. Listrom & Co.,* SEC Release No. 34-19414 (January 10, 1983), where the NASD's findings were set aside because it was not clear that the free-riding interpretation was violated where a best efforts offering took three months to sell, was closed with shares in the hands of restricted accounts, and the shares then traded at a premium. NASD Notice to Members 83-26 (June 1, 1983).

During the period before the registration statement becomes effective, the underwriters may have an expectation that an issue will be hot, but this will not be known as a fact until the stock begins to trade in the after-market. Accordingly, underwriters and dealers for many years incurred a risk when they took indications of interest from persons of the type restricted under the free-riding and withholding interpretation (except as permitted by the normal investment practice exception). It was possible that sales to these persons might be confirmed after pricing notwithstanding that the offering began to trade at a premium in the after-market, thus resulting in a violation of the interpretation. In 1995,[42] however, the NASD amended the interpretation to state that no violation would occur under these circumstances as long as the NASD member canceled the sale and reallocated the security at the public offering price to an unrestricted account prior to the end of the first business day after the date on which secondary market trading began. To assist members in this connection, the NASD introduced in 1996 a new regulatory service called "Compliance Desk." As described in NASD Notice to Members 96-18 (March 1996), the service contemplates that the NASD would monitor trading in the immediate after-market to determine (based on an "analysis of all the facts and circumstances surrounding the first day of trading") whether the new issue is a hot issue. If the NASD determines that the new issue has traded at a premium, it will issue a "hot-issue notification" wire to the participants in the distribution. The participants are then obligated to review their customer allocations to determine whether sales have been made to restricted persons or accounts; if so, they must cancel those trades and reallocate the securities at the public offering price to unrestricted persons or accounts.

• • *NASD Free-Riding Questionnaire.* When the NASD identifies a securities offering as a hot issue, it uses a standard questionnaire to determine whether the managing underwriter and participating underwriters have complied with the interpretation in making sales of the hot issue securities. A form of the

---

42. NASD Notice to Members 95-7 (February 1995).

questionnaire was included in NASD Notice to Members 95-27 (April 1995). It was modified in Notice to Members 96-18 (March 1996) to "clarify" that the interpretation applies to securities received on the exercise of a "Green Shoe" option as well as securities sold short for the account of the syndicate.

• • *Restricted Persons.* The interpretation specifies those persons who are insiders or who are in a position to direct reciprocal business to the member and provides that such persons may not participate in a hot issue except under certain circumstances. First, the obligation to make a bona fide public offering prohibits a member from continuing to hold any of the securities in any of its own accounts. This prohibition is absolute.

Second, other restricted persons include any officer, director, general partner, employee or agent of the member or of any other broker-dealer, or any person associated with the member or with any other broker-dealer.[43] In general, these restrictions also apply to any member of the immediate family of a restricted person. Members of a person's immediate family include parents, mother-in-law or father-in-law, husband or wife, brother or sister, brother-in-law or sister-in-law, son-in-law or daughter-in-law, and children. In addition, the term includes any other person who is supported, directly or indirectly, to a material extent by the restricted person. In the February 1995 amendments, however, the NASD amended the restriction to exclude family members "not supported directly or indirectly to a material extent" by the restricted person if the sale is by a broker-dealer other than that employing the restricted

---

43. "Broker-dealer" for purposes of this restriction excludes an NASD member engaged solely in the purchase or sale of either investment company/variable contract securities or direct participation program securities. Also, the February 1995 amendments exclude from the category of "associated person" a person whose association with an NASD member is limited to "a passive ownership interest in the member of ten percent or less, and who does not receive hot issues from the member in which he or she has the ownership interest; and that such member is not in a position to direct hot issues to such person." NASD Notice to Members 95-7 (February 1995). Finally, the NASD definition of "associated person" is generally confined to *natural* persons. NASD By-Laws, Article I(q).

person and where the restricted person has no ability to control the allocation of the hot issue.[44]

Other restricted persons are a finder with respect to the public offering or any person acting in a fiduciary capacity to the managing underwriter, including, among others, lawyers, accountants and financial consultants, as well as persons supported directly or indirectly to a material extent by any finder or person acting in a fiduciary capacity.

Because they are in a position to provide reciprocal business, the interpretation includes as restricted persons any senior officer of a bank, savings and loan institution, insurance company, registered investment company, registered investment advisory firm, "or other institutional type account," domestic or foreign, or any person in the securities department of, or any employee or any other person who may influence or whose activities directly or indirectly involve or are related to the function of buying or selling securities for, any such institution. Persons deriving material support from these persons are also restricted. Not only are direct sales prohibited, but sales may not be made to any account in which a restricted person has a beneficial interest.

It should be noted that officers, directors, and employees of the issuer itself are not restricted persons, nor is counsel to the issuer, or members of the immediate family of any of these persons.

The February 1995 amendments provided much-needed relief in rights offerings where a restricted person (e.g., a controlling shareholder of a bank who is also a "senior officer" of the bank or otherwise a restricted person) wishes to provide the issuer with a stand-by commitment. Purchases pursuant to a stand-by commitment are no longer subject to the interpretation if the commitment is disclosed in the prospectus for the rights offering, the commitment is the subject of a formal written agreement and the managing underwriter represents in writing that it was unable to find any other purchasers for the securities. Also, any securities purchased are subject to a three-month lockup.

---

44. *Id.*

The February 1995 amendments also provided relief to venture capital investors who are restricted persons but wish to maintain their proportionate interest in an issuer whose securities are the subject of a hot issue. An investor seeking to rely on this relief must have held securities in the issuer for at least one year and must not have increased his or her percentage ownership during the three months preceding the offering. Any securities purchased are subject to a three-month lockup.

• • *Normal Investment Practice.* Except in the case of sales to restricted persons who are officers, directors, general partners, employees or agents of the member or of another broker-dealer, persons associated with them, and members of their immediate family who are in fact supported by them, sales may be made to restricted persons if the member can demonstrate that the securities were sold to them "in accordance with their normal investment practice, that the aggregate of the securities so sold is insubstantial and not disproportionate in amount as compared to sales to members of the public and that the amount sold to any one of such persons is insubstantial in amount." Prior to the February 1995 amendments, normal investment practice meant the history of investment of a restricted person in an account maintained with the member making the allocation; since the amendments, however, a person's investment history includes his or her activity at other firms.

The interpretation states that the previous one-year period of securities activity is the usual basis for determining the adequacy of a restricted person's investment history. In analyzing a restricted person's investment history, the NASD believes that the factors to be considered include the frequency of transactions in the account, the nature and size of the investments, and a comparison of the dollar amount of previous transactions with the dollar amount of the hot issue purchase. The example is given that, if a restricted person purchases $1,000 of a hot issue and his or her account reveals a series of purchases and sales in $100 amounts, the $1,000 purchase would not be consistent with the restricted person's normal investment practice. The interpretation states that the practice of purchasing mainly hot issues would not constitute a normal investment practice.

With respect to the determination of what constitutes a disproportionate allocation, the NASD uses as a guideline 10% of the member's participation in the issue. The requirement of insubstantiality is separate and distinct from the requirement relating to disproportionate allocations and normal investment practices. No specific guidance is given as to what is considered an insubstantial allocation, but the interpretation points out that the term applies both to the aggregate of the securities sold to restricted accounts and to each individual allocation.

• • *Sales to Dealers and Banks.* The interpretation provides that a member may not sell securities that are part of a hot issue at or above the public offering price to any other broker-dealer unless it receives written assurance that the purchase is being made to fill orders for bona fide public customers, other than those falling within the category of restricted persons, at the public offering price as an accommodation to them and without compensation for such. Such circumstances are probably rare.

Hot issues may not be sold to any domestic bank, domestic branch of a foreign bank, trust company, or other conduit for an undisclosed principal, unless the member selling the securities makes an affirmative inquiry as to whether the ultimate purchasers are restricted persons and receives satisfactory assurance that they are not and that the securities will not be sold in a manner inconsistent with the provision relating to the sale to dealers at or above the public offering price. Otherwise, there is a rebuttable presumption that the ultimate purchasers are restricted persons. The member must record on the order ticket or on some other supporting document the name of the person to whom the inquiry was made, the substance of what was said by that person, and what was done as a result thereof. The order ticket or other document must be initialed by a registered representative of the member, and normal supervisory provisions of the member must provide for a "close follow-up and review" of such transactions. Similar inquiries must be made in the case of sales to a foreign broker-dealer or bank that is not participating in the distribution as an underwriter, but in this case the member's supervisory procedures need not provide for a "close follow-up and review." The obligation with respect to foreign broker-dealers or banks can be satisfied with a blanket assurance by means of a Form FR-1.

• • *Investment Partnerships and Corporations.* The interpretation states that a member may not sell hot issue securities to any investment partnership or corporation, domestic or foreign (except companies registered under the 1940 Act), including hedge funds, investment clubs and other like accounts, unless prior to the transaction the member has received a current list of the names and business connections of all persons having any beneficial interest in the account. If this information discloses that any such person is a restricted person, then the sale to that person must be consistent with the interpretation. If the investment vehicle is unwilling to give up this list, the requirement can be satisfied with a written representation of counsel or—since February 1995[45]—the account's independent certified public accountant to the effect that such counsel or accountant reasonably believes that no person with a beneficial interest in the account is a restricted person.

Where a restricted person turns out to have a beneficial interest in an investment partnership or corporation, all is not necessarily lost. The February 1995 amendments to the interpretation codified an earlier NASD-sanctioned "carve-out" procedure pursuant to which the investment partnership or corporation may establish a separate account for its new-issue purchases and exclude restricted persons from participation in this account. The interpretation provides for certain certifications to and by the investment partnership or corporation's accountant, copies of which must be maintained by the NASD member and provided to the NASD upon request.

• • *Issuer-Directed Securities.* Issuer-directed securities are subject to the interpretation if they are directed to restricted persons. Thus, for example, if a bank holding company making a public offering asks the managing underwriter to reserve shares for sale to certain of its officers and employees, including those of its subsidiary bank, the interpretation will apply. Notwithstanding the applicability of the interpretation, sales of

---

45. NASD Notice to Members 95-7 (February 1995).

issuer-directed securities may still be made—without limitation as to amount—to employees or directors of the issuer who do not have the requisite investment history if the securities are subjected to a three-month lockup. Issuer-directed sales to non-employee and non-director restricted persons require the permission of the NASD on the basis of "valid business reasons for such sales" (e.g., sales to suppliers or distributors), demonstration that such sales are insubstantial and not disproportionate to sales to the public and subjecting the securities to a three-month lockup.

The *Papilsky* Rules

Rule 2740 and its companions, Rules 2730 and 2750, are designed to preserve the integrity of the fixed price distribution system that for many years has been the established method of selling securities in underwritten public offerings. These are known as the *Papilsky* rules in honor of Mrs. Paulette Papilsky, the plaintiff in a case that held that, in the absence of a ruling from the SEC or the NASD, an investor's indirect recapture of underwriting discounts and commissions was legal under an earlier version of Rule 2740.

In 1980, the predecessors of Rules 2740 and 2730 were amended and the predecessor of Rule 2750 was adopted as a result of the uncertainties created by this decision. In its current form, Rule 2740 provides in effect that a member of the NASD may not grant or receive selling concessions, discounts or other allowances in connection with the sale of securities that are part of a fixed price offering except as "consideration for services rendered in distribution" and may not grant such concessions, discounts or other allowances to anyone other than a broker or dealer "actually engaged in the investment banking or securities business." A purchaser of the securities, however, may designate that selling credit be given to a broker or dealer that has provided or will provide it with "bona fide research."

Rule 2730 provides that a member engaged in a fixed price offering who purchases or arranges the purchase of securities "taken in trade" shall purchase the securities "at a fair market price" at the time of purchase or shall act as agent in the sale of such securities and charge "the normal commission" therefor. A failure to do so is known as "overtrading." Purchasing the securities at a higher price or selling with a less than normal commission can be an indirect means of granting a discount to the customer. In order to prevent institutional purchasers from recapturing selling concessions by designating an affiliated NASD member to purchase securities for it in a fixed price offering, Rule 2750 provides that a member participating in a fixed price offering may not sell the securities to a "related person."

It should be noted at the outset that the *Papilsky* rules do not require that distributions of securities be structured as fixed price offerings. Rather, as noted by the SEC in the release approving the rules pursuant to Section 19(b), "the provisions of the proposed rule change come into play only after the underwriters have themselves agreed to distribute securities through a fixed price offering."[46]

The SEC has specifically stated that the rule does not prohibit multiple price arrangements. For example, an underwriter may agree with an issuer to offer securities at different prices depending on the amount of securities that the customer is willing to purchase.[47] But if the underwriters voluntarily enter into a price maintenance agreement as one of the terms upon which they will risk their capital, the NASD requires that the agreement be adhered to and that it not be undermined through some subterfuge.

• *Background*

Prior to its amendment in 1980, the predecessor of Rule 2740 provided:

Selling concessions, discounts, or other allowances, as such, shall be allowed only as consideration for services rendered in distribution and in no event shall be allowed to anyone other than a broker or dealer actually engaged in the investment banking or securities busi-

---

46. SEC Release No. 34-17371 (December 12, 1980).
47. *Id.*

ness; provided, however, that nothing in this rule shall prevent any member from selling any security owned by him to any person at any net price which may be fixed by him unless prevented therefrom by agreement.

The rule traces its origin to the Investment Bankers Code approved by President Roosevelt acting under the authority of the National Industrial Recovery Act, as amended in 1934 to include fair practice provisions.[48] Included among the code's rules of fair practice was a rule establishing one price for all investors regardless of the size of the transaction or the importance of the purchaser. In 1935, the rules of fair practice were amended to require an investment banker who received a selling concession to certify that his purchase was solely for the account of clients or, if for his own account, that he intended to redistribute the securities to his clients in the ordinary course of business. This rule was based on the principle that an investment banker is entitled to a selling concession only if it actively participates in the distribution of the securities to others. The original rules of fair practice adopted by the NASD included a provision virtually identical to the predecessor of Rule 2740 as it existed prior to its amendment in 1980.

Prior to its amendment, the predecessor of Rule 2730 provided:

> A member, when a member of a selling syndicate or a selling group, shall purchase securities taken in trade at a fair market price at the time of purchase, or shall act as agent in the sale of such securities.

This rule was designed to prevent overtrading, but as stated by the SEC, as then drafted it "provides little guidance to members or to the NASD in its enforcement efforts in differentiating between a permissible swap and a prohibited overtrade."[49] The predecessor of Rule 2750 was a new provision that had no counterpart in the then existing rules of fair practice, although it was the position of

---

48. *Id.*
49. *Id.*

the NASD that the predecessor of Rule 2740 itself prohibited the use of affiliates to recapture selling concessions.

• • *Pressures by Institutions.* In the release requesting public comment on the proposed *Papilsky* rules,[50] the SEC recognized that the growth of institutional participation in the securities markets had exerted increasing pressure on the fixed price offering system. In the release approving the rules, the SEC observed that when the securities laws were passed in the early 1930s, individual retail investors were the principal customers of securities firms. At that time, the securities industry "performed an intermediation function that, in many cases, extended all the way from the individual investor to the corporate issuer, in the case of securities distributions, and to the specialist's post, in the case of exchange trading."[51] By the 1960s, however, it had become clear that institutional investors, including bank trust departments, insurance companies, mutual funds and pension funds, had made serious inroads, capturing a substantial portion of the intermediation function in that a large portion of the securities issued by corporations, both debt and equity, were being bought by institutional investors acting as financial intermediaries for the individuals whom the securities industry previously had served.

The SEC stated that one of the reasons for this was that "fiduciaries gradually became interested in achieving economic growth in the portfolios they managed instead of concentrating primarily on safety and income." Accordingly, "it became possible for savers to invest in the stock market through a financial intermediary either by creating a trust or by establishing an account managed by a bank or other institutional investor." The SEC stated that the growth of tax-exempt pension funds created large new pools of money available for investment in the securities markets. Bank trust departments, investment advisors and insurance companies began to play a major role in managing the assets of those who received a portion of their compensation in the form of tax-deferred pension benefits. In

---

50. SEC Release No. 34-15807 (May 9, 1979).
51. SEC Release No. 34-17371 (December 12, 1980).

addition, the SEC noted that the explosive growth in mutual funds "brought into the market many investors who, if they had invested directly, would not have been able to achieve a diversified portfolio." The growth in mutual fund investments magnified the trend toward the institutionalization of the securities market.

The desire of institutional investors to lower their transaction costs led to practices that undermined the fixed commission rate system established by the securities exchanges and finally led to the elimination of fixed commission rates on May 1, 1975, known in the industry as "May Day."[52] Institutions were unhappy with a system that required them to pay the same percentage commission on a 50,000-share trade as an individual investor on a 500-share trade. The transaction cost to the broker was substantially the same regardless of the number of shares involved. Thus, exchange members were willing to submit to competitive pressures and to cooperate with their institutional customers in devising methods to evade the anti-rebate rules of the exchanges.

The customer-directed give-up was one device that undermined the fixed rate system. Institutions such as mutual fund managers would direct the executing broker to share its commission with another exchange member that had provided ben-

---

52. Rule 19b-3 under the 1934 Act, adopted by the SEC in January 1975 (SEC Release No. 34-11203 (January 23, 1975)) effective May 1, 1975, prohibits any national securities exchange from adopting or retaining any rule that requires its members to charge fixed commission rates for transactions effected on the exchange or by the use of exchange facilities. As stated in SEC Release No. 34-11203, the practice of fixed commission rates on stock exchanges in the United States originated in the so-called Buttonwood Tree Agreement of 1792, which provided:

> We, the Subscribers, Brokers for the Purchase and Sale of Public Stock, do hereby solemnly promise and pledge ourselves to each other, that we will not buy or sell from this day for any person whatsoever, any kind of Public Stock at a less rate than one-quarter percent Commission on the Specie value, and that we will give a preference to each other in our Negotiations. In Testimony whereof we have set our hands this 17th day of May, at New York, 1792.

efits to the manager by selling fund shares or furnishing research or statistical or advisory services. Reciprocal commission business between exchange members and non-member firms was another device that undermined the system. Then there were exotic schemes such as the "end run" and the "incorporated give-up pocket" where a subsidiary of a mutual fund manager gained membership on a regional exchange in order to recapture commissions.[53]

Schemes used to evade the fixed commission rate structure also were employed in the context of underwritten fixed price offerings. These schemes had the economic effect of affording to institutional and other large purchasers a rebate of some portion of the selling concession. As stated by the SEC:

> Such practices include both direct discounting techniques, such as "overtrading" in swap transactions and certain types of underwriting fee recapture, and indirect compensation arrangements, such as the provision of goods and services in return for so-called "syndicate soft dollars."
>
> In swap transactions, securities are taken in trade from a customer, in lieu of cash, in exchange for the offered securities. A discount from the fixed offering price may be granted to the purchaser of the offered securities where the syndicate member purchases the securities taken in trade at a price exceeding their market value. This "overtrade" is economically equivalent to paying less than the stated offering price for the securities being distributed.
>
> A customer may seek to recapture underwriting fees by designating a broker-dealer affiliate to be included in the selling group. The customer may then purchase the offered security through its affiliate, thereby recapturing the selling concession. Such concession payments to an

---

53. The various schemes to evade the anti-rebate rules of the stock exchanges are described in R. Jennings, H. Marsh & J. Coffee, *Securities Regulation* 556–62 (7th ed. 1992).

affiliate enable the customer to obtain direct discounts from the fixed offering price.

A broker-dealer providing research or other services to a customer may be compensated for those services, at least in part, through purchases by the customer in a fixed price offering. The customer can either purchase the securities directly through the broker-dealer or can contact the managing underwriter and "designate" the dealer to receive credit for the order. In these instances, the dealer is compensated indirectly by receiving "soft dollar" concessions for the research or other services it has provided.[54]

• • *The Papilsky Case.* In 1976, Judge Frankel handed down his decision in *Papilsky v. Berndt.*[55]

The plaintiff, an owner of 40 shares of Affiliated Fund, Inc., then one of the largest mutual funds in the country, brought a derivative action against the fund and its management company, Lord, Abbett & Co., charging violations of fiduciary duties in failing to recapture brokerage commissions, underwriting commissions and tender offer fees for the fund and its shareholders. With respect to the recapture of selling concessions, the plaintiff alleged that Affiliated Fund should have designated Lord Abbett, an NASD member, to receive selling credit when the fund purchased securities in underwritten offerings and that the selling concession so received by Lord Abbett should have been applied to reduce its management fee. Counsel had advised that this would have violated NASD regulations, but Judge Frankel found that, in the absence of a contrary ruling from the SEC or the NASD, underwriting recapture in this manner was available and legal under the predecessor of Rule 2740. He held that a mutual fund advisor would be liable for unrecaptured underwriting discounts unless it established that it fully disclosed to the fund's independent directors that recapture was a possible alternative to other uses of the fees,

---

54. SEC Release No. 34-15807 (May 9, 1979).
55. [1976–1977 Transfer Binder] Fed. Sec. L. Rep. (CCH) ¶ 95,627 (S.D.N.Y. 1976).

and that the directors, as a matter of reasonable business judgment, determined not to seek recapture.[56]

As a result of *Papilsky*, a number of requests were made to the NASD on behalf of mutual fund managers for a ruling on the propriety of recapture under the predecessor of Rule 2740. The NASD responded to these requests in November and December of 1976 by stating that, in its opinion, that rule prohibited underwriting recapture. The SEC wrote to the NASD in February 1977, stating that this interpretation of the rule raised important issues, and that, accordingly, it should be filed as a proposed rule change. After a public meeting with the SEC in May 1977, the NASD agreed to do so.

In July 1978, the NASD made the so-called *Papilsky* filing after first circulating two exposure drafts to its membership. The SEC held hearings on the proposal, and on July 3, 1980 it sent to the NASD a letter requesting that it consider amending the proposals in certain respects.[57] The NASD amended the proposed rule changes, and they were then approved by the membership. The NASD filed its final amended version on September 4, 1980. The proposal was approved by the SEC on December 12, 1980.[58]

• *Analysis of the Papilsky Rules*

Having reviewed the circumstances leading up to their adoption and the purpose that they are intended to accomplish, the *Papilsky* rules and interpretations can now be examined in detail.

• • *Rule 2740 (Selling Commissions, Discounts and Other Allowances).* The basic operative provision designed to assure the integrity of the fixed price distribution system is Rule 2740.

---

56. *See also Moses v. Burgin,* 445 F.2d 369 (1st Cir. 1971), *cert. denied,* 404 U.S. 994 (1971); *Fogel v. Chestnutt,* 533 F.2d 731 (2d Cir. 1975), *cert. denied,* 429 U.S. 824 (1976); *Tannenbaum v. Zeller,* 552 F.2d 402 (2d Cir. 1977), *reversing* 399 F. Supp. 945 (S.D.N.Y. 1975), *cert. denied,* 434 U.S. 934 (1977).

57. SEC Release No. 34-16956 (July 3, 1980).

58. SEC Release No. 34-17371 (December 12, 1980).

This rule provides that, in connection with the sale of securities that are part of a fixed price offering:

> A member may not grant or receive selling concessions, discounts, or other allowances except as consideration for services rendered in distribution and may not grant such concessions, discounts or other allowances to anyone other than a broker or dealer actually engaged in the investment banking or securities business; provided, however, that nothing in this Rule shall prevent any member from (1) selling any such securities to any person, or account managed by any person, to whom it has provided or will provide bona fide research, if the stated public offering price for such securities is paid by the purchaser; or (2) selling any such securities owned by him to any person at any net price which may be fixed by him unless prevented therefrom by agreement.

A related rule, Rule 2420 (Dealing with Non-Members), prohibits NASD members from allowing selling concessions, discounts or other allowances to non-member broker-dealers, except for certain foreign dealers.[59] Thus, the broker-dealers referred to in Rule 2740 must be NASD members or non-member foreign dealers who satisfy the requirements of Rule 2420. It should also be noted that IM-2420-1(d)(2) states that banks and trust companies may not receive selling concessions, discounts or other allowances under Rule 2740 in connection with distributions of securities. This is because banks and trust companies are excluded from the relevant definitions of "broker" and "dealer" in the NASD's By-Laws.

Rule 2740 applies to reallowances as well as to selling concessions. The NASD's interpretation of Rule 2740—IM-2740—provides:

> A broker or dealer who has received or retained a selling concession, discount or other allowance may not

---

59. Rule 2420 also prohibits a member from joining in any syndicate or group with such a non-member in connection with a public offering.

grant or otherwise reallow all or part of that concession, discount or allowance to anyone other than a broker or dealer engaged in the investment banking or securities business and only as consideration for services rendered in distribution.

A member is not his or her brother's keeper, however. The interpretation goes on to state:

A member granting a selling concession, discount or other allowance to another person is not responsible for determining whether such other person may be violating Rule 2740 by granting or reallowing that selling concession, discount or other allowance to another person, unless the member knew, or had reasonable cause to know, of the violation.

Rule 2740 is applicable only to a fixed price offering, which term is defined as follows in Rule 0120:

The term "fixed price offering" means the offering of securities at a stated public offering price or prices, all or part of which securities are publicly offered in the United States or any territory thereof, whether or not registered under the Securities Act of 1933, except that the term does not include offerings of "exempted securities" or "municipal securities" as those terms are defined in Sections 3(a)(12) and 3(a)(29), respectively, of the [Securities Exchange] Act [of 1934] or offerings of redeemable securities of investment companies registered pursuant to the Investment Company Act of 1940 which are offered at prices determined by the net asset value of the securities.

Offerings of exempted securities and municipal securities are excluded because they are largely outside of the NASD's jurisdiction. Mutual fund shares are excluded because Section 22(d) of the 1940 Act expressly prohibits dealers from selling such securities at prices below the public offering price.[60] Wholly foreign offerings are not covered. Thus, in a Eurobond offering made exclusively abroad (even where a portion of the securities are privately placed in the United States), an NASD member participating in the offering may follow the European practice of reallowing a portion of the selling concession to banks that are purchasing for the account of customers.

IM-2740 states that a dealer has rendered services in distribution "if the dealer is an underwriter of a portion of that offering, has engaged in some selling effort with respect to the sale or has provided or agreed to provide bona fide research to the person to whom or at whose direction the sale is made." The interpretation makes the same point in slightly different terms where it states that "nothing in Rule 2740 prohibits a member from providing bona fide research to a customer who also purchases securities from fixed price offerings from the member whether or not there is an express or implied agreement between the member providing the research and the recipient that the member will be compensated for the research in cash, brokerage commissions, selling concessions or some other form of consideration."

The key term is "bona fide research," which is defined as follows in Rule 2740(b):

> The term "bona fide research," when used in this Rule means advice, rendered either directly or through publications or writings, as to the value of securities, the advisability of investing in, purchasing, or selling securities, and the availability of securities or purchasers or sellers of securities, or analyses and reports concerning issuers, industries, securities, economic factors and trends, portfolio strategy, and performance of accounts; provided, however, that investment management or investment discretionary services are not bona fide research.

---

60. See *Spiro Sideris,* 44 S.E.C. 212 (1970).

The meaning of the term "bona fide research" is elaborated upon in IM-2740. It is noted in that interpretation that the Rule 2740(b) definition of bona fide research is substantially the same as the definition of the term "research" in Section 28(e)(3) of the 1934 Act.[61] Interpretations concerning the definition of research under Section 28(e) are referred to for guidance, including SEC Release No. 34-23170 (April 30, 1986).

IM-2740 goes on to make the following observations:

> Moreover, while the provisions in Rule 2740 concerning bona fide research are intended to permit money managers to receive bona fide research from persons from whom securities are purchased, it is not intended to enable a money manager, who is also a member, to view its money management services as bona fide research. Accordingly, the performance of money management or investment discretionary services themselves are expressly excluded from the definition of bona fide research.
>
> Another factor relating to bona fide research is that the research must be "provided by" the member who receives or retains the selling concession, discount or other allowance. Under Section 28(e) of the [Securities Exchange] Act [of 1934], the Commission has stated that the "safe harbor" provided by Section 28(e) only extends to research that is "provided by" the broker to whom brokerage commissions are paid. In determining whether the exclusion for bona fide research under Rule 2740 is available in any given instance, members should refer to the interpretations of the Commission and its

---

61. Section 28(e), which was enacted in 1975 following the elimination of fixed stock exchange commissions, provides that a mutual fund advisor or other fiduciary may cause an account with respect to which it exercises investment discretion to pay a commission in excess of that which another broker would have charged if it determines in good faith that the commission paid is reasonable "in relation to the value of the brokerage and research services provided." Thus, fiduciaries may "pay up" for research.

staff of the similar requirement applicable to Section 28(e).

A member who, directly or through an affiliate, supplies another person with services or products that fail to qualify as bona fide research, or that, in the case of services or products other than bona fide research, are provided to customers for cash or for some other consideration, and also retains or receives selling concessions, discounts or other allowances from purchases by that person, is improperly granting a selling concession, discount or other allowance to that person unless it has been, or has arranged and reasonably expects to be, fully compensated for such services or products from sources other than the selling concession, discount or allowance. The net effect of this is that NASD members simply should not provide these products or services to their customers unless they are prepared to demonstrate that they have been fully compensated for them with consideration other than selling concessions, discounts or other allowances received or retained on the sale of securities in fixed price offerings.

The interpretation states that, in order to demonstrate that the cash or other consideration is full consideration, records should be kept that identify the recipient of the services or products and the amount of cash or other consideration paid or to be paid. The interpretation also states that, unless the amount of cash or other consideration agreed upon appears on its face to be unreasonably low, it will not be necessary to demonstrate that the agreed upon price represented fair market price. There is no requirement that the member charge the same amount to each person to whom it provides the same or similar services or products.

Rule 2740(d) imposes quarterly reporting requirements on members receiving an order designating another broker or dealer to receive credit for a sale. Rule 2740(e) imposes similar record keeping requirements on designees.

NASD rules require that certain agreements be entered into by dealers participating in a distribution. Rule 2740(c) provides:

A member who grants a selling concession, discount or other allowance to another person shall obtain a written agreement from that person that he will comply with the provisions of this Rule, and a member who grants such selling concession, discount or other allowance to a non-member broker or dealer in a foreign country shall also obtain from such broker or dealer a written agreement to comply, as though such broker or dealer were a member, with the provisions of Rules 2730 and 2750 and to comply with Rule 2420 as that Rule applies to a non-member broker/dealer in a foreign country.

Rule 2420(c) requires that, if concessions are allowed to foreign dealers not eligible for NASD membership, "a member shall as a condition of such transaction secure from such foreign broker or dealer an agreement that, in making any sales to purchasers within the United States of securities acquired as a result of such transactions, he will conform to the provisions of paragraphs (a) and (b) of this Rule to the same extent as though he were a member of the [NASD]." It should be noted that any foreign dealer that is registered with the SEC under Section 15 of the 1934 Act is eligible for membership in the NASD.

The practice is to include the agreements required by Rule 2740(c) and Rule 2420(c) in the AAU and the selected dealers agreement. The following is a common form of agreement running from the syndicate members to the managers:

Membership in National Association of Securities Dealers, Inc.; Foreign Underwriters. We understand that you are a member in good standing of the NASD. We confirm that we are actually engaged in the investment banking or securities business and are either (i) a member in good standing of the NASD or (ii) a dealer with its principal place of business located outside the United States, its territories and its possessions and not registered under the 1934 Act who hereby agrees to make no sales within the United States, its territories or its possessions or to persons who are nationals thereof or residents therein (except that we may participate in sales to

Selected Dealers and others under Section 5 of this Agreement). We hereby agree to comply with Rule 2740 of the NASD, and if we are a foreign dealer and not a member of the NASD we also hereby agree to comply with the NASD's interpretation with respect to free-riding and withholding, to comply, as though we were a member of the NASD, with the provisions of Rules 2730 and 2750 and to comply with Rule 2420 as that provision applies to a non-member foreign dealer.

The approval by the SEC of the predecessor of amended Rule 2740 put to rest any question as to whether the NASD is authorized to bring disciplinary proceedings based on violations of the price maintenance provisions of an AAU. In 1945, the SEC had determined that the NASD did not have this power on the basis that an NASD interpretation specifically requiring adherence to price maintenance agreements would be contrary to the provisions of what is now designated as Section 15A(b)(6) of the 1934 Act.[62] This section provides that the rules of the NASD shall not be designed to "impose any schedule or fix rates of commissions, allowances, discounts, or other fees to be charged by its members."

In connection with the adoption of amended Rule 2740, the SEC stated that, regardless of the merits of its analysis in 1945, it was now required to review rules proposed by the NASD under a different standard than was then in effect and that it could now weigh the beneficial purposes of an NASD rule against any burdens on competition. The SEC concluded that it was no longer correct to follow the *per se* approach that it followed in 1945 when it considered irrelevant any beneficial aspects of the NASD's interpretation of its rules.[63]

---

62. *National Association of Securities Dealers, Inc.,* 19 S.E.C. 424 (1945).

63. One author has criticized this position and has called upon the SEC to abrogate the NASD's antidiscounting rules. H.S. Gerla, *Swimming Against*

• • *Rule 2730 (Securities Taken in Trade)*. The improper grant or reallowance of a selling concession or discount may be made indirectly by the use of such devices as "overtrading." This is precisely what Rule 2730 is designed to prevent.

Swapping is a legitimate technique in the sale of underwritten securities. In a swap transaction, securities are taken "in trade" from a customer in exchange for the underwritten securities. This allows an underwriter or dealer to reduce its risk by diversifying its holdings if it is unable to sell the underwritten securities for cash. It permits an institution to purchase securities being offered where it does not have available cash to pay for them or where for other reasons it prefers not to pay cash. Swaps are seldom, if ever, used in connection with common stock offerings. In practice, they are limited to offerings of debt securities or other securities that trade on the basis of yield. In making the trade, if the underwriter or dealer places a higher value on the swapped securities than they are actually worth, then this may be viewed as an indirect rebate of the selling concession. Rule 2730 has provided for many years that securities may be taken in trade only at their fair market price at the time of purchase. It also provides guidance as to what constitutes a fair price.

Rule 2730(a) provides:

> A member engaged in a fixed price offering, who purchases or arranges the purchase of securities taken in trade, shall purchase the securities at a fair market price at the time of purchase or shall act as agent in the sale of such securities and charge a normal commission therefor.

Rule 2730(b)(1) defines "taken in trade" to mean "the purchase by a member as principal, or as agent for the account of another, of a security from a customer pursuant to an agreement or understanding that the customer purchase securities from the member which are part of a fixed price offering." The term "fair market price" is defined to mean a price not higher than the price at which the securities would be purchased in the ordinary course of business by a dealer in such securities in transactions of similar size and having similar characteristics but not involving a security taken in trade. The term "normal commission" is defined in a similar manner.

Rule 2730(c) and its interpretation IM-2730 together establish certain benchmarks, presumptions and recordkeeping obligations relating to what is the fair market price of common stocks and securities other than common stocks. With respect to common stocks, a member is "presumed," and with respect to other securities is "deemed," to have taken them in trade at a fair market price when the price paid is not higher than the highest independent bid at the time of purchase, if bid quotations are readily available. A member is "presumed" to have taken a security in trade at a price higher than the fair market price when the price paid is higher than the lowest independent offer for the securities at the time of purchase, if offer quotations are readily available. If bid and offer quotations are not readily available for the security taken in trade, a member may rely upon quotations for comparable securities. In instances where a member takes securities in trade at a price higher than the highest independent bid and not higher than the lowest independent offer, or when bid and offer quotations are not readily available, there is no safe harbor and there is neither a presumption of compliance or of non-compliance. If the securities taken in trade are common stocks that are traded on an exchange or quoted in Nasdaq, the quotations must be obtained from the exchange or the Nasdaq screen. Quotations for all other securities must be obtained from at least two other dealers. The quotations must be for a transaction of a size corresponding generally to the amount of securities taken in trade.

As of when is the fair market value of the securities taken in trade to be determined? IM-2730 states the NASD's view that swap transactions "that are arranged before the effectiveness of a fixed price offering are not generally viewed as being legally consummated until effectiveness of the fixed price offering." It goes on to state that the fair market price of the securities taken in trade is nonetheless "normally determined at the time of the pricing of the fixed price offering, which occurs on the day before effectiveness usually in the afternoon, and the swap is arranged on the basis of that price." In such cases, according to IM-2730, the determination of the fair market price of the securities taken in trade "may be made as of the time of pricing of the fixed price offering."

The foregoing guidelines obviously predate the use of shelf registration and Rule 430A prospectuses, which make the effective date of the registration statement irrelevant as a guide to the enforceability of a swap. They are clearly correct, however, in focusing on the pricing of the new securities as a better guide to the proper time of valuation than the time of "effectiveness." On the other hand, it is clearly open to a securities firm and a customer to agree that the trade date for the purchase of securities by the securities firm will be a date other than the date of pricing of the new issue. In such a case, the fair market price on the trade date should control for purposes of Rule 2730. The interpretation implies as much when it states that when swaps are agreed to after the effectiveness of the offering (i.e., after pricing), then the fair market price of the swapped securities "must be determined as of the time the transaction is legally consummated," i.e., the trade date.

• • *Rule 2750 (Transactions with Related Persons).* One method that an institution would use to recapture selling concessions was to establish an affiliate as a member of the NASD and to designate the affiliate as the dealer to receive credit for the selling concession. This is what the plaintiff in *Papilsky* claimed that Affiliated Fund should have done.

The predecessor of Rule 2750 was adopted specifically to prohibit recapture through affiliated NASD members. Rule 2750 provides that no NASD member engaged in a fixed price offering of securities shall sell the securities to, or place the securities with, any person or account which is a "related person" of the member unless such related person is itself subject to Rule 2750 or is a non-member foreign broker or dealer who has entered into the agreements required by Rule 2740. A "related person" of a member includes any person or account which directly or indirectly owns, is owned by, or is under common ownership with the member. A person is deemed to own another person if it has the right to participate to the extent of more than 25% in the profits of the other person or owns beneficially more than 25% of the outstanding voting securities of that person.

By virtue of Rule 2750, an NASD member may not participate in an underwriting and sell any of the securities to an institution with which it is affiliated. A member may place securities with a related person, however, if it has made a bona fide public offering of the securities. There can be no claim that a bona fide public offering has been made if the securities immediately trade at a premium in the secondary market. An interpretation to Rule 2750 makes it clear that a sponsor of a unit investment trust will not violate Rule 2750 if it accumulates securities with respect to which it has acted as a member of the underwriting syndicate or selling group if, at the time of accumulation, it intends in good faith to deposit the securities into the unit investment trust at the public offering price and intends to make a public offering of the units.

Underwritings Involving Conflicts of Interest

Rule 2720 imposes a number of special requirements when a member of the NASD participates in a public offering that is deemed under the rule or certain related rules to present a particular kind of conflict of interest. The rule's original concern involved a public offering of the NASD member's own debt or equity securities or those issued by its parent or affiliate. The scope of the rule has been expanded to cover certain other public offerings where similar conflicts of interest may be present.

The principal requirement of Rule 2720 is that the price at which the securities are to be sold to the public be no higher than that recommended by a "qualified independent underwriter." In the case of a debt issue, the yield may be no lower than that recommended by the qualified independent underwriter. To satisfy Rule 2720, the qualified independent underwriter must participate in the preparation of the registration statement and must exercise the usual standards of due diligence with respect thereto.

Independent pricing is not required if the offering is of a class of equity securities for which a bona fide independent market exists both on the date that the registration statement is filed and the date that it becomes effective. Nor is it required if the offering is of a class of securities rated Baa or better by Moody's Investor Services or BBB or better by Standard & Poor's Corporation or is rated in a comparable category by another rating service acceptable to the NASD.

• *Background*

The predecessor of Rule 2720 came into being in the early 1970s when securities firms first began to seek capital from the public, rather than simply relying upon the capital contributed by officers and other employees engaged in the business. This was a time when the securities industry had a real need for additional working capital. Moreover, the industry was beginning to recognize the importance of permanent capital, capital that could not be withdrawn if a large shareholder died or decided to leave the firm.[64]

The first securities firm to have a registered public offering was Grimm & Davis, Inc., which had a combination primary and secondary offering sold on a best efforts basis by D.H. Magid & Co. under a prospectus dated April 23, 1969. This firm was not a member of a securities exchange, but if it had been, its public offering would have been prohibited. At that time, the constitution and rules of the NYSE contained provisions incompatible with public ownership. These provisions included a requirement that every shareholder of a NYSE member firm must be approved by the Board of Governors of the exchange and must agree not to sell or otherwise deal in his stock without the prior approval of the NYSE. The NYSE also required that every holder of voting stock of a member firm be a member or allied member of the NYSE and an officer or employee actively engaged in the business of the member firm.

---

64. An excellent account of this critical period in the history of the securities industry can be found in D.T. Regan, *A View From The Street* (New American Library 1972), particularly Chapter VII.

In 1969, Dan W. Lufkin, Chairman of the Board of Donaldson, Lufkin & Jenrette, Inc. ("DLJ") and a governor of the NYSE, announced to his fellow governors that DLJ intended to file a registration statement for a public offering of its common stock notwithstanding the provisions of the Exchange's constitution and rules.

The firm filed a registration statement on May 22, 1969 naming The First Boston Corporation as its managing underwriter. The firm's preliminary prospectus stated that since its inception in 1959, DLJ had been a member corporation of the NYSE and that the sale of the common stock offered to the public would result in DLJ's being deprived of the privileges of membership unless there were changes in the Exchange's established policies and regulations. It stated that DLJ's ability to avail itself of opportunities for continued growth was a more important consideration than the revenues attributable to NYSE commissions (approximately 63% of its 1968 revenues). The preliminary prospectus went on to state that DLJ was satisfied that significant additions to permanent capital could be obtained most advantageously, if not only, through public financing, and that, accordingly, it had decided to proceed with the offering despite NYSE regulations denying member corporations access to "this otherwise conventional source of capital."

The preliminary prospectus also disclosed that Mr. Lufkin, in his capacity as a NYSE governor, had initiated action for amendments to the constitution and rules of the NYSE to permit public participation in the ownership of equity securities of member corporations. In fact, DLJ delayed its public offering until the NYSE amended its rules to permit public ownership. Pursuant to a prospectus dated April 9, 1970, DLJ made a public offering of 800,000 primary shares through an underwriting syndicate comprised of 90 investment banking firms. Later in 1970, Weeden & Co., a "third market" dealer, had a public offering of 300,000 shares of common stock through a small underwriting syndicate headed by Bache & Co. Incorporated.

Merrill Lynch, Pierce, Fenner & Smith Incorporated had for some time been studying the possibility of going public. As early as 1961, the firm had urged the NYSE to amend its rules by

pointing out the compelling reasons for public ownership.[65]
The firm was determined that, if and when it did go public, it
would "underwrite its own stock," i.e., it would manage the
distribution itself, selling a portion of the shares directly to its
own customers and a portion through a selling group. Its management reasoned that if the firm did not participate in the distribution of its own stock, it would be extremely difficult for its
more than 1.5 million customers to buy shares in the offering.
For them to do so, it would be necessary for them to place their
purchase orders through other brokers. The prospect of its customers opening brokerage accounts at other firms was not to
Merrill Lynch's liking. Moreover, by selling the stock itself,
Merrill Lynch estimated that it would save many millions of
dollars in underwriting costs.

At that time, however, the NASD had a "policy" that prohibited NASD members from participating in the distribution
of their own securities. In 1970, this policy was made a part of
the interpretation with respect to the review of corporate financing.[66] It was represented to be a restatement of the existing
policy of the Board of Governors. It provided in pertinent part
as follows:

> The Board of Governors of the [NASD] has announced
> a policy that a member firm of the [NASD] desiring to
> go to the public market for funds may not underwrite its
> own securities, either directly or indirectly, through a
> parent or subsidiary, or participate in any capacity in
> the distribution of those securities. Where such is done,
> a determination of an unfair or unreasonable underwrit-
> ing arrangement will result.

In September 1970, the Board of Governors of the NASD
appointed a committee to critically examine this policy with a
view towards its relaxation. By the spring of 1971, it was generally known in the securities industry that this policy would
indeed be relaxed and that one of the conditions for self-

---

65. *Id.* at 130.
66. NASD Notice to Members (March 10, 1970).

underwriting would be that the price at which the securities were sold to the public would be subject to the approval of two qualified independent underwriters. They generally were referred to in the industry at that time as "pricers."

Merrill Lynch announced to its shareholders on April 8, 1971 and to the public on April 12, 1971 that it intended to have a public offering of its common stock. At that time, the firm had every reason to believe that the then anticipated change in policy that would permit NASD members to participate in the distribution of their own securities would take the form of a modification of the existing policy statement and that it would be adopted by the Board of Governors without a membership vote. There had been no inkling that the change would require anything more. On April 12, 1971, an article appeared in *The Wall Street Journal* stating that regulation of self-underwriting would be governed by a schedule to the NASD's by-laws that would require the approval of the NASD membership.

Merrill Lynch filed its registration statement with the SEC on April 23, 1971. The preliminary prospectus indicated that the fairness of the public offering price would be passed upon by three independent investment banking firms, one more than it was expected that the NASD would require. At the same time, the registration statement, the preliminary prospectus, and the form of dealer agreement were filed with the NASD's Corporate Financing Department. On May 8, 1971, the NASD issued a Notice to Members entitled "Proposed Amendment To By-Laws and Rules Of Fair Practice (Interpretations) Governing The Distribution Of Securities Of Members." Merrill Lynch then received a letter dated May 11, 1971 from the Director of the Corporate Financing Department stating that, on the basis of the present policy of the NASD prohibiting members from either directly or indirectly underwriting their own securities, the plan of distribution proposed by Merrill Lynch was deemed to be an unfair and unreasonable underwriting arrangement. The letter referred to the proposed amendments, but pointed out that they were subject to a comment period, re-review by the Board of Governors, submission to the membership for vote, and action by the SEC. The letter stated that, in the interim period, the NASD would continue to enforce its existing policy.

Merrill Lynch protested vigorously in a May 14, 1971 letter from its president to the Director of the Corporate Financing Department stating that the distribution arrangements contemplated by the firm conformed in every particular to the new schedule proposed by the Board of Governors. The letter also stated that to ensure that the arrangements were totally fair, registered representatives would receive no production credit nor compensation for any purchases of Merrill Lynch stock made in accounts that they served. On May 27, 1971, Donald T. Regan, then Chairman of the Board of Merrill Lynch, appeared before a subcommittee of the Board of Governors of the NASD and requested that, at the meeting of the Board of Governors scheduled for June 17, 1971, action be taken to permit any NASD member to participate in the distribution of its own securities prior to the adoption of the proposed amendments to the NASD by-laws and the related schedule, provided that the distribution complied with the requirements of the schedule as proposed.

Under date of June 23, 1971, the Committee on Corporate Financing stated that it would raise no objections with respect to the fairness and reasonableness of the distribution arrangements proposed by Merrill Lynch. Thus ended weeks of considerable tension. Through effective advocacy, a problem had been resolved that otherwise would have resulted in an unacceptable postponement of Merrill Lynch's initial public offering.

A Notice to Members dated June 23, 1971 announced that at its June 17 meeting the Board of Governors agreed to modify the interpretation on corporation financing to allow members to underwrite their own securities and that, because of the critical need for permanent capital, members could submit self-underwriting proposals that would be reviewed on an individual basis. Merrill Lynch's registration statement was declared effective on the same day. The public offering price of $28 per share was fixed in accordance with the recommendations of The First Boston Corporation, Lehman Brothers, and Morgan Stanley & Co.

• *Analysis of Rule 2720*

The predecessor to Rule 2720 was adopted in March 1972, nine months after Merrill Lynch went public.[67] Since then, it has been amended several times, and it now applies to NASD members' participation in their own and their affiliates' public offerings of debt or equity securities as well as to offerings as to which they or their affiliates have a "conflict of interest." (A "conflict of interest" is deemed to exist where an NASD member and its associated persons and affiliates beneficially own 10% of more of the issuer's common or preferred stock or subordinated debt.) In addition, as noted earlier under "Venture Capital Restrictions" and "Proceeds Directed to a Member," NASD members are required in these situations to follow Rule 2720's qualified independent underwriter procedures.

The core of Rule 2720 is the requirement that if a member participates in the distribution of its own securities or those of an affiliate (as defined), the offering price may be no higher, or the yield on debt securities no lower, than that recommended by a qualified independent underwriter. (Two are no longer required.) In the case of an offering of securities by a member of the NASD that has not been actively engaged in the investment banking or securities business for at least the past five years, a qualified independent underwriter must manage the offering. These requirements are not applicable if the offering is of a class of equity securities for which there is a bona fide independent market or of a class of securities rated Baa or better by Moody's or BBB by Standard & Poor's or rated in a comparable category by another rating service acceptable to the NASD. In no event may a member participate in the distribution of its own or an affiliate's securities unless a majority of its board of directors or partners have been actively engaged in the investment banking or securities business for at least five years.

To be a qualified independent underwriter, a firm must meet the detailed requirements set forth in Rule 2720. It must not be an affiliate of the issuer or own 5% or more of the issuer's out-

---

67. NASD Notice to Members (March 30, 1972).

standing voting securities. It must have been actively engaged in the investment banking or securities business for at least five years, and it must have been profitable at least three of those five years. A majority of its board of directors or general partners must have been actively engaged in the investment banking or securities business during the preceding five years, and the firm must have been actively engaged in the underwriting of public offerings of securities of a similar size and type during that period. The firm will not be acceptable as a qualified independent underwriter if any person associated with it in a supervisory capacity responsible for organizing, structuring or performing due diligence with respect to corporate public offerings of securities has within the past five years been convicted, enjoined or been subject to certain disciplinary action as a result of a violation of the antifraud provisions of Federal or state securities laws.

The qualified independent underwriter must participate in the preparation of the offering document and must exercise the usual standards of due diligence with respect to the offering. As originally adopted, the predecessor of Rule 2720 required that the qualified independent underwriters be represented by independent legal counsel. This is no longer a requirement, although it is still customary for qualified independent underwriters to retain counsel to assist them in the transaction.

Rule 2720 contains certain disclosure requirements. It also requires that all proceeds from an offering by an NASD member (i.e., a broker-dealer subject to the SEC's net capital rule) be placed in escrow, whether or not the member participates in the distribution. The funds cannot be released from escrow until the member has satisfied the NASD that it meets certain net capital standards. If it does not, the funds must be returned to the investors. Escrow is not required for the sale of securities of a member's holding company parent. Most securities firms that tap the public market on a regular basis do so through a holding company, and accordingly the escrow provision of Rule 2720 has not presented a problem.

A member or a parent of a member that makes a public offering of securities must establish an audit committee within 12 months thereafter and within that period must cause to be elected to its board of directors a public director who serves as a member of the audit committee. A member that makes a distribution to the public of an issue of its securities must send to investors quarterly summary statements of operations and annual certified financial statements. These requirements apply even if the member does not participate in the distribution.

Rule 2720 establishes strict suitability requirements for members underwriting their own securities or those of an affiliate. The suitability determination must be based on information furnished by the customer, and the member must maintain in its files the basis for its suitability determination. A transaction in securities of a member or an affiliate of a member may not be executed by any member in a discretionary account without the prior written approval of the customer. This prohibition is not limited to a member selling its own or its affiliate's securities. It is also applicable to a member selling securities of another member or that member's affiliate.

Notwithstanding the interpretation with respect to free-riding and withholding, Rule 2720(m) permits a member to sell securities issued by it or its parent to its own employees without limitation as to amount and regardless of whether such persons have an investment history with the member. In the case of an offering of equity securities for which a bona fide independent market does not exist, the employees may not sell, pledge or transfer the securities for a period of five months following the effective date of the offering.

The term "affiliate" as used in Rule 2720 is defined as a company that controls, is controlled by, or is under common control with the member. Ownership of a 10% interest creates a presumption of control. Excluded from the category of affiliates are registered investment companies, real estate investment trusts, direct participation programs, and entities issuing financing instrument-backed securities rated investment grade.

Potential Liabilities of Qualified Independent Underwriters

A footnote to Rule 2720 states that, in the opinion of the NASD and the SEC, "the full responsibilities and liabilities of an underwriter" under the 1933 Act attach to a qualified independent underwriter performing the functions called for by the rule. Many practitioners have doubted that a qualified independent underwriter should be liable under Section 11, particularly where the firm performing the pricing function was not a member of the underwriting syndicate and did not otherwise participate in the distribution of the securities. The contrary conclusion would require a considerable stretch of the Section 2(11) definition of "underwriter" to bring within its terms a firm that does no more than recommend the price, perform due diligence and participate in the drafting of the registration statement.

Even assuming that the pricer is an underwriter with Section 11 liability, there remains the question of the extent of this liability. The SEC and the NASD presumably believe that the pricer may be liable for the entire offering. This position would have to ignore, of course, the provision in Section 11(e) to the effect that an underwriter may not be held liable for damages "in excess of the total price at which the securities underwritten by him and distributed to the public were offered to the public." The pricer would argue that it has not "underwritten" any securities in the sense contemplated by Section 11(e).

The issue was first joined in connection with the Merrill Lynch initial public offering. One of the SEC's initial comments on the registration statement was that it should be indicated that the three investment banking firms performing the pricing function "will be deemed to be underwriters" as that term is defined in the 1933 Act and that the fees paid to them may be deemed underwriting compensation. The comment was responded to by including a sentence that stated, "The three firms may be deemed to be 'underwriters' as that term is defined in the Securities Act of 1933, and the amounts paid to these firms for their services may be deemed to be underwriting compensation, but such interpretation is categorically denied by the three firms and ML." The SEC flexed its muscles, and the issue was resolved by deleting the word "categorically." Among the muscle flexing was a demand that the SEC be furnished with an opinion of counsel for Merrill Lynch as to the underwriter status of the three pricers and whether they are "experts" for purposes of Section 11. Counsel rendered an opinion that the firms were neither "underwriters" nor "experts."

The Notice to Members announcing the adoption of the predecessor of Rule 2720 stated that the SEC "has expressed the view that the most important factor involved in its authorization of self-underwritings by members is that the responsibilities and liabilities of underwriters under the Securities Act attach to qualified independent underwriters." For this reason, and because of its recognition that the question had never been adjudicated, the SEC required that a footnote expressing its views be included in the predecessor of Rule 2720 as a condition to not disapproving the self-underwriting proposal. Another condition was that the NASD propose to its membership an amendment to the rule that would bring a firm within the definition of "qualified independent underwriter" only if it "has agreed in connection with the offering in respect to which he is acting as such to undertake the full legal responsibilities and liabilities of an underwriter under the Securities Act of 1933, specifically including those inherent in the provisions of Section 11 thereof."

A provision to this effect is now included in the definition of "qualified independent underwriter" appearing in Rule 2720. Investment banking firms have been able to live with the requirement that they enter into such an agreement as a condition to being a qualified independent underwriter. The agreement customarily is included in the letter recommending the price, but it is entered into with certain qualifications. Thus, a pricing letter from a qualified independent underwriter to an issuer might state as follows:

> [W]e undertake the legal responsibilities and liabilities of an "underwriter" under the Securities Act of 1933, specifically including those inherent in Section 11 thereof. It is specifically understood, however, that we will bear such legal responsibilities and liabilities only to the extent, if any, that a court of competent jurisdiction rules in a judgment which has become final, and not subject to further appeal, that we, in our capacity as a "qualified independent underwriter," bear the legal re-

sponsibilities and liabilities of an "underwriter." We understand that views expressed by, the NASD and the Securities and Exchange Commission indicate that, in acting as a "qualified independent underwriter," we may be deemed to be an "underwriter" within the meaning of the Securities Act of 1933. There are, however, questions of statutory interpretation regarding the underwriter status of a "qualified independent underwriter" which have not yet been judicially determined.

Many prospectuses will state that the qualified independent underwriter may be deemed to be an "underwriter" within the meaning of the 1933 Act, and that the amount paid to it may be underwriting compensation but that these are questions that have not yet been judicially determined. Other prospectuses are silent on the issue.

Unfortunately for the qualified independent underwriter, a recent Seventh Circuit decision provides strong support for the SEC and NASD position. In *Harden v. Raffensperger, Hughes & Co., Inc.*[68] an NASD member had retained Raffensperger, Hughes & Co. ("Raffensperger") to act as its qualified independent underwriter for a $20 million note offering by one of its subsidiaries. Raffensperger did not join the underwriting syndicate and did not offer or sell any notes. Following the offering and the issuer's subsequent bankruptcy, Raffensperger was sued in a class action under Section 11 and related provisions of federal law. The Seventh Circuit affirmed the trial court's denial of Raffensperger's motion for summary judgment.

First, the court held that a qualified independent underwriter is an "underwriter" subject to Section 11 liability even where it is not a syndicate member. The court relied on Section 2(11)'s reference to an underwriter as including anyone who "participates or has a direct or indirect participation" in a registered offering. The court found that Raffensperger had "par-

---

68. 65 F.3d 1392 (7th Cir. 1995), reh. den., 1995 U.S. App. LEXIS 29723 (7th Cir. 1995).

ticipated" in the offering even though it had not purchased, offered or sold any securities.

Raffensperger also argued that because it was not a syndicate member and did not underwrite or sell any securities, its pro rata share of the offering for Section 11(e) purposes was zero. The court found, however, that Raffensperger had acted as a qualified independent underwriter with respect to the entire note offering, thus "perform[ing] the protective function envisioned by the 1933 Congress with respect to the entire . . . distribution." In essence, then, Raffensperger had underwritten and incurred Section 11 liability for all the notes.

If the Seventh Circuit is correct in its holding that a qualified independent underwriter incurs Section 11 liability for the entire offering, then such an underwriter needs to assess this additional risk in making its decision to assume this responsibility and in determining its requirements with respect to compensation and indemnity protection.

Chapter 7

PRIVATE PLACEMENTS

Section 4(2) of the 1933 Act exempts from the registration and prospectus delivery requirements of Section 5 all "transactions by an issuer not involving any public offering." This is the so-called "private offering" or "private placement" exemption. Issuers rely on the exemption for a wide variety of transactions, ranging from the initial sale of "founders' stock" by a new business to a billion-dollar sale of investment-grade debt securities by a "world-class" issuer to literally hundreds of institutional investors. The exemption may also be used for venture capital investments, for acquisitions of closely held corporations where all or part of the consideration is securities of the acquiring corporation, or for sales of limited partnership interests to individual investors.

As in the case of other exemptions from the requirements of Section 5, the person claiming an exemption has the burden of establishing that the exemption is available for the particular transaction. If securities are sold without registration and without a valid exemption, Section 12(a)(1) of the 1933 Act gives the purchaser a right to rescind the transaction for a period of one year after the sale. This right may be exercised against anyone who "sold" the security, which means the passing of title or the solicitation of the sale for the purpose of serving one's own financial interests or those of the securities owner.[1] The seller's good faith belief that the exemption was available is irrelevant, as is the fact that the seller may have provided the purchaser with full and fair disclosure.

The procedures appropriate to establish the exemption will depend on the nature of the transaction. Section 4(2) is self-executing and may be relied upon by an issuer—and its financial intermediaries, if any—on the basis of many decades of court cases, SEC rulings and "lore." In the case of many transactions, however, issuers and financial intermediaries will prefer to rely on SEC rules that provide more certainty than Section 4(2).

Regulation D is the SEC's current set of rules that govern private placements by issuers. When the purchasers are institutional investors, as we will see, Regulation D permits an offering to a potentially indefinite number of institutions.

The field of institutional private placements has been revolutionized since 1990, however, by an SEC rule that does not even apply to a private placement by an issuer. Rule 144A by its terms only permits persons *other than the issuer* to resell "restricted" securities, i.e., securities that they have purchased directly or indirectly from the issuer (or an affiliate of the issuer) in a transaction or series of transactions not involving a public offering. Rule 144A's powerful influence on the market arises from the fact that a financial intermediary can purchase securities from an issuer as principal on a "firm commitment" basis and rely on Rule 144A to resell those securities, subject to a few easily-verified conditions, to a potentially indefinite number of "qualified institutional buyers."

This chapter will describe the history of the Section 4(2) exemption, including the early administrative emphasis on the number of offerees and the Supreme Court's shift of emphasis in *Ralston Purina*[2] to the ability of offerees to "fend for themselves." It will describe how the SEC—usually yielding only reluctantly to the pressure of market realities but sometimes

---

1. *Pinter v. Dahl*, 486 U.S. 622, 642–47 (1988).
2. *SEC v. Ralston Purina Co.*, 346 U.S. 119 (1953).

leading the charge—built on the statutory exemption in ways that would likely have astounded the drafters of the 1933 Act. The SEC's efforts culminated with the adoption of Regulation D in 1982 and Rule 144A in 1990. These rules, which established for all intents and purposes a reliable exemption for sales to institutional investors (not unlike that found in state blue sky statutes[3]), can best be understood in the light of the circumstances that led to their adoption.

Legislative History

The original bill introduced in the House and Senate in 1933, as drafted by Houston Thompson,[4] did not include a private offering exemption as such.[5] It did include an exemption for "the issuance of additional capital stock of a corporation sold or distributed by it among its own stockholders exclusively," where no commission or other remuneration was paid in connection with the sale or distribution. It provided an exemption for isolated transactions, similar to that found in

---

3. The 35 jurisdictions that have adopted the Uniform Securities Act (1956) exempt sales to any bank, insurance company, investment company, pension or profit-sharing trust, "or other financial institution or institutional investor." All other states exempt sales to banks, insurance companies and investment companies, and a number of states simply exempt sales to corporations. The SEC received authority under the Improvements Act to define by rule one or more categories of "qualified purchasers." Securities offered or sold to such qualified purchasers would be exempted from state blue sky registration and qualification requirements. As discussed in Chapter 3, the Improvements Act also preempted such requirements as to a broad range of securities.

4. *See* Chapter 1.

5. H.R. 4314 as introduced by Mr. Rayburn and referred to the House Interstate and Foreign Commerce Committee on March 29, 1933, 73d Cong., 1st Sess. (1933), *reprinted in* 3 Legislative History of the Securities Act of 1933 and Securities Act of 1934, Item 22 (J.S. Ellenberger & Ellen P. Mahar eds., 1973), and S. 875 as introduced by Mr. Robinson and referred to the Senate Judiciary Committee on March 29, 1933, 73d Cong., 1st Sess. (1933), *reprinted in* 3 Legislative History, Item 28. S. 875 was subsequently discharged from the Judiciary Committee and referred to the Banking and Currency Committee on March 30, 1933.

state blue sky laws, which removed from the coverage of the statute:

> Isolated transactions in which any security is sold, offered for sale, subscription, or delivery by the owner thereof, or by his representative solely for the owner's account, such sale or offer for sale, subscription, or delivery not being made in the course of repeated and successive transactions of a like character by such owner for the purpose of engaging in the purchase and sale of securities as a business, and such owner or representative not being the underwriter of such security.

The inadequacy of such an approach is evident today, and it soon became evident to James M. Landis, Benjamin V. Cohen and Thomas G. Corcoran, the draftsmen recruited by Professor Frankfurter to revise the Thompson bill. As Landis recalled in 1959, it was the probing of Middleton Beaman, the chief legislative draftsman for the House of Representatives, to come up with the exact scope of what the statute was intended to cover that led to the Section 4 transaction exemptions:

> "[P]ublic offerings" as distinguished from "private offerings" proved to be the answer. The sale of an issue of securities to insurance companies or to a limited group of experienced investors, was certainly not a matter of concern to the federal government. That bureaucracy, untrained in these matters as it was, could hardly equal these investors for sophistication, provided it was only their own money they were spending. And so the conception of an exemption for all sales, other than by an issuer, underwriter, or dealer came into being, replacing the concept of "isolated transactions" theretofore traditional to blue sky legislation.[6]

---

6. J.M. Landis, *The Legislative History of the Securities Act of 1933*, 28 Geo. Wash. L. Rev. 29, 37 (1959).

The substitute bill introduced in May 1933, as drafted by Landis, Cohen and Corcoran,[7] contained an exemption for "transactions by an issuer not with or through an underwriter." The bill as reported by the House Committee added to this phrase the words "and not involving any public offering."[8] In 1934, the exemption was amended to delete the words "not with or through an underwriter." The Conference Report on this legislation stated clearly the reason for this deletion:

> The Commission has recognized by its interpretations that a public offering is necessary for distribution. Therefore there can be no underwriter within the meaning of the act in the absence of a public offer and the phrase eliminated in the second clause is really superfluous.[9]

The Congress provided no meaningful guidance as to what was contemplated by the term "public offering." The statement is made in *H.R. Rep. No. 85* that the clause in question "exempts transactions by an issuer unless made by or through an underwriter so as to permit an issuer to make a specific or an isolated sale of its securities to a particular person, but insisting that if a sale of the issuer's securities should be made generally to the public that that transaction shall come within the purview of the act."[10] Referring to the exemptions generally, *H.R. Rep. No. 85* stated that the bill "carefully exempts from its application certain types of securities and securities transactions where there is no practical need for its application or where the public benefits are too remote."[11] The Conference Report on the 1933 Act contained a statement that sales of stock

---

7. H.R. 5480 as introduced by Mr. Rayburn and referred to the House Interstate and Foreign Commerce Committee on May 3, 1933, 73d Cong., 1st Sess. (1933), *reprinted in* 3 Legislative History, Item 24.

8. *See* H.R. Rep. No. 85, *supra* note 2, Chapter 1, at 1.

9. H.R. Rep. No. 1838, 73d Cong., 2d Sess. (1934), *reprinted in* 5 Legislative History, Item 20, at 41. This was the conference report accompanying H.R. 9323, 73d Cong., 2d Sess. (1934).

10. H.R. Rep. No. 85, *supra* note 2, Chapter 1, at 15-16.

11. *Id.* at 5.

to stockholders are subject to the 1933 Act "unless the stock-holders are so small in number that the sale to them does not constitute a public offering."[12]

Early Administrative Interpretations

In the first few years following the adoption of the 1933 Act, the emphasis was placed on the number of offerees in applying the private offering exemption. At some point, the number 25 became the test. As early as 1934, Arthur H. Dean made the flat statement that registration is required if securities "are to be sold through the use of interstate commerce or the mails, and are to be offered to more than twenty-five people."[13] Although Dean did not indicate the basis for this statement, it is evident that this well-known securities practitioner had come to believe that this was the test.

The first official reference to the number 25 appears in an early SEC release quoting the text of an opinion of the office of the general counsel of the SEC rendered in the case of a proposed offering of preferred stock to 25 offerees:

> The opinion has been previously expressed by this office that an offering of securities to an insubstantial number of persons is a transaction by the issuer not involving any public offering, and hence an exempted transaction under the provisions of Section [4(2)] of the Securities Act. Furthermore, the opinion has been expressed that under ordinary circumstances an offering to not more than approximately twenty-five persons is not an offering to a substantial number and presumably does not involve a public offering.[14]

Other statements emanating from those administering the statute provided little help in interpreting the scope of the

---

12. H.R. Rep. No. 152, 73d Cong., 1st Sess. (1933), 2 Legislative History, Item 19, at 25.

13. A.H. Dean, *As Amended: The Federal Securities Act,* Fortune, Sept. 1934, at 82.

14. SEC Release No. 33-285 (January 24, 1935).

exemption. In a release in which the Federal Trade Commission (which then administered the 1933 Act) made public abstracts from letters in response to inquiries concerning the application of the statute, the statement was made that an offering by an issuer addressed to its securityholders would be a public offering if the group of securityholders "includes a substantial number of persons."[15] The same release contains a statement that a contemplated offering of stock to 2,450 employees would be regarded as a public offering in that "the word 'public' as used in this provision is not limited to offers which are made indiscriminately and open to anyone."

In SEC Release No. 33-285, after setting forth the 25-person safe harbor, the SEC's general counsel made the point that in no sense was the question of what constitutes a public offering to be determined exclusively by the number of prospective offerees, although this was one factor to be considered. He stressed in this context that the number of offerees "does not mean the number of actual purchasers, but the number of persons to whom the security in question is offered for sale." Other factors considered to be significant were the relationship of the offerees to each other and to the issuer, the number of units offered, the size of the offering and the manner of offering. The general counsel stated that the basis on which the offerees are selected is of the greatest importance:

> Thus, an offering to a given number of persons chosen from the general public on the ground that they are possible purchasers may be a public offering even though an offering to a larger number of persons who are all the members of a particular class, membership in which may be determined by the application of some pre-existing standard, would be a non-public offering.

On the other hand, the general counsel stated that he had "no doubt but that an offering restricted to a particular group or class may nevertheless be a public offering if it is open to a sufficient number of persons." He stated that "an offering to the members

---

15. FTC Release No. 33-97 (December 28, 1933).

of a class who should have special knowledge of the issuer is less likely to be a public offering than is an offering to members of a class of the same size who do not have this advantage." An example would be a group of "high executive officers."

The number of units offered was considered significant because where many units are offered in small denominations, there is "some indication that the issuer recognizes the possibility, if not the probability, of a distribution of a security to the public generally." The size of the offering was considered significant in that small offerings "are less likely to be publicly offered even if redistributed." Finally, the general counsel stated that transactions that are effected "by direct negotiation by the issuer are more likely to be non-public than those effected through the use of machinery of public distribution." With all of these generalities floating about, it is no wonder that in the early years the best conservative advice was to limit the number of offerees to 25.

In SEC Release No. 33-285, the statement was made that there appeared to be developing a general practice on the part of issuers desiring to avoid registration of their securities to seek to dispose of them to insurance companies or other institutions that at the time of purchase state that they are acquiring the securities "for investment and not with a view to distribution." This was the genesis of the "investment letter," i.e., the representation obtained from purchasers in private placements assuring the issuer that they have not, in the words of Section 2(11), purchased the securities "with a view to" their distribution. The representation that the securities have been acquired "for investment" has no statutory underpinnings and, as we will see, can lead to confusion.

In a subsequent release, the SEC's general counsel, after reaffirming that the test for determining whether securities acquired in connection with a private offering could be sold without registration is whether or not they had been acquired with a view to distribution, went on to set forth the factors to be considered in making that determination:

> I wish to make clear, however, that I do not believe the fact that the initial purchaser has stated that his original purchase was for investment and not for resale is neces-

sarily conclusive on this question. In my opinion there should be considered such other factors as: (1) the relation between the issuer and the initial purchaser; (2) the business of the latter, as for example, whether such purchaser is an underwriter or dealer in securities, and, if not, whether the purchase of such a block of securities for investment is consistent with its general operations; and (3) the length of time elapsing between the acquisition of the securities by the initial purchaser and the date of their proposed resale.[16]

In commenting on Rule 142, an obscure rule still on the books that was designed to exclude from the category of underwriters persons whose connection with a distribution of securities is confined to supplying secondary capital by purchasing "for investment" any securities remaining unsold in the hands of underwriters at the conclusion of a public offering,[17] the general counsel made the following observations:

Although it is not impossible to conceive of a situation in which a person who had purchased securities for investment changed his mind in good faith on the next day, and proceeded to dispose of the securities, it must nevertheless be remembered that a state of mind can ordinarily be ascertained only by weighing evidentiary factors, and that a person's actions may be of far greater evidentiary significance than his statements as throwing light on what his state of mind was at a given time. Thus, self-serving statements that a particular purchase was made for investment would carry very little weight in the face of more concrete facts and circumstances inconsistent with such an intention.

Most prominent among the relevant evidentiary factors would undoubtedly be the length of time elapsing between the acquisition of the securities and their pro-

---

16. SEC Release No. 33-603 (December 16, 1935).
17. This rule and Regulation M under the 1934 Act are the only 1933 Act or 1934 Act rules that use the term "for investment."

posed resale. Although retention of the securities for any given length of time would in no event be conclusive, it is obvious that the longer they were held the easier it would be to maintain that they had originally been purchased for investment; and it is my opinion that if they were retained for a period as long as a year that fact would be sufficient, if not contradicted by other evidence, to create a strong inference that they had been purchased for investment. However, such an inference would be rebuttable; for example, it would fall in the face of evidence of a pre-arranged scheme to effect a distribution at the end of the year.[18]

This statement was the source of the one-year holding period rule of thumb that was applied by securities lawyers well into the 1950s.

The *Ralston Purina* Case

The 1953 decision of the United States Supreme Court in *Ralston Purina*[19] had the effect of shifting the emphasis from numbers to the ability of the offerees to fend for themselves.

As described by the district court, the facts of the case were not in dispute.[20] A manufacturer of mixed feeds for poultry and livestock and cereal for human consumption, Ralston Purina Company had been organized in 1894. Since 1942, it had offered stock ownership to employees who could meet its test of "key employees." The company had, from time to time, paid a bonus to certain key employees, and with rare exceptions they had used their bonuses to purchase stock offered to them. The company would make known to managers and heads of departments that stock was available, and the managers were depended upon to select the key employees to whom stock would be made available. The company had approximately 7,000 employees. Purchases were made in 1947 by 243 employees, in 1948 by 20, in 1949 by 414, and in

---

18. SEC Release No. 33-1862 (December 14, 1938).

19. 346 U.S. 119 (1953).

20. 102 F. Supp. 964, 965 (E.D. Mo. 1952).

1950 by 411. For 1951, there were applications to purchase by 165 employees. Although no record was kept of those to whom offers were made and who did not purchase, it was estimated that the offering for the year 1951 had been made to approximately 500 key employees.

The stock was traded in the over-the-counter market, but apparently it was a thin market. One reason given for selling stock directly to employees was that if they attempted to purchase in the open market, the demand would force up the price artificially. At no time was stock sold to employees to procure needed financing. The district court was sympathetic to Ralston Purina's program of stock ownership:

> The sole purpose of the "selection" is to keep part stock ownership of the business within the operating personnel of the business and to spread ownership throughout all departments and activities of the business. No greater tie, to secure loyalty, could be forged between the corporation and its employees than part ownership in the business by the employees. It is an appeal to the employees' self-interest, but a commendable one. Defendant could confine stock offerings to those high in the executive positions but that would not accomplish its long range purpose of bringing from the ranks those who represent good prospects for company management.[21]

The district court held that the private offering exemption had been satisfied.

The Court of Appeals affirmed.[22] In doing so, it was obviously moved by the statement of management as to the reasons for selling stock to employees:

> We feel, sir, that that creates a greater efficiency with the company, because it draws employees of the company closer together. Many of our people come from the rural area, where proprietorship is a matter of great pride to

---

21. *Id.* at 968-69.
22. 200 F.2d 85 (8th Cir. 1952).

them. The fact that they feel that they are owners, at least part owners, in the company, contributes to the morale, and we feel that the idea of breaking down the gap between the ownership and management is something that is highly desirable and something that contributed substantially to the success of the company.[23]

In conclusion, the Court of Appeals stated:

> We sympathize with the efforts of the Commission to restrict the exemption granted by Section [4(2)] to the narrowest possible scope, but we do not think that the intra-organizational offerings of stock by the Company, unaccompanied by any solicitation, which have resulted in a limited distribution of stock, for investment purposes, to a select group of employees considered by the management to be worthy of retention and probable future promotion, is to be excluded from the exemption of nonpublic offerings granted by Congress. There is, we think, virtually no possibility that these offerings, if continued, will frustrate or impair the purpose of the Act.[24]

The Supreme Court disagreed. In his landmark decision, Justice Clark emphasized that among those responding to the offers "were employees with the duties of artist, bakeshop foreman, chow loading foreman, clerical assistant, copywriter, electrician, stock clerk, mill office clerk, audit credit trainee, production trainee, and veterinarian." He quoted the observation of Judge Denman in *Sunbeam Gold Mines*.[25]

> In its broadest meaning the term "public" distinguishes the populace at large from groups of individual members of the public segregated because of some common interest or characteristic. Yet such a distinction is inadequate for practical purposes; manifestly, an offering of securities to all

---

23. *Id.* at 87-88.
24. *Id.* at 93.
25. *SEC v. Sunbeam Gold Mines Co.*, 95 F.2d 699 (9th Cir. 1938).

red-headed men, to all residents of Chicago or San Francisco, to all existing stockholders of the General Motors Corporation or the American Telephone & Telegraph Company, is no less "public," in every realistic sense of the word, than an unrestricted offering to the world at large.

The district court and the court of appeals in *Ralston Purina* had purported to apply the reasoning of *Sunbeam Gold Mines*. The district court stated that this reasoning was "more in harmony with the statute" than the numbers test urged by the SEC in its *Ralston Purina* brief.[26]

Justice Clark stated that the applicability of the private offering exemption should turn on "whether the particular class of persons affected needs the protection of the Act." The basic test, as he saw it, was whether the offerees were "able to fend for themselves." He rejected a numbers test, stating that "the statute would seem to apply to a 'public offering' whether to few or many." He recognized that numbers might have some relevance and could be used for enforcement purposes:

> It may well be that offerings to a substantial number of persons would rarely be exempt. Indeed nothing prevents the commission, in enforcing the statute, from using some kind of numerical test in deciding when to investigate particular exemption claims. But there is no warrant for superimposing a quantity limit on private offerings as a matter of statutory interpretation.

He agreed that some employee offerings may come within the exemption, for example, one made to executive personnel who because of their position have access to the same kind of information that the 1933 Act would make available in the form of a registration statement. But in this case, he concluded that the Ralston Purina employees were not shown to have access to the kind of information that registration would disclose.

Although one may sympathize with the Ralston Purina management, shaking their heads in frustration over the need to ter-

---

26. 102 F. Supp. at 968.

minate a stock purchase program that had been advantageous to the employees, it is hard to quarrel with Justice Clark's analysis. A movement away from the number of offerees as the principal determinant of a private offering made eminent good sense, although one may question Justice Clark's suggestion that an offering to two persons may be public. Based on the reasoning in *Ralston Purina*, it became easier to render opinions on private placements where the number of purchasers was substantially in excess of 25. On the other hand, no one would be shocked or concerned if a promoter were deemed to have violated the 1933 Act by pitching an investment to 20 senior citizens rocking on the front porch of a convalescent home, notwithstanding that the number of offerees was less than 25.

The *Ralston Purina* analysis proved useful in the case of a major privately-owned securities firm which had adopted the practice of permitting employees to purchase stock when they reached a certain management level. Prior to the firm's incorporation, merit was rewarded by promotion to partnership. Following its incorporation, promotions were made first by allowing an executive to purchase nonvoting stock and later, if deemed worthy, to purchase voting stock. When the 1934 Act was amended in 1964 to require 1934 Act registration by issuers with total assets exceeding $1 million and a class of equity securities held of record by 750 or more persons for the first two years of the amendment's operation and 500 or more persons after a two-year phase-in period, the firm found itself in a position where the filing of a Form 10 would be required unless it obtained exemptive relief from the SEC. It applied for and obtained an exemptive order under Section 12(h) of the 1934 Act. In its application, it explained fully the circumstances under which employees were rewarded by allowing them to purchase stock. The SEC granted the 1934 Act exemption and raised no question as to the 1933 Act exemption. The firm's outside counsel rendered to it a Section 4(2) opinion relying upon the reasoning of *Ralston Purina*.[27]

---

27. More recently, in reproposing for comment Rule 701, which exempts offers and sales of securities pursuant to certain compensatory benefit

The *Crowell-Collier* Case

The next major event in the development of the private offering exemption was the publication of the SEC's comments on its investigation of a purported private placement of convertible debentures by The Crowell-Collier Publishing Company.[28]

During 1955 and 1956, Crowell-Collier sold $4 million principal amount of convertible debentures through Elliott & Company, a broker-dealer firm. Crowell-Collier was in need of funds and was being pressured by its banks. In June or early July of 1955, Elliott & Company proposed a plan that contemplated the sale of $3 million of debentures in a private placement and the purchase of another $1 million principal amount by the company's controlling stockholder. On July 6 and 7, Elliott secured commitments from 27 persons, including four broker-dealer firms. It testified in the SEC investigation that no prospects were called who did not purchase. Each of the 27 purchasers represented that it was purchasing the debentures for investment with no present intention of distributing the same. The SEC pointed out that the representation did not run to the underlying common stock as it clearly should have.

Prior to the closing on August 10, 1955, approximately one-third of the 27 purchasers had secured others to join them as participants in their commitments or had secured purchasers of portions of their commitments. The result was that the number of purchasers totaled 88. In February 1956, shortly after the expiration of six months from the closing date, holders of the debentures began to convert them and to sell the common stock

---

plans and contracts relating to compensation, the SEC stated that it "historically has recognized that when transactions of this nature are primarily compensatory and incentive oriented, some accommodation should be made under the Securities Act." SEC Release No. 33-6726 (July 30, 1987).

28. SEC Release No. 33-3825 (August 12, 1957). This transaction also led to disciplinary action under Sections 15(b) and 15A of the 1934 Act against the broker-dealers that participated in the sale of the securities. *See,* e.g., *Elliott & Company,* SEC Release No. 34-5688 (May 7, 1958); *Gilligan, Will & Co.,* SEC Release No. 34-5689 (May 7, 1958); *Dempsey & Company,* SEC Release No. 34-5690 (May 7, 1958).

on the American Stock Exchange. The remaining $1 million principal amount of debentures was not purchased by the controlling stockholder, but was sold by Elliott in May and June of 1956 to 22 purchasers, including three broker-dealer firms, that made the same investment representations as were made in the 1955 transaction. The SEC found that, as a result of these transactions, in the space of 12 months, Crowell-Collier effected a wide distribution of its debentures and common stock.

In the *Crowell-Collier* release, the SEC made a point that had been generally understood but that previously had not been articulated:

> It has been and is the Commission's position that an issuer or an underwriter may not separate parts of a series of related transactions comprising an issue of securities and thereby seek to establish that a particular part is a private transaction if the whole involves a public offering of the securities.

In this case, the transaction as a whole involved a public offering. The principle can be applied conversely. If all resales are limited to persons who could have been participants in the original placement, then the original transaction is entitled to the Section 4(2) exemption.

The *Crowell-Collier* release presented the securities bar with the challenging assignment of advising their clients as to when privately-placed securities could be resold, i.e., when such a sale would not cause the holder of the securities to be deemed an "underwriter" whose presence in the original transaction would vitiate the Section 4(2) exemption. The release contained a statement, however, that the bar came to rely upon for this purpose:

> An exemption under the provisions of Section [4(2)] is available only when the transactions do not involve a public offering and is not gained by the formality of obtaining "investment representations." Holding for the six months' capital gains period of the tax statutes, holding in an "investment account" rather than a "trading account," hold-

ing for a deferred sale, holding for a market rise, holding for sale if the market does not rise, or holding for a year, does not afford a statutory basis for an exemption and therefore does not provide an adequate basis on which counsel may give opinions or businessmen rely in selling securities without registration.

Purchasing for the purpose of future sale is nonetheless purchasing for sale and, if the transactions involve any public offering even at some future date, the registration provisions apply unless at the time of the public offering an exemption is available.

After the *Crowell-Collier* release, the one-year rule of thumb, which had been suggested by the SEC's general counsel, became a two-year rule of thumb that was generally applied by the securities bar in advising with respect to resales of securities initially issued in a private placement.[29]

Pre-Rule 146 Developments

During the 1960s, issuers continued to make private placements, and lawyers continued to grapple with resale issues, with limited interpretive guidance from the SEC. Lawyers worried about such matters as holding periods for privately-placed securities and sales motivated by unforeseen changes in circumstances. In 1962, "an increasing tendency to rely upon the exemption for offerings of speculative issues to unrelated and uninformed persons" prompted the SEC to issue a release pointing out the limitations on the availability of the private offering exemption.[30] This release contained little more than a rehash of statements previ-

---

29. This was based in part on the following statement by Judge Sugarman:

The passage of two years before the commencement of distribution of any of these shares is an insuperable obstacle to my finding that Sherwood took these shares with a view to distribution thereof, in the absence of any relevant evidence from which I could conclude he did not take the shares for investment. No such evidence was offered at the trial.

U.S. v. Sherwood, 175 F. Supp. 480, 483 (S.D.N.Y. 1959).
30. SEC Release No. 33-4552 (November 6, 1962).

ously made by the SEC, but it did flesh out the change in circumstances doctrine that was then an important consideration in determining when resales could be made:

> An unforeseen change of circumstances since the date of purchase may be a basis for an opinion that the proposed resale is not inconsistent with an investment representation. However, such claim must be considered in the light of all of the relevant facts. Thus, an advance or decline in market price or a change in the issuer's operating results are normal investment risks and do not usually provide an acceptable basis for such claim of changed circumstances. Possible inability of the purchaser to pay off loans incurred in connection with the purchase of the stock would ordinarily not be deemed an unforeseeable change of circumstances. Further, in the case of securities pledged for a loan, the pledgee should not assume that he is free to distribute without registration. The Congressional mandate of disclosure to investors is not to be avoided to permit a public distribution of unregistered securities because the pledgee took the securities from a purchaser, subsequently delinquent.

In late 1970, the SEC issued a pronouncement to the effect that it would regard the presence or absence of an appropriate legend and stop-transfer instructions as a factor in considering whether the circumstances surrounding an offering were consistent with the Section 4(2) exemption.[31] By this time, the staff of the SEC was taking the position that no-action letters would not be issued unless the securities had been held for three years or there was a compelling change of circumstances.

In 1972, the SEC adopted Rule 144,[32] which brought objective standards to the question of resales of privately-placed securities. Under Rule 144, a holder of "restricted securities" could begin to sell in "brokers' transactions" after two years, but only in limited amounts and only upon giving public notice

---

31. SEC Release No. 33-5121 (December 30, 1970).
32. SEC Release No. 33-5223 (January 11, 1972).

of a proposed resale. It was no longer necessary to identify a "change in circumstances."[33]

In the early 1970s, a number of judicial decisions were handed down that appeared to limit the availability of the Section 4(2) exemption. In *Lively v. Hirschfeld*[34] the Court of Appeals for the 10th Circuit read *Ralston Purina* as including within a private offering "only persons of exceptional business experience" who are in "a position where they have regular access to all the information and records which would show the potential for the corporation."

In *Hill York Corp. v. American International Franchises, Inc.*,[35] the court said that the fact that the purchasers were sophisticated businessmen was not sufficient to establish the exemption and cited with approval an article indicating that the exemption was limited to those instances "where the number of offerees is so limited that they may constitute a class of persons having such a privileged relationship with the issuer that their present knowledge and facilities for acquiring information about the issuer would make registration unnecessary for their protection."[36]

In *SEC v. Continental Tobacco Company*,[37] the court required that the defendant demonstrate "that each offeree had a relationship with Continental giving access to the kind of information that registration would have disclosed." The judicial in-

---

33. The rule stated explicitly that it was "not the exclusive means" for reselling restricted securities. Over the years, Rule 144 has been amended in important respects. The volume limitation has been increased; the two-year "holding period" has become a one-year period and is now measured from the time the securities were sold by the issuer or its affiliate (rather than from the time of each acquisition by a holder); and all restrictions lapse under certain conditions after the expiration of a two-year holding period. See the discussion in Chapter 1.

34. 440 F.2d 631 (10th Cir. 1971).

35. 448 F.2d 680 (5th Cir. 1971).

36. Orrick, *Non-Public Offerings of Corporate Securities: Limitations on the Exemption under the Federal Securities Act*, 21 U. Pitt. L. Rev. 1, 8 (1959).

37. 463 F.2d 137 (5th Cir. 1972).

sistence on a pre-existing relationship between the offerees and the issuer raised substantial questions as to the availability of the exemption, at least where individual investors were concerned.

These cases involved offers and sales of equity securities to individual investors. Institutional private placements continued with little concern for these decisions, but reliance on Section 4(2) for tax-shelter programs and similar transactions was viewed by some as extremely risky.

Rule 146

Pressure from the financial community, which believed that the judicial trend had impaired the ability of issuers to safely effect private placements, led the SEC in 1974 to adopt Rule 146, which was designed to provide a safe harbor for reliance on the private placement exemption.[38]

Rule 146 was designed to create greater certainty in the application of the Section 4(2) exemption. While stressing that a failure to satisfy all of the conditions of the rule did not raise a presumption that the Section 4(2) exemption was not available and that attempted compliance with the rule did not operate as an election, in that the issuer also could claim the availability of Section 4(2) outside of the rule, the SEC provided in Rule 146 that the private placement exemption would be available if specified conditions were met relating to the manner of offering, the nature of the offerees and purchasers, access to or furnishing of information, limitations on the number of purchasers, and procedures designed to limit subsequent resales.

With respect to the manner of offering, the rule precluded general advertising or general solicitation, including promotional seminars or meetings. The rule, however, did not preclude meetings with qualified offerees to discuss the terms of and to impart information about the offering.

In order to assure that the offerees could fend for themselves (the basic test established by *Ralston Purina*), the rule provided that prior to making any offer the issuer and those acting on its

---

38. SEC Release No. 33-5487 (April 23, 1974).

behalf must reasonably believe either that the offeree "has such knowledge and experience in financial and business matters that he is capable of evaluating the merits and risks of the prospective investment" or that he is "a person who is able to bear the economic risk of the investment." In the jargon of Wall Street, the offeree was required to be either "smart" or "rich." It was not necessary to be both.

The rule imposed somewhat stricter requirements with respect to purchasers as distinguished from offerees. It provided that, prior to making any sale, there must be reasonable belief either that the offeree had the requisite knowledge and experience or that he and his offeree representative together had the requisite knowledge and experience and that, in the latter case, he could bear the economic risk of the investment. Thus, the SEC imposed the requirement that a purchaser be able to bear the economic risk of the investment where it was necessary for him to be guided by the knowledge and experience of an offeree representative. The number of purchasers was limited to 35, but there could be excluded from this number any person who purchased or agreed to purchase for cash, in a single payment or installments, securities in the aggregate amount of $150,000 or more.

It was required that prior to the sale each offeree have access to the same kind of information that would be provided in a 1933 Act registration statement or that he be furnished with that information. A note to the rule made clear that access could exist only by reason of the offeree's "position with respect to the issuer" and that "position" means "an employment or family relationship or economic bargaining power that enables the offeree to obtain information from the issuer in order to evaluate the merits and risks of the prospective investment." A reporting company could satisfy this requirement by delivering to a prospective purchaser its most recent 1934 Act filings. Most issuers that relied on Rule 146 opted for the procedure of delivering 1934 Act materials to prospective purchasers rather than relying on the more subjective access test.

The rule required that the issuer make available to each offeree or its offeree representative the opportunity to ask questions of and receive answers from the issuer or any person acting on its behalf concerning the terms and conditions of the offering and to obtain additional information. A statement to this effect customarily was included in the private placement memorandum. The procedures specified to assure that purchasers were not statutory underwriters included reasonable inquiry to determine whether the purchaser was acquiring the securities for his own account or on behalf of other persons; legends referring to restrictions on transferability; stop transfer instructions; and a written agreement that the securities would not be sold without registration or an exemption therefrom.

As originally adopted, Rule 146 had no reporting requirement. But in 1977, the SEC, referring to abuses of Rule 146, particularly in connection with offerings of oil and gas partnership interests, proposed that reports be required in connection with Rule 146 offerings.[39] The amendment was adopted and a filing on Form 146 was required at the time of the first sale of securities in any offering effected in reliance on the rule.[40]

Two years after the effectiveness of Rule 146, the SEC made a public request for empirical information regarding its operation.[41] The SEC stated that it was "aware of criticism that the Rule is hindering the investment of venture capital, and that as an experiment the Rule is a failure and should be rescinded." The SEC went on to state that, on the other hand, Rule 146 had been criticized by some "as facilitating the fraudulent offering of certain types of securities."

In response to the SEC's request for information, the Committee on Securities Regulation of The Association of the Bar of the City of New York (of which the senior author was then a member) stated, "It is the consensus of this Committee that Rule 146 is serving its purpose well." The Committee stated that it was unaware that the rule was hindering the investment of venture capital and failed to see how Rule 146 could facilitate "the fraudulent offering of certain types of securities." The letter went on to describe how different lawyers viewed Rule

---

39. SEC Release No. 33-5822 (April 18, 1977).
40. SEC Release No. 33-5912 (March 3, 1978).
41. SEC Release No. 33-5779 (December 6, 1976).

146 in the context of private placements of corporate debt securities with institutional investors:

> It is true that certain lawyers experienced in this area believe that Rule 146 provides no substantial benefits and prefer to rely on the traditional standards for private placements developed prior to the adoption of the Rule. *See Section 4(2) and Statutory Law*, 31 Business Lawyer 483 (November, 1975). Other experienced lawyers, including a number of members of this Committee, believe that Rule 146 helps to provide certainty, even in the case of an institutional private placement. Their practice is to render opinions in reliance on Section 4(2), without reference to Rule 146, but to attempt to structure transactions so that they comply with the Rule in all material respects.

The letter also described certain practices that had developed in the investment banking community following the adoption of Rule 146:

> Certain investment banking firms that act as private placement agent follow procedures designed to comply with Rule 146. These firms maintain a list of qualified offerees consisting of institutional investors who, in their opinion, have such knowledge and experience in financial and business matters as to be capable of evaluating the merits and risks of an investment in corporate debt securities and, in addition, are able to bear the economic risk of the investment. Under Rule 146, there is no limit on the number of offerees, provided that each meets this standard. Institutions may be added to or deleted from the list, but, of course, any additional institutions must have the necessary qualifications. To avoid the necessity for limiting the number of actual purchasers, the securities are offered to qualified offerees in minimum amounts of $150,000 for any single purchaser. If the issuer is a reporting company, as is normally the case, before an institution purchases any of the securi-

ties, it is furnished with a copy of the issuer's most recent Annual Report on Form 10-K and each definitive proxy statement, and each report on Form 8-K or Form 10-Q, required to be filed by the issuer since the filing of the Form 10-K. It is also furnished with a description of any material changes in the issuer's affairs which are not disclosed in the above documents. Other information and statements required by Rule 146, such as use of proceeds and a description of the securities, are included in a private placement memorandum. Each offeree is advised by the placement agent that it is afforded the opportunity, prior to purchasing any of the securities, to ask questions of, and receive answers from, the issuer concerning the terms and conditions of the offering and to obtain any additional information, to the extent the issuer possesses the same or can acquire it without unreasonable expense, necessary to verify the accuracy of the information in these documents. Appropriate restrictions are placed on the transfer of the securities.

In addition to providing substantial comfort in traditional types of institutional private placements, Rule 146 procedures of the type described above have facilitated certain types of private placements that were not usually made prior to the adoption of the Rule. For example, since the adoption of Rule 146, there have been an increasing number of continuous offerings of corporate notes which do not meet the requirements of Section 3(a)(3) made to pre-cleared groups of institutional investors in minimum denominations of $150,000 and in conformity with the other requirements of Rule 146.

Regulation D

In view of mixed comments regarding Rule 146, the SEC proposed in 1981 that the rule be superseded by a new Regulation D.[42] Seven months later, Regulation D was adopted in sub-

---

42. SEC Release No. 33-6339 (August 7, 1981).

stantially the form originally proposed.[43] Since its adoption, Regulation D has been amended on several occasions to broaden its scope and improve its operation,[44] and it continues to operate as an important safe harbor under Section 4(2).

Rule 501 of Regulation D defines key terms such as "accredited investor." Rule 502 sets forth general conditions to the exemption, such as integration of other transactions, requirements for the furnishing of specified information, a prohibition of "any form of general solicitation or general advertising" and a requirement that the issuer "exercise reasonable care to assure that the purchasers of the securities are not underwriters" (together with a specification of actions that will establish such reasonable care). Rule 503 provides for a public notice of sales in reliance on the exemption.

Rules 504 and 505 provide exemptions from registration under Section 3(b) of the 1933 Act rather than Section 4(2).[45] Rules 504 and 505 are useful to small businesses and relate to offerings of securities not exceeding $1 million and $5 million, respectively.

Rule 506 of Regulation D embodies the exemption that is of greatest importance for purposes of this chapter. Significantly, it eliminates the offeree qualification requirement of Rule 146 in favor of a general permission to offer and sell to a potentially indefinite number of persons who come within the definition of "accredited investors."

• *General Solicitation or Advertising*

If an offering is to be made in reliance upon Regulation D, then Rule 502(c) requires that "neither the issuer nor any person acting on its behalf" may offer or sell the securities by any form of "general solicitation or general advertising." The rule defines the prohibited activities as including, but not as limited

---

43. SEC Release No. 33-6389 (March 8, 1982).

44. SEC Release No. 33-6437 (November 19, 1982); SEC Release No. 33-6663 (October 2, 1986); SEC Release No. 33-6758 (March 3, 1988); SEC Release No. 33-6825 (March 14, 1989).

45. Section 3(b) permits the SEC to adopt regulations exempting issues in the amount of $5 million or less.

to, advertisements, articles, notices or other communication published in newspapers, magazines or similar media or broadcast over television or radio. It also includes any seminar or meeting whose attendees have been invited by any general solicitation or general advertising.

A notice under Rule 135c is expressly excluded from the prohibition against general solicitation or general advertising for purposes of Regulation D. As discussed in Chapter 1, Rule 135c permits an issuer that files reports under the 1934 Act (as well as certain foreign issuers) to publish a notice of an unregistered offering of securities. The purpose of the rule is to permit issuers that have public reporting responsibilities to give notice of an unregistered offering that may be material to its securityholders. The rule provides that the notice may not be used "for the purpose of conditioning the market in the United States for any of the securities offered." Given this condition, it is probably advisable for the issuer to publish the notice only after the completion of the solicitation phase of the offering or, in the alternative, to take steps to exclude from the offering any potential investors who initiate communication with the issuer or its investment banker after the publication of the notice. On the other hand, it is neither possible nor desirable to lay down rigid rules in this regard. Much might depend, for example, on the business or legal purpose being served by the Rule 135c notice.

Placing a notice on the Internet relating to a Regulation D offering may result in a general solicitation. The SEC staff took this position in October 1995 in response to its own hypothetical involving an issuer's posting of Rule 506 offering materials on the issuer's Website, access to which was conditioned on a user's providing "various information" to the issuer.[46] The staff response may be correct as a technical matter, given the prohibition against a general solicitation. One might question the result, however, if the user had to represent, for example, that he was an accredited investor before gaining access to the Website, and if the Website stated that it was not to be construed as an offer to persons other than accredited investors. On the other hand, the SEC staff re-

---

46. SEC Release No. 33-7233 (October 6, 1995).

cently issued a no-action letter (*IPONET,* available July 26, 1996) approving a broker-dealer's posting of notices of private placements on a Website that is accessible only by means of a password that is made available only to persons who have been qualified by the broker-dealer as accredited investors.

Investment newsletters often publish detailed and highly accurate information on Regulation D offerings while they are in the solicitation stage. The information may even include the name of the placement agent, one or more of the lead investors and the range of "price talk." The information is usually obtained from persons who have been solicited to participate in the offering or who are actually purchasing in the offering. Rule 502(c), as noted above, prohibits general solicitation or general advertising only by the issuer or any person acting on its behalf. Assuming that the publisher of the information relating to the Regulation D offering is not acting in concert with—and has not obtained the information from—the issuer or any person acting on its behalf, there should be no problem under Rule 502(c).

There should be no problem where the information has been obtained from public sources.[47] Conversely, the SEC staff has been unwilling to provide any comfort to publishers who have obtained information from the issuer.[48] Advertisements will be viewed by the staff as inconsistent with the permitted manner of offering, even if they are generic and do not relate to a specific program,[49] as will brochures mailed to a specific interest group.[50] The staff has said that a tombstone advertisement published to commemorate the

---

47. SEC No-action Letter, *Nancy H. Blasberg* (available July 12, 1986); SEC No-action Letter, *Richard Daniels* (available December 12, 1984).

48. SEC No-action Letter, *Merit Communications, Inc.* (available September 7, 1987); SEC No-action Letter, *The Texas Investor Newsletter* (available January 23, 1984); SEC No-action Letter, *Tax Investment Information Corporation* (available February 7, 1983).

49. SEC No-action Letter, *Gerald F. Gerstenfeld* (available December 3, 1985); SEC No-action Letter, *Thoroughbred Racing Stable* (available January 6, 1976); SEC No-action Letter, *Damson Oil Corporation* (available July 5, 1974).

50. SEC No-action Letter, *Aspen Grove* (available December 8, 1982).

successful completion of an offering could run afoul of Rule 502(c), reasoning that where the sponsor or issuer "conducts an ongoing program of private or limited offerings, tombstone advertisements for the completion of each individual offering could be used to solicit investors to the program as a whole."[51]

As noted above, Rule 506 imposes no explicit limitation on the number of offerees or purchasers. There has been concern on the part of some securities lawyers, however, that, if there are too many offerees, there might be deemed to be a general solicitation. In a footnote to the release proposing Regulation D, the SEC warned that, although offers could theoretically be made to an unlimited number of persons, offers to a large number of potential purchasers might involve a violation of the prohibitions against general solicitation and general advertising.[52]

This footnote does not appear in the release adopting Regulation D, although it would be unwise to draw any strong inference from the omission of the footnote that the number of potential investors is irrelevant to the concept of general solicitation. Some securities firms follow the policy of placing a limit on the number of offerees in all Regulation D transactions, while others follow this policy only where individual investors are to be solicited.

Given the large number of persons who may be solicited or even participate in a Regulation D offering, the public disclosure of unregistered transactions made possible by Rule 135c and the ready availability of information on these transactions from third-party sources, it may be that the general solicitation prohibition is simply proving unworkable. Indeed, the SEC requested comment in June 1995 on whether it should modify the general solicitation prohibition.[53] It noted that an ability on the part of issuers to broadly disseminate offering materials to locate potential investors might not compromise investor protection interests in view of the fact that all purchases would continue to meet the requirements of Regulation D. The SEC also requested comment on whether, in view of the language of Section 4(2), it had the statutory authority to eliminate this prohibition. This was, of course,

---

51. SEC No-action Letter, *Alma Securities Corp.* (available August 2, 1982).

52. SEC Release No. 33-6339 (August 7, 1981).

53. SEC Release No. 33-7185 (June 27, 1995).

prior to the Improvements Act's grant to the SEC of broad exemptive authority under the 1933 Act.

• *Number and Nature of Purchasers*

On its face, Rule 506(b)(2)(i) limits the number of purchasers to 35. On the other hand, Rule 501(c)(1)(iv) excludes for purposes of "calculating the number of purchasers under . . . Rule 506(b)" any purchaser who is an accredited investor. This somewhat inelegant drafting technique is the basis for Rule 506's permitting offers and sales to a potentially indefinite number of persons so long as they are "accredited investors."

The term "accredited investor" is defined to include virtually every type of institution that participates in the private placement market, as well as individual investors with substantial income or a large net worth. Thus, the term includes:

- Any bank as defined in Section 3(a)(2) of the 1933 Act or any savings and loan association or other institution as defined in Section 3(a)(5)(A) of the 1933 Act, whether acting in its individual or fiduciary capacity.

- Any broker or dealer registered under the 1934 Act.

- Any insurance company as defined in Section 2(13) of the 1933 Act.

- Any investment company registered under the 1940 Act or a business development company as defined in Section 2(a)(48) of the 1940 Act.

- Any small business investment company licensed by the U.S. Small Business Administration.

- Any plan established and maintained by a state, its political subdivisions, or any agency or instrumentality thereof, for the benefit of its employees, if such plan has total assets in excess of $5 million.

- Any employee benefit plan within the meaning of the Employee Retirement Income Security Act of 1974 if the investment decision is made by a plan fiduciary that is either a bank, savings and loan association, insurance company, or registered adviser, or if the plan has total assets in excess of $5 million or, if a self-directed plan, with investment decisions made solely by persons that are accredited investors.

- Any private business development company as defined in the Investment Advisers Act of 1940.

- Any corporation, partnership, business trust or Section 501(c)(3) organization, not formed for the specific purpose of acquiring the securities offered, with total assets in excess of $5 million. In late 1996, the SEC staff issued a no-action letter (*Wolfe, Block, Schorr and Solis-Cohen* (available December 11, 1996) that permits a "limited liability company" to qualify as an accredited investor under this heading.

- Any director, executive officer, or general partner of the issuer of the securities being offered or of a general partner of the issuer.

- Any natural person whose individual net worth, or joint net worth with that person's spouse, at the time of purchase exceeds $1 million.

- Any natural person who has an individual income in excess of $200,000 in each of the two most recent years or joint income with that person's spouse in excess of $300,000 in each of those years and has a reasonable expectation of reaching the same income level in the current year.

- Any trust with total assets in excess of $5 million, not formed for the specific purpose of acquiring the securities offered, whose purchase is directed by a person who has such knowledge and experience in financial and business matters that he is capable of evaluating the merits and risks of the prospective investment.

- Any entity in which all of the equity owners are accredited investors.

This litany of accredited investors covers a wide range of prospective purchasers. Certainly, in the case of an institutional placement, there is no reason to dip into the 35-purchaser pool, for there are few institutional investors that would not qualify as an accredited investor. In this respect, the 1933 Act now has a *de facto* institutional investor exemption similar to that found in state blue sky laws.

With respect to sales of limited partnership interests or similar investments that are directed to individuals, Regulation D's net worth or income levels are not unduly restrictive. Indeed, it may be argued that investments of this type are not suitable for persons who do not meet either the net worth or income tests for determining who is an accredited investor. Accredited investors need not satisfy any standard of sophistication on the theory that such investors either are presumably sophisticated or have the means to fend for themselves. On the other hand, any non-accredited investor who participates in the transaction must, either alone or with a purchaser representative, have such knowledge and experience in financial and business matters to be capable of evaluating the merits and risks of the prospective investment.

- *Informational Access and Disclosure*

Rule 502(b) does not require that any specific information be furnished if sales are made only to accredited investors. Presumably, such investors have either the sophistication or the means to fend for themselves and to demand and receive such information as they consider necessary. If a sale is made to a person who is not an accredited investor, however, that person must be furnished with the information specified in Rule 502(b) not later than "a reasonable time prior to sale." The information required to be furnished depends upon whether or not the issuer is subject to the reporting requirements of the 1934 Act and upon the size of the offering.

In addition, the non-accredited investor must be afforded the opportunity to ask questions of and receive answers from the issuer regarding the offering and to obtain any additional information that the issuer possesses or can acquire without unreasonable effort or expense that is necessary to verify the accuracy of the information furnished under Rule 502(b).

• *Resale Restrictions*

Rule 502(d) requires the issuer to exercise reasonable care to assure that the purchasers are not underwriters. It also sets up a "safe harbor" by specifying means by which such reasonable care may be demonstrated. These are "reasonable inquiry to determine if the purchaser is acquiring the securities for himself or for other persons," "written disclosure . . . that the securities have not been registered" and therefore cannot be resold without registration or an exemption, and placement of a restrictive legend on the certificate or other document that evidences the securities.

Rule 502(d) states expressly that "[o]ther actions by the issuer may satisfy" the requirement to exercise reasonable care that purchasers are not underwriters. In fact, participants in Regulation D transactions often find it necessary to devise "other actions" to substitute for the "safe harbor" ingredient of a restrictive legend. In the case of offerings of investment-grade fixed-income securities to accredited institutional investors, many securities lawyers believe that an issuer is taking "reasonable care" by obtaining representations from the original purchasers and by making written disclosure that the securities cannot be transferred without an exemption. These lawyers undoubtedly take considerable comfort from the fact that holders of these securities, as a practical matter, generally seek to resell them through broker-dealers who almost invariably inquire as to the origin of the securities and take steps to ensure the availability of an exemption when they effect a resale.[54]

Also, given the increasing preference of issuers and investors alike for book-entry securities, it is obviously ineffective to place a restrictive legend on a global security that disappears into the vault of The Depository Trust Company ("DTC") or a similar institution. Indeed, the SEC in 1993 approved changes to DTC's rules to permit DTC to make Rule 144A-eligible securities eligible for DTC's book-entry settlement services, on

---

54. See the discussion later in this Chapter of "secondary private placements."

the basis of representations from issuers and transfer agents, if the securities were investment-grade debt or were included in an SRO transfer system such as PORTAL.[55] The SEC approved the rule changes on the basis of findings that, among other things, the proposal reduced (presumably to its satisfaction) the potential for unlawful transfers of restricted securities. This finding was in turn based on the representations and undertakings that would be required of issuers and transfer agents when they applied for deposit and book-entry eligibility for a new privately-placed security. It is difficult to conclude that the SEC was not also finding that these procedures were sufficient to constitute reasonable care on the part of the issuer, when it made the initial sale to a placement agent, that the purchasers were not underwriters.

It is probably true that there is no book-entry transaction— even one involving equity securities—where procedures cannot be devised that would constitute "reasonable care" on the part of the participants that the purchasers are not underwriters. Whether these procedures would be acceptable to all participants is, of course, another question.

• *Notice, Disqualification, Blue Sky Requirements*

Rule 503 requires an issuer selling securities in reliance on Regulation D to file with the SEC five copies of a notice on Form D no later than 15 days after the first sale of the securities. In the case of institutional private placements, the Form D filing requirement was often cited as a reason to prefer reliance on Section 4(2) rather than Rule 506. As a result of the 1989 amendments to Regulation D, however, the filing of a Form D is no longer a condition to the establishment of an exemption under Regulation D. This does not mean that the filing requirement is optional. Rule 507 contemplates that the SEC may seek a temporary or permanent injunction against an issuer's violations of the filing requirement. An injunction is a drastic remedy, of course, that a court would be likely to grant for Rule 503 violations only in unusual circumstances. If an injunction were granted, Rule 507 would disqualify the issuer from future

---

55. SEC Release No. 34-33672 (February 23, 1994).

reliance on Regulation D. The SEC could waive such a disqualification upon a showing of good cause.

The North American Securities Administrators Association, Inc., an association of securities administrators from each of the 50 states, the District of Columbia, Puerto Rico, and several of the Canadian provinces, has adopted as an official policy guideline for administering the blue sky laws the "Uniform Limited Offering Exemption." Regulation D has served as the core of the exemption, and Form D was designed to be a uniform notification form that can be filed with the states as well as with the SEC.

On the other hand, the Improvements Act exempted from state blue sky registration and qualification requirements (but not from state notice filing or fee requirements) any security exempted from Section 5 of the 1933 Act pursuant to SEC "rules or regulations issued under section 4(2)." There are also exemptions for securities offered and sold in transactions that are exempt from Section 5 pursuant to Section 4(1) or 4(3), but only if the issuer is a reporting company under the 1934 Act. The result is that state blue sky laws will not hold up a private placement under Regulation D, although the status of traditional "Section 4(2)" private placements is less clear. Secondary market transactions in privately-placed securities of issuers that are not reporting companies under the 1934 Act do not appear entitled to the Improvements Act's benefits, but relatively few states worry about "nonissuer transactions" and in most of these states the participating dealers and institutions will probably be entitled to rely on the regular institutional exemption.

• *Integration*

Rule 502(a) states that all sales that are part of the same Regulation D offering must meet all of the terms and conditions of Regulation D and that offers and sales that are made more than six months before the start of a Regulation D offering or more than six months after completion of a Regulation D offering will not be considered part of that offering, so long as during those six-month periods there were no offers or sales of securities by or for the issuer that are of the same or a similar class as those offered or sold under Regulation D, other than offers or sales of securities under an employee benefit plan. This is merely a safe harbor, and the fact that another offering is made within six months of the Regulation D offering does not necessarily indicate that it is part of that offering. Whether or not separate offerings of securities will be viewed as a single offering (i.e., will be "integrated") depends on the particular facts and circumstances.

The integration problem is not a new one, and it is not unique to Regulation D. In SEC Release No. 33-4552 dealing with the Section 4(2) private offering exemption,[56] the SEC stated that a determination whether an offering is public or private will also include a consideration of the question whether it should be regarded as part of a larger offering made or to be made. In the release, the SEC articulated the factors that it considered relevant to the question of integration: whether (i) the different offerings are part of a single plan of financing, (ii) the offerings involve issuance of the same class of security, (iii) the offerings are made at or about the same time, (iv) the same type of consideration is to be received, and (v) the offerings are made for the same general purpose. These same factors are repeated in a note to Rule 502(a). This note also makes clear that a private placement in the United States will "generally" not be integrated with simultaneous public offerings being made outside the United States effected in compliance with Regulation S.[57]

The five factors stated in SEC Release No. 33-4552 and in the note to Rule 502 provide little help in applying the integration doctrine. The SEC has provided no formal advice as to the weight to be afforded to each of the enumerated factors. Certainly, whether the same type of consideration is received is a meaningless factor. Except in the context of an acquisition, private placements are almost always made for cash. The first and last factors seem to overlap: if the sales are part of a "single plan of financing," then it would appear that they are "made for the same general purpose." If the "sales have been made at

56. SEC Release No. 33-4552 (November 6, 1962).
57. The SEC took the same position in SEC Release No. 33-4708 (July 9, 1964).

or about the same time," it is also likely that they are "part of a single plan of financing."[58] The second factor, namely whether the transactions "involve issuance of the same class of securities," would seem self-evident. There is no basis for integrating a private placement of debt securities with a public offering of common stock. Similarly, if an issuer is having a public offering of subordinated debentures, there should be no reason why it may not concurrently make a private placement of senior debt with a group of insurance companies, even though both offerings are part of a single plan of financing, are made at the same time, involve the same type of consideration, and are made for the same general purpose. As stated by the Director of the SEC's Division of Corporation Finance:

> And, it should be clear why recent structured financing involving side-by-side private and registered offerings do not require integration. In these cases, for example, a single purchaser—a financial institution—buys the entire unregistered senior debt; the senior subordinated unregistered debt is sold to 10 insurance companies and the subordinated debt offered to the public is registered. The validity of the nonregistered offering should be clear but, unfortunately, it is not under current law.[59]

The result may not be clear if one gives too much credence to the SEC's five factors, but no experienced securities practitioner would doubt for a moment the availability of Section 4(2) or Regulation D for the sales to the financial institution and the ten insurance companies. These are simply not the types of transactions that the integration doctrine was designed to reach.

---

58. There have been recent indications that the SEC staff considers the "single plan" and "general purpose" tests to be somewhat more important than the other three tests. As noted, these are often two sides of the same coin. Together with the "at or about the same time" test, they would make a three-sided coin.

59. L.C. Quinn, *Redefining "Public Offering or Distribution" For Today* (speech delivered on November 22, 1986).

Realistically, integration problems seldom arise in the context of two or more institutional private placements. For example, if a private placement of debt securities is made to accredited investors and a second offering of the same type is made shortly thereafter for the same purpose, the two transactions—even if integrated—would still meet the requirements of Regulation D and Section 4(2).

The integration issue has arisen where a company is engaged in a continuous acquisition program, for example, a program by a motel chain to acquire franchisees in exchange for the issuer's common stock. One court refused to apply the integration doctrine where a company made 10 acquisitions involving the issuance of approximately 1.6 million shares of its common stock over a relatively short period of time,[60] but a number of issuers have filed shelf registration statements to cover acquisition programs.

An integration issue may arise where a company is relying on Rule 505 and the question is whether the $1 million limit has been exceeded. This is one reason why it is preferable to structure offerings under Section 506 rather than Section 505. It also may arise where a company is relying on the 35-purchaser test under Regulation D. In this connection, integration was a real concern to promoters offering series of limited partnership interests in oil and gas, real estate and other tax driven ventures. During the period from 1971 through 1979, when the staff ceased giving interpretive advice for no-action rulings on integration questions, a number of conflicting positions were taken in no-action letters and interpretive responses to inquiries from the industry. Would drilling program A be integrated with drilling program B where portions of the properties overlapped? These issues are less relevant today as oil and gas programs have become less common as a result of economic conditions in the industry and tax reform.[61]

---

60. *Bowers v. Columbia General Corp.*, 336 F. Supp. 609 (D. Del. 1971).

61. For a detailed discussion of these issues, *see Integration of Partnership Offerings: A Proposal for Identifying a Discrete Offering,* 37 Bus. Law. 1591 (1982).

Challenging integration problems can arise where an offering starts out as a private placement but evolves into—or is followed by—a registered public offering, and *vice versa*. These problems are discussed below under *Related Private Placements and Public Offerings*.

- *The Substantial Compliance Rule*

The 1989 amendments to Regulation D included the adoption of Rule 508, which provides in effect that minor failures to comply with the technical requirements of Regulation D will not necessarily cause a loss of the exemption. This so-called "innocent and immaterial" defense was long advocated by securities practitioners.

Rule 508 protects an issuer against civil liability under the 1933 Act for a failure to comply with Regulation D in the case of a sale to a particular person if (i) the failure to comply did not pertain to a requirement directly intended to protect that person, (ii) the failure to comply was insignificant with respect to the offering as a whole, and (iii) a good faith and reasonable attempt was made to comply with all applicable requirements of the regulation.

Rule 508 deems the general solicitation prohibition and numerical purchaser limits of Rule 506 to be significant. Under Rule 508, if a provision designed to protect a particular investor is violated, that person could sue for rescission, but other investors in the offering would not have the same right of rescission, unless the violation was significant as to the offering overall.

As originally proposed, Rule 508 would have barred enforcement actions by the SEC. That element of the original proposal generated much opposition by state securities regulators and resulted in the SEC's staff holding joint meetings during the late summer and early fall of 1988 with representatives of the American Bar Association's Section of Business Law and of the North American Securities Administrators Association to seek a workable compromise to preserve Federal-state coordination in the limited offering area. As adopted, Rule 508 specifically states that the failure to comply is actionable by the SEC.

Rule 144A

As noted above, the field of institutional private placements has been revolutionized since 1990 by an SEC rule that by its terms does not even apply to a private placement by an issuer. Rule 144A only permits persons *other than the issuer* to resell securities that they have purchased directly or indirectly from the issuer (or an affiliate of the issuer) in a transaction or series of transactions not involving a public offering. Rule 144A's powerful influence on the market arises from the fact that it permits a financial intermediary who has purchased securities from an issuer in a private placement to make resales of those securities, subject to certain easily-verified conditions, to a potentially indefinite number of "qualified institutional buyers."

The SEC adopted Rule 144A in April 1990.[62] The rule provides a non-exclusive safe harbor from the registration and prospectus delivery requirements of Section 5 of the 1933 Act for resales of certain restricted securities to "qualified institutional buyers" (popularly known in investment banking circles as "QIBs"). The rule provides that sales to QIBs in compliance with the rule are not distributions and that the seller is therefore not an "underwriter." If the seller is not the issuer or a dealer, it can rely upon the Section 4(1) exemption. If the seller is a dealer, it can rely upon the Section 4(3) exemption. Each transaction will be assessed individually. The exemption for an offer and sale under the rule is unaffected by transactions by other sellers.

Rule 144A contains four conditions that are normally subject to easy verification by the person relying on the exemption, i.e., the seller. These are that the restricted security be offered or sold only to QIBs or persons "reasonably believe[d]" to be QIBs, that the seller take "reasonable steps" to ensure that the purchaser is aware that the seller *may* be relying on Rule 144A in making the sale, that the securities not be "fungible" with certain exchange-listed or NASDAQ-quoted securities and that

---

62. SEC Release No. 33-6862 (April 23, 1990). Rule 144A originally was proposed in SEC Release No. 33-6806 (October 25, 1988) and was reproposed in SEC Release No. 33-6839 (July 11, 1989).

the issuer—if it is not a 1934 Act reporting company, an "exempt" foreign private issuer or a foreign government—has committed itself to provide certain "reasonably current" information to a holder or a prospective purchaser. Notably, there is no prohibition relating to "general solicitation."

• *QIB Status*

QIBs are specified types of institutions, acting for their own account or the account of other QIBs, that in the aggregate own and invest on a discretionary basis at least $100 million in securities of non-affiliated issuers.[63] The specified types of institutions include business entities that are corporations, partnerships and business trusts. They also include regulated entities that are insurance companies (including their separate accounts that are not investment companies), registered investment companies, business development companies, licensed small business investment companies, public employee benefit plans, ERISA employee benefit plans and not-for-profit organizations described in Section 501(c)(3) of the Internal Revenue Code.

Banks and savings and loan associations (and certain foreign counterparts) must meet the $100 million test *and* must also meet a $25 million net worth test. Trust funds may qualify as QIBs if their trustees are banks or trust companies and their participants include only public or ERISA employee benefit plans (other than individual retirement accounts or "Keogh" plans). While investment advisers and other entities may qualify as QIBs by aggregating their proprietary securities with the securities owned by managed accounts, it is still necessary for a managed account itself to meet the $100 million test in order to qualify as a QIB.

Less stringent eligibility standards are applicable to broker-dealers registered under the 1934 Act. They are QIBs if on the relevant date they owned or managed on a discretionary basis at least $10 million in securities of nonaffiliated issuers (other

---

63. Securities are to be valued at cost, unless the institution reports its security holdings in its financial statements on the basis of market value and no current cost information has been published, in which case the determination may be based on market value.

than securities that are part of an unsold allotment in a public offering) or if they act in a "riskless principal transaction" on behalf of a QIB.[64] A dealer is deemed to own securities in a trading account as well as those in an investment account. Whether or not it comes within the definition of a QIB, a broker-dealer may act as agent in a sale to a QIB.

In order to rely on the rule, the seller and any person acting on its behalf must offer and sell the securities only to QIBs or to persons whom they reasonably believe to be QIBs. The rule specifies several nonexclusive means of satisfying this requirement. Information concerning the amount of securities owned and under investment management may be determined from the most recently publicly available financial statements or the most recent information appearing in documents filed with the SEC or other governmental agencies or in a recognized securities manual. The seller also may rely on a certification by an executive officer of the prospective purchaser.

Many financial intermediaries have provided questionnaires to their customers who appear to be eligible for QIB status. This is an inefficient means of establishing "reasonable belief." At one point, it appeared that one or more of the rating agencies would list institutions that represented themselves as satisfying the QIB criteria. Such a listing would presumably qualify as either information contained in a "recognized securities manual" or as a "certification" by the investor.

• *Screen-Based and Other "Offers"*

Dealers will frequently want to use proprietary or common carrier electronic communication media (e.g., the Internet) to facilitate Rule 144A offerings by the display of relevant information. If the information is accessible only to QIBs (e.g., by means of a password), electronic display will present no problems under the condition of Rule 144A that offers as well as sales be made only to QIBs or persons reasonably believed to

---

64. A "riskless principal transaction" is defined as "a transaction in which a dealer buys a security from any person and makes a simultaneous offsetting sale of such security to a qualified institutional buyer, including another dealer acting as riskless principal for a qualified institutional buyer."

be QIBs. As noted above, the SEC staff recently agreed that a password-restricted electronic display of information related to private placements did not constitute a "general solicitation." Since general solicitation is a broader concept than "offer," it would clearly follow that a password-protected display should be permissible under Rule 144A if the password were made available only to QIBs. The SEC staff has been unwilling to concede, however, that information may be displayed electronically on any other basis even if the screens contain a legend to the effect that the information is not intended as an offer to any person who is not a QIB.

The SEC staff position on screen-based display of information to non-QIBs overlooks one of the basic distinctions between Rule 144A and Regulation D, i.e., that Rule 144A restricts *offers* to QIBs but does not prohibit *general solicitations*. Even if an Internet communication available to all persons were deemed a general solicitation, it would appear to be a basic principle of contract law that a communication should not be construed as an "offer" if it clearly states that it is not an offer to anyone other than a QIB.

In the case of asset-backed securities, the willingness of dealers to make bids on such securities may depend on the ready electronic availability of performance and related information. In fact, customers who would like the comfort of knowing that a bid is available would be among those most adversely affected by an SEC position that discourages the electronic availability of such information because of the bare possibility that it may be seen by non-QIBs as an incident to its screen-based delivery format.

An offering pursuant to Rule 144A is an unregistered offering within the meaning of Rule 135c, and an issuer that reports under the 1934 Act or is exempt under Rule 12g3-2(b) is entitled to rely on Rule 135c to publish a notice regarding a Rule 144A transaction. When it adopted Rule 135c, the SEC did not amend Rule 144A to exclude a notice pursuant to Rule 135c from the prohibition on offers and sales to persons other than QIBs (as it amended both Regulation D and Regulation S). On the other hand, a notice pursuant to Rule 135c is expressly deemed not to be an "offer" and should therefore not interfere with a Rule 144A transaction.

- *"Fungibility"*

Rule 144A is applicable to both debt and equity securities. It is not available, however, for transactions in securities that, when issued (as opposed to when sold), were of the same class as securities listed on a national securities exchange or quoted in an automated inter-dealer quotation system, such as NASDAQ. Securities quoted in the pink sheets or in the NASD's PORTAL system are not excluded. Securities issued by open-end investment companies and unit investment trusts are not covered by the rule.

Debt securities and preferred stock of different series generally will be viewed as different, non-"fungible" classes of securities for purposes of Rule 144A. Securities that are convertible into securities that are listed or quoted in NASDAQ are treated as securities of the same class as those into which they are convertible unless at the time of issuance the effective conversion premium was at least 10%. Warrants are treated as securities of the same class as the underlying securities unless at the time of issuance they had a term of at least three years and an effective exercise premium of at least 10%. Likewise, securities of the same class as those underlying ADRs that are listed or quoted in NASDAQ are not eligible for resale under the rule.

- *Information Requirement*

If the issuer of the securities is not a reporting company under the 1934 Act and is not a foreign issuer exempt from reporting under Rule 12g3-2(b) (whether on a voluntary basis or otherwise) and is not a foreign government, the availability of Rule 144A is conditioned upon the holder of the securities and the purchaser having the right to obtain specified information from the issuer, upon request, and the purchaser having received that information, if requested. The information required to be furnished, if requested by the purchaser, is a "very brief" and "reasonably current" description of the business of the issuer and its products and services offered; the issuer's most recent balance sheet and profit and loss and retained earnings statements; and similar financial statements for such part of the two preceding fiscal years as the issuer has been in operation.

The rule does not specify the means of establishing the "right" to obtain this information, but the SEC release that adopted Rule 144A suggested that the issuer's obligation could be imposed, *inter alia*, in the terms of the security, by contract (e.g., the purchase agreement), by corporate law, by regulatory requirement or the rules of applicable SROs. Presumably, a representation or undertaking in an offering document would also be sufficient. If reliance is placed on a purchase agreement between the issuer and the underwriters or placement agents where the agreement is governed by non-U.S. law, it would be advisable to determine whether third-party beneficiary rights are recognized under the applicable law.

The SEC staff has advised in several no-action letters that, where a Rule 144A issuer's securities are guaranteed by its parent company, the information requirement depends on the status of the guarantor. *See*, e.g., SEC No-Action Letters, *British Aerospace* (available May 9, 1990), *Schering-Plough Corp.* (available November 21, 1991). Accordingly, the information requirement does not apply where the securities are guaranteed by a parent company that would itself be exempt from the information requirement. If the parent-guarantor would not be exempt, the information required to be supplied would be that of the parent-guarantor.

• *Notice Requirement*

Although Rule 144A imposes no resale restrictions, a seller or any person acting on its behalf must take reasonable steps to assure that the buyer is aware that the seller may rely on the exemption from registration afforded by the rule. Since Rule 144A provides an exemption for what might otherwise be an illegal *offer*, the notice should presumably be given to the prospective purchaser at the time of the offer and not be delayed, for example, until the confirmation of sale is forwarded to the purchaser.

• *PORTAL*

At the same time that it adopted Rule 144A, the SEC approved rules establishing a new NASD marketplace called

PORTAL ("Private Offering, Resale and Trading through Automated Linkages") for the purpose of facilitating transactions in the Rule 144A market by the dissemination of trading information and the availability of an execution capability.[65] PORTAL is a computer and communications facility for primary offering and secondary trading of securities that are eligible for resale pursuant to Rule 144A and that are (a) restricted securities as defined in Rule 144(a)(3) or (b) contractually required to be resold only pursuant to Regulation S, Rule 144A or Rule 144 or in "secondary private placements." Access to PORTAL is currently limited to QIBs, "PORTAL dealers" and "PORTAL brokers."

The prospects for PORTAL's success were undermined from the start by a lapse in communications between the NASD and the SEC. The NASD appears to have anticipated that Rule 144A would *mandate* that resales pursuant to the rule take place in a "closed-loop" system such as PORTAL. As adopted by the SEC, however, Rule 144A contained no such requirement. Under amendments to the PORTAL rules approved by the SEC in December 1993,[66] there is no longer a requirement that PORTAL securities be deposited in and trade through segregated accounts at PORTAL clearing organizations; however, the new rules subject all transactions in PORTAL securities by an NASD member to the PORTAL rules. In addition, in order to improve "protection against leakage," the amendments (a) require that NASD members submit reports containing price and size information relating to PORTAL transactions and indicating whether a purchaser was a QIB or non-QIB with respect to each trade in a PORTAL security, (b) require that all securities included in the PORTAL system be assigned CUSIP numbers that are different from any CUSIP number assigned to unrestricted securities of the same class and (c) permit only legally restricted or "contractually restricted" securities (as defined in the PORTAL rules) to be quoted on the PORTAL system.

---

65. SEC Release No. 34-27956 (April 27, 1990).
66. SEC Release No. 34-33326 (December 13, 1993).

Private Placement Procedures

The procedures appropriate for establishing the private placement exemption will depend on the type of transaction being effected. The most common types of institutional private placement are the following:

- the stand-alone Rule 144A placement with U.S. institutional investors of a large amount of securities of a domestic or foreign issuer, where the methods used to negotiate terms and distribute the securities resemble closely those used in the case of a registered public offering,

- the continuous "Section 4(2)" or "restricted" program, following Regulation D or Rule 144A procedures, involving either commercial paper that does not qualify for the Section 3(a)(3) exemption or MTNs, which in either case are continuously sold to institutions, and

- the traditional stand-alone private placement of debt securities with a relatively small number of institutional purchasers.

The type of private placement that involves the most risk and requires the most carefully structured offering procedures is an offering pursuant to Regulation D of limited partnership interests or other equity securities in a market that consists largely of individuals rather than institutions.

• *Rule 144A Private Placement*

There are two types of Rule 144A offering: Rule 144A-only offerings and Rule 144A-eligible offerings. Both commence as private placements from an issuer to an intermediary such as a securities dealer; the difference lies in the permitted resales of the securities.

Rule 144A-only offerings generally provide that any resales of the securities (until the securities become freely tradeable under Rule 144 or registered under the 1933 Act) may be made only pursuant to Rule 144A. Rule 144A-only offerings also generally provide that investors that initially purchase the securities from the issuer or the intermediary must be QIBs, although some Rule 144A-only offerings permit accredited investors that are not QIBs to purchase securities in the initial placement.

In Rule 144A-eligible offerings, the terms of the securities are drafted to permit resales pursuant to Rule 144A. However, resales of the securities pursuant to some or all of the other available 1933 Act exemptions (e.g., Regulation S or a secondary private placement) are also available.

The SEC reports periodically to Congress on developments in the Rule 144A market. In its last report dated July 20, 1994 (which was based on information from the adoption of Rule 144A in April 1990 through the end of 1993), the SEC identified 709 transactions under Rule 144A by 625 issuers involving an aggregate of more than $91 billion of securities. Nearly half of the issuers were non-U.S. issuers, who accounted for approximately 28% of the dollar amount of securities sold in the United States in reliance on the rule.

Rule 144A transactions by foreign issuers involved more than $6 billion of common equity securities and more than $18 billion of debt securities. U.S. issuers were involved in few common stock transactions, undoubtedly because of the unavailability of Rule 144A for offerings of "fungible" securities, but U.S. issuers did complete transactions involving nearly $12 billion of convertible debt or preferred stock and more than $50 billion of debt securities (including more than $10 billion of asset-backed securities).

Rule 144A transactions are increasingly being used for offerings of high yield debt securities of U.S. companies and, to a lesser extent, non-U.S. companies. In the first quarter of 1997 alone, $17.8 billion of high yield debt was placed pursuant to Rule 144A, more than double the amount placed in the first quarter of 1996. Some sources expected that Rule 144A offerings in 1997 would account for two-thirds of all high yield offerings.

• • *Rule 144A Debt Offering.* Except for the fact that they are by definition directed at a more limited universe of investors, Rule 144A transactions in debt securities have come to resemble closely their SEC-registered counterparts. Indeed, it might not be an overstatement to assert that for at least some securities the public and Rule 144A markets have merged for all practical and economic purposes. Some investment banks have combined or closely aligned their public and private origination groups in order more effectively to compete for issuers' business. Even on the "buy side," many investors have become so accustomed to the aftermarket liquidity made possible by Rule 144A that they regard the security's designation as "Rule 144A-eligible" as more of a technicality than a distinction of economic importance.

As in a public offering, the issuer will work with its U.S. counsel, its investment banker and its counsel, and its independent accountants to prepare the purchase agreement and the offering materials. The purchase agreement's representations and warranties, covenants and agreements, closing conditions and indemnification and contribution arrangements will usually reflect the investment banker's standard format. Of course, the offering materials will not be subject to the regulatory review process involved in an SEC-registered public offering, but marketing considerations and the disclosure policies of the investment banker will raise many similar drafting issues.

For example, a non-U.S. issuer's investment banker will generally determine in consultation with the issuer what U.S. dollar convenience translations and what U.S. "gaap" reconciliation items, if any, would be desirable for the marketing and sale of the security. In the case of high yield debt, it may be desirable to include forecasts or projections in the offering materials.

With all the strengths and weaknesses inherent in the comparison, due diligence on a Rule 144A debt offering resembles in many ways the due diligence process followed on registered public offerings. If the debt is investment-grade, due diligence on a Rule 144A placement will parallel that associated with an investment-grade shelf takedown (see Chapter 8) with the important reservations that there will not have been an initial filing with the SEC nor an opportunity for designated purchasers' counsel to perform any "continuous due diligence" on the issuer. On the other hand, if the debt is less than investment-grade, due diligence may be quite extensive, depending on the investment banker's familiarity with the issuer and the rating agencies' views of trends in the issuer's credit standing.

Since the Supreme Court's decision in *Gustafson*, an intermediary's liability for disclosure deficiencies in a private placement has been determined under Rule 10b-5 rather than under Section 12(a)(2) of the 1933 Act. Rule 10b-5, of course, requires a demonstration of *scienter* on the part of the defendant, i.e., either intentional fraud or, according to most courts, "recklessness." Section 12(a)(2), on the other hand, which most investment bankers and securities lawyers assumed for many years would determine an intermediary's liability, is a "negligence-based" remedy because its due diligence defense requires the exercise of "reasonable care."

For this reason, investment bankers' due diligence procedures for private offerings (including, since 1990, Rule 144A transactions) were established on the assumption that the securities firm would have to prove a lack of negligence, i.e., that it had acted in the exercise of reasonable care. *Gustafson* meant that such firms now had to establish only the absence of intentional fraud or reckless misconduct. While this difference might appear to justify some modifications in traditional procedures, there are some downside risks:

–   Plaintiffs' lawyers are skilled in alleging—with the benefit of hindsight—that securities firms were "reckless" in ignoring "red flags" or other indications that an issuer had undisclosed problems.

–   The document alleged in *Gustafson* to be a "prospectus" was the purchase agreement itself rather than an offering document. This might be the basis for a factual distinction in future litigation, despite the majority opinion's strong language suggesting that its holding is of general application.

–   Modifications to traditional procedures might make it more difficult to give the issuer's accountants the representation contemplated by SAS 72 regarding the underwriter's use of due diligence procedures in a non-

registered offering that are substantially equivalent to
those used in a registered offering.

–   All participants should be aware of the possibility that
state law may provide remedies that go beyond Rule
10b-5. Indeed, plaintiffs' lawyers appear to be relying
more heavily on state law remedies since the enactment
of the Reform Act.

The pressures on investment bankers to alter traditional due
diligence procedures are, of course, external rather than internal.
The premium placed on speed in order to lock in a transaction
means that there is often simply little time for the usual inquiries,
opinions or comfort letters. Also, issuers often object to the cost or
inconvenience of these basic due diligence methods.

The book-entry settlement facilities of DTC will be available for debt securities that are eligible for resale pursuant to
Rule 144A and that are either investment-grade or, if non-investment grade, are PORTAL-eligible.

The SEC staff takes the position that an offering of securities pursuant to Rule 144A may constitute a "distribution" for
purposes of the SEC's anti-manipulation rules if the transaction is distinguishable from ordinary trading transactions by
reason of its "magnitude" and the presence of special selling
efforts and selling methods. Investment-grade debt securities
are not subject to the relevant rules. The effect of the anti-manipulation rules for offerings of non-investment-grade debt
securities is that the investment bankers will be unable to commence making a market in the new securities until the completion of the distribution. In 1993, the SEC exempted all Rule
144A-eligible securities of foreign governments or foreign private issuers that were offered or sold in the U.S. to QIBs in
exempt transactions.[67] As part of its adoption in 1996 of Regulation M, the SEC extended this exemption to U.S. issuers as
well.[68]

---

67. SEC Release No. 34-33138 (November 3, 1993).
68. See the discussion in Chapter 4.

• • *Rule 144A Common Equity Offering.* As noted above, Rule 144A is not available for a security that is "fungible" with a security listed on a U.S. securities exchange or quoted in NAS-DAQ. This means that U.S. issuers have not been able to rely significantly on Rule 144A for the purpose of offering their common stock. They have, however, been able to rely on the rule for significant offerings of convertible securities, often on a "bought deal" or "overnight" basis, where the conversion premium is sufficiently high to overcome the fungibility problem. Non-U.S. issuers, on the other hand, have found Rule 144A highly useful in making placements in the United States of convertible securities or American Depository Shares representing their ordinary shares, either on a stand-alone basis or as part of a global offering. See Chapter 9 for a discussion of global offerings.

Due diligence procedures in connection with a non-U.S. issuer's Rule 144A equity offering are quite similar to those followed in connection with registered public offerings. The offering document will normally not include a numeric or quantitative reconciliation of the issuer's financial statements to U.S. "gaap" since this will often have been the single most significant obstacle to the issuer's engaging in an SEC-registered transaction. It is common, however, for the document to provide a narrative description of the major differences between U.S. "gaap" and the local accounting principles used to prepare the financial statements included in the document.

An equity offering under Rule 144A requires the non-U.S. issuer to deposit its securities with the custodian bank, which will in turn issue its American Depository Receipts ("ADRs") to the investment bank or banks engaged by the issuer to distribute the ADRs. This transaction usually relies on the Section 4(2) exemption. The investment bank or banks will then rely on Rule 144A in making resales of the ADRs.

There is no U.S. exchange listing in the case of a Rule 144A ADR offering, although corresponding depositary receipts may be listed on a European exchange such as the Luxembourg Stock Exchange or quoted on a European facility such as the Stock Exchange Automated Quotation System ("SEAQ") of the London Stock Exchange. In addition, the Rule 144A ADRs will typically be designated for trading in the PORTAL system in order to make them eligible for book-entry settlement.

Generally, Rule 144A ADR facilities permit new deposits of underlying ordinary shares by QIBs or offshore purchasers who have bought such shares in the secondary market and who are willing to accept restricted ADRs in exchange. This is unnecessary, of course, where the issuer also has an unrestricted facility. As in the case of other "restricted" securities, Rule 144(k) will permit the ADRs to be publicly offered and sold without registration upon the lapse of two years from the sale of the ADRs by the issuer or its affiliate. For this reason, a Rule 144A ADR facility is generally structured so as to permit neither the issuer nor any affiliate to deposit additional shares into the facility following the offering.

The SEC has issued guidelines relating to the situation where an issuer has concurrent restricted and unrestricted ADR facilities. This might arise, for example, where an issuer completes a Rule 144A offering either before or after it establishes a "Level One" facility for the convenience of the public holders of the same class of the issuer's underlying securities. The SEC's concern arises from the possibility of "leakage" between a restricted and an unrestricted facility as well as from the prospect of "automatic fungibility" where depositary receipts offered outside the United States in reliance on Regulation S become eligible for resale into the United States. The guidelines were issued in *Depositary Receipts* (available April 14, 1993) and rely on the SEC's power to control whether and when a Form F-6 registration statement becomes effective. (As discussed in Chapter 9, a Form F-6 registration statement is required for an unrestricted program.)

The guidelines require that Rule 144A ADRs be distinguished from Regulation S depositary receipts and from unrestricted depositary receipts by a different name and CUSIP number. Deposits into and withdrawals from the restricted facility are subject to certification requirements. Depositors of securities into a Regulation S facility must certify that they are not an affiliate of the issuer and that the securities are not restricted securities. Finally, a Form F-6 registration statement may not be filed covering a new unrestricted facility or a new Regulation S facility until 40 days after consummation of the Regulation S offering.

• *Continuous Private Placement Programs*

Traditionally, institutional private placements were effected as discrete offerings with a single closing. In the mid-1970s, a number of commercial paper dealers began to sell commercial paper that did not qualify for the Section 3(a)(3) exemption (see Chapter 10) to institutional investors in ostensible reliance upon Section 4(2). Because commercial paper programs require the continuous issuance of new notes to replace maturing notes, these "Section 4(2)" or "restricted" programs represented private placements made on a continuous basis over an extended period of time. "Section 4(2)" eventually came also to be relied upon for continuous offerings of medium-term notes (see Chapter 8) where the Section 3(a)(3) exemption was not available because the notes had maturities in excess of 270 days.

• • *Continuous Offering Procedures for Restricted Commercial Paper.* Originally, these programs were effected in accordance with procedures designed to comply in all material respects with the provisions of Rule 146, other than the requirement that a report be filed on Form 146. (See the discussion above under *Rule 146.*) Subsequently, these procedures could be simplified with the adoption of Regulation D. In either case, the dealer[69] did not sell the notes in reliance upon Rule 146 or Regulation D or even Section 4(2) itself—all of which are issuers' exemptions—but in reliance upon the dealer's exemption under Section 4(3). This analysis is based on the assumption that there is no "public offering" or "distribution" within the meaning of Section 4(3) when the dealer offers and sells the notes in accordance with Section 4(2), Rule 146 or Regulation D.

In contrast to other types of private placement, Rule 144A is not relied upon as often as Regulation D in the case of continuous "restricted" commercial paper programs. Non-QIBs make up a significant part of the universe of buyers in these programs, and dealers are reluctant to give up this segment of the market.

Section 3(a)(3) commercial paper programs are often conducted without benefit of a formal agreement between the

---

69. Most commercial paper programs are conducted by two or more dealers on behalf of an issuer, and references to "dealer" should be understood to include references to "co-dealers" unless the context otherwise requires.

dealer and the issuer. From the early days of "restricted" programs, however, it was recognized that there should be a clear understanding between the issuer and the dealer as to the procedures to be followed in making offers and sales under the program. The procedures proposed to be followed by the dealer were therefore set forth in a formal "dealer agreement." Just as in the case of underwriting agreements (see Chapter 2), there are variations among the various dealers' standard form of agreement. An industry association is working on a model form of agreement for both Section 3(a)(3) and Section 4(2) programs.

A dealer agreement will contain customary representations and warranties by the issuer, undertakings by the issuer to inform the dealers of material developments on an ongoing basis, and formal conditions to the commencement of the program. There is less uniformity on the inclusion of issuer indemnity and contribution undertakings. Some dealers make the not unreasonable assumption that an issuer's indemnity obligation will not be worth very much if the issuer defaults on its commercial paper (the point being that litigation will arise in connection with commercial paper only if it is not paid at maturity, while litigation will often arise in connection with common stock or long-term debt at a time when the issuer is still perfectly solvent).

The principal purpose of the dealer agreement in a "restricted" program is to formalize the procedures to be followed in offering and selling the issuer's notes. As noted above, the dealer will be relying on the Section 4(3) exemption and not on Regulation D. Since the issuer will neither solicit investors nor pass title to the notes to investors, it would appear that the issuer has no real stake in whether or not the dealer has a good exemption. On the other hand, the issuer is relying on Regulation D to sell the notes to the dealer. The issuer will therefore want to know that it has exercised "reasonable care" to assure that the dealer will not be acting as an "underwriter" in reselling the notes.

The dealer will also want the issuer to agree to the reasonableness of the procedures that the dealer proposes to follow. Moreover, the issuer's counsel will customarily be asked to deliver an opinion *to the dealer* that the offer and sale of the notes in the manner contemplated by the dealer agreement will be entitled to a private placement exemption (the exact expression of this opinion varies a great deal). Finally, the dealer will want to demonstrate to the issuer great concern about the adequacy of the procedures to achieve the exemption if for no other reason than to head off a request from the issuer that the dealer indemnify it against any loss arising out of the exemption's proving to be unavailable. (Such a request would be rather pointless, of course, since the issuer's maximum exposure in that event would be the obligation to prepay its own short-term notes.)

The dealer agreement will usually specify that notes will be sold in minimum denominations or amounts of $250,000. In a book-entry settlement environment, of course, minimum denominations are a fiction. The useful purpose of the undertaking, however, is to reinforce the "non-public" nature of the program by requiring each investor's investment decision to be in a significant amount. In view of this purpose, the authors do not believe it is necessary to provide (as some agreements do) that each person for whom a fiduciary is acting must also be purchasing the minimum amount of notes.

The universe of eligible buyers is a frequent source of confusion and disagreement. The commercial paper market is primarily institutional, and the dealer agreement will typically restrict offers and sales to QIBs and institutional accredited investors. Some dealers, however, will want to be able to offer and sell notes to those of their customers who are "sophisticated" individual investors. This is sometimes permitted in the agreement, but there is a lack of uniformity on who is deemed to be a "sophisticated" individual investor. Some agreements require only a minimum net worth (usually well in excess of the accredited investor minimum for "natural persons" of $1,000,000), while others require a pre-existing relationship and a dealer determination of investment sophistication. The latter requirements deserve some discussion.

"Pre-existing relationship" is a concept sometimes relied upon to show the absence of a general solicitation in the context of a private offering directed at individual investors. As discussed below in connection with such offerings, however, the existence of a pre-existing relationship is not the only means by which one can demonstrate the absence of a general solicitation. If a dealer wishes to offer "restricted" commercial paper to its *customers* who are high net worth individuals, this clearly satisfies the test (even on the assumption the test has any applicability in a private commercial paper program designed to comply with Regulation D).

The requirement that a dealer make a determination of investor sophistication is really a throwback to Rule 146. Unlike the requirements of that rule, however, it is irrelevant under Regulation D whether or not an investor is "sophisticated" so long as the investor is an "accredited investor." Moreover, sophistication has nothing to do with whether or not a general solicitation is taking place. To be sure, a judgment about sophistication is appropriate as part of the dealer's discharge of its obligation to its customer to recommend suitable investments, but this obligation does not concern the issuer and does not belong in the dealer agreement.

Dealers and issuer (or their respective counsel) also disagree from time to time about whether or not the dealer should abide by a ceiling on the number of investors who can participate in the program. Like the "minimum denomination" requirement discussed above, a ceiling on the number of offerees serves the purpose of reducing the likelihood that a program will involve a general solicitation; in the context of a predominantly institutional offering, however, the analysis should focus on the manner of offering rather than on numbers. In the early days of restricted commercial paper programs, some dealer agreements provided for a flexible ceiling where the maximum number of offerees increased with the size of the program. For a $1,000,000,000 program, for example, the dealer could approach as many as 750 offerees. Such arbitrary limits are unnecessary in the context of a commercial paper program structured in accordance with Regulation D and directed at institutional accredited investors or high net worth individuals.

Lawyers advising dealers also disagree as to whether dealers should be in a position at any given time to identify all persons to whom notes have been offered. Those lawyers who believe that this is necessary rely on court decisions and SEC statements in *amicus* briefs to the effect that an offering cannot qualify for a private placement exemption unless evidence can be produced of the exact number and identity of all offerees. The private placements under attack in the cited court decisions or SEC proceedings, however, usually involve somewhat careless large-scale solicitations of individual investors to purchase a speculative security. In addition, the availability of an exemption usually had to be tested under the subjective standards of Section 4(2), since the issuers or their agents had either not attempted to take advantage of Rule 146 or Regulation D or were held to have failed in the attempt. Under Regulation D, as discussed above, the *number* of offerees is arguably relevant to whether or not there is a general solicitation; on the other hand, arbitrary limits should be unnecessary in the context of a restricted commercial paper program directed at institutional accredited investors and high net worth individuals. (It follows that one should not have to be able to fix the exact number of offerees; the ability to approximate the number by reference to mailing, facsimile or courier records should suffice.) The *identity* of the offerees at any given time is, of course, relevant to whether or not the investors are accredited investors. Again, however, it should be possible to establish this fact without knowing the name and address of each offeree by reference to common business records such as standard mailing lists.

If the proceeds are to be used to purchase or carry securities, the dealer agreement may also contain a requirement, arising out of the Federal Reserve Board's Regulation T, that the dealer may act as principal in resales of notes only where the buyer is a QIB; otherwise, the dealer must act as agent. The problem arises most frequently where the issuer is using the proceeds of the program to finance a stock acquisition, a purpose for which restricted commercial paper programs are a swift and efficient vehicle. Regulation T governs extensions of credit by broker-dealers and, among other things, prohibits broker-dealers from extending unsecured credit that is to be used for the purpose of purchasing, carrying or trading in securities. Traditionally, the Federal Reserve Board does not regard *public* offerings of commercial paper or debt securities (e.g., a firm commitment underwriting of an issuer's debt securities) as an extension of credit by the underwriter or dealer. The problem arises when the dealer wishes to act as principal in purchasing restricted commercial paper from the issuer for purposes of resale to the dealer's customers. This practice, while customary in the commercial paper market, was deemed by the staff of the Federal Reserve Board in 1984 to constitute a prohibited "extension" of credit because the dealer became the owner of the issuer's commercial paper for some period of time before it was sold to an investor.[70] The Board modified this position somewhat in 1990 by permitting the dealer to act as principal if it purchased debt securities for resale pursuant to Rule 144A.[71] Out of concern that they might otherwise be held to be violating Regulation X (which prohibits persons from receiving the benefit of certain credit that the lender is prohibited from extending), dealer agreements in these situations therefore require the dealer to act as agent except in selling to QIBs. Commercial paper dealers are understood to be attempting to persuade the Board's staff to extend the 1990 interpretation to all sales to accredited institutional investors.

Commercial paper notes are traditionally issued in bearer form, and they are ordinarily negotiable instruments under the Uniform Commercial Code. One might, therefore, conclude that particularly stringent resale restrictions would be appropriate in order to demonstrate reasonable care that the dealer and subsequent purchasers were not acting as "underwriters." In fact, however, commercial paper presents few challenges arising out of resale activity. First of all, most investors hold notes until maturity. Second, in those cases where an investor has an

---

70. Staff Opinion of December 11, 1984 (Federal Reserve Regulatory Service ¶ 5-606.4). At the time, Regulation T also sharply restricted a broker-dealer's "arranging" of credit for securities purposes. Acting as agent in a private placement for this purpose, however, was deemed to constitute "investment banking services" not subject to the arranging prohibition. Effective July 1, 1996 the arranging prohibition was eliminated for all situations except where the broker-dealer willfully arranges credit that violates any margin rule applicable to the lender or borrower. Federal Reserve Docket No. R-0772, 61 F.R. 20386 (May 6, 1996).

71. Interpretation of the Federal Reserve Board, Federal Reserve Regulatory Service ¶ 5-470.1 (July 16, 1990).

unanticipated need for liquidity, it will almost invariably seek a bid from one of the dealers on the program. The dealers are the natural buyers for the paper in view of their familiarity with the issuer and the issuer's credit, and they have a natural outlet for the repurchased paper, i.e., they can simply resell under the program. Third, the fact that most commercial paper transactions are settled by book-entry rather than by the issuance of physical notes makes it difficult for an investor to sell or even pledge a note outside the program. These considerations should be of significant importance in deciding what resale restrictions are appropriate for a restricted commercial paper program.

In particular, the considerations mentioned above do have significance for a traditional device for preventing resales that might destroy the basis for the private placement exemption, i.e., restrictive legends. In traditional private placements, prospective investors received warnings about restrictions on resale from three separate sources: the offering materials (the "private placement memorandum" or "PPM"), the purchase contract and the physical certificate relating to the security that was being offered and sold. In addition, the documents stated that the investor would be deemed to have agreed to the restrictions in the event that it purchased notes.

In restricted commercial paper programs, there is no written purchase contract that binds the purchaser of notes, and it is useless to place a restrictive legend on a "master" commercial paper note that is being deposited with DTC for purposes of facilitating book-entry settlement of notes. Moreover, DTC sometimes objects to particular forms of restrictive legend placed on the master note. This leaves the private placement memorandum as the only vehicle for providing notice to the investor of restrictions on resale and for obtaining the investor's deemed agreement to abide by such restrictions.

The authors believe that it is sufficient to rely on the private placement memorandum as a vehicle for disclosing and obtaining agreement to restrictions on resale. They also believe there is no need to place an overly-restrictive legend on a master note deposited with DTC.

Wherever its location, the restrictive legend serves to reinforce that the notes are available only to specified categories of investor. In addition, the legend states that in the event the holder wishes to resell the note it must do so in accordance with specified procedures. At one time, legends often required the holder to resell the note only to the dealer from which it had been purchased. More recently, legends permit the holder to sell back to the issuer, any dealer designated by the issuer or directly to a QIB in a Rule 144A transaction.

The format of the private placement memorandum relating to restricted commercial paper is undergoing significant change. At one time, dealers distributed annual, quarterly and special memoranda relating to each issuer's restricted or Section 3(a)(3) program. The memoranda often contained long extracts from the issuer's reports filed with the SEC under the 1934 Act. Dealers generally believed that the memoranda served to protect them against lawsuits from investors in the event of a default by the issuer. Over time, it came to be recognized that a lawsuit was as likely to be based upon allegations of inadequate "due diligence" or investigation by the issuer as on allegations of false or incomplete disclosure. Moreover, it came to be recognized that investors could easily themselves obtain the issuer's 1934 Act reports, either electronically or directly from the issuer, and perform an independent credit analysis.

Many dealers are accordingly adopting an abbreviated commercial paper offering memorandum format that contemplates only "bare bones" information about the commercial paper program (size of program, denominations, form and ratings), with a reference for further information to the issuer or its 1934 Act reports. In the case of a restricted program, of course, the memorandum also contains the restrictive legend.

Questions also arise from time to time relating to dealers' screen-based solicitation efforts. Many commercial paper dealers communicate with their commercial paper buyer customers by screen-based displays. These enable the potential buyer efficiently to examine the notes that the dealer is offering for sale. So long as the screens are available—by password or otherwise—only to investors who are eligible to purchase paper under the dealer agreement, the screens present no problem. If they are more broadly available, e.g., to all Internet users, this can amount to a general solicitation under Regulation D in violation of the dealer agreement. This is not a sensible result, of course, particularly if the screen carries a legend to the effect that it is not intended as an offer to or solicitation of anyone who is not an eligible purchaser.

• • *Integration.* The question of integration must be faced when an issuer decides to commence a "restricted" program at the same time that it is issuing commercial paper in reliance on Section 3(a)(3). The problem can also arise in reverse order. In either case, it is likely that there will be an overlap in the maturities of the notes issued in the separate programs.

The staff of the SEC has issued a number of no-action letters permitting simultaneous offerings of commercial paper under Section 3(a)(3) and private placements of notes with overlapping maturities. In the first of these, the issuer represented that different securities dealers would be used in connection with the sale of the commercial paper and the private placement of notes with maturities ranging from 30 days to seven years.[72] The issuer also represented that controls would be established to insure that proceeds from the sale of the commercial paper would be used to finance only current transactions and that the proceeds from the private placement would be used to finance only non-current transactions.

The staff has taken a similar no-action position with respect to the simultaneous sale through the same dealer of commercial paper and the private placement of notes with maturities ranging from 30 days to 270 days.[73] There the issuer represented that it had in effect controls to assure that proceeds from the sale of its commercial paper would be used exclusively for current transactions and that the proceeds from the private placement would be used exclusively for transactions that were not current. The issuer agreed to deposit the proceeds from the private placement in a different bank from that utilized for the deposit of proceeds from the sale of its commercial paper. The issuer stated that it expected that the two offerings would have

---

72. SEC No-action Letter, *Pittsburgh National Corp.* (available August 15, 1977).

73. SEC No-action Letter, *NCNB Corp.* (available April 27, 1978).

some overlap because of the sale of commercial paper to institutions that also participated in the private placement.

The SEC's staff also took a favorable no-action position where an issuer contemplated a simultaneous offering of commercial paper and a private placement of promissory notes with maturities ranging from 30 days to one year.[74] Again, the issuer represented that the proceeds from the two offerings would be used for current transactions and non-current transactions, respectively. The issuer represented that the private placement would be to major corporate and other institutional investors in the national market, whereas the commercial paper would be restricted primarily to a predominantly regional market.

An integration problem can arise if an issuer decides to convert a commercial paper program from a Section 3(a)(3) program to a Section 4(2) program. This occurred in the case of a joint venture that issued three series of commercial paper notes, each guaranteed by one of the three joint venturers. The notes were issued without registration in reliance upon an opinion of counsel based on a number of no-action letters that recognized that the Section 3(a)(3) exemption would be available for commercial paper issued to provide interim financing of capital expenditures where permanent financing was to be obtained within a reasonable time after the completion of construction. The opinion was conditioned on the understanding that the commercial paper program would not be continued beyond a specified date. In view of the success of the commercial paper program and the then existing relationship between interest rates in the commercial paper market and interest rates for long-term indebtedness, the issuer sought a means of extending the commercial paper program beyond the time originally contemplated.

The issuer's commercial paper dealer, Goldman Sachs Money Markets Inc., had established procedures under Section 4(2) designed to provide an exemption from registration for the sale of commercial paper that did not meet the requirements of

---

74. SEC No-action Letter, *First & Merchants Corp.* (available July 27, 1978).

Section 3(a)(3). These procedures were embodied in an agreement that Goldman Sachs proposed to enter into with the issuer. The decision was made to convert the program to one made in reliance on Section 4(2). The problem was integration. If the Section 4(2) program was merely a continuation of the Section 3(a)(3) program, the public nature of the Section 3(a)(3) program could taint the availability of Section 4(2).

The commercial paper market is essentially an institutional market. It was, therefore, possible that the Section 3(a)(3) program did not in fact involve a public offering. Counsel advised the issuer that, although the existing commercial paper program had been instituted in reliance upon Section 3(a)(3), if, in fact, it had been conducted in a manner that satisfied Section 4(2), then it would not affect the availability of the private placement exemption for the notes proposed to be issued in accordance with Section 4(2) procedures.

Counsel reviewed the program as theretofore conducted and was able to conclude that the private placement exemption had in fact been available. This conclusion was based on the following findings set forth in its opinion letter:

> To determine whether, in our opinion, the XYZ commercial paper program has in fact been conducted as a private placement, we have examined records made available to us by Goldman setting forth the potential investors to whom offers of XYZ commercial paper were made and the identity of each purchaser of Notes of each series since the commercial paper program was instituted in April 1983. These records indicate that since the institution of the commercial paper program, 41 investors have owned Series A Notes, 23 investors have owned Series B Notes and 13 investors have owned Series C Notes. Each of these investors appears to be an "accredited investor" within the meaning of Regulation D under the Securities Act. Goldman has advised us that the only sales of less than $200,000 of the Notes were made to the following investors: in Series A, to affiliates of two large insurance companies; in Series B, to a large union pension fund, to a university and

to a large cash management fund; in Series C, to affiliates of a large union pension fund. Chemical Bank has advised us that there have been no exchanges of Notes for Notes of smaller denominations.

We have also discussed with representatives of Goldman the manner in which the Notes have been offered for sale. We are satisfied that the Notes have not been offered "by any form of general solicitation or general advertising" within the meaning of Regulation D under the Securities Act.

On this basis, the Section 4(2) program went forward as planned.

An integration problem can also arise if an issuer wishes to conduct simultaneously a "restricted" commercial paper program and a registered MTN program where the maturities of the MTNs overlap with those of the commercial paper notes. (The same problem can arise if an issuer conducts simultaneously a restricted MTN program and a Section 3(a)(3) commercial paper program.) Overlapping maturities should not in isolation present a problem if the programs can be distinguished in other ways, e.g., by the use of proceeds. If this is not the case, the issuer should undertake that it will not issue MTNs with a maturity of less than a specified period at any time while it is issuing "restricted" commercial paper. The period should be specified with a view to establishing a reasonable distinction between the MTNs and the commercial paper in the light of the investor base and market conditions.

• • *Continuous Offering Procedures for Restricted MTNs.* MTNs emerged during the 1980s as a major source of funding for U.S. and non-U.S. corporations. One reason for the growth of the market was the willingness of major U.S. investment banks to commit resources to assist in primary issuance and to provide secondary market liquidity. Another significant reason was the SEC's adoption of Rule 415 in March 1982 (see Chapter 8). Shelf registration made it possible for issuers to take advantage of brief "window periods" of attractive interest rates by selling registered securities on very short notice.

U.S. issuers will normally elect to set up their MTN programs on a shelf-registered basis. For non-U.S. issuers, however, registered public offerings are not so easy. It is true that non-U.S. issuers that wish to make an SEC-registered offering of investment-grade debt are not required to provide the geographic market and industry segment information normally associated with a registered public offering (see Chapter 9). They are still required, however, to reconcile certain financial statement information to U.S. "gaap." This requirement has served as an obstacle to many non-U.S. issuers who otherwise would have set up a public MTN program in the U.S. Also, for reasons related to the Investment Company Act of 1940, a public MTN program might not be possible for a non-U.S. issuer's U.S. finance subsidiary where the parent company is unwilling or unable to provide an unconditional guarantee of the subsidiary's MTNs.

It is possible, of course, for non-U.S. issuers to avoid the reconciliation and related SEC disclosure requirements by selling MTNs on a private placement basis. Unlike the situation in the restricted commercial paper market with its shorter maturities, however, non-U.S. issuers for many years believed there would be a significant illiquidity premium associated with the private placement of MTNs.

Following the SEC's adoption of Rule 144A, an alternative market was effectively created that enabled non-U.S. corporations to access U.S. capital markets without having to comply with SEC accounting and related requirements and without having to pay a material liquidity premium. Non-U.S. issuers responded to Rule 144A by dramatically increasing their sale of MTNs in the U.S. private market.

Private MTN programs involve the initial issuance of MTNs (a) to a dealer acting as principal or (b) through a dealer, acting as agent, to QIBs or institutional accredited investors. As in the case of Rule 144A private placements discussed above, the issuer's exemption for its sales to or through dealers may be Section 4(2) or Regulation D, while the dealer buying as principal will resell to QIBs under Rule 144A and to institutional accredited investors under Section 4(3) by analogy to Regulation D. Investors who wish to resell will be able, of course, to do so in reliance on Rule 144A (or any other available exemption permitted under the terms of the program).

Given that the offering procedures for a private MTN program will generally restrict offerees and purchasers to QIBs or institutional accredited investors, no particular disclosure is required to be delivered to investors to perfect the private placement exemption. For marketing reasons, however, substantial disclosure about the issuer and, if the issuer is a U.S. finance subsidiary, the non-U.S. parent is customarily provided in a private placement memorandum. The disclosure in the memorandum about the issuer (or its parent) is normally greater than that required for a commercial paper program but less than that required for a registered offering and will depend on the business of the issuer (or its parent) and the credit ratings assigned to the notes. The SEC disclosure rules often serve as a guide to what is disclosed in the memorandum. The differences between the issuer's home country accounting and U.S. "gaap" are usually described only in narrative form. The typical memorandum will also contain a general description of the MTNs (including any affirmative and negative covenants and the events of default), private placement legends and disclosure about resale and other transfer restrictions (including the availability of Rule 144A) and the availability of the issuer to answer questions and to provide further documents to the extent it can do so without unreasonable effort or expense. The memorandum will need to be updated from time to time, depending on the degree to which the MTN program involves a continuous offering. Pricing supplements reflecting the specific terms of an MTN takedown are generally delivered to investors.

If the MTNs are to be eligible for Rule 144A, of course, the issuer (and, in the case of a guaranteed U.S. finance subsidiary, the non-U.S. parent) will have to meet the information requirement of Rule 144A(d)(4). For non-reporting issuers, the information requirement will probably be met either by a contractual undertaking as contemplated by Rule 144A(d)(4) or by filings with the SEC under Rule 12g3-2(b).

Qualification of an indenture under the 1939 Act is not required for a private MTN program; however, issuers that expect to eventually register their programs under the 1933 Act may use an indenture that can be qualified under the 1939 Act so that all their U.S. MTN notes of the same rank will be offered on the same terms and provisions. Normally, issuers of private MTNs issue notes pursuant to an agreement with an issuing and paying agent that does not assume the fiduciary obligations of a trustee under the 1939 Act. These agreements are largely standardized. Because of the absence of express fiduciary obligations, the issuing and paying agents charge less for their services than trustees. The agreement will include guidelines to be followed by the issuing and paying agent in connection with transfers of outstanding MTNs; these procedures are designed to preserve the private placement exemptions on which the program is built.

The distribution agreement for a private MTN program will contain representations and warranties by the issuer about its business, its financial condition and the MTN program that will be deemed to be updated as of the time of each sale and issuance of MTNs. Closing conditions, including officers' certificates, comfort letters and opinions of counsel, as well as the requirement for periodic delivery of such documents, are also specified. The agreement will provide for indemnity and contribution by the issuer to the investment bank intermediary in the event of material misstatements or omissions in the disclosure document.

If the proceeds of the MTN program are to be used to finance the purchase or carrying of securities, the same Regulation T considerations apply as discussed above in connection with continuous offerings of restricted commercial paper.

Privately offered MTNs are eligible for DTC book-entry settlement if they are PORTAL-eligible or, if not PORTAL-eligible, if they are investment grade.

In all other material respects, a private MTN program is administered in the same manner as a registered MTN program. As in the case of Rule 144A offerings, dealers will want to display information about the program on their private or common carrier screen-based information networks. If this is the case, steps must be taken to avoid a "general solicitation" (e.g., by making access dependent on a password) or an "offer" to non-QIBs.

• *Stand-Alone Institutional Placements*

Private placements with insurance companies and other institutional investors became the preferred method of financing in the years immediately following the adoption of the 1933 Act.[75] At that time, many companies were reluctant to register securities under the 1933 Act for fear of the liabilities that might be incurred under Section 11. They therefore resorted to transactions qualifying for the private offering exemption, and an institutional private placement market developed.

Traditional private placements have declined in relative importance for several reasons:

– Many issuers and investors have become impatient with the delay, expense and inconvenience associated with negotiating the detailed terms and covenants that traditionally characterize this market.

– In today's Rule 415 environment, the registration of debt securities is a relatively easy procedure.

– Even where a registered public offering is not possible (e.g., because speed is particularly important or where SEC accounting requirements cannot be immediately complied with), many issuers have the option of an offshore offering pursuant to Regulation S or an "underwritten" Rule 144A placement.

– There is increasing competition from loan syndication groups, which are housed not only at commercial banks but also at the major investment banking firms.

• • *Procedures.* An issuer that decides to make a private placement generally will work with an investment banking firm to line up the purchasers. After reviewing market conditions and preparing a term sheet, the investment banker's private placement department will contact insurance companies, public and private pension funds and other institutions in an effort to place the issue. Potential purchasers will be circled, and the

---

75. C. Rodgers, *Purchase by Life Insurance Companies of Securities Privately Offered,* 52 Harv. L. Rev. 773 (1939).

institution that will purchase the largest amount of securities will be designated as the lead lender. The lead lender will select counsel for the purchasers, generally a firm with which it has worked extensively in the past and that is familiar with its preferred form of documentation.

Counsel for the purchasers will prepare the initial draft of the purchase agreement and related note, and the issuer's counsel will work with his client and the investment banking firm in preparing the private placement memorandum. Generally, this will consist of a term sheet and the issuer's 1934 Act reports, but no particular form of disclosure is required if sales are made exclusively to accredited investors. The interest rate and similar economic terms will have been fixed at this point, even though the closing is not scheduled to take place until some time in the future.

Depending on the creditworthiness of the issuer, it may be required to negotiate and agree to various financial covenants. Limitations may be placed on the amount of additional debt that it may incur, and the incurrence of funded debt on a subsidiary level may be prohibited entirely. There may be limitations on the incurrence of liens and the disposition of assets. The payment of dividends may be limited to earnings subsequent to the date of the transaction plus a cushion in an amount to be negotiated. There may be limitations on the type of investments that the issuer may make.

The purchase agreement and related note may contain detailed representations by the issuer as well as affirmative covenants (e.g., to maintain the issuer's existence, to maintain its properties, to keep proper books and records and to comply with applicable laws). The issuer may be required to agree to deliver periodic financial information to the purchasers so long as the securities are outstanding. Private placements of this type often are the subject of intense negotiation between counsel for the purchasers and counsel for the issuing corporation. The lead lender has a strong bargaining edge. Many lead lenders are unyielding in their demands. Here the golden rule applies: "He who has the gold makes the rules."

A draft of the documents will be delivered to each of the prospective purchasers and in all likelihood will be reviewed by a member of the legal department of each. If there are 50 purchasers, comments on the documents can be expected from 50 different lawyers or lending officers. The job of collecting comments will fall upon special counsel for the purchasers. It is a time-consuming task, and when all comments are received, there may be a further round of negotiations. A separate purchase agreement will be entered into with each purchaser, but their terms will be identical.

It is easy to understand why issuers and investors would prefer the relative speed and simplicity of an offshore offering or an "underwritten" Rule 144A transaction to the expensive, time-consuming and onerous procedure described above. In an effort to protect their market, several law firms that specialize in this type of transaction have recently developed "model" documentation that is intended to alleviate some of these problems.[76]

• • *Investment Representations.* In an institutional private placement, it has been customary for the loan agreement to contain a representation by the lender that it is purchasing the securities for investment and not with a view to distribution "but subject nevertheless to any requirement of law that the disposition of its property shall at all times be within its control." This proviso tracks language that once appeared in Section 78 of the New York Insurance Law.[77] Institutional investors will resist any suggestion that a legend be placed on the notes that they purchase. Their investment portfolios may be subject to review by state regulatory authorities, and legends may be questioned by the state examiners. When Rule 146 required legends, some lawyers made efforts to overcome this resistance. But since the adoption of Regulation D, where a legend is only one means of

---

76. There has been a recent movement towards more standardized documentation. *See* American College of Investment Counsel, Transaction Process Enhancement Committee, *Private Placement Process Enhancements* (January 1995) and *Guide to Amendments* (January 1996).

77. Prior to its amendment in 1983, Section 78 provided that an insurer could not enter into "any agreement to withhold from sale any of its property" and that "[t]he disposition of its property shall be at all times within the control of its board of directors, in accordance with its charter and by-laws." With the amendment of Section 78 (now recodified as Section 1441), the proviso is no longer necessary, if indeed it was ever required.

demonstrating that a purchaser is not an underwriter, legends are generally thought to be unnecessary in an institutional placement of debt securities.

• • *Availability of Section 4(2) Exemption.* An institutional private placement will satisfy the requirements of Section 4(2) since the issuer will be selling securities directly to the investors or through a financial intermediary acting as agent.[78] It generally will be able to satisfy the requirements of Regulation D as well. Each purchaser is a sophisticated investor. It has the bargaining power to fend for itself. Like the mutual funds in *Value Line Fund, Inc. v. Marcus*,[79] they are "sophisticated, knowledgeable, experienced institutional investors with great resources, and plainly [are] 'able to fend for themselves.' " The notes will be placed through direct negotiation, and there will be no general solicitation or general advertising. Although, as will be seen, a secondary market exists in privately placed debt securities, institutions simply do not purchase debt securities with a view to distribution. Although counsel generally will obtain a representation from the investment banker that placed the issue with respect to the number of offerees, numbers are not a significant factor in the case of an institutional placement. The opinion rendered at the closing with respect to the availability of the Section 4(2) exemption is a relatively easy opinion for counsel to give. The SEC has never challenged an issuer's reliance on Section 4(2) in the case of a private placement with insurance companies and other institutional investors, and the authors are not aware that the exempt status of such a transaction has ever been the subject of litigation under the 1933 Act.

• • *Secondary Private Placements.* A large and active secondary market exists for privately placed debt securities. If an

---

78. *See Institutional Private Placements under the Section 4(2) Exemption of the Securities Act of 1933*, 31 Bus. Law. 515 (1975); R.H. Kinderman, Jr., *The Private Offering Exemption: An Examination of Its Availability Under and Outside Rule 146*, 30 Bus. Law. 921 (1975).

79. [1964-1966 Transfer Binder] Fed. Sec. L. Rep. (CCH) ¶ 91,523 at 94,970 (S.D.N.Y. 1965).

institution that has purchased debt securities in a private placement decides that it would like to sell all or part of its position,
it will be relatively easy for it to find one or more other institutional investors to take over its position at a price related to the
then current market price for similar debt securities. The "secondary private placement" is likely to be made through a securities dealer, frequently the firm that arranged the initial private
placement and is therefore familiar with its terms. If the dealer
is not familiar with the transaction, it will have to obtain and
review the relevant documentation in order to be sure of what
it is buying (and what it will reoffer to its customers).

In reselling the securities to the dealer, the institution will rely
upon the exemption provided by Section 4(1) of the 1933 Act,
which applies to "transactions by any person other than an issuer,
underwriter or dealer." The seller is not an underwriter because
the original transaction did not involve a distribution; in addition,
the seller will represent to the dealer that it has not offered the
securities for resale except to the dealer and, if applicable, a specified number of other institutions (i.e., it has not engaged in any
"general solicitation"). The dealer will also obtain representations from the purchasing institution to the effect that it will not
resell except in reliance on an exemption under the 1933 Act. The
dealer itself will not engage in any general solicitation, and on this
foundation it will rest its claim to the dealer's exemption provided
by Section 4(3). Since the purchaser will be an institution that
could have participated in the original private placement, the issuer's original Section 4(2) exemption remains intact when the transaction is viewed as a whole in a manner consistent with the
Crowell-Collier analysis.

Because the selling institution in a "secondary private
placement" is relying on Section 4(1) by analogy to principles
underlying Section 4(2), this type of transaction is sometimes
referred to as a "Section 4(1-1/2)" transaction.[80] The use of
the term "Section 4(1-1/2)" confuses the issue. The institu-

80. C.W. Schneider, *Section 4(1-1/2)—Private Resales of Restricted or Control Securities,* 49 Ohio St. L.J. 501 (1988); Olander & Jacks, *The Section 4(1-1/2) Exemption—Reading Between the Lines of the Securities Act of 1933,* 15 Sec. Reg. L.J. 339 (1988); ABA Committee Report, *The Section*

tional seller has a clear Section 4(1) exemption, the intermediary has a Section 4(3) exemption, and the issuer retains its Section 4(2) exemption. There is no need to resort to "half measures" in making the 1933 Act analysis.

Even if the original transaction did not involve reliance on Rule 144A, it may be that the institutional seller and the intermediary dealer may be able to rely on Rule 144A as a basis for their respective sales if the requirements of that rule—particularly that the dealer and the new purchasers be QIBs—are met.

• *Regulation D Placements with Individual Investors*

Where the market for securities being sold in reliance on Regulation D is comprised of individuals rather than institutions, more elaborate procedures are required. For the most part, this has been the market for limited partnership offerings such as real estate syndicates, oil and gas drilling programs, research and development partnerships, and offerings involving investments in such assets as race horses and precious coins. At one time, most of these offerings provided some tax benefits. Doctors, dentists, lawyers, business executives, and professional athletes sought to shelter their income from taxation by investing in these programs. Even after tax reform eliminated most of the tax benefits, wealthy individuals continued to invest in similarly structured private placements promising potential economic benefits.

• • *General Solicitation and Prior Relationships.* With respect to offerings of this type, the SEC's Division of Corporation Finance, in determining what constitutes a general solicitation, has underscored the existence and substance of pre-existing relationships between the issuer, or the securities firm acting as its agent, and the persons being solicited.[81] Earlier,

---

"4(1-1/2)" Phenomenon: Private Resales of "Restricted" Securities, 34 Bus. Law. 1961 (1979).

81. *Kenman Corporation,* SEC Release No. 34-21962 (April 19, 1985) (administrative proceeding against a broker-dealer that made a promotional mailing in connection with two limited partnership offerings to a list of persons who had invested in prior offerings by the broker-dealer, a list of executive officers of 50 Fortune 500 companies, a list of physicians in

the staff had taken the position that efforts by a dealer to identify prospective offerees by arranging for third-party intermediaries to provide the names of persons believed to be suitable offerees would constitute a general solicitation.[82] Subsequently, however, the staff agreed that an unsolicited recommendation by a qualified offeree that an offer be made to another previously unidentified person and the subsequent solicitation of that person did not violate Rule 146; nor did receiving recommendations from intermediaries of prospective offerees for subsequent offerings not in progress or contemplated.[83]

The emphasis on pre-existing relationships has been principally in the context of offerings to individual investors. No one can quarrel with the view that cold-calling is inappropriate where limited partnership interests or other equity securities are being sold to individuals in reliance on Section 4(2). But for institutional private placements, the existence or non-existence of a pre-existing relationship with the offerees should not be a matter of concern.[84]

More recently, the SEC has tempered its views on this subject. In SEC Release No. 33-6825,[85] it stated with respect to Rule 508 that "if an offering is structured so that only persons with whom the issuer and its agents have had a prior relationship are solicited, the fact that one potential investor with whom there is no such prior relationship is called may not necessarily result in a general solicitation." And the SEC stated in

---

California, and a list of presidents of certain listed companies); SEC No-action Letter, *Mineral Lands Research & Marketing Corporation* (available December 4, 1985); SEC No-action Letter, *Woodtrails-Seattle, Ltd.* (available August 9, 1982).

82. SEC No-action Letter, *Arthur M. Borden* (available September 15, 1977).

83. SEC No-action Letter, *Arthur M. Borden* (available October 6, 1978).

84. *But see* SEC No-action Letter, *Webster Management Assured Return Equity Management Group Trust* (available February 7, 1987) (no-action letter refused because there would be no prior relationship with the offerees who would be pension, profit-sharing and other employee benefit trusts).

85. SEC Release No. 33-6825 (March 14, 1989).

note 12 to this release, "The staff has never stated, and it is not the case, that prior relationship is the only way to show the absence of a general solicitation."

A number of broker-dealers have sought the staff's blessing for programs designed to enable their registered representatives to identify and solicit prospective offerees in a manner consistent with the staff's views on prior relationships. A program devised by Bateman Eichler, Hill Richards, Incorporated contemplated the mailing of an introductory letter and a questionnaire to no more than 50 professionals such as lawyers, accountants and corporate executives. If questionnaires were returned, the registered representatives would follow up to obtain additional financial and personal data. These people then would be considered eligible offerees in private placements of the type in which the person had indicated an interest and which were considered to be suitable for him. It was stipulated that no offering materials would be sent to a prospective offeree for at least 45 days after the original mailing to him. The staff responded that the program itself did not constitute an offer to sell securities and that subsequent offers to persons identified through the program would not be viewed as a general solicitation "provided a substantive relationship has been established with the offeree between the time of the initial solicitation and the later offer." The staff said that such a relationship could be established if the information furnished to Bateman Eichler provided it with "sufficient information to evaluate the prospective offeree's sophistication and financial circumstances."[86]

At the same time, the staff responded to a request by E.F. Hutton & Company for confirmation that its procedures for the private placement of direct participation programs did not constitute a general solicitation.[87] The staff concluded that substantive relationships would be considered to have been created between Hutton and persons who within the preceding three years had invested in a public or private program sponsored by

---

86. SEC No-action Letter, *Bateman Eichler, Hill Richards, Incorporated* (available December 3, 1985).

87. SEC No-action Letter, *E.F. Hutton & Company* (available December 3, 1985).

Hutton and for whom Hutton had on file a current completed suitability questionnaire and a new account form. It also agreed that substantive relationships could be established through responses to Hutton's suitability questionnaire if the response provided "sufficient information to evaluate the prospective offerees' sophistication and financial circumstances." In this case, the staff found Hutton's forms to be lacking. It went on to stress that the relationship must be established prior to the time that the broker-dealer begins participating in the particular Regulation D offering.

The staff has been reluctant to pass on the sufficiency of specific questionnaires submitted to it for approval. It has been willing to go no further than to say that "a satisfactory response by a prospective offeree to a questionnaire that provides a broker-dealer with sufficient information to evaluate the respondent's sophistication and financial situation will establish a substantive relationship."[88]

• • *Number of Offerees.* None of the letters from the SEC's staff relating to pre-existing relationships raised the issue of the number of offerees. In the *Woodtrails* no-action letter,[89] the number of prior investors to whom the offer was to be mailed totaled 330. In the past, however, tax shelter programs and other limited partnership offerings have been made to a sufficiently large number of individual investors to raise questions in the financial community as to whether these offerings were appropriately made in reliance upon the private placement exemption. This was particularly so where the offering was meeting with little success and it was necessary for the dealer to reach out to a wider and wider group of potential investors.

• • *Procedures and Controls.* It may be instructive to review the procedures and controls adopted by a major securities firm for Regulation D offerings of corporate equity securities and limited partnership interests to sophisticated high net worth individuals and smaller institutions and where solicitations are

88. SEC No-action Letter, *H.B. Shaine & Co., Inc.* (available May 1, 1987).
89. *Supra* note 81.

made by registered representatives in branch offices and not exclusively by representatives of the firm's private placement department. The procedures for private placements of this type must be more highly structured than in the case of private placements where investment bankers are selling debt securities of Fortune 500 companies to large institutional clients. In accordance with the firm's policy, each offering is made pursuant to procedures set forth in an extensive memorandum. The procedures are designed not only to assure compliance with Regulation D but also to satisfy the suitability standards imposed by the NASD and the stock exchanges. Each offering is under the supervision of a special compliance unit that is responsible for assuring that the procedures are followed. In addition, the firm's internal legal department is consulted at all stages of an offering on questions involving the procedures.

The procedures emphasize that offers may be made only to high net worth individuals who are accredited investors as defined for purposes of the particular offering *and* who alone or with a purchaser representative not affiliated with the firm have sufficient financial sophistication and expertise to evaluate the risks and merits of the investment. They also warn against any form of publicity, general seminars or advertising (including unrestricted *internal* communications vehicles such as "squawk boxes"). They also emphasize the importance of maintaining strict control over offering procedures.

The compliance procedures describe three basic stages of an offering: (1) designation of participating sales representatives, (2) designation of eligible offerees and (3) solicitation of eligible offerees. The compliance unit maintains logs that record information relevant to each of the three stages.

• • • *Designation of Participating Sales Representatives.* The compliance unit is responsible for informing branch office managers of an offering. The materials used for this purpose emphasize the high suitability standards that apply to the transaction, the necessity of restricting the manner in which clients are solicited (to avoid any "general solicitation"), the responsibility of the manager for approving sales representatives who may participate in solicitation efforts as well as in supervising those representatives on an ongoing basis and, finally, the requirement that all persons solicited have a pre-existing substantive relationship with the firm (as well as with their representative) for at least six months. The nature of this relationship is not defined, but it must be sufficient to permit the firm and the representative to assess whether an investment in the program would be suitable for the client. The compliance unit initially proposes sales representatives to the manager, who may delete names or propose additional names. The manager must sign and submit to the compliance unit the final list of participating representatives. The compliance unit then forwards preliminary materials—for internal use only—to the participating representatives.

Materials provided to the managers and participating representatives include an information bulletin about compliance procedures, a compliance statement and offeree qualification statement, a schedule of each manager's and representative's responsibilities, and Blue Sky materials.

• • • *Designation of Eligible Offerees.* Each participating representative must submit to his manager the names of those clients nominated by the representative as eligible offerees. The representative must support each nominee with an offeree qualification statement signed by the representative; this statement contains information about the nominee's financial standing, investment sophistication and pre-existing relationship with the representative and the firm. The manager must be satisfied about the nominee's qualifications, including the suitability of the offering for the nominee. Grounds for a finding of non-suitability for otherwise-qualified nominees might include the nominee's possible need for liquidity or the fact that the nominee is invested disproportionately in speculative holdings. The manager must confirm or delete each nominee proposed by the representative. Each representative's final list of eligible offerees is submitted to the compliance unit, which reviews the nominations and supporting information. Any need for additional information is referred back to the manager or representative; other questions are referred to internal counsel. Final lists of eligible offerees are confirmed to the manager and representative and a copy retained by the compliance unit.

• • • *Solicitation of Eligible Offerees.* In general, representatives and managers are not directly involved in the distribution of offering materials to eligible offerees or the solicitation of subscriptions. A representative who has been successful in nominating clients as eligible offerees may request a copy of the private placement memorandum for his or her internal use. Neither the private placement memorandum nor any other soliciting material may be copied or reproduced in any manner. The representative may then request that the compliance unit send solicitation materials (the private placement memorandum and a retail investor disclosure statement) to the client. The compliance unit does so after checking for possible Blue Sky problems. If an offeree is using a purchaser representative, the compliance unit also sends a set of solicitation materials to the purchaser representative.

If an eligible offeree indicates interest in making an investment, the representative will ask the compliance unit to set up a meeting with the principals on whose behalf the securities are being offered. If an eligible offeree decides to participate, the representative requests that the compliance unit send subscription documents to that person for execution and return to the representative. The representative makes a further suitability review, countersigns the subscription documents and signs a purchaser suitability questionnaire and (if applicable) a questionnaire submitted by a purchaser's representative. These steps constitute a representation that the representative believes the investment is suitable for the client, that the representative has a reasonable basis for believing all representations and statements by or about the client and that all required solicitation procedures have been followed. The manager must in turn review each subscription with the representative and be satisfied as to these matters; the manager must then initial the subscription documents and the purchaser suitability questionnaire (and, if applicable, the purchaser representative's questionnaire) and forward these to the compliance unit. A representative of the compliance unit reviews the documents for compliance with the required procedures and consults internal counsel as appropriate. Internal counsel also reviews all purchaser representatives' questionnaires to confirm the suitability of the representative (in which case the client may appoint a new representative but may not elect to proceed without one).

• • • *Closing Procedures.* Prior to each closing of a private offering, the compliance unit reviews subscription documents for proper execution, cross-checks for Blue Sky compliance, confirms receipt by the representative and client of all disclosure documents, sends subscription documents to the firm's bankers for the transaction (who will forward them to issuer's counsel for review), confirms acceptance of the subscription to the representative and the client and assures that the relevant files are complete.

Related Private Placements and Public Offerings

We discussed above the integration problem in the context of two or more private offerings, where the object of analysis is to determine whether the offerings should be viewed as a single offering. The integration problem can also arise in the context of a private offering and a related registered public offering. The consequences of integration in this context are, of course, much more severe. Since it is unlikely that a private offering can survive being integrated with a public offering, the result may be that the private offering has lost its exemption. In addition, the making of private offers before the filing of a registration statement may be viewed as "gun-jumping."

For many years, securities lawyers were able to provide their clients with reliable advice on when and how a private offering's exemption might be endangered because of a contemporaneous SEC-filed registration statement. More recently, this has become a more difficult task for two principal reasons. First, as the discussion above should demonstrate, the traditional distinctions between the public and private markets are blurring. Investment bankers may act as agent today in selling a tranche of *registered* securities "off the shelf" to a single buyer, while tomorrow they may act as principal in making a private placement of *restricted* securities to a potentially indefinite number of investors. In addition, investors who used to be happy with "demand" or "piggyback" registration rights for their restricted securities are more often insisting on a currently effective resale registration statement or a covenant to file one within a specified period of time. Second, the SEC staff has abandoned to some degree its former flexibility and pragmatism in this area—an ability, as Professor Loss has observed, "to separate the big from the small potatoes"[90]—in an apparent effort to prevent "end runs" around the 1933 Act's liability provisions. (There were reports in early 1997, however, that the SEC staff was reconsidering its views in this area.)

There are several frequently-occurring situations in which it is necessary to decide whether a private offering's exemption is endangered by a related registered public offering. These include: (1) an unsuccessful—or disguised—attempt at a private offering followed by a registered public offering, (2) an unsuccessful registered public offering followed by a private offering, (3) a private offering with immediate or delayed registration of the purchased securities for resale and (4) a private offering followed by the issuer's exchange offer of registered securities for the restricted securities.

• *Private Offering Followed by Public Filing*

In a not infrequent situation, an issuer and its investment banker will commence work on a private offering and conclude, after unsuccessful solicitation efforts, that the transaction can only be effected by means of a registered public offering. Fortunately, an SEC rule applicable to this situation has been around since 1935. Rule 152 provides:

> The phrase "transactions by an issuer not involving any public offering" in Section 4(2) shall be deemed to apply to transactions not involving any public offering at the time of said transactions although subsequently thereto the issuer decides to make a public offering and/ or files a registration statement.

This rule was originally adopted to allow "those who have contemplated or begun to undertake a private offering to register the securities without incurring any risk of liability as a conse-

---

90. L. Loss & J. Seligman, 2 *Securities Regulation* 1114 (3d ed. 1989).

quence of having first contemplated or begun to undertake a private offering."[91]

While the rule and its explanation appear simple enough on the surface, the SEC staff has recently taken the position that the rule does not apply where the private offering and the public offering are in effect the "same" transaction. According to the staff view, this would constitute "gun-jumping" in violation of Section 5.

There are two ways of making sure, of course, that a registered offering is not the "same" offering as a previous private offering. One way is to abandon the private offering. While the staff does not dispute that it is possible to abandon a private offering and start up a *new* registered offering, it has not offered any guidance on what facts and circumstances will support this distinction. For example, how much time must elapse between the "abandonment" of the private offering and the filing of a registration statement? Must the issuer refuse to return the calls of the investors who indicated interest in participating in the transaction?

The other way to make sure that the registration statement represents a "new" offering is to complete the private offering. But what is "completion?" The SEC staff appears to concur that it is possible to plan a transaction from the beginning on the basis that investors will agree to purchase securities in a private offering on the understanding that the issuer will file and cause to become effective a registration statement covering their resales (a so-called PIPE or "private investment, public equity" transaction). According to the 1990 *Black Box* no-action letter,[92] Rule 152 is available for this situation where the purchasers are obligated to complete the transaction subject only to the satisfaction of specified conditions that are not within their control.

Suppose, however, that it has become clear to the issuer that the transaction must be registered but the issuer is unable— perhaps because of a shortage of time—to negotiate definitive purchase agreements before filing a registration statement. In the *Black Box* letter, the SEC staff "for policy reasons" acqui-

---

91. SEC Release No. 33-305 (March 2, 1935).

92. SEC No-action Letter, *Black Box Incorporated* (available June 26, 1990). *See also* SEC No-action Letter, *Squadron Ellenhoff* (available February 28, 1992).

esced in a financially troubled issuer's filing a registration statement before reaching definitive agreements with not more than 35 QIBs and seven other institutional investors. In a subsequent letter,[93] the staff explained *Black Box* as having been based not on the financial condition of the issuer but rather on "the nature and number of the offerees." It also stated that the *Black Box* "policy position" was "narrowly construed by the staff" and limited to situations where the unregistered offering was made only to QIBs and "no more than two or three large institutional accredited investors."

What happens if the issuer is not willing to abandon its prospective investors, if it is not able to negotiate definitive agreements and if the investors are not of the "super-heavyweight" character involved in *Black Box*? It may be a sufficient indication of a "new" offering if the issuer genuinely intended to proceed with a private offering and only subsequently decided that it was necessary to turn to the public alternative. There is support in *Black Box* for this proposition, but the staff is reluctant for obvious reasons (relating to the SEC's Division of Enforcement not being fond of having to prove an issuer's state of mind) to confirm it. What does one do, for example, with the situation where an issuer decides in effect to "test the waters" with investors under cover of a purported private placement, where the real purpose is to lay the groundwork for a registered public offering? Notwithstanding that such offers might constitute "gun-jumping" if a registration statement covering the "same" offer is subsequently filed, the SEC recognizes that such "test the waters" activity may be consistent with investor protection. Accordingly, it proposed in June 1995[94] the adoption of a rule that would expressly permit such activity by nonreporting companies. Solicitation activity would have to terminate upon the filing of a registration statement, and sales of securities could not commence until 20 days after such termination. The release proposing the rule noted difficulties that might arise if the issuer decided to abandon a public offering in favor of a private

---

93. *Squadron Ellenhoff* (available February 28, 1992).

94. SEC Release No. 33-7188 (June 27, 1995). Proposed new Rule 135d was based on a 1992 SEC initiative applicable to small offerings under Regulation A.

offering where its "test the waters" activity had amounted to a general solicitation; in that event, the issuer might have to wait six months or restructure its offering to avoid "integration."

Rule 152 has even broader application than described above. Thus, where an issuer planned a registered public offering within four months after a private placement, the staff took a no-action position under Rule 152.[95] The staff has reaffirmed this position even where the issuer contemplated the subsequent public offering at the time of the private placement.[96] Of course, even where Rule 152 does not apply, the issuer may be able to fall back on the five-part "facts and circumstances" test (discussed above under "Regulation D—Integration") to support a conclusion that the private offering and the public offering are not the same transaction.

• Public Filing Followed by Private Offering

The SEC staff takes the position that "[t]he filing of a registration statement for a specific securities offering (as contrasted with a generic shelf registration) constitutes a general solicitation for that securities offering rendering Section 4(2) unavailable for the same offering."[97] The staff position would doom, of course, any attempt to withdraw a registration statement and proceed with a private offering of the same securities. Particularly for smaller companies, the staff position can amount to playing financial Russian Roulette: once it files its registration statement, it assumes the risk that if the public market becomes unavailable to it because of market conditions or disclosure problems, then it will not have the private markets available either (subject possibly to the *Black Box* "super-heavyweight" exception discussed above).

---

95. SEC No-action Letter, *Verticom, Inc.* (available February 12, 1986).

96. *See* SEC No-action Letter, *Vintage Group, Inc.* (available May 11, 1988); SEC No-action Letter, *Immune Response Corp.* (available November 2, 1987); SEC No-action Letter, *Vulture Petroleum Corporation* (available February 2, 1987); SEC No-action Letter, *BBI Associates* (available December 29, 1986).

97. E.g., 1 Practising Law Institute, *The SEC Speaks in 1997* 376 (1997).

In the authors' view, the staff position elevates form over substance. Even though the public has a form of access to the 1933 Act filing by means of EDGAR and SEC copying facilities, the issuer should still be able to take into account such factors as the reason for the abandonment of the public offering, whether the registration statement is still on file, and—most important—whether the filing was a "quiet" filing, i.e., where no preliminary prospectuses were circulated and where no marketing efforts took place. In this last respect, the staff position is particularly unfair when one considers that U.S. IPO candidates are not permitted to make "confidential" filings of the kind available to every foreign issuer and to some U.S. issuers engaged in acquisitions.

There are several alternatives available to an issuer that finds itself in the position of having filed, but being unable to proceed with, a public offering. First, the issuer can try to structure a private offering that differs sufficiently from the offering contemplated by the registration statement to support advice from counsel that it is prudent to proceed with the private offering. Second, the issuer can wait for six months by analogy to Regulation D. Third, if the reason for the failure to proceed with the public offering is related to market conditions rather than SEC comments on the registration statement, the issuer can elect to proceed with a "private" offering on a registered basis. Under current staff positions,[98] even a small group of individual or institutional purchasers will not be deemed presumptive underwriters if and when they attempt to resell.

• *Private Offering with Concurrent or Future Registration*

It is commonplace today for purchasers of privately-placed securities to bargain for the ability to make prompt resales of their securities pursuant to an effective registration statement. There are two conceptual problems under the 1933 Act in connection with the registration of the privately-placed securities. The first is that there may be an integration problem if the private offering is not "complete" prior to the filing of the regis-

---

98. *See*, e.g., SEC No-action Letter, *American Council of Life Insurance* (June 10, 1983).

tration statement. The *Black Box* letter discussed above is support for the proposition that Rule 152 is available even where the private placement is not closed prior to the filing of the registration statement as long as the only conditions to the investors' commitments are ones that are beyond their control. After the registration statement is filed, there can be no renegotiation of the investors' commitments. In addition, Rule 152 may not be available for new investors after the filing of the registration statement.

The second conceptual problem relates to the capacity in which the registered securities are to be sold. The staff takes the position that if offers are made and commitments obtained in reliance on the private placement exemption prior to the filing of the registration statement, then the registration statement should cover resales by the purchasers and not the initial issuance of securities to the purchasers. The significance of this distinction is that the securities are "restricted securities" in the hands of the purchasers and that the broker-dealers through whom they resell pursuant to the registration statement may therefore be acting as underwriters with corresponding Section 11 liabilities.

Where the private placement investors are willing to close prior to the filing or effectiveness of a registration statement, they may nevertheless bargain for terms that obligate the issuer promptly to file and obtain the effectiveness of a registration statement. The terms may also create an inducement for the issuer to follow through on this commitment, e.g., an increased interest rate if the registration statement is not filed or does not become effective within a stated period of time.

• *Registration Rights Agreement*

Investors have traditionally bargained for an agreement by the issuer to register the new securities as promptly as practicable or on a "demand" or "piggyback" basis. Under the typical registration rights agreement, the holders of a specified amount of the securities may demand registration at the company's expense ("demand" rights). There may be a cutoff period when the registration rights expire. In some cases, registration rights may be exercised only once, and in other cases, the holders will be entitled to demand registration on more than one occasion. The purchasers of the securities also may be granted incidental or "piggyback" registration rights, so that if the issuer files a registration statement covering securities of the same class, the holders will be entitled to include their shares in the registration statement. The agreement may require them to sell in the offering through the same underwriters that the issuer is using in order to assure an orderly distribution. They may be required to refrain from making any sales until a specified period of time after the completion of the distribution. The issuer may agree to indemnify any brokers or dealers ("underwriters") through whom the holders may resell their securities. The terms of any registration rights agreement will vary from transaction to transaction.[99]

The registration statement filed by the issuer will state that the selling securityholders may sell from time to time on terms to be determined at the time of sale and that the selling securityholders and any broker-dealers that participate with them in the distribution of the securities may be deemed to be underwriters within the meaning of the 1933 Act. The holders of the securities at the time the registration statement becomes effective must be named in the prospectus. In some cases, this information has been difficult to obtain, but the SEC has held its ground and will generally require this information.

One of the disadvantages of registration rights for an issuer is that the registration statement will have to be "evergreen" until the holders have completed their sales, i.e., the prospectus will have to be updated and the registration statement possibly amended in order to reflect new developments. For an issuer eligible to use Form S-3, of course, the burden will be considerably less.

Purchasers of privately-placed warrants or convertible securities also commonly bargain for registration rights for the common stock underlying the warrants or convertible securities. Their expectation is that they will hold the warrants or convertible securities until it appears advantageous to exercise or convert and that they will then receive registered common

---

99. For a thorough discussion, see Carl W. Schneider, "Registration Rights Agreements—Variables and Practical Considerations," *The Corporate Counsel* (March-April 1996).

stock that they may freely resell into the public market. The SEC staff does not appear to agree. The staff position is that an investor must receive *restricted* common stock upon exercise or conversion of a restricted security.

In the case of a convertible security, the exchange is exempt under Section 3(a)(9) of the 1933 Act so that it is at least not necessary to repeat the formalities of the original private placement. In the case of a warrant, however, a new private placement exemption must be established to support the issuance of the common stock upon exercise of the warrant. This may not be easy where the holders of the warrant are no longer accredited investors or otherwise do not measure up to private placement requirements.

Of course, the issuer may register the common stock for resale by the exercising or converting holder. The holder is no worse off as a result, but the issuer must maintain an "evergreen" registration statement as described above.

• *Private Offering Followed by Exchange Offer*

The registration-for-resale procedure described above offers potential liquidity to the holder of privately-placed securities, but it has the disadvantage that the securities are still "restricted securities" in the hands of the investor until they are actually sold pursuant to the registration statement. This has the effect of limiting the group of institutional investors who for legal or policy reasons may be unable to purchase restricted securities even with registration rights. On the other hand, a procedure that enabled the investors to *exchange* the restricted securities for registered securities would promote a broader institutional market and increase liquidity for the securities, thus resulting in cost savings to the issuer. Another advantage for the issuer would be that it would not have to maintain an "evergreen" shelf registration statement for the period of time it took for the investors to sell their securities.

In fact, the SEC staff has published several interpretive letters[100] that permit an issuer and the purchasers of its privately-

---

100. The original letter was *Exxon Capital Holdings Corp.* (available May 13, 1988). Other significant letters include *Brown & Wood LLP* (avail-

placed securities[101] to agree that the issuer will effect a post-closing exchange offer for the privately-placed securities. The exchange offer will be registered on Form S-4 and will offer substantially identical securities that the purchasers will be able to resell without delivering a prospectus. The letters are generally conditioned on (a) the holder not being an affiliate of the issuer, (b) the holder having acquired the new securities in the ordinary course of its business, (c) the holder having no arrangement or understanding with any person to participate in a distribution of the new securities and (d) the holder not having purchased the "old" securities directly from the issuer to resell pursuant to Rule 144A or any other available exemption under the 1933 Act. The last condition, of course, essentially prevents a broker-dealer from taking advantage of the interpretive position to sell securities left over from the original placement ("unsold allotments").

Before effectiveness of the exchange offer registration statement, it is necessary to provide the staff with a supplemental letter stating that the exchange offer is being registered in reliance on the staff position set forth in the interpretive letters. The letter must also contain prescribed representations, including the absence of any arrangements for the distribution of the registered securities to be issued in the exchange offer.

The no-action letters take the position that the person acquiring the "new" securities from the issuer in the exchange

---

able February 7, 1997); *Grupo Financiero InverMexico, S.A.* (available April 4, 1995); *K-III Communications Corp.* (available May 14, 1993); *Corimon C.A. S.A.C.A.* (available March 22, 1993); *Vitro, S.A.* (available November 19, 1991); *Epic Properties, Inc.* (available October 21, 1991); *Warnaco, Inc.* (available October 11, 1991); *Morgan Stanley & Co., Inc.* (available June 5, 1991); and *Mary Kay Cosmetics, Inc.* (available June 5, 1991).

101. The earlier letters were limited to debt and preferred stock. Other letters have covered depositary shares representing common stock of non-reporting non-U.S. companies, on the theory that the exchange offer technique offers these companies a "stepping stone" approach to the U.S. public equity markets. The *Brown & Wood LLP* letter in early 1997 confirmed the availability of the technique for "capital securities" (also known as "trust" or "hybrid" preferred securities).

offer is not an "underwriter" with respect to such securities even though the securities are "purchased from . . . [the] issuer with a view to . . . the distribution" thereof. Broker-dealers, however, are not so lucky. In 1993, the staff issued a letter[102] that required any broker-dealer participating in the exchange offer to be described in the exchange offer prospectus as possibly being a "statutory underwriter" and to deliver a prospectus on any resales of the registered securities. The staff appears to be troubled by the absence of any financial intermediary with Section 11 liabilities in a transaction where a placement of securities pursuant to Rule 144A is followed quickly by a registered exchange offer.

Section 11(d)(1)

Section 11(d)(1) of the 1934 Act restricts a broker-dealer's extension or arranging of credit on a security that is part of a "new issue" in the "distribution" of which the broker-dealer is participating or has participated as a member of a selling syndicate or group. (There is no reason to assume that a "selling syndicate or group" cannot consist of a single broker-dealer.) If Section 11(d)(1) applied to private placements, a broker-dealer could not extend or arrange credit for the purchaser and might be unable to arrange for delayed settlements beyond 35 days after purchase.

The term "distribution" is not defined in Section 11(d)(1) or the SEC's rules under that section, but it is generally agreed that the prohibition does not apply to private placements under Section 4(2) of the 1933 Act or Rule 506 of Regulation D.[103] The SEC took the position when it adopted Rule 144A that it would be prepared to consider providing "interpretive relief . . . in appropriate circumstances." Given the purpose of Section 11(d)(1), which is to prevent broker-dealers from dumping securities into customers' margin accounts, the authors do not believe the SEC could successfully maintain that the prohibition applies to Rule 144A transactions.

---

102. *Shearman & Sterling* (available July 2, 1993).

103. *See* C.F. Rechlin, *Securities Credit Regulation* § 9.03[2] (1995).

Chapter 8

SHELF REGISTRATIONS—RULE 415

If an issuer expects to be making frequent public offerings of its securities, and especially if it is eligible to use Form S-3 or Form F-3, it will probably decide to file a shelf registration statement as permitted by Rule 415 under the 1933 Act. A shelf registration statement covers securities that are not necessarily to be sold in a single discrete offering immediately upon effectiveness, but rather are proposed to be sold in a number of tranches over a period of time or on a continuous basis.

Issuers used shelf registration during the period from January 1992 through December 1995, on a value-weighted basis, for approximately one-half of all their underwritten offers of preferred stock and approximately 40% of all their underwritten offers of corporate debt.[1] Shelf registration was used over this period for only approximately 10% of all underwritten offers of common stock, but there is evidence that issuers are increasingly using shelf registration for this purpose. For example, takedowns from shelf registrations amounted in 1992 to 3% of all underwritten offers of additional common stock, but

---

1. *Report of the Advisory Committee on the Capital Formation and Regulatory Processes* (July 24, 1996), Appendix A at 15. All of the statistics in this paragraph are taken from the report.

these offerings increased to 9% in 1993 and to 15% in each of 1994 and 1995. One explanation for issuers' increased interest in the use of shelf registration to sell common stock may be the opportunity to use an unallocated shelf (as discussed below) to mitigate any "overhang" effect; it appears that some 80% of the common stock sold using shelf registration from 1992 through 1994 had been registered on an unallocated basis.

If a qualified issuer decides to take the shelf route, it will register a specified dollar amount of securities pursuant to Rule 415. Since 1992, U.S. issuers eligible to use Form S-3 have been permitted to register both debt and equity securities on the same registration statement on an unallocated basis, i.e., without specifying the principal amount of debt and the amount of shares of equity securities being registered.[2] (In 1994, this privilege was extended to non-U.S. issuers eligible to use Form F-3.[3]) In the aggregate, the amount of securities that may be registered is supposed to be limited to that which "is reasonably expected to be offered and sold within two years from the initial effective date of the registration."

Issuers eligible to use Form S-3 or Form F-3 may offer their securities either on a continuous or delayed basis. For example, either immediately or at some time after effectiveness, when market conditions appear favorable, the issuer may request proposals or bids from one or more underwriters for the sale of, e.g., $150 million principal amount of debt securities of a specified maturity or range of maturities. The issuer weighs the various proposals and decides to accept terms that include, by way of illustration, a 6% coupon, a seven-year maturity and a specific price to public and underwriting discount. The securities are then "taken off the shelf," i.e., the issuer and the underwriters sign a terms agreement that is based on a full-scale underwriting agreement that was previously filed as an exhibit to the registration statement, and the terms of the securities and the underwriting arrangements are set forth in a supplement to the basic prospectus that is filed with the SEC under Rule 424(b)(2) by the close of business on the second business day after pricing. There is no need for the SEC to take any action.

---

2. SEC Release No. 33-6964 (October 22, 1992).
3. SEC Release No. 33-7053 (April 19, 1994).

Three months later, when the issuer needs funds or simply wishes to take advantage of a perceived "market window," it may repeat the process, this time ending up with a $100 million issue of five-year notes with a specified coupon, public offering price and underwriting discount. It may issue additional securities from time to time until all of the registered securities have been sold, at which time it may file a new shelf registration statement. With the availability of the unallocated shelf procedure, the issuer has the ability to move rapidly with great flexibility to take advantage of market opportunities.

The use of Form S-3 or Form F-3 greatly simplifies a shelf registration program because the issuer can incorporate its 1934 Act reports by reference rather than amend or supplement the registration statement and prospectus each time a material event occurs. The rule does not require, however, that an issuer be eligible to use Form S-3 or Form F-3 in order to take advantage of shelf registration for purposes other than "delayed" offerings. For example, shelf registration is available to any issuer for "continuous" offerings of securities such as in the case of MTN programs, discussed below.

Shelf registrations were also used by issuers of mortgage related securities long before Rule 415, and the technique continues to be used to register billions of dollars of asset-backed securities each year.

Rule 415 specifically permits shelf registration of secondary offerings by selling securityholders from time to time on a securities exchange or otherwise at prices current at the time of sale. This technique also predates Rule 415 by many years.

Rule 415 permits shelf registration of securities offered under a dividend or interest reinvestment plan or an employee benefit plan; securities to be issued upon the exercise of outstanding options, warrants or rights or upon the conversion of other outstanding securities; securities that have been pledged as collateral; and ADSs registered on Form F-6.

Shelf registration has made it possible for issuers to use highly efficient methods of distributing securities, but Rule 415 did not come about without controversy. As will be seen, the SEC did not escape criticism and opposition as it sought to adapt its rules and policies to evolving practices in the securities markets.

The process by which the SEC sought to deal with registration "for the shelf" began in the 1930s. The way that the law has developed in this area is not unlike that described by Professor Lon Fuller in his jurisprudence classes at the Harvard Law School. As an example of how the law responds to the realities of life, Professor Fuller would point to the flagstone paths laid out on the Cambridge Common. If the otherwise law-abiding citizens of Cambridge consistently strayed from the paths designated for their use, wearing away the grass as they followed a more convenient route from one point to another, the city fathers simply would pave over the paths that they had created. The SEC has followed similar pragmatic principles in coping with shelf registration, and Rule 415 can be viewed as a pavement that has been laid to widen and improve an already existing path.

The Evolution of Shelf Registrations

Section 6(a) of the 1933 Act provides, "[a] registration statement shall be deemed effective only as to the securities specified therein as proposed to be offered."[4] Shortly after the adoption of the 1933 Act, the SEC had occasion to interpret this sentence and took the position that it permitted the registration only of securities intended to be offered presently (i.e., soon) and not those intended to be offered at some remote future date.[5] The SEC's theory was that, if securities are registered for future distribution, prospective investors relying on the registration statement may receive stale information. Among the amendments to the 1933 Act proposed in 1941[6] was a modification of Section 6(a) to permit registration for the shelf. This amendment was opposed by the SEC and was never enacted.

---

4. For a discussion of the legislative history of Section 6(a), *see* S. Hodes, *Shelf Registration: The Dilemma of the Securities and Exchange Commission*, 49 Va. L. Rev. 1106, 1108–15 (1963).

5. United Combustion Corp., 3 S.E.C. 1062 (1938); Shawnee Chiles Syndicate, 10 S.E.C. 109 (1941).

6. H.R. 4344, 77th Cong., 1st Sess. (1941); S. 3985, 76th Cong., 3d Sess. (1940).

• *Traditional Shelf Registrations*

In time, the SEC backed away from a rigid interpretation of Section 6(a), and it had become established by the early 1960s that certain types of offerings could be covered by shelf registration statements.[7] For the most part, these were offerings that by their very nature were required to be put on the shelf. The following minute of a June 8, 1961 meeting of the SEC summarized the status at that time:

> Discussion also was had concerning the general problem involved in the registration of stock which was not to be made the subject of an offering in the immediate, foreseeable future. Mr. [Manuel F.] Cohen suggested that the Commission should continue the practice of permitting registration (a) in the American Marietta type of case in which a reasonable number of shares were being registered for future issuance under a continuing program for the issuance of stock in connection with the acquisition of other companies by purchase or merger; (b) in cases involving "private placements" under circumstances which suggest the necessity for registration; (c) where there was a likely distribution within the reasonable future upon conversion of privately placed debentures and similar situations in which the Commission insisted upon registration, including the issuance of options and stock to underwriters; (d) for sale of shares by "controlling" persons of acquired companies following transactions falling within Rule 133; and (e) where there was a representation that the shares were otherwise proposed for distribution within a reasonable period after the effective date of registration. However, he further suggested that registration for cash sale would not be in order, whether for new or control shares, if there was no bona fide intention to sell within a reason-

---

7. *See generally* C. Israels, *S.E.C. Problems of Controlling Stockholders and in Underwritings* 182 (Practising Law Institute Transcript 1962).

able period but only at some indefinite future period and eventuality.

Charles E. Shreve, general counsel of the Division of Corporation Finance, described the SEC's position in somewhat more pragmatic terms:

> The policy of the Commission is to afford the opportunity for registration where it seems consistent with the Congressional intention of having you register offerings proposed to be made. Sometimes the line is not easy to draw. It is not possible under § 6(a) to register all of the outstanding stock simply because someday somebody might want to sell it. On the other hand, it is recognized that sales are not always made by a conventional offering. Controlling persons who must register the securities when they want to sell to the public, may want to sell by normal market trading transactions. That may take a matter of months. If they seem to have a real present intention of selling a designated maximum amount of stock in that way, we say "All right; go ahead and register."[8]

One type of shelf transaction that the SEC had no intention of permitting was one in which an issuer, as opposed to a selling shareholder, sought to register a block of shares to be sold for cash from time to time in the future.[9] One that slipped through the cracks, however, was a prospectus dated August 5, 1966 of Industrial Electronic Hardware Corp. covering 100,000 shares of common stock offered by the issuer "from time to time, for a maximum period of two years, in brokerage transactions on the American Stock Exchange or otherwise at prices then current on that Exchange." As a rule, this type of transaction was not permitted.

• • *Continuous Acquisition Programs.* The use of shelf registration statements to cover shares of common stock to be is-

---

8. C. Israels & G. Duff, *When Corporations Go Public,* 115–16 (1962).
9. C. Israels, *supra* note 7, at 208.

sued in future acquisitions was to all intents and purposes mandated by the SEC in the late 1950s and early 1960s. At that time, a number of companies launched programs that contemplated future acquisitions of privately owned companies on a more or less regular basis. Each separate acquisition might qualify as a private placement, but applying its integration doctrine (see Chapter 7), the SEC took the position that the transactions were sufficiently interrelated as to require registration of the shares to be issued. Of necessity, the registered shares were kept on the shelf until the closing of each particular transaction. One example of this type of shelf registration was the prospectus dated February 24, 1961 of American-Marietta Company covering nearly 5 million shares of common stock to be issued from time to time in the acquisition of other businesses. Prospectuses of this type came to be known as "American Marietta-type" prospectuses, as indicated by Mr. Cohen's reference in the above quoted SEC minute.

Other early examples of shelf registrations designed for acquisitions were the February 28, 1961 prospectus covering 95,000 shares of common stock of Sports Arenas, Inc. and the May 14, 1963 prospectus of Holiday Inns of America, Inc., which stated, "The Common Stock is to be offered from time to time in connection with acquisition by the Company of licensee-owned Holiday Inns and in isolated instances for motel properties owned by non-licensees."

• • *Sales Following Private Placements.* The most common type of shelf registration was one covering securities issued in a private placement to persons wishing to be in a position to resell if they should choose to do so. Frequently, the transaction would have involved the acquisition of a privately owned company in exchange for the acquiring company's shares. The registration statement would be filed pursuant to a registration rights agreement or simply because the issuer was willing to accommodate the holders of the securities.

Prior to the adoption of Rule 144 in 1972,[10] there was substantial uncertainty as to when and under what circumstances a

10. SEC Release No. 33-5223 (January 11, 1972).

person acquiring securities in a private placement could resell them without being deemed a statutory underwriter. The holder may have signed an investment letter stating that he had not purchased the securities "with a view to distribution," the key words in the Section 2(11) definition. But conduct inconsistent with this representation, such as a sale shortly after the acquisition, could lead to the conclusion that the seller was indeed an underwriter and that accordingly the securities should have been registered to cover his sale.

In some private acquisition transactions, not all of the stockholders were willing to give investment representations. The solution in some cases was to register the securities for the shelf to enable the holders to sell from time to time at prices prevailing at the time of sale. The SEC was willing to allow these registration statements to become effective without any representation from the holders that they had an immediate intention to sell. An October 4, 1961 prospectus of Universal Match Corporation is an apt illustration. There the statement is made:

> On June 30, 1961, the Company acquired all the outstanding capital stock of Reflectone Electronics, Inc., a Connecticut corporation, in exchange for 120,000 shares of the Company's common stock. As to 84,000 of said shares, the recipients represented to the Company that they were acquiring said shares for investment and not for distribution. No such representation was made with respect to the remaining 36,000 shares which are covered by this Prospectus and which may be sold by the holders thereof as set forth on the cover page of this Prospectus.

• • *Shares Issued Upon Conversions of Privately Placed Securities.* Section 3(a)(9) of the 1933 Act exempts the issuance of common stock upon the conversion of outstanding convertible debentures or preferred stock but does not exempt the resale of that stock. Rule 155, adopted by the SEC in 1962[11] but subsequently rescinded, provided in effect that the public sale

---

11. SEC Release No. 33-4450 (February 7, 1962).

of shares acquired upon conversion of a privately placed security would require registration unless the shares were not acquired with a view to distribution. Unlike Rule 144, which now permits tacking in these circumstances, under Rule 155 the holding period for the underlying shares began upon conversion and not when the convertible securities were purchased. In the 1960 release reproposing Rule 155, the SEC indicated its willingness to be flexible in its interpretation of Section 6(a) in the context of resales of privately placed convertible securities or the shares into which they were converted.[12]

• • *Underwriters' Stock and Warrants.* The SEC has consistently taken the position that cheap stock and immediately exercisable warrants sold to underwriters in connection with a public offering of securities should be registered at the same time as the securities to be offered to the public. In a published response to an inquiry regarding underwriters' warrants, where it was stated that for tax reasons none of the warrants or the underlying stock would be reoffered for at least six months after the effective date of the registration statement, the SEC said that, since it was not contemplated that the warrants or the underlying stock would be distributed immediately, the registration statement should contain an undertaking to file a post-effective amendment that would disclose the terms of the distribution.[13] Amended prospectuses covering the resale of underwriters' warrants or stock were permitted to provide for sales on a delayed or continuous basis.

• • *Resales Following Rule 133 Transactions.* Prior to the adoption of Rule 145 in 1972,[14] a merger or similar transaction requiring a vote of stockholders was not deemed to involve a "sale" of the securities issued in exchange for shares of the acquired corporation. The "no sale theory" was upheld by the Court of Appeals for the Ninth Circuit in the famous *Leland Stanford*

---

12. SEC Release No. 33-4248 (July 14, 1960). Rule 155 was originally proposed in SEC Release No. 33-4162 (December 2, 1959).

13. SEC Release No. 33-3210 (April 9, 1947).

14. SEC Release No. 33-5316 (October 6, 1972).

decision[15] and was codified when Rule 133 was adopted in 1951.[16] But abuses arose. Controlling stockholders would arrange questionable mergers to "free up" large blocks of stock.

In *Great Sweet Grass*,[17] the SEC held that Rule 133 could not be relied upon where there was a preexisting plan to use the stockholders of an acquired corporation as a conduit in distributing a block of stock to the public. In *SEC v. Micro-Moisture Controls, Inc.*,[18] the court held that, where the persons negotiating a merger had such control over the process as to make the stockholder vote a mere formality, there was no "corporate action" on which Rule 133 was premised, and registration would be required.

In 1959, the SEC amended Rule 133[19] to spell out the circumstances under which the stockholders of an acquired corporation would be deemed underwriters in reselling the securities received in the acquisition transaction. Registration of any resales would be required if the issuer had made arrangements with an underwriter to purchase the securities issued to the stockholders of the constituent corporation. Absent such arrangements, only the constituent corporation and its affiliates (those in a control relationship with it) would be considered underwriters if they acquired their securities with a view to distribution. The rule excluded from the term "distribution" brokerage transactions of the type then permitted by Rule 154, the predecessor to the current Rule 144.

At the same time as it amended Rule 133, the SEC adopted Form S-14, which permitted an issuer whose shares were listed on an exchange to file with a prospectus consisting of the proxy statement used in the acquisition transaction with a wraparound spelling out the plan of distribution. One issuer, Schering-White

---

15. *National Supply Co. v. Leland Stanford Junior Univ.*, 134 F.2d 689 (9th Cir. 1943), *rev'g* 46 F. Supp. 389 (N.D. Cal. 1942).

16. SEC Release No. 33-3420 (August 2, 1951).

17. *In re Great Sweet Grass Oils Ltd.*, 37 S.E.C. 683 (1957).

18. 148 F. Supp. 558 (S.D.N.Y. 1957) (preliminary injunction), 167 F. Supp. 716 (S.D.N.Y. 1958) (permanent injunction), *aff'd sub. nom. SEC v. Culpepper*, 270 F.2d 241 (2d Cir. 1959). *See also U.S. v. Crosby*, 294 F.2d 928 (2d Cir. 1961).

19. SEC Release No. 33-4115 (July 16, 1959).

Laboratories, had been permitted to use this type of wraparound prospectus prior to the adoption of Form S-14.[20] Form S-14 required an undertaking to update the registration statement to comply with Section 10(a)(3) of the 1933 Act for a period of 24 months after its effective date. Implicit in the adoption of Form S-14 was a waiver in this context of any restriction that Section 6(a) might impose upon registration for the shelf.

In the years following the amendment of Rule 133, there were occasions when registration for the shelf was all but insisted upon by the SEC. An Allied Chemical Corporation prospectus dated February 28, 1963 covering 2.5 million of the 6.3 million shares of common stock issued a year earlier upon the acquisition of Union Texas Natural Gas Corporation contained the following statement on its cover page:

> This Prospectus relates to an aggregate of 2,595,511 shares of the Common Stock of Allied issued upon the merger to the stockholders of Union Texas listed under the heading "Certain Stockholders of Union Texas" in this Prospectus. Such stockholders were unwilling to represent that they were acquiring such shares for investment. Allied understands that, under such circumstances, the Securities and Exchange Commission takes the position that such stockholders may be "underwriters" as such term is defined in the Securities Act of 1933; and, accordingly, such shares have been registered. Allied disclaims that such stockholders are "underwriters" under such Act or that sales of such shares by them will constitute a public offering of such shares by Allied.

Shelf-type prospectuses have been used to cover resales by certain stockholders of companies acquired in a registered exchange offer. The SEC has taken the position that those stockholders of the target company who negotiated the exchange offer will be considered underwriters in reselling the securities acquired by them in exchange for those of the acquired com-

20. C. Israels, *supra* note 7, at 211–12. This is the transaction referred to in SEC Release No. 33-3846 (October 10, 1957).

pany. There are numerous examples of exchange offer prospectuses that contain a paragraph at the foot of the cover page to the effect that the prospectus may also "be used to cover resales of shares acquired in the exchange offer by those persons who may be deemed to be underwriters in making such sales."

• • *Stock Option Plans.* One type of shelf registration not referred to by Mr. Cohen in his June 8, 1961 presentation to the SEC was a Form S-8 registration statement covering shares that could be issued from time to time under an employee stock option plan or other type of employee benefit plan. By the very nature of these plans, the securities are registered for sale at some unspecified time in the future. With respect to resales of the registered shares by officers deemed to be in control of the issuer, there always has been some question as to whether a prospectus designed for an employee offering is suitable to cover resales to the public. At one point, the SEC permitted the Form S-8 prospectus to be used for resales if beefed-up in certain respects. Instruction C to the form now provides that the Form S-8 prospectus is not available for this purpose but that resales under Rule 415 may be made with a separate prospectus filed as part of the Form S-8 registration statement. The prospectus may be prepared in accordance with the requirements of Form S-3. Resales are permitted without limitation if the issuer meets the registrant requirements of that form; if that is not the case, then the amount of securities proposed to be sold during any three-month period by any person may not exceed the amount provided for in Rule 144(e).

• • *Pledged Securities.* Another type of shelf registration not referred to by Mr. Cohen is one covering securities pledged by a control person or a statutory underwriter as collateral for a loan. Unless it makes a private sale or sells under Rule 144, the creditor foreclosing on the collateral may have to comply with the registration and prospectus delivery requirements of Section 5 of the 1933 Act.[21] A pledgee, of course, does not gener-

---

21. *SEC v. Guild Films Co., Inc.* 178 F. Supp. 418 (S.D.N.Y. 1959), *aff'd,* 279 F.2d 485 (2d Cir. 1960); *In re Skiatron Electronics and Television Corp.,* SEC Release No. 33-4282 (October 3, 1960).

ally take securities as collateral with a view to selling them. It makes a secured loan with the full intention that interest and principal will be paid at the required time. If, however, the borrower does not meet its obligations, the lender wishes to be in a position to foreclose on the collateral and to sell it promptly. Registration of pledged securities to deal with this contingency has been permitted by the SEC without question and with little, if any, concern over the language of Section 6(a).

• *"90-Day Undertakings"*

In addition to the undertaking to update the registration statement specifically called for by former Form S-14, the SEC sometimes required similar undertakings to justify the use of shelf registration. In 1961, the SEC began to call for so-called "90-day undertakings." These undertakings required a registrant to file a post-effective amendment disclosing such current information as would have been required in the filing of a new registration statement if the first offering of the securities took place more than 90 days after the effective date of the registration statement.

In attempting to be flexible, the SEC received a certain amount of criticism from those who believed that Section 6(a) should be strictly construed. One commentator complained that the Commission was in effect "disregarding the thrust of section 6(a), which ensures current information by prohibiting shelf registration; at the same time it is stepping outside the governing statute by administratively requiring the issuer to incorporate an undertaking to update the registration statement.[22] The same person concluded that "[p]roper enforcement of the Securities Act requires that Section 6(a) not be emasculated by allowing the filing of post-effective amendments in lieu of strict adherence to congressional intent that securities not be registered unless they are presently intended to be offered for sale."[23] Other commentators questioned the SEC's authority to

---

22. S. Hodes, *supra* note 4, at 1140.
23. *Id.* at 1148.

require undertakings in the absence of a statute conferring this power.[24]

• *The Hazel Bishop Case*

In June 1960, Hazel Bishop Inc. filed a registration statement relating to 1.1 million shares of its outstanding common stock. This represented approximately 61% of the number of shares outstanding, and the registration statement named 70 selling stockholders who might offer shares from time to time at prices current at the time of sale through brokers on the American Stock Exchange, in the open market, or otherwise. An amendment filed in October 1960 increased the number of shares to 1.3 million and the number of selling stockholders to 112.

Shortly thereafter, the SEC initiated proceedings under Section 8(d) of the 1933 Act to determine whether a stop order should be issued suspending the effectiveness of the registration statement. In issuing a stop order, the SEC found that the registration statement contained numerous false and misleading statements, including deficiencies in the financial statements.[25] More significantly, the SEC raised fundamental questions with respect to a massive uncoordinated distribution of this type.

It first questioned the efficacy of Rule 153, which permits the prospectus delivery requirements of the 1933 Act to be satisfied as between brokers in a transaction on a national securities exchange by delivering copies of the prospectus to the exchange. The SEC noted that members of the exchange may or may not request copies for their own use or for delivery to customers and that there was a real danger that the information contained in the registration statement might not in fact come to the attention of brokers and dealers or buyers of the securities and that the public would not be aware of the material facts pertaining to Hazel Bishop and the circumstances of the distribution. The SEC stated:

---

24. A.H. Dean, *Twenty-Five Years of Federal Securities Regulation by the Securities and Exchange Commission,* 59 Colum. L. Rev. 697, 726 (1959).
25. *Hazel Bishop Inc.,* SEC Release No. 33-4371 (June 7, 1961).

We believe that it would be highly prejudicial to the protection of investors and the public interest generally if the massive distribution here proposed by a large group which numbers among it the controlling persons of Hazel Bishop should be initiated through the facilities of the Exchange unless prior thereto facts of this case are given a much wider public distribution than is likely to result from the mere delivery of copies of the prospectus to the Exchange. Accordingly, it is our view that prior to the final effective date of this registration statement, the public interest requires the transmittal by registrant of our opinion accompanied by an adequate prospectus to all of the selling stockholders and the members of the Exchange community.

The SEC also noted that in a conventional distribution of securities the activities of underwriters are governed by the underwriting documents which provide "a controlled procedure designed to bring about an orderly marketing of the security free of practices prohibited by the statutes or rules as manipulative, deceptive or fraudulent, or otherwise unlawful." The SEC noted that here there were at least 112 selling stockholders and that no procedures had been established to coordinate their activities or guard against unlawful practices such as bids and purchases in violation of Rule 10b-6.

The SEC also expressed concern that there might be written communications that violated the prohibitions of Section 5 of the 1933 Act. It observed that one of the selling stockholders was the specialist in the common stock of Hazel Bishop and expressed skepticism as to how a specialist could properly discharge its function and at the same time comply with Rule 10b-6 and the other applicable provisions of the 1934 Act. The SEC concluded:

In summary, we think that under the factual situation here presented the potentialities for violations of the law, witting or unwitting, on the part of those who are about to offer their stock on the basis stated are so grave that consistent with our obligations under the Exchange

Act, they should be called to the attention of the selling stockholders, the issuer, the Exchange, the existing stockholders of Hazel Bishop and the general public.

Shortly after this decision was handed down, the stop order was lifted and an amended registration statement became effective. In order to meet the problems raised by the SEC's opinion, the selling stockholders and Hazel Bishop entered into an agreement designed to assure compliance with the 1934 Act, with particular reference to Rules 10b-2, 10b-6 and 10b-7. The company instructed its transfer agent to honor requests for transfer only for those selling stockholders who were signatories to this agreement. Hazel Bishop sent a copy of the SEC's opinion and the final prospectus to all members of the NASD and the American Stock Exchange and recommended that they not execute any orders without confirming that the selling stockholder had signed the requisite agreement. The notice to dealers stated that "any broker who acts for any of the selling shareholders named in the Registration Statement must be furnished by such selling shareholders with copies of the Prospectus to enable him to deliver a prospectus to the buying broker, who may be required to deliver a copy of its prospectus to its customer." The notice to dealers also contained warnings with respect to compliance with Rules 10b-2, 10b-6 and 10b-7.[26]

---

26. The following year, the SEC issued a stop order suspending the effectiveness of a registration statement filed by American Finance Company, Inc. covering an offering of units, on the basis of misleading statements and omissions with respect to, among other matters, a proposed offering by a group of selling stockholders, 17 in number. The prospectus disclosed that the Lomasney underwriting firm was to purchase 60,000 shares at an advantageous price for its own account and for the account of favored customers. These shares were included in the registration statement, and the prospectus stated that they would be reoffered subsequently pursuant to an appropriately supplemented prospectus furnishing additional information. "However," said the SEC, "the prospectus does not inform prospective investors of the possible effects on the market in the common stock, following the completion of the sale of the Units, of a subsequent distribution of the 60,000 shares, which is a very large number of shares in relation to the 75,000 shares that will be available for trading on the comple-

In a subsequent shelf offering of outstanding shares of common stock of Thompson-Starrett Companies, Inc., additional steps were taken to coordinate the distribution. There it was provided in the agreement between the company and the selling stockholders that only a broker authorized by the issuer could be used to effect sales and that no sales could be made other than on the American Stock Exchange. The agreement also provided that all sell orders must be at a specified price or prices not lower than the last reported bid price nor higher than the higher of either the last reported asked price or the last reported sales price on the American Stock Exchange prior to the receipt of the order by the broker. The agreement further provided that neither a "market" nor a "stop loss" order could be entered and that an order could be given to a broker on a discretionary ("not held") basis.[27]

The SEC formalized its position with respect to uncoordinated distributions by publishing a speech delivered by Chairman William J. Cary to the Practising Law Institute in which he outlined the administrative procedures developed by the SEC to control offerings of this type.[28] These procedures were further codified when the SEC adopted its Guide 53.[29]

Guide 53 applied to a registered "at the market" offering by selling stockholders who included insiders or substantial holders, involving a substantial amount of securities in relation to the securities of the class outstanding (more than 10%), the absence of a

---

tion of the sale of Units." The SEC went on to say, "In view of the large number of shares proposed to be offered in relation to the limited floating supply of shares, the apparent lack of cohesiveness in the selling group and the absence of a prior market, the registration statement should have identified the sellers and their relationships to each other, registrant and Lomasney, and should have disclosed that such distribution would not be coordinated or controlled by a managing underwriter and that the selling group had not provided the contractual safeguards for the protection of buyers and sellers usually provided in a conventional distribution." *In re American Finance Co., Inc.*, 40 S.E.C. 103, 1050–51 (1962).

27. *See* Yerkes, *Shelf Registrations: The Role of the Broker-Dealer*, 29 Bus. Law. 397, 409 (1974).

28. SEC Release No. 33-4401 (August 3, 1961).

29. SEC Release No. 33-4936 (December 9, 1968).

professional underwriter to act for the group and the absence of a conventional underwriting agreement. The guide stated that where these elements were present and there was a limited group of selling stockholders or several groups of related stockholders, then contractual arrangements should be entered into between the members of the respective groups and the issuer requiring compliance with the SEC's anti-manipulative rules (namely, not to buy other securities of the same class or solicit purchases by others) until the offering by all members of the group was completed and to inform the exchange, the brokers and the selling stockholders in the group when the distribution by the respective members of the group was over.

The guide provided that, where there is a large group of unrelated sellers and agreements are thus not feasible, the issuer should notify the sellers of the applicable SEC rules and regulations. It also stated that, under a single registration statement, some stockholders might be required to enter into agreements while notification of others might be sufficient. These arrangements were required to be disclosed in the registration statement.

Guide 53 was ultimately replaced by the provision in Rule 461 that provides that one of the bases on which the SEC may refuse to accelerate the effectiveness of a registration statement is "whether, in the case of a significant secondary offering at the market, the registrant, selling securityholders and underwriters have not taken sufficient measures to assure compliance with Rules 10b-2, 10b-6 and Rule 10b-7 under the Securities Exchange Act of 1934." As a general matter, the problem of uncontrolled or uncoordinated distributions has not been a significant issue in recent years.

• *Guide 4*

In 1968, the SEC codified its position with respect to shelf registration statements as Guide 4 to its guides for the preparation and filing of registration statements.[30] The circumstances under which shelf registrations would be permitted were those previously mentioned: a continuous acquisition program, Rule

---

30. *Id.* These guides were initially proposed in SEC Release No. 33-4890 (December 20, 1967).

155 situations, resales of securities acquired in a Rule 133 transaction, pledged securities, securities purchased by underwriters in connection with public offerings, and securities to be offered pursuant to options, warrants or rights.

Guide 4 also permitted securities to be shelf-registered if a representation were made that they would be publicly offered within a reasonable period of time after the effective date of the registration statement or if, because of particular circumstances, effective control over the resale of the securities by other persons would be difficult to maintain. The guide noted that where securities are so registered they could not be sold at a time when the prospectus had not been kept up to date in accordance with Section 10(a) of the 1933 Act. It also noted that registration statements of this character may involve questions arising under Rules 10b-2, 10b-6 and 10b-7 under the 1934 Act.

• *Further Developments*

The adoption of Rule S-16, which originally was applicable only to brokerage transactions on an exchange, facilitated the development of shelf registrations for secondary offerings. The issuer could use a short-form registration statement that could be continuously updated by the filing of 1934 Act reports, thus easing the burden on the issuer and placing it in a position where it might be more inclined to accommodate selling securityholders. As previously noted, the SEC began in the mid-1970s to permit the registration on Form S-1 or Form S-7 of MTNs proposed to be offered on a continuous basis by finance companies and bank holding companies. Also, a number of institutions, including the Bank of America, were permitted to shelf-register mortgage pass-through securities to be sold in direct sales, sales on an agency basis, or offerings through syndicates organized by specified managing underwriters. The stage was set for the SEC to play out the drama that led to the adoption of Rule 415.

The Adoption of Rule 415

Rule 415 came into being as a result of efforts by the staff of the SEC to improve the integrated disclosure system. As part of that process, the SEC conducted a comprehensive review of all of the guides for the preparation and filing of registration statements. As a result of its reevaluation of Guide 4, the SEC published for comment, as proposed Rule 462A, a comprehensive position with respect to shelf registration statements.[31] In addition to blessing traditional shelf registrations, the proposed rule would have permitted shelf registration of primary offerings of debt and equity securities that an issuer reasonably expected to offer over the next two years.

Proposed Rule 462A drew little attention, perhaps because it was buried in a release in which the SEC proposed for comment the reorganization of Regulation S-K, the elimination or incorporation of all the guides (except those pertaining to specific industries) into Regulation S-K or Regulation C and certain revisions to the general rules and regulations under the 1933 Act. It was a massive document of which the shelf rule was only a small part. Several of those who commented on the proposed shelf rule were concerned that it had not received widespread attention from issuers and investment bankers because it appeared in the middle of a lengthy release. These commentators recommended that the proposal be republished for comment in a separate release in order that it might receive the careful consideration that it deserved. Thus, the SEC reproposed Rule 462A in a separate release and in a somewhat revised form.[32]

As the investment banking community focused on the proposed shelf rule, a Chicken Little reaction set in. Here was a proposal that some believed could undermine the traditional manner in which securities had been distributed to the public— fixed price offerings through underwriting syndicates. Efforts to persuade the SEC to postpone the rule's adoption were led by Morgan Stanley & Co. Incorporated, which stated in a letter to the SEC dated February 2, 1982: "Implementation of the Rule as proposed may produce fundamental structural changes in the capital raising process with undesirable consequences

---

31. SEC Release No. 33-6276 (December 23, 1980).
32. SEC Release No. 33-6334 (August 6, 1981).

that have not been explored, either in the Commission's release or in the comment letters submitted." Morgan Stanley went on to predict that the proposed rule "could substantially impair the process by which most of the long-term private capital has been raised in this country—fixed price public offerings by syndicates of securities firms." Goldman, Sachs & Co., in a letter dated January 7, 1982 from its co-senior partner, John C. Whitehead, also expressed concern over the proposed shelf rule.

In recognition of the concerns expressed by the securities industry, the SEC adopted the shelf rule (redesignated Rule 415) in March 1982 on a temporary basis.[33] The SEC proposed to experiment with its use and announced that during the period before November 1982 it would hold public hearings to explore the rule's impact and to give interested parties further opportunities to express their views.

The period immediately following the adoption of Rule 415 was marked by a flurry of activity on Wall Street. Each of the major investment banking firms produced its own thick brochure explaining how the rule would operate. These brochures were in the hands of clients and prospective clients within days following the announcement of the rule's adoption. Lawyers worked around the clock to produce standard forms of indentures, underwriting documents and prospectus disclosure that their investment banking clients could use to demonstrate to corporate issuers that they were ready to move full steam ahead in assisting them in establishing shelf programs. At the same time that they were seeking to persuade issuers that their services were essential in this new era, the investment banks were preparing for presentations at the SEC hearings, presentations that would raise concerns as to the rule's impact on the healthy functioning of the capital markets.

Some of the principal players under Rule 415 were among its most vocal critics. John Whitehead of Goldman Sachs was quoted in *Fortune* as saying that he did not have any problem with his firm's willingness to make use of the new rule. "We adapt to the ground rules whether or not we like them," he ex-

---

33. SEC Release No. 33-6383 (March 3, 1982).

plained. "We've been very active under 415. That's where I get my information that it's bad for investors."[34] Firms with fewer blue chip clients than Morgan Stanley or Goldman Sachs welcomed Rule 415 as providing an opportunity to make inroads into their competitors' investment banking relationships.

In a March 1982 release, the SEC scheduled the hearings for June and framed the issues to be considered.[35] The SEC stated that it would examine the extent to which structural changes in public offerings were due to factors extrinsic to the adoption of Rule 415, such as volatile markets and interest rates, the role played by institutional investors in the securities markets, quick financings made possible by short-form registration statements, and the significance of "market windows." The SEC stated that it would pay particular attention to the effects of Rule 415 on fixed price public offerings and the practice of syndication. The entire tone of the release suggested that the SEC believed that the problems that concerned the investment banking community did not stem from Rule 415 but rather from other economic forces. This certainly was the view of certain key members of the staff.[36]

Written and oral presentations were made at the June 28 hearings. Issuers gave their strong support to Rule 415. Citicorp, which had filed the first registration statement under Rule 415 (a Form S-3 covering $500 million of notes), made a particularly eloquent presentation. A number of the major investment banking firms reiterated the concerns previously expressed, including the difficulty of performing due diligence and the impact of Rule 415 on syndicates and fixed price offerings.

John H. Gutfreund, the chairman of Salomon Brothers, argued convincingly that knowledge of the calendar for debt financings is an important factor in pricing an issue. "The

---

34. A.F. Ehrbar, *Upheaval In Investment Banking*, Fortune (August 23, 1982). *See also* N. Osborn, *The Furor Over Shelf Registration*, Institutional Investor (June 1982).

35. SEC Release No. 33-6391 (March 12, 1982).

36. *See* Remarks of Lee B. Spencer, Jr., Director, Division of Corporation Finance, before the University of Southern California School of Accounting's SEC and Financial Reporting Institute (May 7, 1982).

concept of a financing calendar, or some mechanism to provide notice to the market of imminent new issues," he said, "is central to the supply and demand judgments which all investors must undertake in securities evaluation." This information, according to Mr. Gutfreund, was almost as important as disclosure concerning the issuer itself. With respect to disclosure and due diligence, Mr. Gutfreund expressed the view that the effective due diligence that uncovered the problems of Penn Central before its demise in 1970 (see Chapter 5) would have been impossible in the context of an instantaneous shelf offering.

Several persons testifying at the hearing urged the SEC to increase the amount of information required to be included in an S-3 prospectus. In addition, the Securities Industry Association and others urged the SEC to relieve underwriters of responsibility for documents incorporated by reference. The most far-reaching relief urged at the hearings for the problems presented by fast time schedules, however, was the introduction of a mandatory "cooling-off" period for many primary distributions. Numerous regional firms appeared at the hearing and testified that as a result of Rule 415 they had been unable to participate in syndicates in which they normally would have been included. Also, the NASD was particularly concerned about the impact of the rule on fixed price offerings, a method of distributing securities that had been strongly praised by the SEC in the *Papilsky* hearings.[37]

In September 1982, the SEC, with three commissioners sitting, voted to extend Rule 415's effectiveness through December 31, 1983.[38] Chairman Shad had recused himself from the proceedings, and there was one vacancy at the time. The extension was intended to "provide a greater opportunity to study the operation and impact of Rule 415 through what might be a full financial cycle." Commissioner Barbara Thomas wrote a 36-page dissent stating that shelf registrations should not be permitted for offerings of equity securities and that a two-day notice period should be required for debt offerings not registered on Form S-3.[39]

---

37. *See* Chapter 6.

38. SEC Release No. 33-6423 (September 2, 1982).

39. For an analysis and rebuttal of Commissioner Thomas's position, *see* B. Banoff, *Regulatory Subsidies, Efficient Markets, and Shelf Registra-*

The SEC again solicited comment on Rule 415 and its operation in order to provide those affected with one last opportunity to express their views before final action was taken.[40] In November 1983, the SEC adopted Rule 415 on a permanent basis, but in deference to the concerns expressed about the rule, it limited shelf registration to either "traditional" offerings or, in the case of "primary" offerings, to those made on Form S-3.[41] This limitation caused no great stir since most of the primary shelf filings that had been made since the adoption of the rule on a temporary basis had used this form.[42] The SEC also responded to concerns about due diligence and the quality of disclosure by expressing its conviction that new methods of "anticipatory" and "continuous" due diligence were being developed as an adequate substitute for traditional due diligence. Some of these methods, referred to by issuers during the hearings, included the appointment of a single law firm to act as underwriters' counsel, the holding of "drafting sessions" on 1934 Act reports in which prospective underwriters and their counsel could participate and the holding of "periodic due diligence sessions" between issuers and prospective underwriters either periodically or "at any time."

Commissioner Thomas stuck by her guns and continued to express the view that Rule 415 should not be applicable to primary offerings of equity securities. The chairman of the SEC, John R. Shad, filed a special concurring opinion in which he took issue with the SEC's inventory of techniques of "continuous" and "anticipatory" due diligence, finding them to be of

---

tion: An Analysis of Rule 415, 70 Va. L. Rev. 135 (1984). For a critique of the Banoff article, *see* M. Fox, *Shelf Registration, Integrated Disclosure, and Underwriter Due Diligence: An Economic Analysis,* 70 Va. L. Rev. 1005 (1984). *See generally* ABA Committee on Federal Regulation of Securities, *Report of Task Force on Sellers' Due Diligence and Similar Defenses Under the Federal Securities Laws,* 48 Bus. Law. 1185 (1993).

40. SEC Release No. 33-6470 (June 9, 1983).

41. SEC Release No. 33-6499 (November 17, 1983).

42. The limitation did, however, raise the question whether continuous MTN offerings by issuers not eligible to use Form S-3 were "traditional" offerings or "primary" offerings.

"limited practical value" in view of the need for issuers and underwriters to spend "hundreds of thousands of hours annually" in meetings on the speculative possibility that an offering would occur. The chairman predicted that such meetings would soon be attended only by "junior observers, rather than qualified participants."

Expansion of Eligibility to Use Form S-3 and Form F-3

Notwithstanding the SEC's permanent adoption of Rule 415 in 1983, shelf registration would not have become a powerful financing tool without an expansion of a U.S. issuer's ability to use Form S-3 and a non-U.S. issuer's ability to use Form F-3. As noted above, clause (x) of Rule 415 permits the registration of securities to be sold on a "continuous or delayed basis" but limits registration for this purpose to offerings on Form S-3 or Form F-3. An issuer not eligible to use these forms may register securities pursuant to clause (ix), which permits continuous offerings (such as MTNs) but not delayed offerings (such as periodic takedowns). Such an issuer will also not have the convenience of automatic updating by means of incorporating by reference its 1934 Act reports.

The SEC began in 1981 to lay the foundation for the use of Form S-3 to support shelf registration by republishing the new form for comment.[43] As originally proposed,[44] the predecessor to Form S-3 (like its immediate predecessor, Form S-16) would have been available for a primary offering only on condition that the offering be underwritten. If maintained, this requirement would have forced shelf offerings into an impractical long-form registration format with continuing updating obligations. Fortunately for the future of shelf registration, however, the SEC in 1981 followed the advice of commenters and decided not to repropose the requirement.

In October 1992, the SEC adopted amendments to Form S-3[45] that had the effect of expanding the number of companies

---

43. SEC Release No. 33-6331 (August 6, 1981).
44. SEC Release No. 33-6235 (September 2, 1980).
45. SEC Release No. 33-6964 (October 22, 1992).

eligible to use shelf registration for primary offerings. The amendments, among other things, reduced an issuer's required reporting history under the 1934 Act from 36 months to twelve months and reduced the equity "float" requirement from $150 million to $75 million. They also eliminated the three million share trading volume test. The form was also amended to include investment-grade asset-backed securities as an additional category of transactions eligible to use Form S-3 and, consequently, shelf registration.

The SEC adopted amendments to Form F-3 in April 1994[46] that expanded the use of Form F-3 and, consequently, shelf registration for eligible non-U.S. issuers. The amendments shortened the minimum reporting history requirement from 36 months to twelve months (provided the issuer has filed at least one annual report) and reduced the minimum public float requirement from $300 million to $75 million.

There is an exemption from the NASD's filing requirements for securities registered on Form S-3 and Form F-3 and offered pursuant to Rule 415.[47] Oddly enough, however, this exemption applies only if the issuer meets the standards for the use of the respective forms as they were in effect prior to October 21, 1992. The NASD believes in its wisdom that the premise of the exemption, i.e., that S-3 and F-3 issuers can be presumed to have enough bargaining power to resist unfair arrangements, may not be justified under the new standards adopted by the SEC in 1992.

The SEC's expansion of Form S-3 and Form F-3 as a vehicle for delayed or continuous offerings has been a principal driving force behind the shelf registration phenomenon.

The Impact of Rule 415

In the end, the adoption of Rule 415 was inevitable. Issuers needed capital in large amounts and on a regular basis. Given increasingly volatile market conditions, there was a premium on speedy and reliable access to the markets during periods of

---

46. SEC Release No. 33-7053 (April 19, 1994).
47. Rule 2710(b)(7)(C)(i).

perceived opportunity. Issuers and investment bankers were no longer willing to tolerate unpredictable delays arising from SEC administrative practices. Even those who most opposed Rule 415 because of its consequences for disclosure and verification agreed that issuers would, if the rule were not adopted, make increased use of the Eurodollar market where "bought deals" were the rule. Indeed, some of the larger firms that opposed Rule 415 were nevertheless among those that found the rule most attractive because it enabled them to offer their clients options in both markets.

Important changes had taken place in the way that securities were distributed well before the adoption of Rule 415. One of the most significant developments was the action taken by the SEC in April 1978 in extending the availability of Form S-16 to underwritten primary offerings.[48] The result was to speed up the registration process, first to approximately one week and later to a matter of days. The old practices of allowing a month or more to elapse between the filing of a registration statement and its effective date and allocating upwards of a week to form a syndicate and sell the issue fell by the wayside in the case of high-grade debt and equity securities. A consequence was a reduction in the amount of time available for underwriters to perform due diligence. The due diligence concerns expressed in the Rule 415 hearings were the same concerns that previously had been expressed in the context of Form S-16.[49]

The development in the Euromarket of "bought deals," deals in which underwriting commitments would be made with no prior marketing efforts, led to increasing pressure for more rapid access to the United States markets. In Europe, where there are no requirements that securities be sold pursuant to an effective registration statement, the traditional method of selling debt securities through underwriting syndicates following a marketing period largely had been replaced by instantaneous sales to banks or other financial institutions that would bid for

---

48. SEC Release No. 33-5923 (April 10, 1978).

49. *See* C. Johnson, *Expanded Use of Form S-16; Guide 42,* Tenth Annual Institute on Securities Regulation 39 (Practising Law Institute Transcript 1979).

the securities on a firm basis and resell them in whatever manner they chose.[50] Issuers thus avoided the market risk inherent in the former practice of pricing an issue after a two-week selling period.

As bought deals became increasingly prevalent in the Euromarket, United States investment bankers sought ways to fit this concept within the framework of an offering registered under the 1933 Act.

The discipline of fixed-price offerings also began to erode before the adoption of Rule 415. Debt securities purchased in the Euromarket pursuant to bought deals generally are not reoffered at a fixed price. Instead, as stated in Morgan Stanley's February 2, 1982 letter to the SEC, sales are made first at discounted prices to large investors willing to act promptly, then the balance is hedged in the options or futures market, and a portion is offered to retail buyers at higher prices.

Although the NASD's *Papilsky* rules[51] prohibit sales at a discount in a fixed-price offering except to an NASD member (or certain foreign dealers) for services actually performed in the distribution of the securities, there is no requirement that a public offering of securities be made at a fixed price. If there is no agreement with the issuer to reoffer the securities at a fixed price or if the prospectus does not indicate that they are to be so offered, then the *Papilsky* rules do not apply. Indeed, there is nothing to prevent an investment banker from offering registered securities at different prices to institutions and retail purchasers.

The complaints voiced to the SEC about Rule 415's adverse consequences for disclosure and due diligence were therefore directed largely at the wrong target. Underwriters' ability to engage in due diligence investigations prior to an offering had already been weakened by the introduction of the integrated disclosure system and an added premium on speedy access to markets. It came to be questionable whether the underwriter any longer "sponsored" an issue in a meaningful

---

50. *See generally* N. Adam, *Behind the Bravado of the Bought Deal,* Euromoney (August 1980).

51. Rules 2730, 2740 and 2750. *See* Chapter 6.

way, as opposed to delivering pricing advice and distribution services. Changes in SEC review practices, volatile market conditions and severe competition among underwriters also adversely affected disclosure and due diligence.

An ABA task force summarized these developments:

> For underwriters, the effect of the changes described above was to accelerate the transition from "relationship" to "transactional" investment banking. The traditional underwritten public offering by a reporting company—sometimes referred to as that "high ceremony of capitalism"—degenerated in the space of a few years into a series of bargain-basement brawls, characterized by abbreviated and sporadic opportunities for investigation and successive sales by different underwriters of large amounts of securities on the basis of identical disclosure documents. The finely-honed prospectus—"the best record of our due diligence," in the view of many underwriters—was replaced by a multi-document "offering package" consisting of documents that had been filed by the issuer at varying times for varying purposes (e.g., periodic reporting, Form 8-K reporting, proxy solicitation) and large portions of which were beyond the underwriters' capacity to influence, that were often delivered constructively (i.e., not at all) to the buyer, and that especially in the case of continuous offerings were subject to automatic change whenever the issuer filed a 1934 Act report. Indeed, it was no longer clear what the underwriter's goal was to be in sorting out the accuracy of different documents prepared at different times.[52]

Whether these developments are viewed as beneficial to issuers or detrimental to the capital markets, they represented significant changes in the distribution process that had come about

---

52. ABA Committee on Federal Regulation of Securities, *Report of Task Force on Sellers' Due Diligence and Similar Defenses Under the Federal Securities Laws*, 48 Bus. Law. 1185, 1186–87 (1993).

independently of Rule 415. These practices had been changing in any event, but Rule 415 raised the consciousness of issuers to the possibilities of change. Investment bankers responded by intensifying their efforts to be innovative. They also realized that to compete effectively they must be willing to commit large amounts of capital. Growing capital requirements led to a renewed interest in public ownership by privately-owned securities firms, an increase in public financing by the major firms (often at the holding company level under their own debt shelf registration statements), and a willingness by a number of securities firms to be acquired by larger companies (not always in the securities business) that were in a position to provide needed capital.

One of the authors and a partner concluded in an article published shortly after Rule 415 was adopted on a temporary basis:

> Whether shelf registrations become the norm or most companies decide to "shelve the shelf rule," changes in traditional underwriting practices are likely to continue in the new rule 415 environment. Bought deals and other alternatives to fixed-price syndicated offerings did not require the adoption of rule 415. What really matters is the climate for change resulting from the financial community's reaction to the rule. Even if the SEC rescinds or amends rule 415 (and rescission seems unlikely), it cannot turn back the clock to the time when it was assumed without question that a fixed-price syndicated offering was the only proper way to distribute securities.[53]

Operation of Rule 415

If an issuer qualifies for the use of Form S-3 or Form F-3 and decides to file a shelf registration statement, it determines the dollar amount of securities to be registered and checks the box on the facing sheet of the registration statement to indicate

---

53. C. Johnson & K. Cote, *The New Shelf Registration Rule*, 15 Rev. Sec. Reg. 925, 934 (1982).

that the filing is being made under Rule 415. The registration statement must contain the undertakings described below. The SEC may or may not review the document. If the registration statement covers an at-the-market offering of equity securities, other substantive requirements must be met.

• *Securities Covered by Rule 415*

Securities may be registered under the 1933 Act for an offering to be made on a continuous or delayed basis in the future if the registration statement pertains only to securities specified in one of the eleven clauses of Rule 415(a)(1), i.e., (i) securities to be offered or sold by a person other than the issuer or an affiliate, (ii) securities to be offered and sold pursuant to a dividend or interest reinvestment plan or employee benefit plan, (iii) securities to be issued upon the exercise of options, warrants or rights, (iv) securities to be issued upon the conversion of other securities, (v) securities pledged as collateral, (vi) depositary receipts registered on Form F-6, (vii) mortgage-related securities, (viii) securities to be issued in business combinations, (ix) securities "the offering of which will be commenced promptly, will be made on a continuous basis and may continue for a period in excess of 30 days from the date of initial effectiveness," (x) securities "registered (or qualified to be registered) on Form S-3 or Form F-3 . . . which are to be offered and sold on a continuous or delayed basis" by or on behalf of the issuer or an affiliate and (xi) common stock to be offered and sold on a delayed or continuous basis by an investment company that makes periodic repurchase offers.

The most significant applications of Rule 415 for corporate finance purposes are described in clauses (ix) and (x).

Note that clause (vii) covers only mortgage-related securities, which would exclude other categories of asset-backed securities such as those backed by credit card receivables and auto loans. The instructions to Form S-3, however, expressly make investment grade asset-backed securities eligible to use Form S-3. Offerings of these securities are therefore eligible under clause (x) of Rule 415(a)(1) to be registered for offer and sale on a continuous or delayed basis.

• *Amount and Type of Securities Registered*

Rule 415 limits the amount of securities that an issuer may register for offering on a delayed or continuous basis (i.e., pursuant to clauses (viii), (ix) and (x)) to those that it reasonably expects to sell within two years. The SEC will defer to the issuer's judgment in this respect, and it has not been known to second-guess an issuer that does not manage to sell all of the shelf registered securities within the two-year period. The expiration of the two-year period will not terminate the registration of securities that remain unsold.

The two-year limitation does not apply to offerings of mortgage-related securities. For no apparent reason other than historical, it does apply to offerings of securities backed by assets other than mortgages, e.g., credit card or other receivables. The limitation also applies to MTN programs and other traditional shelf offerings that "will be commenced promptly, will be made on a continuous basis and may continue for a period in excess of 30 days from the date of initial effectiveness." These may include, in the words of the 1983 release that adopted Rule 415 on a permanent basis, "customer purchase plans; exchange, rights, subscription and rescission offers; offers to employees, consultants or independent agents; offerings on a best efforts basis; tax shelter and other limited partnership interests; commodity funds; condominium rental pools; time sharing agreements; real estate investment trusts; farmers' cooperative organizations or others making distributions on a membership basis; and continuous debt sales by finance companies to their customers."[54]

In the case of debt securities offered on a continuous or delayed basis, an issuer is required to disclose a dollar amount to be offered. Because of the continuous offering requirement of clause (ix), it is customary for such offerings to specify the terms and conditions of the securities being registered (typically MTNs), including various interest rate and currency options. In the case of issuers eligible to make offerings on a delayed basis pursuant to clause (x) of the rule, the practice is

---

54. SEC Release No. 33-6499 (November 17, 1983).

to specify a dollar amount of generic debt and describe various categories of debt securities that may be issued (without any obligation to allocate as among these categories).

In the case of common stock or preferred stock, the amount of securities to be offered may be specified in terms of the number of shares.

U.S. issuers since 1992 and non-U.S. issuers since 1994 may elect to register both debt and equity securities on the same shelf registration statement without specifying the principal amount of debt or the number of shares of equity securities being registered. Thus, an issuer registering securities "for the shelf" on Form S-3 or Form F-3 may disclose in its base prospectus the various types of securities covered by the registration statement (both debt and equity), but it does not have to identify the specific amount of each category to be offered.

It should be noted that the use of the "generic" or "unallocated" registration statement is limited to sales pursuant to Rule 415(a)(1)(x), i.e., sales by the issuer or an affiliate. The technique is not available for secondary market sales by non-affiliates. The reason for the limitation is obscure, and the SEC has received several recommendations that it be abolished.

Item 512 of Regulation S-K requires the issuer to undertake to file a post-effective amendment to deregister any securities that remain unsold at the termination of the offering, but the authors are not aware of any issuer that has done so for reasons related to this requirement. Prior to the sale of all of the registered securities, the issuer may file a new registration statement covering additional securities to be sold from time to time. The securities remaining from the prior registration statement and the newly-registered securities may be offered pursuant to a common prospectus under Rule 429. Additional securities may generally not be registered by means of a post-effective amendment to an existing registration statement.[55]

---

55. Rule 413 under the 1933 Act provides:

Except as provided in Sections 24(e)(1) and 24(f) of the Investment Company Act of 1940, the registration of additional securities of the same class as other securities for which a registration statement is al-

• *Documentation*

As part of the initial registration of shelf-registered securities, basic documents are filed with the SEC. The base prospectus, which generally permits broad variations on the securities that can be issued, is prepared by the issuer and its counsel, and frequently with the collaboration of a law firm designated by the issuer to represent future underwriters. The base prospectus, of course, forms the principal part of the registration statement. In the case of debt or asset-backed securities, an open-ended indenture that permits the issuance of numerous types of debt or asset-backed securities is normally qualified under the 1939 Act and filed as an exhibit to the registration statement. In the case of preferred stock, a form of charter amendment required to establish the basic terms of the preferred stock is filed as an exhibit to the registration statement. In other cases, such as the registration of rights or warrants, the documents creating the securities are also filed as exhibits. The form of underwriting agreement, if any, or the form of distribution agreement relating to MTNs is also included as an exhibit to the registration statement.

An issuer will usually try to satisfy itself that its documents are satisfactory to at least some of the underwriters with whom it expects to do business on the basis of the shelf registration statement. Occasionally, an underwriter will raise objections to a feature of one of the key documents, e.g., to the "market out" clause of the underwriting agreement. If the issuer wants the underwriter to participate in its offerings, it may negotiate the offending clause. If the issuer believes that it has a large enough "stable" of underwriters who are satisfied with the documents as they stand, the issuer will refuse to negotiate. Of course, it may change its mind at some point in the future depending on the performance of the other underwriters.

When a financing opportunity arises, the issuer will be able to move quickly because of the availability of registered securities and prenegotiated agreements. A terms agreement under

---

ready in effect shall be effected through a separate registration statement relating to the additional securities.

the underwriting agreement previously filed with the SEC (or, alternatively, a terms agreement that incorporates the underwriting agreement) will be executed and delivered as the basis for the contract between the issuer and the underwriters who make a successful proposal. The terms of the new securities, the underwriting arrangements and any "material changes" in the issuer's affairs (as required by Item 11 of Form S-3) are set forth in a prospectus supplement that is delivered to investors together with the base prospectus, and the securities are issued pursuant to preestablished procedures with the underwriters or selling agent and, in the case of debt securities, the trustee. Although the prospectus supplement and, in some cases, final forms of the securities or related documents are filed with the SEC at the time of a "takedown," the SEC does not ordinarily review these filings.

Questions sometimes arise as to whether the terms of a particular security have been adequately foreshadowed in the base prospectus as to justify the mere filing of a prospectus supplement rather than a post-effective amendment. In connection with "novel or unique" securities or other product areas that raise these questions, it may be prudent to consult with the SEC staff to ensure that it has no objections to the prospectus supplement approach.

• *Shelf Updating Procedures*

There are limits on the degree to which the SEC's rules permit a shelf registration statement to be updated by means of incorporation by reference of the issuer's 1934 Act filings. In certain situations, the SEC insists on an opportunity to review new information before an offering can proceed, and in other situations the new information must be incorporated by reference in a particular manner.

Item 512(a) of Regulation S-K implements these SEC policies by requiring specific undertakings from issuers that file registration statements under Rule 415. These undertakings require that certain updating be accomplished by means of a post-effective amendment to the registration statement. Unlike mere prospectus supplements, post-effective amendments are subject to SEC review (which may require 48 hours or longer) and must be declared effective before the related prospectus may be used in confirming sales. Moreover, another undertaking specifies that any post-effective amendment starts the clock running anew for purposes of the statute of limitations contained in Section 13 of the 1933 Act.

Pursuant to the undertakings, a post-effective amendment must be filed to incorporate information into the registration statement that is for the purpose of:

- including any prospectus required by Section 10(a)(3) of the 1933 Act (which provides that any prospectus used more than nine months after the effective date of a registration statement must contain information as of a date not more than 16 months prior to its use);

- reflecting in the prospectus any facts or events arising after the effective date of the registration statement (or the most recent post-effective amendment) that, individually or in the aggregate, represent a "fundamental change" in the information set forth therein; and

- including any material information with respect to the plan of distribution not disclosed in the registration statement or any material change to such information.

Item 512 specifies that the first two undertakings do not apply to registration statements on Form S-3 or Form F-3 if the relevant information is contained in a 1934 Act report that is incorporated by reference in the registration statement. The SEC has said that a "fundamental change" is something more than a "material change" and has given examples of the differences. It has stated that, while many variations and matters such as operating results, properties, business, product development, backlog, management, and litigation ordinarily would not be fundamental, major changes in the issuer's operations, such as significant acquisitions or dispositions, would require the filing of a post-effective amendment. Also, any change in the business or operations of the registrant that would necessitate a restatement of the financial statements would be a fundamental change. But as material changes, to say nothing of fundamental changes, will be included in regularly filed 1934 Act reports (with accompanying press releases), it has not been necessary for issuers or their counsel to trouble themselves with close calls as to what is fundamental rather than simply material.[56]

As originally adopted, the required undertaking to file a post-effective amendment to reflect a change in the plan of distribution ended with the words "including (but not limited to) any addition or deletion of a managing underwriter." Rule 405 contained a broad definition of the term "managing underwriter," but the staff construed it sensibly to cover only an underwriter who actually performed a management function. Primarily because of this undertaking, the early shelf registration statements named a number of potential managing underwriters.

The undertaking operated in a rather strange fashion. If a registration statement contemplated offerings directly by the issuer or through three named investment banking firms or underwriting syndicates managed by one or more of them, the members of a syndicate managed by any one or more of the designated firms could be named in a sticker, and a post-effective amendment would not be required. If a firm not previously named were to co-manage a syndicate with one or more of the named underwriters, no post-effective amendment would be required even if the new firm acted as the book-running manager. But if that firm acted as the sole manager of a subsequent offering, a post-effective

---

56. It should be noted that the "fundamental" as opposed to "material" dichotomy adopted by the SEC to determine when a post-effective amendment will be required flies in the face of the traditional analysis that a post-effective amendment should be used to change or correct a statement in an effective registration statement while a supplement should be used to reflect a development that has occurred after the registration statement has become effective. Professor Loss's classic example is that if a registration statement discloses that the issuer owns 500 acres of timberland and a subsequent survey shows that it owns only 250 acres, then a post-effective amendment is required to correct the error. If, however, the registration statement correctly discloses that the issuer owns 500 acres, and after effectiveness, a forest fire destroys the timber on half of these acres, then a supplement filed under Rule 424 is the proper means of reflecting this material, perhaps fundamental, change in the registrant's affairs. 1 L. Loss & J. Seligman, *Securities Regulation* 550–51 (3d ed. 1989).

amendment would be required even though it had been named in the previous supplement and even though its management of the earlier offering would have satisfied the SEC's rationale for requiring a post-effective amendment, namely, the need to create a "pause" in the process to "facilitate underwriter involvement with the registration statement when such a material change in the plan of distribution occurs."

What would happen if an unnamed firm initiated a "bought deal" and did not invite a named firm to act as a co-manager? Initially, the staff had no ready answer and determined to proceed on a case-by-case basis to resolve questions of this type.

In its September 2, 1982 release extending the effectiveness of Rule 415, the SEC noted that two principal interpretive questions had arisen in the course of administering Rule 415. These were (1) determining those circumstances in which a person would be deemed to be a managing underwriter and (2) whether it was necessary under particular circumstances to proceed by means of a post-effective amendment or a prospectus supplement. Recognizing that a post-effective amendment would often have adverse consequences for a transaction, the SEC amended Rule 415 to delete the requirement to undertake to file a post-effective amendment to reflect the addition or deletion of a managing underwriter. This action made it unnecessary to name any underwriters in the first place and afforded issuers the flexibility of doing deals quickly with whatever firm might come along and offer attractive terms.

Currently, issuers avoid problems under the third undertaking by describing the plan of distribution in the base prospectus in terms that are as broad as possible.

A further undertaking relates to the incorporation by reference of the issuer's annual report on Form 10-K filed under the 1934 Act. This document, which constitutes the principal part of any registration statement on Form S-3, need not be filed as part of a post-effective amendment. The issuer must undertake, however, that, for purposes of the statute of limitations contained in Section 13, each filing of a Form 10-K that is incorporated by reference will be deemed to be a new registration statement relating to the offered securities and that the initial bona fide offering of such securities is deemed to commence as of the time of such filing. The effect of the undertaking, of course, is to make the issuer and other persons who may be named as defendants under Section 11 potentially liable under that section for the registration statement as updated by the Form 10-K. No such undertaking applies to the incorporation by reference of the issuer's quarterly reports on Form 10-Q, and there would appear to be no Section 11 liability for such reports.

• *At-The-Market Equity Offerings*

Under Rule 415, certain requirements must be met in the case of a shelf registration statement pertaining to an issuer's at-the-market offering of equity securities. The requirements apply to an offering of equity securities by an issuer "into an existing trading market for outstanding shares of the same class at other than a fixed price on or through the facilities of a national securities exchange or to or through a market maker otherwise than on an exchange." To effect this type of offering, the registrant must qualify for Form S-3 or Form F-3. Where voting stock is registered, the amount registered for the purpose of the at-the-market offering may not exceed 10% of the aggregate market value of the registrant's outstanding voting stock held by non-affiliates (calculated as of a date within 60 days prior to the date of filing). Finally, the offering must be made through one or more named underwriters acting as principal or as agent for the issuer.

Shelf Filings by Foreign Governments or Political Subdivisions

Rule 415 does not provide for registration on a delayed or continuous basis of securities issued or guaranteed by a foreign government or one of its political subdivisions. As discussed in Chapter 9, these issuers are not eligible to use Form F-3. Instead, they register their securities under Schedule B to the 1933 Act. They are not subject to the continuous reporting requirements of the 1934 Act unless they choose to list their securities on an exchange. Nonetheless, the SEC has adopted procedures that allow "seasoned" foreign governments to file shelf registrations in a manner similar to that specified in Rule 415. Even before Rule 415 was first proposed, the Kingdom of Sweden was permitted to register for shelf debt securities to be

sold from time to time in the United States. The base prospectus contained the same type of political, economic, and statistical information contained in prospectuses previously used by
the Kingdom in selling its debt securities. The registration statement contemplated the filing by post-effective amendment of
preliminary and final prospectus supplements, similar to a Form
S-16 prospectus, for each issue. According to the correspondence with the SEC permitting the filing, the procedure was
designed to provide Sweden with substantially the same benefits as a Form S-16 registrant.[57]

The SEC followed up with a release setting forth the views
of the Division of Corporation Finance on the use of registration statements for delayed offerings by foreign governments.[58]
In effect, the SEC invited other foreign governments that previously had filed registration statements to follow the same procedures as those developed for the Kingdom of Sweden.

In September 1982, at the same time that it extended the
effectiveness of Rule 415, the SEC published a revised staff
interpretation regarding foreign government shelf registration
statements.[59] When the SEC adopted Rule 415 on a permanent
basis in November 1983, it reaffirmed the September 1982 staff
position and concluded that it allowed seasoned foreign governments to use the shelf registration procedure in a manner substantially similar to that specified in Rule 415.

The shelf procedure continued to be applicable to seasoned
foreign governments and their political subdivisions, i.e., those
that had registered securities (or guarantees of the securities of
others) within the past five years and had not defaulted in the
payment of principal or interest.[60] The original procedure required the annual filing of a registration statement of securities

---

57. SEC No-action Letter, *Kingdom of Sweden* (available September 10,
1980).

58. SEC Release No. 33-6240 (September 10, 1980).

59. SEC Release No. 33-6424 (September 2, 1982).

60. This definition had first been established in SEC No-action Letter,
Republic of Venezuela (available November 24, 1980). An otherwise "non-
seasoned" non-U.S. governmental issuer wishing to conduct a delayed or
continuous offering may satisfy the seasoning requirement by first filing a

to be offered on a "firm commitment" basis during a period of 12 months from the effective date. Under the revised procedure, foreign governments could register an amount reasonably expected to be offered and sold within two years, the same amount that could be registered under Rule 415. The requirement of a firm commitment underwriting was later eliminated. The original procedure contemplated two supplements, a preliminary supplement and a final supplement that would contain the pricing information, and that the base prospectus containing the Schedule B information would accompany both the preliminary supplement and the final supplement. Under the revised procedure, if the registrant had previously furnished a person with a copy of its base prospectus, it need only deliver prospectus supplements to that person. The supplements were required to state that a copy of the base prospectus would be furnished promptly, without charge, upon request.

The Division of Corporation Finance has no objection to an issuer's including in the base prospectus all the information included in the prospectus supplements under the original procedure except for "price, maturity, and related information." That information can be furnished by means of a Rule 424 sticker instead of in a post-effective amendment. A condition to using this procedure is that the base prospectus be "adequately disseminated to the public" a reasonable period of time before the offering.

The SEC has issued no-action letters to several "seasoned" Schedule B issuers[61] in which it has allowed these issuers to use a special procedure to update their registration statements and to comply with the disclosure requirements under the 1933 Act. Under this procedure, the issuer voluntarily files an annual

---

registration statement for a discrete offering of securities. It may then file a shelf registration immediately following completion of the first offering.

61. E.g., United Mexican States (February 25, 1994), Nacional Financiera, S.N.C. (July 5, 1994), Kreditanstalt für Wiederaufbau and Kfw Int'l Finance Inc. (July 18, 1994), Republic of Portugal (July 22, 1994), Japan Dev. Bank, et al. (August 3, 1994), Ontario Hydro (October 31, 1994), Commonwealth of Australia (April 4, 1995), Government of Victoria and Treasury Corp. of Victoria (June 23, 1995).

report on Form 18-K and amendments to the annual report on Form 18-KA. These filings are then incorporated by reference into the issuer's Schedule B registration statements, including its shelf registrations.

The annual Form 18-K includes all information required by the form and any additional information required to be included in a Schedule B registration statement together with any other information deemed material to investors. The Form 18-KA amendments are filed as necessary and include, for example, such information as the interim financial reports of the issuer, its annual budget and any additional information deemed necessary or appropriate for disclosure purposes.

When the registration statement is filed under Schedule B, the base prospectus incorporates by reference the most recently filed Form 18-K, including all amendments. Incorporation of the filed Form 18-K and any Form 18-KA effectively relieves the issuer of the need to file annual post-effective amendments to its shelf registration statement.

Conventional Debt and Preferred Stock Shelf Registrations

A Rule 415 shelf registration is a vehicle ideally suited to issuers of investment-grade debt securities eligible to use Form S-3 or Form F-3 that seek access to the capital markets on a regular basis. It is also well suited to continuous MTN offerings, which will be examined later in this chapter.

Market overhang is not a significant factor for high-grade debt, and the ability to move quickly to take advantage of market windows is important in the debt market. The same can be said for straight preferred stock, and a significant number of issuers have registered preferred stock to be sold off the shelf. Rule 415 does not require an investment-grade rating as a condition to filing, but the rule has not been used as often by issuers of high-yield securities. Many of these issues are sold under Rule 144A, often on a one-shot basis with a heavy degree of marketing.

Once a company decides to file a shelf registration statement covering its debt securities or straight preferred stock, there are certain procedures to be put in place and numerous documents to be drafted. The key to the process is to provide for maximum flexibility and the ability to accomplish a take-down from the shelf in a matter of hours. If the proper structure is created, there should seldom be a need for a post-effective amendment when the securities are sold.

If the company has a significant relationship with an invest-ment banking firm, it may be helpful to bring it into the loop at an early stage to take advantage of its expertise. Many issuers will not do so in the interest of maintaining their own indepen-dence or in order to keep the playing field level for all potential underwriters.

It is strongly recommended that a law firm be designated as counsel for the underwriters or other purchasers of the securi-ties. If a firm is appointed to act in this capacity, it should be allowed to participate in the establishment of the program. Such participation will facilitate the first takedown, which would oth-erwise be held up while counsel became familiar with the rel-evant disclosure and documentation.

• *Securities To Be Registered*

The company should review its financial needs and make a reasoned estimate of the amount of securities that it expects to sell over the next two years. While the SEC is not likely to second guess a registrant, there is no reason to go overboard. Remember that the filing fee for a billion dollar shelf is more than $300,000. On the other hand, a shelf covering less than $150 million of debt securities is hardly worth the effort.

The question sometimes arises whether immediate take-downs from a shelf registration statement are permitted. At one point, the SEC condemned the use of shelf registration for the purpose of "procedural convenience," i.e., the ability to facili-ate an immediate securities offering by having a registration statement become effective \ ithout all required information.[62] The SEC's objections lost their force with the adoption of Rule 430A, and the SEC has since confirmed that immediate take-downs are permissible. The registration statement at the time it becomes effective, however, must include all material informa-

---

62. SEC Release No. 33-6499 (November 17, 1983) (text at note 31).

tion to the extent it is known or reasonably available to the issuer. "Accordingly, if an offering of securities is certain at the time the shelf registration statement becomes effective, the relevant information (e.g., description of securities, plan of distribution and use of proceeds) must be disclosed with respect to the securities subject to the immediate takedown . . ."[63]

• *Plan of Distribution*

Rule 415 merely sets forth a procedure for registering securities. It does not mandate any particular method of distribution. Many issuers file shelf registrations with no intention of selling securities other than in conventional underwritings managed by their traditional investment banker. They have been successful in the past in raising funds in this fashion, and they see no reason to change simply because they are using a shelf registration statement. Although there is no longer any legal reason to name potential underwriters in the base prospectus, some issuers will name their traditional banker as a potential underwriter while maintaining the flexibility of using another firm. In a traditional type of underwritten transaction off a shelf, the deal will be structured, there will be price talk with potential purchasers, and the underwriters will build a book, all before an underwriting commitment is made.

For the more frequent issuers, the so-called "commodity" issuers of debt securities, the process is far less refined. An assistant treasurer may place phone calls to the capital markets desks of three or four underwriting houses and solicit bids for an amount of securities with a specified maturity. In some cases, the amount and maturity will be left open. A response will be expected within the hour. The firms will go through an exercise that they refer to as a "fire drill," calling upon the resources of sales, trading, and syndicate personnel in coming up with a bid. The best bid may not be the winner. Issuers have been known to shop bids.

The winning bidder will have entered into a bought deal; it will have agreed to purchase the securities before beginning its marketing efforts. It may have tested the market a bit, but it

---

63. SEC Release No. 33-7168 (May 11, 1995) (text following note 39).

will not have built a book before agreeing on a price. It may get together a small group of major bracket New York-based firms to join in a syndicate to spread the risk. But, in any case, it must scurry around and try to unload the securities at a profit. In all likelihood, the securities will wind up in the hands of a small number of institutional investors.

There is fierce competition for bought deals among the top New York-based firms. The spreads are thin. In some swap-driven transactions, underwriters have been known to bid with a negative spread in order to obtain the fee for arranging the currency or interest rate swap.

There have been bids that would appear to make little economic sense. The bidder may have been seeking to buy an introduction to a potential corporate client. Or it may have been trying to build its position in the published standings or "league tables."[64] It may be that its primary interest was in having its name appear in a tombstone advertisement along with a top-grade issuer.

In doing bought deals, the risk-reward ratio is weighted heavily on the risk side. Without an accurate forward calendar to rely upon, underwriters are unable to gauge the potential supply of debt securities coming to market, an important consideration in making a pricing decision. Some bought deals have resulted in spectacular, well-publicized losses for the firms involved. In other cases, they have generated windfall profits as the market took a sudden favorable turn after the underwriting commitment was made.

Deals may be done without an issuer soliciting bids. In the Rule 415 environment, issuers are besieged with creative financing proposals to be done off the shelf. Many of the ideas are good ones that fit the issuer's needs. This is one of the reasons why flexibility is essential, not only with respect to timing but also with respect to the terms of the securities. As stated in an article on innovative debt securities:

---

64. One widely-followed version of such tables is compiled periodically by *Investment Dealers' Digest.*

It became customary for lawyers to receive urgent calls from investment bankers to the effect that "We have a purchaser for $20 million zero-coupon debt of X Corporation. Can this be done today off X Corporation's shelf?" Or "We have a swap for 100 million New Zealand dollars. Can New Zealand dollar denominated securities be issued under Y Corporation's shelf? And can we sell them in Europe in bearer form?" Perhaps neither shelf was drafted with zero-coupon or foreign currency denominated bearer debt securities expressly in mind, but with sufficient flexibility in the documents the transaction could go forward.[65]

Direct sales to institutional investors without the use of an underwriter has not become an accepted method of distribution. Perhaps issuers realize that if they bypass the traditional distribution channels, those channels may not be around when they need them. An exception that proves the rule was a Dutch auction in 1982 of $135 million of debt securities of Exxon Corporation.[66]

However the securities are marketed in fact, the plan of distribution set forth in the base prospectus should be drafted so broadly that the undertaking to file a post-effective amendment

---

65. N.D. Slonaker & L.M. Wiltshire, *Innovative Debt Securities,* 20 Rev. Sec. & Com. Reg. 89, 90 (1987).

66. The mechanics of a Dutch auction are described in a 1977 SEC no-action letter issued to a subsidiary of Exxon Corporation. Each bidder, including institutions and individuals as well as broker-dealers, indicates the amount of debt securities to be purchased and the yield. "After closing the invitation period, the bids are listed in ascending order of yields. The bid with the lowest yield is accepted first, and then other bids at successively higher yields are accepted up to those bids with the highest yield required to reach the total amount of the offering. The highest accepted yield is the yield at which all of the bonds are awarded. Upon determination of the yield, the interest rate and price are fixed by the issuer. The securities will be awarded to the successful bidders at a uniform price based on the accepted yield." SEC No-action Letter, *Exxon Corporation* (available May 9, 1977). *See also* SEC No-action Letter, *Salomon Brothers* (available August 22, 1985).

to reflect a material change in the plan of distribution will never come into play.

• *The Indenture and the Description of the Securities*

A single shelf registration statement may cover both senior and subordinated debt securities, and a single trustee may serve for the holders of both classes of securities unless and until there is a default.

Indentures for shelf programs should be open-ended. There should be no limitation on the amount of debt securities that may be issued thereunder. The indenture will set forth the terms and provisions that are common to all of the securities that may be issued. It should be drafted in such a way that when each series of debt is issued a supplemental indenture will not be required. Rather, the terms of each series should be permitted to be set forth in an officer's certificate delivered to the trustee. The variable terms also will be set forth in the body of the securities.

The indenture should be drafted so broadly that any conceivable type of debt can be issued thereunder. It should provide for original issue discount securities (zero coupon obligations or those bearing a rate of interest below market rates). In the case of a deep discount security, the full principal amount will not be payable upon the acceleration of maturity (in the event of default or the operation of some other indenture provision), and the indenture should provide that, in such case, the amount payable will be included in the terms of the security. The indenture should provide that the securities may be issued in registered form or in bearer form with coupons attached. This will accommodate sales in the Euromarket and elsewhere outside of the United States. Provision should be made for obligations denominated in foreign currencies as well as United States dollars. The indenture should permit the issuance of floating rate obligations, as well as those with a fixed interest rate. It should be broad enough to allow puttable bonds and securities with extendible maturities.

In dealing with separate series of obligations under a single indenture, care should be taken to assure that action by the holders of debt of a particular series is sufficient in appropriate cases and that the holders of other series of debt need not be involved. For example, an amendment of the indenture should require the consent of the holders of a specified percentage of the debt securities of each series affected thereby. Likewise, in the event of default with respect to debt securities of a particular series, only the holders of that series of debt should have rights with respect to the declaration of acceleration, rescission of any declaration of acceleration, and waiver of events of default. The indenture should permit an existing series of obligations to be reopened, so that additional securities of the same series can be issued at a later date. For example, in May 1989, Merrill Lynch & Co., Inc. issued two series of Floating Rate Renewable Notes and a month later reopened the two series and offered additional notes with identical terms and provisions. Reopening an existing series is a rare occurrence.

The base prospectus will contain a description of the debt securities and the indenture or indentures under which they are to be issued. It will refer to the prospectus supplement for a description of the terms of the securities of the particular series to which it relates: their designation (e.g., by coupon and maturity); any limit on the aggregate principal amount; the percentage of their principal amount at which the securities will be issued and, in the case of original issue discount securities, the principal amount payable upon acceleration of maturity; the date or dates on which the securities will mature or the manner in which those dates are determined; the rate or rates per annum (which may be fixed or variable) at which the securities will bear interest, if any, or the method of determining the rate or rates; the date from which interest, if any, will accrue, the dates on which interest will be payable, and the record dates for interest payment dates; the dates, if any, on which, and the price or prices at which, the securities will, pursuant to any mandatory sinking fund provisions, or may, pursuant to any optional sinking fund provisions, be redeemed by the issuer, and the other detailed sinking fund provisions; the date, if any, after which, and the price or prices at which, the securities may, pursuant to any optional redemption provisions, be redeemed at the option of the issuer or of the holder and the other detailed terms and provisions of any optional redemption, including any remarketing arrangements; the form (registered or bearer or both) in which the securities may be issued and any restrictions applicable to the exchange of one form for another and to the offer, sale and delivery of the securities in either form; whether and under what circumstances the issuer will pay additional amounts in respect of any securities held by a person who is not a U.S. person in respect of specified taxes, assessments or other governmental charges and whether the issuer has the option to redeem affected securities rather than pay such additional amounts; whether the securities are to be issued initially or permanently in the form of a global security and, if so, the identity of the depositary for the global security; and the currency, currencies or currency units for which the securities may be purchased and in which they are payable.

• *Preferred Stock*

Preferred stock must be authorized by the issuer's certificate of incorporation. The amount authorized must be a fixed amount, and it may be increased only by action of the board of directors, a stockholder vote and the filing of a certificate of amendment. A charter provision of the type that had been customary long before the adoption of Rule 415 that authorizes the issuance of preferred stock in series should provide the necessary flexibility for a preferred stock shelf program. The terms of each particular series must be set forth in a certificate of designation filed with the secretary of state of the state in which the issuer is incorporated. This requirement will not impede a takedown under a shelf, for the certificate of designation need only be filed prior to the closing at which the securities are issued.

• *Board Authorization*

Before a shelf program can be implemented, the issuer's board of directors must meet to authorize the issuance of the securities to be registered, the filing of the shelf registration statement, the execution of the indenture, and the other matters that customarily are found in a carefully prepared set of resolutions for a financing. A shelf program could not function, however, if it were necessary for the board to meet, even by telephone, each time securities are taken off the shelf. To permit expeditious takedowns, the board must delegate to a special committee, or preferably to specified officers, the authority to determine the amount of securities for each tranche and the terms of the securities to be sold.

When Rule 415 was first adopted, there was some question as to the extent to which boards of directors would be willing to give up control over specific issues of debt securities. As debt shelf registration statements have become commonplace, this concern has faded, and boards of major companies seem quite comfortable in delegating to senior officers discretion as to the timing, size and terms of debt issues. Lawyers practicing in the area of corporate finance likewise are comfortable that, as a matter of state law, a board of directors can delegate borrowing authority to individuals holding specified offices in the corporation and that these officers may be authorized by the board to redelegate this authority to subordinates under their direction. Indeed, in the case of MTNs, which are sold on a continuous basis, it is not unusual for the pricing of individual notes to be the responsibility of an employee other than a senior officer. The pricing of debt should be contrasted to the pricing of an issue of common stock. Most lawyers take the position that the pricing of a common stock issue may be delegated by the board only to the executive committee or to a special committee of directors authorized by statute. (This does not preclude delegation by reference to current market prices.)

The creation of a series of preferred stock requires action by the board of directors or at least a special committee of the board. This is because the applicable corporate statute will require a certificate of designation adopted by the board. Perhaps the board will allow the corporate officers to authorize a preferred stock tranche under the issuer's shelf registration, but any such action must be subject to formal corporate action before the stock can be issued.

• *Underwriting Documents*

All of the investment banking firms that are players in the shelf arena have in place master AAUs, so that no agreement need be signed by the underwriters when a syndicate is put together to take securities off the shelf. When Rule 415 first was adopted on a temporary basis and it was necessary for issuers to name a number of potential managing underwriters in order to avoid the delay inherent in a post-effective amendment, it became the custom to enter into a basic underwriting agreement with the underwriters named in the prospectus and to use a terms agreement for each takedown. The underwriting agreement with the form of terms agreement attached would be filed as an exhibit to the registration statement, and it was unnecessary to make a subsequent filing when the terms agreement was filled in and signed. In many cases, these underwriting agreements continue to operate.

An issuer that has not named underwriters in its shelf prospectus also will file a standard underwriting agreement as an exhibit to its registration statement, but it is not pre-signed. Rather, the underwriting agreement with the filled-in terms is signed at the time that the underwriters commit to purchase the securities. There is little difference in the two procedures. Whether the managing underwriter signs a terms agreement, having previously signed an underwriting agreement, or whether it signs an underwriting agreement with the terms attached, a single signature will be required when the takedown is made, and the transaction can be completed just as expeditiously whichever procedure is followed.

The terms of the underwriting agreement will be basically the same as those found in the issuer's pre-Rule 415 underwriting agreements. The closing will be set for three business days after the takedown from the shelf or such longer period as may be agreed to pursuant to the SEC's "T+3" rule (see Chapter 3). The standard legal opinions, comfort letter and officer's certificate will be required as conditions to closing. In the case of a bought deal, there may be no comfort letter at the time that the underwriting agreement is signed, but only at the closing. This differs from the standard practice in conventional underwritten offerings. The underwriting agreement will contain the usual indemnification and contribution provisions.

An "out" clause that has become quite customary in underwriting agreements for shelf programs that was not in vogue prior to the adoption of Rule 415 is one that allows the underwriters to terminate their commitment if the issuer's debt securities are downgraded by one of the rating agencies. Underwriting agreements may also permit the underwriters to terminate their obligation to purchase the securities if any facts come to their attention that lead them to believe that the prospectus is false or misleading. It is quite common for the issuer to agree with the underwriters that it will not issue any similar securities under its shelf until the closing or the earlier sale of the securities by the underwriters.

There have been some complaints that designated underwriters' counsel has little leverage in negotiating the terms of the underwriting agreement. This complaint simply reflects the fact that a lawyer has little leverage in negotiations if he or she does not have a client at the table. Some underwriters simply will not bid on an issuer's securities if they are unhappy with the underwriting terms (e.g., the "market out" or the indemnity or contribution provisions). If they would otherwise be interested in bidding, they will often inform the issuer of the source of their concern. The issuer may ignore this concern if it believes that enough other firms are participating to guarantee vigorous competition. If it concludes at some point that it can use the services of the excluded firm in order to reinvigorate competition, it may volunteer a modification that will bring the excluded firm back into the fold.

• *Disclosure and Due Diligence*

The ABA's Federal Regulation of Securities Committee appointed a task force in 1990 to study the effect of shelf registration, integrated disclosure and related developments on underwriters' ability to perform due diligence sufficient to sustain a defense under Section 11 or Section 12(a)(2) of the 1933 Act. The task force described in depth in the following excerpt from its report[67] the disclosure and due diligence process associated with shelf takedowns of investment grade debt securities:

The issuers eligible to use rule 415 for primary shelf offerings on a delayed basis are those eligible to use

---

67. ABA Committee on Federal Regulation of Securities, *Report of Task Force on Sellers' Due Diligence and Similar Defenses Under the Federal Securities Laws*, 48 Bus. Law. 1185, 1218–24 (1993) (some footnotes omitted).

Forms S-3 and F-3 . . . As such, the issuers for the most part are established companies about which there is relatively wide dissemination of the information contained in the 1934 Act reports. The debt securities of most shelf issuers are rated by the rating agencies.

The buyers of shelf-registered debt securities are almost exclusively institutional investors. As in the secondary market, decisions to buy are made on the basis of yield (premium over Treasury securities of comparable maturity), rating information, and the name of the issuer. The name of the issuer is particularly important in the case of investors such as insurance companies with internal credit evaluation capabilities and well-defined procedures for approving issuers' securities for purchase. Where the investor has previously approved the name, securities of the issuer are treated more or less as commodities with yield and rating information becoming the key ingredients to a purchase decision. Where an issuer's name is relatively new or little-known in the debt markets, one or more investment banking firms may work with investors' credit analysts or investment committees to explain the issuer's credit and seek to have the name approved.

The disclosure document for a shelf offering is the short-form basic prospectus contained in the registration statement, as supplemented at the time of the offering by a prospectus supplement that describes the offered securities and, to the extent necessary, updates previously reported information concerning the issuer. The basic prospectus incorporates by reference the issuer's 1934 Act reports filed prior to and subsequent to the registration statement's effective date.

Although there is considerable variation, most prospectus/prospectus supplement combinations contain, at most, very abbreviated financial and business disclosure concerning the issuer. Frequently, the prospectus/prospectus supplement combination will contain only a table of selected financial information and a very brief business description. Less frequently there will be a management's discussion and analysis ["MD&A"] or an MD&A summary. Financial statements rarely are included. Accordingly, normally most, if not all, of the key information for an informed credit decision—the financial statements, the complete MD&A and the full description of the issuer's business—are in the incorporated documents. The incorporated documents are, of course, equally available to the buyers of the securities and the potential underwriters on an ongoing basis.

While practice varies, potential underwriters sometimes are invited to review and comment on shelf registration statements prior to their filing. In such cases, the underwriters have the opportunity to review, on a more traditional time schedule, the disclosures included and incorporated by reference in the registration statement and to make adjustments to the sum total of the disclosures contained therein through adjustments to the registration statement. Frequently, however, potential underwriters are not invited to participate in the filing of a shelf registration statement, and obviously they are not invited when they have not been identified (which very frequently is the case).

Following effectiveness of the shelf registration statement, there is considerable variation in the ongoing business relationships between the issuer and potential underwriters and in the access that is afforded underwriters to perform an ongoing investigation in anticipation of shelf takedowns. As to ongoing business relationships, there is a whole spectrum of possibilities. In some cases, the issuer of shelf-registered debt securities will tend to be in more or less continuous consultation with one or a small group of investment banking firms and, as market conditions warrant, sell a portion of the registered securities through one or more such firms on a negotiated basis. In other cases, the issuer will invite a relatively large number of investment banking firms (i) to make proposals from time to time with respect to the type of shelf-registered security that may be sold on favorable terms under current market conditions or (ii) bid, in an auction-like process, for a security identified in advance by the issuer. In still other cases, an issuer may respond favorably to an unsolicited proposal from an investment banking firm that may or may not have a pre-existing relationship with the issuer. Because market conditions change rapidly, the time between presentation of a proposal and a commitment to proceed can be a few hours or even minutes.

Importantly, the use of bid-like procedures has transformed shelf underwriting into a transaction-oriented business as opposed to a relationship-oriented business. Attendant to this, there is a reduced level of familiarity between many underwriters and issuers and, realistically, a substantially reduced level of influence that these underwriters may bring to bear on the disclosures made in the issuer's disclosure documents, particularly in the circumstance where the underwriter has not participated in the preparation of the registration statement or, as discussed *infra*, the incorporated documents. The underwriter functions less as a trusted adviser and more as a trader. Competition among underwriters is fierce and, realistically, issuers have little incentive to cooperate with any one underwriter who raises a disclosure concern or who insists on its "standard" documentation or closing conditions. Shelf takedowns may occur months after the effective date of the shelf registration statement, and there may be long periods when there are no offerings taken off a shelf registration statement. New underwriters may become involved, having no history with the issuer or the registration statement.

There is a range of practices by which issuers permit underwriters to conduct updating due diligence investigations following the effective date of the registration statement. Some issuers stay in relatively frequent communication with one or a small number of prospective underwriters for the purpose of providing them with a more or less continuous flow of information about the issuer and its financing needs. Frequent issuers may hold annual or even quarterly "due diligence" meetings with prospective underwriters. Other issuers provide prospective underwriters with relatively little information on a continuous basis, although the issuers' periodic reports under the 1934 Act are of course available for review. When a decision is reached to proceed with a particular offering, there is usually a "due diligence" conference call involving representatives of the issuer and of the underwriters (or, if there are many underwriters, the lead or managing underwriters). Where due diligence investigations were performed at the time of filing of the registration statement and at periodic intervals thereafter, this conference call may merely serve to update the underwriters with respect to the most current information. In circumstances where no investigation was performed at the time of filing of the registration statement and/or periodically thereafter, however, this conference call may serve as the underwriters' sole investigation, at least during the issuer's current reporting period. Underwriters are making more frequent use of their equity analysts and credit departments as a means of identifying "red flags" relating to a particular issuer.

Following effectiveness, identified potential underwriters sometimes may be invited to comment on drafts of documents prepared for the purpose of subsequent filing and incorporation by reference, although frequently and perhaps routinely they are not afforded this opportunity. As a practical matter, many issuers are unwilling to discuss unfiled draft 1934 Act reports with a group of potential underwriters out of concern that leaks of such information will occur and affect trading in the issuer's securities. While issuers may be willing to discuss draft reports with an underwriter with whom they have a long-term relationship, many issuers view the risk of such discussions with other potential underwriters as an unwarranted risk.

In the case of most issuers utilizing the shelf takedown method of distribution, the issuer or the prospective underwriters, assuming they are a relatively small and discrete group, will designate one law firm to act as counsel for the underwriters of the shelf-registered securities on the occasion of each particular offering. The underwriters of each particular offering are responsible for paying this law firm's fees and disbursements, including those associated with the "startup" and maintenance of the shelf facility. The use of one counsel typically serves to provide continuity throughout the life of the shelf registration. Designated underwriters' counsel may review and participate in the filing of the registration statement. On an ongoing basis, the designated counsel may or may not be afforded an opportunity to comment on drafts of the issuer's annual, quarterly and other reports before they are filed with the SEC. It will participate in any annual or quarterly "due diligence" meetings, if the issuer arranges for any, again at the expense of the underwriters of future takedowns. Counsel's activity in this regard will otherwise be confined to updating its document review at the time of a particular underwriting and participating in any "due diligence" conference call or meeting relating to the particular underwriting.

The continuity provided by designated underwriters' counsel serves an important "bridging" function in linking the due diligence efforts of successive underwriters. For example, where the underwriter of a particular takedown is an investment banking firm that has not acted recently as underwriter for the issuer, the underwriter naturally takes a degree of comfort from counsel's ability to describe, for example, the areas of investigation that received emphasis on prior offerings. The new underwriter is then able to allocate its due diligence resources accordingly.

There are severe limitations, however, on what counsel can do in the absence of an underwriting client. An underwriter is more often better equipped from the standpoint of business and financial expertise to identify the weak points in an issuer's business and financial condition and to assess the adequacy of an issuer's disclosure in this regard. And whatever counsel's degree of activity on a particular takedown or even between takedowns, it is still the underwriter that is exposed to liability and that has the burden of establishing a "due diligence" defense.

During the period between pricing and closing, the "winning" underwriter and its counsel may still conduct due diligence. As a practical matter, of course, the underwriter's only recourse if a disclosure problem is identified during this period is to decline to go forward, relying on such "outs" in the underwriting agreement as the absence of a clean opinion of issuer's counsel or underwriters' counsel. Underwriters are reluctant to pull deals, however, especially if significant effort has been invested in the transaction or there is a danger that the issuer might accuse the underwriter of reneging on its commitment. For this reason, an underwriter will call off the deal only in the event of a very clear and serious disclosure problem.

Although it may seem too obvious to require special mention, any inquiries made between pricing and closing are part of the underwriter's "investigation" for purposes of the due diligence defense. It is true that, as to underwriters, the accuracy of the registration statement is assessed for section 11 purposes as of the date of pricing (date of purchase by the underwriter), but this is irrelevant. What is important is that the underwriter retains the ability not to close if its inquiries turn up a significant disclosure problem.

Competition among prospective underwriters to offer the issuer the best "all-in" cost of funds on any particular offering has led to pressure on underwriters' compensation in shelf-registered debt offerings. The disclosed "spread" for a particular offering may not tell the whole story, given the possibility of market losses in the event that the security was priced away from the market. The frequent practice of "at-the-market" offerings, combined with the frequent use of swaps or other derivative products in connection with an offering, also makes it difficult to quantify the degree to which under-writers are making or losing money in shelf-registered offerings.

Pressure on underwriting compensation has also led to pressure on underwriters' ability to pay their coun-sel's fees. This has led, in turn, to a not undesirable review of what areas counsel reasonably should exam-ine in a particular offering. In equity transactions, for example, counsel may no longer routinely do the work necessary to be able to give a validity opinion on all of the issuer's outstanding stock. Despite *BarChris*, even the reading of the issuer's and its subsidiaries' minute books is not immune from analysis on a cost-benefit basis.

In the rule 415 environment of shelf-registered take-downs, underwriters face two practical problems in establishing a due diligence defense under section 11. The first problem relates to the opportunity for and scope of due diligence. When the issuer is in continuous consultation with one or a small group of potential un-derwriters prior to an offering, there sometimes will be time for the underwriters to perform a due diligence investigation of the issuer's current affairs prior to a take-down much in the same manner as would be done prior to a traditional "stand-alone" offering, even where significant time has elapsed from the time of filing of the registration statement or where new underwriters are involved. But other than in this fairly limited circum-stance, when an issuer requests proposals from prospec-tive underwriters, the deadlines are such that the prospective underwriters have little or no opportunity to perform "traditional" due diligence before responding to the request. Realistically, a prospective underwriter interested in making a proposal will be able to review the issuer's 1934 Act reports, consult its equity analyst who follows the issuer, check available information on the issuer's ratings, and assess the issuer's and its man-agement's reputation for avoiding surprises. Of course, the issuer will as a condition of closing be responsible for confirming specific representations and warranties and for furnishing an opinion of its counsel and a "comfort letter" from its accountants; designated underwriters' counsel also will deliver an opinion. To the extent that the opinions cover disclosure matters, they are more qualified than in the case of matters such as due incorporation or the validity of the registered securities.

The task will be easier to the extent that the prospective underwriter has taken advantage of opportunities provided by the issuer for "continuous due diligence" or to the extent that designated underwriters' counsel has been able to review documents between offerings on behalf of underwriters to be designated in the future. (The value of such procedures varies: as was predicted during the debate that led up to the adoption of Rule 415, they suffer from a high degree of abstraction because of the absence of an actual offering and an actual client.) While it is possible to conduct these review procedures—and possibly conduct some face-to-face meetings with the issuer's management—after the underwriter agrees to "take down" the securities and prior to the closing of the transaction, whatever is discovered will have to be extraordinarily significant to justify the dissemination of supplemental disclosure (which will be strongly resisted by the issuer) or cancellation of the underwriter's commitment (which will—especially if issuer's counsel is able to "give the opinion"—expose the underwriter to accusations of reneging and the risk of litigation).

The second problem relates to the content of the registration statement and the underwriter's responsibilities for that content. Under section 11, the liability of the issuer, directors, signing officers and experts is measured as of the registration statement's effective date. Their responsibility with respect to subsequently filed and incorporated 1934 Act reports is presumably subject to section 12(2) [now Section 12(a)(2)]. Under section 11(d), the liability of a securities firm that becomes an underwriter after the effective date is measured at the time the securities firm becomes an underwriter, which may be months after the effective date. By this time the registration statement also will consist of subsequently filed and incorporated reports on Forms 10-Q and 8-K or, in the case of certain foreign private issuers, Form 6-K. Information contained in the registration statement may be out of date, and some such information will not have been updated in all cases by the subsequently filed and incorporated reports. Some information also will have been superseded by issuer announcements and analyst reports.

There is no clear test for the purpose of underwriters' due diligence as to what constitutes the "registration statement" for section 11 purposes at its "effective date", i.e., the date the underwriters become underwriters. In one case, the district court held that, for purposes of issuer liability, accuracy was to be "assessed as of the effective date of the allegedly misleading part of the Registration Statement. For most disclosures that date was . . . [the effective date], but for after-incorporated documents it was the date they were filed."[68] It is easier to express the distinction than it is to find it in practice, however, and underwriters still are forced in many cases to dissipate their limited due diligence resources on documents that no longer correspond to the "mix" of information on the basis of which investors buy the securities. Indeed, the idea of the "registration statement" as the defining document for liability and due diligence purposes is at odds with the SEC's premise of an "efficient capital market."

It should not be overlooked that the rating agencies play a key role in the success of a shelf program covering debt securities or straight preferred stock. They have adapted their procedures to the realities of Rule 415. They will now assign a rating to all of an issuer's debt securities of a specified ranking,

---

68. *Wielgos v. Commonwealth Edison Co.*, 688 F. Supp. 331, 338–40 (N.D. Ill. 1988), *aff'd on other grounds*, 892 F.2d 509 (7th Cir. 1989).

whereas in the days before Rule 415 they would only rate a specific issue. An issuer that expects to successfully carry on a shelf program must establish its credibility with the rating agencies and maintain an open line of communications with the persons responsible for its rating. Periodic rating agency presentations are essential. Investors rely on ratings. So do the people on the capital markets desk that buy the deals. In many respects, the analysis of the rating agencies is more important to them than whatever due diligence their firms may perform. This is one reason for the provision found in shelf underwriting agreements permitting termination in the event of a downgrading.

The question has been raised as to the obligation of underwriters' counsel to confer with a underwriter about to do a bought deal if there is a close call on an item of disclosure and the decision is made—by the issuer and its counsel and by underwriters' counsel—that the disclosure will not be made. The problem is more theoretical than real. Counsel should always be sure that his or her client is aware of any set of facts that gives rise to a close disclosure problem or, for that matter, any set of facts that is disclosed but that may have escaped the client's attention. But the client will not be interested in whether or not the set of facts is disclosed, provided that underwriters' counsel is still willing to render the usual disclosure opinion to the effect that anything that has to be disclosed has in fact been disclosed. Where underwriters' counsel believes that a disclosure should be made and the issuer does not agree, he or she always has the option of withholding or qualifying the disclosure opinion. In situations like this, however, it is important to remember who the real client is. It is probably not the underwriter's representative on the capital markets desk. Even if underwriters' counsel could catch such an individual's attention in the clamor of a trading room, he or she would be in no position to evaluate the business risk and decide whether or not to do the deal. In this instance, the person to contact is the firm's in-house investment banking counsel.

One overlooked phenomenon of shelf registration is that, given volatile market conditions, it can actually raise the quality of due diligence. If a shelf registration statement is filed with a view to effecting a number of future conventional under-writings, the prospective underwriters and their counsel may be in a better position to perform due diligence than if they were not called in until the issuer was ready to do the deal. If an issuer decides to file a shelf so that it will be in a position to have an underwritten offering when a window opens in the debt market, it is in a planning mode. It is far better to work on a registration statement under these circumstances than to be called by an investment banking client on a Monday afternoon and be told that all hands must be in Toledo on the following morning because the company wants to file a registration state-ment on Thursday for a debenture offering to be priced the fol-lowing Monday for effectiveness on Tuesday. It would be far better for all concerned if the company had gone the shelf route and had begun its preparations weeks earlier.

Medium-Term Note Programs

MTNs need not have medium terms. Indeed, the prospec-tuses under which they are sold generally provide that they may have maturities of from nine months to 30 years. MTN pro-grams were first used by finance company subsidiaries of auto-mobile manufacturers to "match fund" automobile loans to dealers and consumers with liabilities of similar maturities and were designed to fill the gap between commercial paper with its maximum maturity of nine months and the minimum prac-ticable maturity of underwritten debt securities (usually in the area of three years).

MTNs were developed by the commercial paper depart-ments of the investment banks, rather than by bankers working in their general corporate finance departments. This is why, even today, MTN programs are frequently promoted and ad-ministered by a specialty group within an investment banking firm, rather than by those bankers who would be called upon to handle a standard underwritten offering of notes or debentures. MTNs are distinguished from other securities not so much by their terms but by the way that they are marketed using tech-niques familiar to commercial paper dealers. The settlement procedures for MTNs also have been borrowed from the world of commercial paper.

MTNs were first developed in the early 1970s when finance companies, traditional issuers of commercial paper, sought to extend the maturities of their paper in order to better match the maturities of their consumer and commercial loans. They came to their commercial paper dealers for help. It was clear that maturities could not be extended beyond 270 days while still relying on the Section 3(a)(3) exemption under which these companies had been issuing their paper. So notes with longer maturities began to be issued in continuous Section 4(2) programs of the type described in Chapter 7. The next development came in the mid-1970s, when a number of finance companies persuaded the SEC to allow them to conduct their programs under a registration statement. As the notes were sold on a continuous basis, the very nature of the programs demanded a shelf registration statement.

Form S-16, the predecessor of Form S-3, was available for primary offerings only if there was a firm commitment underwriting. MTNs, for the most part, were originally sold on an agency basis, and accordingly, the issuers that registered their programs prior to the adoption of Form S-3 were required to file on Form S-1 or Form S-7. This proved to be cumbersome. The related prospectuses tended to be long and required the continuing expense of periodic revision and reprinting since current financial and other information could not be incorporated by reference to 1934 Act filings. The most common procedure followed was to set forth in the prospectus the interest rates for specified ranges, or "bands," of maturities and to change the rates as required by market conditions. Originally, the SEC required a post-effective amendment for this purpose, but in time it permitted interest rates to be changed with a sticker mailed after the fact for filing pursuant to Rule 424.

MTN programs normally provide the flexibility to issue securities with maturities that range from nine months to 30 years or more, although they are usually issued with maturities of two to five years. MTNs are generally sold on a principal or agency basis from a dealer's trading desk with three business-day settlement in same day funds. Payment of principal and interest due at maturity is made in same day funds. Book-entry only MTN programs, with payments through DTC, have become standard.

While the traditional MTN is a fixed-rate, nonredeemable senior debt security, almost all programs provide the flexibility to issue other types of debt securities (e.g., floating rate, zero coupon, amortizing, multi-currency or indexed MTNs). Many MTN programs now offer the flexibility to issue subordinated MTNs. For floating rate MTNs, the most common interest rate indices include LIBOR, bank prime rates, commercial paper composite rates, certificate of deposit composite rates, federal funds rates and Treasury bill rates.[69] Many MTN programs permit takedowns that are denominated in non-U.S. currencies. Most MTN programs are rated investment-grade by at least one nationally recognized rating agency.

While finance companies were the initial users of MTN programs, such programs provide an easy means for many other types of issuers to access the capital markets. MTN programs have been developed to securitize mortgage loans (both fixed and floating rate) and other financial assets, including mortgage-backed securities. Equipment trust certificates have also been marketed on a continuous basis as MTNs.

Despite the availability of registration, some corporate issuers continue to sell MTNs in continuous Section 4(2) programs. A more recent phenomenon has been the reliance on Section 3(a)(2) for note programs conducted by domestic banks and branches and agencies of foreign banks. Branches and agencies of foreign banks adopted these programs with increasing frequency following the reaffirmation by the SEC in September 1986 of the position that it had taken previously on a case-by-case basis that branches and agencies of foreign banks are the functional equivalent of domestic banks and should be treated as such for purposes of Section 3(a)(2).[70]

---

69. Since floating rate MTNs are often issued in connection with interest rate swaps or with interest rate risk insurance strategies, the interest rate indices for floating rate MTNs generally follow the definitional conventions of the International Swap Dealers Association, Inc.

70. SEC Release No. 33-6661 (September 23, 1986).

Traditionally, bank financing had been effected on the holding company level, but as the rating agencies came to view some banks as stronger credits than their holding company parents, it made sense to have the bank as the obligor. Some banks chose to have their obligations classified on their call reports as certificates of deposit, but for a variety of reasons, institutional investors preferred to purchase obligations having the characteristics of corporate notes. As there is no real economic distinction between a certificate of deposit and a note, the banks were able to have their cake and eat it too by calling their obligations "deposit notes." Several offerings of these instruments have been made without an offering circular or other documentation, but for the most part deposit note programs have all of the characteristics of corporate MTN programs, except that the notes are not registered with the SEC.

• *Documentation*

Once established, an MTN program allows the issuer to offer and sell a wide range of debt securities, in varying amounts and maturities, without the need to go through the registration process for each issuance. Each sale requires only that (1) the terms of the sale be agreed upon at pricing (this is frequently done orally with written confirmation) and, in the case of certain principal takedowns, that an update of the most recently delivered comfort letter, legal opinions and officers' certificate be provided, (2) a copy of the existing prospectus and a pricing supplement relating to the sale be delivered to the purchaser, (3) an MTN, either in global or certificated form, be completed by the trustee or issuing and paying agent, as the case may be, upon the issuer's instructions, and (4) a copy of the pricing supplement be filed with the SEC under Rule 424.

Traditionally, the pricing supplement for an MTN offering would include specific selling price information only in the case of agency transactions. In the case of principal takedowns, the supplement might set forth an initial public offering price (subject to its being varied at the election of the broker-dealer) or it might simply state the price at which the broker-dealer had purchased the MTNs from the issuer and that the broker-dealer intended to reoffer the MTNs "at the market." Each purchaser would, of course, receive a confirmation setting forth the exact price paid by that purchaser.

An indenture must be qualified under the Trust Indenture Act of 1939 in respect of shelf-registered MTNs (except in the case of a non-U.S. governmental issuer registering pursuant to Schedule B of the 1933 Act). The trustee under an indenture can be qualified after the securities are registered under the 1933 Act, and it is possible to qualify an indenture with one trustee that relates to both senior and subordinated debt securities. There are two types of indenture normally used for MTN programs, one being restricted to MTNs and the other permitting the issuance of any type of debt security. Both are open-ended in that they do not limit the amount of debt securities that can be issued. The terms of both forms are generally standard, while certain provisions (such as the negative pledge and other covenants, events of default and consolidation and merger provisions) will vary depending on the issuer and its undertakings under outstanding borrowing documents.

One advantage of an indenture not restricted to MTNs is that it permits the issuance of many varieties of debt securities that are limited only in that they must be debt securities. This advantage, however, is available as a practical matter only to issuers eligible to use Form S-3 or Form F-3 since the offering would otherwise not be able to take advantage of delayed offerings under clause (x) of Rule 415(a)(1).

Each investment bank has its own form of agreement providing for the distribution of MTNs to or through one or more dealers by the issuer, although the forms used by the investment banks that participate most actively in the market have become similar in many respects. The issuer will enter into one distribution agreement that will be signed by all the investment banks it has appointed as dealers for the MTNs, and this agreement will govern all sales by these firms acting as principal or agent. The agreement contains basic representations and warranties by the issuer about its business, its financial condition and the MTN program; these representations and warranties will be deemed to be updated as of the time of each sale and issuance. Closing conditions, including officers' certificates, comfort letters and opinions of counsel, as well as the requirement for periodic delivery of officers' certificates, comfort letters and opinions of counsel, are specified. The agreement also contains indemnity and contribution undertakings by the issuer against liabilities arising out of any material misstatement or omission in the prospectus.

Because of the continuous nature and many variables of an MTN program, the issuer will provide for administrative procedures to clarify its role, that of the trustee or issuing and paying agent and the dealers in connection with the offer, sale, issuance, settlement and maturity of the MTNs. Other standard agreements required in connection with an MTN program include an Interest Calculation Agreement between the issuer and the calculation agent (usually the trustee or the issuing and paying agent) that calculates the interest on floating rate MTNs and an Exchange Agency Agreement between the issuer and the exchange rate agent (again, usually the trustee or the issuing and paying agent) that acts in connection with any currency exchange that may be required pursuant to the terms of any MTNs payable other than in U.S. dollars or with an option for payments in U.S. dollars.

• *Registration under Rule 415*

MTN issuers eligible to use Form S-3 or Form F-3 may file a shelf registration statement under clause (x) of Rule 415(a)(1), permitting continuous or delayed offerings. MTN issuers not eligible to use Form S-3 or Form F-3 are limited to continuous offerings under clause (ix). There is more flexibility under clause (x) in being able to issue debt securities generally or even equity securities from a shelf registration statement that permits either continuous or delayed offerings. Moreover, the incorporation by reference advantage offered by Form S-3 and Form F-3 is significant in that it avoids the need for a lengthy prospectus and frequent post-effective amendments. Issuers have, to be sure, registered MTN programs on Form S-1 or Form F-1, but the process requires close coordination between the drafting of 1934 Act reports and the maintenance of the 1933 Act prospectus and registration statement.

It will be recalled that the SEC, in adopting Rule 415 on a permanent basis in 1983, limited the use of shelf registration for "primary" transactions to issuers eligible to use Form S-3. Other issuers could use shelf registration only for "traditional" transactions. MTN programs, of course, are both "traditional" and "primary." It did not take long for the SEC to question whether an issuer not eligible to use Form S-3 could use shelf registration for an MTN program.

A finance company subsidiary of a major insurance company had registered its MTN program on Form S-1 since it was not a 1934 Act reporting company at the time of the original filing. When the company filed its first annual post-effective amendment after the 1983 release, the SEC examiner questioned whether the notes could continue to be registered under Rule 415.

Counsel for the issuer and counsel for the agents were of the opinion that this continuous offering satisfied the requirements of subsection (ix) of the rule. The basis for this opinion was set forth in a letter to the examiner which stated as follows:

> Before filing the Registration Statement Amendment, we, together with counsel for the prospective agents, gave careful consideration to the requirements of Release No. 33-6499. This offering is a traditional shelf registration under paragraph (a)(1)(ix) of revised Rule 415 as set forth and explained in Release No. 33-6499. Paragraph (a)(1)(ix) permits registration of securities "the offering of which will be commenced promptly, will be made on a continuous basis and may continue for a period in excess of 30 days from the date of initial effectiveness." This type of offering is permitted whether or not the issuer qualifies for Form S-3. The Notes have been, and will continue to be, offered precisely in this manner. Of the $200,000,000 of Notes originally registered, an aggregate of $9,000,000 have been sold on a "best efforts basis" in four separate transactions through December 31, 1983, and the remaining $191,000,000 will be priced and sold from time to time with adjustments in pricing occurring as market conditions dictate, which may be weekly or daily. Such

a pattern of continuous distribution of debt securities meets the requirements of paragraph (a)(1)(ix).

Release No. 33-6499 makes it clear that the Commission intended to limit the use of Rule 415 to primary offerings of securities qualified to be registered on Form S-3 or Form F-3 and to "traditional shelf offerings." In the mid-1970s, long before the adoption of Rule 415, the Commission began to permit offerings of debt securities pursuant to shelf registrations by finance companies and finance subsidiaries of industrial companies that borrowed frequently in the capital markets. A number of these companies filed shelf registration statements covering offerings from time to time of medium-term notes with varying maturities and interest rates. These offerings were made directly or through investment banking firms acting as agent or as principal. The distinguishing feature of these offerings was that they were made on a continuous basis rather than on a delayed basis as is often the case with Rule 415 filings.

Among the traditional shelf registration statements covering medium-term notes was a $200,000,000 medium-term note filing on Form S-7 made by Ford Motor Credit Company in March 1973. Other companies that filed for continuous offerings of medium-term notes prior to the adoption of Rule 415 were Clark Equipment Credit Company, Associates Corp. of North America, Commercial Credit Company, Sears Roebuck Acceptance Corporation, Montgomery Ward Credit Corp. and General Motors Acceptance Corporation. The enclosed excerpt from *Moody's Bond Record* for December 1981 shows a separate grouping entitled "Medium-Term Notes (SEC Shelf Registrations)" demonstrating that this type of offering was widely used prior to the adoption of Rule 415.

The type of offering being made by the Issuer is exactly the type of traditional shelf registration that the Commission intended would continue after the adoption of the amendments to Rule 415. The purpose of offering in this manner is to enable the Issuer to match capital demands with portfolio holdings, an objective that the Commission recognized in Release No. 33-6499 requires the use of a shelf registration statement. If the Commission were to take the position, despite the clear language of paragraph (a)(1)(ix) of revised Rule 415, that the Issuer may not distribute the Notes in the manner contemplated, then the Issuer would be placed at a severe competitive disadvantage with respect to other finance companies and would, as a practical matter, be unable to offer the Notes publicly.

The amendment to the registration statement was declared effective with no further delay, and deals continued to be done off the issuer's shelf.

• *Procedures*

MTNs will be offered off the dealers' trading desks in much the same manner as commercial paper. The market for MTNs, like commercial paper, is investor driven. The dealers will continuously offer the MTNs through electronic posting procedures on a "maturity band" basis (e.g., 6% for maturities from two years to three years from date of sale), and within this maturity range the investor, the dealer and the issuer will tailor the exact maturity to specific investment and funding requirements. As in the case of shelf-registered debt securities, the investor is primarily interested in (other than maturity) rating information, the name of the issuer and the yield (premium over Treasury securities of comparable maturity). While the dealer's traditional obligation was to distribute the securities on a "best efforts" basis, the depth of the MTN marketplace and competitive pressures now usually result in dealers' taking down securities as principal on a more or less regular basis. Whether it is acting as agent or principal, the MTN dealer is generally regarded as an "underwriter" for Section 11 purposes.

The buyers of MTNs are to a large measure also the buyers of underwritten corporate debt securities, consisting of institutional investors such as banks and bank trust departments, insurance companies, pension funds, mutual funds, investment advisers, nonprofit corporations, state and local governments, and corporations. The average transaction in an MTN program is usually in excess of $2 million.

- *Disclosure and Due Diligence*

The ABA task force report on sellers' due diligence defenses described the MTN disclosure and due diligence process as follows:[71]

> While the degree of disclosure about the issuer and its business, and the scope of its financial statements, that are actually contained in an MTN prospectus (as opposed to being incorporated by reference) vary among issuers, prospectuses used in very active MTN programs often contain only the ratio of earnings to fixed charges required by Item 3 of Form S-3 and rely entirely upon incorporated 1934 Act filings. Prospectuses seldom are distributed to prospective purchasers before they make an investment decision; rather, the supplemented prospectus is usually delivered with the confirmation.
>
> Agents for MTN programs operate on the basis of documentation that is similar to that used for rule 415 shelf takedowns. The underwriting agreement often is referred to as a distribution agreement, to reflect the fact that it provides for the named agents to sell MTNs on a best efforts agency basis or to buy the MTNs as principal and resell them, usually "at the market." Because it is not practical to deliver closing documents at the time of each sale of MTNs, distribution agreements usually provide for an initial "paper" closing at which legal opinions, accountants' "comfort letters," officers' certificates and other traditional closing documents are delivered. The issuer's representations and warranties are deemed to be reaffirmed as of the time of each sale and settlement of an MTN. Additional legal opinions, comfort letters and officers' certificates are usually required

---

71. ABA Committee on Federal Regulation of Securities, *Report of Task Force on Sellers' Due Diligence and Similar Defenses Under the Federal Securities Laws*, 48 Bus. Law. 1185, 1226–27 (1993) (some footnotes omitted).

on a periodic basis (generally each quarter) as the prospectus is amended, whether by the filing of 1934 Act documents that are incorporated by reference pursuant to Item 12 of Form S-3 or otherwise. Issuers agree to amend the prospectus as required and to alert the agents if disclosure problems arise.

Agents usually request the right to review the issuer's 1934 Act periodic reports before they are filed, but have little meaningful influence over the content of such filings. As a practical matter, their only option is to resign from the program. Agents' purchases as principal also are subject to customary termination provisions, such as material adverse changes in the issuer's business or financial condition, a downgrading of the securities or their being put on a "watch list" by a rating agency, and other "market outs." Indemnification and contribution agreements are identical to those contained in standard underwriting agreements.

Because each agent controls its own selling efforts and presents all offers within posted rates directly to the issuer, MTN programs usually do not have a "lead agent" or "lead manager" responsible for sponsoring and coordinating the offering. (If there is a lead agent, the designation only serves to determine the order of listing on the prospectus cover and in the tombstone advertisement and the style of the documentation.) Some issuers allow limited "reverse inquiry," i.e., an investor may be allowed to purchase MTNs from the issuer either directly or through a broker-dealer not designated as an agent in the prospectus.

Because agents must reckon with the possibility of losing a significant amount of MTN sales to "reverse inquiry" by investors or non-designated broker-dealers, they typically prevail upon the issuer to pay a portion of their expenses associated with the transaction. This usually includes the fees and disbursements (up to a predetermined amount) of the law firm that is designated by the issuer as "agents' counsel." Issuers correctly regard this expense as affecting their "all-in" cost of funds raised through the MTN program, and there is considerable pressure on law firms to keep down their quoted and actual charges. To the extent that counsel's charges exceed what the issuer is willing to reimburse, the agents of course must pick up the difference.

The initial due diligence investigation usually is conducted by designated agents' counsel and all agents. Additional due diligence sessions with the issuer and its representatives take place when the prospectus is periodically updated or 1934 Act documents are being prepared for filing and incorporation by reference. Despite the predictable schedule for the filing of an issuer's 1934 Act reports, the agents' need to maintain continuous sales under an ongoing program often imposes considerable time pressure on the agents and their counsel to review these reports and reach conclusions, if any, as to the adequacy of the issuer's disclosure. An agent's due diligence often is supplemented by its corporate credit department, which generally monitors the credit of issuers and even may establish position limits on principal purchases and secondary market positions.

• *Section 11(d)(1)*

As discussed in Chapter 3, Section 11(d)(1) of the 1934 Act prohibits the extension of credit by a broker-dealer on a new issue of securities. The restriction also applies to certain transactions in the after-market for a period of 30 days after the broker-dealer was a participant in the distribution of the securities. A broker-dealer will be considered a participant in the distribution of a new issue as long as it continues to be "a party to an executory agreement to purchase or distribute such issue." The staff of the SEC took the position in 1986 that a broker-dealer acting as an agent in an MTN program could not extend credit on the notes, even those that were issued 30 days prior to the proposed extension of credit, on the theory that the distribution agreement constituted an executory agreement to distribute the notes.[72] Fortunately, the staff reversed its posi-

---

72. SEC No-action Letter, *Goldman, Sachs & Co.* (available December 4, 1986).

tion in a 1990 no-action letter[73] in which it appeared to take the position that, because the financial terms of MTNs are tailored to the individual needs of customers, each tranche can be considered as a separate distribution under Section 11(d)(1).

Of course, a dealer would still be unable to extend credit to a customer unless the MTNs were "OTC margin bonds" under Regulation T. This requires, among other things, that an MTN be part of an issue that has not less than $25 million outstanding. The staff of the Federal Reserve Board took the oral position in 1991 that MTNs of "similar investment characteristics" would meet the $25 million test from and after the issuance of MTNs in that aggregate amount pursuant to an issuer's shelf registration statement, without regard to whether particular tranches were denominated as the same or separate series, had fixed or floating interest rates, were denominated in U.S. dollars or other currencies, or were indexed to different indices.

Common Stock Shelf Registrations

• *Primary Offerings*

Issuers were quick to see the advantages of shelf registration as a vehicle for distributing debt securities, but they warmed more slowly to shelf registration as a vehicle for primary distributions of common stock. Rapid access to the market is generally less important for common stock offerings than for straight debt, and the advantages of a shelf registration may be outweighed by the detrimental effects of a large block of stock overhanging the market. Public utilities are possible exceptions in that they issue common stock frequently and their stock prices depend primarily on the relationship between their dividend rates and the yield on fixed-income securities. Indeed, a few utilities have adopted so-called "dribble plans."

As noted earlier, some of the "overhang" concern may have been dissipated by the recent availability of the "universal" shelf registration statement that covers an amount of securities

---

73. *Kidder, Peabody & Co. Incorporated* (August 16, 1990).

that need not be allocated between debt and equity.[74] Indeed, there were reports in 1996 of a number of large "block trades" of common stock taken down from an issuer's shelf registration statement. In these so-called "equity takedowns," the banker commits to buy the securities from the issuer at a fixed price agreed upon after the close of the market; it then resells to institutional clients before the opening of the market on the next day. There is no road show and no book-building process. Obviously, the banker incurs a significant risk that it will be unable to resell the securities at a profit. For this reason, offerings of this type are generally limited to better-known issuers with well-known investment stories and a relatively liquid common stock. Real estate investment trusts, or REITs, have recently found this technique attractive because of their high capital needs (arising from purchases of new properties) and the tax law requirement that they pay high dividends to their stockholders.

• *Investment Companies*

Rule 415 specifically is not applicable to a registration statement pertaining to redeemable shares issued by an open-end management company, a so-called mutual fund. Although mutual funds offer their shares on a continuous basis, they operate under their own set of rules promulgated under the 1940 Act. Rule 24f-2 under the 1940 Act permits open-end funds to register an indefinite number of shares and to file an annual notice showing the number of shares sold, accompanied by the requisite registration fee. Closed-end funds, however, are permitted to use Rule 415, and a number of fixed-income funds have relied on the rule for continuous offerings of their shares.

Closed-end investment companies are not eligible to register on Form S-3. Rather, they use Form N-2. This form covers regis-

---

74. There were reports in 1996 that some investment bankers still "recommend[ed] against use of even the unallocated shelf for common stock offerings, except where the issuer is large enough to be less susceptible to market overhang or where the issuer already has disclosed their [*sic*] intention to raise significant equity capital." *Report of the Advisory Committee on the Capital Formation and Regulatory Processes* (July 24, 1996), Appendix A at 19.

tration both under the 1933 Act and the 1940 Act. Thus, they do not come under subsection (x) of Rule 415, which permits primary offerings only by Form S-3 or Form F-3 issuers. Instead, certain fixed-income funds have relied for their continuous offerings on subsection (ix), which permits shelf filings for securities "the offering of which will be commenced promptly, will be made on a continuous basis and may continue for a period in excess of 30 days from the date of initial effectiveness." The continuous offerings made by these funds are not "at-the-market offerings" and thus are not subject to the limitations on such offerings imposed by Rule 415. Rather, the shares are continuously offered at prices equal to the fund's then current net asset value per share. Not only are the shares not offered at the market, but, as the prospectuses state, there is not expected to be any secondary trading market for the shares of these fixed-income funds. Thus, the problem of market overhang that has previously been discussed in the context of common stock shelf registrations is not present in offerings of this type.

Where continuous offerings have not been preceded by a firm commitment underwriting, a single prospectus has been used, even where there is first an invitation for subscriptions. Where there is a firm commitment underwriting, however, a separate prospectus is used for that offering and a newly dated prospectus is used for the continuous offering. In some cases, the original registration statement covering the underwritten offering does not cover the continuous offering, and a new registration statement is subsequently filed for this purpose. In other cases, two forms of prospectus are included in a single registration statement that is used to register the shares for the underwritten offering (including the overallotment option) and the continuous offering.

Certain closed-end funds that make periodic repurchase offers pursuant to Rule 23c-3 under the 1940 Act are eligible to rely on subsection (xi) of Rule 415 to offer their shares on a continuous basis. This subsection has not been widely used for this purpose.

• *Non-Underwritten Registered Equity Secondaries*

As previously mentioned, shelf registrations frequently are used to cover offerings of outstanding common stock by control persons or statutory underwriters where sales are to be made from time to time at market prices current at the time of sale. These are traditional shelfs, and there are a number of legal issues and marketing considerations that arise in the context of this type of offering. While bought deals and large debt underwritings receive the press coverage and merit the tombstone advertisements, shelf secondaries continue to be handled in substantial volume with little if any publicity.

The prospectus delivery requirements of the 1933 Act can be satisfied in the case of a regular way sale on an exchange by delivering copies of the prospectus to the exchange pursuant to Rule 153. The theory is that physical delivery to the broker on the other side of the transaction is unnecessary because the broker can get a copy of the prospectus from the exchange library. Will the buying broker do so? Probably not. Will he even know that he is buying registered securities? Again, probably not, although at one time the American Stock Exchange had a requirement that the order tickets covering sales of stock under a shelf prospectus be marked "dist" for distribution.

Rule 153 is applicable only to transactions between brokers on an exchange. If the shares are being sold by means of a spot secondary after the close of the exchange or in a block trade, the securities firm handling the transaction will be dealing directly with the purchasers, and a copy of the prospectus must be delivered to them with their confirmation. (Of course, any institution whose mailroom receives a confirmation will usually forward the confirmation for processing while dropping the prospectus into the wastebasket.) In the case of a sale to another dealer through NASDAQ, or otherwise in the over-the-counter market, physical delivery of the prospectus is likewise required because Rule 153 currently applies only to transactions on an exchange.[75] When the dealer purchasing the shares

75. One of the authors proposed many years ago that the NASD adopt a rule similar to Rule 153 that would dispense with the need for over-the-counter dealers to deliver prospectuses among themselves. J. McLaughlin, *"Ten Easy Pieces" for the SEC*, 18 Rev. Secs. & Comms. Reg. 200, 201 (1985). Whatever difficulties may have existed at the time, there can hardly be any remaining valid objection to dispensing with such deliveries in view

receives the prospectus, must it redeliver it to its customer, assuming that it finds its way out of the mail room? The registered shares will simply become part of the dealer's inventory, indistinguishable from any other shares of the same issuer. As the dealer continues to make a market, there is no way of pointing to any particular shares in its inventory and saying that these are the registered shares and that they are being resold to an identified buyer. The fact of the matter is that the prospectus will not be redelivered to an ultimate investor but may also wind up in the wastebasket.

A dealer that sells shares under a shelf registration statement for a control person or a statutory underwriter will itself be deemed an underwriter. It is customary for shelf prospectuses to so state. A dealer that buys the registered shares from the dealer handling the sale will not be deemed an underwriter so long as it is operating in the ordinary course of its business and has not entered into any special arrangements with the selling stockholders or the dealer on the sell side of the trade. The SEC has addressed this issue in the context of primary at-the-market offerings under Rule 415. The following statement in the release reproposing Rule 415 sets forth principles that are equally applicable to secondary offerings:

> Accordingly, an exchange member or specialist effecting a transaction in the shelf-registered security with an underwriter who is in privity with the registrant generally would not be deemed to be an underwriter if the member or specialist performed its usual functions and had not entered into any special selling arrangements with the registrant or the underwriter. The same would be true in the case of an over-the-counter market maker who did not buy from the registrant. In a similar vein, a broker-dealer could solicit buy orders from its customers for a security subject to such a shelf registration statement without being deemed an underwriter of that

---

of the ready availability of prospectuses on EDGAR or by other electronic means, and the fact that every over-the-counter dealer by definition has access to a computer and a modem.

security upon executing the trade, as long as such broker-dealer limited itself to its ordinary business activities and had no special arrangements with the underwriters or issuer.[76]

As previously noted, most of the early shelf offerings were handled as regular way brokerage transactions. When Form S-16 was first adopted in 1970, it was available for secondary offerings only if they were effected "in the regular way" on a stock exchange. Form S-16 was a convenient device for issuers required to file shelf registration statements to meet their obligations under registration rights agreements, and regular way sales were specified in these filings as the plan of distribution. In 1972, Form S-16 was amended to eliminate the requirement that sales be made only "in the regular way" on an exchange, thus opening the door for more efficient distribution methods for shelf offerings on Form S-16.

By the early 1970s, the block trader had come into his/her own. All of the major securities firms had established block trading departments and were committing large amounts of capital to facilitate trades of large blocks of stock. Today, block trades make up a major portion of the trading volume on the principal exchanges. If a firm is approached by a customer wishing to sell a substantial number of listed shares, say more than 10% of the daily trading volume, a block trade usually will be the most-cost-effective method of effecting the sale. If there is institutional interest in the stock and the number of shares involved bears a reasonable relationship to that interest, then the firm's block trading department will be in a position to quickly and efficiently place the shares with institutional buyers, usually few in number. In most cases, the transaction price is set at a discount from the last sale price on the exchange. The firm lines up interest in the block and makes a firm bid to the seller. It sells the shares as agent, but will position a portion of the block if necessary to meet its commitment to its customer. The trade is crossed on the floor of the exchange and is printed on the tape.

---

76. SEC Release No. 33-6334 (August 6, 1981).

The block trade became the preferred method of sale for outstanding shares covered by shelf registration statements, although off-board secondary offerings frequently were used for sales off the shelf where warranted by size or investor interest. In a spot secondary, other securities firms are invited to participate in the distribution, and a selling concession is offered. In the 1970s, a number of firms organized sales units that would monitor shelf filings and approach the named sellers in an effort to convince them to use the services of the firm in selling their shares. A major part of the pitch would be the firm's distribution capacity and its willingness to commit its capital to make a firm bid.

A firm handling a shelf offering may have entered into negotiations with the customer before the registration statement was filed, especially where the firm has a role in placing the securities with the customer or in advising on a merger or similar transaction in which the customer receives the shares. More often, the firm may be presented with a registration statement that has already been declared effective. If it does have the opportunity to participate in the drafting of the prospectus, it has the advantage of assuring that the plan of distribution is appropriately set forth. In some cases, the proposed method of distribution will be fixed and can be described with precision in the prospectus. In other cases, it may be advisable to draft the plan of distribution to provide for the widest latitude. If a dealer is chosen to handle a sale after the registration statement has been declared effective, and the plan of distribution does not contemplate the block trade or the off-board secondary that it has proposed to its customer, then it will be necessary to file a post-effective amendment to the registration statement.

A firm selling common stock for a customer under circumstances that may make it a statutory underwriter should also be concerned about its potential liabilities under Section 11. Many firms will not act for a customer in this capacity unless the customer can deliver an indemnity agreement from the issuer. If the customer's shares originated in a private placement or in a merger or similar transaction, the customer or his or her counsel may have bargained for such an indemnity. The dealer will want to review the terms of the issuer's undertaking and bargain for the widest indemnity contemplated by those terms. If the indemnity does not measure up to the dealer's standards, it may decline to execute the transaction.

Indemnities, of course, are vulnerable to SEC or judicial scrutiny as well as to the issuer's possible insolvency. The dealer's better course of action is to try to establish a due diligence defense. The issuer is highly unlikely to be willing to afford the dealer an opportunity to ask questions—much less to make suggestions about the quality of the issuer's disclosure. There is no reason, however, why the dealer should not seek out its research analyst who follows the issuer to inquire about his or her views on the stock and on whether any surprises are expected to occur in the near future.[77]

The Presumptive Underwriter Problem

Beginning in the 1960s, the SEC took the position that a purchaser of a relatively large amount of securities covered by a registration statement would be presumed to be an underwriter and thus required to redeliver a current prospectus in making resales.[78] The presumptive underwriter doctrine began as SEC lore (not law). It is alluded to in the 1969 *Wheat Report*.[79]

The theory was that a distribution of securities had not been completed while they were still in the hands of a large purchaser and that the disclosures required by the 1933 Act should be provided to the "ultimate" purchasers. Surely (went the theory) disclosure to the "ultimate" investors could not be avoided by registering securities for sale to a single institution that might turn around the next day and sell them to the public without delivering a prospectus. But where should the line be drawn? With respect to offerings of common stock, the traditional presumptive underwriter doctrine had been that anyone

77. *See* ABA Committee on Federal Regulation of Securities, *Report of Task Force on Sellers' Due Diligence and Similar Defenses Under the Federal Securities Laws*, 48 Bus. Law. 1185, 1229 (1993).

78. *See generally* C. Nathan, *Presumptive Underwriters*, 8 Rev. Sec. Reg. 881 (1975).

79. Wheat Report, *supra* Chapter 1, note 24, at 272, note 22.

who purchased more than 10% of an offering would be deemed an underwriter unless the number of shares purchased was relatively small in relation to the number outstanding.[80] With respect to fixed-income securities, the SEC took a somewhat more liberal stance, and in one case, took a no-action position with respect to a purchaser of 14% of a registered offering of nonconvertible preferred stock.[81]

The presumptive underwriter doctrine generated considerable concern in the context of shelf offerings, particularly with respect to bought deals. Assume that an issuer filed a registration statement under Rule 415 covering $500 million of its debt securities to be sold in several tranches. If a single institutional investor bought an entire series of $100 million of debt through an underwriter, could it freely resell the securities at any time without delivering a current prospectus? In applying the presumptive underwriter doctrine, should one look to the total amount of securities covered by the shelf registration statement or to the amount of securities sold in each discrete offering?

Lee B. Spencer, Jr., then the Director of the SEC's Division of Corporation Finance, was determined to make Rule 415 work. In connection with the rule's adoption, he advised the financial community that the staff was no longer applying the presumptive underwriter doctrine, at least insofar as it embodied any automatic percentage test. Rather, he said, the staff would examine all of the facts and circumstances surrounding the purchase of a large block of securities to determine whether the purchaser should be deemed an underwriter in making resales. Among the circumstances to be considered were the amount of securities purchased in relation to the amount outstanding, whether the purchaser was likely to hold for the long pull, and the length of time that the securities were owned before the resale took place.

A determination of a purchaser's status as an underwriter would thus depend on subjective factors. The real thrust of the SEC's revised position was that it would not deem a purchaser

---

80. SEC No-action Letter, *Hercules, Inc.* (available October 2, 1972).

81. SEC No-action Letter, *Jersey Central Power & Light Company* (available January 22, 1975).

an underwriter unless (with the benefit of hindsight) it appeared to be acting as a conduit for the issuer to avoid delivery of a current prospectus to the ultimate purchasers.

Institutions had lingering concerns despite Mr. Spencer's statement that "[w]e are going to give that doctrine the full funeral rites it so richly deserves."[82] In time, however, these concerns diminished, and institutions now purchase securities off the shelf with little, if any, fear that they will be considered underwriters in making resales. The SEC helped matters when it issued the American Council of Life Insurance no-action letter, in which Mr. Spencer agreed with counsel's view that "insurance companies and similar institutional investors generally should not be deemed underwriters under Section 2(11) with regard to the purchase of large amounts of registered securities provided such securities are acquired in the ordinary course of their business from the issuer or underwriter of those securities and such purchasers have no arrangement with any person to participate in the distribution of such securities."[83] The real comfort, however, has come from the fact that Rule 415 has operated for many years now without the SEC raising underwriter concerns with respect to resales of securities taken off the shelf.

Regulation M

For many years after the adoption of Rule 415, the SEC applied a "single distribution" analysis to shelf registration statements for purposes of its antimanipulation rules (primarily Rule 10b-6) discussed in Chapter 4. Under this approach, each takedown from a shelf was deemed to be part of a "distribution" for Rule 10b-6 purposes if the aggregate amount of securities registered on the shelf was sufficient to constitute a distribution for such purposes. The effect of this approach was that all participants in the distribution were subject to Rule

---

82. W.J. Williams, Jr., *Problems in the Application of the 1933 Act and Rules Thereunder to Shelf Offerings,* Fourteenth Annual Institute on Securities Regulation 117 (Practising Law Institute Transcript 1983).

83. SEC No-action Letter, *American Council of Life Ins.* (available May 10, 1983).

10b-6 for the life of the shelf, but with exceptions for certain bids or purchases outside specified "cooling-off" periods.

The SEC's "single distribution" analysis arose largely out of the SEC's concern, discussed earlier in this Chapter, regarding shelf registration statements covering sales by numerous unaffiliated selling securityholders. Treating these sales as a single distribution, however, meant mandating coordination where there would otherwise be no reason for coordination. Recognizing that this approach was counterproductive, the SEC soon relaxed its position so that the restrictions of Rule 10b-6 ordinarily applied to an individual selling shelf stockholder only when that person was offering or selling securities from the shelf. A broker-dealer effecting such sales would be subject to the rule only where it was involved in a distribution based on the amount of securities that it was asked to sell (or foreseeably would be asked to sell) as well as on the basis of the methods used to sell the securities.[84]

From the standpoint of issuers' offerings of shelf-registered securities, the primary significance of the single-distribution theory was that it was necessary to determine whether specific prospective underwriters had "continuing agreements" with the issuer to sell the registered securities. If so, the underwriter would be deemed to have commenced its participation in the distribution when it entered into the agreement and would be subject to Rule 10b-6 restrictions in respect of each takedown.

The SEC effected a major simplification of the rules in this area when it abandoned the single-distribution approach as part of its adoption of Regulation M in late 1996. Under the new approach, each takedown off a shelf is to be individually examined to determine whether the offering constitutes a distribution (i.e., whether the takedown satisfies the magnitude criterion and the special selling efforts and selling methods criterion). As to the second of these criteria, the Regulation M Release states that the issuer's description in the shelf registration statement of a variety of potential selling methods will not cause, by itself, any sales off the shelf to be treated as a distri-

---

84. SEC Release No. 34-23611 (September 11, 1986).

bution unless the underwriter "in fact uses special selling efforts or selling methods in connection with particular sales off the shelf, and the sales are of a magnitude sufficient to demonstrate the existence of a distribution."[85]

In the Regulation M Release, the SEC also confirmed its earlier position that "[i]n those situations where a broker-dealer sells shares on behalf of an issuer or selling security holder in ordinary trading transactions into an independent market (i.e., without any special selling efforts) the offering will not be considered a distribution and the broker-dealer will not be subject to Rule 101." It added a caveat, however, that the result would likely be different where the broker-dealer had a sales agency agreement that provided for "unusual transaction-based compensation," even if the securities were sold in ordinary trading transactions.[86]

---

85. Regulation M Release, *supra* Chapter 4, note 1, at note 47.
86. *Id.* (text following notes 47 and 48). See the discussion in Chapter 4.

Chapter 9

INTERNATIONAL FINANCINGS

The 1980s and 1990s have been marked by a dramatic growth in the size and importance of international securities markets. For many U.S. issuers, the markets outside the United States have become an important source of capital that they can tap relatively quickly and with a minimum of disclosure formalities.[1] On the other hand, foreign issuers also frequently find it advantageous—for reasons we shall discuss—to offer their securities in the U.S. markets.[2] Finally, many U.S. and foreign issuers have become accustomed to offer their securities in "global offerings" directed simultaneously to investors in the U.S. and offshore markets.

The fortunate beneficiary of the growth of international securities markets is the investor, for whom the U.S. and offshore

---

1. U.S. issuers publicly sold more than $56.3 billion of debt securities in international markets during 1996, an increase of more than 30% over 1995. *Investment Dealers' Digest* (January 13, 1997) at 46.

2. Non-U.S. issuers publicly sold more than $90.4 billion of debt securities in the United States during 1996, nearly twice as much as in 1995. Non-U.S. issuers publicly sold more than $19 billion of equity securities in the United States in 1996, nearly twice as much as in 1995. *Investment Dealers' Digest* (January 13, 1997) at 48.

557

markets are becoming, for many purposes, indistinguishable. On the equity side, U.S. and foreign investors alike have the capability of analyzing investments in markets around the world.[3] On the fixed-income side, they monitor interest rate and currency developments as a basis for determining their relative involvement in dollar-denominated or non-dollar-denominated fixed-income investments. On both the equity and fixed-income sides, investors look to securities firms on a global basis to provide deep and liquid secondary markets in many securities as well as to offer the ability to hedge all or a portion of the risk inherent in a single instrument or market sector.

There are many reasons for the globabilization of securities markets. A few might include the ability of investment bankers to access favorable financing opportunities for issuers in diverse markets; financial innovation and particularly the development of sophisticated devices to hedge against interest rate and currency risk; advances in telecommunications and computer technology that make it possible for securities firms to "pass the book" around the world for trading purposes; the deregulation of exchange controls and capital markets; the development of book-entry clearance and settlement facilities; improved transparency and liquidity in the worldwide secondary markets; and the creation of global research capabilities by many of the world's leading securities firms.

The institutionalization of the securities markets has been a significant factor as well. There is increased interest on the part of portfolio managers, both domestic and foreign, in securities issued outside of their own countries, both for reasons of risk diversification and a search for superior returns.[4] The growth of global investment companies that invest on a worldwide basis, as well as the introduction of numerous "country funds" (U.S. closed-end investment companies that invest in the securities markets of specific countries), have also contributed to the increase in holdings of foreign securities by U.S. investors.

---

3. According to the SEC, the capitalization of the U.S. equity market was $8 trillion at the end of 1995 compared to a worldwide $16.5 trillion. *1995 Annual Report* 27.

4. For example, foreign investment by U.S. private sector pension funds grew from an estimated $3.3 billion in 1980 to over $381.0 billion in 1996.

The federal securities laws have their clearest application when an issuer—domestic or foreign—is offering securities into the United States. Their application has been less clear where the securities are offered, at least initially, outside the United States. In these cases, while the SEC has acknowledged that the federal securities laws are not intended to protect persons outside the United States, it has nevertheless worried that securities offered in an ostensibly "offshore" transaction may be intended to find their ultimate home in the United States.

This chapter will discuss the SEC's efforts over the last three decades to spell out the circumstances under which a U.S. or foreign issuer may make an "offshore" offering without violations of the registration requirements of the 1933 Act. It will also discuss the particular problems a foreign issuer must overcome when it wishes to make a registered public offering in the United States.[5] Finally, we will discuss the challenges of a "global" offering—i.e., a public offering outside the United States together with a simultaneous public or private offering in the United States.

Offshore Offerings and the 1933 Act

• *Interest Equalization Tax*

As the European economy recovered in the years following World War II, a European capital market developed in the early 1960s which provided a source of funds for U.S. corporations. During the 1950s, the strength of the dollar in the foreign exchange markets caused U.S. goods to become less competitive, resulting in a outflow of dollars to Europe. At the same time, U.S. companies increased their overseas investment in manufacturing facilities. The sale of debt securities by foreign issuers in the U.S. market further contributed to the outflow of dollars. By the end of the 1950s, the U.S. balance of payment deficit had become a matter of concern, and in 1963 the Con-

---

5. Chapter 7 describes private placements in the United States by U.S. and non-U.S. issuers.

gress imposed the Interest Equalization Tax ("IET"),[6] a tax on the value of foreign debt or equity securities acquired by U.S. persons.

The IET was designed to make foreign investment less attractive and thus to discourage foreign borrowing in the United States. The implementation of the IET caused non-U.S. borrowers to turn to the Euromarket as a source of funds. The money was there, including the large pool of dollars that had grown from the dollar outflow during the preceding decade. These funds came to be known as Eurodollars, dollars held by non-residents of the United States, usually on deposit with European banks and held by those banks in their New York branches, subsidiaries, or correspondent banks.

Continuing balance of payment deficits led to restrictions on overseas direct investment by U.S. corporations. Under controls imposed in 1968 and administered by the Office of Foreign Direct Investments, U.S. corporations were forced to finance their foreign operations in foreign markets. Eurobond issues by these companies increased from $527 million in 1967 to more than $1.9 billion in 1968.[7]

As U.S. issuers began to sell debt securities in the Euromarket, partly in response to the direct investment guidelines, questions arose as to the application of the 1933 Act to such transactions. The registration provisions of Section 5 of the 1933 Act apply to any offer or sale of a security involving interstate commerce or the use of the mails ("jurisdictional means") unless an exemption is available. Since "interstate commerce" is defined in Section 2(7) of the 1933 Act to include "trade or commerce in securities or any transportation or communication relating thereto . . . between any foreign country and any State, Territory, or the District of Columbia," the registration provisions of the 1933 Act might be construed to reach any offer or sale of securities—even to foreign investors—if the offer or sale involved even incidental use (e.g., by the issuer or by underwriters) of U.S. jurisdictional means.

---

6. Interest Equalization Tax Act of 1963–64, Pub. L. No. 88-563, 78 Stat. 809 (repealed 1976).

7. F.G. Fisher, *International Bonds* 21 (Euromoney 1981).

Although it might well have taken enforcement action in the event of a sale to dealers in a foreign country with a view to resale in the United States, the SEC had little inclination to test its jurisdiction where a domestic issuer effected a distribution exclusively abroad. A vague theory existed at the time that a Section 4(2) exemption would be available to this type of transaction in that the term "public offering" should be read to mean "public offering in the United States." But prior to 1964, the SEC had not fully articulated its position, and as Eurodollar offerings proliferated, many felt that it was time for the SEC to do so.[8]

• *Release 33-4708*

In 1964, a Presidential Task Force chaired by Henry H. Fowler delivered its Report on Promoting Increased Foreign Investment in United States Corporate Securities and Increased Foreign Financing for United States Corporations Operating Abroad (the "Fowler Task Force Report"). One of the recommendations of the Fowler Task Force Report was that the SEC clarify the circumstances under which 1933 Act registration would not be required in connection with public offerings of securities outside the U.S. to foreign purchasers. In response to this recommendation, the SEC on July 9, 1964 published Release No. 33-4708 ("Release 4708") in which it acknowledged that *"the registration requirements of Section 5 of the Act are primarily intended to protect American investors"* (emphasis added). The release then noted that the SEC:

> had not taken any action for failure to register securities of United States corporations distributed abroad to foreign nationals, even though use of jurisdictional means may be involved in the offering. It is assumed in these situations that *the distribution is to be effected in a manner which will result in the securities coming to rest abroad.* . . . Apart from [a situation involving a distribution through a Canadian stock exchange that might be

---

8. For a discussion of this subject with extensive citations, *see* Comment, *Extraterritorial Effect of the Registration Requirements of the Securities Act of 1933,* 24 Vill. L. Rev. 729 (1978–1979).

expected to flow into the hands of American investors or a situation involving an offer targeted toward American investors living abroad], . . . it is immaterial whether the offering originates from within or outside of the United States, whether domestic or foreign broker-dealers are involved and whether the actual mechanics of the distribution are effected within the United States, *so long as the offering is made under circumstances reasonably designed to preclude distribution or redistribution of the securities within, or to nationals of, the United States.* (Emphasis added).

In response to another Task Force recommendation, the release also stated that the SEC would not integrate an offering made abroad with a simultaneous private placement in the United States of the same security. "Generally, transactions otherwise meeting the requirements of . . . [Section 4(2) of the 1933 Act] need not be integrated with simultaneous offerings being made abroad and, therefore, are not subject to the registration requirements of the Act solely because a foreign offering is being made concurrently with the American private placement which otherwise meets the standards of the exemption."

As noted above, the IET represented at the time of the publication of Release 33-4708 a significant economic disincentive for U.S. investors to acquire securities of foreign issuers. The SEC staff subsequently regarded the IET as a factor to be taken into account in deciding whether to grant no-action letters on the need to register offerings made abroad.[9] While the IET was in effect, the principles of Release 33-4708 were relied on primarily for sales abroad of Eurodollar obligations issued by a foreign finance subsidiary (or an "80-20" U.S. finance subsidiary) of a U.S. corporation, guaranteed by the parent and often convertible into the parent's common stock. Where the U.S. parent or a domestically incorporated subsidiary was the issuer of the obligations, an elec-

---

9. E.g., SEC No-action Letter, *Intercontinental Hotels Corp.* (available August 11, 1971). Although Release 33-4708 specifically refers only to U.S. issuers, the SEC staff also applied it to offerings by foreign issuers. *See*, e.g., *Vizcaya International N.V.* (April 4, 1973), *Republic of Iceland* (March 19, 1971).

tion could be made to have the obligations treated as those of a foreign issuer whose acquisition by a U.S. person would be subject to the IET.[10]

• *Debt Financings After Elimination of IET*

In January 1974, the IET was reduced to zero,[11] and one of Release 33-4708's important underpinnings was accordingly eliminated. With respect to a Eurodollar financing made shortly after the elimination of the IET in accordance with offering procedures that had then become standard, the SEC's staff took a no-action position on the offering itself but expressly refused to take a position as to when and under what circumstances the securities could be resold in the United States or to U.S. nationals.[12]

Securities lawyers soon developed elaborate procedures designed to substitute for the IET in meeting the objectives of Release 33-4708 regarding non-distribution of securities to U.S. investors. Many of these procedures were the subject of SEC no-action letters, including *Pacific Lighting Corporation* (available June 13, 1974) and *The Singer Company* (available September 3, 1974). The procedures were considerably simplified in a no-action letter relating to *The Procter & Gamble Company* (available February 21, 1985). By the mid-1980s, the substance of the procedures generally in effect (subject to variations as a result of the preferences of individual securities firms and their counsel and the circumstances of particular cases) could be summarized as follows:

1. Invitation Telexes. Invitation telexes to prospective underwriters and dealers stated that the securities to be distrib-

---

10. Committee on Taxation of International Finance and Investment of New York State Bar Association, Tax Section, *Report on International Finance Subsidiaries*, 28 Tax. L. Rev. 443, 509 (1973).

11. Exec. Order No. 11,766 (1974), reprinted in [1974] U.S. Code Cong. & Ad. News 8260. The Interest Equalization Tax Act was repealed by the Tax Reform Act of 1976, Pub. L. No. 94-455, 90 Stat. 1520.

12. SEC No-action Letter, *Sperry Rand Corporation* (available March 1, 1974). *See also* SEC No-action Letter, *American Motors Corporation* (available January 24, 1974).

uted ("distribution securities") would not be registered under the 1933 Act and that they would not be offered, sold or delivered in the U.S. or to U.S. persons as part of the distribution.

2. Contractual Restrictions. Underwriters and dealers would agree (a) not to acquire distribution securities for the account of a U.S. person, (b) not to sell distribution securities in the U.S. or to U.S. persons (or to others for reoffering in the U.S. or to U.S. persons), (c) as to securities of the same class acquired otherwise than in connection with the distribution, not to offer or sell such securities in the U.S. or to U.S. persons prior to 90 days after completion of the distribution, as determined by the lead managing underwriter, (d) in connection with sales of distribution securities, to deliver confirmations stating (i) that the securities had not been registered under the 1933 Act, (ii) as to non-dealer purchasers, the substance of the foregoing restrictions and (iii) as to dealer purchasers, that the purchaser represented that it would comply with the foregoing restrictions and would deliver similar confirmations to persons to whom it sold the distribution securities.[13]

3. Disclosure. The offering circular or prospectus would state (a) that the distribution securities were unregistered and could not be sold in the U.S. or to U.S. persons, (b) that the securities would initially be represented by a temporary global security exchangeable for definitive securities (i) not earlier than 90 days after the date certified by the lead managing underwriter as the date of completion of the distribution and (ii) upon certification of non-U.S. beneficial ownership and (c) that non-complying offers or sales in the U.S. or to U.S. persons might violate U.S. law.

4. "All-Sold" Telexes. Underwriters and dealers would agree to confirm to the lead managing underwriter, upon request, that they had sold all allotted securities in compliance with the foregoing restrictions.

5. Delivery of Securities. The securities would be initially represented by a temporary global security that would be ex-

---

13. Questions might have been raised—but never were, so far as the authors are aware—as to the efficacy under local law of deeming purchasers of securities to have "agreed," by accepting a security, to observe restrictions on the disposition of such security.

changeable for definitive securities only under the circumstances described above.

6. Press Releases and Advertising. Press releases and tombstone advertisements would state that the securities had not been registered under the 1933 Act and that they could not be sold in the U.S. or to U.S. persons as part of the distribution. Tombstones would customarily not be published until the closing date or such later time as the lead managing underwriter believed the distribution to have been completed.

Release 33-4708 did not contemplate international equity offerings,[14] and the SEC could be expected to be more concerned about the potential for resale of equity securities into the U.S. than in the case of debt offerings. Subsequent to the elimination of the IET, however, the SEC issued a number of no-action letters relating to equity offerings where it considered the procedures adequate to prevent resales into the United States.[15] These procedures became so well known that even foreign issuers making international equity offerings incorporated similar restrictions into their offering procedures, including complex confirmation delivery undertakings designed to avoid sales in the U.S. or to U.S. persons. Oddly enough, similar offerings of U.S. issuers did not always require these undertakings, but they did contemplate an absolute prohibition of U.S. sales for a period of one year as opposed to a 120-day prohibition for the non-U.S. issuers.

---

14. Because of the flow-back potential, the October 1972 sale in Japan of 700,000 shares of common stock of General Telephone & Electronics Corp. (the first equity offering by a United States company in Japan) was registered under the 1933 Act as well as under the Japanese securities law Also, G.D. Searle & Co. registered all of the common stock that it offered outside of the United States in an October 24, 1974, exchange offer for shares of Gold Cross Hospital Supplies Limited, an English company.

15. E.g., SEC No-action Letter, *Foote, Cone & Belding Communications Inc.* (reconsidered June 21, 1976); SEC No-action Letter, *Hexalon Real Estate, Inc.* (available July 1, 1977); SEC-No-action Letter, *Sulpetro International, Ltd.* (available August 25, 1977); SEC No-action Letter, *RSA Corporation* (available January 3, 1978); SEC No-action Letter, *American Eastern Real Estate and Investment Corporation* (available November 27, 1978).

In 1985 the SEC issued a no-action letter to InfraRed Associates Inc.,[16] a U.S. issuer that proposed to make an initial public offering through a U.K. underwriting firm to investors outside North America. The letter was issued after some negotiation, and it noted "particularly that securities may be transferred to or for the benefit of North American persons only after a twelve month period following the end of the offering, and then only if (i) the securities are duly registered under the [1933] Act, and any applicable securities laws of any state of the United States ('State Act'); (ii) an exemption from registration under the [1933] Act and any applicable State Act is available and InfraRed has received an opinion of counsel to such effect reasonably satisfactory to it; or (iii) such securities are sold on the London Stock Exchange in accordance with procedures approved by the London Stock Exchange." The *InfraRed* letter was unusual in implying the SEC staff's agreement that a specific method of resale was available to purchasers of the securities offered abroad.

- *Dissatisfaction with Release 33-4708*

By the mid-1980s, it was becoming apparent that Release 33-4708 had some serious conceptual shortcomings and that the procedures it had spawned were overly complex, subject to breaking down in practice and designed primarily for the convenience of counsel in rendering legal opinions:

1. It was unclear exactly what the SEC had done in Release 33-4708. While the SEC acknowledged in the release and in subsequent no-action letters that it was possible to effect a foreign distribution without 1933 Act registration, it generally (with rare exceptions such as the *InfraRed* letter mentioned above) carefully reserved its position on when (if ever) the distributed securities could be resold in the U.S. or to U.S. persons. Because this ambiguity was built into the procedural structure, holders of (and would-be dealers in) securities distributed abroad in compliance with the release and the no-action letters were in some ways in a worse position than holders of (and would-be dealers in) securities *illegally* distrib-

---

16. SEC No-action Letter, *InfraRed Associates, Inc.* (available October 14, 1985).

uted in the U.S. At least, these securities could be resold in reliance on Section 4(3)(A) commencing 40 days after the commencement of the illegal distribution.

2. The definition of "U.S. person" for purposes of the release and the related procedures was customarily taken as "any national or resident of the United States, any corporation, partnership or other entity created or organized in or under the laws of the United States or any political subdivision thereof, or any estate or trust which is subject to United States federal income taxation regardless of the source of its income." It was often difficult for underwriters and dealers to apply this definition to particular customers, e.g., foreign branches of U.S. banks and insurance companies.[17] The definition was derived from tax requirements applicable in the fixed-income area, however, and it resisted attempts at modification despite its having no necessary relevance to the purposes of the 1933 Act. More important, it was becoming less clear that the 1933 Act should prevent U.S. persons located abroad from purchasing securities involved in offshore distributions. For one thing, it was difficult (if not impossible), in the case of equity securities listed on a foreign exchange (as in the case of the *InfraRed* letter), to prevent U.S. persons from simply purchasing the distributed securities in the secondary market. For another, prohibiting sales to U.S. persons had the potential for depriving U.S. investors of important opportunities.

3. Despite the premise of the release that the registration provisions of the 1933 Act are primarily concerned with the protection of U.S. investors, the release implied that offers and sales in the geographic U.S. are prohibited. This leaves unclear the status of non-U.S. investors whose accounts are managed by U.S. investment advisers, U.S.-based international organiza-

---

17. The SEC took the position, however, that a branch or agency of a U.S. bank or insurance company operating outside of the United States for valid business reasons and subject to local regulation would not be viewed as a U.S. person and could thus be offered unregistered securities. SEC No-action Letter, *Foreign Agencies and Branches of United States Banks and Insurance Companies* (available February 25, 1988).

tions and approaches to U.S. corporations regarding investments by their foreign affiliates.

4. On its face, the release set forth only an interpretation of the 1933 Act. While the release was codified in the Code of Federal Regulations, it was not clear that persons relying on the release could do so as if it were a "rule or regulation" within the meaning of Section 19(a) of the 1933 Act.[18]

5. The determination whether a distribution has been "completed" is customarily left to the lead manager of an issue, who must certify such completion as a condition of the exchange of temporary global securities for definitive securities. Obviously, the lead manager is at the mercy of the information provided by the underwriters. What would happen if an underwriter were to misrepresent the state of its position?

6. Also, counsel would customarily require as a condition of a legal opinion regarding the non-applicability of the registration provisions of the 1933 Act that the lead manager certify to such counsel one of (or some combination of) the propositions that (a) the lead manager has no reason to believe that the contractual restrictions would be disregarded so that a distribution would take place in the United States and (b) the lead manager was of the opinion that the offering was being made "under circumstances reasonably designed to preclude distribution or redistribution of the securities" in the United States or to U.S. persons. Responsible counsel obviously requires some factual basis for such an opinion, but it is not clear whether the requested certifications did not in effect beg the question as to which counsel was being asked to opine.

7. It was unclear under the release and the procedures whether a breakdown of the procedures in any one trade would "taint" the entire transaction.

• *Evolution of a Territorial Approach*

During the 1980s, the SEC began to take a new look at the growing internationalization of the capital markets with a view to assuring that its rules did not unnecessarily impede multina-

---

18. Compare *Gerstle v. Gamble-Skogmo, Inc.*, 478 F.2d 1281 (2d Cir. 1973), with *Colema Realty Corp. v. Bibow*, 555 F. Supp. 1030 (D. Conn. 1983).

tional offerings. It came to recognize that the United States was facing serious competition from a largely unregulated transnational financial market. In its *1987 Internationalization Report,* the SEC staff noted that securities markets around the world were changing as foreign issuers expanded their use of U.S. capital markets, domestic issuers accessed foreign markets and both debt and equity offerings were made on an international basis. "As a result of these offerings," the staff observed, "the lines of demarcation between domestic and international capital markets are beginning to blur and domestic markets are facing serious competition from a largely unregulated, transnational financial market." In addition, questions concerning the reach of Section 5 of the 1933 Act had "resulted in complex and costly offering procedures to assure that registration provisions do not apply [to an offering], as well as the exclusion of United States persons from various offshore investment opportunities." At the same time, the ability of U.S. investors (particularly institutions) to purchase securities in foreign secondary markets meant that they were likely to be disadvantaged when the foreign issuers engaged in rights offerings or exchange offers.[19]

The fact that U.S. institutional investors were beginning to chafe at SEC policies relating to the jurisdictional reach of Section 5 was a new phenomenon in 1987. For example, Peter C. Clapman of College Retirement Equities Fund ("CREF") stated to the SEC at its 1987 roundtable on the internationalization of securities markets that CREF was being deprived of the opportunity to invest in attractive foreign new issues.[20] Investing in France was a case in point:

The focus of the new issue problem now turns to France and the new privatization issues. These are issues of

19. *1987 Internationalization Report* at III-311.

20. Statement of Peter C. Clapman, Senior Vice President and Associate General Counsel, Teachers Insurance & Annuity Association—College Retirement Equities Fund, to the SEC Roundtable on Internationalization of Securities Markets (February 17, 1987), *1987 Internationalization Report* at V B-115, 121.

stock of companies presently owned by the French government being sold mostly to the French public, with a small amount of stock available to non-French citizens. Such stock has been and is likely to be attractively priced. It is difficult to obtain such stock. An American must take [the] initiative to find out about it—who the underwriters are. Because CREF has been in the French market since 1978, we should normally be able to acquire some shares. A limited amount is available to foreigners—but until now—not to Americans. Why? The French government and French issuers were concerned about doing a private placement with American institutions because of perceived fear of the SEC. Americans were, of course, free to buy in the aftermarket—after the benefits of the bargain were enjoyed by all others. Hopefully, the SEC will address this issue shortly. Until then, Americans will continue to have difficulty.

The SEC did address the issue and granted to CREF a no-action letter that made clear that equity securities issued as part of the French privatization program could be sold to U.S. institutions in reliance upon the private placement exemption and that these institutions could freely resell the securities on the *Bourse* in Paris without inquiring as to the identity of the purchasers. The institutions would agree not to resell within the United States or knowingly to a U.S. national. The SEC's staff also agreed that the French issuers would not be required to comply with any additional procedures in the foreign offerings as a result of the U.S. private placement.[21]

In the *1987 Internationalization Report*, the SEC staff suggested that a territorial approach to the registration provisions of the 1933 Act would be consistent with its purpose and with "comity principles. . . . Such an approach recognizes the primacy of the laws in which a market is located. As investors

---

21. SEC No-action Letter, *College Retirement Equities Fund* (available February 18, 1987). In a subsequent letter, the SEC confirmed the first CREF letter in regard to foreign issuers' rights offerings and exchange offers. SEC No-action Letter, *College Retirement Equities Fund* (available June 4, 1987).

choose their markets, they would choose the laws applicable to such markets."[22]

• *Adoption of Regulation S*

Regulation S was first proposed in June 1988.[23] As suggested in the *1987 Internationalization Report*, the proposed rule was based on a territorial approach to Section 5. "Under such an approach, the registration of securities is intended to protect the U.S. capital markets and all investors purchasing in the U.S. capital market, whether U.S. or foreign nationals. Principles of comity and reasonable expectations of participants in the global market justify reliance on laws applicable in jurisdictions outside the United States to define disclosure requirements for transactions effected offshore. . . . [T]his territorial approach to the application of the registration provisions would not affect the broad reach of the antifraud provisions of the federal securities laws."[24]

Regulation S was adopted in final form in April 1990 with its territorial philosophy intact.[25] The regulation consists of a general statement of the applicability of the registration provisions of the 1933 Act, and it also consists of two nonexclusive safe harbors for the extraterritorial offer, sale and resale of securities.

---

22. *1987 Internationalization Report* at III-317. The new approach had been foreshadowed in a November 1986 speech by Linda C. Quinn, then director of the SEC's Division of Corporation Finance. She observed that it may have been "appropriate before the Euromarket, London, Japan and others evolved into major markets, for the Commission to suggest that securities offered to a U.S. citizen anywhere in the world should comply with the Securities Act. But if this was ever warranted, it surely is not today."

23. SEC Release No. 33-6779 (June 10, 1988) (Proposing Release).

24. *Id.* (footnotes omitted). Unlike Release 33-4708, Regulation S recognized no distinction between Canada and other parts of the world. The Proposing Release stated that given the dramatic changes in the world capital markets since 1964, the SEC was no longer of the view that the Canadian markets should be singled out for special treatment under Section 5. *Id.* at note 64.

25. SEC Release No. 33-6863 (April 24, 1990) ("Adopting Release"). The rule had been reproposed for comment in SEC Release No. 33-6838 (July 11, 1989).

• • *General Statement.* The general statement, contained in Rule 901, defines the terms "offer," "offer to sell," "sell," "sale" and "offer to buy" as used in Section 5 of the 1933 Act as including only "offers and sales that occur within the United States" and as not including offers and sales "that occur outside the United States." The Adopting Release states that the determination "as to whether a transaction is outside the United States will be based on the facts and circumstances of each case. If it can be demonstrated that an offer or sale of securities occurs 'outside the United States,' the registration provisions of the Securities Act will not apply, regardless of whether the conditions of the safe harbor are met. For a transaction to qualify under the General Statement, both the sale and the offer pursuant to which it was made must be outside the United States."[26]

• • *Safe Harbors.* The more useful part of Regulation S consists of the two safe harbors. The *issuer safe harbor* in Rule 903 deems certain offers or sales by an issuer or a distributor (or any affiliate or person acting on their behalf) to be outside the United States for purposes of Rule 901 (i.e., the general statement). The *resale safe harbor* in Rule 904 is available for certain offers and sales outside the United States by all persons other than those covered by Rule 903 (except for certain officers and directors of an issuer).

Each of the safe harbors is subject to the general conditions relating to the presence of an "offshore transaction" and the absence in the United States of "directed selling efforts."

• • *Offshore Transaction.* An offer or sale of securities is made in an "offshore transaction" if (i) the offer is not made to a person in the United States (other than a distributor) and (ii) at the time the buy order is originated, the buyer is outside the United States or the seller and any person acting on his behalf reasonably believes that the buyer is outside the United States. There are two alternatives to the second requirement. For purposes of the issuer

---

26. As proposed, the general statement would have included a list of factors to be considered in determining whether an offer or sale occurred outside the United States. Commenters generally opposed such a list as more harmful than helpful. Adopting Release (text following note 28).

safe harbor, it is sufficient if the transaction is executed in, on or through a physical trading floor of an established foreign securities exchange. For purposes of the resale safe harbor, it is sufficient if the transaction is executed in, on or through the facilities of a "designated foreign securities market"[27] and neither the seller nor any person acting on its behalf knows that the transaction has been prearranged with a buyer in the United States.

Notwithstanding these provisions, offers and sales of securities specifically targeted at identifiable groups of U.S. citizens abroad, such as members of the armed forces serving overseas, are not deemed to be made in "offshore transactions." On the other hand, offers and sales to certain persons not considered to be "U.S. persons" (see below) are permitted even though these persons are physically located in the United States.

As noted in the Adopting Release, "[a]ctivities specifically excluded from the definition of directed selling efforts also will not be deemed offers in the United States" for purposes of the offshore transaction requirement.

• • *Directed Selling Efforts.* The term "directed selling efforts" means "any activity undertaken for the purpose of, or that could reasonably be expected to have the effect of, conditioning the market in the United States for any of the securities being offered in reliance on . . . Regulation S." The principal problems under this definition relate to advertising, quotation services and research.

• • • *Advertising.* The definition of "directed selling efforts" includes the placement of an advertisement in a publication with a general circulation in the United States that refers to the Regulation S offering.[28] On the other hand, the definition

---

27. As defined in Rule 902(a)(1). The SEC or its staff had designated by April 1997 a total of 26 offshore markets as "designated offshore securities markets" for this purpose. Additional markets may be so designated by the Division of Corporation Finance, acting pursuant to delegated authority, on the basis of criteria specified in Rule 902(a)(2).

28. A publication has a general circulation in the United States if it either (a) is printed primarily for distribution in the United States or (b) has had, during the preceding 12 months, an average circulation in the United

specifically excludes certain forms of advertisement. It is permissible to place an advertisement required to be published under U.S. or foreign law or regulation that contains no more information than legally required and contains a statement that the securities have not been registered under the 1933 Act and may not be offered or sold in the United States (or, if applicable, to a U.S. person) without registration or an exemption. It is also permissible to place a limited tombstone advertisement in a foreign publication if less than 20% of the foreign publication's circulation (calculated by aggregating its U.S. and "comparable" non-U.S. editions) is in the United States.[29]

• • • *Quotations.* According to the Adopting Release, distribution in the United States of a broker-dealer's quotations for a security offered in reliance on Regulation S could be construed as directed selling efforts. Rule 902(b)(6) provides, however, that this will not be the case with U.S. distribution of a foreign broker-dealer's quotations by a third-party system that distributes quotations "primarily in foreign countries" if two conditions are met: (1) that the system not permit transactions between foreign broker-dealers and persons in the United States and (2) that contacts not be initiated within the United States or with U.S. persons beyond those permitted under the SEC's safe harbor rule for foreign broker-dealers (i.e., Rule 15a-6 under the 1934 Act).

• • • *Research.* According to the Adopting Release, the "[d]istribution or publication in the United States of information, opinions or recommendations concerning the issuer or any class of its securities could constitute directed selling efforts,

---

States of 15,000 or more copies per issue. Where a foreign publication produces a separate edition with a general circulation in the United States, only the U.S. edition will be considered a publication with a general circulation in the United States if the affiliated non-U.S. editions together do not meet the definition when the U.S. edition is disregarded. Rule 902(k).

29. Rule 902(b)(4) specifies the permitted content of the tombstone, which the Adopting Release describes as similar to that permitted under Rule 134. The rule also prescribes certain legends that must be included. For a discussion of what editions of a foreign publication are "comparable" for purposes of a tombstone advertisement, *see* the Adopting Release at note 55.

depending on the facts and circumstances." As to reporting issuers only, however, the Adopting Release carves out of "directed selling efforts" the publication of information, opinions and recommendations that essentially meet the requirements of Rule 139(b) under the 1933 Act.[30] There is no parallel treatment, however, to permit research material on issuers qualifying for Forms S-3 or F-3 to come within the more liberal provisions of Rule 139(a). Moreover, there is no relief whatsoever for non-reporting issuers. In fact, the Adopting Release addresses the SEC's expectation that the effect on the market of information, opinions or recommendations relating to non-reporting issuers may be "more significant due to the possible absence of other publicly available information about the issuer," and it recommends that "[d]istributors and their affiliates should exercise even greater caution . . . concerning non-reporting issuers or their securities." As one of the authors observed several years ago:

> In the U.S. domestic market, it is probably not really significant that Rule 139 does not apply to non-reporting issuers. At any given time, the number of non-reporting companies that are about to file registration statements is quite small; the likelihood that securities analysts will be writing about such companies in the "regular course of their business" is even smaller.
>
> On the other hand, the number of non-reporting issuers making offshore distributions in reliance on Regulation S is likely to be extremely large. It includes all foreign sovereign governments, many international organizations and an even larger number of foreign private issuers. The securities of many of these issuers are owned extensively by U.S. investors and are followed closely by U.S. securities analysts. Foreign sovereign debt, for example, often provides a convenient vehicle

---

30. I.e., "reasonable regularity," "normal course of business," reference to a "substantial number" of other companies or a "comprehensive list" of recommended securities, no "materially greater space or prominence" and no more favorable opinion or recommendation.

for acting upon conclusions regarding foreign exchange and interest rate outlooks. U.S. investors are also important buyers of the equity securities of non-reporting foreign private issuers, in U.S. markets as well as abroad, and many U.S. broker-dealers' research departments follow such stocks either in the United States or through their overseas affiliates. An interpretation of "directed selling efforts" that would inhibit the flow of research material on these issuers to U.S. investors would either prejudice U.S. investors (or encourage them to rely on foreign analysts), or seriously undermine the usefulness of Regulation S.[31]

Indeed, the SEC subsequently amended Rule 139 to extend its benefits to many non-reporting foreign private issuers, and the amendment is undeniably helpful in the case of an SEC-registered offering by such an issuer.[32] The SEC has done nothing, however, to ensure the continuity of research in the United States while such an issuer is making an offshore offering in reliance on Regulation S.

• • • *Miscellaneous Activities.* In the Adopting Release, the SEC tried to provide comfort that the prohibition on directed selling efforts would not prevent an "isolated, limited contact with the United States,"[33] the dissemination of "routine information of the character and content normally published by a company, and unrelated to a securities offering," the conduct of "bona fide journalistic activities" or the flow of "normal corporate news." It is also made clear in the Adopting Release

31. Joseph McLaughlin, *"Directed Selling Efforts" Under Regulation S and the U.S. Securities Analyst*, 24 Rev. of Secs. & Comms. Reg. 117, 120 (1991).

32. SEC Release No. 33-7053 (April 19, 1994). The rule was further amended in 1995 to clarify that its benefits are available for qualifying foreign private issuers' initial public offerings in the United States. SEC Release No. 33-7132 (February 1, 1995).

33. Such a contact, however, might constitute an offer in the United States for purposes of the offshore transaction requirement. Adopting Release at note 60.

that it is permissible to initiate selling efforts *from the United States* so long as they are directed abroad.

In response to complaints by U.S. journalists that they were being excluded from foreign issuers' news conferences, Preliminary Note 7 to Regulation S specifically states that nothing in the regulation "precludes access by journalists for publications with a general circulation in the United States to offshore press conferences, press releases and meeting with company press spokespersons in which an offshore offering or tender offer is discussed, provided that the information is made available to the foreign and United States press generally and is not intended to induce purchases of securities by persons in the United States or tenders of securities by United States holders in the case of exchange offers." As discussed below under "Global Offerings by Foreign Corporations—Foreign Publicity," the SEC in late 1996 proposed the adoption of a new Rule 135e that would exclude from the definition of "offer" for Section 5 purposes certain offshore activities involving "journalists."

Not long after the adoption of Regulation S, a listed U.S. company completed an offshore convertible debt offering in reliance on the new regulation. It not unreasonably concluded that its U.S. stockholders might want to know about the offering and accordingly filed a report of the transaction on Form 8-K. The SEC staff criticized the issuer in strong terms on the theory that the report on Form 8-K amounted to directed selling efforts in respect of the convertible offering. This position was untenable from the beginning, and the SEC eventually amended the definition of directed selling efforts in 1994 to exclude notices in accordance with Rule 135 or newly-adopted Rule 135c.[34]

• • • *Extent of Prohibition.* The prohibition on directed selling efforts applies for the entire period that the issuer, the distributors, their affiliates and any persons acting on their behalf are offering and selling the securities and for any additional "restricted period" described below. Any violation of the prohibition on directed selling efforts by any of these persons pre-

---

34. SEC Release No. 33-7053 (April 19, 1994).

cludes reliance on the safe harbor *by any person*. Importantly, however, "[o]ffering activities [in the United States] in contemporaneous registered offerings or offerings exempt from registration will not preclude reliance on the safe harbors."[35]

• • *Issuer Safe Harbor.* Rule 903 provides a safe harbor for offers and sales of securities by an issuer, a distributor, their respective affiliates or any person acting on their behalf. A particular offering will be eligible to qualify for one of the three channels provided by the safe harbor. Each channel requires compliance with a set of conditions that are more or less restrictive according to the potential of the particular offering for flowback to the United States and the potential harm to investors if such flowback were to occur.[36]

• • • *Category 1 Transactions.* The conditions relating to the presence of an offshore transaction and the absence of directed selling efforts in the United States are the only conditions that must be met for "Category 1 transactions," i.e., those referred to in Rule 903(c)(1). These include: (a) offerings by foreign issuers that reasonably believe at the start of their offering that there is no "substantial U.S. market interest" (popularly known as "SUSMI") in the security being offered,[37] (b)

---

35. Adopting Release at note 47.

36. In the case of offerings of debt securities that are fully and unconditionally guaranteed as to principal and interest by the issuer's parent company, Rule 903(c)(5) provides that the relevant category is determined by the status of the guarantee and not by the status of the guaranteed security.

37. SUSMI exists with respect to a class of equity securities if U.S. exchanges and inter-dealer quotation systems constituted the single largest market for such securities in the last fiscal year (or the period since the issuer's incorporation) *or* 20% or more of all trading in such securities took place during such period on U.S. exchanges and inter-dealer quotation systems and less than 55% of such trading took place in or through the market facilities of a single foreign country.

SUSMI exists with respect to a class of debt securities if *all* of the following conditions apply: (a) the issuer's debt, preferred and asset-backed securities are held of record by 300 or more U.S. persons, (b) $1 billion or more of such securities is held by U.S. persons and (c) 20% or more of the outstanding amount of such securities is held by U.S. persons.

"overseas directed offerings" by foreign issuers and, in certain cases, by U.S. issuers,[38] (c) securities backed by the full faith and credit of a foreign government and (d) certain employee benefit plans of foreign issuers.

• • • *Category 2 Transactions.* Category 2 includes all transactions by U.S. or non-U.S. reporting issuers[39] and any debt[40] transactions by a non-reporting foreign issuer. Transactions covered by Category 2 require the imposition of specified selling restrictions as well as compliance with the two general conditions. In the case of reporting issuers, the selling restrictions "are designed to protect against an indirect unregistered public offering in the United States during the period the market is most likely to be affected by selling efforts offshore. In the event flowback of reporting issuers' securities does occur after the restricted period, the information relating to such securities publicly available under the Exchange Act generally

---

38. An "overseas directed offering" is an offering of securities "directed into a single country other than the United States to the residents thereof and that is made in accordance with the local law and customary practices and documentation of such country." Rule 902(j)(1). U.S. issuers may take advantage of the overseas directed offering option only if the offering is limited to non-convertible debt, preferred stock or asset-backed securities that are denominated in a currency other than U.S. dollars and that are neither convertible into U.S. dollar-denominated securities nor linked to U.S. dollars in a manner that has the effect of converting the securities into U.S. dollar-denominated securities. On the other hand, the securities may be combined with interest rate or currency swaps that are "commercial in nature." Rule 902(j)(2). The distinction between "linkages" and "swaps commercial in nature" is sometimes elusive in practice.

39. A reporting issuer must be obligated to file 1934 Act reports and have filed all required 1934 Act reports for a period of twelve months prior to the Regulation S offering (or such shorter time the issuer was required to file reports). Foreign issuers that file pursuant to Rule 12g3-2(b) are not reporting issuers for Category 2 purposes. A foreign issuer for whose securities there is no SUSMI may, of course, proceed under Category 1.

40. "Debt" for Category 2 purposes includes non-participating preferred stock and asset-backed securities "because of the similarity of the market for these securities to the debt market." Adopting Release at notes 106–08.

should be sufficient to ensure investor protection." In the case of debt transactions by foreign issuers, the SEC expects the restrictions to provide adequate protection against an indirect U.S. distribution "because of the generally institutional nature of the debt market and the trading characteristics of debt securities."

The restrictions for Category 2 transactions include restrictions on particular offers and sales ("transactional restrictions") and "offering restrictions."

Transactional restrictions require that the securities sold under Regulation S prior to the expiration of a 40-day restricted period not be offered or sold to or for the benefit or account of a U.S. person. (No certification to this effect is required by Regulation S, although in the case of debt securities a certification may be required for tax purposes as discussed below.) In addition, a distributor selling securities to another distributor or to a dealer or any person receiving a selling concession or similar compensation must include in any confirmation sent prior to the expiration of the 40-day restricted period a notice stating that the purchaser is subject to the same restrictions on offers and sales that apply to the distributor.[41] Importantly, non-compliance with a transactional restriction precludes reliance on the safe harbor by the person who failed to comply as well as its affiliates and persons acting on their behalf, but such non-compliance does not affect anyone else's ability to rely on the safe harbor.[42]

The 40-day restricted period is defined in Rule 902(m) by reference to the later of the date upon which the securities were first offered to persons other than distributors in reliance upon Regulation S or the date of closing of the offering. In the case of a continuous offering, the restricted period commences "upon completion of the distribution of such tranche, as deter-

---

41. Unlike the no-action letters issued under Release 33-4708, it is not necessary to seek to create a binding agreement to abide by the restrictions. Screen-based confirmations or other notices may be used, including a summary notice if all subscribers to a screen-based system are provided with a key that includes the full text of a notice. Adopting Release at note 129.

42. Adopting Release at note 109.

mined and certified by the managing underwriter or person performing similar functions;"[43] however, in the case of a continuous offering of non-convertible securities "in identifiable tranches" (e.g., MTNs), the restricted period for a tranche commences upon the manager's certification of the completion of the distribution of that tranche. Significantly, all offers and sales by a distributor of an unsold allotment are deemed to be made during the restricted period. After the expiration of the restricted period, the securities (other than unsold allotments) are no longer subject to restrictions.

The term "U.S. person" is defined in Rule 902(o). Unlike the no-action letters issued under Release 33-4708, residence in the U.S. rather than U.S. citizenship is the principal factor in determining the status of a natural person under Regulation S. Thus, the Adopting Release illustrates, a French citizen resident in the United States is a U.S. person. The following persons other than natural persons are also "U.S. persons" for purposes of Category 2:

- Any partnership or corporation organized or incorporated under the laws of the United States. According to the Adopting Release, however, "[a]n entity organized under foreign law by a U.S. person principally for the purpose of investing in unregistered securities is a U.S. person unless organized and owned by accredited investors (as defined in Regulation D) who are not natural persons, estates or trusts." Moreover, a branch or agency of a foreign entity is treated as a U.S. person if it is located in the United States. Branches and agencies of U.S. banks and insurance companies located outside the United States are not treated as U.S. persons if they operate for valid business reasons, are engaged in the banking or insurance business and are subject to "substantive local banking or insurance regulation."

---

43. Special conditions apply in the case of a continuous offering of securities to be acquired upon the exercise of warrants.

- Any trust of which any trustee is a U.S. person, except that a U.S. professional fiduciary may act as trustee if another trustee who is not a U.S. person has sole or shared investment power and no beneficiary of the trust (and no settlor of a revocable trust) is a U.S. person. (Note that the presence of U.S. persons as beneficiaries is irrelevant if there is no U.S. person acting as trustee.)

- Any estate of which any executor or administrator is a U.S. person, except that a U.S. professional fiduciary may act as executor or administrator if another executor or administrator who is not a U.S. person has sole or shared investment power and the estate is governed by foreign law.

- Any non-discretionary account or similar account (other than an estate or trust) held by a dealer "or other fiduciary" for the benefit or account of a U.S. person.

- Any discretionary account or similar account (other than an estate or trust) held by a dealer "or other fiduciary" that is a U.S. person, unless the person exercising investment discretion is a professional fiduciary and the account is held for the benefit or account of a non-U.S. person.

Certain multilateral organizations with significant operations in the United States are expressly excluded from the definition of U.S. person. These include the United Nations, the International Monetary Fund, the World Bank, certain regional development banks "and any other similar international organizations, their agencies, affiliates and pension plans."

Contacts with U.S. professional fiduciaries acting with investment discretion for the accounts of non-U.S. persons, in their capacities as such, and with multinational organizations excluded from the definition of U.S. person, are also excluded from the definition of "directed selling efforts." Offers and sales to such persons are also deemed to be made in offshore transactions.

Offering restrictions are procedures intended to ensure compliance with the transactional restrictions and must be adopted for the entire offering by the issuer, the distributors, their affiliates and any persons acting on their behalf. The restrictions require distributors to contract that all their offers and sales will be made in accordance with the safe harbor, any other available exemption or pursuant to registration under the 1933 Act. In addition, all offering materials and documents (other than press releases) used in connection with offers and sales prior to the expiration of the restricted period must disclose that the securities have not been registered under the 1933 Act and may not be offered or sold in the United States or to a U.S. person (other than a distributor) unless registered or entitled to an exemption from registration. This disclosure must appear at specified places in the prospectus or offering circular and in all advertisements. Unlike the transactional restrictions, failure to implement the offering restrictions will preclude the availability of the safe harbor for *all* parties.

• • • *Category 3 Transactions.* Category 3 includes all transactions not covered by Categories 1 or 2, including those presumed to be most at risk for "flowback" into the United States (e.g., debt or equity offerings by non-reporting U.S. issuers or equity offerings by foreign issuers where SUSMI exists for such securities). Category 3 transactions must meet the general conditions relating to the presence of an offshore transaction and the absence of directed selling efforts and must comply with more extensive offering restrictions than in the case of Category 2 transactions.

One such offering restriction is that any distributor selling securities to another distributor or to a dealer or any person receiving a selling concession or similar compensation must include in any confirmation sent prior to the expiration of the restricted period (40 days or one year, as noted below) a notice stating that the purchaser is subject to the same restrictions on offers and sales that apply to the distributor.

In the case of debt securities, the offering restrictions also require that (a) any offer or sale prior to the end of a 40-day restricted period not be made to a U.S. person or for the account or benefit of a U.S. person (other than a distributor) and (b) the securities be represented by a temporary global certificate that cannot be exchanged for definitive securities until the expiration of the 40-day restricted period and until certification of beneficial ownership of the securities by non-U.S. persons (or by any U.S. person who purchased the securities in an exempt transaction).

In the case of equity securities, the offering restrictions also require a *one-year* restricted period and satisfaction of *all* of the following additional conditions:

- The purchaser (other than a distributor) must certify that it is not a U.S. person and is not acquiring the securities for the account or benefit of a U.S. person (or that it acquired the securities pursuant to an exemption),

- The purchaser (other than a distributor) must agree to resell only in accordance with Regulation S, pursuant to registration under the 1933 Act or in reliance on an exemption,

- In the case of a U.S. issuer, the securities must contain a legend to the effect that transfer is prohibited except in accordance with the provisions of Regulation S (which presumably includes transfers pursuant to registration or in reliance on an exemption), and

- The issuer is required by contract or charter or by-law document to refuse to register any transfer of securities not in accordance with the provisions of Regulation S (except that if the securities are in bearer form or foreign law prohibits such refusal, then other reasonable procedures may be implemented to prevent any impermissible transfer).

• • *Resale Safe Harbor.* In addition to the safe harbor for issuer and distributor transactions, Regulation S provides a safe harbor for resales by persons other than the issuer, any distributor, any of their respective affiliates (except an officer or director who is an affiliate solely by virtue of such position) or any person acting on their behalf.

The resale safe harbor requires compliance with the general conditions requiring the presence of an "offshore transaction" and the absence of directed selling efforts in the United States by the seller, any affiliate or any person acting on their behalf. An "offshore transaction" for this purpose is defined, however, to require that the buyer be outside the United States or that the seller and any person acting on his or her behalf reasonably believe this to be the case. In the alternative, the transaction must be executed on or though a "designated offshore securities market"[44] without any knowledge on the part of the seller or any person acting on his or her behalf that the transaction has been pre-arranged with a buyer in the United States.

Additional conditions apply to resales by certain affiliates or securities professionals. If a person is an affiliate of an issuer or a distributor solely because he or she holds the position of an officer or director, then that person may rely on the resale safe harbor if he or she pays no more than the "usual and customary broker's commission that would be received by a person executing such transaction as agent." A dealer or other person receiving selling compensation in connection with the offering may rely on the safe harbor to resell securities prior to the expiration of the restricted period if neither the seller nor any person acting on its behalf knows the offeree or buyer to be a U.S. person[45] and if a confirmation or other notice of applicable restrictions is sent to any purchaser known to be another securities professional.

• • *Private Placements in United States Concurrent with Public Offerings Abroad.* Like Release 33-4708 before it, Regulation S expressly contemplates that a private placement in the United States may take place at the same time as an offshore public offering in reliance on the safe harbor.[46] Also, a preliminary note to Regulation D states that Regulation S may be relied upon for offers and sales of securities outside of the United States even if coincident offers and sales are made in accordance with Regulation D inside the United States.

---

44. *See* note 27, *supra.*
45. There is no "duty of inquiry." Adopting Release at note 140.
46. Adopting Release at note 47.

In recent years, it has become commonplace to provide for a U.S. private placement in connection with an international public offering of debt or equity securities. Sales in these private placements generally have been limited to institutions that qualify as QIBs under Rule 144A. In some cases, sales to institutional accredited investors may also be permitted.

The U.S. private portion of the transaction is generally coordinated by the managing underwriters, and individual underwriters and dealers are not permitted to sell any securities in the United States without coordinating with the managers.

• • *Convertible Securities.* According to the Adopting Release, convertible securities are generally treated for purposes of the issuer safe harbor and the applicable restricted periods like the security into which they are convertible. However, where the securities are not convertible before any applicable restricted period would have ended if the underlying securities had themselves been offered and sold under the issuer safe harbor, then the restricted period is determined by reference to the convertible security. "Thus, an offering of convertible debt securities by a foreign issuer with substantial U.S. market interest in its debt and equity securities would fall within the second category of the issuer safe harbor if the debt securities are not convertible for 13 months but would fall within the third issuer safe harbor category if the debt securities were convertible after 11 months." For purposes of determining SUSMI, the measurement is made both by reference to the convertible security and the underlying security. If SUSMI exists in either case, it exists with respect to the convertible securities.

The issuance of common stock upon conversion of debentures is exempt pursuant to Section 3(a)(9) of the 1933 Act, which exempts exchanges by an issuer with its own securityholders. According to the Adopting Release, where such a conversion takes place during the applicable restricted period, the securities issued on conversion will be restricted only for the remainder of the restricted period.[47]

---

47. Adopting Release at note 75.

• • *SEC Concerns with "Abusive" Regulation S Transactions.* Preliminary Note 2 to Regulation S states that neither the general statement nor any of the safe harbors is available "with respect to any transaction or series of transactions that, although in technical compliance with . . . [the] rules, is part of a plan or scheme to evade the registration provisions of the [1933] Act." In mid-1995 the SEC published an interpretive release setting forth its views "concerning problematic practices under Regulation S" and requesting comment as to whether Regulation S should be amended "to limit its vulnerability to abuse."[48] The SEC stated that it had learned that some market participants were conducting placements of securities purportedly offshore under Regulation S "under circumstances that indicate that such securities are in essence being placed offshore temporarily to evade registration requirements with the result that the incidence of ownership of the securities never leaves the U.S. market, or that a substantial portion of the economic risk relating thereto is left in or is returned to the U.S. market during the restricted period, or that the transaction is such that there was no reasonable expectation that the securities could be viewed as actually coming to rest abroad." These transactions, the SEC concluded, were of the kind "that run afoul of Preliminary Note 2" and would therefore not be covered either by the general statement in Rule 901 or by the safe harbors in Rule 903.

The release went on to describe transactions such as "parking" securities with offshore affiliates of the issuer or a distributor, the use of non-recourse promissory notes expected to be repaid with the proceeds of a resale of the Regulation S securities into the U.S. market, fees paid or discounts granted to induce the purchaser to hold the securities for the restricted period, and short selling or other hedging having the effect of transferring the risk of ownership of the securities back to the U.S. market.

The SEC asked for comment on whether Regulation S should be amended in certain respects to deter the perceived abuses. Proposed amendments included an extension of the re-

---

48. SEC Release No. 33-7190 (June 27, 1995).

stricted periods, the exclusion of certain discounted offers from the safe harbor, a prohibition of "risk shifting transactions" during the restricted period and a prohibition of the use of certain types of non-recourse or other types of promissory notes.

In late 1996 the SEC adopted rules to require U.S. companies reporting under the 1934 Act to report unregistered sales of equity securities. It did so in the belief that this would discourage abusive practices under Regulation S. In general, exempt sales of equity securities were required to be reported on Form 10-Q; equity securities offered in reliance on Regulation S, however, would have to be reported on Form 8-K within 15 days of the "sale."[49]

The SEC followed up on this rulemaking by proposing additional rule changes in early 1997. These changes would lengthen to *two years* the restricted period for equity securities of U.S. issuers (or non-U.S. issuers for whom the principal market is in the United States). They would also classify securities sold pursuant to Regulation S as "restricted securities" and preserve the status of such securities as restricted securities even if resold offshore pursuant to the resale safe harbor. The proposals would also prohibit the use of promissory notes as payment for these securities and require purchasers to agree not to engage in certain hedging transactions.[50]

• *Eurobonds*

Eurobonds are debt securities that are underwritten by international syndicates and sold—and subsequently traded—in significant measure outside the country in whose currency the securities are denominated. The equity counterpart to the market for "Eurobonds" is the market for "Euroequities." As the SEC pointed out in its 1987 staff report on the internationalization of the securities markets, "[t]he prefix 'Euro-' is somewhat of a misnomer today. Originally, the market was centered in London and existed throughout Europe. In recent years, how-

---

49. SEC Release No. 34-37801 (October 10, 1996). There was no elaboration in the release as to whether "sale" for this purpose meant the date of offering or the date of closing.

50. SEC Release No. 33-7392 (February 20, 1997).

ever, with the advent of financial deregulation worldwide, the Euromarkets have greatly exceeded their original boundaries, have no national boundaries and are used by borrowers and lenders on a worldwide basis."[51]

Eurobonds are frequently denominated in dollars, in which case they are called Eurodollar obligations. Eurobond offerings are to be distinguished from those international bond transactions where an issuer sells securities denominated in the currency of another country through a syndicate of underwriters based primarily in that country. An example would be a sale by a Finnish issuer of bonds denominated in German marks directed to the German market and underwritten by a syndicate of German banks and German branches of international banks.

• • *Syndicate Procedures.* The procedure traditionally followed for an offering of bonds in the Euromarket prior to the advent of "bought deals" was to issue a press release on "launch day" and, at the same time, invite the underwriters and selling group members by telex; to fix the terms of the issue on "offering day;" and to close approximately two weeks later.[52] The bought deal was first used extensively in early 1979,[53] and, since that time, it has become the norm for straight debt financings. Now, the traditional procedures are used principally for offerings of bonds with an equity kicker.[54]

In the case of a bought deal, the offering is launched with the transmittal of a telex from the lead manager to those investment firms that are invited to become part of the "management group." Unlike the traditional practice, there rarely will be separate underwriting or selling groups. At the time that the telex is sent, the terms of the obligations have been fixed, including their maturities and the rate of interest to be paid annually (as opposed to semi-annually as is customary in the United States). The telex will set forth the underwriting commission and the amount of the praecipuum to be paid out of the underwriting commission to the lead

---

51. *1987 Internationalization Report* at III-4 note 2.
52. F.G. Fisher, *Eurobonds* 74 (Euromoney 1988).
53. *Id.* at 16.
54. *Id.* at 73.

manager. The co-managers are asked to accept the invitation by sending to the manager a telex in a prescribed form not later than a specified number of days following the transmittal of the invitation telex. Unlike the practice in the United States, the managers usually will assume with each other on a joint and several basis the responsibility for subscribing to the entire issue. The telex also will set forth the amount of the selling concession, the issue price and the other terms of the securities, including any cross-default provision and redemption provisions.

The managers will enter into a subscription agreement or underwriting agreement with the issuer anywhere from two weeks to a month later, and at the same time they will enter into an agreement among managers. The offering circular will be dated the same date. The closing will take place a week or two later.

The offering circular may contain a caveat to the effect that the distribution and the offering of the securities in certain jurisdictions may be restricted by law and that persons into whose possession the offering circular comes are required to inform themselves about and to observe any applicable restrictions.

London is the center of Eurobond activity, and each manager will represent, and the offering circular will so state, that it has not and will not offer or sell the securities in the United Kingdom, by means of any document, other than to persons whose ordinary business activities involve them in acquiring, holding, managing or disposing of investments (whether as principal or as agent) (except in certain circumstances that would not constitute an offer to the public within the meaning of the Companies Act of 1985 and certain regulations thereunder). Each manager will also comply with all applicable provisions of the Financial Services Act of 1986 with respect to anything done in, from or otherwise involving the United Kingdom, and it will also issue or pass on in the United Kingdom any document relating to the offering only to certain sophisticated investors.

Eurodollar obligations may be issued under an indenture with an indenture trustee, as in the case of a U.S. offering. More frequently, however, they will be issued under a fiscal agency agreement. In the latter case, the fiscal agent will not assume a fiduciary obligation to the holders of the securities. Eurodollar obligations are generally issued in bearer form. As will be seen, however, the issuance of bearer bonds by U.S. corporations requires compliance with certain procedures under the Internal Revenue Code.

The securities will be listed in Luxembourg or London in order to make them eligible for investment by certain institutions. The principal reason for listing is to broaden the market for the securities. Residents of certain countries are prohibited by exchange control regulations and other restrictions from owning foreign securities unless they are listed. Some institutions have a policy of buying only listed bonds.[55]

• *EuroMTNs*

As we have seen, frequent issuers of debt securities in the U.S. market recognize that shelf registration offers advantages of cost, speed and flexibility over stand-alone SEC-registered debt offerings. It should, therefore, be no surprise that continuous issue programs have become an important factor in international debt financing. While the Eurobond market is still larger in terms of outstandings ($2 trillion in Eurobonds at the end of 1995 compared to half a trillion in EuroMTNs), the EuroMTN market grew at a compound rate of 69% a year between 1990 and 1994 compared with 13% a year for the Eurobond market.[56] Growth in the market has been fueled principally by deregulation that has permitted issuers to access funds in currencies other than U.S. dollars, frequently in combination with a currency swap that would produce the desired currency at a cost savings. In 1991, for example, EuroMTN tranches were issued in eight currencies; by 1996, EuroMTNs were denominated in 32 currencies.[57]

U.S. issuers have recently accessed the EuroMTN market as an alternative to their U.S. funding sources. While some U.S. government-sponsored enterprises have been able to launch global programs because of their exemption under the 1933 Act, most U.S. issuers rely on Regulation S as a basis for the

---

55. *Id.* at 105.

56. *Ten Years Old—And A Prosperous New Year for EuroMTNs?* Corporate Finance (January 1996) at 22.

57. *A Vision of the Future*, Euromoney (March 1996) at 114.

exemption of their EuroMTN program from the registration requirements of the 1933 Act.

• *Eurocommercial Paper*

Like the EuroMTN market, the Eurocommercial paper market is generally thought to have started in 1986. The market has recently grown to more than $100 billion, the bulk of which is attributable to between 350 and 400 rated programs.[57] The advantages of Eurocommercial paper include a cost-effective source of funding, the ability to raise funds in a variety of currencies (often accompanied by currency swaps), the low cost of establishing a program and the ability to use proceeds for any purpose (in contrast to the U.S. requirement that commercial paper be used for "current transactions"). Also, a Eurocommercial paper program can serve as an introduction to the capital markets and an introduction to investors for lesser-known credits. For example, Eurocommercial paper is frequently the precursor of a EuroMTN program.[58]

U.S. issuers of Eurocommercial paper can find an exemption from the registration requirements of the 1933 Act either in Regulation S or, if the maturity and "current transactions" standards are met, in Section 3(a)(3) of the 1933 Act. See Chapter 10.

Tax Considerations

The structure of an offering of Eurodollar obligations by a U.S. issuer is driven by U.S. tax considerations as well as by Regulation S. U.S. corporate debt obligations sold in the Euromarket are traditionally in bearer form, although this is becoming less uniform in the case of securities targeted to institutions. The primary tax concerns relate to (a) the "TEFRA D" sanctions on issuers of bearer obligations sold to U.S. investors and (b) a U.S. issuer's obligation to make gross-up payments to compensate holders for the imposition of U.S. withholding taxes.

58. *More Potential Still for the Euro CP Market*, Corporate Finance (July 1996) at 10.
59. *Id.*

• *TEFRA D Issuer Sanctions*

The Tax Equity and Fiscal Responsibility Act of 1982 added Sections 163(f) and 4701 to the Internal Revenue Code, which provide sanctions for any person who issues "registration-required obligations" in bearer form to U.S. persons (the "issuer sanctions"). The issuer sanctions deny a deduction for interest payments on such obligations (Section 163(f)(1)) and subject the issuer to an excise tax equal to the product of 1% of the obligation's principal amount and the number of calendar years to maturity (Section 4701(a)).[60] The purpose of the issuer sanctions is to prevent U.S. taxpayers from acquiring bearer obligations, thereby facilitating their avoidance of U.S. federal income taxes.

Section 163(f)(2)(B) (commonly known as the "Eurobond exception") provides an exception from the issuer sanctions for a bearer obligation that (a) is sold under arrangements reasonably designed to ensure that it will be sold (or resold in connection with its original issue) only to non-U.S. persons, (b) the interest on which is payable only outside the United States and its possessions and (c) has a legend on its face that any U.S. person who holds the obligation will be subject to limitations under the U.S. income tax laws, including the limitations provided in Sections 165(j) and 1287(a) (the "holder sanctions").[61]

Shortly after the SEC adopted Regulation S, the Treasury issued new regulations applicable to debt instruments issued under the Eurobond exception on or after September 7, 1990. Previously, an issuer could establish the Eurobond exception by following procedures designed to comply with Release 33-4708 and relying on an opinion of counsel that the 1933 Act was not appli-

---

60. For purposes of these provisions, the term "registration-required obligation" means any obligation (including any obligation issued by a governmental entity) other than an obligation that (i) is issued by a natural person, (ii) is not of a type offered to the public, (iii) has a maturity (at issue) of not more than one year, or (iv) is an obligation described in Section 163(f)(2)(B). Section 163(f)(2)(A).

61. The holder of a registration-required obligation issued in bearer form is denied a loss on the sale or exchange of the obligation (Section 165(j)) and is denied capital gain treatment on any gain on the obligation (Section 1287).

cable because the securities were intended for distribution to persons who were not U.S. persons. The old Treasury regulations looked to SEC standards to determine whether the Eurobond exception was available. The new regulations established an exemption, known as the "D Exemption," that stands on its own. The exemption cannot be established simply by complying with Regulation S. Thus, the procedures for a Eurobond financing must be established with two sets of regulations in mind.

The first requirement for the establishment of the D Exemption is that neither the issuer nor any distributor may offer or sell the obligation during a 40-day restricted period to a person who is within the United States or its possessions or to a "U.S. person." A distributor must covenant that it will not do so and must establish procedures designed to ensure that its employees are aware of the restrictions. The restricted period is essentially the same as that provided for in Regulation S, but the definition of "U.S. person" is different. While Regulation S excludes citizens residing abroad from the definition of U.S. person, Section 7701 of the Internal Revenue Code defines a U.S. person to include any citizen of the United States.

Notwithstanding the tax definition of U.S. person, the D Exemption contains one substantial concession to the liberalized overseas sales provisions of Regulation S. A bearer obligation can be sold to a U.S. person outside of the United States if that person buys and holds the obligation through a foreign branch of a U.S. financial institution, including a U.S. bank or securities firm. Direct sales to foreign branches of U.S. financial institutions are permitted as well, as are sales to international organizations such as the World Bank.

A second requirement is that neither the issuer nor a distributor may deliver the obligation within the United States in connection with a sale that occurred during the 40-day restricted period. There is also a certification requirement. Except in the case of offshore offerings targeted to a single foreign country, a certificate must be provided to the issuer on the earlier of the date of the first interest payment or the date of delivery by the issuer of the obligation in definitive form. The certificate must state that the obligation is owned by a non-U.S. person or by an exempt U.S. person, including a foreign branch of a U.S. financial institution and a U.S. person who acquired the obligation through a foreign branch of a U.S. financial institution and holds it there on the date of certification. This certification requirement has the effect of preventing reporting companies from taking full advantage of the liberalized procedures permitted under Regulation S.

An obligation issued in bearer form may be converted to registered form in order to permit its resale into the United States or to a U.S. person. But once an obligation is in registered form, it may not be converted to bearer form for sale to a foreign person. The retention in the new regulations of the prohibition of two-way convertibility has been criticized by the financial community as a serious impediment to the creation of a truly global market.

Debt obligations issued with a maturity of less than one year are not subject to the issuer sanctions or holder sanctions.

• *Withholding Taxes and Gross-Up Obligations*

Compliance with the TEFRA D regulations will exempt a U.S. issuer's obligation from U.S. federal withholding tax, backup withholding tax and information reporting. If an obligation with a maturity of 183 days or less is sold to a non-U.S. person, however, the obligation will be subject to backup withholding and information reporting unless the issuer receives an Internal Revenue Service Form W-8 (Certificate of Foreign Status) from the beneficial owner. The issuer can avoid having to collect Form W-8s if the obligation is issued under specific guidelines. U.S. issuers in the Euromarket will nevertheless agree, subject to certain limitations and exceptions, to pay to a foreign holder of their debt securities such additional amounts as may be necessary so that every net payment of principal and interest on the securities, after deducting or withholding for or on account of any present or future U.S. tax or other governmental charge imposed upon the holder or by reason of the making of such payment, will be not less than the amount provided for in the obligations and the related coupons. This "gross-up" agreement protects the holder against a change in U.S. tax law that would subject it to a withholding tax. If it appears that the additional amount will be payable, the issuer will have the right to redeem the obligations, in whole but not in part, upon notice, at a redemption price equal to the principal amount of the debt together with accrued interest.

Common Stock Issues by U.S. Issuers Through U.S. and International Syndicates

A portion of any common stock offering registered under the 1933 Act may find its way into the hands of foreign investors. For larger offerings, the underwriters frequently conduct road shows in Europe and Asia as well as in major cities in the United States, and for years foreign underwriters have been included in U.S. underwriting syndicates. Sometimes the foreign underwriters would be listed separately in the "Underwriting" section of the prospectus.

Beginning in 1986, the practice developed in connection with large SEC-registered common stock offerings of having a separate international syndicate to market a portion of the offering. The first deal to have dual syndicates is believed to have been the January 15, 1986 offering of common stock of The Black & Decker Corporation where 6.5 million shares were solely underwritten by Salomon Brothers Inc. and two million shares were underwritten by an international syndicate represented by Salomon Brothers International Limited. In addition to (or in lieu of) an international syndicate, there may be a group of underwriters responsible for sales in specific regions or countries.

The agreement entered into between the U.S. underwriters and the international underwriters provides for sales between the two syndicates in amounts that may be mutually agreed upon at the initial public offering price less the selling concession. In anticipation of this need for flexibility and fungibility, all of the shares included in the offering are registered under the 1933 Act by means of a single registration statement. The two prospectuses will be identical except for the cover page, the "Underwriting" section, and the back cover page. The international prospectus will also include a section on U.S. tax considerations. The alternate pages for the international prospectus will be set forth in the registration statement following the U.S. prospectus.

The underwriting arrangements for the foreign tranche are essentially the same as those for the domestic tranche and, accordingly, the international underwriters will enter into an underwriting agreement at the same time as the U.S. underwriters, and the closings will be held concurrently.

As there are two separate underwriting agreements, a decision must be made as to the extent to which the two offerings are interdependent. Should the U.S. underwriters be required to close if for some reason the foreign underwriters fail to do so? In the Black & Decker offering, neither closing was conditioned upon the other. In other offerings, the U.S. underwriters may have the right to terminate the U.S. underwriting agreement, and the international underwriters may have the right to terminate the international purchase agreement, if the closings under each of these agreements did not occur concurrently. In other cases, the closing of the larger offering (where there is a significant disparity in the size of the international and U.S. offerings) may be a condition to the closing of the smaller offering, but the reverse will not be true. This is all a matter of business judgment and may depend in part on the extent to which the proceeds of one or both offerings are required for a particular purpose.

In this type of transaction, efforts are made to keep the two offerings separate and distinct. The international underwriters will agree that they are not purchasing any shares of common stock for the account of any U.S. person and that they will not offer or sell any common stock or distribute the prospectus to any person within the United States or to any U.S. person. The U.S. underwriters will make the same agreement with respect to persons other than U.S. persons. The agreement between the two syndicates will contain provisions providing for the coordination of their activities. The manager of the U.S. syndicate will have full control of stabilizing activities, but stabilization will be for the account of both syndicates.

SEC-Registered Offerings by Foreign Private Issuers

Historically, the United States has been an important source of equity capital for foreign private issuers through the sale of shares represented by American depositary receipts ("ADRs").

The United States also provides a market in which debt securities may be offered by foreign private issuers and by foreign governments or international organizations. While non-U.S. issuers often prefer to tap the U.S. capital markets by means of private placements, they are also able and willing to use the U.S. public markets when it is in their interest to do so. A foreign issuer selling securities to the public in the United States must, of course, comply with the registration and prospectus delivery obligations imposed by the 1933 Act. As we will see, the SEC has been assiduous (up to a point) in encouraging foreign issuers to access the U.S. public markets, accommodating them in various ways, including the availability of registration forms that are tailored to the special circumstances of non-U.S. issuers. The SEC has even modified the continuous reporting requirements of the 1934 Act, which apply to any issuer that enters the U.S. public markets, to accommodate the needs of non-U.S. issuers.

• *American Depositary Receipts*

There is nothing that prevents a U.S. person from owning shares of a foreign company. Direct ownership is inconvenient, however, and the American Depositary Receipt ("ADR") was developed to mitigate this inconvenience.[62] An ADR is a negotiable receipt, resembling a stock certificate, that is issued by a U.S. bank to evidence shares of a foreign company that have been deposited with it and that are held at its branch office in the country of origin. The shares underlying the ADRs are called American Depositary Shares or ADSs. When an ADS represents a single share, there is virtually no distinction between it and the share that it represents. The ADS concept becomes especially useful, however, when the foreign shares trade in their local market at a price that is far lower than that to which U.S. investors are accustomed. On occasion, an ADS

---

62. *See generally* J.W. Royston, *The Regulation of American Depositary Receipts: Americanization of the International Capital Markets*, 10 N.C.J. Int'l L. & Com. Reg. 87 (1985); R.E. Moxley, *The ADR: An Instrument of International Finance and a Tool of Arbitrage*, 8 Vill. L. Rev. 19 (1962).

will represent a fraction of a foreign share, thus effectively splitting a high priced stock.

The use of ADRs simplifies the ownership of foreign shares by U.S. investors. Settlement is easier, especially if the ADRs are listed on the New York Stock Exchange or the American Stock Exchange or traded on NASDAQ. If the investor purchased the ordinary shares in the issuer's home country, the investor would have to purchase foreign currency in order to make payment for the shares. Also, settlements are routinely late in many foreign countries.

Custody and notice arrangements can also present problems for purchasers of ordinary shares. In some countries, for example, shares are customarily in bearer form. Issuers rely on advertisements in local newspapers to notify stockholders of dividend payments. Where ADRs are issued to represent bearer shares, the depositary will be responsible for collecting the dividend, converting it into dollars and paying it to the registered holder of the ADR (who may, of course, be the investor's broker-dealer). The depositary will perform a similar function in the case of stock dividends and rights offerings.

Morgan Guaranty Trust Company of New York takes credit for initiating and developing the concept of ADRs. It claims to have issued the first ADR in 1927 for Selfridge Stores, now a part of Sears Holdings p.l.c.[63] On the other hand, Irving Trust Company (now merged into The Bank of New York) testified to the SEC that it had been issuing ADRs against shares of Roan Antelope Copper Mines since 1926.[64] Nearly 70 years later, there were more than 1200 ADR programs.[65] In 1980, ADRs representing 350 million shares were traded. This volume ballooned to more than 5.6 billion shares in 1996.[66]

---

63. *American Depositary Receipts* (Morgan Guaranty Trust Company of New York Brochure).

64. *Official Report of Proceedings Before the SEC in the Matter of Conference on American Depositary Receipts* 7 (June 20, 1955) [hereinafter *ADR Proceedings*].

65. The Bank of New York, *Depositary Receipts (ADRs and GDRs) January 1, 1996 through June 30, 1996.*

66. *Id.*

ADRs are invariably the vehicle used in connection with an SEC-registered public offering by a non-U.S. issuer. A program set up for this purpose is called a "Level 3" program. Less frequently, a non-U.S. issuer will set up an ADR program solely for the purpose of listing the ADRs on a U.S. exchange or having them quoted on NASDAQ. A program set up for this purpose is called a "Level 2" program. Both Level 2 and Level 3 programs require extensive disclosure on the part of the non-U.S. issuer. Most ADR programs are set up at the "Level 1" stage, i.e., an ADR that trades in the over-the-counter "pink sheet" market.

A program at the Level 1 stage can be unsponsored or sponsored by the issuer. The growing trend is for issuers to establish sponsored facilities. An unsponsored program may come into being when interest in a foreign company develops in the U.S. market and a bank, probably at the suggestion of a broker-dealer, responds with an ADR program to facilitate trading. The depositary simply asks the foreign company for its approval in establishing the ADR program. In an unsponsored program, the investors bear the cost of the ADR facility. In a sponsored ADR program, the issuer pays the depositary for administrative and stockholder-related expenses and will undertake to provide the depositary with financial information and other materials for dissemination to the holders of the ADRs.

When the 1933 Act was adopted, a substantial number of ADR facilities were in place. The question then arose whether additional ADRs could be issued without going through the registration process. At that time, Section 3(a)(1) of the 1933 Act provided an exemption for securities that had been sold or disposed of by the issuer in a bona fide offer to the public prior to 60 days after the enactment of the statute. Early on, the SEC took the position that where an ADR facility had been established prior to the Section 3(a)(1) cutoff date and where prior to that date the offer to issue ADRs against a deposit of shares outstanding on that date had been made, registration of the ADRs was not required even though they were issued after the cutoff date.[67] The SEC also permitted the issuance of ADRs

---

67. Moxley, *supra* note 62, at 29.

against shares issued by way of a stock dividend on shares outstanding prior to the cutoff date.[68] Subsequently, depositary
banks and their counsel persuaded members of the SEC's staff
that, where underlying shares could be sold in the United States
without registration in reliance upon what is now the Section
4(1) exemption, they could be made the subject of ADRs on the
theory that the ADRs themselves were entitled to the Section
3(a)(2) exemption as securities issued by a bank.[69]

The legal status of ADRs continued to be fuzzy into the
mid-1950s. In 1955, Irving Trust Company announced that it
would issue ADRs against 34 selected foreign securities.[70]
When Guaranty Trust Company became aware of the new program, its counsel called the director of the Division of Corporation Finance to request an opinion similar to the one that was
reported to have been given to Irving. The response was that he
was not familiar with the matter but that he would look into it.
Later that day, he advised counsel that he was concerned about
various problems connected with the program and that the entire matter was to be brought before the SEC. He further stated
that, until the SEC had taken some action, he regarded it inadvisable for a bank to proceed with a general issue of ADRs.
When Irving Trust Company learned of this, it quite naturally
was distressed. One can imagine the reaction of its officers to
the fact that counsel for Guaranty Trust Company had mucked
up its program by raising the issue with the SEC.

The next development was an all-day conference at the SEC
on June 20, 1955 among four of the commissioners, members
of the staff, representatives of the major New York City banks
that issued ADRs and the banks' counsel. As a result of this
conference and subsequent discussions with the staff, the SEC
determined that ADRs were not entitled to the Section 3(a)(2)
exemption. Instead, it adopted a simplified registration form
that would enable banks to issue ADRs without undue difficulty or expense.[71] The result was Form S-12,[72] which could

---

68. ADR Proceedings, *supra* note 64, at 32.
69. *Id.* at 8 and 42.
70. *Id.* at 7.
71. Moxley, *supra* note 62, at 29.

be used to register ADRs where the holder was entitled to withdraw the underlying securities at any time and where the deposited securities, if sold in the United States, would not be subject to the registration provisions of the 1933 Act. The form provided that the prospectus could be the ADR itself and that the only items of information required to be set forth were the terms of deposit, a description of any fees or charges that could be imposed on a holder, the name and address of the depositary, and a statement as to the availability for inspection of reports and communications emanating from the issuer of the underlying securities.

The form stated that the entity created by the agreement for the issuance of the ADRs was deemed to be the issuer of the ADRs for purposes of the 1933 Act. It provided that the registration statement was to be signed by the depositary bank in the name and on behalf of this fictitious entity. But the form specifically stated that the depositary itself would not be deemed an issuer, a person signing the registration statement, or a person controlling an issuer. By this device, the SEC made the issuance of ADRs possible without subjecting the depositary bank to potential liabilities under Section 11 of the 1933 Act.

(It was not argued in 1955, nor has it been argued since, that ADRs are not securities separate and apart from the underlying shares. But if shares of a foreign corporation can be sold in the United States without registration in reliance upon the exemptions provided by Section 4(1) and Section 4(3) of the 1933 Act, why should the ADRs representing them be subject to registration any more than the actual stock certificates? The functions performed by the depositary bank are custodial and ministerial, and the holder of the ADR may take possession of the underlying shares at any time. If an ADR is a separate security, why not a monthly statement received from a brokerage firm showing the ownership of securities in a securities account and held by the broker in street name?)

---

72. SEC Release No. 33-3593 (November 17, 1955), proposed in SEC Release No. 33-3570 (August 31, 1955).

In 1983, the SEC adopted a new form for registering ADSs represented by ADRs.[73] This is designated Form F-6. It is available where deposited securities are sold in a transaction registered under the 1933 Act or in an exempt transaction. The issuer of the deposited securities must be a reporting company under Section 13(a) or Section 15(d) of the 1934 Act or be exempt under Rule 12g3-2(b), unless the issuer of the deposited securities concurrently files a registration statement on another form covering the deposited securities. As in the case of Form S-12, the prospectus may take the form of the ADR itself.

In 1991 the SEC issued a major release on the ADR market in which it requested information and comment on three principal regulatory areas: (1) whether the substantive disclosure required by Form F-6 was sufficient for the protection of investors, (2) whether depositaries and/or issuers of deposited securities should be required to assume responsibility for the disclosures in a Form F-6 registration statement and to accept 1933 Act liabilities for such disclosures and (3) what information regarding the ADRs themselves should be provided or made available to investors and which market participants should be responsible for providing or making available such information.[74]

- *1933 Act Registration*

In November 1982, the SEC adopted an integrated disclosure system for foreign private issuers.[75] The 1933 Act registration forms for these issuers, Forms F-1, F-2, and F-3, roughly parallel

---

73. SEC Release No. 33-6459 (March 18, 1983).

74. SEC Release No. 33-6894 (May 23, 1991).

75. SEC Release No. 33-6437 (November 19, 1982). The term "foreign private issuer" is defined in Rule 405 under the 1933 Act as any foreign issuer other than a foreign government except an issuer meeting the following conditions: (1) more than 50% of the outstanding voting securities of such issuer are held of record either directly or through voting trust certificates or depositary receipts by residents of the United States; and (2) any of the following: (i) the majority of the executive officers or directors are U.S. citizens or residents, (ii) more than 50% of the assets of the issuer are located in the United States, or (iii) the business of the issuer is administered in the United States. For the purposes of this definition, the term "resident"

Forms S-1, S-2, and S-3 in the domestic system. Form F-1 must be used where the issuer does not qualify for the use of either Form F-2 or Form F-3. To be eligible to use Form F-3, a foreign private issuer must either (a) be registering investment grade debt securities (non-convertible debt securities rated in one of the four highest rating categories by at least one nationally recognized U.S. rating organization) or (b) have an aggregate market value world-wide of its common equity held by non-affiliates that is the equivalent of $75 million or more. It also must have been subject to, and must have complied with, the reporting requirements of the 1934 Act for at least twelve months prior to the filing of the registration statement. In addition, the registrant and its subsidiaries must not, since the end of the last fiscal year for which an annual report on Form 20-F has been filed, have failed to make any required preferred stock dividend or sinking fund payment or defaulted on payment of any material indebtedness or long-term lease rentals.

A majority-owned subsidiary of a foreign private issuer may use Form F-3 to register non-convertible securities even though the subsidiary does not itself meet the requirements of the form, if the parent is eligible to use Form F-3 and fully guarantees the securities as to principal and interest. This exception is useful in those cases where non-U.S. companies offer guaranteed securities through U.S. subsidiaries for tax, legal investment or other reasons.

As in the case of domestic issuers, the staff is prepared to meet with non-U.S. issuers and their advisers in a pre-filing conference for the purpose of discussing anticipated disclosure or accounting problems. In an effort to accommodate non-U.S. issuers, the SEC also informally permits such issuers to make a "confidential" filing of the registration statement for the purpose of comment by the staff. Not only is such a filing confidential, since it does not appear in the public file, but the filing does not even require payment of the filing fee. The staff attempts to provide comments on such filings within the same 30-day period applicable to formal filings.

---

as applied to securityholders means any person whose address appears on the records of the issuer, the voting trustee or the depositary as being located in the United States.

As discussed above, a foreign private issuer selling its shares in a public offering directed to the U.S. market in the form of ADSs represented by ADRs must file a registration statement covering the underlying shares and must also cause the depositary bank to file a registration statement on Form F-6 covering the ADSs. A foreign private issuer that is making a public offering of its debt securities in the United States must also file a registration statement on the appropriate form; in addition, it must qualify an indenture under the Trust Indenture Act of 1939.

In addition to the same persons that are required to sign the registration statement of a domestic issuer, the registration statement of a foreign private issuer must be signed by its authorized representative in the United States.[76] The forepart of the prospectus should set forth information concerning the enforceability in the issuer's home jurisdiction of civil liabilities under the Federal securities laws. The prospectus also should state that substantially all of the issuer's directors and officers, and certain experts named in the registration statement, reside outside of the United States and, as a result, it may not be possible for investors to effect service of process within the United States upon such persons.

• *Disclosure*

The disclosure required of foreign issuers filing a registration statement on Form F-1 largely parallels that required of domestic companies filing on Form S-1. Transactional information required to be set forth in the prospectus (e.g., summary information, risk factors, use of proceeds, determination of offering price, dilution, selling securityholders, plan of distribution and description of registered securities) is specified in Items 1 through 10 of Form F-1. Information about the issuer that Form F-1 requires to be included in the prospectus is specified by reference to Part I of Form 20-F, which is the foreign issuer's counterpart to Form 10-K.

Item 1 of Form 20-F requires a description of the issuer's business. In addition to a description of the issuer's principal

---

76. As a person signing the registration statement, the authorized representative is subject to liability under Section 11 of the 1933 Act.

products and services, its principal markets and its methods of distribution, the issuer must break down total sales and revenue during the past three fiscal years by categories of activity and geographical markets (with sales to unaffiliated customers and sales transfers to other categories of activity of the issuer shown separately). A "relatively homogeneous activity which contributes significantly to total sales and revenue" is to be considered as a separate category of activity.

Item 2 requires a description of the location and general character of the issuer's principal properties. Unlike a U.S. issuer, a non-U.S. issuer need not describe its properties by industry segment.

Other items of Form 20-F require (3) a description of legal proceedings, (4) the disclosure of information relating to controlling persons, (5) the nature of the trading market for each class of securities to be registered, (6) any home country restrictions on the export or import of capital, including exchange controls, and any limitations on the right of nonresident or foreign owners of securities to hold or vote those securities and (7) local taxes applicable to U.S. securityholders and the terms of any tax treaty.

Item 8 of Form 20-F requires a tabular presentation of selected financial information (balance sheet and income statement) for each of the last five years (and for any applicable interim periods). The table must be presented in the same currency, and on the same basis of reconciliation, as the issuer's financial statements in the prospectus. If the issuer's financial statements are not presented in U.S. dollars, the issuer must also disclose a recent exchange rate and provide a five-year history of exchange rates. A dividend table must be provided if equity securities are being registered, and the dividends must be stated in both local currency and in U.S. dollars.

Item 9 requires a Management's Discussion and Analysis of its liquidity, capital resources and results of operation. In the case of a non-U.S. issuer, this will include a discussion of relevant governmental fiscal, monetary or political policies or other factors that have affected or could materially affect the issuer's operations or an investment by U.S. investors.

Item 10 requires an identification of directors and executive officers, including any family relationships. Item 11 requires disclosure of the compensation paid to directors and officers as a group. Information as to individual compensation is required of a non-U.S. issuer only if it otherwise makes this information publicly available.

Item 12 requires information on outstanding options on the non-U.S. issuer's securities, including those held by directors and officers as a group. Again, individual information is required if it is otherwise made public. Item 13 requires the disclosure of certain transactions between the non-U.S. issuer and its directors, officers and significant securityholders, but only to the extent the information is disclosed to stockholders or otherwise made publicly available.

• *Financial Statement Requirements*

It is generally advisable to discuss any accounting questions with the SEC before the registration statement is filed, even on a "confidential" basis. The SEC has in the past shown some flexibility with non-U.S. issuers and required less than full compliance with some of the financial disclosure requirements where the issuer was able to demonstrate that historical compliance was impractical and that systems were in place that would assure future compliance.

• • *Reconciliation to U.S. "gaap."* The financial statement requirements for Form F-1 are specified by reference to Items 17 and 18 of Form 20-F. In either case, the issuer is required to furnish financial statements for the same fiscal years required of a U.S. issuer. The statements must "disclose an information content substantially similar to financial statements that comply with United States generally accepted accounting principles and Regulation S-X." They may be prepared according to U.S. "gaap" or, alternatively, on the basis of another "comprehensive body of accounting principles" if accompanied by a discussion of the material variations between the two systems, including a quantification of such material variations by means of a reconciliation in a specified format of net income and balance sheet line items.

The "reconciliation" requirement is a matter of particular concern to many non-U.S. issuers. In April 1994, the SEC amended Form 20-F to permit first-time non-U.S. private issuers to reconcile the required financial statements and selected financial data for only the two most recent fiscal years and any interim periods, rather than five years as previously required. In each subsequent year, an additional year of reconciliation is required. In addition, the SEC determined in 1994 to accept (without reconciliation to U.S. gaap) cash flow statements and information relating to hyperinflation and business combinations presented in accordance with standards of the International Accounting Standards Committee.[77]

Despite these accommodations by the SEC, there remain many non-U.S. issuers that are unwilling to provide the U.S. gaap reconciliation that Form F-1 and Form 20-K require for a U.S. listing, a NASDAQ quotation or a registered public offering. For one thing, the reconciliation effort involves significant time and expense. For another, reconciled numbers can be confusing to the issuer's home country tax authorities, labor unions and stockholders.

Many non-U.S. issuers do provide U.S. gaap reconciliations, of course. If these numbers were really of value to U.S. investors, one would expect considerable attention to be paid to the announcement of the U.S. gaap numbers as well as any possible effect of these numbers on the issuer's stock price. In fact, the authors are not aware of a single situation where this has been the case. Most non-U.S. issuers' stock prices are set by supply and demand in the home country, and analysts who follow non-U.S. issuers necessarily rely on the issuer's home country financial statements. U.S. investors necessarily follow suit, suggesting that the reconciled numbers are not really "material" in a conventional securities law sense. The same conclusion is suggested by the fact that non-U.S. issuers who offer securities to U.S. investors under Rule 144A are hardly ever called upon to provide reconciled numbers.

---

77. SEC Release Nos. 33-7053 (April 19, 1994), 33-7117 (December 13, 1994) and 33-7119 (December 13, 1994).

There is considerable support internationally for the development of "international accounting standards" under the auspices of the International Accounting Standards Board, which has undertaken to issue such standards by the early part of 1998. The SEC and the Financial Accounting Standards Board profess to be supportive of this process, but both bodies have institutional agendas that may conflict with their willingness to embrace international standards within the near future.

• • *Geographic Market and Industry Segments.* The principal difference between Items 17 and 18 of Form 20-F is that Item 17 does not require the information on geographic market and industry segments called for by U.S. accounting standard SFAS 14. A non-U.S. issuer is entitled to follow Item 17 if it is making a public offering of investment grade non-convertible debt securities or if it is simply listing its securities without making a simultaneous public offering. In all other cases, the non-U.S. issuer must comply with Item 18.

While Item 18 usually imposes a heavier burden on foreign issuers, compliance will afford issuers (if otherwise eligible) full access to the benefits of the short-form registration statements. In view of the full access that Item 18 affords, the SEC advises issuers in the general instructions to Form 20-F to consider the benefits of the availability of short-form registration statements in determining which financial statements to include in their annual reports.

• • *Interim Financial Information.* For the purpose of "reduc[ing] the impediments to foreign issuers making securities offerings in the United States," the SEC amended Section 3-19 of Regulation S-X in November 1993[78] to accommodate the many non-U.S. issuers whose periodic reporting requirements do not extend to quarterly reports. In lieu of requirements that often forced non-U.S. issuers into "blackout" periods, the new rules require audited balance sheets for each of the two most recent fiscal years and audited statements of income and changes in financial position for each of the three preceding fiscal years. If an issuer's registration statement becomes effec-

---

78. SEC Release No. 33-7026 (November 3, 1993).

tive during the first six months of its fiscal year, however, and if the audited balance sheet for the previous fiscal year is not available, Section 3-19 permits the issuer to rely on the audited balance sheets for the two preceding years if the issuer also includes an audited or unaudited balance sheet as of a date within ten months of the effective date. No relief is provided if the filing becomes effective during the second six months of the fiscal year; in addition, if the filing becomes effective during the last two months of the fiscal year, the issuer must also include an audited or unaudited balance sheet as of some date during the fiscal year. In certain rights offerings to stockholders, reinvestment plans or offerings of securities upon conversion or exercise of other securities, the balance sheet may be as old as one year at the time of effectiveness.

In addition, the November 1993 amendments relaxed the reconciliation requirement for interim financial information made available by the non-U.S. issuer on a more frequent basis than required by Section 3-19 of Regulation S-X and, therefore, required to be included in the registration statement. In lieu of a reconciliation to U.S. gaap, the rule now requires only a narrative disclosure and quantification of material variations not previously disclosed or quantified.

The SEC in December 1994 adopted amendments to Rule 3-20 of Regulation S-X to allow a non-U.S. issuer greater flexibility in selecting the reporting currency it uses in SEC filings.[79] Under the amendments, an issuer can state amounts in its financial statements in any currency that it deems appropriate. The same release streamlined the reconciliation requirements for issuers with operations in countries with hyperinflationary economies.

• *Continuous Reporting Under the 1934 Act*

As a result of Section 12(b) of the 1934 Act, an issuer that lists its securities on a U.S. securities exchange must register the listed class of securities under the 1934 Act. By registering a class of securities under the 1934 Act, an issuer ordinarily becomes subject to the reporting, proxy, Williams Act, insider

---

79. SEC Release No. 33-7117 (December 13, 1994).

reporting and short-swing profit recapture provisions of the 1934 Act, as well as to the Foreign Corrupt Practices Act. As discussed below, however, foreign issuers with a class of securities registered under the 1934 Act are exempted by SEC rule only from the proxy provisions of Section 14 and from all provisions of Section 16 (insider reporting and short-swing profit recapture).[80]

The SEC's 1964 *Special Report of Special Study of Securities Markets* recommended in Chapter IX that issuers of unlisted securities having 300 or more "equity securityholders of record and/or known beneficial holders" be made subject to Sections 13, 14 and 16 of the 1934 Act. The study did not consider the implications of this recommendation for foreign issuers whose securities were held by U.S. investors.

The Securities Acts Amendments of 1964 amended the 1934 Act to require for the first time that certain issuers register securities under the 1934 Act and comply with 1934 Act reporting requirements even though the issuers had not listed any securities on a national securities exchange and had not had a registration statement become effective under the 1933 Act. As it passed the Senate, the bill would have exempted all foreign securities (and related ADRs) from the registration and reporting requirements unless the SEC should find by rule or order that a "substantial public market" existed in the U.S. for the equity securities of an issuer (or class of issuers) and that continued exemption would not be "in the public interest or consistent with the protection of investors."[81] This approach was based on the premise that, while U.S. investors in foreign securities ought in principle to be afforded the same protections as were provided for investors in domestic securities, their interests would be adversely affected if foreign securities could not trade at all in U.S. markets. The Senate approach also had the support of the SEC, which believed that enforcement of the registration and reporting requirements of the 1934 Act against for-

---

80. In addition, as a result of Section 15(d) of the 1934 Act, any issuer that makes a registered public offering of securities under the 1933 Act becomes subject to the continuous reporting requirements of the 1934 Act.

81. S. Rep. No. 88-379 at 29 (1963).

eign issuers outside the jurisdiction of the United States (at least those who had not voluntarily sought funds in the U.S. capital markets or a listing on an exchange) would present serious practical difficulties.[82]

On the House side, however, the Senate approach was politically unacceptable to a number of key Congressmen, as evidenced by the following colloquy between SEC Commissioner Manuel F. Cohen and Representative John D. Dingell of Michigan:[83]

> MR. DINGELL. I am talking about the philosophy of the thing. Here you have corporations which are held abroad which have no real interest in the American investor who seek merely to market their securities on terms and under conditions which are most advantageous to them and to get the American dollar under the best circumstances and who really frankly don't give a damn about the American investor. Now, isn't that correct?
>
> MR. COHEN. Well, I don't know that I want publicly to subscribe to that latter part of your statement.
>
> MR. DINGELL. Let's put it on the other hand.
>
> You don't deny that this is so or in many instances would be so, do you, sir?
>
> MR. COHEN. Now, if you are talking in terms of the sale of securities by an issuer seeking funds from the American public, I want to emphasize again, although I don't want to appear argumentative, that registration is required. This provision relates to outstanding securities in the hands of the public.
>
> MR. DINGELL. I don't really care about that. I think we are nitpicking on that particular point. I am talking about the broad matter of public policy. You have already conceded the broad matter of public policy that the American investor should have a higher quality and quantity of protection from foreign issues than he should have from

---

82. *Id.* at 29-31.

83. *Hearings Before a Subcommittee of the Committee on Interstate and Foreign Commerce,* 88th Cong., 1st Sess. 1286 (1964).

issues of corporations which do business and which are owned by citizens of the United States.

MR. COHEN. I agree to that; yes, sir.

MR. DINGELL. All right.

So, it appears to me, very frankly, gentlemen, that this is a rather extraordinary provision of law and it appears to me that it is a substantial diminution in the quality of protection which is afforded to American investors.

The final legislation therefore reversed the Senate position; Section 12(g)(1) as enacted made no distinction between securities of foreign or domestic issuers, but Section 12(g)(3) authorized the SEC by rule or order to exempt any foreign security from the registration requirement.[84] The SEC also received broad power in new Section 12(h) to exempt securities from the provisions of Sections 12(g), 13, 14, 15(d) and 16 of the 1934 Act.

The SEC had opposed the House version of the bill because of what it saw as enforcement problems, possible harm to existing trading markets in foreign securities and its perceived need for greater flexibility. Its first action was to exempt all foreign securities and related ADRs so that no foreign issuer would be required to register until April 30, 1966 (in the case of an issuer whose fiscal year was the same as the calendar year).[85] During the next fourteen months, the SEC studied how best to bring foreign issuers under the 1964 amendments. In November 1965, it noted that its study had "revealed continuing improvement in the reporting of financial and economic information by foreign issuers." Relying in part on this perceived improvement, the SEC at the same time proposed rules that would have required previously non-reporting and unlisted foreign issuers subject to Section 12(g) and having a class of securities held of record by 300 or more U.S. residents to register such securities on a new Form 20 by supplying "certain information, documents and reports which they are either required to make public abroad or which they transmit to their security-holders." (The computation of record holders was to include as

84. H.R. Rep. No. 88-1418 at 11 (1964).
85. SEC Release No. 34-7427 (September 15, 1964).

separate holders the aggregate number of customers on whose behalf a broker-dealer, bank or other nominee held a foreign private issuer's securities; the nominee was "expected" to inform the issuer on request of the number of separate accounts.) The SEC justified the 300-holder breakpoint on the basis that "the existence of 300 holders resident in the United States indicates a sufficient public interest in a foreign security to warrant registration *by the issuer* . . ." (emphasis added). ADRs were to be exempted but not the underlying shares.[86]

A proposed amendment to Rule 3a12-3—which exempted certain foreign issuers from Sections 14(a) and 16 of the Act—would have made these provisions wholly applicable to North American issuers (including Canadian and Mexican companies) as well as to foreign issuers having more than half of their stock held by U.S. residents or whose principal business was conducted in the U.S. Other foreign issuers would have been exempt from the proxy solicitation rules only if they kept their U.S. solicitation efforts within prescribed limits. The SEC's rule package also contemplated a procedure by which the SEC would identify foreign issuers it thought were subject to the registration requirement and invite them to state why registration was not required; non-responding issuers or those whose responses were unsatisfactory would be put on a "list," and broker-dealers would be required to inform their customers of the foreign issuers' non-compliance with the registration requirement.

Comments on the 1965 proposals—including comments from the U.K. and Canadian governments, supported by the International Law Committee of The Association of the Bar of the City of New York[87]—criticized them as improper under international law. The committee believed there was no problem under international law in an SEC requirement that foreign issuers comply with SEC regulations "to the extent that foreign issuers 'voluntarily' accept the jurisdiction of the Commission, for example, by listing their securities on a stock exchange in the United States or by publicly selling their securities in the United States . . ." On the other hand,

---

86. SEC Release No. 33-7746 (November 16, 1965).
87. 21 *The Record* 240 (1966).

the committee noted that "[h]ow United States shareholders acquired their shares in these foreign issuers is irrelevant in determining the applicability of the Act—that is, the fact that United States persons acquired shares in the foreign corporation through their own actions and with no encouragement or assistance from the foreign corporation does not affect the applicability of the Act . . ."

The committee cited Section 18(b) of the 1965 *Restatement (Second), Foreign Relations Law of the United States* as standing for the proposition that, as a matter of United States "municipal law," the United States could exercise its "legislative jurisdiction" over persons outside the United States who engaged in conduct that had a "substantial effect" within the United States and "a direct causal relationship." Merely having 300 stockholders in the United States did not, in the committee's view, meet this test. The committee drew an analogy to due process standards imposed by the U.S. Supreme Court on a state's attempt to assert personal jurisdiction over nonresident defendants. The committee believed a non-U.S. corporation, neither listing nor selling securities in the U.S., could not be subject to U.S. jurisdiction under the "standard" that looks to "some act by which [the foreign corporation] purposefully avails itself of the privilege of conducting activities within the forum state [asserting jurisdiction], thus invoking the benefits and protections of its laws."[88]

The committee was less concerned about the imposition on foreign issuers generally of registration and reporting requirements than it was about the potential application to foreign issuers—especially Canadian and other North American issuers—of U.S. proxy (Section 14) and insider trading (Section 16) regulation. As to the latter, it suggested that the SEC might "diminish the seriousness of the violation of international law" by adopting a rule that would exempt foreign "companies which voluntarily furnish [to the SEC] substantially the information required" by the SEC's proposed rules, "even though the fundamental problem of the extent of United States jurisdiction would remain."

Commenters also believed that the proposals would likely have the effect of retarding foreign countries from adopting im-

---

88. *Id.* at 251, quoting *Hanson v. Denckla*, 357 U.S. 235, 253 (1958).

proved corporate and securities laws. After extending the temporary exemption for foreign securities for another year,[89] the SEC requested foreign issuers subject to Section 12(g) and having more than 300 U.S. resident holders of equity securities to furnish it with certain home country information. In August 1966, the SEC published a list of 80 companies that it believed had complied with its request and a list of 32 companies that had not furnished information to the SEC pursuant to its request. It stated that it thought such lists would be "useful" to broker-dealers in making recommendations to their customers.[90]

In April 1966, the SEC adopted amendments to Rule 3a12-3 providing for full exemptions from Sections 14 and 16 for foreign issuers unless they were North American companies or what the SEC later referred to as "essentially United States companies" (i.e., companies that had more than 50% of their voting securities held of record directly or indirectly by U.S. residents *and* either their business was administered principally in the U.S. or 50% or more of their directors were U.S. residents).[91]

In April 1967, the SEC referred to the information provided by foreign issuers and its study of improvements in the reporting of financial information by foreign issuers. It concluded that "the continuing improvement in the quality of the information now being made public by foreign issuers, together with the improvement which may reasonably be expected to result from recent changes and current proposals for change in relevant requirements, warrants the provision of an exemption from Section 12(g) for those foreign companies which have not sought a public market for their securities in the United States through public offering or stock exchange listing." The exemption—set forth in Rule 12g3-2(b)—required the foreign issuer to furnish to the SEC information it was required to make public abroad or transmit to its securityholders and to identify the information as being furnished for the purpose of claiming the exemption. This information would not be deemed "filed" with the SEC, and the issuer would, therefore, not be subject to potential liability under Section 18 of the

---

89. SEC Release No. 34-7867 (April 21, 1966).

90. SEC Release No. 34-7934 (August 10, 1966).

91. SEC Release No. 34-7868 (April 21, 1966).

1934 Act. (There was no mention of Rule 10b-5.) Canadian and other North American issuers were eligible to take advantage of the new exemption, in which case they would not be subject to the proxy rules (Section 14) or the insider trading and reporting rules (Section 16).[92]

As originally adopted, Rule 12g3-2 required a list identifying the information furnished and provided that, if the issuer had prepared an English translation or version of a document, it should furnish that translation or version rather than the original language document. A foreign language document nevertheless could satisfy the requirements of the rule. Some issuers shipped off to the SEC crates of foreign language documents with no identifying list.[93]

Rule 12g3-2(b)(4) therefore currently provides:

> Press releases and all other communications or materials distributed directly to securityholders of each class of securities to which the exemption relates shall be in English. English versions or adequate summaries in English may be furnished in lieu of original English translations. No other documents need be furnished unless the issuer has prepared or caused to be prepared English translations, versions, or summaries of them. If no English translations, versions, or summaries have been prepared, a brief description in English of any such documents shall be furnished. Information or documents in a language other than English are not required to be furnished.

The SEC did not adopt proposed special rules for broker-dealers who dealt in foreign securities. It noted that information concerning certain foreign issuers might not be available in the U.S. and that broker-dealers should take this into consid-

---

92. SEC Release No. 34-8066 (April 28, 1967). Professor Loss suggests that the SEC's "shift . . . from the special registration procedure it had originally proposed [for foreign private issuers] to the technique of a conditional exemption" was "presumably for psychological reasons." 2 Loss & Seligman 782 (3d ed. 1989).

93. Jennings & Marsh, *Securities Regulation* 1593-94 (6th ed. 1987).

eration "in deciding whether they have a reasonable basis for recommending these securities to customers."[94]

Rule 12g3-2(b) was an exemption, of course, only from the registration requirements of Section 12(g). An issuer whose securities were listed on a U.S. securities exchange was required to register these securities under Section 12(b). An issuer whose securities were unlisted, however, was eligible for the Rule 12g3-2(b) exemption notwithstanding the number of U.S. holders or the volume of trading in the over-the-counter market.

Only four years after the adoption of the Rule 12g3-2(b) exemption, the NASD initiated its automated interdealer system for electronically disseminating quotations known as NASDAQ. By the early 1980s the SEC had come to the conclusion that "trading on NASDAQ is substantially the same as trading on an exchange,"[95] and it proposed in October 1982 an amendment to Rule 12g3-2(b) that would have made that rule's exemption unavailable for foreign private issuers whose securities were traded in NASDAQ.[96] In support of its proposal, the SEC cited an issuer's necessary involvement in applying for a NASDAQ "listing," the payment of fees and the meeting of specific standards as evidence of "voluntary" entry into the U.S. capital markets.[97] The effect of the proposal was to force affected foreign issuers to choose between registering their securities under Section 12(g) or "delisting" their securities from NASDAQ and leaving them to trade in the "pink sheets."

As might be expected, comment was overwhelmingly critical of the SEC proposal. Predicted consequences of a shift to "pink

---

94. The history of the 1964 legislation makes clear, however, that if a foreign issuer subject to Section 12(g) does not comply with the SEC's registration and reporting requirements, this will not of itself mean that trading in its securities in the United States will be illegal or that broker-dealers trading in these securities will have civil liability as a result. H.R. Rep. No. 88-1418 at 11 (1964).

95. SEC Release No. 33-6493 (October 6, 1983).

96. SEC Release No. 33-6433 (October 28, 1982).

97. The SEC candidly admitted, however, that many foreign issuers had in fact not taken any action in support of a NASDAQ listing for their securities; the relevant obligations had been undertaken, and the fees paid, by the depositary banks that issued the related ADRs.

sheet" trading included "increased price spreads, decrease in information, price quotes not carried in newspapers, less liquid market[s] and fewer institutions in the market, absence of NASD surveillance, and delays in execution of transfers."[98] One commenter estimated that these factors could cause a price drop of 20%. In view of these concerns, the SEC decided to strike a "pragmatic balance" and apply only prospectively its view that foreign issuers of NASDAQ securities should be regarded as "voluntarily seeking U.S. trading markets." It accordingly "grandfathered" indefinitely those non-Canadian foreign private issuers that were in compliance with the Rule 12g3-2(b) exemption as of October 5, 1983 and quoted in NASDAQ as of that date. Securities of Canadian issuers were "grandfathered" only until January 1986, in view of what the SEC described as recent "hot-issue" problems involving Canadian securities.

Once a non-Canadian foreign private issuer becomes subject to the reporting requirements of the 1934 Act by listing its securities on a U.S. exchange or NASDAQ or by registering securities under the 1933 Act, the applicable reporting forms are an annual report on Form 20-F and interim reports on Form 6-K. Form 20-F also is used by foreign issuers for the initial registration of their securities pursuant to Section 12(b) or Section 12(g). Canadian issuers that have securities listed on a U.S. exchange or quoted on NASDAQ, or that exceed the Section 12(g) threshold of equity securities held of record by U.S. residents, must also use these forms unless they are eligible to use Forms 40-F or 6-K (which apply only to certain Canadian issuers under the SEC's Multijurisdictional Disclosure System applicable to Canadian issuers).

• *Multijurisdictional Disclosure System*

In 1991, the SEC and the Canadian Securities Administrators adopted a multijurisdictional disclosure system ("MJDS") for use by the United States and each of the provinces and territories of Canada.[99] The MJDS was developed to allow quali-

---

98. SEC Release No. 33-6493 (October 6, 1983).

99. SEC Release No. 33-6902 (June 21, 1991); *National Policy Statement No. 45—Multijurisdictional Disclosure System*, 14 OSC Bull. 2889 (June 28, 1991).

fied companies in the United States and Canada to make public offerings and file periodic reports in both countries while being regulated only in their home country. The MJDS allows Canadian issuers to register securities under the 1933 Act by means of a Canadian prospectus (with certain additional U.S. disclosures) using a "wrap-around" 1933 Act registration form. These public offerings may be made in conjunction with a contemporaneous Canadian public offering or the public offering may be made only in the United States. The MJDS is available to Canadian private issuers and crown corporations.

Under the MJDS, specific registration forms are available for Canadian issuers. Form F-9 is used to register investment grade debt securities, while Form F-10 is used to register equity or non-investment grade debt securities. F-7 is used for rights offerings. Unlike Forms F-1, F-2 and F-3, the SEC staff will not review registration statements filed pursuant to the MJDS, absent special circumstances, and such registration statements are effective immediately upon filing or, for U.S.-only offerings registered on Forms F-9 and F-10, at some later date as specified by the Canadian issuer. The principal jurisdiction in Canada designated by the issuer is responsible for conducting any review of the filings. On the other hand, the MJDS offering remains subject to the SEC's authority to issue a "stop order" if the SEC believes such an order is in the public interest and necessary for the protection of investors.

Since the adoption of the MJDS for Canadian issuers, the SEC has occasionally referred to the MJDS as a first step in responding to the internationalization of the capital markets. The SEC has also expressed interest in extending the MJDS concept to include foreign countries other than Canada.

Sales in the United States by Foreign Governments and Their Political Subdivisions

Foreign governments and their political subdivisions frequently borrow in the U.S. capital markets through the issuance of debt securities. Although securities issued or guaranteed by the United States and its instrumentalities are exempt from the registration requirements of the 1933 Act, a similar exemption is not

afforded to securities issued or guaranteed by foreign governments.[100] At or about the time that the 1933 Act was adopted,
American investors held more than $1.5 billion dollars of de-
faulted foreign government bonds,[101] and Congress could hardly
be expected to provide an exemption for these securities from the
registration requirements of the new 1933 Act.

• *1933 Act Registration*

Section 7 of the 1933 Act requires any "foreign government,
or political sub-division thereof" registering securities under the
1933 Act to follow the disclosure requirements of Schedule B to
the 1933 Act. The SEC has never adopted registration forms for
these issuers comparable to those it has adopted for private issuers
(e.g., S-1, S-2, S-3, F-1, F-2 and F-3), and non-U.S. governmental
issuers therefore continue to be guided by the statutory disclosure
requirements of Schedule B as well as by SEC review policy and
the self-enforcing policing mechanisms of the securities markets.

The term "political subdivision" is not defined in the 1933 Act,
and the SEC has not developed express criteria for determining
whether or not a particular issuer is a "political subdivision" for
purposes of Schedule B. The SEC has, however, issued a number
of no-action letters and provided informal advice on Schedule B
eligibility. These letters and informal advice suggest the following:

–   First, the SEC is more likely to allow a non-U.S. is-
     suer to file a Schedule B registration statement if the
     issuer is formed by governmental action for the pur-
     pose of performing governmental functions delegated
     to it, or if the issuer is formed pursuant to an agree-

---

100. Section 304(a)(6) of the Trust Indenture Act of 1939 exempts from
the provisions of that statute "any note, bond, debenture, or evidence of
indebtedness issued or guaranteed by a foreign government or by a subdivision, department, municipality, agency, or instrumentality thereof."

101. According to a key Senate report, about $4.9 billion of foreign
government securities were outstanding as of March 1, 1934 of which about
$1.5 billion were in default. These securities included national govern-
ments, states, provinces, departments and municipalities. S.Rep. 1455 pursuant to S.Res.84 (72d Cong.) and S.Res. 56 and S.Res. 97 (73d Cong.)
(June 6, 1934) at 91.

ment among countries to serve their joint interests. In some cases, however, the SEC may require that the registration statement also be signed by the government or governments for which the issuer is performing such functions.

–   Second, the SEC has issued favorable letters only to issuers that in effect have the credit support of a government, either by operation of law or in the form of an unconditional guarantee or pursuant to call provisions applicable to subscribed but unpaid capital. In one case, this included back-to-back lending arrangements pursuant to which the government undertook to pay principal and interest on the same terms as the issuer's borrowing. In the case of an express guarantee, of course, the guarantee will have to be registered as a separate security, and the government will have to sign the registration statement.

–   Third, each of the issuers in the favorable no-action letters had legal immunities and exemptions commonly associated with governmental bodies, agencies and instrumentalities.

Whether or not an issuer with an ambiguous status is entitled to follow Schedule B is usually discussed with the SEC in a pre-filing conference. At such a conference, the issuer should be prepared to provide the SEC with detailed information about the issuer and its relationship to a government.

Schedule B requires the disclosure of specified information about the issuer (including a governmental guarantor, if applicable), the offering and the underwriters. The required information includes the use of proceeds, the amount and nature of funded debt, any defaults on external debt within the past 20 years, receipts and expenditures, legal matters and information relating to the offering. Rules 490 through 493 modify certain Schedule B requirements applicable to outstanding debt, underwriting arrangements and legal matters.

Schedule B does not require audited financial statements, but the SEC usually requires a Schedule B issuer to include in the registration statement any financial statements that it otherwise publishes. Reconciliation to U.S. "gaap" is not required, but the SEC may require such explanation of the financial statements as it believes may be appropriate for U.S. investors.

The fact that Schedule B specifies only minimal disclosure does not mean that no other disclosure is required. Underwriters, investors and the SEC expect substantial additional disclosure, including in the case of a sovereign country information regarding its geography, population and political system, its economy, monetary system, foreign trade and balance of payments, foreign exchange, public finance, public debt and other relevant matters. An issuer other than a government or political subdivision will provide additional information concerning its business, financial condition and results of operations.

Take, for example, the February 3, 1994 prospectus covering the first U.S. public offering by the People's Republic of China. The offering involved U.S. $1 billion of ten-year bonds. The prospectus provided information on the issuer's geography, population, governmental structure, international relations and membership in international organizations. It then described the country's economy, including economic reforms, major economic indicators, environment, employment and wages, foreign investment and securities markets. The prospectus discussed the country's foreign trade and balance of payments, including its most favored nation status with the United States and its intentions regarding its status as a contracting party to the General Agreement on Tariffs and Trade. Information was provided on the country's balance of payments and official international reserves. The prospectus described the country's public finances, including the budget process, revenues and expenditures (on-budget and off-budget) and plans for fiscal reform. The prospectus included a section on the country's legal system, including the role of the courts, access to the courts by foreign persons and the enforceability of foreign judgments and arbitration awards. As contemplated by Schedule B, there was a description of the country's internal and external public debt.

The prospectuses of other foreign governments follow the same format. These documents are marvelous sources of information, whether or not one is interested in buying the securities.

• *Consent to Service and Sovereign Immunity*

It is customary for a foreign governmental issuer to appoint an agent in the United States on whom process may be served in an action based on the issuer's securities; however, this appointment does not usually extend to actions brought against the issuer under the securities laws. It is also customary for a foreign governmental issuer to waive its sovereign immunity, but again not with respect to alleged securities law violations. The waiver of sovereign immunity in respect of the foreign governmental issuer's securities may not be strictly necessary. The Foreign Sovereign Immunities Act of 1976 ("FSIA")[102] provides that a foreign government is not immune from the jurisdiction of U.S. courts in an action based upon "commercial activity carried on in the United States by the foreign state; or upon an act performed in the United States in connection with a commercial activity of the foreign state elsewhere; or upon an act outside the territory of the United States in connection with a commercial activity of the foreign state elsewhere and that act causes a direct effect in the United States." The FSIA defines "commercial activity" by reference to "the nature of the course of conduct or particular transaction or act, rather than by reference to its purpose," and the U.S. Supreme Court held in 1992 that a foreign state's issuance of debt obligations was "commercial activity" for purposes of enforcement under the FSIA of a breach-of-contract claim.[103] In the same case, the Court also held that a unilateral rescheduling of debt obligations payable in New York was sufficient to cause a "direct effect" in the United States.

There is no direct authority as to whether a foreign governmental issuer may claim sovereign immunity with respect to the federal securities laws. If the issuance of debt securities in the U.S. markets is "commercial activity" under the FSIA for purposes of a breach-of-contract action, it is difficult to see why the conclusion should be any different where the claim is based on, e.g., insufficient disclosure. It is also possible that a foreign governmental issuer's registration of its securities under the

---

102. 28 U.S.C. § 1605(a)(2) (1994).
103. *Republic of Argentina v. Weltover, Inc.*, 112 S. Ct. 2160 (1992).

1933 Act might be held to constitute an implied waiver of any such immunity.

The following excerpt from a People's Republic of China prospectus relates to jurisdictional matters:

> China is a foreign sovereign state. Consequently, it may be difficult for investors to obtain or realize upon judgments of courts in the United States against China. China will irrevocably submit to the jurisdiction of any state or federal court in the Borough of Manhattan, The City of New York in any action arising out of or based on the Securities brought by any holder of a Security (other than any action arising out of or based on United States federal or state securities laws). In addition, China will irrevocably waive, to the fullest extent permitted by law, any immunity, including foreign sovereign immunity, from jurisdiction to which it may otherwise be entitled in any action arising out of or based on the Securities (other than any action arising out of or based on United States federal or state securities laws) brought in any state or federal court in the Borough of Manhattan, The City of New York or in any competent court in China; provided, however, China will not waive its sovereign immunity with respect to the assets necessary for the proper functioning of China as a sovereign power, including military assets, and including real property and buildings and the contents thereof owned by the Ministry of Foreign Affairs and located outside of China. Because China has not waived its sovereign immunity in connection with any action arising out of or based on United States federal or state securities laws, it will not be possible to obtain a United States judgment against China based on such laws unless a court were to determine that China is not entitled under the Foreign Sovereign Immunities Act of 1976 (the "Immunities Act") to sovereign immunity with respect to such action. Furthermore, under the Immunities Act, execution upon the property of China in the United States to enforce a judgment is limited to an execution

upon property used for the commercial activity on
which the claim is based, and China has not waived any
immunity which may otherwise be available to it with
respect to the execution of any judgment. China has
been advised by its PRC counsel, the Law Department
of the Ministry of Finance, People's Republic of China,
that there is doubt as to the enforceability in China of
any actions to enforce judgments of United States courts
arising out of or based on the Securities, including judgments arising out of or based on the civil liability provisions of United States federal or state securities laws,
primarily because there is no treaty or other arrangement or basis for reciprocal enforcement of judgments
between China and the United States. China has also
been advised by its PRC counsel that there is doubt as
to the enforceability in original actions brought in PRC
courts of the civil liability provisions of United States
federal or state securities laws. See "Description of
Debt Securities—Governing Law; Consent to Service"
and "Description of Warrants—Governing Law; Consent to Service".

As noted in Chapter 8, the SEC has made the benefits of
shelf registration available to "seasoned" foreign governmental entities.

• 1934 Act Registration and Reporting

Section 15(d) of the 1934 Act, which applies the continuous reporting requirements to issuers that have sold securities
under a registration statement, expressly excludes foreign governments and political subdivisions from its coverage. As governments do not issue equity securities, they will not be caught
up by Section 12(g). A foreign government will, therefore, become subject to the registration and reporting requirements of
the 1934 Act only if it voluntarily lists its debt securities on a
national securities exchange or has them traded on NASDAQ.
In that event, it would file a registration statement on Form 18
in connection with its listing application. Thereafter, it would
file annually on Form 18-K. In the case of a sovereign issuer,

these forms require disclosure regarding gold reserves, import and export information and the balance of international payments for the most recent fiscal year. (As discussed in Chapter 8, a foreign governmental issuer may also decide voluntarily to file reports in order to facilitate shelf registration.)

Rights Offerings

As noted by the SEC in its 1991 release on "cross-border rights offers,"[104] while rights offerings are no longer common in the United States they are still used in many countries as a means of raising equity capital. Many countries, especially in the European Union, have corporation law or exchange listing requirements that require preemptive rights. A proposed European Union directive would also require public companies issuing shares for cash in most cases to offer the shares to existing holders on a preemptive basis.

Rights offerings create problems, however, under the U.S. securities laws:

> U.S. investors, particularly those holding over-the-counter securities, are often excluded from or cashed out of[104] these rights offerings because of foreign issuers' reluctance to comply with the disclosure requirements and accounting rules applicable to Securities Act registration statements, or to incur the obligation to file periodic reports under the Exchange Act required of those who conduct public offerings in the United States. There have even been instances where foreign issuers which are already reporting companies under the Exchange Act

---

104. SEC Release No. 33-6896 (June 4, 1991).

105. "Where there is a trading market for the rights in the issuer's home country, the issuer may cash out its U.S. shareholders by causing the rights that would otherwise be distributed to them to be sold in the open market on their behalf. U.S. investors that are cashed out generally do not receive the full benefit of the offering, however, as they are usually responsible for selling expenses and other transaction costs, including underwriters' commissions. Exchange rate fluctuations may also affect net proceeds." *Id.* at note 14.

have excluded their U.S. shareholders from rights offerings, purportedly because of concerns with U.S. processing time at both the federal and state levels.

The exclusion or cashing out of U.S. investors not only denies these investors a potentially valuable investment opportunity, but may also subject them to substantial dilution. Depositary banks for American Depositary Receipts ("ADRs") estimate that in 1990 alone, U.S. investors that own foreign securities in the form of ADRs were excluded from more than 25 rights offerings and cashed out of approximately 60 such transactions.[106]

The cash-out procedure described above by the SEC has been around at least since 1947. "[O]n the principle that it is no sin to be practical, especially if the letter of the law can be satisfied at the same time, the SEC has permitted Canadian and other non-American corporations to send their subscription rights into this country with substantially the following legend attached":[107]

The shares of the company are not registered under the United States Securities Act of 1933. The shares referred to in the annexed warrants are being offered in Canada but not in the United States of America. The offering to which the said warrants relates is not, and under no circumstances is to be construed as, an offering of any shares for sale in the United States of America, or the territories or possessions thereof, or as a solicitation therein of an offer to buy any of the said shares. The company will not accept subscriptions from any person, or his agent, who appears to be, or who the company has reason to believe is, a resident of the United States of America. The company is informed that there is no objection to a United States shareholder selling this warrant in Canada.

---

106. *Id.* (some footnotes omitted).
107. 2 Loss & Seligman, *Securities Regulation* 760–61 note 43 (3d ed. 1989).

The SEC stated in connection with a 1947 rights offering by Royal Dutch Petroleum Company that it would interpose no objection if brokers or dealers purchased subscription rights from U.S. residents and sold them outside of the United States.[108]

As noted above, the SEC issued a no-action letter to CREF in 1987 that made it clear that CREF and other U.S. institutional investors could exercise rights to purchase shares of foreign corporations as part of a U.S. private offering.[109] The CREF letter, of course, did not solve the problem for the non-institutional holder of foreign shares. Accordingly, in the 1991 release quoted above, the SEC proposed "[t]o facilitate the extension of rights offerings to U.S. investors and to encourage foreign authorities to prohibit discriminatory treatment of U.S. investors" by proposing a small issue exemption under Section 3(b) of the 1933 Act for specified equity rights offerings not exceeding $5 million in the United States. It also proposed a new registration form that would allow the use of home country disclosure documents in the case of larger equity rights offerings as well as a relaxation of the requirements for use of Form F-3 in connection with the registration of rights offerings and other specified transactions. The SEC explained the proposed relief as based on the premise that "the interests of those U.S. investors that have already made an investment in a foreign issuer, frequently on the bases [sic] solely of disclosure required by foreign law, would be better served by facilitating the extension of rights offerings of additional securities to them than by insisting on U.S. disclosure."[110]

The SEC has taken no action on the 1991 proposals. It may be that some of the pressure has been taken off by the CREF letter and the subsequent adoption of Rule 144A, which makes it possible for a foreign issuer to include U.S. stockholders in a rights offering if the participants are limited to QIBs and the other requirements of the rule are satisfied. Since the rule does not exempt offers and sales by an issuer, it would be necessary

---

108. SEC Release No. 33-3266 (November 25, 1947).

109. SEC No-action Letter, *College Retirement Equities Fund* (available June 4, 1987).

110. *Id.*

to engage an intermediary—such as a U.S. broker-dealer—who would buy rights from the U.S. stockholder for the purpose of exercising them and selling the new shares to such of the U.S. stockholders as are QIBs. Obviously, the process would be more costly to stockholders than being able to participate directly. Also, the stock they receive would be "restricted stock" under Rule 144 (but the stock may be resold abroad in a transaction that qualifies for Rule 904).

It may also be that many U.S. institutions have found a way to participate in rights offerings through accounts maintained with, and securities held through, foreign banks or foreign offices of U.S. banks and broker-dealers.

Global Offerings by Foreign Corporations

There is a special set of problems that must be faced in connection with international offerings by foreign issuers where a portion of the shares are to be sold in the United States. These problems are particularly acute where the offering arises out of a foreign privatization and it becomes necessary to coordinate the mechanics of the home country offering, the international offering (outside the United States) and the U.S. offering. In this type of transaction, it is often necessary to accommodate certain aspects of the U.S. federal securities laws to offering practices customary outside the United States.

• *1933 Act Registration*

A decision that must be made by a foreign issuer and its legal advisers is the number of shares to be registered under the 1933 Act. Should the issuer register only those shares to be purchased by the U.S. underwriting syndicate, should a certain number of additional shares be registered to provide for the possibility of additional shares flowing into the United States, or should the entire issue be registered?

In 1977, Her Majesty's government sold a large block of ordinary shares of The British Petroleum Company Limited ("BP") by means of two underwritten offerings. The principal market for the shares was in London, although ADRs were also traded on the NYSE. On June 14, 1977, the government announced a share offering to the public in the United Kingdom and elsewhere outside North America, but reserved the right to withdraw some of the shares for an offering in the United States and Canada. Purchasers were required to represent that they were not North American persons. Several days after the termination of this offering, 13,357,000 ADSs representing an equal number of ordinary shares were offered in the United States and Canada under a prospectus dated June 27, 1977. These represented shares withdrawn from the offering outside of North America. In addition to the shares represented by ADRs, 13,339,000 of the 53,428,591 shares sold outside of North America were covered by the registration statement.

In 1979, there was a public offering of an even larger block of BP ordinary shares. This time, the offering was made only in the United Kingdom, although nationals and residents of other countries were not precluded from purchasing so long as they met certain conditions, including payment in pounds sterling. Although (unlike the sale in 1977) there was to be no offering in the United States, the shares were registered under the 1933 Act in view of the close relationship between the United Kingdom and the U.S. markets for the BP shares. This was a time when the SEC was less accommodating to foreign issuers than it is today, and one can imagine the discussions with the SEC's staff that led to the decision to register under the 1933 Act even though there was to be no U.S. distribution.

In the massive BP offering that took place in October 1987, the registration statement covered 670 million ordinary shares, 610.8 million shares representing those to be sold to underwriters for resale under ADRs to purchasers in the United States and Canada and an additional number of shares that, according to the facing sheet of the Form F-3, had been offered and sold outside the United States but that might be resold from time to time in the United States during the distribution. Here the decision was made to register some additional shares to cover sales in the United States in the after-market. The cost of registering the entire offering would have been prohibitive. As it was, the filing fee was $807,153.

The pattern has developed—at least where there is no preexisting substantial U.S. interest in the foreign shares—of registering with the SEC the number of shares to be offered and sold in the United States plus an additional 10% to 15% of such shares. The primary purpose of registering shares in excess of those expected to be sold in the United States is to cover transfers from the international underwriters to the U.S. underwriters to meet varying levels of demand in different markets.[111] During the first 40 days following the commencement of the offering, registration of the excess shares is also deemed (albeit by means of a considerable leap of faith) to cover for purposes of Section 4(3)(A) of the 1933 Act the resale of shares in the United States by non-U.S. dealers who purchase shares from non-U.S. investors in a foreign secondary market.

• *Form and Delivery of Prospectus*

Where all or part of a global offering is registered under the 1933 Act, the question arises whether the form or forms of prospectus covering sales outside the United States must be filed as part of the U.S. registration statement. Also, must a prospectus meeting the requirements of the 1933 Act be delivered to foreign purchasers?

Section 5(b)(1) of the 1933 Act could be read as requiring that if a registration statement is filed with respect to a security, the prospectus covering that security, wherever used, must meet the requirements of Section 10(a).

This issue arose in 1973 in connection with an offering exclusively to Japanese investors of shares of Fundamerica of Japan, Inc., a U.S. mutual fund organized to invest in U.S. securities. In discussions with the SEC staff, it was agreed that the fund need not register shares to be offered exclusively in Japan where resales to U.S. persons were prohibited. However, the Japanese Ministry of Finance insisted on registration under the 1933 Act as well as under the comparable Japanese statute.

---

111. These transfers take place pursuant to marketing agreements that divide the offering into markets for which particular syndicates are responsible. The agreements also permit the global coordinator of the offering to move shares from one syndicate to another and generally to make determinations relating to the offering that are commonly performed by a book-running managing underwriter in the United States.

This resulted in an apparent conflict between the U.S. requirement that a prospectus covering registered securities must comply with Section 10(a) of the 1933 Act and the Japanese requirement that only the statutory Japanese prospectus could be used in that country. To allow the offering to proceed, the SEC adopted Rule 434C,[112] which provided, in effect, that a prospectus required by the Japanese laws covering securities that are also registered under the 1933 Act is deemed to meet the requirements of Section 10(a) when the offering in Japan is to persons who are not nationals or residents of the United States. This rule was subsequently rescinded by the SEC as "unnecessary or obsolete" as part of a general overhaul of its regulations.[113] Apparently, no one then on the staff could figure out what this rule was all about and what purpose it served.

The technique is often used of including more than one form of prospectus in the registration statement. This is usually accomplished by including the form of cover page to be used abroad (e.g., with the names of the international syndicate managers in lieu of the U.S. managing underwriters) and other relevant portions of the international prospectus (e.g., the tax section and the section describing the international underwriters).

Even if a prospectus meets or is deemed to meet the requirements of the 1933 Act, is it necessary—as a matter of U.S. law—to deliver the prospectus to a foreign investor with or before the confirmation of sale? As a theoretical matter, the position could be taken that shares offered abroad are registered only for the purpose of sale into the United States and that, consistent with Regulation S, the SEC is not interested in extending the prospectus delivery requirements of Section 5 to transactions outside of the United States. As a practical matter, however, the answer is likely to be that U.S. underwriters will include a copy of the relevant prospectus when they confirm sales to non-U.S. buyers, while non-U.S. underwriters will comply only with the prospectus delivery requirements (if any) imposed by their home country and the home country of the buyer.

---

112. SEC Release No. 33-5365 (February 7, 1973).
113. SEC Release No. 33-6383 (March 3, 1982).

• *Section 11 Liability*

If a non-U.S. purchaser can identify his or her purchased shares as having been registered under the 1933 Act, does it follow that the non-U.S purchaser has Section 11 remedies against the non-U.S. issuer, the U.S. and non-U.S. underwriters and all other persons named in Section 11? It can be argued that the provision of Section 11 that limits an underwriter's liability to the "total price at which the securities underwritten by him and distributed to the public were offered to the public" should be construed to refer to the public in the United States.[114] If the argument holds in this context, as it should, persons named in Section 11 as potential defendants should have no liability under that section to non-U.S. purchasers. The argument is weaker for avoiding liability under Section 12(a)(2), but the fact that such liability is limited to the "seller" should mean that the recourse of non-U.S. investors under that section will be limited to the foreign underwriters or dealers from whom they purchased.

• *Underwriting Practices*

Differences between underwriting practices in a foreign country and those in the United States can give rise to substantial difficulties as evidenced by the problems that arose in connection with the October 1987 global offering of BP shares by Her Majesty's government.

Prior to the offering, the government owned approximately 31.5% of the outstanding BP shares, with the balance held by members of the public. The shares were traded in London in the form of ordinary shares and ADSs. In addition, ADSs were listed and traded on the NYSE in the form of ADRs. The shares also were traded on the Tokyo Stock Exchange. As part of its continuing program of privatization, Her Majesty's government determined to sell its remaining BP shares. At the same time, BP proposed to sell additional shares to the government,

---

114. J.R. Stevenson & W.J. Williams, Jr., "United States Legal Aspects of International Securities Transactions," *A Lawyer's Guide to International Business Transactions*, Part III, Folio 5, 51 (2d ed. 1980).

which would be included with its own holdings as part of the offering.

The worldwide combined offering had a value of approximately $13 billion. The plan was for the major portion of the shares to be sold to retail subscribers and eligible BP employees in the United Kingdom at a price representing a discount from the market price. Existing holders of BP shares and ADSs were also to be offered the opportunity to subscribe in the offering on a priority basis. A "pathfinder" prospectus was released in the United Kingdom on September 25, 1987, and registration statements were filed with the SEC on the same date. The remainder of the combined offering, designated the international offer, was to be made to institutions in the United Kingdom and through syndicates of underwriters in the United States, Canada, Japan and continental Europe.

The key dates in any equity offering in the United Kingdom are "impact day," "application day," and "allocation day." In the case of the retail offering of BP shares in the United Kingdom, impact day was October 15, 1987. At that time, the offering price was fixed and the retail offer commenced. Applications in the retail offering, together with payment, were required to be submitted by application day, which was October 28, 1987. The basis of the allocation was to be announced on October 30, 1987. The stockholder offer was to follow a slightly different schedule. Pursuant to that offer, holders of BP shares on September 30, 1987, and holders of ADSs on October 14, 1987, were to be offered the opportunity to subscribe at the same price as that fixed for the retail offer.

The combined offering was underwritten on impact day. At that time, the United Kingdom underwriters entered into a standby underwriting commitment covering the shares proposed to be sold in the retail offer, those to be sold to United Kingdom institutions, and those covered by the stockholder offer outside the United States, Canada and Japan. The international underwriters, including the U.S. underwriters, Goldman, Sachs & Co., Morgan Stanley & Co. Incorporated, Salomon Brothers Inc., and Shearson Lehman Brothers Inc., entered into an underwriting agreement at the same time. This differed from the procedure followed in the 1977 BP offering where the U.S.

underwriters did not commit until allocation day. In the case of the 1987 offering, the registration statement covering the shares to be purchased by the U.S. underwriters was not to become effective until after allocation day, almost two weeks after the underwriting agreement was signed.

The commitment was made on the basis of the price in pounds sterling with payment to be made in dollars, on the basis of the exchange rate on the date of closing. The underwriters were thus protected against exchange rate fluctuation. They were not protected, however, against a turn in the stock market. Their commitment was firm, and they were required to close even if the registration statement had not yet become effective. Pursuant to the underwriting agreement, the four U.S. underwriters had the authority to form a broad syndicate of underwriters in the United States, and these underwriters were to be substituted and take up a portion of the commitments of the four underwriters who signed the underwriting agreement.

Between the execution of the underwriting agreement and the date that the registration statement was to be declared effective, share prices in London and in other world markets fell dramatically, reaching a climax in the October 19 crash. Between the close of business on October 14, 1987, when the fixed price was established at 3.30 pounds sterling per share, a 6% discount from the closing price, the price of the BP shares in London fell from 3.52 pounds to 2.62 pounds at the close of business on October 29, 1987. During the same period, the price of an ADS on the NYSE fell from 69-3/4 to 55-3/4. The underwriters were faced with a disaster. There was no market out in the underwriting agreement, and there was no way that the U.S. underwriters would be able to form a syndicate of substitute underwriters to share the loss.

As reported in *The New York Times* on October 21, there was speculation in London that the BP offering might be withdrawn, but that morning the Chancellor of the Exchequer made a public statement that the deal would go forward on schedule, even though it was expected to result in losses to the underwriters of as much as 500 million pounds. On October 26, representatives of the underwriters met with government officials to urge them to postpone the sale. But Prime Minister Margaret

Thatcher held firm, and the deal went forward. The U.S. under-writers proceeded to offer the shares pursuant to a prospectus dated October 30, 1987. The public offering price was substantially less than the price paid by them for the ADSs.

As a concession, on October 29, 1987, the Chancellor of the Exchequer announced that the Bank of England would make an offer to purchase installment payment shares at 70 pence per share. The offer was made on November 6, 1987, and was to extend at least until December 11, 1987. This would serve to limit the potential losses of the purchasers of the BP shares and ADSs and would help to provide an orderly after-market. The SEC accommodated the offer by granting exemptions under the Williams Act and under Rules 10b-6 and 10b-7.

• *Foreign Publicity*

Under the 1933 Act, publicity in advance of or during a distribution of securities is strictly limited. A television program advertising a securities offering or a newspaper advertisement not meeting the requirements of Rule 134 would be viewed as attempts to condition the market and therefore as illegal prospectuses. Similarly, a news item inspired by the issuer may result in an illegal prospectus. This is generally not the case abroad. Articles in the press with respect to an issuer and a proposed offering of its securities frequently appear in London and in other markets, often inspired by press releases emanating from the issuer. Officers of foreign companies have no qualms about talking to the press in anticipation of a securities offering.

These activities during a global offering, a portion of which is to be made in the United States, have been a matter of some concern to the staff of the SEC. In particular, foreign privatizations tend to be accompanied by extraordinary advertising campaigns in the home country, and some of this publicity inevitably finds its way into the United States where it may "condition the market." In addition, foreign publicity relating to tender offers may raise questions under the Williams Act.

Even apart from the sometimes aggressive publicity efforts associated with privatizations and related global offerings, many non-U.S. issuers have persuaded themselves in recent years that they should adopt "self-help" measures to alleviate the SEC's perceived concern even with relatively routine publicity. Accordingly, these issuers would regularly exclude journalists for publications with a significant U.S. circulation (whether the publication were U.S.-based or foreign-based) from their press conferences, from meetings with issuer representatives and from press materials released offshore where a current or proposed securities offering or tender offer was to be discussed.

When the SEC adopted Regulation S in 1990, it stated in Preliminary Note 7 that nothing in the new rules precluded access by journalists to press conferences, press releases and meetings with issuer representatives where information is made available to the foreign and U.S. press generally "and is not intended to induce purchases of securities by persons in the United States or tenders of securities by United States holders in the case of exchange offers." Furthermore, the staff stated in a 1990 no-action letter[115] that the SEC's rules "are not intended to limit or interfere with news stories or other bona fide journalistic activities, or otherwise hinder the flow of normal corporate news." The same letter stated that access by journalists need not be limited where information about a tender offer is being made available "to the foreign and U.S. press generally and is not intended to induce participation in the offer by U.S. holders."

Congress directed the SEC in the Improvements Act to address the applicability of the securities laws to foreign press conferences and foreign press releases. Even before the President signed the legislation, however, the SEC proposed in late 1996 the adoption of a new Rule 135e that would exclude from the definition of "offer" for Section 5 purposes certain foreign activities involving "journalists" (a term not defined).[116] The proposed rule would permit an issuer or selling securityholder or their "representatives" to provide journalists with access to press conferences held outside the United States, meetings with issuer or selling securityholder representatives conducted outside the United States or written press related materials released outside the United

---

115. SEC No-action Letter, *Reuters Holding plc* (available March 6, 1990).

116. SEC Release No. 33-7356 (October 10, 1996).

States, even if these activities included a discussion of a current or proposed offering of securities. The offering would have to take place at least partially outside the United States, and both U.S. and foreign journalists would have to be provided with access to the activities. In addition, where the offering was conducted at least partially in the United States *or* where the issuer was a U.S. issuer, then certain notices would have to be included regarding the unregistered nature of the offering. The definitions of "general solicitation or general advertising" and "directed selling efforts" would also be amended to exclude communications that met the requirements of the proposed rule, and the tender offer rules would be similarly amended insofar as they apply to foreign private issuers.

Significantly, the availability of the new rule would not be conditioned on intent or any other subjective element. While asking for comment on this point, the SEC expressed its belief that a "purely objective test" was necessary in order to achieve the purposes of the safe harbor. On the other hand, the proposed rule would not extend to analysts' reports.

In mid-1995, Deutsche Telekom AG ("DTAG") recognized that its privatization and its proposed initial public offering (scheduled at the time to commence in the spring or summer of 1996) would attract close coverage by the general interest and financial press both within and outside Germany. The reasons for such coverage would include DTAG's stature as one of the most important enterprises in Germany, its key role in the telecommunications industry, its proposed joint ventures with other large telecommunications companies and the fact that its offering would represent the largest offering by far in the history of the German financial markets.

For these reasons, DTAG anticipated that it might not be possible to keep all activity that could be construed as "offering activity" outside the United States prior to the formal commencement of the offering. Accordingly, its counsel proposed to the SEC staff[117] guidelines that would govern publicity, the

---

117. SEC No-action Letter, *Deutsche Telekom AG* (available June 13, 1995).

release of information and contact with investors by or on behalf of the issuer, the underwriters, relevant agencies of the German government and other participants in the offering.

During a period scheduled to end at least three months prior to the commencement of the offering ("Stage One"), DTAG could communicate freely with persons in the United States on matters unrelated to the offering. It could communicate freely with the U.S. press as to the offering (as long as information were also made generally available to the non-U.S. press), engage in "image" advertising (without referring to the offering and without making any projections) and make normal releases of information about DTAG (including responding in limited fashion to unsolicited inquiries about the offering from potential investors in the United States). The limits of activity in respect of research reports by broker-dealers or banks were to be the subject of future guidelines.

"Stage Two" would commence at the expiration of Stage One and would last until the commencement of the offering. During this period, the usual 1933 Act restrictions on publicity would be applicable.[118] Finally, the usual restrictions on publicity would apply during the period from the commencement of the offering until its completion.

In light of the "exceptional circumstances" described in DTAG's letter, the SEC staff responded that it would not recommend enforcement action if DTAG and participants in the offering were to proceed as set forth in the guidelines.

• *Foreign Research*

The distribution of research in connection with a securities offering is strictly controlled in the United States, but this is not the case in most of the rest of the world. In fact, it is quite common for non-U.S. underwriters to publish research reports

---

118. The DTAG letter also contemplated the possible filing of a "pink herring" preliminary prospectus, i.e., a document that would not contain all of the information normally included in a registration statement and that would not be generally distributed. The purpose of the filing would be to make possible oral communications and meetings that would otherwise constitute "gun jumping."

prior to or even during a public offering. There is nothing wrong with this practice from the standpoint of the U.S. securities laws as long as the research material can be prevented from being delivered into the United States. Assurances on this point are hard to come by, however, and U.S. underwriters understandably worry that the leakage into the United States of foreign-originated research will cause the SEC to delay an offering (or worse). U.S. underwriters are also concerned about the content of such research material, both from a theoretical point of view (false or misleading statements in the research material might encourage foreign investors to file lawsuits in U.S courts) or a practical point of view (foreign underwriters may be achieving an unfair competitive advantage in making sales based on the research material).

Rules 138 and 139 under the 1933 Act provide significant relief for persons who wish to disseminate research reports on U.S. issuers that are involved in registered public offerings. Until recently, these rules were available only for research material on issuers that were reporting companies under the 1934 Act. By definition, non-U.S. issuers making global equity offerings were seldom reporting companies, and these rules were therefore unavailable. In 1994, the SEC amended both rules to extend their benefits to research on foreign private issuers without regard to their reporting history under the 1934 Act as long as their securities had traded for a period of at least twelve months on a "designated offshore securities market" as defined in Regulation S.[119]

The 1995 amendments to Rules 138 and 139 did not benefit providers of research on privatization candidates, who by definition did not meet the twelve-month seasoning requirement. On the other hand, the main function of research—to provide continuous information to investors about securities that are traded in the market—is by definition inapplicable to privatization candidates. The SEC might not have reacted favorably to a suggestion that it permit research on a privatization candidate prior to or during an initial public offering, but a 1996 no-

---

119. *See* note 32, *supra.*

action request on behalf of Deutsche Telekom AG[120] presented the question in a much more favorable context: i.e., that of research on an entire industry.

DTAG's letter pointed out that U.S. investors had a legitimate interest in receiving research on the global telecommunications industry and that such research would be incomplete unless it discussed DTAG. The letter proposed guidelines under which any prospective underwriter that had an established history of covering the telecommunications or a related industry could distribute research in the ordinary course of business to persons to whom such research had customarily been provided. The research would have to focus generally on the industry or specifically on one or more companies competing with or engaged in business ventures with DTAG and would have to avoid giving DTAG any materially greater space or prominence. The research would have to avoid detailed financial or business information relating to DTAG, financial projections (with certain exceptions), nonpublic information and any specific discussion of the proposed offering.

The SEC staff responded that it would not recommend enforcement action if prospective underwriters and other participating broker-dealers were to publish industry reports in conformity with the stated guidelines.

As noted above, the SEC's proposed Rule 135e did not extend to analysts' reports. The significance of the proposed rule, however, is probably less in its proposed coverage than in its representing for all practical purposes an acknowledgment by the SEC that the evolution of communications technology and the blurring of geographic boundaries has progressed to the point where regulation of communications as "offers" under the federal securities laws is simply no longer feasible. And if this is true for international communications, it is undoubtedly also true for purely domestic communications such as corporate Websites, broker-dealer research, electronic databases and other methods of disseminating information to the market place. The best solution may be a significant deregulation of "offers" in general.

---

120. SEC No-action Letter, *Deutsche Telekom AG* (available June 14, 1996).

• *Regulation M*

It will generally be the case, where a non-U.S. issuer is making a public offering in the United States, either that the issuer's securities already have an established trading market in the issuer's home country or that such a market rapidly develops following the commencement of the offering. The SEC staff has traditionally taken the position that its anti-manipulation rules apply to trading activity *anywhere in the world* if a distribution is taking place in the United States. This position meant, of course, that SEC rules such as Rule 10b-6 could apply to bids and offers for the issuer's securities by distribution participants (or their affiliates) in the normal course of their business in the issuer's home country. SEC rules such as Rule 10b-7 could also apply to stabilizing activity or to attempts (such as by means of research reports) to "induce" someone to purchase the issuer's securities, whether or not such activity was permitted in the home country.

Rules 10b-6 and 10b-7 have been replaced by provisions of Regulation M. See the discussion in Chapter 4.

• *Installment Payment Offerings*

Securities sold in global offerings, particularly in connection with privatizations, often provide for installment payments by the purchasers of the securities. As discussed in Chapter 3, Section 11(d)(1) of the 1934 Act prohibits a broker-dealer from extending or arranging for the extension of credit "on" securities that are part of a "new issue" in the distribution of which the broker-dealer was a participant. By selling installment payment securities, a U.S. underwriter might be viewed as arranging an extension of credit in violation of this prohibition. The SEC has been willing, however, to take a no-action position under Section 11(d)(1) in situations where the Federal Reserve Board would not raise objections under Regulation T.[121]

---

121. SEC No-action Letter, *British Petroleum Company p.l.c.* (available October 1, 1987); SEC No-action Letter, *Morgan Stanley & Co. Inc.* (available November 26, 1984) (British Telecommunications plc offering).

The position of the Federal Reserve Board in this area has been expressly motivated by a desire to accommodate foreign governments that are in the process of privatizing state-owned issuers.[122] In 1995, the Board proposed to amend the arranging prohibition of Regulation T to permit broker-dealers to effect the sale of a foreign security offered on an installment basis if no more than 15% of the offering were offered to U.S. persons. The amendment was not adopted when the Board in 1996 dramatically curtailed the scope of the arranging prohibition. As matters now stand, a U.S. underwriter may sell an installment payment security except in those relatively rare cases where the issuer's extension of credit violates the relevant margin rule to which the issuer is subject. Where the rare problem arises, the Board staff will likely entertain a request for relief, particularly where the transaction involves a privatization and the portion of the offering sold in the United States is relatively small.

---

122. *See* C.F. Rechlin, *Securities Credit* § 4.03[3] (1996).

Chapter 10

COMMERCIAL PAPER

The term "commercial paper" is generally used to describe a short-term unsecured financing vehicle that is extensively relied upon by major financial institutions, industrial and commercial enterprises and governmental entities. From the issuer's point of view, commercial paper is a flexible and low-cost alternative to bank borrowing.

Commercial paper is purchased almost exclusively by institutional investors. From the investor's point of view, commercial paper is an alternative to one of the other so-called "money market" instruments, i.e., U.S. Treasury bills, discount notes of U.S. government agencies, negotiable certificates of deposit and bankers' acceptances. In recent years, however, commercial paper has grown faster than the overall market, rising from 23% of money market instruments in 1970 to 42% in 1996.[1] With the decline of short-term large-denomination certificates of deposit, commercial paper has become particularly attractive to money market funds. Other important buyers of commercial paper are bank trust departments, insurance companies, pension funds, corporations, and state and local governments.

---

1. Federal Reserve Bank of New York, U.S. Bureau of Public Debt (as reported by Goldman, Sachs & Co., July 1996).

Traditional commercial paper can have a maturity of up to nine months, but in practice maturities are generally concentrated in the range of from one to 45 days with an average of 30 days.[2] Maturities can be tailored to meet investor needs so that, for example, if an investor has $50 million that it wishes to invest for 23 days, it should be able to find one or more dealers that act for one or more issuers willing to sell 23-day paper. Conversely, an issuer that needs $50 million for 23 days can ordinarily obtain these funds by calling its dealers during the morning of the day on which it needs the funds. (Unlike bank borrowing facilities, commercial paper programs do not usually require advance notification.)

Issuers in the U.S. commercial paper market have traditionally been highly-rated borrowers, but credit-enhancement devices such as bank letters of credit have been used to allow other borrowers to gain access to this market. The role of independent rating agencies increased dramatically following the Penn Central default in 1970. Their role further increased as money market funds became major purchasers of commercial paper; these funds are subject to the SEC's Rule 2a-7 under the 1940 Act, which restricts their ability to purchase lower-grade commercial paper. One of the two leading rating agencies reported in late 1995 that 90% of the commercial paper rated by it was in the top or "Prime-1" category. Another 9% was in "Prime-2;" less than one-half of 1% was in "Prime-3;" and commercial paper rated "not prime" accounted for only 0.05% of rated commercial paper.[3]

Commercial paper is normally sold at a discount from the face or principal amount of the transaction, with the discount

---

2. The Federal Reserve Bank of New York collects and publishes information on commercial paper rates, maturities and amounts outstanding. On March 26, 1997, the preliminary weighted average maturity of total outstanding commercial paper reported to the Bank was 39.14 days. Current information can be found on the Bank's Website at www.ny.frb.org, which is the source (unless otherwise stated) of statistics in this chapter relating to the commercial paper market.

3. Moody's Investors Service, *Commercial Paper Defaults and Rating Transitions, 1971–1995* at 7 (December 1995).

representing an interest component to be paid to the investor at maturity. Traditionally, commercial paper took the form of a short-term negotiable promissory note issued in bearer form. Book-entry commercial paper was introduced by DTC in 1990 and has quickly come to dominate the market.

The U.S. commercial paper market is primarily a U.S. dollar market, but programs have been established that are denominated in other currencies.

Characteristics of the Market

The commercial paper market has grown dramatically over the past 25 years, with U.S. outstandings rising from approximately $33.5 billion in December 1970 to approximately $730 billion by mid-1996.[4] A money market had become established in New York City by the middle of the 19th century, but the commercial paper market really did not come into its own until the 1960s when monetary restraints restricted the availability and increased the cost of bank financing, thus forcing issuers to find alternative sources of short-term funds.

Direct issuers, as opposed to those that sell through dealers, accounted for roughly 30% of the market in mid-1996, as measured by the amount of commercial paper outstanding. There are approximately 45 direct issuers that are, for the most part, large financial companies such as General Electric Capital Corporation. These issuers have commercial paper programs of sufficient size to justify the cost of establishing their own placement facilities. The remaining 70% represents the dealer market, where commercial paper is sold through dealers.

The dealer market consists principally of a few major players and a larger number of smaller investment and commercial banks. It is highly competitive. At one time, some dealers (notably Goldman, Sachs & Co.) insisted that an issuing client sell its paper exclusively through them. Other dealers, of course, tried to persuade issuers that their interests were better served by having two or more dealers compete on the basis of perfor-

---

4. Federal Reserve Bank of New York, as reported by Goldman, Sachs & Co. (July 1996).

mance. Goldman Sachs changed its policy in late 1987, and multiple dealerships are now more common.

High interest rates and volatility in the long-term bond market during the 1980s contributed to the growth of commercial paper as a financing alternative. A chief financial officer who is not willing to issue long-term debt securities at a fixed rate has the option of issuing floating rate obligations (or one of the more innovative financial instruments that have been developed in recent years) or of entering the commercial paper market. A commercial paper program can have the same economic effect as a long-term floating rate obligation. Although commercial paper notes have short maturities, in the typical program, new notes are issued to replace maturing notes on a continuous basis. Thus, an issuer can maintain a fixed amount of paper outstanding for as long as it considers advisable and market conditions permit. If the market remains stable and the issuer's credit rating remains strong, the size of its commercial paper program can be increased or decreased at will.

Historically, commercial paper programs have had a cost advantage over bank borrowings. Another advantage is that loan covenants are not required in the establishment of a commercial paper program. There are also less tangible factors at work in an issuer's decision to tap the commercial paper market. For one thing, it is clearly advantageous to have the alternate source of funding that commercial paper represents. For another, a commercial paper program enables an issuer to broaden its investor base and to cultivate relationships with a wide range of institutional investors.

The market for commercial paper is largely institutional. The principal investors are money market funds, bank trust departments, insurance companies, foreign central banks, pension funds and other managed accounts, and corporate treasury departments. The proliferation of money market funds has been a significant factor in the growth of the commercial paper market. There are an estimated 10,000 buyers of commercial paper, with the most active 20% of accounts representing about 80% of the demand.

Investors rely heavily on ratings assigned by Moody's Investors Service and Standard & Poor's Corporation in evaluating commercial paper issuers.[5] Those issuers that do not qualify for an investment grade rating may enhance the credit of their paper with a bank letter of credit (less often, an insurance company surety bond is used for this purpose). Most issuers maintain unused bank lines in an amount equal to their outstanding paper (subject to seasonal fluctuations) in order to demonstrate to the market and the rating agencies their ability to liquidate their obligations should market conditions prevent refinancing through the issuance of new notes.

Dealers' Role

For those issuers that do not wish to administer their own programs, commercial paper dealers provide an important service. The sponsoring dealer provides advice in establishing the program and in dealing with the rating agencies. For an issuer entering the market for the first time, the dealer will seek to create investor interest through discussions between its sales force and representatives of potential buyers, written memoranda to investors, and, in some cases, road shows or face-to-face meetings with groups of potential investors.

Commercial paper dealers generally act as principals. They purchase notes from issuers and resell them to investors. They do attempt, however, to line up purchasers in advance and will take into inventory only that amount of paper as is necessary to accommodate the financings needs of their issuer clients. Investors usually hold commercial paper to maturity, but dealers stand ready in practice to provide liquidity to those investors to whom they originally sold the paper. In recent years, however, both investors and dealers have been more willing to trade in the secondary market.

Dealers are compensated through a small markup (historically 1/8 of 1% per annum, but now often less for larger programs) on the paper they place with investors or, alternatively, by periodically charging a fee to the issuer based on the amount of commercial paper outstanding. Traditionally, dealers have

---

5. Moody's highest commercial paper rating is Prime-1, and Standard & Poor's is A-1.

looked on a commercial paper relationship with an issuer as a "door opener" to other investment banking assignments.

Mechanics

Transactions in the U.S. commercial paper market usually take place between 8:00 a.m. and 12:00 noon, New York City time (the normal trading hours for most U.S. commercial paper), and transactions are settled by 3:00 p.m. on the same day. Purchases and payments at maturity are both effected in same day funds.

The mechanics of a commercial paper program are handled by an issuing and paying agent, which is usually a money center bank with a special department established to perform this function. The advent of book-entry commercial paper has largely eliminated the cumbersome and expensive procedures associated for so many years with physical notes.[6] In a book-entry environment, the issuing and paying agent issues and holds in custody for DTC two master notes, one for discounted commercial paper and one for interest bearing commercial paper. These two master notes represent all the commercial paper issued or to be issued by the issuer. The amount of commercial paper represented by the master notes will fluctuate with entries by the agent on the master notes and into DTC's electronic system as new paper is issued and outstanding paper is paid at maturity. All commercial paper issued in book-entry form is tracked by DTC through CUSIP numbers, which are assigned by the CUSIP Service Bureau of Standard & Poor's Rating Services (a division of the McGraw Hill Companies, Inc.). DTC processes the operational aspects of a commercial paper program in accordance with an agreement, or "letter of representations," among the issuing and paying agent and DTC.

1933 Act Considerations

Registration under the 1933 Act is impracticable in the case of short-term obligations that are being issued, repaid and re-

---

6. Book-entry programs usually allow for the issuance of physical commercial paper in the event of a disruption of the DTC system.

placed with new obligations on a continuous basis. The SEC registration fee is based on the offering price of the specific securities to be issued, rather than the maximum dollar amount to be outstanding at any one time, thus making the cost of registration prohibitive for commercial paper. For example, if a $200 million program were established and $200 million of 30-day notes were issued each month over a 24-month period, $4.8 billion of notes would have to be registered with a registration fee of nearly $1.5 million. Thus, commercial paper is never registered under the 1933 Act but always is issued in reliance upon one of the statutory exemptions from registration, usually the Section 3(a)(3) exemption available to most commercial paper.

Where the paper is backed by a letter of credit issued by a U.S. bank or a regulated domestic branch or agency of a foreign bank, it is exempt under Section 3(a)(2), which exempts securities guaranteed by a bank, whether or not it also is exempt under Section 3(a)(3). As discussed in Chapter 7, commercial paper can also be issued in reliance upon the Section 4(2) private offering exemption. If commercial paper is exempt under any of these provisions, it also is exempt from the requirements of the Trust Indenture Act of 1939.

• *Section 3(a)(3) Commercial Paper Exemption*

Section 3(a)(3) exempts from the registration and prospectus delivery requirements of Section 5 of the 1933 Act:

Any note, draft, bill of exchange, or bankers' acceptance which arises out of a current transaction or the proceeds of which have been or are to be used for current transactions, and which has a maturity at the time of issuance of not exceeding nine months, exclusive of days of grace, or any renewal thereof the maturity of which is likewise limited[.]

• • *SEC Release No. 33-4412.* In construing Section 3 (a)(3), it is important to consider SEC Release No. 33-4412 (September 20, 1961) in which the SEC stated:

The legislative history of the [1933] Act makes clear that Section 3(a)(3) applies only to prime quality negotiable commercial paper of a type not ordinarily purchased by the general public, that is, paper issued to facilitate well-recognized types of current operational business requirements and of a type eligible for discounting by Federal Reserve banks.

Although there is no difficulty in applying the nine-month maturity requirement, since most commercial paper has a maturity of less than 45 days, the SEC stated in this release that "obligations payable on demand or having provision for 'automatic roll over' " would not satisfy the nine-month standard. The fact that it is customary to issue new commercial paper to refinance maturing paper does not create a problem in this context since the "roll-over" is not automatic but is in the discretion of the issuer and its commercial paper dealer.[7]

• • *The Prime Quality Standard.* With respect to the "prime quality" standard, an investment grade rating from one or more of the recognized rating agencies should be sufficient. If an issuer defaults on its commercial paper, however, a court may well apply hindsight and hold that the obligations could not possibly have been of prime quality.[8] In appropriate cases, the staff of the SEC has been willing to concur that the Section 3(a)(3) exemption is available even though the commercial paper is not rated.[9]

Defaults on commercial paper have been rare in recent years, thanks in large part to the market's development of an "orderly exit" mechanism for weakening credits. First of all,

---

7. *Compare* SEC No-action Letter, *A.G. Becker Paribas Inc.* (available July 2, 1984), in which the staff of the SEC refused to approve an arrangement under which an issuer would have the option of issuing "delayed delivery" notes to the dealer at the maturity of the original paper. The staff viewed the arrangement as in effect allowing the issuer to extend the maturity of the original paper.

8. *See* the discussion below under "Liabilities on Default—Section 12(a)(1)."

9. E.g., SEC No-action Letter, *Southeast Banking Corp.* (available November 21, 1989); SEC No-action Letter, *Lyondell Petrochemical Co.* (available July 19, 1989); SEC No-action Letter, *Russell Corp.* (available September 22, 1988).

commercial paper investors' aversion to risk typically leads to a reduction in outstandings as and when an issuer is downgraded. Moody's suggests that an average U.S. issuer's outstandings could be expected to fall by 10% if it is downgraded from Prime-1 to Prime-2. Furthermore, "[a] transition from Prime-2 to Prime-3 has typically been associated with a 34% decline in outstandings and a transition from Prime-3 to Not Prime has typically been accompanied by a 52% decline in outstandings."[10] As explained by Moody's, the market compels an issuer whose credit is weakening to reduce or eliminate its reliance on commercial paper financings. "This process usually begins long before access to alternative forms of liquidity, such as bank lines, are denied to a company."[11] Firms in this situation must replace the maturing commercial paper with alternative and presumably more expensive and less convenient forms of financing that are more consistent with its declining fortunes.

• • *Offers to the Public.* It is true that commercial paper is a type of instrument "not ordinarily purchased by the general public," but this does not mean that the paper must be privately offered if the Section 3(a)(3) exemption is to be available. Such a restriction would make Section 3(a)(3) redundant in view of the exemption in Section 4(2) for private offerings generally.[12] Suggestions to the contrary by the SEC have been based on the following quotation in SEC Release No. 33-4412, which improperly attributes to Section 3(a)(3) language in the Senate Report on a bill offered by the Senate and rejected by the Congress:

Thus the Senate Report on the Securities Act of 1933 explained the purpose of Section 3(a)(3) as follows:

---

10. Moody's Investors Service, *Commercial Paper Defaults and Rating Transitions, 1972–1995* at 14 (December 1995). The board of directors of a money market fund is required under Rule 2a-7(c)(5)(i) to reassess promptly whether a downgraded portfolio security "continues to present minimal credit risks." The reassessment is not required if the security is sold (or matures) within five business days of the downgrading.

11. *Id.* at 13.

12. 3 Loss & Seligman, *Securities Regulation* 1192 note 143 (3d ed. 1989).

> Notes, drafts, bills of exchange, and bankers' acceptances which are commercial paper and arise out of current commercial, agricultural, or industrial transactions, and which are not intended to be marketed to the public, are exempted ... It is not intended under the bill to require the registration of short-term commercial paper which, as is the usual practice, is made to mature in a few months and ordinarily is not advertised for sale to the general public.
>
> (S. Rep. No. 47 on S. 875, 73rd Cong., 1st Sess. (1933), pp. 3–4.)

The dots inserted by the SEC in the above-quoted portion of its release reflect the omission of the words "(sec. 2(a))," which referred to a provision in the rejected Senate bill which excluded the following from the definition of the term "security":

> Notes, drafts, bills of exchange, or bankers' acceptances which are commercial paper and arise out of current commercial, agricultural, or industrial transactions or the proceeds of which have been or are to be used for current commercial, agricultural, or industrial purposes *when such paper is not offered or intended to be offered for sale to the public.* (emphasis added)

It is clear that the language of the Senate report, which the SEC stated was applicable to Section 3(a)(3), related not to Section 3(a)(3) in the form adopted, but rather to a completely different bill which expressly limited the commercial paper exclusion to paper which is not offered to the public. The deletion of this limitation from the 1933 Act as finally adopted indicates a legislative intent to exempt commercial paper meeting the Section 3(a)(3) tests whether or not it is offered to the public.

In an action against Perera Company, Inc., the SEC sought to enjoin the sale of short-term paper on the ground that the Section 3(a)(3) exemption was not available where sales are made to the general public. The defendant was a company engaged in the purchase and sale of foreign currency, and in the course of its business it sold its short-term notes to finance its currency purchases. The notes had maturities of less than nine months, and the SEC did not contend that they were issued to finance other than current transactions. However, the notes were sold in small denominations and were advertised for sale to the general public.

Relying on SEC Release No. 33-4412, the SEC took the position that notes that are sold on the public market do not come within the Section 3(a)(3) exemption, thereby excluding the notes issued by Perera. The defendant contended that, not only did its notes fall within the express language of Section 3(a)(3), but also the only language in SEC Release No. 33-4412 that supported the SEC's position was the above quotation from the Senate report on the bill that never passed. In a procedural decision relating to a protective order sought by the SEC to prevent the taking of the deposition of a staff member instrumental in formulating SEC Release No. 33-4412, the court stated that "the S.E.C. appears suspect in the formulation of the release in issue. . . ."[13]

Perera was not decided on its merits; rather, the defendant agreed to a settlement without admitting any violations.[14] Perera agreed that it would not sell its notes in denominations of less than $2,500 and that it would not make use of pamphlets, brochures or other written forms of solicitation or advertisements in the offer and sale of its notes, except that order forms could be sent to present and former holders of Perera notes and, in addition, could be enclosed with statements of account or statements of transactions in foreign exchange. It was stipulated that the order forms would state that the notes were not offered pursuant to a registration statement and would be accompanied by Perera's most recent financial statement.

The significance of this settlement is that, although Perera agreed to limit the form of written solicitations that it would use, it was not prevented from continuing to offer to the general public short-term promissory notes in denominations of at least $2,500. If the SEC had been correct in its contention that the Section

---

13. *SEC v. Perera Company, Inc.*, 47 F.R.D. 535, 537 (S.D.N.Y. 1969).
14. [1969-1970 Transfer Binder] Fed. Sec. L. Rep. (CCH) ¶ 92,764 (S.D.N.Y. August 3, 1970).

3(a)(3) exemption is not available for sales to the public, it could not properly have entered into such a stipulation.

Nevertheless, in deference to the SEC's views on "public" offerings of commercial paper under Section 3(a)(3), commercial paper generally is offered only to institutional investors and substantial individual investors. Commercial paper usually is issued in minimum denominations of $100,000 or more to assure that all purchasers are substantial commercial paper investors and thus not members of the general public. The SEC, however, has specifically taken a no-action position with respect to the sale of commercial paper in minimum denominations of $25,000, provided all of the provisions of the exemption are otherwise met.[15]

More recently, the SEC staff took a no-action position that permitted "limited advertising" of a commercial paper program.[16] General Electric Capital Corporation ("GECC"), then and now the largest direct issuer of commercial paper, reported to the SEC that it regularly received unsolicited calls from sophisticated institutional investors expressing an interest in purchasing commercial paper of GECC or its affiliates. The only way that it could reach these potential investors would be to retain one or more commercial paper dealers—at considerable cost—or to advertise. GECC discussed the Senate Report language quoted above and concluded that advertising would be consistent with the exemption as long as it appeared in *The Wall Street Journal* or in publications directed primarily at institutional investors and as long as the advertising stated that the commercial paper was offered only to sophisticated institutional investors. The staff took a no-action position. The authors do not understand the GECC letter to stand for the proposition that commercial paper must be offered and sold only to institutional investors; rather, the letter stands for the proposition that it may be prudent to impose such a limitation if one intends to advertise a program.

---

15. SEC No-action Letter, *Merrill Lynch, Pierce, Fenner & Smith Incorporated* (available September 5, 1972). *See also* SEC No-action Letter, *Southeast Banking Corp* (available November 21, 1989); SEC No-action Letter, *Hughes Supply, Inc.* (available October 4, 1988).

16. SEC No-action Letter, *General Electric Capital Corp.* (available July 13, 1994).

• • *Eligibility for Discounting.* In a letter dated February 20, 1980 to the General Counsel of the Board of Governors of the Federal Reserve System, the then General Counsel of the SEC stated that the SEC's staff was no longer requiring that commercial paper be eligible for discounting at a Federal Reserve Bank as a condition for granting no-action requests under Section 3(a)(3). Since the Federal Reserve Banks no longer discount commercial paper, this is not a surprising conclusion.

• • *The Current Transaction Test.* The "current transaction" test is the most difficult and subjective requirement to be applied in determining whether commercial paper is exempt under Section 3(a)(3). In SEC Release No. 33-4412, the SEC stated, in the context of its then requirement that the paper be of a type eligible for discounting, that, under the regulations of the Board of Governors of the Federal Reserve System, it was permissible to discount a negotiable note that:

> has been issued, or the proceeds of which are to be used in producing, purchasing, carrying or marketing goods or in meeting current operating expenses of a commercial, agricultural or industrial business, and which is *not* to be used for permanent or fixed investment, such as land, buildings, or machinery, *nor* for speculative transactions or transactions in securities (except direct obligations of the United States government) . . . . [emphasis in original].

The SEC further stated in this Release that the current transaction standard is not satisfied where the proceeds from the issuance of the paper

> are to be used for the discharge of existing indebtedness unless such indebtedness is itself exempt under Section 3(a)(3); the purchase or construction of a plant; the purchase of durable machinery or equipment; the funding of commercial real estate development or financing; the purchase of real estate mortgages or other securities; the financing of mobile homes or home improvements; or the purchase or establishment of a business enterprise.

• • *The Concept of Commercial Paper Capacity.* Since the publication of SEC Release No. 33-4412, the staff of the SEC has issued numerous no-action letters in which it has recognized that an issuer need not trace the proceeds of a commercial paper program into identifiable current transactions. Rather, the current transaction requirement will be satisfied as long as the amount of commercial paper outstanding at any one time does not exceed the dollar amount of current transactions eligible to be financed.

In taking no-action positions based on this formula approach, the SEC has not inquired into an issuer's cash or cash equivalents, its investment portfolio, or the size of its borrowings under bank lines. The principle has been firmly established that dollars are fungible and that there is no requirement that the proceeds from the sale of commercial paper be segregated for a particular purpose or that they be traceable to a particular use.

In 1986, the staff of the SEC took the unusual step of expressly endorsing the balance sheet formula approach advocated by counsel in his no-action request and the related concept of "commercial paper capacity."[17] Normally, the staff will respond to a no-action request with a short statement that no enforcement action will be recommended, but in this case the staff went on to make the following observations:

> In reaching this conclusion, the Division [of Corporation Finance] concurs in your view that the balance sheet test as applied in your letter is an appropriate measure of commercial paper capacity. More specifically, we agree that:
> 1. The Company may measure its commercial paper capacity by determining the capital it has committed to current assets, as defined in your letter for the purposes of Section 3(a)(3), and to the expenses of operating its business over the preceding 12-month period. If the transaction giving rise to the asset is a current transaction, it may be funded with commercial paper.

---

17. SEC No-action Letter, *Westinghouse Credit Corp.* (available May 5, 1986).

2. Since the emphasis of the balance sheet test is on the capital committed to, or funds invested in, certain assets, what is important in measuring the Company's commercial paper capacity is not so much the means by which capital is committed but the current character of the underlying asset. Current transactions giving rise to specific assets on the balance sheet may be defined for purposes of Section 3(a)(3) by reference to the following concepts:

(a) Means of Commitment. Capital may be committed to Section 3(a)(3) current assets by means of purchasing as well as directly originating the funding vehicles;

(b) Characterization of Asset. The nature of the underlying asset determines the relevant time period for evaluating whether or not the asset is a current asset for commercial paper purposes;

(c) Portion Financing. The relevant current portion (for purposes of Section 3(a)(3)) of capital committed to an asset will be credited toward the Company's commercial paper capacity irrespective of whether it is the only portion, the next portion or the final or remaining portion of capital invested in such asset. Capital becomes a current asset on the balance sheet of the Company for Section 3(a)(3) purposes when its maturity is certain and close enough to payoff that it can be viewed as attributable to a current transaction.

While the concept endorsed by the staff was expressed in the context of finance company paper, it is equally applicable to other types of issuers.

The importance of this concept cannot be overemphasized. It is the key to applying the current transaction test under Section 3(a)(3). Indeed, if it had been necessary to demonstrate that specific funds were allocated to a particular purpose, as originally had been feared,[18] the commercial paper market never would have grown in the dramatic fashion that it has.

---

18. A.H. Dean, "The Federal Securities Act: I" 51–52, *Fortune* (August 1933). (Dean wrote, "Inasmuch as most corporations do not 'earmark' the proceeds arising from various sources, it may be difficult to prove that

• • *Role of No-Action Letters.* The concept of commercial paper capacity took on even greater importance when the SEC staff in the late 1980s determined not to issue further no-action letters on the subject of current transactions for Section 3(a)(3) purposes. Up to that time, the staff had issued literally scores of letters, many of which sought to extend "laundry lists" of purposes that had been approved in earlier letters. The authors understand the staff to have become concerned that these letters were getting out of hand. In addition, the staff became concerned during this period about the role of an issuer's bank lines in determining whether the issuer's commercial paper was of the requisite "prime quality."

The staff has not issued any no-action letters on the current transactions test since 1990. The older letters have not been withdrawn, however, and securities lawyers still consult them as a supplement to the "commercial paper capacity" test when preparing to opine on the availability of the Section 3(a)(3) exemption.

• • *Financing of Inventories and Accounts Receivable.* The financing of inventories and accounts receivable by an industrial or commercial enterprise has long been recognized by the SEC as satisfying the current transaction test. The following is a typical factual presentation in seeking a no-action letter on this basis:

> The proceeds from the sale of the Notes . . . will not exceed the amounts required to support current transactions. Accordingly, the amount of the Notes sold in reliance upon Section 3(a)(3) and outstanding at any particular time will be limited to the sum of the Company's consolidated inventory and accounts receivable, which, at March 31, 1985, was $1.946 billion.[19]

---

the proceeds of commercial paper have been or are to be used for current transactions.")

19. SEC No-action Letter, *Atlantic-Richfield Co.* (available July 22, 1985). *See also* SEC No-action Letter, *Johnston Coca-Cola Bottling Group, Inc.* (available May 17, 1989); SEC No-action Letter, *Russell Corp.* (avail-

• • *Payment of Operating Expenses.* The staff of the SEC has been willing to take no-action positions where it is represented that the commercial paper proceeds will be used to pay ordinary operating expenses. This use of proceeds does not lend itself to a balance sheet formula approach, but rather a formula based on past levels of operating expenses. In some cases, the operating expenses providing commercial paper capacity have been stated to be those for the preceding 12 months.[20]

Generally, where the payment of operating expenses is listed as a current transaction, other uses that do lend themselves to a balance sheet approach, such as the carrying of inventories and accounts receivable or short-term lending activities, also are cited in the no-action request.[21] In one case, the issuer stated in its request that, in addition to financing inventory and current accounts receivable, it would use the commercial paper proceeds to pay such operating expenses as "federal, state and local income, property, franchise and other taxes, salaries, legal accounting and audit expenses, travel expenses, and retirement benefits."[22] In another no-action request, the operating expenses to be financed were stated to include interest on indebtedness and deposits and dividends on the outstanding common and preferred stock of the issuer or its subsidiaries.[23]

---

able September 22, 1988); SEC No-action Letter, *American Crystal Sugar Co.* (available November 13, 1987).

20. E.g., SEC No-action Letter, *The Black & Decker Corp.* (available July 12, 1989); SEC No-action Letter, *United Cable Television Corp.* (available December 30, 1987).

21. E.g., SEC No-action Letter, *Turner Broadcasting System, Inc.* (available November 7, 1989); SEC No-action Letter, *Hughes Supply Inc.* (available October 4, 1988).

22. SEC No-action Letter, *General Host Corp.* (available February 3, 1986). *See also* SEC No-action Letter, *J.B. Hunt Transport, Inc.* (available August 8, 1989).

23. SEC No-action Letter, *Southeast Banking Corp.* (available November 21, 1989). *See also* SEC No-action Letter, *National Community Banks, Inc.* (available July 13, 1989); SEC No-action Letter, *MNC Financial, Inc.* (available September 9, 1988).

• • *Carrying Finance Company Receivables.* Finance companies, such as General Motors Acceptance Corporation and Ford Motor Credit Company, are major issuers of commercial paper, with billions of dollars of notes outstanding at any one time. The types of activities in which finance companies engage have long been recognized as satisfying the current transaction test, and most finance companies have not found it necessary to seek no-action letters from the staff of the SEC.

In SEC Release No. 33-401 (June 18, 1935), the SEC published an opinion of its then General Counsel to the effect that the proceeds of commercial paper notes of the type normally issued by finance companies may be regarded as used for current transactions if the issuer is in the business of making loans on or purchasing notes, installment contracts or other evidences of indebtedness and the proceeds are used for such purposes in the usual course of business. This position was reaffirmed by the SEC in SEC Release No. 33-4412, in which it stated that "short-term paper issued by finance companies to carry their installment loans" is a type of security that has usually been considered to fall within the terms of Section 3(a)(3).[24]

• • *Lending Activities of United States Bank Holding Companies and Foreign Banks.* The staff of the SEC has issued numerous no-action letters relating to commercial paper issued by United States bank holding companies for the purpose of financing their own current operating requirements and the various lending activities of their banking subsidiaries.

Bank holding companies, unlike their bank subsidiaries, may not rely on the Section 3(a)(2) exemption available to regulated banks. Examples of permitted uses applicable to bank holding companies include funding (whether directly or through participations) of commercial, consumer, construction and mortgage loans having maturities not greater than five years and factoring and capital goods financing. Commercial paper may be used to fi-

---

24. *See also* SEC No-action Letter, *Kerr-McGee Credit Corp.* (available October 12, 1987; SEC No-action Letter, *Dana Credit Corp.* (available May 16, 1986); SEC No-action Letter, *Westinghouse Credit Corp.* (available May 5, 1986).

nance loans with remaining terms of five years or less even though their original terms may have been much longer. In addition, commercial paper proceeds may be used to carry long-term mortgage loans pending their packaging and sale to permanent mortgage investors.[25] Similar no-action letters have been issued to savings and loan associations.[26]

Many foreign banks have issued commercial paper in the United States in reliance upon the Section 3(a)(3) exemption. For the most part, these banks have not sought no-action letters from the SEC but have relied upon opinions of U.S. counsel as to the availability of the exemption. In the usual opinion of this type, counsel recites that the bank requires funds for its short-term lending activities, states the current dollar amount of commercial, consumer and other loans having maturities of not greater than five years, and concludes that the current transaction test will be met as long as the amount of commercial paper outstanding at any one time does not exceed the dollar amount of the bank's loans maturing within five years. In the usual case, qualified loans far exceed the amount of commercial paper proposed to be outstanding at any one time.[27]

• • *Financing of Leasing and Related Activities.* In the past, the staff of the SEC was willing to grant no-action letters that were quite liberal with respect to the terms of leases proposed to be financed with the commercial paper proceeds. An example is a 1980 letter in which the staff took a no-action position where a leasing company represented that it intended to limit the amount of notes sold in reliance upon the Section 3(a)(3) exemption and outstanding at any particular time to the amount of its operating expenses for the preceding 12 months

---

25. *See* SEC No-action Letter, *Southeast Banking Corp.* (available November 21, 1989); SEC No-action Letter, *National Westminster Bancorp Inc.* (available September 29, 1989); SEC No-action Letter, *Huntington Bancshares Inc.* (available May 1, 1987).

26. E.g., SEC No-action Letter, *Imperial Savings Assoc.* (available September 21, 1988).

27. A no-action position was taken in this context in SEC No-action Letter, *Chase Manhattan Corp. (Canadian Subsidiary)* (available July 2, 1984).

plus the sum of its net investment in direct finance leases of non-permanent equipment with original terms of seven years or less; its investment in operating leases covering equipment which had an original estimated economic life of nine years or less; secured loans having original terms of seven years or less on equipment which had an original estimated economic life of nine years or less; interim financing loans for temporarily "warehousing" equipment; and "floor plan" loans to affiliated equipment dealers.[28]

Other early no-action letters covered commercial paper issued to finance the acquisition of equipment of a non-permanent nature to be leased or sold under conditional sale contracts for periods of up to five years and, in some cases, seven years.[29]

In 1985, the SEC's staff tightened up its position with respect to leasing activities.[30] A bank holding company, after discussion with the staff, undertook to exclude any leases with terms in excess of five years. This reflected the staff view that the terms of the underlying leases supporting commercial paper qualifying for the Section 3(a)(3) exemption should not exceed five years.[31] The staff also has issued letters relating to the interim financing of equipment to be leased to clients of leasing companies without any limitation on the term of the lease.[32]

---

28. SEC No-action Letter, *GATX Leasing Corp.* (available June 23, 1980).

29. SEC No-action Letter, *Cummins Financial, Inc.* (available July 2, 1984); SEC No-action Letter, *Goldman, Sachs & Co.* (available May 21, 1984); SEC No-action Letter, *Centerre Bancorporation* (available November 7, 1983); SEC No-action Letter, *E.F. Hutton Credit Corp.* (available September 11, 1983); SEC No-action Letter, *Greyhound Corp.* (available March 12, 1982); SEC No-action Letter, *Seafirst Corp.* (available February 14, 1980).

30. SEC No-action Letter, *Landmark Banking Corp.* (available March 14, 1985).

31. SEC No-action Letter, *MNC Financial Inc.* (available September 9, 1988).

32. SEC No-action Letter, *Evans Railcar Leasing Co.* (available February 27, 1981); SEC No-action Letter, *Ryder Truck Rental, Inc.* (available

• • *Financing of Insurance Operations.* A comprehensive discussion of the current transaction test as it applies to the business of insurance is found in correspondence between the SEC's staff and counsel for Nationale-Nederlanden N.V., a Dutch holding company whose subsidiaries are engaged primarily in the insurance business.[33] The insurance holding company's request stressed that the commercial paper was being issued to bridge short-term timing differences between the receipt of premiums and other operating revenues and current cash requirements. The request proposed a formula under which the commercial paper outstanding at any one time would not exceed 75% of the amount by which life insurance premiums receivable within the following nine months, together with the principal of, and interest on, loans, and net rentals receivable during the same period, exceeded short term indebtedness other than the commercial paper. The request went on to characterize the commercial paper as being issued in order to "premature" premiums and other revenues receivable within nine months.[34]

• • *Financing of Broker-Dealer Operations.* The staff has issued a number of no-action letters under Section 3(a)(3) to securities firms and their holding company parents. Current transactions in the securities industry have been considered to include the financing of receivables arising in connection with margin indebtedness owed by customers and accounts that are payable by other broker-dealers and financial institutions in connection with securities borrowed and failed to deliver.[35]

January 18, 1980); SEC No-action Letter, *Pullman Leasing Co.* (available May 29, 1979).

33. SEC No-action Letter, *Nationale-Nederlanden N.V.* (available August 28, 1981).

34. *See also* SEC No-action Letter, *Pacific Mutual Life Insurance Co.* (available May 13, 1988); SEC No-action Letter, *The Travelers Corp. and The Travelers Insurance Co.* (available November 4, 1982); SEC No-action Letter, *The Mutual Benefit Life Insurance Co.* (available February 8, 1982); SEC No-action Letter, *Equitable Life Assurance Society of the United States* (available April 7, 1980 and June 23, 1980).

35. SEC No-action Letter, *Morgan Keegan, Inc.* (available November 10, 1986); SEC No-action Letter, *Robert W. Baird & Co. Inc.* (available

The staff also has taken a no-action position with respect to any and all receivables from customers, and not just margin indebtedness, where it was represented that these receivables are typically payable within one year.[36] The carrying of inventories of obligations issued or guaranteed by the U.S. government or its agencies and of money market instruments with maturities of not more than one year from the date of their purchase also have been considered current transactions within the meaning of Section 3(a)(3).[37] The carrying of inventories of other debt and equity securities, at least in amounts necessary to satisfy customers' orders, also has been considered a current transaction.[38]

As indicated above, the staff of the SEC has been willing to take no-action positions where it is represented that commercial paper proceeds will be used to pay ordinary operating expenses. Several of the no-action letters issued to securities firms refer to operating expenses such as payroll, employee travel, rent, and similar items, in addition to current items that can be derived from the balance sheet.[39] The *Merrill Lynch* letter also refers to such operating expenses as taxes, retirement benefits, legal, accounting and audit expenses and advertising costs.

•• *Investments in Money Market Obligations.* A number of issuers have instituted commercial paper programs to generate funds to invest in short-term money market obligations, including

---

March 26,1986); SEC No-action Letter, *Shearson/American Express Holdings Inc.* (available June 11, 1984); SEC No-action Letter, *Shearson American Express Inc.* (October 4, 1982).

36. SEC No-action Letter, *Merrill Lynch & Co., Inc.* (available May 17, 1985).

37. SEC No-action Letter, *Robert W. Baird & Co. Inc.* (available March 26, 1986); SEC No-action Letter, *Morgan Keegan, Inc.* (available November 10, 1986); SEC No-action Letter, *Merrill Lynch & Co., Inc.* (available May 17, 1985).

38. SEC No-action Letter, *Morgan Keegan, Inc.* (available November 10, 1986); SEC No-action Letter, *Merrill Lynch & Co., Inc.* (available May 17, 1985).

39. SEC No-action Letter, *Morgan Keegan, Inc.* (available November 10, 1986); SEC No-action Letter, *Robert W. Baird & Co. Inc.* (available March 26, 1986).

securities issued by the U.S. government or its agencies, bankers' acceptances, bank certificates of deposit and commercial paper of other issuers. Under certain market conditions, the yield that can be derived from investments in obligations of this type may be higher than the rate that the issuer must pay on its own commercial paper. In these cases, the maturities of the money market obligations are matched against the maturities of the commercial paper, thereby, in effect, creating an arbitrage.

In a series of no-action letters beginning in the early 1970s, the staff of the SEC approved the investment of commercial paper proceeds in money market obligations such as short-term certificates of deposit or commercial paper of other issuers. Initially, the no-action letters covered cases where the issuer periodically had excess liquidity and not where the issuer proposed to sell its commercial paper for the purpose of generating funds for investment in money market obligations.[40]

In 1976, the staff for the first time found the current transaction test to have been met where commercial paper was to be issued by a bank holding company to generate funds for investment.[41] There the holding company stated that it would invest the proceeds "in short-term direct obligations of the United States and in obligations of other issuers where the periods to maturities of such obligations from the dates of investment therein are not more than nine months." There was no suggestion that the investments would be made only to utilize temporary cash surpluses.[42]

---

40. *See,* e.g., SEC No-action Letter, *Hospital Corp. of America* (available August 20, 1979); SEC No-action Letter, *First Kentucky National Corp.* (available June 21, 1976); SEC No-action Letter, *Horizon Bancorp* (available May 3, 1976); SEC No-action Letter, *Texas American Bancshares, Inc.* (available November 11, 1974); SEC No-action Letter, *The Fort Worth National Corp.* (available January 3, 1973).

41. SEC No-action Letter, *BancOklahoma Corp.* (available March 1, 1976).

42 . *See also* SEC No-action Letter, *Pan American Banks Inc.* (available May 28, 1984); SEC No-action Letter, *Crocker National Corp.* (available November 15, 1982); SEC No-action Letter, *Interstate Financial Corp.*

In 1983, for the first time, the staff took a no-action position on the issuance of commercial paper by an industrial company for the express purpose of funding an arbitrage program.[43] The Kellogg Company, a manufacturer and marketer of convenience food products, stated in its no-action request that its current transactions might include investments in short-term financial instruments having a term to maturity at the time of purchase not in excess of 12 months, including United States government and federal agency obligations; municipal notes rated "AA" or better; certificates of deposit; bankers' acceptances and other commercial bank obligations; and commercial paper of other issuers having a rating of A-1, P-1, or F-1. The no-action request went on to state that the maturity of the commercial paper issued by Kellogg would "fall within five business days of any reset or other change in the interest rates of financial instruments . . . purchased or carried . . . with funds allocable to the proceeds of the Paper, or within five business days of the maturity dates of such instruments where such maturity dates have not been preceded by an interest rate change."

The staff took a similar no-action position the following year.[44] Counsel to the issuer stated that commercial paper notes would be issued as part of Gillette's "cash management program" and that the proceeds would be invested in

> high grade debt securities, United States and foreign bank time deposits, bankers' acceptances or bank certificates of deposit which, at the time of their purchase, have remaining maturities not in excess of twelve months or in certain diversified, open-end investment companies . . . which invest only in United States dollar denominated money market instruments[.]

While taking a no-action position on the program in general, the staff expressly refused to take a no-action position on

---

(available October 11, 1982); SEC No-action Letter, *Exchange National Corp.* (available February 8, 1982).

43. SEC No-action Letter, *Kellogg Co.* (available October 7, 1983).

44. SEC No-action Letter, *The Gillette Co.* (available May 15, 1984).

the investment in money market funds because interests in such investment companies are equity securities.

The staff also took a no-action position under Section 3(a)(3) with respect to a program initiated by Goldman, Sachs & Co. under which its commercial paper clients would invest all or a portion of the proceeds from the sale of their commercial paper in secured obligations of Goldman Sachs with maturities matching the commercial paper notes, each obligation bearing interest at a rate equal to the discount rate at which the corresponding commercial paper note was issued plus a spread to be determined by agreement between the issuer and Goldman Sachs.[45]

• • *Interim Construction Financing.* In SEC Release No. 33-4412, the SEC stated that the current transaction standard would not be satisfied where the proceeds from the sale of commercial paper were to be used for "permanent or fixed investment, such as land, buildings, or machinery" or for "the purchase or construction of a plant" or "the purchase of durable machinery or equipment." Subsequent to that release, however, the staff recognized that, under certain circumstances, interim financing of permanent improvements would qualify as a current transaction. In 1972, the staff granted a no-action letter under Section 3(a)(3) covering the interim financing of hotel construction when accompanied by a take-out commitment for permanent financing.[46] The staff then took a no-action position with respect to the use of proceeds by a real estate developer to finance building and land improvements accompanied "in most instances" by take-out commitments for permanent financing.[47]

In July 1979, a major commercial paper dealer applied for and was granted a generic no-action letter covering commercial paper to be issued to finance, on an interim basis, the construction of a plant or other capital assets where the construction period would

---

45. SEC No-action Letter, *Goldman, Sachs & Co.* (available May 15, 1986).

46. SEC No-action Letter, *Marriott Corp.* (available March 10, 1972).

47. SEC No-action Letter, *Kaiser Aetna* (available February 7, 1974).

not exceed three years, even in cases where there was no take-out commitment for permanent financing.[48] Counsel argued in the no-action request that alternative methods of permanent financing, namely bank borrowings under an existing line of credit, the use of internally generated funds, or subsequently arranged financing, are as suitable as a take-out commitment for permanent financing to retire commercial paper. The staff agreed with respect to "internally generated funds or subsequently arranged financing in the case of issuers which, by virtue of their outstanding credit position, appear to clearly have the ability to retire the commercial paper as indicated."

Subsequently, the staff issued no-action letters covering commercial paper used to finance the construction of a common carrier pipeline system[49] and improvements to or extensions of an existing pipeline system.[50] In neither case was there a take-out commitment for permanent financing.

In the first case, it was represented to the staff that it was expected that the commercial paper would be retired with funds derived from operations or through the issuance of long-term debt obligations in the private placement market "within a reasonable period after the completion of the improvement or extension being financed, which period is not expected to exceed twelve months." In the other case, it was represented that the financial objective was that by the end of the construction period the debt portion of the capital cost of the pipeline would be financed by securities with the longest available maturities that could be obtained at acceptable interest rates and that, in any event, the issuer did not expect to issue any commercial paper to finance or refinance the construction costs of the pipeline after a specified date approximately two and one half years after the date of the letter.

---

48. SEC No-action Letter, *A.G. Becker Inc.* (available September 24, 1979).

49. SEC No-action Letter, *Cortez Capital Corp.* (available August 18, 1982).

50. SEC No-action Letter, *Colonial Pipeline Co.* (available September 18, 1981).

The staff also took a no-action position where it was represented that commercial paper issued to provide interim financing for restaurant development would be retired no later than 36 months after completion of the particular project being financed.[51] No-action requests by bank holding companies frequently included, among other uses of proceeds, loans for interim construction financing.[52]

Goldman, Sachs & Co., one of the largest commercial paper dealers, demonstrated in the early 1980s the usefulness of the commercial paper market as a source of construction financing by selling commercial paper to finance the construction of its headquarters building at 85 Broad Street.

• • *Financing of Public Utility Operations.* For several decades, major electric and gas public utilities were engaged in continuous construction programs, including the construction of large nuclear facilities. Traditionally, public utilities had financed their construction programs through the sale of first mortgage bonds and equity securities with commercial paper providing interim financing.

In 1973, Consolidated Edison Company of New York, Inc., in seeking a no-action letter covering the issuance of commercial paper in an amount not to exceed its utility receivables and fuel inventory, specifically addressed the issue of tracing proceeds to construction. The utility's order from the New York State Public Service Commission made reference to so-called "arrearage" financing, in which short-term credit (bank loans or commercial paper) would be used to meet construction requirements with permanent financing undertaken to pay off the short-term debt only when the amount outstanding approached the magnitude of the desired permanent financing. Also, the utility's mortgage bond

---

51. SEC No-action Letter, *McDonald's Corp.* (available June 25, 1982). *See also* SEC No-action Letter, *Hawaiian Electric Industries, Inc.* (available March 28, 1985); SEC No-action Letter, *Olympia & York Properties* (available October 29, 1984, *reconsidered* November 20, 1984).

52. E.g., SEC No-action Letter, *National Westminster Bancorp Inc.* (available September 29, 1989); SEC No-action Letter, *First Fidelity Bancorporation* (available July 28, 1988).

prospectus stated that the net proceeds from the sale of the bonds would be used in part "to repay from time to time at or before maturity short-term obligations incurred as a result of the Company's construction program." The no-action request conceded that it might be argued that the statements in the Public Service Commission order and the prospectus had identified the proceeds of the commercial paper as being used for plant construction, at least on a temporary basis, pending refunding through permanent financing. This did not present a problem to the SEC's staff, and a no-action letter was issued based on a formula tied to receivables and fuel inventory.[53]

The SEC staff has issued letters that permit a public utility or its holding company to issue commercial paper up to an amount equal to the greater of (a) 25% of consolidated operating revenues during the past 12 months or (b) the sum of receivables and fuel inventory.[54] Another formula that has been acceptable to the staff is to limit the amount of outstanding commercial paper to the greater of 25% of gross revenues for the past 12 months or 50% of gross revenues for the preceding six months.[55] Other utilities have been granted no-action letters where the request stated that the commercial paper would be issued to carry accounts receivable and fuel inventories, to meet current operating requirements and to finance construction on an interim basis.[56]

---

53. SEC No-action Letter, *Consolidated Edison Co. of New York, Inc.* (available February 22, 1973).

54. SEC No-action Letter, *Hawaiian Electric Industries, Inc.* (available March 28, 1985); SEC No-action Letter, *Dominion Resources, Inc.* (available October 28, 1983); SEC No-action Letter, *Minnesota Power and Light Co.* (available November 8, 1971).

55. SEC No-action Letter, *New Jersey Natural Gas Co.* (available September 6, 1976).

56. SEC No-action Letter, *Peoples Gas Light and Coke Co.* (available September 28, 1989); SEC No-action Letter, *Lee County Electric Cooperative, Inc.* (available May 13, 1988); SEC No-action Letter, *PaineWebber Inc.* (available October 21, 1985); SEC No-action Letter, *Public Service Company of New Mexico* (available June 29, 1984); SEC No-action Letter, *Tucson Electric Power Co.* (available April 22, 1983).

• • *Nuclear Fuel Financing.* A number of public utilities have financed nuclear fuel by leasing the fuel from a special purpose corporation or trust established to issue commercial paper. The proceeds from the commercial paper issued by the special purpose entity are used to purchase nuclear fuel materials in process or finished nuclear fuel assemblies and in some cases contract rights pertaining to nuclear fuel. Where nuclear fuel materials are purchased, the proceeds also are used to pay the costs of processing and fuel assembly fabrication.

The period from the acquisition of nuclear fuel materials through the expiration of the fuel's usefulness is known as the "nuclear fuel cycle," and the commercial paper proceeds are used to finance the fuel in various stages throughout this cycle. In the original no-action letters relating to nuclear fuel financing, it was stated that the nuclear fuel cycle (the period of time that the issuer would own the nuclear fuel in the reactor or the materials from which it was processed) would not exceed 60 months.[57]

Subsequently, the staff found acceptable financing over a nuclear fuel cycle that would normally be six and one-half years but initially would be 11-1/2 years because of delays in the construction of the nuclear facility.[58] Even later, the staff took a no-action position where it was represented that for an operating reactor the complete nuclear fuel cycle would be a period of between 61 and 85 months when reloading of the fuel is involved or a period of between 68 and 92 months when preparation of the initial core is involved.[59]

---

57. SEC No-action Letter, *Duke Power Co.* (available August 9, 1979); SEC No-action Letter, *A.G. Becker Inc.* (available January 16, 1978); SEC No-action Letter, *Lehman Commercial Paper Inc.* (available October 3, 1977).

58. SEC No-action Letter, *Mid-Michigan Energy Co.* (available September 8, 1980). *See also* SEC No-action Letter, *Illinois Power Co.* (available March 6, 1981).

59. SEC No-action Letter, *Goldman, Sachs & Co.* (available May 21, 1984). *See also* SEC No-action Letter, *Security Pacific Merchant Banking Group* (available May 23, 1988), which contemplated a nuclear fuel cycle of between 48 and 84 months, and SEC No-action Letter, *Renaissance Energy Corp.* (available December 29, 1989), in which note proceeds were to

• • *Acquisition Financing.* From time to time, issuers have sought to use commercial paper to finance acquisitions, either directly or by repaying bank debt incurred for that purpose. In other cases, issuers have sought to increase a commercial paper program at or about the time an acquisition is being made. SEC Release No. 33-4412 made clear that the current transaction standard is not satisfied where the proceeds from the issuance of commercial paper are to be used for the purchase or establishment of a business enterprise. Moreover, while interim financing of construction may satisfy Section 3(a)(3), the SEC staff's position on interim financing of acquisitions has not been consistent.[60]

On the other hand, it can be argued that an issuer that has sufficient inventories and accounts receivable to support a commercial paper program of a certain size should not be precluded from instituting or increasing such a program simply because it will use otherwise available funds to acquire another company. The *Consolidated Edison* letter discussed above strongly supports the position that a formula approach is acceptable even if the purpose or motive underlying the issuance of commercial paper is the financing of a noncurrent transaction.

The no-action letter most frequently cited in support of the proposition that a recent acquisition that requires financing should not affect the availability of an otherwise supportable Section 3(a)(3) exemption is a 1981 letter issued to Fluor Corporation covering a commercial paper program that it planned to institute shortly after it acquired St. Joe Minerals Corporation.[61] Whether or not a need to refinance the acquisition was a

---

be used to purchase nuclear fuel for resale to The Detroit Edison Company.

60. Three letters were issued in 1983 only after the requesting issuers deleted references to acquisition financing. SEC No-action Letters, *Liberty National Corp.* (available May 6, 1983), *Continental Bancorp, Inc.* (available February 17, 1983), *Florida Coast Banks, Inc.* (available September 12, 1983). *But see Bank of Boston Corp.* (August 28, 1989) (approving as a current transaction the acquisition by a bank holding company of "banks and other entities" for a period ending on the earlier to occur of 270 days or the obtaining of permanent financing).

61. SEC No-action Letter, *Fluor Corp.* (available December 18, 1981).

motivating factor in the establishment of the commercial paper program is not evident from the text of the request. In the no-action request, however, it was stated quite clearly that the proceeds would not be segregated but would become part of Fluor's general funds and that accordingly it would not be practicable to trace specific dollars from the proceeds to specific applications. It was represented that the aggregate principal amount of commercial paper to be outstanding at any time would not exceed the sum of Fluor's consolidated accounts receivable, contract work in progress and inventories. The no-action request included a table setting forth on a combined basis the current asset accounts (more than $940 million) of Fluor and St. Joe as of various dates. In effect, the SEC staff took a no-action position with respect to a commercial paper program in the magnitude of close to $1 billion within months following a very major acquisition by Fluor.

Whenever there is any doubt about an issuer's commercial paper capacity when the primary purpose of issuance is to fund an acquisition, it is preferable to consider a "restricted" or "Section 4(2)" program in lieu of a Section 3(a)(3) program. As discussed in Chapter 7, restricted programs are relatively easy to establish and permit an issuer to use the proceeds of the program for any purpose. In addition, the cost of such programs is usually comparable to that of a Section 3(a)(3) program.

• • *Issuer's Repurchase of Securities.* An issuer should be entitled to rely on the Section 3(a)(3) exemption to issue commercial paper where it has sufficient commercial paper capacity and the proceeds will be used in part to finance a stock repurchase program. In *Bank of Boston Corp.* (available August 28, 1989), the staff approved as a current transaction in and of itself the financing of a stock repurchase program for a period ending on the earlier to occur of 270 days or the obtaining of permanent financing.

• • *Financing by Foreign Governmental Entities.* A foreign governmental entity may finance its short-term needs through the issuance of notes in the United States in reliance upon Section 3(a)(3). In 1982, the City of Gothenburg, Sweden, received a no-action letter relating to short-term notes that it proposed to issue in order to finance the operation of a municipal electric utility.[62] In its request, the City's counsel referred to an unpublished 1962 exchange of correspondence with the SEC relating to the City of Montreal. In that situation, the staff had advised that the exemption was not available because the notes to be sold would not be discountable by the Federal Reserve Bank (which it was then advised could only discount notes arising out of commercial transactions), and because certain of the proposed uses of the proceeds were not within the contemplation of the current transactions standard contained in Section 3(a)(3). Counsel argued that the Montreal precedent was not relevant because there the proceeds were to be applied to non-commercial purposes, such as the financing of maintenance of sidewalks, streets and public places, anticipation of tax revenues, and other purposes for which Montreal was authorized to borrow pending the sale of long-term obligations. Counsel stressed that in the case of Gothenburg the proceeds were to meet the current operating expenses of the city's public utility operations. The no-action letter was granted without any reference to these distinctions.

Two other no-action requests submitted on behalf of sovereign governments also stressed the commercial nature of the proposed use of proceeds. The request of the Kingdom of Denmark referred to certain state enterprises, including railways, the postal and telegraph services (which also provide long-distance telephone services), seaports, airports, forests, a ferry and the company through which trade between Denmark and Greenland is conducted. It was represented that Denmark would limit the amount of its commercial paper so that at no time would the aggregate amount outstanding exceed the sum of the then dollar equivalent of the current accounts receivable of these state enterprises, their depreciation and amortization charges for the preceding year, their inventories and their requirements for salaries, pension payments, rental and general office expenses. On this basis, the staff granted the no-action request.[63]

---

62. SEC No-action Letter, *City of Gothenburg* (available March 5, 1982).

63. SEC No-action Letter, *Kingdom of Denmark* (available May 13, 1985).

The staff subsequently issued a no-action letter to the Kingdom of Spain on the basis that the aggregate amount of commercial paper outstanding would not exceed the amount of the current advances to state enterprises engaged in such activities as the operation of railroads, coal mining, metallurgy, maritime shipping, airline transportation and telecommunications. In addition, the outstanding paper would not exceed the sum of the U.S. dollar equivalents of these enterprises' accounts receivable, depreciation expenses and inventories and wage-related expenditures.[64]

In view of the advice by the General Counsel of the SEC in 1980 that the staff no longer requires commercial paper to be eligible for discounting, there was no reason to have emphasized in these no-action requests the commercial nature of the use of proceeds. A foreign governmental issuer may issue short-term promissory notes in reliance upon Section 3(a)(3) to finance current transactions, whether or not they are of a commercial nature. This is confirmed by a no-action letter issued in 1986 to Lehman Commercial Paper Incorporated allowing its sovereign clients to issue commercial paper to finance current governmental expenditures or to retain the proceeds as part of their foreign exchange reserves.[65]

Nothing in Section 3(a)(3) limits that exemption to programs that are designated as "commercial paper" or requires that an issuer elect to rely on that exemption. Indeed, it is not even necessary that the foreign governmental issuer ever have heard of Section 3(a)(3). In the normal situation, of course, a foreign governmental issuer of short-term debt obligations will not be selling these obligations into the United States. It is often the case, however, that U.S. securities firms wish to trade these obligations in the United States or to sell them to their U.S. customers. There is no reason why a dealer may not rely on the exemption for these purposes if it can confirm that the debt obligations meet the requirements of Section 3(a)(3) as described above. In this connection, it should be possible to verify the issuer's "commercial paper capacity" by reference to its public accounts.

---

64. SEC No-action Letter, *Kingdom of Spain* (available August 1, 1985).

65. SEC No-action Letter, *Lehman Commercial Paper Inc.* (available December 1, 1986).

• *Section 3(a)(2) Bank Support Exemption*

Commercial paper backed by letters of credit of domestic banks have long been viewed by the staff of the SEC as exempt under Section 3(a)(2) on the basis that letters of credit are in effect guarantees and that the commercial paper they support are therefore exempt as securities guaranteed by a bank.[66] It is immaterial for this purpose whether the letter of credit is attached to the notes or the bank issues a master letter of credit or whether the letter of credit runs to a depository bank or directly to the holders of the notes.[67]

Where commercial paper is backed by a letter of credit and is therefore exempt under Section 3(a)(2), there is no need to be concerned as to whether the current transaction test is satisfied. Nor is there a need to be concerned with the nine-month limitation of Section 3(a)(3), although for marketing reasons "Section 3(a)(2) paper" usually has the same terms and is sold in the same manner as Section 3(a)(3) paper.

Foreign banks' U.S. branches and agencies received numerous no-action letters to the effect that commercial paper backed by their letters of credit is also entitled to the Section 3(a)(2) exemption. These letters were issued on the premise that the nature and extent of the supervision in a particular state, and the manner in which the branch or agency is regulated, permitted reliance upon the Section 3(a)(2) exemption.[68]

---

66. SEC No-action Letter, *Underwood Neuhaus & Co. (Allied Bank of Texas)* (available February 21, 1985); SEC No-action Letter, *Chase Manhattan Bank, N.A.* (available July 2, 1979); SEC No-action Letter, *Security Pacific National Bank* (available June 26, 1978 and October 2, 1978); SEC No-action Letter, *Mason-McDuffie* (June 20, 1975); SEC No-action Letter, *Chemical Bank/Lomas & Nettleton Mortgage Investors* (available December 1, 1971); SEC No-action Letter, *United California Bank* (available April 15, 1971).

67. SEC No-action Letter, *Goldman, Sachs & Co.* (available July 10, 1978). For bankruptcy law reasons, however, letters of credit are usually direct-pay (i.e., the letter of credit bank pays holders of maturing commercial paper, and the issuer reimburses the bank through a reimbursement agreement).

68. SEC No-action Letter, *Fuji Bank Ltd.* (available September 17, 1984); SEC No-action Letter, *The Toronto-Dominion Bank (Hiram Walker*

In a 1986 release,[69] the SEC reviewed the history of its no-action positions with respect to Section 3(a)(2) and determined to formalize its position on the application of that section to securities issued or guaranteed by foreign banks' U.S. branches and agencies. It stated that the exemption would be available provided that the nature and extent of federal or state regulation and supervision of the particular branch or agency is "substantially equivalent" to that applicable to federal or state chartered domestic banks doing business in the same jurisdiction. The SEC stated that this determination was the responsibility of issuers and their counsel and that no-action letters on this subject would no longer be granted.

If a letter of credit is viewed as a security separate from the underlying obligation which it supports, then it must independently find its own exemption under the 1933 Act. In seeking a no-action letter with respect to letters of credit issued by the home office (not a branch or agency) of a bank based in the Netherlands to back short-term promissory notes issued by certain commercial and industrial customers, counsel took the position that the letters of credit should be exempt from registration based upon the Section 3(a)(3) exemption. Counsel assumed that the exemption under Section 3(a)(3) would be available for the notes alone and then framed the issue as whether the addition of the letter of credit supporting such notes would require registration of either the notes or the letter of credit. Counsel pointed out that no-action letters covering parent guarantees of a subsidiary's commercial paper had been granted on the basis that the essential characteristics of the guarantees were derived from the notes which they supported.[70]

Commercial Paper, Inc.) (available July 6, 1984); SEC No-action Letter, *Industrial Bank of Japan, Ltd.* (New York Agency) (available February 10, 1984); SEC No-action Letter, *National Westminster Bank, Ltd.* (available November 30, 1981); SEC No-action Letter, *Mitsui Bank, Ltd. (New York Branch)* (available November 30, 1981).

69. SEC Release No. 33-6661 (September 23, 1986).

70. *See* SEC No-action Letter, *U.S. Pioneer Electronics Corp.* (available August 13, 1979); SEC No-action Letter, *Mitsui & Co. (Canada), Ltd.* (available September 5, 1974).

Counsel argued that letters of credit issued by a foreign bank should be regarded in the same way. In addition, counsel argued that the letters of credit viewed alone should qualify for the Section 3(a)(3) exemption in that they would have the same duration as the underlying notes and that, although not technically notes, they came within the spirit of the Section 3(a)(3) exemption. The staff took a no-action position, but subject to the condition that the commercial paper notes backed by the letters of credit would be limited to those issued by U.S. customers of the foreign bank.[71] In a subsequent letter issued to a bank in Finland, however, the staff took a no-action position even though it was stated that the bank's letters of credit would back commercial paper of U.S. and non-U.S. issuers.[72]

Commercial paper sometimes is backed by a surety bond written by an insurance company. In such cases, the commercial paper itself must be exempt under Section 3(a)(3) and the surety bond, if deemed a separate security, will be entitled to the exemption provided by Section 3(a)(8), which exempts: "Any insurance or endowment policy . . . issued by a corporation subject to the supervision of the insurance commissioner, bank commissioner, or any agency or officer performing like functions, of any State or Territory of the United States or the District of Columbia."[73] Unlike a letter of credit issued by a domestic bank or a domestic branch or agency of a foreign bank, a surety bond cannot create an exemption for underlying commercial paper that is not itself exempt.[74]

The disparity in treatment of obligations guaranteed by banks and those guaranteed by insurance companies drew complaints from the insurance industry, notwithstanding the fact

---

71. SEC No-action Letter, *Amsterdam-Rotterdam Bank N.V.* (available October 14, 1980).

72. SEC No-action Letter, *Saastopankkien Keskus-Osake-Pankki* (available October 24, 1988).

73. *See* SEC No-action Letter, *Lehman Commercial Paper Inc.* (available October 3, 1977). *See also* SEC No-action Letter, *Financial Security Assurance Inc.* (available October 24, 1988).

74. SEC No-action Letter, *Insurance Co. of North America* (available September 26, 1983).

that banks are extensively regulated on the federal level while insurance companies are regulated only on the state level. In Section 105 of the Government Securities Act of 1986,[75] however, Congress directed the SEC to conduct a study of the Section 3(a)(2) exemption, including its impact on competition between banks and insurance companies in providing financial guarantees. The SEC's report[76] recognized the existence of a competitive disparity and recommended that Congress eliminate the Section 3(a)(2) exemption for securities backed by bank guarantees and also grant general exemptive authority to the SEC. Congress did not act in response to the SEC report, and support for raising insurance company guarantees to the level of bank guarantees evaporated as several insurance companies began to encounter well-publicized financial difficulties.

• *Section 4(2) Continuous Private Placement Programs*

An issuer whose commercial paper that does not meet the Section 3(a)(3) requirements and that is unable or unwilling to obtain a bank letter of credit may still take advantage of the commercial paper market by setting up a "restricted" or "Section 4(2)" commercial paper program. This type of program is discussed in Chapter 7.

"Restricted" commercial paper programs present special challenges for registered open-end investment companies, particularly money market funds. Because the SEC considers restricted securities to be "illiquid" assets, open-end investment companies must generally avoid investing more than 15% of their assets in such securities.[77] Money market funds are sub-

---

75. Pub. L. No. 99-571.

76. *Report by the United States Securities and Exchange Commission on the Financial Guarantee Market: The Use of the Exemption in Section 3(a)(2) of the Securities Act of 1933 for Securities Guaranteed by Banks and the Use of Insurance Policies to Guarantee Debt Securities* (August 28, 1987).

77. "The usual limit on aggregate holdings by an open-end investment company of illiquid assets is fifteen percent of its net assets." Guide 4 to the Guides to Form N-1A, as amended in SEC Release No. IC-18612 (March 12, 1992)).

ject to a 10% limit.[78] On the other hand, the SEC permits an open-end fund's directors to determine that Rule 144A and foreign securities are liquid. In a 1994 interpretive letter, the SEC staff concurred in a commercial paper dealer's views that a fund's board of directors might determine that non-Rule 144A "restricted" commercial paper was also liquid for purposes of the percentage limitation so long as it was rated in one of the two highest rating categories. The board was also required to "consider the trading market for the specific security, taking into account all relevant factors."[79]

1940 Act Considerations

As discussed in Chapter 3, any issuer that holds significant amounts of "securities" as defined by the 1940 Act may be viewed as an investment company for purposes of that statute. Among the commercial paper issuers most likely to fall under this definition are issuers of asset-backed securities, broker-dealers, banks and insurance companies.

The status under the 1940 Act of issuers of asset-backed securities is discussed in Chapter 14.

As for broker-dealers, banks and insurance companies, there are express exemptions in the 1940 Act for *U.S.* issuers engaged in these businesses as well as for their holding companies.[80] The status of foreign banks and insurance companies, however, has not always been clear.

In late 1978, a Swedish commercial bank entered the United States commercial paper market without seeking exemptive relief under the 1940 Act. Through a series of circumstances, the

---

78. SEC Letter dated December 9, 1992 to Matthew P. Fink, President, Investment Company Institute.

79. SEC No-action Letter, *Merrill Lynch Money Markets, Inc.* (available January 14, 1994).

80. 1940 Act, § § 3(c)(2), 3(c)(3), 3(c)(6). The SEC has taken the interpretive position that U.S. branches and agencies of foreign banks are "banks" for purposes of the 1940 Act for the limited purpose of issuing securities in the United States. SEC Release No. IC-17681 (August 17, 1990).

staff of the SEC became aware of this and questioned whether the bank might be deemed an investment company. When made aware of the problem, the bank withdrew from the market.

The question was raised because the principal assets of commercial banks are consumer and commercial loans represented by some form of note or other evidence of indebtedness. If the evidences of indebtedness representing these loans were to be considered investment securities and if they amounted to more than 40% of the bank's assets (which would almost always be the case), then the bank would be deemed an investment company unless it could demonstrate that it was primarily engaged in a business other than that of owning or holding such securities.

The status of foreign banks under the 1940 Act became somewhat of a legal *cause celebre* following the staff's challenge to the Swedish bank's commercial paper program. In February 1979, five New York City law firms submitted to the staff of the SEC a draft of a letter setting forth legal arguments to the effect that foreign commercial banks should not be deemed to be investment companies. This letter was prepared following a meeting between representatives of these firms and the SEC staff at which the legal issues were fully aired. The staff did not respond to the letter but advised that the best course for a foreign bank to follow would be to assume that it was an investment company (without so admitting) and to seek an exemption from the provisions of the 1940 Act pursuant to Section 6(c).

In April 1979, the SEC began granting exemptive orders permitting foreign banks or their finance subsidiaries to sell their debt securities in the United States without registering as investment companies under the 1940 Act. These exemptions became routine, and the SEC codified them in 1987 by adopting Rule 6c-9 (which also permitted the sale of nonvoting preferred stock). Subsequently, the SEC granted a number of individual exemptive orders under Section 6(c) of the 1940 Act permitting foreign banks to sell their equity securities in the United States.

The SEC treated foreign insurance companies in similar fashion, granting individual exemptive orders permitting the sale of both debt and equity securities.

In 1990, the SEC proposed to extend the scope of Rule 6c-9 to cover foreign banks' equity securities and to exempt foreign insurance companies (and their finance subsidiaries) on the same basis as foreign banks and their finance subsidiaries.[81] In response to comments, the SEC decided in 1991 to abandon Rule 6c-9 in favor of a new Rule 3a-6, which specifically excludes foreign banks and insurance companies from the 1940 Act's definition of investment company.[82] As a result, these entities' holding companies are now also excluded under Rule 3a-1 and their finance subsidiaries are excluded under Rule 3a-5. In addition, the 1991 rulemaking resolved a longstanding anomaly by amending Rule 3a-5 to extend it to cover finance subsidiaries of foreign banks and insurance companies owned or controlled by foreign governmental entities.

There were two other consequences to the 1991 exclusion of foreign banks and insurance companies from the 1940 Act's definition of investment company. First, U.S. investment companies were no longer restricted by Section 12(d)(1)(A) of the 1940 Act from buying the securities of foreign banks and insurance companies (which were no longer "investment companies"), and Rule 12d1-1 (which had been adopted in 1990 to permit such investments) was accordingly rescinded. Second, because Section 12(d)(2) of the 1940 Act limits investment companies' acquisition of U.S. insurance company securities in excess of a specified level, Rule 12d2-1 was adopted to define "insurance company" for this purpose as including a foreign insurance company—thus preserving equal treatment for foreign and domestic insurance companies in terms of the eligibility of their securities for purchase by U.S. investment companies.

• *Finance Subsidiaries*

Most commercial paper programs established by foreign issuers have used a U.S. finance subsidiary to issue the commercial paper with an unconditional guarantee of the parent backing the subsidiary's obligation. The proceeds are advanced to the parent or to the parent's operating subsidiaries. U.S. fi-

---

81. SEC Release No. IC-17682 (August 17, 1990).
82. SEC Release No. IC-18381 (November 4, 1991).

nance subsidiaries are used primarily for marketing purposes, in that certain institutional investors are limited by corporate policy or otherwise in the amount of foreign securities that they may purchase.

Rule 3a-5 under the 1940 Act is intended to exclude from the definition of investment company any issuer that is organized primarily to finance the business operations of its parent company or a company controlled by its parent company. If the finance subsidiary's debt securities or preferred stock are "issued to or held by the public," they must be unconditionally guaranteed by the parent company. In addition, at least 85% of the proceeds of the offering must be advanced to the parent company or a company controlled by the parent company "as soon as practicable" but in any event not more than six months after receipt of such proceeds. To avoid temptation, the rule limits the types of securities that the finance subsidiary may hold as temporary investments.

A guarantee of preferred stock need extend only to dividends that have been declared and, in the event of liquidation, to the lower of the liquidation preference plus accumulated and unpaid dividends or the subsidiary's remaining assets after the satisfaction of prior claims.[83] A support or "keepwell" agreement does not currently satisfy the "unconditional guarantee" condition of the rule,[84] although the SEC has issued Section 6(c) exemptive orders in the case of support agreements where regulatory requirements prevented the parent companies from issuing a guarantee.[85] On the other hand, a guarantee is not required if the finance subsidiary sells its securities by means

---

83. SEC No-action Letter, *Chieftain International Funding Corp.* (available November 3, 1992).

84. Rule 3a-5(a)(7) permits a parent company that is a foreign bank as defined in Rule 3a-6 to satisfy the guarantee requirement by issuing a letter of credit that meets specified conditions.

85. SEC Release No. IC-15388 (October 31,1986) (application); SEC Release No. IC-15430 (November 21, 1986) (order); SEC Release No. IC-14964 (February 28, 1986) (application); SEC Release No. IC-15014 (March 25, 1986) (order).

of a private placement[86] or pursuant to Regulation S[87], even if the securities are eligible for resale under Rule 144A.[88]

In addition to Rule 3a-5, finance subsidiaries engaged exclusively in the issuance of notes with a maturity of no more than nine months may be eligible to claim an exclusion under Rule 3a-3. This exclusion is available, however, only if the parent company does not fall within the statutory definition of investment company or is excluded by Rule 3a-1.

• *Structured Financing Vehicles*

Structured financing vehicles may be established for the purpose of holding and financing a wide variety of tangible or intangible assets. The 1940 Act aspects of these vehicles are considered in Chapter 14.

Eurocommercial Paper

The U.S. securities law aspects of Eurocommercial paper are considered in Chapter 9.

Liabilities on Default

In the case of common stock or long-term debt obligations, there is always a risk that the value of the security may decline at any time because of earnings disappointments, rating changes or other adverse developments. An underwriter of common stock or long-term debt securities may face litigation risk under these circumstances. The underwriter may be comforted to a degree by the knowledge that it will surely have the company of the issuer as a co-defendant in any litigation and even by a reasonable expectation that the issuer will pay the costs of defense and settlement pursuant to the usual indemnification arrangements.

---

86. SEC No-action Letter, *Econo Lodges of America, Inc.* (available December 22, 1989).

87. SEC No-action Letter, *Societe Generale and SGA Societe Generale Acceptance N.V.* (available February 14, 1992).

88. SEC No-action Letter, *Sony Capital Corp.* (available April 27, 1992).

The risk associated with a short-term obligation such as commercial paper is not that the value of the instrument will decline prior to maturity as the result of adverse developments. Rather, the risk is that the "orderly exit" mechanism described earlier will not work in time and that the issuer will be forced to default on outstanding paper. A default of this kind is usually quickly followed by a filing under the Bankruptcy Code and the prospect of a total loss of principal for investors who are not accustomed to regarding commercial paper as an investment associated with risk of this kind.

In the event of a default by an issuer of commercial paper, holders will have to wait in line in bankruptcy court in order to recover anything from the issuer. Since commercial paper is typically unsecured, they will be waiting at the end of the line (just before the holders of equity securities). If they believe their investment was induced by false or misleading disclosure, they may make claims against the rating agencies or the issuer's independent accountants.

If they purchased the paper from a dealer, however, the holders have available an additional "deep pocket." The dealer's potential liability under these circumstances can be for the entire amount of the issuer's defaulted commercial paper. In the case of a multi-hundred million dollar program, this can lead to a serious weakening of the dealer's own financial standing. It is this potential for catastrophic liability that motivates dealers to take great pains to examine the 1933 Act status of their issuers' commercial paper programs, to monitor their issuers' creditworthiness and to urge the issuers to exit the market by drawing down on bank lines if there are signs of a deteriorating credit situation.

A dealer's potential liabilities can arise under Sections 12(a)(1) and 12(a)(2) of the 1933 Act, under Rule 10b-5, under corresponding provisions in state securities laws, or on the basis of common law fraud. Obviously, there are no Section 11 liabilities since commercial paper is not registered under the 1933 Act.

- *Section 12(a)(1)*

If commercial paper is sold without an available exemption from the registration requirements of Section 5 of the 1933 Act, then any purchaser may rescind the transaction as against any "seller" for a period of one year. Under the U.S. Supreme Court's decision in *Pinter v. Dahl*,[89] a dealer that passes title to the investor or that solicits the transaction for pecuniary reasons would appear to be a "seller" for this purpose.

It is therefore vital for a dealer to have confidence in the exemption under which it is selling the issuer's commercial paper. As we have seen, the Section 3(a)(3) exemption requires that the issuer use the proceeds of the sale of commercial paper for "current transactions." It is standard for a dealer at the commencement of a program to obtain an opinion from the issuer's counsel as to the availability of the exemption, but this opinion usually assumes that the proceeds will be used for stated purposes. Even if the opinion is required to be updated at future intervals, it is unlikely to provide specific factual comfort. Since a dealer has few alternative means of verifying that the issuer is in fact using the proceeds of the program for current transaction purposes, the dealer is necessarily at the issuer's mercy on this important part of the exemption.

It is not entirely clear that a court would visit the drastic rescission remedy on a dealer that had been lied to by an issuer about its use of the proceeds of the program for current transactions. On the other hand, it is clearly advisable for the dealer to take some precautions. In this connection, the concept of "commercial paper capacity" is again likely to be of significant help. A dealer can relatively easily—and therefore should—monitor an issuer's use of commercial paper against the information contained in the issuer's financial statements. And even though the concept of "commercial paper capacity" is based on SEC staff advice, a dealer ought to have a reasonable chance of persuading a court that the concept's origins and longevity make it eligible for the "good faith reliance" protection of Section 19(a) of the 1933 Act.[90]

Another potential vulnerability for the dealer lies in the Section 3(a)(3) exemption's dependence, at least under the SEC's Re-

---

89. 486 U.S. 622 (1988).

90. Compare *Gerstle v. Gamble-Skogmo, Inc.*, 478 F.2d 1281, 1293-94 (2d Cir. 1973), with *Colema Realty Corp. v. Bibow*, 555 F. Supp. 1030, 1040 (D.Conn. 1983).

lease 33-4412, on the "prime quality" of the commercial paper at the time of issuance. There are some cases under Rule 10b-5[91] that suggest a "Catch-22" outcome on this point: if an issuer of commercial paper defaults on the paper, then that paper could not have met the "prime quality" test at the time of its issuance.

Whatever the validity of these cases for Rule 10b-5 purposes, they should not control on the availability of the 1933 Act exemption. It should be sufficient for the latter purpose that the paper was rated "prime" at the time of its issuance by any of the major rating agencies and that the dealer had no reason to question that rating.

The vagaries of the Section 3(a)(3) exemption suggest that it would be in the interest of dealers to rely less on Section 3(a)(3) and more on Section 3(a)(2) and "restricted" or Section 4(2) programs. In particular, dealers can have a higher degree of confidence that 1933 Act exemptions are in fact available where the program is based on Rule 144A or procedures that parallel Regulation D. This does not mean, however, that a dealer cannot argue—even after an issuer's default—that a program should be regarded as having been entitled to a private placement exemption even where it was run for many years as a Section 3(a)(3) program. If the commercial paper was in fact sold to institutional accredited investors who did not (and were not likely to) act as underwriters in making resales, the program's entitlement to a private placement exemption may be sufficiently strong to withstand a rescission claim.

• *Antifraud Remedies*

Even if an exemption from 1933 Act registration can be established for the defaulted commercial paper, the dealer is still exposed to liability under the antifraud remedies. The scope of this liability will depend on the manner in which the commercial paper was offered and sold. The two major remedies are Section 12(a)(2) of the 1933 Act and Rule 10b-5 under the 1934 Act. In general, a dealer should prefer to be subject to liability

---

91. *Zeller v. Bogue Electric Manufacturing Corp.*, 476 F.2d 795, 800 (2d Cir.), *cert. denied,* 414 U.S. 908 (1973). *See also Sanders v. John Nuveen & Co.*, 463 F.2d 1075, 1079 (7th Cir.), *cert. denied* 409 U.S. 1009 (1972).

only under Rule 10b-5, which requires reliance by the plaintiff as well as *scienter* (i.e., intentional or reckless misconduct) by the defendant. By contrast, Section 12(a)(2) is a negligence-based remedy.

Section 3(a)(2) commercial paper, for example, is expressly excluded from liability under Section 12(a)(2). A holder of defaulted Section 3(a)(2) commercial paper must therefore proceed under Rule 10b-5.

Under the U.S. Supreme Court's *Gustafson* decision, discussed in Chapters 5 and 7, the Section 12(a)(2) remedy applies only to public offerings. A dealer that has sold commercial paper sold under a private placement exemption should therefore be subject only to Rule 10b-5 liability. On the other hand, as suggested above for Section 12(a)(1) purposes, the fact that a program was conducted in ostensible reliance on the Section 3(a)(3) exemption should not foreclose the dealer from demonstrating retroactively that the paper was in fact offered other than "publicly." Whether this will be sufficient under *Gustafson* to limit the plaintiff to Rule 10b-5 remedies is, of course, an open question.

• • *Section 12(a)(2).* Section 12(a)(2) permits a buyer of a security to rescind his purchase as against any person who offered or sold the security "by means of a prospectus or oral communication" that contained an untrue statement of material fact or omitted to state a material fact necessary in order to make the seller's statements, "in the light of the circumstances under which they were made, not misleading." The seller has a defense based on a showing that the seller did not know and, in the exercise of "reasonable care" could not have known, of the relevant untruth or omission. Since the enactment of the Reform Act, a plaintiff's recovery under Section 12(a)(2) is subject to reduction for any amount shown to be attributable to reasons unrelated to the asserted untruth or omission.

A claim under Section 12(a)(2) can take two forms in a commercial paper case. First, the plaintiff may rely on an allegedly false or misleading disclosure document used in connection with the sale. Second, the plaintiff can rely on asserted implied representations by the dealer to the effect that it believed that the commercial paper issuer was creditworthy *and* that this belief was based on a reasonable investigation.

The format of commercial paper disclosure documents can affect an investor's ability to make the first form of claim described above. If the documents contain (or incorporate by reference) all of the issuer's 1934 Act reports, for example, the plaintiff may be able to find (with the aid of hindsight) some incorrect statement or an omission that made a statement misleading. The plaintiff's task is usually even easier if the dealer, in preparing the disclosure document, excerpted information from the issuer's public reports or edited or summarized some of this information. On the other hand, if the documents contain only "bare bones" information about the commercial paper program (size of program, denominations, form and ratings), with an reference to the issuer or its 1934 Act reports for further information, it will be much harder for the plaintiff to point to deficiencies in the document. It will also be harder for the investor to claim that the commercial paper was sold to him "by means of" a specific document or communication, which is an essential element of Section 12(a)(2), or on the basis of an implied recommendation by the dealer.

There appears to be a trend among dealers toward "bare bones" offering documents in commercial paper programs. There are probably two reasons why this did not happen at an earlier date. First, many dealers were influenced by the terms of the SEC's 1974 settlement of injunctive proceedings against Goldman, Sachs & Co. arising out of the Penn Central bankruptcy and commercial paper default.[92] These terms contemplated that the dealer would provide investors with information relating to the creditworthiness of the issuer. It was common knowledge at the time that the SEC's Division of Enforcement expected the settlement to establish a standard of commercial paper disclosure comparable to that required by the 1933 Act.

Second, the SEC began to amend its 1934 Act reporting forms in the early 1970s to require much more extensive information about an issuer's business and financial condition. The

---

92. *SEC v. Goldman, Sachs & Co.*, SEC Litigation Rel. No. 6349 (May 2, 1974) (S.D.N.Y. Docket No. 74 Civ. 1916 (HRT)).

availability of informative 1934 Act reports made it easier for dealers to include these reports (or excerpts from the reports) as part of their commercial paper disclosure materials. The incentive to do so was probably influenced by the fact that investors did not have ready access to 1934 Act reports except from the issuer or an intermediary such as a dealer.

Conditions have changed significantly in the past few years regarding the availability of 1934 Act reports. All such reports are now readily available to investors through electronic and other sources. Moreover, investors in commercial paper are typically sophisticated investors who have access to this information as well as the ability to analyze it and make their own credit judgments. Finally, the market has come to rely to a much greater degree on the rating agencies.

Accordingly, commercial paper dealers are more likely to minimize their litigation exposure by adopting a disclosure document format that limits disclosure to the "bare bones" of the program and refers the investor to the issuer or an electronic data base for the issuer's 1934 Act and other public reports.

The second form of Section 12(a)(2) exposure described above is more difficult for a dealer to mitigate. It is based on the concept that a dealer in commercial paper makes an implied representation regarding its belief in the issuer's creditworthiness and, further, that this belief is based on a reasonable investigation. To be sure, the determination of what is a "reasonable" investigation will depend on the facts.

In an extended series of cases decided between 1972 and 1981,[93] purchasers of defaulted commercial paper sued the dealer who had marketed it. At a time when the plaintiff's case was based on Rule 10b-5, a panel of the Seventh Circuit referred to the dealer as the "exclusive underwriter" of the paper and noted that:

---

93. *Sanders v. John Nuveen & Co., Inc.*, 524 F.2d 1064 (7th Cir. 1975) (*Sanders II*), *vacated and remanded on other grounds*, 425 U.S. 929 (1976), *on remand*, 554 F.2d 790 (7th Cir. 1977) (*Sanders III*), *rehearing denied*, 619 F.2d 1222 (7th Cir. 1980) (*Sanders IV*), *cert. denied*, 450 U.S. 1005 (1981).

An underwriter's relationship with the issuer gives the underwriter access to facts that are not equally available to members of the public who must rely on published information. And the relationship between the underwriter and its customers implicitly involves a favorable recommendation of the issued security. Because the public relies on the integrity, independence and expertise of the underwriter, the underwriter's participation significantly enhances the marketability of the security. And since the underwriter is unquestionably aware of the public's reliance on his participation in the sale of the issue, the mere fact that he has underwritten it is an implied representation that he has met the standards of his profession in his investigation of the issuer.[94]

Ultimately, the case became one under Section 12(a)(2) of the 1933 Act, but the Seventh Circuit adhered to the previous panel's conclusion (when the case was based on Rule 10b-5) that the dealer had not made a "reasonable investigation" of the issuer because it had not reviewed the issuer's tax returns and its accountant's work papers. In response to the dealer's argument that the previous panel had confused the "reasonable investigation" standard of Section 11 with the "reasonable care" defense of Section 12(a)(2), and that by so doing it had held the dealer to a standard higher than that imposed in a Section 11 case, the Seventh Circuit concluded that it could "find no significance in this difference in language [i.e., "reasonable investigation" as opposed to "reasonable care"] in the case at bar."[95] It also suggested that it did not regard it as "at all clear" that there was always a higher standard in a Section 11 case.[96]

The Supreme Court denied a writ of *certiorari* over a dissent by Justices Powell and Rehnquist, who noted that the SEC had filed a brief in the Seventh Circuit arguing that it would "undermine the Congressional intent . . . if the same degree of investigation were to be required to avoid potential liability

---

94. 524 F.2d at 1069–70 (footnotes omitted).
95. 619 F.2d at 1228.
96. *Id.*

whether or not a registration statement is required."[97] The dissenting Justices were particularly troubled by the Seventh Circuit's having "denied" the dealer the "right to rely on 'the authority of an expert' "—i.e., the issuer's auditors in this case—that it would have had if the commercial paper had been registered under the 1933 Act.[98]

In *University Hill Foundation v. Goldman, Sachs & Co.,*[99] one of the cases involving Penn Central's 1970 default on its commercial paper, Judge Lasker concluded that it would be "inappropriate to import wholesale to the commercial paper context" the duties imposed on an underwriter under Section 11. He also rejected a reading of *Sanders* as "establishing an inflexible rule that an investigation which fails to include first hand verification of an issuer's financial condition is *per se* unreasonable." Rather, a commercial paper dealer's obligations under Section 12(a)(2) should be analyzed in terms of:

> a close consideration of the facts of the relationship between Penn Central and Goldman, Sachs, the latter's access to information, the nature of the data it relied upon and the presence or absence of "warning signals" . . . Based on the role it played in marketing Penn Central notes, Goldman, Sachs' credit investigation must be judged by a fairly rigorous standard. . . . [I]t singlehandedly directed the entire distribution campaign and was the exclusive source of the notes for all would-be purchasers. Not only was its relationship to the Penn Central management, therefore, uniquely close, but its implicit warrant of the soundness of its basis for recom-

---

97. 450 U.S. at 1009 (quoting Brief of SEC, filed in *Sanders III*).

98. *Id.* at 1009–10. The ABA Task Force on Sellers' Due Diligence Defenses and Similar Defenses Under the Federal Securities Laws (of which one of the authors was co-chair) agreed with the dissenting Justices that *Sanders* should be confined to its facts and expressed the belief that the current Supreme Court would recognize the significant distinction between "reasonable investigation" and "reasonable care" that the words of the statute imply. 48 Bus. Law. 1185, 1238–39 (1993).

99. 422 F. Supp. 879 (S.D.N.Y. 1976).

mending the notes was correspondingly far greater than that of an ordinary broker-dealer. . . .[100]

Ultimately, Judge Lasker held that there had been sufficient "storm warnings" about Penn Central's financial condition that should have led Goldman Sachs to make further inquiries, to require access to internal records and projections, and to verify them. Its failure to do so, the court concluded, made its ongoing credit investigation unreasonable and its representation to the purchaser untrue within the meaning of Section 12(a)(2).[101]

• • *Rule 10b-5.* Rule 10b-5 applies only to misstatements or omissions made in connection with the purchase or sale of a "security." Unlike the 1933 Act, Section 3(a)(10) of the 1934 Act specifically excludes from the definition of a security "any note which has a maturity at the time of issuance of not exceeding nine months." If the definition were applied literally, there could be no liability under Rule 10b-5 in a commercial paper case. As noted above, however, the Second Circuit has held that a short-term note is not excluded from Rule 10b-5 unless it meets the general notion of commercial paper reflected in SEC Release No. 33-4412, including the prime quality requirement. In view of the U.S. Supreme Court's recent emphasis on the text of federal statutes, the Second Circuit position may be open to question.[102]

---

100. *Id.* at 900–01.

101. *Id.* at 902. Under this analysis, a dealer that has breached its implied representation about the reasonableness of its credit investigation—which creates the false statement that Section 12(a)(2) requires—presumably does not get a second chance to argue the same point as an affirmative defense under Section 12(a)(2).

102. The courts that considered whether Penn Central notes were securities either did not reach the issue by finding no Section 10(b) liability or followed the criteria in SEC Release No. 33-4412 and found the notes lacking in one or more respects and thus subject to the 1934 Act. *See Franklin Savings Bank of New York v. Levy,* 551 F.2d 521, 527-28 (2d Cir. 1977); *University Hill Foundation v. Goldman, Sachs & Co.,* 422 F. Supp. 879, 905 (S.D.N.Y. 1976); *Mallinckrodt Chem. Works v. Goldman, Sachs & Co.,* 420 F. Supp. 231, 239-41 (S.D.N.Y. 1976); *Alton Box Board Co. v. Goldman, Sachs*

From the dealer's point of view, it is not very important whether or not the plaintiff can bring a claim under Rule 10b-5 as well as under Section 12(a)(2). This was not the case, of course, when the statute of limitations for actions brought under Rule 10b-5 was thought to be longer than that allowed for Section 12(a)(2) actions. On the other hand, Rule 10b-5 is likely be the only federal remedy available to a plaintiff for purposes of proceeding against non-"seller" potential defendants such as accountants or rating agencies. (This is not to say that such a plaintiff could not use Rule 10b-5 to reach the issuer of the commercial paper, but an issuer that cannot pay its commercial paper at maturity is likely to be in Bankruptcy Court by the time litigation is commenced.)

& Co., 418 F. Supp. 1149, 1157-58 (E.D. Mo. 1976), rev'd 560 F.2d 916 (8th Cir. 1977); Welch Foods, Inc. v. Goldman, Sachs & Co., 398 F. Supp. 1393, 1397-99 (S.D.N.Y. 1974).

Chapter 11

INNOVATIVE FINANCING
TECHNIQUES

Innovation in the financial markets is spurred in the first instance by competition among investment banking firms. While always fierce, this competition has intensified in recent years as a result of the Rule 415 environment and the breakdown in traditional investment banking relationships. Volatile markets also play an important role in forcing investment bankers to develop innovative debt and equity securities that will better serve the needs of potential issuers, whether or not traditional clients of the firm, as well as the interests of the firm's investor customers.

Even as markets return to relative stability, innovation remains the keynote of investment banking. The major firms have formed product development departments that work with securities lawyers to create new financial instruments. One way of enabling issuers to finance at a lower all-in cost is through the use of tax benefits, and for this reason tax counsel plays a significant role in the process. Good accounting advice is also essential. The process is highly market-oriented with new products being designed not only to serve the needs of issuers but also to meet the demands of portfolio managers and other investors.

Investment bankers like to package new instruments in exotic formats with fancy names that are often formulated to create a catchy acronym. Merrill Lynch's Treasury Investment Growth Receipts were known as "TIGRs" and were followed by "LYONS," "PRIDES" and "STRYPES." Other firms have comparable products and acronyms. The trademark bar has been an unintended beneficiary of Wall Street's creativity.

The financial community's response to the changing needs of issuers and investors has, of course, not been limited to the development of innovative securities products. These products occupy only a portion of the spectrum of derivative products that Wall Street has developed in recent years. For example, swap contracts also play an important role for many issuers and investors, whether the contracts are keyed to interest or currency rates or commodity or equity prices. Caps, floors and collars are also part of the corporate treasurer's and institutional investor's arsenals, along with options on commodities, currencies and equities. Exchange-traded futures and options provide additional alternatives.

The ABA Section on Business Law's Committee on Developments in Business Financing publishes annually a useful review of innovative financial products.

For any innovative product, there are certain key questions that the securities lawyer must address. These may arise from the point of view of the issuer of the product or from that of the broker-dealers who will be selling the product and maintaining a secondary market. To start with, all of the participants in the transaction are obviously interested in whether the product should be treated as a security within the meaning of the 1933 Act. As discussed in Chapter 1, the line between securities and non-securities is not always so clear. If the product is to be treated as a security, however, is it to be registered with the SEC? If not, what exemption is available? Is the product a futures contract or option subject to the Commodities Exchange Act? What disclosure obligations will arise, either regarding the issuer or the product itself?

From the standpoint of the broker-dealer, how will the product be marketed, and what information will be supplied to the sales force? If the product must be carried in inventory for a time, what will be the impact on the broker-dealer's regulatory net capital? Is the product eligible for margin credit? May it be the subject of repurchase agreement financing? How will transactions be cleared and settled?

From the issuer's standpoint, does it have systems in place that are adequate to measure its exposure under the product? Does the issuer plan to engage in any hedging activity as a result of the offering? How will the issuer treat the product and any related hedging activity for financial reporting purposes?

This chapter will examine innovative products that generally fall on the securities side of the line and the regulatory issues that surround them. Securities with voluntary conversion features or issued with warrants attached are discussed in Chapter 12.

Deep Discount and Zero Coupon Obligations

The yield on a debt security is a function of both the stated interest rate and the price at which the security is sold to the investor. Thus, debt securities that are sold at a discount from their face amount may carry an interest rate below that which the market would require if they were sold at par. If a debenture with a specified rating and maturity would require a 10% interest rate to receive market acceptance if offered at par, then an 8% coupon would only be acceptable if the debenture were offered at a price sufficiently below par. The lower the interest rate, the greater must be the discount from the face amount.

The ultimate deep discount instrument is the zero coupon obligation, a debt security that bears no interest at all. Commercial paper is generally a zero coupon obligation, although it is not thought of as such. It generally does not bear interest but is sold to investors at a discount from its principal amount. Because of the short maturities of commercial paper, the discount is relatively small. Where long-term zero coupon obligations are issued, however, the discount from par will be substantial.

• *Tax Considerations*

If a debt security is sold to the public at a substantial discount, the original issue discount ("OID") provisions of Sections 1271–1273 and Section 1275 of the Internal Revenue Code and the regulations thereunder will come into play.

• • *Definition of OID.* Publicly offered debt securities potentially subject to the OID provisions include any obligation with an original term of more than one year from the date of original issue, other than U.S. savings bonds and small personal loans made between individuals.

OID on obligations of these types is equal to the excess of the "stated redemption price at maturity" over the "issue price." The stated redemption price of a debt instrument is equal to the sum of all payments provided by the debt instrument other than "qualified stated interest" payments. The term "qualified stated interest" generally means stated interest that is unconditionally payable in cash or property (other than debt instruments of the issuer) at least annually at a single fixed rate. For example, in the case of a zero coupon obligation, the stated redemption price would be simply the stated face amount. However, varying rates of interest, or multiple payments of principal, bring more complex rules into play. The "issue price" of an obligation sold to the public for cash is the initial offering price to the public (excluding dealers and brokers) at which price a substantial amount of the debt instruments was sold. There is no guidance as to what is a "substantial amount," but most firms look to the price at which the first 10% or 20% of the obligations are sold.

OID may be ignored by holders if it is less than one-quarter of 1% of the stated redemption price at maturity multiplied by the number of complete years to maturity.[1] For example, the holder of a 10-year bond with an issue price of more than $97.50 would not be subject to the OID rules. Note that, if a bond closing is on June 3, 1997, and the bond matures on June 1, 2007, the bond is only a nine-year bond for this purpose and, thus, an issue price of, say, $97.60 would make holders of the bond subject to the OID rules.

• • *Consequences of OID.* If OID exists, the holder must accrue currently, in all periods during which the obligation is held, the OID allocable to such periods. While the allocation of OID to particular periods is complex, it is basically a "constant yield" method from the issue date to the maturity date with the yield being based upon compounding at the close of each "accrual period." An "accrual period" may be of any length and may vary

---

1. Issuers, however, can still take an interest deduction for the *de minimis* OID under Section 163 of the Internal Revenue Code.

over the term of the instrument, provided that each accrual period is no longer than one year and each scheduled payment of principal and interest occurs either on the first or last day of an accrual period. If a holder purchases a debt instrument for an amount that is greater than its adjusted issue price as of the purchase date and less than or equal to the sum of all amounts payable on the debt instrument after the purchase date other than qualified stated interest, it will be able to reduce the amount of OID that it must include in its gross income with respect to such debt instrument for any taxable year (or portion thereof in which it holds the debt instrument) by the portion of the excess properly allocable to the period. If a holder purchases a debt instrument for an amount that is greater than the sum of all amounts payable on the debt instrument after the purchase date other than qualified stated interest, then it will not be required to include any OID in income. If the holder purchases the bond for less than the issue price, plus accrued discount to date, the difference is not subject to the OID rules but instead is subject to the market discount rates, which are similar in some cases. Any OID accrued by the holder increases its tax basis in the obligation.

• • *Reporting of OID.* An issuer is required to report OID accruing to a holder of its debt on Form 1099 in the same manner as interest. Of course, since the issuer has no way of knowing the price paid by a particular holder, the Form 1099 is only accurate as to a holder who has purchased the obligation at a price equal to or below the issue price, plus accrued discount to date. All other holders must make their own adjustments, based on their own purchase date and purchase price.

The issuer is required by regulation, in the case of instruments that are not publicly offered, to legend a debt instrument by stating on the face of the instrument that the instrument has OID and either (i) set forth on the face of the debt instrument the issue price, the amount of OID, the issue date, the yield to maturity and certain other additional information in the case of certain types of instruments or (ii) provide the name or title and either the address or telephone number of a representative of the issuer who will, beginning no later than 10 days after the issue date, promptly make available to holders upon request the information described above.

A penalty of $50 per obligation will be imposed on the issuer for a failure to comply other than for reasonable cause. In the case of instruments which are publicly offered and which have OID, the issuer must file an information return with the Internal Revenue Service in the form prescribed by regulations (Form 8281 as of November 1996). The penalty for failure to comply, absent reasonable cause, is 1% of the aggregate issue price, not to exceed $50,000 per issue.

• Bankruptcy and Events of Default

If a bankruptcy proceeding is commenced in respect of the issuer of a deep discount or zero coupon obligation, the claim of the holder is limited under Section 502(b)(2) of the Bankruptcy Code to the initial public offering price of the obligation plus that portion of the OID that is amortized from the date of issue to the commencement of the bankruptcy proceeding. If there is an event of default under the terms of the obligation or the governing indenture and this is followed by an acceleration of the maturity of the obligation, the indenture will usually provide that the holders will receive an amount of principal equal to the sum of the initial public offering price plus that portion of OID attributable to the period from the date of issue to the date of acceleration.

• Accounting Treatment

Under U.S. gaap, a holder of an obligation purchased with OID normally must report as an item of income for financial accounting purposes the portion of the discount attributable to the applicable reporting period. The calculation of this attributable income is made in accordance with the "interest method," which corresponds generally to the method provided by the 1982 Tax Act. The issuer reports amortization of debt discount as an item of interest expense on the same basis. The debt is carried on the issuer's balance sheet at par, less the unamortized debt discount, with appropriate details in the notes to its financial statements. The normal footnote presentation is to list all issues of long-term debt at their stated principal amounts and subtract the aggregate debt discount from the subtotal of the principal amounts to arrive at the net amount reflected on the balance sheet. An alternative presentation is to state the amount of discount separately for each issue.

• Deep Discount Obligations

There are cost savings to an issuer of deep discount debt securities. Less cash is taken in at the outset than would be the case if the debt were issued at par, but smaller periodic cash interest payments are required. Amortization of OID is a non-cash expense, but it is deductible for tax purposes. The return that the issuer can earn on the tax benefits is taken into account in determining the cost of borrowing.

With deep discount obligations, the holder receives cash based on the stated below-market interest rate but is taxed on the basis of that amount plus the amortized OID computed by the constant interest method. A deep discount obligation can be structured so that the investor receives cash interest payments in an amount at least sufficient to cover the required tax payments.

Debt securities may be sold at a discount from their face amount not because the interest rate is below market but because the initial interest payment is deferred until a specified date in the future. Securities of this type can be used effectively by a company financing a leveraged buyout that needs all the cash that it can conserve in the early years but projects that it will be able to pay interest at a market rate when it begins to realize the cost savings from the operating efficiencies that it plans to institute.

• Zero Coupon Obligations

Zero coupon obligations are debt securities that do not bear any interest but, instead, are sold at a discount from par that is sufficient to provide the investor with a yield to maturity based on market rates at the time of issue. Because the holder must pay taxes even though it receives no cash until maturity, zero coupon obligations are designed primarily for the tax-deferred market, i.e., pension plans, IRAs and Keogh plans.

Notwithstanding the tax disadvantages, many taxpaying institutions and individuals look on zero coupon bonds as convenient vehicles for acting on their views on the direction of interest rates. If such an investor believes that bond prices are about to rise, there is tremendous leverage in buying a 30-year zero at a very low price.

Zero coupon obligations are used by money managers to eliminate reinvestment risk. In the case of conventional interest-bearing investments, the holder bears the risk that future interest payments may be reinvestable only at a lower rate. With zero coupon obligations, this risk is eliminated. The rate at which accrued interest is compounded is determined at the time of issuance and is built into the amount of the discount. Investment managers seeking to "immunize" their portfolios are willing to accept a lower yield in return for this certainty and convenience. Another highly important feature of zero coupon obligations is call protection, which assures the permanence of the investment. These advantages inure to the benefit of the issuer in the form of lower borrowing costs.

Some of the advantages of zero coupon obligations were highlighted in a ditty sung some years ago at the annual dinner meeting of the investment banking division of a major underwriting firm. The words were sung to the melody of "The Battle Hymn of the Republic:"

> Mine eyes have seen the glory of the zero coupon bond;
> It saves the client basis points over current coupon ones;
> It gives the buyer call protection and reinvestment break;
> And the firm goes marching on.

In purchasing a zero coupon obligation with a long maturity, an investor must be satisfied that the issuer will be able to make payment when the obligation becomes due. In the case of an interest bearing obligation, the investor at least is receiving interest on a periodic basis. With a zero, the investor receives no cash until maturity. For this reason, there is virtually no market for non-convertible zeros that are not rated investment grade. (Convertible zero coupon bonds in the form of "LYONs" are discussed in Chapter 12.)

- *Stripped Treasury Obligations*

With the growth of professionally managed pension funds and the demand for quality investments that would eliminate reinvestment risk and provide call protection, what could be more appealing than a zero coupon *U.S. Treasury* obligation? Of course, no responsible government would issue an instrument that would saddle a future generation with a large balloon payment while the current generation received a free ride with respect to interest payments. But the right to receive the interest payment that comes due on a Treasury obligation ten, fifteen or twenty years hence has all of the economic characteristics of a zero coupon obligation.

The Treasury and the Federal Reserve Bank of New York initially opposed the idea of stripping and selling Treasury coupons because of perceived disruptive market effects. The stripping that had taken place had been done on an informal ad hoc basis, and there was no secondary market for the stripped coupons.

In the middle of 1982, after months of study of the economic, tax and regulatory ramifications, Merrill Lynch announced a major new program under which the interest and principal components of U.S. Treasury obligations would be sold separately to the public through the use of deposit receipts. By purchasing from Merrill Lynch an instrument called Treasury Investment Growth Receipts (or "TIGRs"), investors would be purchasing zero coupon Treasury obligations. Tax counsel advised Merrill Lynch that TIGRs would be taxed in the same way as any other zero coupon obligation. Merrill Lynch also received opinions of counsel that TIGRs were not securities separate and apart from the underlying Treasury obligations and, thus, were exempt from registration under Section 3(a)(2) of the 1933 Act, which exempts obligations of the United States, and that the custodial arrangement did not constitute an investment company under the 1940 Act.

Other investment banking firms quickly established deposit receipt programs based on the TIGR format. These included the Certificates of Accrual on Treasury Securities (or "CATS") program of Salomon Brothers and the Treasury Receipt (or "TR") program sponsored by Goldman, Sachs & Co. and others.

These programs were highly successful, not only for the investment banking firms and their clients, but also in terms of assisting the Treasury in marketing long-term obligations at more favorable rates than would otherwise have been available. The programs were so successful, in fact, that the Treasury, which had originally viewed stripping with skepticism, decided to "move in." On January 15, 1985, the Secretary of the Treasury announced a new program, to be known as Separate Trading of Registered Interest and Principal of Securities (or "STRIPS"), pursuant to which the principal and interest payments on certain Treasury securities would be made available for separate trading in the book-entry system. This program enabled investors to purchase Treasury obligation principal and interest payments in the secondary market as zero-coupon securities, without the necessity of a custody arrangement.

The STRIPS program has eclipsed the private sector programs, and new treasury receipts are no longer being created by the investment banks. The concept, however, has been extended to municipal bonds that have been defeased with U.S. government obligations, and bankers continue to explore other potential stripping opportunities.

There were lessons learned in connection with the private sector stripping programs that continue to be useful today. It would, therefore, be useful to review the mechanics of stripping and how these mechanics affected the analysis of securities law issues.

• • *Structure.* The mechanics of stripping are quite simple. Treasury obligations of a single issue were purchased in the secondary market or directly in a Treasury auction by an investment banking firm and placed into a custody account with a bank. Upon deposit of the obligations into the custody account, the custodian bank delivered to the investment banker receipts for the component parts, acknowledging that the obligations would be held by the custodian for the benefit of the beneficial owners. The investment banking firm then sold the receipts to investors. The receipts were freely transferable instruments, and the custodian bank served as the transfer agent and registrar.

The custodian bank would hold the Treasury obligations pursuant to the terms of a custody agreement that provided that the custodian must hold the obligations solely for the benefit of the beneficial owners, i.e., the holders of the receipts, and must apply all moneys received on the Treasury obligations on account of principal and interest to the related receipts. The custody agreement also provided that the holders of the receipts, as the owners of direct interests in the underlying Treasury obligations, had all of the rights and privileges of owners of transferable Treasury securities, except that the custodian had the exclusive right to hold the underlying Treasury obligations on behalf of the owners of the receipts. The custodian held the Treasury obligations in book-entry form with a Federal Reserve Bank.

The custody agreements also typically provided that the obligations and moneys in the custody account could not be subject to any right, charge, security interest, lien or claim of any kind in favor of the custodian and that the custodian had no authority or power to assign, transfer, pledge or otherwise dispose of any of the assets in the custody account to any person other than the holders of the receipts.

• • *Securities Law Considerations.* For purposes of the 1933 Act and state blue sky laws, the receipts were not looked upon as securities separate from the underlying Treasury obligations, which were themselves exempt from registration. The "separate security" concept can, however, be somewhat tricky. If, for example, a diversified portfolio of United States government and agency obligations were placed in a unit investment trust, the trust certificates would have to be registered as securities separate from the exempt underlying obligations. In that case, there would be a pooling arrangement. This would not be so, however, for a mere custodial arrangement involving a single Treasury obligation.

Similarly, under the 1940 Act, no investment company would be created by a custodial arrangement if the custody agreements were structured so that the receipts represent a direct interest in the interest or principal component of the underlying Treasury obligations, and no pooling, participation arrangement or investment discretion were involved that might be deemed to give rise to a separate security and thereby an investment company. The custodial arrangement would be purely administrative and mechanical in nature. It would no more create a separate security than would leaving securities in street name with a broker. The arrangement would be structured so that the holder of the receipt could proceed directly against the Treasury if necessary to enforce the obligation. The custodian would add no value to the transaction, and there would be no "common enterprise" involved in the arrangement.[2]

Although the SEC staff did not take a no-action position with respect to any of the Treasury stripping programs, the principles for determining whether a stripping program results in the creation of a separate security were formulated by the staff in a letter from the Division of Market Regulation to the Municipal Securities Rulemaking Board addressing whether receipts sold pursuant to a stripped coupon municipal bond program were subject to the MSRB's rules.[3] While the letter to the MSRB purported to express no view regarding whether the stripped coupon arrangement created a separate security, the conclusion that they constituted "municipal securities" under the 1934 Act necessarily determined that no separate security was created by virtue of the stripping and custody arrangement. The analysis undertaken in the *MSRB* letter parallels the analysis required to determine whether a particular stripping and custody arrangement involves the creation of a separate security under the 1933 Act or an investment company under the 1940 Act.

The conclusions set forth in the *MSRB* letter were conditioned upon the program sponsor's obtaining an opinion of counsel as to the accuracy of representations in the offering circular that owners of the stripped coupon securities would have all the rights and privileges of owners of the underlying municipal securities; that each receipt holder, as the real party in interest, would have the right, upon default of the underlying municipal securities, to proceed directly and individually against the issuer of the securities; and that the holder of a receipt would not be required to act in concert with other holders

---

2. *See SEC v. W.J. Howey Co.*, 328 U.S. 293 (1946).

3. SEC No-action Letter, *Municipal Securities Rulemaking Board* (available January 19, 1989). *See also* SEC No-action Letter, *Financial Security Assurance Inc.* (available March 30, 1988); SEC No-action Letter, *Financial Guaranty Insurance Company* (available February 15, 1989); SEC No-action Letter, *Merrill Lynch, Pierce, Fenner & Smith Inc.* (available September 26, 1990).

or the custodian. The conclusions also were conditioned upon the following factors: each receipt would represent the entire interest in a discrete, identified interest payment or principal payment on the underlying municipal security; the custodian bank would perform only clerical or ministerial services on behalf of the receipt holders; neither the custodian nor the sponsor would guarantee or otherwise enhance the creditworthiness of the underlying municipal security or the stripped coupon security; the custodian would undertake to notify holders in the event of a default and to forward to them copies of all communications from the issuer of the underlying municipal security to the bondholders; an opinion of counsel would be provided indicating that the underlying municipal securities would not be considered assets of either the sponsoring firm or the custodian bank; and other factors would not be present, such as re-marketing agreements, that would require the investors in the stripped coupon securities to rely upon the sponsor to obtain the benefit of their investment.

Similar conditions have formed the basis for the no-action positions of the Division of Corporation Finance and the Division of Investment Management with respect to whether custodial receipts for bonds insured in the secondary market constitute separate securities.[4] The SEC staff has also issued a number of favorable no-action responses with respect to primary participation programs to which the issuer of the underlying security is a party.[5]

---

4. SEC No-action letter, *Financial Security Assurance Inc.* (available March 30, 1988); SEC No-action letter, *Financial Guaranty Insurance Company* (available February 15, 1989).

5. SEC No-action Letter, *Best Products Co., Inc.* (available February 11, 1980) (master note arrangement); SEC No-action Letter, *Prudential-American Securities Inc.* (available January 26, 1975) (aggregation arrangement involving bankers' acceptances); SEC No-action Letter, *Blyth Eastman Dillon & Company* (available May 21, 1975) (commercial paper safekeeping and hypothecation plan); SEC No-action Letter, *Bankers Trust Company* (available July 4, 1972) (sale of depository receipts for underlying bankers' acceptances); SEC No-action Letter, *Kelling & Co., Inc.* (available October 22, 1984) (certificates of participation in municipal leases); SEC No-action Letter, *Lincoln Federal Savings and Loan Association* (available January 8,

The analysis that the receipts are not securities separate from the underlying obligations is not impacted by the fact that the Treasury is not specifically a party to the custody arrangements and has no knowledge of the identity of the beneficial holders of the receipts. Under the Federal Reserve book-entry system, substantially all Treasury payments are made through layers of nominee and subnominee accounts, and there is no knowledge on the part of the Treasury as to the identity of the beneficial owner, much less any specific acknowledgment of its obligations to a specific beneficial owner. The book-entry system necessarily contemplates the existence of non-registered owners of Treasury securities. Customers holding book-entry Treasury securities in their securities accounts with brokers have no alternative but to hold the securities in street name form. In the case of book-entry securities, there is no registered certificate for the broker to deliver to the customer. The custodial arrangements pursuant to which TIGRs, CATS and TRs were issued can be viewed as nothing more than a formal street name arrangement.

If the Treasury should default on its obligation with respect to a receipt, only the beneficial owner, as the real party in interest, would be entitled to proceed directly against the United States. In such proceedings, the holder of the receipt obviously would have to establish that it is the beneficial owner of the principal or interest payment evidenced by the receipt on the basis of traditional principles of principal and agency law. The Treasury regulations with respect to the book-entry system do not deal explicitly with the rights of beneficial owners upon default. While the regulations are not explicit, they certainly contemplate that the beneficial holder, as the real party in interest, has the right to proceed directly against the government upon default. On the other hand, if the Treasury makes full payment on an obligation into the book-entry system, it has satis-

---

1985) (pooling of customers' funds in money market deposit accounts); SEC No-action Letter, *E.F. Hutton & Company Inc.* (available March 28, 1985) (units of participation in FSLIC-insured certificates of deposit); SEC No-action Letter, *United Financial Banking Companies, Inc.* (available May 11, 1988) (master note commercial paper program).

fied its obligation, and if the payment does not reach the beneficial owner, the owner has a cause of action against someone for wrongful conversion of its funds. The custodial or agency risk of wrongful conversion does not create a separate security or interpose another obligor (or a joint obligor) with respect to the securities. If this were the case, all government obligations held in street name accounts would be subject to losing their exempt status under the Federal securities laws.

• • *Certain Bankruptcy Considerations.* Neither creditors of the investment banking firm sponsoring the receipt program nor creditors of the custodian could attach receipts held by investors in the event of bankruptcy or receivership of the sponsor or the custodian. The receipts evidence ownership by the holder of a direct interest in a specified component part of the underlying Treasury obligations with no separate security being created. Assuming that the receipt was held by someone other than the sponsoring investment banker or the custodian, the receipts would not constitute "property of the estate" of either the sponsoring investment banker or the custodian and, therefore, would not be subject to the claims of their creditors. The transfer of the receipt by the sponsoring investment banker, as a dealer, to the investor would not be voidable by the trustee as a preferential transfer unless such transfer were made to satisfy an antecedent debt, which is not the case in the ordinary and customary sale of the receipts to investors by the sponsoring investment banker or other dealers.

• • *Sales Abroad.* In at least two cases, receipts representing the interest and principal components of bonds issued by entities other than the Treasury have been sold in the Euromarket. These were receipts relating to debt obligations issued by the International Bank for Reconstruction and Development and debt obligations issued by the Inter-American Development Bank. In both cases, it was provided in the governing instruments that, in the event that the debt were accelerated, payments to the holders of the receipts would be made in proportion to the respective amortized face amounts of the receipts outstanding at the time of acceleration. Thus, in the event of acceleration, the custodian would be required to restructure the rights of the holders of the receipts and allow them to participate on a proportionate basis in the pool of funds available for payment.

This degree of potential participation by the custodian raises a question as to the status of the receipts as separate securities for purposes of the 1933 Act and the 1940 Act. In both of these cases, however, the receipts were sold exclusively outside of the United States. The custodian in one case was the Cayman Islands branch of a U.S. bank, and in the other case it was the branch of a U.S. bank located in Jersey in the Channel Islands.

• • *Corporate and Municipal Obligations.* Questions have been raised as to the possibility of stripping corporate obligations. This would not be feasible unless the custodial arrangements provided for a restructuring of the rights of the holders of the certificates in the event of bankruptcy, as in the case of the certificates sold abroad. In the absence of a provision of this type, the sale of a future interest payment makes sense only where the credit is as ironclad as the U.S. Treasury. If, for example, a corporation were to file for bankruptcy or if its debt were accelerated as a result of a covenant violation, the future interest payment could simply disappear. Under the Bankruptcy Code, a claim for unmatured interest is not "allowable." There is always a risk in buying corporate obligations, but there is no way that an investor should accept the risk that its right to receive payment, in the event of the issuer's bankruptcy, may not even be allowable.

The programs involving custodial receipts for components of stripped municipal bonds have been limited to those where the bonds had been defeased with U.S. Treasury obligations (thus making them virtually risk free) or where high-grade bonds are not redeemable prior to maturity and there is no provision for acceleration of maturity in the event of default. These limitations reduce the risk of total loss that otherwise would be faced by the owner of a coupon component in the event of redemption or acceleration of maturity prior to the due date of the interest payment.

When TIGRs were first developed, the separate security analysis was viewed as precluding an arrangement whereby the custodian would be required to allocate proceeds in the event of bankruptcy, at least if the receipts were to be sold in the United States. But there have been a number of recent developments that would indicate otherwise. The SEC has issued exemptive orders with respect to stripped bond custody receipt programs in which the custodian was provided with the power to allocate proceeds upon acceleration in proportion to the relative present values of each outstanding receipt at the time of payment. The orders were conditioned upon the receipts being offered only to institutional investors in minimum amounts of $150,000.[6]

In certain transactions, the custodian has been given authority to allocate proceeds upon default. The question of default was addressed in the following fashion in a Fannie Mae offering circular:

> If Fannie Mae defaults on any of the Principal Obligations or Interest Obligations underlying the Fannie Mae STRIPS, the custodian will notify the owners of the Fannie Mae STRIPS of (a) the Bonds affected thereby, (b) the date and nature of the default, (c) the face amount and number of Fannie Mae STRIPS to which such default relates, and (d) any other information the custodian deems appropriate. If the funds received by the custodian in respect of any Principal Obligation or Interest Obligation are insufficient to pay in full the Fannie Mae STRIPS evidencing ownership thereof, the custodian shall apply such funds to make payment pro rata among all the owners of such Fannie Mae STRIPS.

In the stripped coupon municipal security area, there has been even greater evolution in this regard, and the *MSRB* letter indicates an acceptance of certain of these provisions. Stripped municipal custody arrangements typically contain provisions such as the following taken from an offering circular dated December 23, 1988 relating to PRAMS, i.e., Prudential-Bache Securities Inc.'s Receipts of Accrual on Municipal Securities, Series 14, relating to The City of New York General Obligation Bonds, Fiscal 1989 Series A due August 15, 2005:

---

6. *See The First Boston Corp.*, SEC Release No. IC-15741 (May 15, 1987).

In the event of receipt of moneys or other property after (i) the acceleration of the maturity of a Municipal Security, or (ii) any bankruptcy, insolvency or reorganization proceedings or arrangement with creditors which results in the cancellation of, or a change in the payments to be received by a holder of a Municipal Security, the custodian shall promptly give notice to the holders of the PRAMS then outstanding and unpaid. Such notice shall state that, not later than ninety (90) days after the receipt of such moneys or other property, the custodian shall distribute such moneys or other property in accordance with the characterization given such payment by the issuer of, or trustee for, the Municipal Securities. Amounts so characterized as principal shall be distributed, pro rata, to holders of Corpus PRAMS or Converting PRAMS; amounts so characterized as interest shall be distributed to holders of Strip PRAMS and, in some cases, Converting PRAMS in order of maturity in chronological order from the first to mature to the last. In the event that no characterization is made or the characterization is not clear, the custodian shall bring an action in a court of competent jurisdiction within the State of New York seeking to have such court determine the relative rights of the holders of PRAMS to any such payments. The expenses of such action incurred by the custodian shall be paid by the holders of the PRAMS to the extent of the payments received by the custodian.

Extendible and Adjustable Rate Securities

Investment bankers have devised a variety of securities for the purpose of reducing the risk in issuing fixed-rate, long-term debt in an uncertain interest rate environment. These securities—notes with extendible terms, obligations with adjustable interest rates, preferred stock with dividends reset through auction procedures—have been customized to satisfy the needs of the issuer and the appetite of investors.

• *Extendible Notes*

Extendible notes are those that have a fixed interest rate (or a specified spread over an index) for an initial period, say one or three years, at the end of which the issuer may reset the rate or spread for a specified period based on current market conditions. At this point, the issuer may have the option to redeem the notes at par, although redemption provisions will vary from instrument to instrument. After receiving notice of the new interest rate or spread and the new interest period, holders may elect to have the notes repurchased by the issuer at par.

Extendible notes were first conceived in the early part of 1982, a time when many issuers were trying to bridge a period of anticipated high interest rates. They provided issuers with the opportunity to finance at short-term rates while retaining the flexibility to extend the financing if market conditions were favorable at the end of each reset period. It is true that the same objectives could be accomplished by simply issuing one- or three-year notes from time to time, but extendible notes are more economical in that there is only a one-time underwriting cost.

Xerox Credit Corporation was the first issuer to have its extendible notes reach the first extension date. Prior to the mailing of the rate differential notice to the holders of the notes, the corporation's general counsel wrote to the SEC seeking concurrence in his opinion that the annual rate-fixing would not require a new registration under the 1933 Act. He contended that the interest rate adjustment was a change in one term of the security accomplished in the manner expressly provided for at the time the security was issued and that accordingly the resetting of the interest rate should not be viewed as the issuance of a new security. Even if it were so viewed, he argued, the transaction should be considered an exchange of securities with existing securityholders and thus exempt under Section 3(a)(9). The staff of the SEC agreed and issued the requested no-action letter.[7]

As these instruments evolved, remarketing agreements became the norm. The securities and the indentures under which they are issued permit the issuer to elect to designate a purchaser (an investment banking firm) to purchase and remarket the securities on its behalf. Although the securities are pur-

---

7. SEC No-action Letter, *Xerox Credit Corporation* (available June 16, 1983).

chased by the investment banker, the staff of the SEC views the issuer's relationship to the transaction to be such as to require reregistration, just as would be the case if the issuer purchased the securities itself and reissued them. For an issuer that has in place a shelf registration covering a sufficient amount of debt securities, this should create no mechanical or timing problems, although the principal amount of securities being remarketed will be applied against the total amount registered and remaining available under the shelf. A post-effective amendment to the shelf would not be required if the method of distribution is set forth in sufficiently broad terms. No further action would be required under the 1939 Act in connection with the remarketing. If the issuer does not have a shelf in place, a new registration statement will be required and care should be taken to allow sufficient time for possible full review by the staff of the SEC. The remarketing agent must deliver a current prospectus when it resells the securities.

Some instruments have been designed to avoid the necessity of registration by structuring the remarketing as a secondary offering on behalf of the holders of the securities who no longer desire to hold them at the new interest rate. Under this approach, the holders bear the risk that it will not be possible to remarket the securities at the new interest rate. On the other hand, the investment banking firm that sets the rate has every incentive to set it at a level that will ensure a successful remarketing.

• *Investor Puts*

A security related to the extendible note is the debt security sold with an investor put, i.e., an option on the part of the investor to elect to have the debt security paid prior to its stated maturity. The reason for the put feature is usually to reduce the investor's interest rate risk, but in the case of weaker credits it may also serve to reduce the investor's credit risk.

• *Adjustable Rate Debt Securities*

Floating rate notes have become commonplace, although there are still securities professionals who can recall when they were a novelty. The base rate for these instruments can be any verifiable rate. In November 1994, for example, Dean Witter, Discover & Co. sold $500,000,000 of three-year floating rate notes in an underwritten public offering; a portion of the notes paid interest at a spread over the federal funds rate, and the remainder of the notes paid interest at a spread over LIBOR. The applicable rate from time to time was to be determined by a calculation agent, who happened to be the trustee under the indenture under which the notes were issued. As is common in the case of floating rate notes, little was left to the calculation agent's discretion: the LIBOR rate was to be ascertained from a designated Telerate screen, and the federal funds rate was to be ascertained from a daily publication of the Board of Governors of the Federal Reserve System.

Money market funds are among the principal purchasers of floating rate notes and their close relatives, variable rate notes. (Variable rate notes adjust their interest rate at set dates, such as the last day of a month or calendar quarter.) In either case, a fund that holds itself out as a "money market" fund must meet the requirements of the SEC's Rule 2a-7 under the Investment Company Act of 1940. The rule requires a money market fund to conform to limitations on the maturity of each individual investment as well as on the average maturity of its entire portfolio of investments. For the purposes of the rule, however, the maturity of a floating rate or variable rate note can be "shortened" if the fund has a unconditional right to "put" the security or otherwise to obtain principal and interest within stated periods.

Prior to the adoption of the current version of Rule 2a-7, funds and dealers tried to make do with "conditional dealer undertakings." In a letter to the SEC[8] requesting a no-action position on these undertakings, counsel for Goldman, Sachs & Co. stated that its client had become "increasingly aware of the expectation of many market participants, including pension funds, mutual funds, corporate treasurers departments and other institutional investors in fixed income securities, for a degree of liquidity in their investments which may not necessarily result from ordinary dealer and market-making activities," particularly in view of the pricing anomalies to which adjustable rate securities were often subject.

---

8. SEC No-Action Letter *Goldman, Sachs & Co.* (available October 19, 1989).

Counsel sought approval of a proposal whereby Goldman Sachs would undertake to certain institutional customers, on an ad hoc basis and at their request, to repurchase their adjustable rate securities at par, subject to certain conditions. These undertakings would be in writing and would be subject to the conditions that, on the date of purchase, in the sole judgment of the dealer, no adverse change, or potentially adverse change, existed in the financial condition or business of the issuer; no downgrading in the ratings of any debt securities of the issuer by any nationally recognized statistical rating agency would have occurred and no such agency would have under review a possible downgrading of such securities; normal market conditions existed; and the dealer would have available appropriate maturity limits and credit facilities to make the purchase.

The issue, of course, was whether a conditional undertaking of this type made by Goldman Sachs or any other dealer would be viewed as a security issued by the dealer that would have to be registered under the 1933 Act. Counsel argued that these undertakings were not securities and that, even if they were, the dealer could rely on the Section 4(2) private offering exemption. Significantly, counsel did not express a flat opinion on the matter. The Division of Corporation Finance responded that it was unable to advise that it would not recommend enforcement action if Goldman Sachs made conditional undertakings to repurchase securities, as described, without registering them under the 1933 Act, absent an exemption. It also noted that it would generally not express a view on the availability of the Section 4(2) exemption to particular transactions.

These conditional repurchase undertakings had been "floating" around the financial community for many years. The securities bar had viewed them with discomfort. However conditional, a repurchase obligation of this type looks, smells and tastes like a security. The client response has been that "everyone else is doing it." The fact that the undertakings were provided on a selective basis was a further source of concern. If they were available to those purchasers who asked for them, shouldn't all purchasers be told that they were available? In one instance where they were put to the test, counsel for the issuer and the selling agent agreed that the following form of notice could be mailed to all purchasers of adjustable rate notes along with the prospectus and the confirmation:

> In connection with our sale to you of the principal amount set forth in the enclosed confirmation of Adjustable Rate Notes (the "Notes") of XYZ Corporation ("XYZ"), we wish to advise you as follows. Although not obligated to do so, we intend to make a trading market in the Notes and believe that we have sufficient capital so that there will be liquidity in that market. The terms of the Notes have been designed with the intention that they will trade at par on the first date of each interest period. Although we can give no assurances to this effect, we would anticipate that given the continuing creditworthiness of XYZ and the existence of reasonably orderly markets, we would be willing to give you a par bid for your Notes on the first day of any interest period should you wish to sell them at that time, subject, of course, to internal credit approvals and our then applicable position limitations. In accommodating your desire to sell your Notes, we would need at least four business days' notice prior to such date of your intention to sell.

Why did Goldman Sachs approach the SEC anticipating, as it must have, the response that it received? One can only speculate, but it may be that it decided that since "everyone else is doing it" it was time to bring the practice out in the open and provide a level playing field for all underwriters of adjustable rate notes.

• *Variable Coupon Renewable Notes*

Variable coupon renewable notes (or "VCRs") are a variation on the standard extendible notes. They generally have a one-year maturity but provide for an automatic 91-day extension on the maturity date and at the end of each succeeding quarter, unless the holder elects to have the notes mature. The interest rate is reset weekly based on a spread over the 91-day Treasury bill rate. If the holder chooses to terminate the automatic extension, it will receive a new note with a fixed maturity date 273 days after the end of the current dividend period. The new note will provide for a spread over the Treasury bill rate that is significantly less (perhaps 50 basis points) than that provided for in the original note. This provides a disincentive to elect to have the notes mature. The underwriter is paid an annual fee based on the principal amount of notes that remain outstanding, thus providing it with an incentive to maintain an active secondary market into which a holder can sell if it wishes to terminate its investment rather than elect to have the notes mature.

• *Increasing Rate Notes*

Increasing rate notes have been used in connection with acquisition financing. The interest rate does not change in relation to an index but rather according to a pre-determined timetable. These notes are usually intended to provide interim financing. The threat of a periodic increase in the interest rate on the notes is intended to encourage the borrower to pay off the notes at the earliest possible date (either by obtaining permanent financing or by selling off assets). The increased interest rate is also intended to compensate the lenders for the increased risk of their investment in the event that the issuer is unable to pay off the notes as contemplated. As a reverse twist, there are also debt securities that are privately sold with a commitment to register the securities under the 1933 Act or to exchange the securities for securities registered under the 1933 Act; the securities provide for an increase in their interest rate if the registration statement is not filed or does not become effective by a specified date (see Chapter 7).

• *Adjustable Rate Preferred Stock*

Interest received by an investor from a corporate borrower is subject to Federal income tax to the full extent of the interest payment, but a corporation that receives dividends from another U.S. corporation is entitled to the dividends-received deduction (currently 70% of the amount of the dividend). Preferred stock can thus be an attractive investment for a corporation. While theoretically junior in rank to a note or a debenture, the preferred stock of a high-grade issuer frequently can be issued with a dividend rate lower than the interest rate that the market would demand for that issuer's debt securities. As dividends paid are not deductible by the issuer, this type of financing is particularly attractive to issuers that have a low marginal tax rate.

In the early 1980s, a number of major issuers sold floating rate preferred stock with the dividend rate reset for each quarterly dividend period to the highest of the Treasury bill rate, the 10-year constant maturity rate for Treasury obligations and the 20-year constant maturity rate, plus or minus a specified number of basis points. These rates were defined as the arithmetic average of the two most recent weekly per annum discount rates for three-month Treasury bills, 10-year average yields and 20-year average yields, all as published by the Federal Reserve Board during the calendar period immediately prior to the last 10 calendar days in the month preceding the new quarterly dividend period. Unlike the holders of extendible notes, the holders of these issues of preferred stock were not afforded the right to have their stock repurchased. The stock was not redeemable for five years, after which it was redeemable at a premium for the next five years and at par thereafter.

• *Dutch Auction Preferred Stock*

As the investment bankers exercised their creativity, the accepted instrument became a preferred stock where the dividend rate was reset every 49 days or, in some cases, for a dividend period elected by the holder or specified by the issuer. These securities came to be known generically as "Dutch auction" preferred stock.[9]

Usually, each share has a liquidation preference of $100,000 per share, and the shares are offered at that price. If the charter specifies the par value and liquidation preference at, say, $100 per share, the shares may be offered in units, each consisting of 1,000 shares, resulting in the desired $100,000 offering price. Thus, for example, a $75 million offering would involve only

---

9. In the flower markets of Holland, batches of flowers are auctioned in a fashion that is unique. There is no opening bid that is raised by others until no one is willing to bid any higher. Rather, a large dial visible to all is set at an unrealistically high price and slowly winds down until a buyer shouts out his acceptance. Thus, there is only one bid, the winning bid.

750 shares. The intended market is large corporate buyers, those that can react intelligently to the auction process.

Dividends on the shares are cumulative from the date of original issue and are payable commencing on a specified date and on each specified day of the week that is the last day of successive periods thereafter (usually 49-day periods), subject to certain exceptions. The dividend rate for the initial dividend period is fixed, and the applicable rate for each succeeding dividend period is determined on the basis of orders placed in an auction conducted on the business day preceding the commencement of the applicable 49-day dividend period. The auction will be conducted by the bank serving as transfer and paying agent, in its capacity as auction agent. In each auction, each existing holder will indicate its desire to either continue to hold shares without regard to the rate that results from the auction, continue to hold shares if the rate that results from the auction is equal to or greater than the rate bid by that holder, or sell shares without regard to the rate that results from the auction. Potential holders may participate in the auction by offering to purchase shares if the rate that results from the auction is equal to or greater than the rate that it has bid. Hold orders, bids and sell orders may be submitted for different numbers of shares held by an existing holder, and existing holders may participate as potential holders by bidding for additional shares.

The rate determined by an auction may not be higher than the maximum rate, which is a rate, determined by reference to the credit rating of the shares, that is a percentage of the 60-day "AA" composite commercial paper rate. The range of percentages will vary with the issuer. If the issuer fails to make timely payment of the full amount of a dividend, the rate will not be based on an auction but instead will be the maximum percentage of the commercial paper rate or some other index such as LIBOR.

If sufficient "clearing bids" exist (i.e., the number of shares subject to bids by potential holders is at least equal to the number of shares subject to sell orders by existing holders), the applicable rate for the dividend period will be the lowest rate specified in the submitted bids which, taking into account such rate and all lower rates bid by existing holders and potential holders, would result in existing holders and potential holders owning all of the shares available for purchase in the auction. If sufficient clearing bids do not exist, the applicable rate will be the maximum rate on the auction date, and in that event, existing holders who have submitted sell orders will not be able to sell in the auction all shares subject to their sell orders. If all existing holders submit (or are deemed to have submitted by virtue of their failure to act) hold orders, the applicable rate will be a low percentage (e.g. 59%) of the "AA" composite commercial paper rate.

Each prospective purchaser of securities of this type, including purchasers in the original offering and participants in any auction, is required to sign and deliver to a broker-dealer (who will deliver copies to the auction agent) a "master purchaser's letter" in which the prospective purchaser agrees, among other things, to abide by the results of the auctions, that the shares may be transferred only pursuant to a bid or a sell order placed in an auction, or to or through a broker-dealer, or to a person that had delivered, or caused to be delivered on its behalf, a signed copy of a master purchaser's letter to the auction agent. In the case of all transfers other than those pursuant to auctions, the auction agent must be advised of the transfer. The master purchaser's letter also contains an agreement that the shares shall be represented by a global certificate registered in the name of DTC's nominee and that the purchaser's ownership of the shares will be maintained in book-entry form for the account of the DTC participant named as the purchaser's agent in the master purchaser's letter.

As noted above, auction rate preferred stock is particularly attractive to issuers in a tax position in which they do not need the deduction available to interest payments. An issuer that anticipates a change in its tax status may decide to issue auction rate preferred stock exchangeable at its option after a specified date for debt securities with an interest rate fixed pursuant to auction procedures. The exchange would be covered by the Section 3(a)(9) exemption.

In connection with a 1984 offering of Money Market Cumulative Preferred Stock, or MMP (Shearson Lehman's trademarked designation of preferred stock with dividend resettings through the auction process) by American Express Company, counsel sought assurance from the SEC that a new registration statement or a post-effective amendment to the original registration statement would not be required each time that the dividend rate was changed through the auction process. The concern was that, because of the periodic auction, the issuer might be deemed to be engaged in a continuous distribution of its securities that required continuous registration. Counsel stated that the auction is essentially a mechanism to reset dividend rates and to allow the shares to trade at par in the auction. In addition, counsel argued that the transactions involved in the auction should best be viewed as secondary market transactions in securities the distribution of which has been completed. The staff of the SEC agreed.[10]

The auction process does not always work as planned. For example, an article in the October 2, 1989 issue of *The Wall Street Journal* reported that an auction relating to the preferred stock of Tucson Electric Power Company short-circuited when too few bids were entered for the securities. The cap on the interest rate and a drop in the company's credit rating kept the buyers away. It was reported that the provision limiting the dividend rate to 130% of the "AA" composite commercial paper rate made the yield on the securities noncompetitive. As a result, existing holders entering sell orders in the auction were stuck with the securities until the next successful auction, unless they decided to dump them in the market at a loss.

• *Remarketed Preferred Stock*

In the case of remarketed preferred stock, the dividend is not reset by an auction process but by the investment banking

---

10. SEC No-action Letter, *Simpson Thacher & Bartlett (Lehman Brothers Kuhn Loeb Incorporated)* (available May 20, 1984). The staff took the same position in SEC No-action Letter, *City Capital Funding, Inc.* (available November 12, 1984) where identical securities were involved and the only difference was that the issuer was not an established company but rather a newly formed finance subsidiary of a savings and loan association. This position was expressly conditioned upon counsel's representation that the issuer would continue to file, pursuant to Section 15(d) of the 1934 Act, all applicable reports required under Section 13(a).

firm acting as remarketing agent. The dividend rate for the initial dividend period will be fixed at the time of sale. In some cases, the investor will be entitled to choose the initial dividend period from two or more periods specified in the prospectus. At the end of the initial dividend period and each successive dividend period, a holder may elect either to tender its shares at the $100,000 initial sale price or to hold them at the new applicable dividend rate and elect either a 7-day or a 49-day dividend period or one of such optional dividend periods as may have been specified by the issuer. The applicable dividend rates for the subsequent dividend periods will be those rates determined by the remarketing agent in advance of each dividend period to be the lowest rates that will enable it to remarket tendered shares at a price of $100,000 per share. As in the case of auction rate preferred stock, there is a cap on the dividend rate, which will float with the "AA" composite commercial paper rates and may vary depending on the rating assigned to the shares.

Indexed Debt Instruments

Beginning principally in June 1986 with an issue of oil indexed notes by The Standard Oil Company of Ohio (prospectus supplement dated June 19, 1986), many issuers have sold debt instruments, including certificates of deposit, where the amount of principal payable at maturity and/or the interest rate is tied to the performance of a commodity, a stock or bond index, a foreign currency or the rate of inflation. By providing the investor with a play on the price movement of the underlying commodity or index, the issuer could attach a lower fixed interest rate to the obligation. At the same time, it would ordinarily hedge its risk with respect to the commodity or index to which the obligation was tied.

Some of these so-called "hybrid" instruments raised a regulatory issue, i.e., whether they were the economic equivalent of commodity option contracts or futures contracts subject to the jurisdiction of the Commodity Futures Trading Commission (the "CFTC") and thus prohibited as off-board transactions under the Commodity Exchange Act (the "CEA") and the regulations thereunder.[11]

• *The Regulatory Structure*

Section 4(a) of the CEA provides that it is unlawful to enter into a commodity futures contract that is not made "on or subject to the rules of a board of trade which has been designated by the Commission as a 'contract market' for such commodity." Prior to the amendments to the CEA effected by the Futures Trading Practices Act of 1992,[12] the CFTC had no power to grant exemptions from this "exchange-trading" requirement. The 1992 legislation authorized the CFTC to exempt any agreement, contract or transaction (or any class thereof) from any of the requirements of the CEA.

Futures contracts are contracts for the purchase or sale of a commodity for delivery at a specified time in the future at a price that is established when the contract is made. Both parties to the contract are obligated to fulfill the contract at the agreed price, but contracts providing for delivery may usually be closed out by paying the price differential. Thus, a speculator in commodity futures need not wind up with a pile of soybeans on his front lawn.

Futures contracts are undertaken principally to assume or shift price risk without transferring title to the underlying commodity. The contracts have standard terms. There are margin requirements, and clearing organizations match trades and guarantee counterparty performance.

Prior to the early 1970s, trading in the pits of the commodity exchanges was limited to trading in contracts for physical commodities—wheat, cotton, pork bellies, frozen concentrated orange juice, and the like. In 1974, the CEA was amended to broaden the definition of "commodity" to include not only physical commodities but also all "services, rights, and inter-

---

11. For comprehensive outlines on this subject, see A.R. Pietrzak & M.S. Sackheim, *CFTC Exemption Procedures for Novel Derivative Transactions*, 26 Rev. Sec. & Com. Reg. 121 (July 1993), and G.K. Palm & D.R. Crawshaw, *Recent Developments In Hybrid Instruments and Privately Issued Warrants* (Practising Law Institute Course Handbook for New Financial Instruments and Techniques 1989).

12. Pub. L. 102–546, 106 Stat. 3590 (1992).

ests in which contracts for future delivery are presently or in the future dealt in." At the same time, Congress created the CFTC to assume the functions previously performed by the Department of Agriculture, functions that were no longer thought appropriate for the department as futures markets expanded beyond physical commodities into financial instruments.

During the 1970s, the Chicago Mercantile Exchange developed under the leadership of Leo Malamed a market for futures contracts on foreign currencies, Eurobonds, U.S. Treasury obligations and broad-based stock indices. A major event was the introduction in April 1982 of the S&P 500 futures contract, an instrument that played a major role in the events of October 1987.[13] It was not long before other index futures contracts and stock index options came to be traded under the jurisdiction of the CFTC.

Although futures contracts on physical commodities may be performed by delivery of the commodity, this is not the case with cash-settled contracts based on indexes or other financial instruments. Most trading on United States commodities exchanges is now in contracts of this type.[14]

In 1980, the SEC and the CFTC became embroiled in a dispute over which agency had jurisdiction over options on GNMA pass-through certificates. While litigation was pending, the chairmen of the two agencies (John R. Shad of the SEC and Phillip Johnson of the CFTC) reached an accord to the effect that jurisdiction over options follows jurisdiction over the instruments on which the options are written. The SEC took jurisdiction over options on securities, and the CFTC took jurisdiction over options on futures contracts (including futures contracts based on securities indices). The courts, however, held that the agencies could not alter their jurisdiction by mutual agreement and that options on GNMA pass-throughs came within the jurisdiction of the CFTC.[15] Congress then passed legislation that codified the Shad-Johnson accord.

---

13. *See* T. Metz, *Black Monday* (Wm. Morrow & Co. 1988).

14. 1995 CFTC Ann. Rep. at 95-96.

15. *Chicago Board of Trade v. SEC*, 677 F.2d 1137 (7th Cir.), *vacated as moot*, 459 U.S. 1026 (1982).

The CEA now provides in Section 2(a)(1)(B) that the CFTC has no jurisdiction over any option on one or more securities (as defined in the 1934 Act), including any group or index of such securities, or any interest therein or based on the value thereof. It further provides that the CFTC has exclusive jurisdiction over contracts for future delivery based on a group or index of securities as well as options on such contracts.[16] Thus, the CFTC has the authority to regulate the trading of futures contracts (including futures on securities) and options on futures contracts. The SEC has authority to regulate the trading of securities and options on securities.[17]

• *CFTC Reaction to Hybrids*

When the CFTC became aware of Sohio's 1986 offering of oil indexed notes, it reportedly began an investigation but decided that it would not take any action. It did not, however, publish an opinion setting forth its reasoning. The Sohio notes did not bear interest. One series matured in 1990 and the other in 1992. They were issued in units with 15-year debentures carrying a 6.30% coupon. Beginning on January 1, 1990, in the case of the 1990 notes, and on April 1, 1991, in the case of the 1992 notes, they were redeemable at the option of the holder twice a month at their principal amount plus a premium calculated under a formula based on the amount by which crude oil futures prices on the New York Mercantile Exchange exceeded $25 per barrel, up to a maximum of $40 per barrel.

One basis for concluding that the CFTC did not have jurisdiction over the Sohio notes was that, even if they had features

---

16. The 1982 legislation also added to the definition of "security" in Section 3(a)(10) of the 1934 Act the words: "any put, call, straddle, option, or privilege on any security, certificate of deposit, or group or index of securities (including any interest therein or based on the value thereof), or any put, call, straddle, option, or privilege entered into on a national securities exchange relating to foreign currency."

17. *Chicago Mercantile Exchange v. SEC*, 883 F.2d 537 (7th Cir. 1989). In this case, Judge Easterbrook held that "index-participations"—contracts of indefinite duration based on the value of a basket of securities which the SEC had permitted to be traded on securities exchanges—were futures contracts subject to the jurisdiction of the CFTC.

similar to commodity options or futures, the determination should be made on the basis of whether the units were predominantly debt or predominantly options or futures. One way to determine this was to calculate what each unit would sell for in the market if it did not have the index feature. On this basis, the index feature was worth about 27% of the unit, thus making the instrument predominately debt.[18]

In the fall of 1986, the CFTC appointed an "off-exchange task force" to consider the issue of hybrids. Over the next year, a number of indexed deals were done, some in reliance on oral no-action advice from members of the staff of the CFTC serving on the off-exchange task force. Salomon Inc issued $100 million of Standard & Poor's 500 Index Subordinated Notes due 1990 under a prospectus dated August 21, 1986. These bore the acronym SPINS. In March 1987, The Chase Manhattan Bank, N.A. began to offer certificates of deposit that were also linked to the Standard & Poor's 500 Index.

Under an offering circular dated March 12, 1987, Student Loan Marketing Association sold three-year obligations linked to the Australian dollar, which provided for the payment at maturity of the United States dollar equivalent of A$1,452 for each $1,000 principal amount of notes. The obligations, which were known as Principal Exchange Rate Linked Securities, or PERLS, bore an above-market interest rate because of the expectation that the Australian dollar would decline as against the United States dollar over the life of the notes.

Several months later, Sallie Mae sold "Reverse PERLS," linked to the yen under an offering circular dated May 6, 1987. This issue was structured so that, for each $1,000 of face value, the amount paid at maturity five years hence would be $2,000 minus the United States dollar equivalent of ¥138,950. Thus, holders of the notes would receive an amount of principal greater than the face amount if, at maturity, the United States dollar had appreciated against the Japanese yen and a lesser amount (to a minimum of zero) if it had depreciated.

---

18. E.R. Schroeder, *Commodity Indexed Debt Securities*, 19 Rev. Sec. & Com. Reg. 204, 205 (1986).

In September 1987, The Chase Manhattan Corporation issued "Reverse SPINS,"[19] under which the additional amount payable at maturity increases as the Standard & Poor's 500 Index decreases. Merrill Lynch & Co., Inc. then came out with an issue of zero coupon obligations called LYONs that were tied to the NYSE Index.[20]

In August 1987, hybrids received a jolt when the CFTC served subpoenas on Wells Fargo Bank, N.A. with respect to its gold indexed certificates of deposit and on The Chase Manhattan Bank with respect to oil indexed swaps. Wells Fargo subsequently consented to an injunction. The CFTC ceased providing informal advice, and during this period the only hybrids that were issued were those tied to stock indexes. Issuers felt comfortable that options on a basket of securities or a stock index were securities and, thus, not subject to the jurisdiction of the CFTC.

In December 1987, the CFTC issued a so-called "advance notice of proposed rulemaking," which discussed the treatment of hybrids.[21] The proposals were viewed by the securities industry as establishing inappropriately difficult requirements for exclusion from CFTC regulation. Moreover, the language of the notice explaining the proposals raised questions as to whether or not certain transactions widely viewed as outside of the CFTC's jurisdiction, such as interest rate swaps, might be viewed as commodity instruments by the CFTC. This led to an avalanche of negative comments from the financial community and from other government agencies, including the SEC, the Treasury and the Comptroller of the Currency.

From the publication of the advance notice until the summer of 1988, the staff of the CFTC declined to take no-action positions with respect to hybrids, thus chilling the development of creative indexed instruments.

At a meeting with representatives of the Corporate Finance Committee of the Securities Industry Association on June 2,

---

19. Prospectus supplement dated September 14, 1987.

20. Prospectus dated October 2, 1987. See Chapter 12 for a description of LYONs.

21. 52 Fed. Reg. 47022 (December 11, 1987).

1988, CFTC Chairman Wendy L. Gramm expressed surprise at the forceful response to the advance notice from the SIA and other commentators. She said that, since the release had been nothing more than an advance notice of proposed rulemaking, the CFTC had not expected such a fuss. Further, she noted that, although the SIA and others had requested that the release be withdrawn, technically there was nothing to be withdrawn as no rules had been proposed.

After a period of further study, Chairman Gramm began to express in public pronouncements a more open attitude toward the position of the financial community on hybrid instruments. Later in the summer of 1988, the off-exchange task force once again began to provide no-action advice, both orally and through letters and written advisories. Merrill Lynch & Co., Inc. received oral clearance for an issue of Dollar BILS, which it sold under an August 22, 1988 supplement to its generic debt shelf. These were 10-year non-redeemable obligations issued at par that provided for no periodic payments of interest. At the stated maturity, a holder would receive an amount equal to the principal of the Dollar BIL plus interest, if any, based on the increase in the value of a portfolio of more than 300 high-quality corporate bonds with maturities of at least 15 years comprising a Merrill Lynch index over its value on the date of the prospectus.

Three letters were issued by the off-exchange task force that took no-action positions on Reverse PERLS.[22] The position also was then taken that the inflation indexing feature of an issuer's notes resulted in option characteristics that were *de minimis*.[23] No-action positions also were taken by the CFTC with respect to senior subordinated debentures providing for

---

22. CFTC Interpretative Letter 88-10 (June 20, 1988); CFTC Interpretative Letter 88-11 (July 13, 1988); CFTC Interpretative Letter 88-12 (July 22, 1988). The third letter stated that it would be unnecessary to obtain no-action advice as to future issues of this type if the CFTC were given two days' advance notice and the security clearly met a list of specified criteria. This position also was set forth in an Advisory of July 26, 1988.

23. CFTC Interpretative Letter 88-16 (August 26, 1988).

additional interest tied to increases in the price of natural gas[24] and gold indexed certificates of deposit.[25]

- *The Interpretation and the Rules*

At a January 5, 1989 meeting, the CFTC approved the publication of a release setting forth proposed rules with respect to hybrid instruments that "combine characteristics of commodity option contracts with debt or depository interests"[26] and an interpretation with respect to other hybrids that "combine characteristics of futures contracts or commodity options with debt or depository interests."[27]

The reason for the dual approach to the problem was the difference between the statutory treatment of futures contracts under Section 4(a) of the CEA and options under Section 4c(b).

The CFTC did not have the statutory authority to permit off-board dealing in futures. If it were to permit hybrids that combined characteristics of futures contracts with debt or depository instruments, then it would have to let go of its jurisdiction; it would have to take a definitional approach through a statutory interpretation and say that certain hybrids simply were not covered by the statute. With respect to hybrids with certain option characteristics, however, the CFTC could proceed by way of rulemaking. Section 4c(b) gives it this authority. The CFTC could permit off-board transactions in hybrids with option features while still retaining jurisdiction over these instruments.

- • *The Interpretation.* The CFTC invited comment on the interpretation, but unlike the proposed rules it did not require further adoption or ratification. It remained on the books as promulgated in January 1989 until April 1990, when it was reissued with certain modifications and clarifications to conform to the rules adopted in July 1989 and to respond to comments received by the CFTC.[28] The hybrid instruments, which the interpretation states are not within the coverage of the CEA or the

---

24. CFTC Interpretative Letter 88-17 (September 6, 1988).
25. CFTC Interpretative Letter 88-18 (September 23, 1988).
26. 54 Fed. Reg. 1128 (January 11, 1989).
27. 54 Fed. Reg. 1139 (January 11, 1989).
28. 55 Fed. Reg. 13582 (April 11, 1990).

regulations of the CFTC, are debt, preferred equity or depository instruments that are indexed to a commodity on no more than a one-to-one basis; limit the maximum loss on the instrument; have a significant "commodity-independent yield;" do not have a commodity component that is severable from the instrument; do not call for delivery of a commodity by means of an instrument specified in the rules of a designated contract market; and are not marketed as being or having the characteristics of a futures contract or commodity option.

The one-to-one limitation means that if the instrument has an interest rate indexed to or calculated by reference to the price of a commodity or provides for a principal payment so indexed or calculated, the percentage change in the interest rate for any interest payment period or the commodity-dependent principal payment may not exceed the percentage change in the commodity price to which it is indexed. The interpretation gives the example of a depository instrument with interest payments indexed to the price of gold. The fixed interest yield is 8% per annum, or $80 for each $1,000 of principal amount. The commodity-dependent interest payment is calculated by dividing the commodity-independent interest payment by $500 and then multiplying this quotient by the difference between the spot price of gold at the time of the interest payment and $500, if the spot price exceeds $500; otherwise, there is no adjustment. This instrument meets the one-to-one requirement because a 1% rise in the price of gold will result in an 80-cent commodity-dependent interest payment, which is 1% of the $80 commodity-independent interest payment.

The interpretation spells out the manner in which the maximum loss provision operates. In the case of a hybrid instrument bearing interest indexed to the price of a commodity, the maximum loss on each coupon or interest payment may not exceed the commodity-independent interest. The gold indexed obligations described above meet this test because in no event will the holder receive less than 8% per annum. In the case of a hybrid where the principal payment at maturity is linked to the price of a commodity, the maximum loss to the purchaser may not exceed the face value or initial purchase price of the instrument, whichever is higher. In any event, the issuer must receive full payment for the instrument upon its issuance, and the provisions of the instrument may not require the holder to pay any additional sums during the life of the instrument or at maturity.

The interpretation elaborates on the requirement that the instrument have a significant commodity-independent yield, i.e., the yield to maturity due solely to commodity-independent payments. In order to limit the commodity-dependent yield, the commodity-independent yield must equal at least 50%, but no more than 150%, of the estimated annual yield at the time of issuance for a comparable non-hybrid instrument. The interpretation states that the application of this standard under the assumption of an interest rate of 10% means that coupon instruments issued at par with a maturity of up to one year could have a commodity component accounting for approximately 5% of the issue price. For those with a maturity of five years, the commodity component could be approximately 20%, ten years approximately 30% and long-term no more than 50%. The interpretation, which sets forth a formula that can be used as guidance in fashioning various instruments, has become particularly important because the CFTC cannot exempt a transaction from the provisions or prohibitions of Section 2(a)(1)(B)(v) of the CEA. For example, single-equity futures products are illegal *per se*. The interpretation, however, provides a vehicle pursuant to which hybrid instruments satisfying its criteria may be viewed as "excluded" from regulation under the CEA. Trading in these instruments may therefore take place without obtaining an exemption from the CFTC.[29]

• • *The 1989 Rules.* The CFTC's initial rules on hybrids with commodity option components were adopted in July 1989.[30] As adopted, they were somewhat less restrictive than those proposed the preceding January. The rules contained requirements, similar to those of the interpretation, that the commodity component be non-severable, that the instrument not

---

29. *See*, e.g., Letter dated September 22, 1993 from Acting CFTC Chairman Bair to SEC Chairman Levitt (single equity-linked debt securities); CFTC Interpretive Letter No. 94-32, Comm. Fut. L. Rep. (CCH) ¶ 26,042 (Feb. 4, 1994); and CFTC Interpretive Letter No. 94-93, Comm. Fut. L. Rep. (CCH) ¶ 16,249 (July 27, 1994).

30. 54 Fed. Reg. 30684 (July 21, 1989).

provide for settlement in the form of a delivery instrument, and that it not be marketed as, or as having the characteristics of, a futures contract or a commodity option. In the unlikely event that the instrument failed to qualify under the interpretation for any one of these reasons, then it would fail to qualify under the rules as well. The rules made it clear (as did the interpretation) that an instrument would not be viewed as having been marketed as having the characteristics of a futures contract or a commodity option to the extent that it were necessary to describe the functioning of the instrument or to comply with applicable disclosure requirements.

The enactment of legislation in 1992 granting the CFTC exemptive authority over hybrid instruments resulted in the adoption of a new set of rules.

• • *The 1993 Rules.* Pursuant to the exemptive authority provided to the CFTC under the Futures Trading Practices Act of 1992, the CFTC adopted in 1993 a new Part 34, entitled "Regulation of Hybrid Instruments," concerning hybrid instruments that are debt or equity securities or depository instruments.[31] The 1993 rules replaced the original 1989 hybrid rules. While the 1989 rules applied only to instruments with option components because of the then existing limit on CFTC exemptive authority, the new rules apply to instruments with futures or options components or both. Under new Part 34, a test is used to determine the predominant nature of the instrument. A debt or equity security or depository instrument for which the sum of the commodity-dependent components is less than the commodity-independent value of the commodity-independent component is exempt from most CEA provisions, including the CEA's exchange-trading requirement, if it also meets other specified criteria. The CFTC has referred to this as the "predominance test." The theory is one of functional regulation—only those hybrid instruments that are "predominantly" commodity options or futures instruments should be subject to the CEA's exchange-trading provisions.

---

31. 58 Fed. Reg. 5580 (Jan. 22, 1993), reproduced at Comm. Fut. L. Rep. (CCH) ¶ 25,538. Part 34 is retroactive to October 23, 1974.

To qualify as an exempt hybrid instrument under new Part 34, the following conditions must also be satisfied:

(1) an issuer must receive full payment of the hybrid instrument's purchase price, and a purchaser or holder of a hybrid instrument may not be required to make additional out-of-pocket payments to the issuer during the life of the instrument or at maturity;

(2) the instrument may not be marketed as a futures contract or commodity option, or, except to the extent necessary to describe the functioning of the instrument or to comply with applicable disclosure requirements, as having the characteristics of a futures contract or a commodity option;

(3) the instrument may not provide for settlement in the form of a delivery instrument that is specified as such in the rules of a designated contract market; and

(4) the instrument must be initially issued or sold subject to applicable federal or state securities or banking laws to persons permitted thereunder to purchase or enter into the instrument.

An exemption under the Part 34 rules is self-executing, not requiring any notice or filing with the CFTC. Pursuant to Section 4(c) of the CEA, pursuant to which the Part 34 rules were adopted, the CFTC may also exempt any agreement, contract or transaction (or class thereof) that is otherwise subject to the section 4(a) exchange-trading requirement, from being required to be transacted on a futures exchange and from any other provision of the CEA (except the provisions of section 2(a)(1)(B)). The CFTC must affirmatively conclude that such transaction (a) must be entered into between "appropriate persons" as defined in section 4(c)(2) and (b) not have a material adverse effect on the ability of the CFTC or any futures exchange to discharge its regulatory duties.

• *Certain Observations on Hybrids*

Congress' grant of exemptive authority to the CFTC in 1992 and the adoption of the Part 34 hybrid rules in 1993 brought to an end a period of regulatory uncertainty that had been frustrating to the securities industry.

The hybrid saga is an example of the efforts that frequently are required for deals to get done. When legitimate financial transactions of a particular type run into regulatory roadblocks, it often is necessary to call upon the resources of industry organizations and bar association committees to bring about their removal. Individual efforts frequently are not sufficient. Hundreds of comment letters went into the framing of the hybrid interpretation and rules. The Securities Industry Association played a role, as did the bar associations. If a deal runs into a snag that has implications for the securities industry as a whole, it is advisable to call upon the good offices of the SIA (or, in the case of debt or asset-backed securities, of PSA The Bond Market Trade Association). Let the regulators know that the industry is interested and that the position that they are taking has broad policy implications.

Sometimes the most expeditious manner of dealing with the problem is through an ad hoc committee of interested lawyers. This was the approach that was taken when the Federal Reserve Board staff took the position that delayed delivery arrangements for debt underwritings involved an extension of credit under Regulation T (as discussed in Chapter 3). The same approach was taken when the SEC took the position that foreign banks seeking to sell their commercial paper in the United States were investment companies subject to the 1940 Act (as discussed in Chapter 10). It may take time, as was the case with hybrids, but with the proper approach, the regulatory hurdles can be cleared.

Currency Exchange Warrants

Currency exchange warrants entitle the holders to receive from the issuer upon exercise (in the case of a put warrant) the cash settlement value in U.S. dollars of the right to sell a specified amount of a specified foreign currency or currency units for a specified amount of U.S. dollars. Call warrants relate to the right to purchase the currency.

As mentioned in Chapter 8, some issuers have registered currency exchange warrants under their generic shelf registration statements. They are contractual obligations issued under the terms of a currency warrant agreement entered into with a bank that acts as warrant agent. They are typically exercisable at any time prior to expiration. The issuer will use a portion of the proceeds from the sale of the warrants to hedge its currency risk at a cost below the amount of those proceeds, thus lowering its all-in borrowing cost.[32]

Bear, Stearns & Co. Inc. was the principal architect of this financial product. The basic legal structure for currency exchange warrants is set forth in an interpretative letter from the staff of the SEC to the AMEX and counsel for Bear Stearns. The thrust of this letter is that the warrants are securities subject to the sole jurisdiction of the SEC. The SEC viewed them as "the economic equivalent of a long-term put option on a foreign currency." Section 3(a)(10) of the 1934 Act includes in the definition of "security" an option entered into on a national securities exchange relating to a foreign currency. Section 4c(f) of the CEA provides, "Nothing in this Act shall be deemed to govern or in any way be applicable to any transaction in an option on foreign currency traded on a national securities exchange." If not traded "on" a national securities exchange, currency options—which are also considered to be "commodity" options—are subject to the jurisdiction of the CFTC. The warrants were to be listed and registered for trading on the AMEX. Bear Stearns and the AMEX represented to the SEC their belief that "the primary market for secondary trading in the warrants will be on the AMEX with virtually all transactions effected on the floor of the AMEX, and do not expect significant off-exchange trading to occur in the warrants." The interpretative letter stated that the possibility of some off-exchange trading would not affect the status of the warrants as securities traded on a national securities exchange.

The SEC's interpretative letter contemplated that the warrants would be publicly offered as part of a unit consisting of a $1,000 medium-term note and 20 currency warrants immediately separable upon the initial public offering and that the

---

32. N.D. Slonaker & L.M. Wiltshire, *Innovative Debt Securities*, 20 Rev. Sec. & Com. Reg. 89, 96 (1987).

notes and units, as well as the warrants, would be listed. In the offerings that have been made, the notes and warrants have been offered separately, and not as units, in order to avoid any problem under the CEA that might result from the trading of units off the exchange prior to the separation of the components. Arrangements should be made for the listing to be effective when the warrants are first sold to the public.

The first offering of currency exchange warrants in the United States was an offering by General Electric Credit Corporation under a prospectus dated June 10, 1987 of $100 million of three-year notes and 2 million Japanese Yen Currency Exchange Warrants with an expiration date five years out. Other issuers followed with sales of notes and warrants tied to the yen or the deutsche mark. Citicorp had an offering under a July 9, 1987 prospectus of 2 million foreign exchange warrants that were not accompanied by an offering of debt securities.

The way that these instruments operate can be better understood by examining a specific transaction. Ford Motor Credit Company sold $100 million of 8.95% notes due 1991 and 2 million Japanese Yen Currency Exchange Warrants under a prospectus dated July 14, 1988. The notes and warrants were offered separately, and not in units, but the note and warrant offerings were each contingent upon the consummation of the other. Each warrant entitled the holder to receive from Ford Motor Credit the cash value in U.S. dollars of the right to purchase U.S. $50 at a price of ¥6989, representing an exchange rate of ¥139.78 per U.S. $1.00. The warrants were exercisable at any time until the fifth business day preceding their July 15, 1991 expiration date. In the event that the warrants were delisted from, or permanently suspended from trading on the AMEX, and not accepted at the same time for listing on another national securities exchange, the expiration date of the warrants would be the date that delisting or permanent suspension became effective. This provision was designed to preserve the status of the warrants as securities. If not exercised, the warrants would be deemed automatically exercised on July 15, 1991 or any earlier expiration date. A warrantholder could exercise no fewer than 2,000 warrants at any one time, except in the case of automatic exercises.

The Ford Motor Credit warrants were sold at a price of $2.375 per warrant. The prospectus pointed out that this price was considerably in excess of the price that a commercial user of Japanese yen might pay in the interbank market for a comparable option involving significantly larger amounts of underlying currencies. At the time of offering, the offered spot rate of Japanese yen for U.S. dollars was ¥133.06 = U.S.$1.00. The spot exchange rate of the Japanese yen as compared to the U.S. dollar determines whether the warrants have a cash settlement value at any time prior to their expiration. The warrants were out-of-the-money when originally sold and would have a cash settlement value in excess of zero only if the Japanese yen depreciated against the U.S. dollar to the extent that one U.S. dollar were worth more than the ¥139.78 strike price. The prospectus explained that the cash settlement value would be a dollar amount which is the greater of zero and the amount computed by subtracting from 50 an amount equal to 50 times a fraction, the numerator of which is the strike price and the denominator of which is the spot exchange rate of Japanese yen for U.S. dollars at 10:00 a.m. on the date of exercise.

The prospectus stated in a risk factors section that investors should be aware that it is not possible to predict how the warrants will trade in the secondary market or whether the market will be liquid or illiquid. It went on to state that it is possible that the trading value of a warrant may decline even if there is a decrease in the value of the Japanese yen as compared to the U.S. dollar and that, in addition to the relationship between the strike price and the exchange rate, a number of additional factors could affect the trading value of the warrants. The prospectus stated that, if the volatility of the exchange rate increases, the trading value of the warrants can be expected to increase, and that, if volatility decreases, the trading value of the warrants can be expected to decrease. It also pointed out that, as the time remaining to the expiration date decreases, the trading value is expected to decrease, and that, if Japanese yen interest rates increase relative to U.S. dollar interest rates, the value of the Japanese yen relative to the U.S. dollar in the forward market can be expected to decrease with a consequent effect on the trading value of the warrants.

Stock Index Warrants

Another type of freestanding indexed warrant has been used. These are put warrants on the Nikkei and other stock exchange indices. Among the issuers were Salomon Inc (tombstone advertisement dated January 18, 1990) and Bankers Trust New York Corporation (tombstone advertisement dated February 1, 1990). In each of these cases, the warrants were sold independently of a debt financing. They expired in two years.

Debt Securities with Embedded Options

It sounds exotic to describe a debt security as having an "embedded option," but nothing could be simpler. A convertible security (as discussed in Chapter 12) contains an embedded "call" option in the form of a privilege on the part of the holder to convert the security into the issuer's common stock. Obviously, the holder will do so only if the value of the common stock received at the time of conversion is in excess of the principal amount of the debt security. At the same time, the holder is under no compulsion to convert just because this is the case. Rather, the holder may choose to defer conversion since the option represented by the conversion feature will continue—like other options—to have "time value."

All straight debt securities that permit the issuer to redeem the securities prior to their maturity date can also be said to have an embedded call option, i.e., the issuer has a contractual right to "call" on the holders to deliver back the security in exchange for cash in the amount of the agreed-upon redemption price. Presumably, the issuer will take advantage of this right if interest rates decline subsequent to the issuance of the security. In that case, the issuer will be able to borrow money more cheaply elsewhere and use the proceeds to redeem the more expensive debt securities. Of course, purchasers of debt securities are aware of this possibility, and they often bargain for protections such as a minimum number of years before the issuer may redeem the bonds, a redemption "premium" that makes it more expensive for the issuer to redeem the securities in the early years of their life and (on some occasions) a prohibition on redemption with the use of money borrowed at a cheaper cost.

More recently, companies have issued debt securities with embedded "put" options, i.e., a privilege on the part of the holder to elect to deliver the security at agreed-upon intervals in exchange for payment of the agreed-upon "put" price. Presumably, the holder will take advantage of this right if interest rates increase subsequent to the issuance of the security. In that case, the holder will be able to reinvest elsewhere at a better rate the cash received from the issuer. Credit considerations may also play a role.

Options are seldom without cost, whether embedded or not. The purchaser of a convertible bond "pays" for the option on the common stock by accepting a lower coupon rate on the convertible securities. The issuer of a redeemable security pays for the right to redeem the bond by paying a higher coupon rate. The buyer of a "puttable" bond pays for the privilege by accepting a lower coupon rate.

When an issuer registers its convertible securities with the SEC under the 1933 Act, it also registers at the same time the securities into which the convertible securities are convertible. As discussed in Chapter 12, this is because the offering is deemed to involve the underlying securities as well as the convertible securities (at least if the convertible securities are immediately convertible, which is usually the case). Even though the purchaser is also paying for the embedded call option represented by the conversion privilege (and even though options on securities are defined as securities for all purposes of the 1933 Act), no one has argued that the issuer should also be registering the embedded call option as a separate security. In this respect, the offering is unlike an offering that might be economically and functionally equivalent to a convertible security offering, e.g., an offering of straight debt or preferred securities with attached warrants to purchase common stock, in which case (as discussed in Chapter 12) the warrants would have to be registered as a separate security. The difference, of course, is that the warrants will usually trade separately at some point, while the conversion feature in a convertible security usually remains embedded for the life of the security.

In the case of a redeemable security, the embedded option is really being purchased by the issuer from the purchaser of the redeemable security. More precisely, one might say that the issuer has "retained" the privilege of calling back the securities and paid for this privilege by paying a higher coupon rate. No one has suggested, however, that there would be any point in worrying about whether or not the holders' options should be registered under the 1933 Act.

In the case of puttable securities, the issuer is "selling" an option to the buyers of the securities. The question, therefore, arises whether the put should be separately registered along with the securities. As in the case of convertible securities, however, the option usually remains embedded for the life of the security. It would be pointless to register the put as a separate security.

There is no reason, however, why an issuer of redeemable securities should not be able to "detach" or "strip out" its right to redeem the securities. In a 1993 transaction, an issuer did precisely this in connection with the issuance of underwritten notes. The issuer's right to redeem the notes after two years was stripped out in the form of "option purchase rights" that were sold in a Rule 144A transaction to QIBs. Upon exercise of the option purchase rights and deposit of the principal amount of the notes, the QIBs would be deemed to have purchased the notes from the holders of the notes (presumably in reliance on the Section 4(1) exemption). At this time, of course, the QIBs would be the owners of non-redeemable notes with a remaining life to maturity of eight years.

The fact that it was deemed necessary to sell the option purchase rights in a Rule 144A transaction suggests that the rights were assumed to be separate securities upon their being stripped out of the notes. Indeed, it was necessary to persuade the SEC staff that there should be no "integration" between the public sale of the notes and the private sale of the rights. No consideration appears to have been given, however, to whether the separate securities represented by the rights were securities "issued" by the holders of the notes rather than securities issued by the issuer of the notes.

The issuer was also able to persuade the staff that the deemed sale of the notes by the holders thereof to the QIBs who were exercising their option purchase rights was a secondary market transaction exempt under Section 4(1) and not a distribution by the issuer.[33] The technique of "stripping out" the issuer's right to redeem debt securities has also been applied to municipal securities.

Inflation-Indexed Debt Securities

An early example of an inflation-indexed debt security was an issue of one-year Inflation Indexed Notes paying interest quarterly at the rate of 2.15% per annum sold by Federal National Mortgage Association under an offering circular dated July 19, 1988. Under the terms of the instrument, the principal was revalued on each interest payment date with reference to the consumer price index.

In early 1997, the U.S. Treasury sold its first inflation-indexed bonds. The principal amount of these bonds was also adjusted based on changes in the Consumer Price Index–Urban over time, while interest on the bonds accrued at a fixed rate based on the adjusted principal amount of the bonds. Within a few days, eight other corporate and quasi-governmental issuers had sold debt securities at interest rates—not principal amounts—that were linked to the Consumer Price Index–Urban.

Inflation-indexed debt securities are attractive for issuers whose revenues tend to rise with inflation, such as commodity producers or utilities. Other issuers may prefer to swap their way out of the inflation risk, and these issuers may find an inflation-indexed financing more cost effective than a straight debt financing, even after taking into account the cost of the swap.

The future of this type of instrument remains to be seen, at least in a time of relatively mild inflationary pressures.

---

33. It was also necessary to persuade the staff that the transaction was a proper use of the issuer's shelf registration statement. The issuer took the position that the registration statement contemplated the sale of redeemable securities and that the option purchase rights should be viewed as an assignment of the redemption rights.

Trust Preferred Securities

"Trust preferred securities" are corporate securities that have characteristics that are common both to preferred stock and corporate debt securities. There are many different structures and variations in economic terms, but the common denominator is that the issuer—subject to proposed changes in the tax laws—is able to take a tax deduction for payments on the securities (something that is not possible in the case of dividends on preferred stock) while the securities are treated for purposes of the issuer's credit standing—and sometimes for regulatory purposes—as the equivalent or near-equivalent of equity securities.

In the case of conventional preferred stock, issuers rely on the fact that eligible corporate investors are entitled under current federal income tax law to deduct 70% of the dividends that they receive on corporate equity securities. This deduction (called the dividends received deduction or "DRD") appeals to many tax-paying institutional investors. It also results, of course, in the issuer being able to offer the preferred stock at a lower cost of funds.

Unlike interest on debt, however, dividends on DRD preferred stock are not tax-deductible to the issuer. For many issuers, a combination of the tax-deductibility associated with interest payments and the "equity credit" associated with preferred stock will provide a better capital-raising alternative than either DRD preferred stock or straight debt securities.

A popular structure for preferred securities of this kind is Trust Originated Preferred Securities or "TOPrS", developed by Merrill Lynch in early 1995. TOPrS are issued by a Delaware statutory business trust sponsored by a corporate issuer (or one of its subsidiaries) that owns at least 3% of the total capital of the trust. The trust issues the TOPrS and then lends the proceeds of its capital-raising activity (including the TOPrS) to the issuer and takes back a long-term subordinated deferrable interest debenture whose maturity and terms match those of the TOPrS. The debenture may or may not be convertible into the issuer's common stock or exchangeable for common stock of another issuer.

The corporate issuer also guarantees the trust's payments of distributions on the TOPrS, as well as payments upon redemption of the TOPrS or liquidation of the trust, out of funds held by the trust.

Under the corporate tax rules in effect at least through the early part of 1997, the issuer receives a tax deduction for its interest payments to the trust as the holder of the debenture. On the other hand, holders of the TOPrS are deemed to receive interest payments from the trust. Therefore, they are not eligible to take advantage of the DRD.

The debenture held by the trust generally has a maturity of 30 years, with the corporate issuer having the option in certain offerings to extend this maturity for another 19 years. (There is no limit on the life of the debenture if it is issued by a non-U.S. company.) The corporate issuer typically has the right to cause a redemption of the TOPrS after a specified number of years or prior to such time in the event of certain adverse tax or regulatory events (e.g., a change in tax law that would disallow the issuer's tax deduction or, in the case of a bank holding company, the failure of the debenture to qualify as Tier 1 capital). The TOPrS will be subject to redemption upon the earlier of the stated maturity or redemption of the debentures.

TOPrS, like most preferred securities of this kind, have an interest deferral feature. This allows the corporate issuer, under certain circumstances, to defer interest payments on the debenture and the trust, in turn, to defer distributions on the TOPrS for up to five consecutive years. The potential deferral of interest payments is similar to a corporation's ability to defer dividends on traditional preferred stock. It is, of course, quite unlike an issuer's inability to defer interest payments in the case of traditional straight-debt securities—at least, not without causing a default. A potential disadvantage for holders of TOPrS if payments are deferred is that they must, nevertheless, accrue the payments for tax purposes.

An alternative structure, known as Monthly Income Preferred Securities or "MIPS", was developed by Goldman, Sachs & Co. in 1993. It uses a special purpose corporation or partnership. Another Goldman Sachs product, known as Quarterly Income Preferred Securities or "QUIPs", uses a trust structure similar to TOPrS. Some investors find partnership structures less attractive than a trust in that they receive a more cumbersome Schedule K-1 for tax reporting purposes rather than a Form 1099.

Although trust preferred securities resemble long-term equity capital, a leading rating agency has stated that it does not assign "an absolute percentage of 'equity credit' " to an instrument for analytic purposes. Rather, the agency views a specific instrument "within the context of the issuer's overall credit fundamentals."[34]

Trust preferred securities received a boost in late 1996 when the Federal Reserve Board approved their use as a means of adding to a bank holding company's Tier 1 capital. To qualify, the securities had to provide for a minimum five-year consecutive deferral period on distributions to holders of the preferred securities. In addition, the intercompany loan was required to be subordinated to all other subordinated debt of the bank holding company and to have the "longest feasible maturity." The Board's approval took into consideration the fact that bank holding companies seldom (if ever) suspend their preferred dividends for as much as five years. In addition, other regulated entities such as insurance companies had been able to use similar securities for capital-boosting purposes.

Between the date of the Board's approval and early February 1997, approximately $28.6 billion of trust preferred securities (known in this context as "capital securities") were issued in approximately 111 transactions. In early February 1997, however, the Clinton Administration's budget proposals included a provision that would eliminate the tax advantages of these securities.

An example of a TOPrS financing is the $500,000,000 offering in January 1996 by TCI Communications Financing I, a Delaware business trust (the "Trust") controlled by TCI Communications, Inc., a 1934 Act-reporting company engaged in the cable television business ("TCI"). The Trust issued 20,000,000 TOPrS at a price of $25 each for gross proceeds of $500 million. The

---

34. Moody's Investors Service, *Moody's Assesses Hybrid Securities* (June 1996) at 7.

Trust used the proceeds of the TOPrS to invest in an equivalent principal amount of TCI's 8.72% Subordinated Deferrable Interest Notes (the "Notes"). Holders of the TOPrS received cash distributions that corresponded to the quarterly interest payments on the Notes. TCI also guaranteed the Trust's payment of distributions out of funds held by the Trust as well as payments on liquidation of the Trust or the redemption of the TOPrS. TCI retained the right to defer interest payments on the Notes for up to 20 consecutive quarters, in which case distributions on the TOPrS would also be deferred. During any deferral of interest payments, distributions on the TOPrS would nevertheless continue to accrue with interest, compounded quarterly. Holders were cautioned in the prospectus supplement that they would not have the right to appoint any representative or trustee or otherwise act to protect their interests during any such deferral and also that they would be required to include the deferred interest income in their taxable income.

- *1933 Act Considerations*

In contemplation of the issuance of TOPrS from time to time, a shelf registration statement was filed covering $1 billion of TOPrS together with the related TCI debentures and guarantees. The Trust, three similar trusts and TCI all signed the registration statement as co-registrants. Form S-3 was used in reliance on TCI's eligibility to use that form, the deemed status of the Trust as a majority-owned subsidiary of TCI and the deemed equivalence of TCI's obligations to a guarantee of the TOPrS. No separate financial statements for the Trust were included in the registration statement in reliance on Staff Accounting Bulletin 53.

(Hybrid preferred securities are frequently offered to QIBs pursuant to Rule 144A as well as to offshore investors in reliance upon the safe harbor afforded by Regulation S. The question arises under Regulation S as to the "category" in which the offering belongs for purposes of determining the duration of the required "offerings restrictions." If the preferred securities were regarded as equity securities of a non-reporting U.S. issuer (i.e., the issuing trust), they would be Category 3 securities subject to a one-year restricted period and other conditions. This is an unreasonable result if the underlying debt securities would themselves be Category 2 securities subject to a 40-day restricted period. To be sure, Rule 903(c)(4) would permit non-participating preferred stock to be treated for this purpose as debt securities subject to Category 3, but this would still require compliance with some onerous conditions. A more promising solution is afforded by Rule 903(c)(5), which permits reliance on a parent company's guarantee of an issuer's "debt securities" to determine the appropriate category. The authors believe that hybrid preferred securities are similar enough to debt securities to justify reliance on this approach, but the point has not been raised with the SEC staff.)

- *1934 Act Considerations*

The Trust would not have ongoing reporting and disclosure obligations under the 1934 Act in reliance on Staff Accounting Bulletin 53 and the deemed equivalence of TCI's obligations to a guarantee of the TOPrS. (There are numerous no-action letters approving this conclusion, usually on condition that the reporting issuer's financial statements contain specific disclosures regarding the preferred securities and the relationship of the trust to the reporting issuer.)

Moreover, the Trust was not viewed as subject to the 48-hour prospectus delivery obligation imposed by Rule 15c2-8(b) on underwriters of securities of non-reporting issuers. Again, the basis for this conclusion was the fact that investors were relying on TCI's obligations, and that TCI was itself a reporting company.

- *1939 Act Considerations*

All of the following were qualified as indentures under the Trust Indenture Act of 1939: (a) the Trust's declaration of trust, pursuant to which the TOPrS were issued, (b) the indenture pursuant to which the Notes were issued and (c) TCI's guarantee.

- *1940 Act Considerations*

The Trust was exempt from the requirements of the 1940 Act in reliance on Rule 3a-5, a rule normally applied for the purpose of exempting finance subsidiaries. To qualify for Rule 3a-5, it was necessary to assume (among other things) that the Trust could be treated as a "corporation" and that the TOPrS could be treated as non-voting preferred stock issued by the "finance subsidiary." The SEC staff acquiesced in these assumptions.

Mandatorily Convertible Instruments

Mandatorily convertible securities can offer issuers a number of advantages. In their most basic form, an issuer will issue a debt security or preferred stock that is mandatorily convertible within a specified number of years into the issuer's own common stock. The technique serves as a means of persuading a rating agency that the issuer will definitely receive equity capital within a specified number of years. It also offers the issuer a means of selling its common stock now at a minimum price. In return, the investor will expect to receive a higher return than is available on the common stock.

It is only a short step to issuing a debt security or preferred stock that is mandatorily convertible (or, more precisely, exchangeable) into the common stock of a subsidiary of the issuer. And it is only a short additional step to the underlying security being common stock of a company in which the issuer has a minority position. Also, in these cases, the issuer is using the mandatorily convertible security as a means of obtaining cash now—without having to pay any taxes—and at the same time ensuring that it will receive at least a minimum price for the underlying stock that it owns. (This is sometimes referred to as "monetizing" a minority participation in another company.) As a variation, the issuer may reserve the right to pay cash at the time of conversion in lieu of delivering actual shares, thereby giving it the option of retaining the shares indefinitely or even exposing itself to market risk if it decides to sell the shares prior to the security's maturity.

• *Conversion into Company's Own Common Stock*

In 1988, Morgan Stanley developed a product known as Preferred Equity Redemption Cumulative Stock (or "Percs"). Percs were slow in gaining popularity, in part because of a lack of interest on the part of U.S. companies in the 1988–90 time period in issuing new equity securities. Eventually, issuers became interested in the product, which offered the assurance of an eventual issuance of common stock upon mandatory conversion within three years. In turn, the issuer would pay the investor a higher dividend than that available on the issuer's common stock, and the investor would accept a cap on the common stock's appreciation potential. The product is similar from the investor's standpoint to a purchase of common stock and a simultaneous writing of a call option on the stock. The investor receives more income but limits its participation in a potential increase in the market price of the stock.

Percs have been useful to issuers that have had to reduce the dividend on their common stock. In 1988, Avon Products, Inc. wanted to cut the generous dividend on its common stock without upsetting those of its stockholders for whom a high yield was important. In exchange for up to 25% of its common stock, it therefore offered Percs with a yield equivalent to the pre-cut common stock yield but with a cap on upside potential. In 1994, Times Mirror Company settled a lawsuit arising out of a proposed 80% cut in its dividend by agreeing to issue up to $350 million in Percs. In 1995, Sun Company, Inc. wanted to avoid a major shift in its stockholder base as a consequence of its plans to cut its common stock dividend. It therefore offered its stockholders a choice between participation in an exchange offer of Percs-like "Targets" or in a Dutch auction tender offer for the common stock.

While investors may be willing to accept the modified equity exposure inherent in a mandatorily convertible instrument, market-makers usually prefer to hedge this risk. The natural way for a market-maker to hedge its holdings of a convertible instrument is to make short sales of the underlying common stock, assuming that it is possible to borrow the stock for the purpose of making deliveries to settle the short sales. Where the stock available to be borrowed is in short supply, some market-makers have entered into agreements with the issuer of the stock underlying the mandatory convertible instrument that entitle them to borrow the underlying stock for this purpose. The SEC staff takes the position that a market-maker who intends to deliver such stock to settle a short sale must deliver a prospectus to the person on the other side of the short sale. This is, of course, contrary to the position taken by the authors in Chapter 13 to the effect that there should be no obligation to deliver a prospectus in this situation.

Securities firms have developed several different types of mandatorily convertible preferred securities. They differ in how any appreciation in the common stock is shared between the issuer and the investor. Salomon Brothers developed Dividend Enhanced Convertible Stock (or "Decs") in 1993, and Merrill Lynch introduced Preferred Redeemable Increased Dividend Equity Securities (or "Prides") in the same year. Morgan Stanley offered a revised Percs product in 1994 called Participating Equity Preferred Stock (or "Peps"). Salomon Brothers also offers a debt variety of Decs that is denominated Debt Exchangeable for Common Stock.

• *Conversion into Another Company's Common Stock*

An issuer may wish to "monetize" all or a portion of its holding in another publicly-held company. It may do so by issuing a mandatorily convertible debt or preferred security that converts into the common stock of the other company, generally within three to five years. The issuer may intend that the stock be delivered or it may retain the right to pay the holders cash at maturity. For credit rating reasons, the issuer may commit to deliver cash only if it is able to raise the cash by selling its own equity securities within a specified period. The advantages of the transaction for the issuer are the immediate receipt of cash, the guarantee of a minimum price for its stock position in the other company and the deferral of capital gains taxes until the stock is actually delivered. The issuer may also retain an interest, depending on the price terms of the transaction, in the underlying stock's upside potential before maturity.

• *Equity-Linked Notes*

An issuer of a mandatory convertible debt security need not own the underlying common stock. As a matter of contract, an issuer may sell its debt securities that will be discharged at maturity not by payment or conversion into the issuer's or another company's stock but rather by the delivery of stock of a completely unrelated company (or by the payment of cash in an equivalent amount). A number of investment banking firms have created equity-linked products of this kind, e.g., Bear Stearns (ELKS), Salomon Brothers (YEELDS) and Lehman Brothers (CHIPS). The issuer of the debt security may be an affiliate of the investment banking firm or it may be a third-party issuer.

Equity-linked notes may be mandatorily exchangeable or only at the option of the holder. A mandatorily exchangeable security exposes the holder to loss of principal, while the holder of an optionally exchangeable security may choose to receive the principal amount or redemption price of the note in cash.

• *1933 Act Considerations*

Because the linked issuer is not involved in the transaction, it will obviously not be willing to register the shares of its stock that may be delivered at the maturity of the equity-linked note. On the other hand, such registration should not be required since the issuer of the note will obtain the stock on the open market. Assuming that the issuer is not an affiliate of the issuer of the underlying securities, the only 1933 Act registration obligation will, therefore, relate to the notes themselves.

Obviously, however, the investor is also interested in disclosure about the issuer of the underlying securities. Therefore, the question remains whether, and to what extent, the issuer of the equity-linked note should include in its prospectus any disclosure about the issuer of the linked securities.

An issuer would understandably be reluctant to include such disclosure, even if it were available from the linked issuer's public filings, because of its concern that it would become liable under Section 11 of the 1933 Act or otherwise for deficiencies in these filings. Accordingly, it became the practice for issuers of equity-linked notes to include only a very brief description of the linked issuer's business, a reference to the availability of its filings under the 1934 Act and a history of the linked issuer's stock price and (in some cases) dividend payments.

The SEC staff acquiesced for a number of years in this practice. It subsequently began to draw a distinction, however, between offerings in which the linked issuer was eligible to register primary offerings of its securities for cash on Form S-3 or Form F-3 and those offerings in which this was not the case. In the SEC staff's view, complete financial statement and non-financial statement disclosure about the linked issuer was material to investors at the time of the initial sale of the equity-linked notes and on a continuous basis until exchange or payment. Where the linked issuer was not eligible to use Form S-3 or Form F-3, then the issuer of the equity-linked security would have to include in its prospectus all of the information about the linked issuer that the latter would have to include in its own prospectus if it were to make an offering of its own.

In no-action correspondence in mid-1996, the staff was persuaded that sufficient market interest and publicly available information could be assumed to be available where the linked issuer (as an alternative to being eligible to use Form S-3 or Form F-3) met a national securities exchange's listing criteria applicable to the underlying issuer in the case of a listing of equity-linked notes. In the case of the American Stock Exchange, for example, those criteria would require either (a) a minimum market capitalization of $3 billion and at least 2.5 million shares traded during the past 12 months, (b) a minimum market capitalization of $1.5 billion and at least 20 million shares traded during the past 12 months or (c) a minimum market capitalization of $500 million and at least 80 million shares traded during the past 12 months.[35]

• *Due Diligence*

The issuer of the equity-linked notes, its directors and signing officers and any underwriters will have the usual Section 11 liability for disclosures and omissions relating to the note issuer. In addition, any underwriter may have Section 12(a)(2) liability for any statements made to purchasers of the notes—whether these statements relate to the issuer of the notes or the issuer of the linked security. An underwriter would have the benefit of the "reasonable care" defense under Section 12(a)(2) in resisting claims by purchasers that statements made to them were materially untrue or misleading. To invoke this defense successfully, an underwriter will have to exercise due diligence that is reasonable under the unique circumstances of this type of offering. Since it cannot expect the cooperation of the linked issuer, an underwriter will have to review the linked issuer's periodic reports, consult its analyst

35. SEC No-action Letter, *Morgan Stanley & Co., Inc.* (available June 24, 1996).

for his or her views on the linked issuer's common stock and otherwise inquire into the existence of any "red flags" that should be investigated or, if investigation is not feasible, should call for the offering to be abandoned.

As noted above, neither the note issuer nor any underwriter will have any reason to expect the linked issuer's cooperation in its due diligence effort. The linked issuer has no prospect of economic benefit from the transaction, and it may even perceive the transaction as prejudicial to its own ability to issue equity. The question remains as to whether an underwriter should ask the linked issuer to cooperate, e.g., by answering a few questions on the telephone or in a brief meeting. If there were no downside to this inquiry, it might be prudent to make it. On the other hand, the linked issuer could easily, whether or not in good faith, sabotage the offering by suggesting that it was aware of material, adverse and undisclosed information that it was not yet prepared to disclose. In view of this potential interference with the offering from a person having no stake in it, and in view of the unlikelihood under the best of circumstances of obtaining the linked issuer's cooperation, there appears to be no point in asking the linked issuer to cooperate in the due diligence effort.[36] This does not mean, of course, that an underwriter might not wish as a business courtesy to inform the linked issuer of the planned offering in advance of its being publicly announced.

• *Listing*

Equity-linked notes are often listed on a national securities exchange or quoted on NASDAQ. Each of the NYSE, the AMEX and NASDAQ has detailed listing requirements for such securities.

An important reason for listing is often the need to take advantage of the federal preemption of state bucket shop and usury laws contained in Section 28(a) of the 1934 Act. Section

---

36. *Cf. Feit v. Leasco Data Proc. Eq. Corp.*, 332 F. Supp. 544, 581–83 (S.D.N.Y. 1971) (dealer-managers found to have established due diligence defense under Section 11 when facts indicated that officer of target company would not cooperate by providing data on "surplus surplus" and that an estimate should therefore not be included in the prospectus).

28(a) requires that an instrument be "traded pursuant to rules and regulations of a self-regulatory organization" that are filed with the SEC pursuant to Section 19(b) of the 1934 Act. In the case of Rule 144A securities, therefore, a listing on PORTAL would also qualify the security for Section 28(a) preemption.

• *Off-Balance Sheet Monetizations (STRYPES)*

An issuer with a stock position that it would like to "monetize" may not be in a position to issue its own mandatorily convertible securities for that purpose. Nevertheless, such an issuer can still achieve its objectives if it can find another issuer willing to issue its securities that are mandatorily convertible into the securities held by the first issuer.

A popular vehicle for this purpose uses a security known as Structured Yield Product Exchangeable for Stock (or "STRYPES"), developed by Merrill Lynch & Co., Inc. The basic STRYPES product is a Merrill Lynch debt security with a three- to five-year maturity that bears interest at a fixed rate, payable quarterly. It is discharged by the delivery of shares of the underlying security or, at the issuer's option, cash. The number of shares or the amount of cash is fixed by a formula based on the average price of the underlying security over a 20-day trading period. The holder has no choice but to receive the shares or cash; it therefore faces the possibility of a loss of principal. On the other hand, the holder is buying the shares at today's price and will receive an enhanced return over the period until maturity of the STRYPES.

The owner of the underlying shares receives a number of advantages from the STRYPES transaction. It is "selling" the underlying shares at today's price, but the cash election makes it possible to retain the shares if it wishes to do so. It can also maintain voting rights, collect dividends and defer the payment of taxes.

The STRYPES issuer's obligation to deliver the underlying security or cash is hedged by entering into a forward purchase contract with the owner of the underlying security. The contract may be "pre-paid" (i.e., the owner of the underlying security receives cash up front) or settled at the maturity of the

STRYPES. In the case of a pre-paid forward purchase, the issuer of the STRYPES will retain the present value of the coupon payments on the STRYPES, or the owner of the underlying security will agree to make periodic payments to the STRYPES issuer equal to the coupon payment on the STRYPES.

The agreement usually leaves the owner free to sell the underlying security if it wishes to do so, without prejudice, of course, to its obligation to deliver the shares or cash at the maturity of the STRYPES. It will provide for anti-dilution adjustments similar to those associated with convertible securities.

• • *1933 Act Considerations.* The issuer of the STRYPES will usually do so from a registration statement on Form S-3. If, as is often the case, it is not certain that the owner of the underlying security is not in "control" of the issuer of the underlying security, of if the underlying securities are "restricted securities" within the meaning of Rule 144, it will also be necessary for the underlying security to be registered at the commencement of the transaction. Each issuer will file its separate registration statement or take advantage of a previously-filed and effective shelf registration. There will be a single common prospectus that consists of a prospectus relating to the STRYPES that is attached to a prospectus for the underlying security. The STRYPES prospectus will include information about the STRYPES issuer that is consistent with a debt takedown by that issuer. The issuer of the underlying security will usually be eligible to use Form S-3 or Form F-3, in which case the information on this issuer contained in the STRYPES prospectus will be limited to a brief description of the issuer, recent market prices of the underlying security and a statement that the issuer is a reporting company under the 1934 Act whose filings are available from the SEC. There is also a reference to the attached prospectus of the issuer of the underlying security, but it is stated that the attached prospectus is not a part of the STRYPES issuer's prospectus or incorporated by reference therein.

If the underlying security is not a "restricted security" and its owner is not in "control" of its issuer, then Section 4(1) of the 1933 Act will make it unnecessary for the underlying security to be registered at the commencement of the transaction. In this case, the extent of disclosure in the STRYPES prospectus relating to the issuer of the underlying security will vary depending on marketing considerations.

The STRYPES issuer and the issuer of the underlying security will file their respective prospectuses with the SEC under Rule 424(b). After extensive discussions with the SEC, it appears settled that there is no obligation to deliver a prospectus relating to the underlying securities at the time the STRYPES mature (so long as the issuer of the underlying securities has a class of securities registered under the 1934 Act throughout the life of the STRYPES).

• • *Liability Considerations.* The issuer of the STRYPES will normally not be concerned about civil liability for its own disclosure, but it may be less sure about its liability as an issuer for the disclosure provided to investors by the underlying issuer. None of this disclosure is included in the STRYPES issuer's registration statement, so there should at least be no question of Section 11 liability.

The underwriter of the STRYPES will certainly be deemed a "seller" of the underlying securities for purposes of Section 12(a)(2) liability. The underwriting agreement will call for representations and warranties, legal opinions and a comfort letter that are consistent with a secondary offering.

• • *Listing.* STRYPES are listed with the NYSE or AMEX or quoted on NASDAQ. As discussed above, one of the principal purposes of listing or quotation on NASDAQ is to take advantage of the federal preemption of state bucket shop and usury issues contained in Section 28(a) of the 1934 Act. Each of the exchanges and NASDAQ has special listing standards for equity-linked debt securities, and STRYPES are considered to fall into this category.

Short Sales Against the Box

Securities offerings almost invariably involve "long" sales, i.e., the issuer delivers newly-issued securities to the underwriters or purchasers, or the selling securityholders deliver securities owned by them. There is no reason, however, why a selling securityholder should not be able to deliver securities borrowed from another person. From the investor's point of view,

after all, the origin of the securities being purchased is immaterial. It is no different in the secondary market, where any investor purchasing securities may in fact be purchasing
securities that the seller has borrowed from another source.

The technique of agreeing to sell securities and meeting
one's delivery obligation by the use of borrowed securities
while retaining an equivalent "long" position is known as
"selling short against the box." Its most common purpose is to
postpone the realization of a taxable gain. Under principles in
effect for many years, a seller of securities "short against the
box" does not realize gain for tax purposes until the transaction is closed out by the delivery of securities to the lender.
These securities can come from the original "long" position or
represent other securities purchased for the purpose in the open
market.

In the November 1995 initial public offering of The Estée
Lauder Company Inc., two of the selling shareholders borrowed the shares they were selling from certain family members and family trusts. According to the Prospectus:

> In each case, the lending stockholders will receive from
> the borrowing stockholders amounts equal to dividends
> and other distributions that would have been paid on the
> borrowed shares, plus a customary fee, and such bor-
> rowing stockholders would be obligated to repay the
> borrowing by delivering to the lending stockholders
> shares equal in number to the borrowed shares three
> business days after demand by the lending stockhold-
> ers. The borrowing stockholders' obligation will be se-
> cured by a pledge to the respective lending stockholders
> of an equal number of shares of Class A Common Stock
> owned by the borrowing stockholders.

It should be noted that the lenders were persons related to
the selling stockholders. It was therefore possible to inquire
into their ownership of the shares being loaned to the selling
stockholders. In addition, the customary selling stockholders'
representations in the underwriting agreement were replaced by
representations to the effect that the lending stockholders had
good and valid title to the shares to be sold by the borrowing

stockholders. Counsel for the selling stockholders delivered opinions to the effect that the underwriters received valid title to the shares, free and clear of any encumbrances, assuming that they were purchasers for value in good faith under the Uniform Commercial Code.

The "short against the box" technique was proposed to be abolished as part of the Clinton Administration's 1998 budget proposals released in February 1997. Under the proposals, a taxpayer would be required to recognize gain (but not loss) upon entering into a "constructive sale" of any appreciated position in stock, debt or partnership interests. A "constructive sale" would occur when the taxpayer (or possibly a related person) "substantially eliminates" risk of loss and opportunity for gain by entering into one or more positions with respect to the same or substantially identical property. Thus, a taxpayer holding appreciated stock that entered into a short sale with respect to the same or substantially identical stock would recognize gain on the appreciated stock position. The same result will follow under the proposals in the case of "equity swaps," the grant of call options or the purchase of put options where there was a "substantial certainty" that the option would be exercised, and in the case of transactions that were "marketed or sold" as substantially eliminating the risk of loss and opportunity for gain, regardless of whether the transaction involved the same or substantially identical property. Many of the key terms in the proposals are left undefined.

Chapter 12

CONVERTIBLE SECURITIES, WARRANTS AND UNDERWRITTEN CALLS

A corporation raising capital through the issuance of fixed-income securities—whether debt securities or preferred stock—may seek to reduce its cost of funds by providing investors with an "equity kicker." The corporation may accomplish this by issuing debt securities or preferred stock that are convertible at the holder's election into the corporation's common stock at a conversion price above the market price prevailing at the time that the fixed-income securities are offered. The convertibility feature is the economic equivalent of a call option on the common stock for the life of the convertible security. It therefore has value, and this value is reflected in the investor's willingness to accept a lower current return in the form of interest or dividend payments.

An issuer may be less concerned about lowering its interest payment costs than about demonstrating to its creditors or to the rating agencies that its convertible securities will in fact become equity securities rather than remain in the form of preferred stock or a debt obligation. The key to this treatment may be to issue *mandatorily convertible* securities, i.e., securities that will become common stock whatever the price performance of the common stock in the open market or the preferences of the holder. The conversion may be triggered either because the issuer's common stock price exceeds a certain level or simply by the passage of a specified period of time. Unlike the buyer of traditional convertible securities, who in effect purchases a call option on the underlying common stock, the buyer of mandatorily convertible securities is in effect selling a put option to the issuer. Just as the buyer of traditional convertible securities expects to pay for the call option by receiving a lower current return, the buyer of mandatorily convertible securities expects to be compensated for the sale of the put option by receiving a higher current return.

Another financing alternative is the simultaneous issuance of debt securities with warrants to buy the issuer's common stock. Warrants are nothing more than a long-term call option on the underlying common stock. They will usually trade separately from the debt securities, will have a fixed life and will entitle the holders to purchase for cash a specified number of shares of common stock at the warrant exercise price.

A corporation may also issue debt securities or preferred stock that are exchangeable at a fixed price for common stock of another corporation. In the case of either convertible or exchangeable securities, if the market price of the underlying security increases sufficiently, the issuer may call the convertible or exchangeable security for redemption, thereby economically forcing conversions or exchanges into the underlying security.

The terms of convertible or exchangeable debt securities will be set forth in an indenture or supplement to an indenture between the issuer and a bank acting as trustee. The terms of convertible or exchangeable preferred stock will be set forth in a certificate of designation filed as a charter document. The terms of warrants will be set forth in a warrant agreement between the issuer and a warrant agent (usually a bank).

Convertible Securities

Holders of convertible debt securities are entitled prior to maturity, but subject to prior redemption, to convert their debentures into shares of common stock at a specified conversion price. In the case of convertible preferred stock, there is usually no maturity date, in which case the conversion privilege will continue indefinitely, subject to the issuer's right to call the shares for redemption. The conversion price, like the interest or dividend rate, will be determined at the time the debentures are offered for sale and typically will be fixed at a substantial premium (e.g., 15% to 20%) over the current market price of the common stock. (Convertible securities are, therefore, sometimes described as a means of "issuing stock at a premium over market.") Like the other economic terms of the security, the premium is a matter for negotiation between the issuer and the underwriters.

The conversion price usually does not change over the life of the securities, except to the extent that it is adjusted pursuant to anti-dilution provisions to reflect such events as stock splits, stock dividends, and distributions of rights or warrants permitting the holders to purchase common stock at less than the market price current at that time. Occasionally, however, convertible securities will be issued under terms that include a "step-up" in the conversion price at stated intervals over the security's life.

Conversely, an issuer may wish to provide investors with "downside protection" by agreeing to issue additional shares if the underlying security is selling below an agreed-upon threshold. For example, Microsoft Corporation—which pays no dividends on its common stock—publicly offered in December 1996 a series of 2-3/4% Convertible Exchangeable Principal-Protected Preferred Shares. This security offered investors a current return and the guarantee of receiving common stock or cash having a value not less than the value of the common stock on the issuance date of the preferred shares; in return, however, the investor's opportunity for equity appreciation was capped at 28%.

Issuers have also elected to issue convertible debentures that embody "reset" features that contemplate a reduction in the conversion price to reflect declines in the market price of the underlying security. For example, a number of Japanese issuers responded in 1996 to investor anxiety about the Japanese stock market by issuing convertible securities with an annual reset feature, i.e., the conversion price adjusted each year to the prevailing average price of the issuer's American Depositary Shares (if lower than the immediately prior conversion price), but not lower than a stated dollar amount per ADS.

Even without such features, an issuer—for example, an issuer of convertible preferred securities on which there are substantial dividend arrearages—may attempt to "induce" conversions by offering to holders the opportunity to convert and receive additional amounts of the underlying security.

Convertible securities generally provide for interest or dividends payable at periodic intervals at a fixed interest or dividend rate. "LYONs," as discussed below, are zero-coupon securities that provide the investor with a fixed rate of return, although it is not payable in cash on a current basis. Some companies have issued adjustable rate convertible securities.

The market price of a convertible security will fluctuate with the price of the issuer's common stock as well as in response to the changing market environment for fixed-income securities. The influence of the common stock price on the price of the convertible security will be greater to the extent that the security is "in-the-money," i.e., where the current market price of the underlying common stock exceeds the conversion price. In general, convertible securities neither appreciate nor depreciate quite in line with the equity markets; on the other hand, if the equity and bond markets are down in the same year, this can mean that convertibles will underperform the equity markets (but not necessarily the bond markets). Holders of convertible securities may realize gains or losses either by selling the securities or by converting them and selling the common stock.

The size of the convertible market is prodigious. In early 1996, the size of the global convertible market was estimated at $376 billion. About one-half of this was represented by Japanese issues, while about $110 billion was represented by U.S. domestic issues. A significant part of the U.S. domestic market is represented by convertible securities offered and sold pursuant to Rule 144A.

• *Debenture and Preferred Stock Provisions*

Convertible debentures are usually subordinated to the issuer's senior debt. They are purchased more for the equity play than for the below-market rate of interest that they bear. Convertible preferred stock generally will rank on a parity with the issuer's other preferred stock.

Convertible debentures usually are long-term instruments with maturities of 20 or 25 years, but the indentures may provide for

mandatory annual sinking fund payments that are designed to retire a specified percentage of the issue prior to maturity.

Convertible securities, whether debentures or preferred
stock, usually are redeemable, in whole or in part, at the option
of the issuer, at declining redemption prices. For example,
where the coupon on the debenture is 6.75%, the indenture
might provide that in the first year the redemption price will be
par plus a premium of 6.75%. The redemption premium might
decline incrementally over the next 10 years, and the debentures might thereafter be redeemable at par. It is also possible
that the indenture will not allow any redemption at the option
of the issuer until the securities have been outstanding for a
stated number of years or until the underlying stock has traded
above a specified price level for a stated period of time. Alternatively, the issuer might agree to a "soft-call" provision that
gives it the right to call the security at any time in the first three
years if the underlying security rises a specified amount above
the conversion price, a lesser amount in the second year and a
lower amount in the third year. This provides flexibility to an
issuer with high-growth expectations while compensating the
investor as if the security had a certain number of years of
"hard-call" protection.

There is no end to the types of bells and whistles that can be
attached to a convertible security. For example, a corporation may
sell securities on a "delayed convertibility" basis where the securities are not immediately convertible and no conversion price is
immediately specified. Rather, the issuer has the right to set the
conversion price and trigger the convertibility feature at a time of
its choosing (but prior to an "outside" date). The conversion price
would normally have both a floor and a ceiling but would otherwise be set as a percentage of the closing price of the underlying
security over a stated number of trading days prior to the time of
determination of the conversion price.

In some cases, the governing instrument will provide that
the corporation may lower the conversion price for a period of
time, thus allowing it to induce conversions without calling the
securities. This amounts to holding a "fire sale" for a limited
period of time, and if a holder does not convert while the sale is

going on, the conversion price of his securities will revert to the original level when the sale is over.

The indenture under which convertible debentures are issued must provide for the possibility that the issuer will be acquired by another corporation. In that event, what will happen to the conversion privilege? The governing indenture should provide, in effect, that, in the case of any consolidation or merger involving the issuer of the common stock into which the securities are convertible as a result of which holders of the issuer's common stock become entitled to receive stock, securities or other property or assets (including cash) with respect to or in exchange for their common stock, or any sale or transfer of all or substantially all of the assets of that issuer, the holders of the convertible debentures then outstanding will be entitled thereafter to convert their debentures only into the kind and amount of securities, cash and other property receivable by the holders of the common stock upon the consummation of the transaction. The provision should operate to place the holders of the convertible debentures in a position where upon conversion they will receive whatever they would have received if they had converted their debentures immediately prior to the consolidation, merger, sale or transfer. A provision of this type may not be appropriate for convertible preferred stock, which will be governed by the merger agreement just like any other equity security.

Care must be taken that the provision is worded so as to operate effectively in the case of a reverse triangular merger where a subsidiary of the acquiring company merges into the target company and the target company maintains its corporate identity. The drafter should avoid the language found in older indentures that excludes "a consolidation or merger in which the company is the continuing corporation."

The indenture should provide specifically for an acquisition transaction where the consideration payable to the holders of the common stock is cash. In the case of a cash acquisition, the holders of the convertible securities should be entitled to convert their securities only into cash. An indenture of Collins Radio Corporation was found to be ambiguous, and the case remanded for a jury determination of the parties' intent, where the applicable provision referred to conversion into "the kind and amount of shares of stock and other securities and property receivable upon such consolidation, merger, sale, conveyance, transfer or disposition" and did not refer specifically to cash.

The result was remedied on rehearing (cash after all is property), but it is best to leave nothing to chance.[1]

A number of issuers have sold convertible exchangeable preferred stock. These securities are exchangeable in whole, but not in part, at the option of the issuer on any dividend payment date beginning on a date one to three years out for the issuer's convertible subordinated debentures bearing an interest rate equal to the dividend rate on the preferred stock. Under Delaware law, the exchange feature should be viewed as a redemption of the preferred stock in exchange for debentures, rather than as a conversion of the preferred stock into debentures. Section 151(b) of the Delaware General Corporation Law provides that stock with a liquidation preference may be redeemable for "cash, property or rights, including securities of the same or another corporation." On the other hand, Section 151(e) only contemplates the conversion of stock into other stock of the same corporation, whether at the option of the corporation or the holder or upon the happening of a specific event.

- *1933 Act Considerations*

Common stock of a corporation issued upon conversion of its debentures or preferred stock is exempt from registration under Section 3(a)(9) of the 1933 Act in that it constitutes a "security exchanged by the issuer with its existing securityholders exclusively" where no remuneration is paid for soliciting the exchange. In other words, when the holder of the debenture or preferred stock surrenders it for conversion into shares of the issuer's common stock, an exchange of securities takes place and the Section 3(a)(9) exemption is applicable. The only instance in which this would not be the case is in the context of an underwritten call where the standby underwriters solicit conversions and a portion of their standby fee is considered to have been paid for making the solicitations.

---

1. *Broad v. Rockwell International Corporation*, 614 F.2d 418 (5th Cir. 1980), *rev'd on rehearing en banc*, 642 F.2d 929 (5th Cir. 1981).

A public offering of convertible securities requires registration of the underlying common stock if, as is customary, the securities are immediately convertible. The legal basis for this is found in the 1933 Act definition of "offer" and "sale." Section 2(3) provides:

> The issue or transfer of a right or privilege, when originally issued or transferred with a security, giving the holder of such security the right to convert such security into another security of the same issuer or of another person, or giving a right to subscribe to another security of the same issuer or of another person, which right cannot be exercised until some future date, shall not be deemed to be an offer or sale of such other security; but the issue or transfer of such other security upon the exercise of such right of conversion or subscription shall be deemed a sale of such other security.

By negative implication, the reverse is true. If a corporation offers debentures or preferred stock immediately convertible into common stock, it is deemed to be offering the underlying common stock at the same time. It should be stressed, however, that the common stock is registered only for purposes of the original distribution of the convertible securities and that registration of the common stock is not a prerequisite for the availability of the Section 3(a)(9) exemption when the securities are converted. The conversion is an exempt transaction. Thus, for example, if the conversion feature were delayed and the securities by their terms were not convertible until six months after issuance, Section 3(a)(9) would apply to conversions even though the common stock had never been registered.

When a registration statement is filed covering convertible securities, it is not possible to specify the number of shares of common stock into which they are convertible, as this will be a function of the conversion price. The conversion price will not be fixed until the securities are ready to be sold (which may be after the effective date if Rule 430A is used). Accordingly, it is customary for the grid on the facing sheet of the registration statement that sets forth the amount of securities to be registered to contain a footnote reference providing for the registration of "such currently indeterminate number of shares of common stock as may be required for issuance upon conversion of the debentures [or preferred stock] being registered hereunder." This will be sufficient to register the requisite number of shares of common stock, and it is not customary to specify the actual number of shares in the pricing amendment or Rule 424 prospectus when the conversion price is finally determined. The actual number of shares into which the securities are originally convertible is not relevant in calculating the registration fee.

Some facing sheets will contain, in addition to the above-quoted footnote language, the words "including such additional shares as may be issuable as a result of adjustments to the conversion price." This additional language does no harm, but it is not required. First of all, the additional shares would be required to be registered only if the anti-dilution provisions of the indenture became operative while the debentures were still being distributed. The underlying common stock is registered only for purposes of the original distribution of the debentures in that, as discussed above, their issuance upon conversion is exempt under Section 3(a)(9). But even if the anti-dilution provisions kicked in before the distribution was completed, the additional shares of common stock would be deemed registered by virtue of Rule 416(a) under the 1933 Act, which provides:

> If a registration statement purports to register securities to be offered pursuant to terms which provide for a change in the amount of securities being offered or issued to prevent dilution resulting from stock splits, stock dividends or similar transactions, such registration statement shall, unless otherwise expressly provided, be deemed to cover the additional securities to be offered or issued in connection with any such provision.

Questions have been raised as to the necessity of registering common stock underlying convertible debentures offered solely outside the United States, in that after the applicable restricted period, the debentures may be acquired by U.S. residents. The issuance of common stock to a U.S. person upon conversion of his debentures should be exempt under Section 3(a)(9) whether or not the common stock was originally registered, but prior to the adoption of Regulation S the resale restrictions for common stock sold abroad were more restrictive than for sales of fixed income securities (see Chapter 9). There was a concern, accordingly, that a sale of debentures with a conversion price not significantly in excess of the current market price might be viewed as a device to avoid the more restrictive provisions. On the other hand, this was not considered a problem if the market price of the common stock were reasonably stable and the conversion price was at least 10% above the market price at the time of sale.

Under Regulation S, the determination of the applicable restricted period for convertible securities is generally that of the underlying security. Harsh consequences can be avoided, however, by delaying the convertibility feature until after the expiration of that period. As the release adopting Regulation S stated by way of illustration, "an offering of convertible debt securities by a foreign issuer with substantial U.S. market interest in its debt and equity securities would fall within the second category of the issuer safe harbor [40 day restricted period] if the debt securities are not convertible for 13 months but would fall within the third issuer safe harbor category [one year] if the debt securities were convertible after 11 months."[2]

At one time, tax considerations required that a foreign finance subsidiary be the primary obligor on convertible debt securities sold abroad. A corporation organized under the laws of the Netherlands Antilles was customarily used for this purpose. The parent would guarantee the obligations, and the securities would be convertible into shares of common stock of the parent. The Section 3(a)(9) exemption was considered unavailable because of the lack of corporate identity between the parent issuer of the common stock and the subsidiary issuer of the debentures. In this type of

---

2. SEC Release No. 33-6863 (April 24, 1990) (text following note 76). For purposes of Regulation S, whether or not there is "substantial U.S. market interest" or "SUSMI" in a convertible security is determined both by reference to the convertible security and the underlying security. In other words, if SUSMI exists in either security, there is SUSMI in the convertible security.

transaction, it was customary to delay the conversion privilege for nine months and to register the underlying common stock on Form S-16 prior to the time that the debentures became convertible. A number of issuers that had been maintaining current registration statements to cover conversions of securities issued by foreign finance subsidiaries have been able to convince the staff of the SEC that they should no longer be required to do so, where a relatively small amount of securities was outstanding.[3]

Liquid Yield Option Notes

A special type of convertible debt instrument devised by Merrill Lynch Capital Markets is the "Liquid Yield Option Note" with the acronym "LYON." LYONs are zero coupon obligations, i.e., they do not bear interest, but rather are issued at a deep discount from their face amount. Each $1,000 principal amount of LYONs is convertible into a specified number of shares of common stock at any time prior to maturity.[4]

Holders of LYONs may require the issuer to repurchase the securities on a specified date (often seven years after issuance) at a price equal to the issue price plus accrued original issue discount to that date. The issuer has the option of paying the purchase price in cash, with shares of its common stock based on the then current market price, or with notes maturing on the same date as the LYONs bearing interest at a rate designed to have them trade at par. The issuer must give the holders of the LYONs notice of the method of payment 20 business days prior to the purchase date. If payment is to be made by the delivery of common stock or notes, when the actual number of shares of common stock or the interest rate on the notes is determined, this information must be published in a newspaper of national circulation. A holder of LYONs

---

3. SEC No-action Letter, *National Can Corporation* (available September 22, 1983); SEC No-action Letter, *Baxter Travenol Laboratories Inc.* (available July 8, 1983); SEC No-action Letter, *American Motors Corporation* (available July 8, 1982).

4. Salomon Brothers underwrote an offering of a similar type of zero coupon convertible debt security for Berkshire Hathaway Inc. (prospectus dated September 21, 1989), but of course it was not called a LYON.

who has elected to have his securities purchased may withdraw his election on or prior to the purchase date.

LYONs are redeemable at the option of the issuer at redemption prices that are equal to their issue price plus accrued original issue discount to the date of redemption. During the first two years that they are outstanding, however, they are not redeemable unless the price of the common stock trades at a specified level for a specified period prior to the mailing of the notice of redemption.

When the holder of a LYON exercises his conversion privilege, he will not receive any cash payment representing accrued OID. The issuer's delivery to the converting holder of the fixed number of shares of common stock into which the LYON is convertible will satisfy its obligation to pay the principal of the LYON, including the accrued OID attributable to the period from the date of issue to the conversion date. Thus, while the conversion rate (i.e., the number of shares of common stock into which each $1,000 principal amount of LYONs are convertible) remains fixed, because the OID is deemed to be paid upon conversion, the economic effect is that the conversion price increases as OID accrues. In other words, for conversion to make economic sense, the market price of the common stock must continuously increase to compensate for the accrual of OID.

Under the Clinton Administration's budget proposals of February 1997, OID and interest deductions on LYONs and similar products would be deferred until payment. "Payment" for this purpose would not include delivery of equity of the issuer or a related party or payment in an amount of cash that was fixed with reference to the value of such equity.

• *1933 Act Registration Issues*

In the case of LYONs, where the repurchase price may be paid with common stock or notes, the practice initially was to have the registration statement cover an indeterminate number of shares and an indeterminate principal amount of notes. Again, registration of these securities was for purposes of the original distribution of the LYONs, and it was not considered necessary to deliver a current prospectus in connection with the put procedures. Because the put is not exercisable until a date certain in the future, an analogy may be made to a delayed conversion feature and an argument constructed that the stock and notes issuable by the corporation to satisfy the put need not be registered in the first instance. The staff of the SEC eventually took the position that the stock and the notes need not be registered, and it became the practice not to register them.

• *1934 Act Issues*

Issuers have frequently obtained from the SEC exemptions under former Rule 10b-6 and Rule 13e-4 (the issuer tender offer rule) as well as no-action positions under Rule 10b-13. Regulatory relief was readily granted.[5]

The problem under Rule 10b-6 arose out of a rather strained reading of the rule. The reasoning was that as a consequence of the issuer's determination to proceed with the LYONs offering and because of the possibility that the issuer might issue common stock or notes pursuant to the repurchase option, it was engaged in a distribution for Rule 10b-6 purposes of each of the LYONs, the common stock and the notes. Further, it was reasoned that the repurchase option constituted a bid by the issuer for the LYONs, a bid that needed an exemption in order to be permissible prior to the termination of the distribution of the LYONs.

Under the Regulation M Release, neither the writing of a put option nor the maintenance of a short put position is deemed to be a continuing bid for the underlying security. This would suggest that the repurchase option should not constitute a bid for the LYONs. If it did, of course, then Rule 102's prohibition on bids during the distribution would apply to the LYONs as well as to the common stock and the notes (since these are "reference securi-

---

5. E.g., SEC No-action Letter, *Maxus Energy Corporation* (available February 9, 1989); SEC No-action Letter, *International Minerals & Chemical Corporation and IMC Fertilizer Group, Inc.* (available November 4, 1988); SEC No-action Letter, *Waste Management, Inc.* (available October 25, 1988); SEC No-action Letter, *Triton Energy Corporation* (available August 29, 1988).

ties"). In those cases where the common stock was eligible for the $1,000,000 ADTV/$150 million public float exception and where the notes were entitled to the investment grade exception, no exemption would be necessary. In other cases, a new exemption or no-action letter would be necessary since Regulation M does not preserve prior exemptions and no-action positions.

The SEC has also taken the view that the offer to purchase LYONs pursuant to the repurchase option constitutes an issuer tender offer pursuant to Rule 13e-4. This rule requires the issuer to publish, send or give to securityholders the information required by certain items of Schedule 13e-4, including the consideration being offered in the tender offer. The exemptive orders permit the commencement of a tender offer pursuant to the repurchase option without stating the number of shares of common stock that persons tendering their LYONs will receive or the interest rate on the notes. In addition, the SEC expressed the view that the terms of the option provisions set forth in the registration statement may constitute a public announcement of a tender offer within the meaning of Rule 10b-13. This rule prohibits a person making a tender offer for an equity security from purchasing that security otherwise than pursuant to the tender offer from the time the offer is publicly announced until it expires. The typical LYON no-action position permits purchases of the subject securities prior to the publication of the number of shares to be issued to satisfy the put or the interest rate on the notes to be issued for that purpose.

In April 1989, the staff of the SEC issued a letter to Shoney's, Inc. in which the relief from Rule 10b-6, Rule 13e-4 and Rule 10b-13 took the form of no-action positions on each of the rules, rather than exemptive relief as to Rule 10b-6 and Rule 13e-4. The staff has rendered informal advice that if a transaction comes within the terms of the Shoney's no-action letter, it is not necessary to seek relief from the SEC, and a number of LYONs deals have been done in reliance upon this advice.

Exchangeable Debentures

A corporation that owns shares of common stock of another publicly owned company may issue debentures exchangeable at a fixed price for all or a portion of those shares. In financial parlance, these are called exchangeable debentures to distinguish them from debentures convertible into the stock of the issuer.

The only difference between an exchangeable debenture and a convertible debenture is that, in the case of the former, holders are entitled to acquire stock of an entity other than the issuer of the debt securities. Otherwise, the legal structure is substantially identical. The shares for which the debentures are exchangeable must be placed in escrow with a depositary bank under an arrangement that will keep them out of reach of the issuer's creditors. But the same anti-dilution provisions apply and the same potential exists for forcing exchanges by calling the debentures for redemption.

The issuance of exchangeable debentures is a less common transaction than the issuance of debentures convertible into stock of the same issuer, but it is an equally effective device for reducing the issuer's cost of borrowing.

This financing vehicle may be used if a corporation has made an investment in the stock of another corporation and wishes to hold it in anticipation of an increase in its market price. While continuing to own the stock, the corporation may use it as a means of raising funds at favorable interest rates. If the investor corporation determines that it would be willing to sell the stock if the price increases to a certain level, then it makes economic sense for it to issue debt securities exchangeable for the stock at a price that would enable it to call the debt securities and force exchanges when the price of the stock reaches the target level.

The transfer of stock to the holder of the debentures upon exercise of the exchange privilege does not come within the provisions of Section 3(a)(9) because the issuer of the debt securities and the issuer of the stock are different entities. The exchange transaction, however, will be exempted under Section 4(1) as a transaction by "any person other than an issuer, underwriter or dealer" unless the common stock is a "restricted security" in the hands of the issuer of the debentures. The Section 4(1) exemption may also not be available if the issuer of the debentures is in a control relationship with the issuer of the common stock, but as will be seen, it may be possible to structure a transaction that will satisfy the 1933 Act even if it cannot be demonstrated to the satisfaction of the SEC that no control relationship exists. If the stock is not a restricted security and a control relationship does not exist, then it is not necessary to register the common stock either in connection with the initial sale of the debentures or in connection with the exchange of the debentures for the underlying shares.

In most cases, exchangeable debentures have been issued in circumstances in which it was not necessary to register the underlying stock. These transactions generally will proceed on the basis of an opinion of counsel to the effect that the underlying shares are not restricted securities and that a control relationship does not exist between the issuer of the debentures and the issuer of the shares.

In 1971, International Paper Company obtained a no-action letter from the SEC permitting it to issue debentures exchangeable for common stock of C.R. Bard, Inc. without registration of the Bard shares, even though it owned 17% of the outstanding Bard common stock.[6] The SEC previously had been unwilling to conclude that International Paper was not in a control relationship with Bard and expressed concerns as to whether International Paper should be deemed a statutory underwriter with respect to its Bard shares in that it had acquired them approximately two and one-half years previously in connection with the acquisition of a company that the staff considered to be in control of Bard.[7] International Paper had no representation on the board of directors of Bard; the family of Harris L. Willets owned more than 19% of the outstanding Bard common stock and was recognized to be in control; and, after a request to do so, Bard had refused to register the common stock underlying the exchangeable debentures. As part of its no-action request, International Paper agreed to relinquish its voting rights to the Bard common stock and to have the escrow agent agree to vote the shares in escrow in proportion to the votes cast by all other shareholders. The registration statement

---

6. SEC No-action Letter, *C.R. Bard, Inc.* (available November 8, 1971).

7. SEC No-action Letters, *C.R. Bard, Inc.* (available June 28, 1971 and October 4, 1971).

covering the International Paper debentures contained information with respect to Bard obtained from filings with the SEC under the 1934 Act. The debentures were not exchangeable for a year after issuance, and it was pointed out to the staff that at the time the debentures could be exchanged for Bard shares, International Paper would have held them for four years.

Assuming that the issuer of the debentures is in a control relationship with the issuer of the underlying shares, registration of the shares would be required in connection with the underwriting of the debentures if the debentures are immediately exchangeable. Registration would not be required for this purpose, however, if the exchange privilege is delayed. The distinction is found in the definition of "offer" and "sale" in Section 2(3) of the 1933 Act. Under this provision the offer and sale of the debentures would not be deemed an offer or sale of the underlying shares if the exchange privilege "cannot be exercised until some future date."

If the debentures are immediately exchangeable for the common stock, their issuance would be deemed an offer of the common stock for or on behalf of a controlling shareholder by the underwriters of the debentures. This would make the underwriters of the debentures underwriters of the common stock, thereby requiring registration of the common stock. Section 2(11) of the 1933 Act defines the term "underwriter" to include any person who offers or sells for an issuer in connection with the distribution of any security, and for purposes of this definition, the term "issuer" includes a person in a control relationship with the issuer. If, however, the debentures are not exchangeable for the common stock until some date in the future, it is clear that the common stock need not be registered to permit the underwriting of the debentures.

If the exchange privilege is delayed, the question then arises whether the common stock need be registered at the time that it is actually issued in exchange for the debentures. A strong argument can be made that the common stock need not be registered to cover an exchange when the delayed exchange privilege becomes effective. The fact that the issuer of the debentures may be in a control relationship with the issuer of the underlying shares is relevant only for purposes of determining whether the underwriters of the debentures are also underwriters of the common stock underlying the debentures. Under the 1933 Act, a controlling person is deemed an issuer only for purposes of defining who is an underwriter. Under the 1933 Act, a controlling person may offer securities directly to the public without registration so long as there is no intermediary involved in the transaction who might be deemed an underwriter. This will be the case when the delayed exchange privilege becomes effective. At that point, no investment banking firm will be involved in the transaction and the issuer will be dealing directly with the public in exchanging the common stock for its debentures. If this is a correct interpretation of the law, then registration of the common stock would not be required even when the debentures become exchangeable.

This analysis has not been tested with the staff of the SEC, and it is not supported by any no-action letters issued in the context of exchangeable debentures or in the analogous context of subsidiary debt convertible into shares of its parent. But if the occasion should arise where there is a substantial question of control and the issuer of the shares underlying the debentures is unwilling to register them, the possibility of a delayed exchange privilege and reliance on the Section 4(1) exemption for the actual exchanges could be the solution to the problem. Here a conference with the staff would be in order, but a no-action request should not be submitted unless there is reasonable assurance that the response will be favorable.

If the relationship between the issuer of the exchangeable debentures and the issuer of the common stock is reasonably cordial, the issuer of the shares may be willing to register them. Of course, if the control relationship really exists, the issuer may be forced to register. This, after all, is the real test of control: the power to compel registration. Registration should not be burdensome if the issuer of the stock is eligible to use Form S-3 for the purpose of the original offering of the exchangeable security as well as for the exchanges. Moreover, for purposes of the instructions to Form S-3, the exchangeable debentures should be viewed as convertible securities, and if the issuer meets the reporting requirements Form S-3 should be available to register securities to be offered upon the exchange of outstanding exchangeable securities issued by an affiliate of the issuer even if the issuer of the common stock does not meet the other tests for the use of Form S-3.

Stock Purchase Warrants

Stock purchase warrants are securities that entitle the holder to purchase from the issuer shares of its common stock at an agreed upon cash price at any time prior to their expiration. Unlike a convertible or exchangeable debenture, where the conversion or exchange privilege is simply one of the terms of the instrument, warrants can be traded as separate securities. One of the drawbacks of warrants is that they require an "evergreen" prospectus that will be delivered to the holder upon the exercise of his warrant.

• *Units of Debt Securities and Warrants*

An issuer can reduce its cost of funds when issuing debt securities by issuing units consisting of debentures and warrants to purchase common stock of the issuer. The warrants will have a limited life (frequently five years), and the exercise price will be fixed at a premium to the market price of the common stock at the time of sale. The purchaser of the debentures will have an equity play not unlike that afforded to a purchaser of convertible securities. The terms of the offering may be such that the warrants may not be separated from the debentures prior to a specified date, or earlier if the managing underwriter determines that a separate trading market will not interfere with the success of the distribution of the units.

Warrants are issued under a warrant agreement with a bank or trust company acting as warrant agent. The warrants should contain anti-dilution provisions similar to those used for convertible securities and should also provide for the possibility of a merger or other acquisition involving the issuer.

When units are offered in reliance on Regulation S, the applicable restricted period for the units is determined by reference to the constituent security that triggers the longest restricted period. If the constituent securities can be separately traded immediately after issuance of the units, however, then separate restricted periods may be applied "to the extent feasible."[8]

• *Warrants Offered with High Yield Bonds*

Warrants also have been sold to purchasers of high yield bonds (usually in connection with a leveraged buyout), not for the purpose of reducing interest costs, but rather to provide an equity incentive to purchase the debt securities. These warrants have been issued at a nominal price and are exercisable at a price far below the real value of the common stock.

Some warrants that have been offered in this context have been exercisable at a nominal consideration or for no consideration at all. For example, warrants to purchase over 47 million shares of common stock of RJR Holdings Corp. offered under a prospectus dated May 12, 1989 through Drexel Burnham Lambert along with high-yield debt securities of RJR Holdings Capital Corp. were sold for a penny per warrant and were exercisable at seven cents per share. Warrants to acquire shares of common stock of Ann Taylor Holdings, Inc. that were offered under a July 14, 1989 prospectus with debt securities of Ann Taylor, Inc. were sold for $1.04 per warrant, but they entitled the holders to acquire shares of common stock for no additional consideration. The prospectus stated, "In determining that no additional consideration would be payable upon the exercise of the Warrants, Holdings and Merrill Lynch considered, among other things, that the provisions of Section 3(a)(9) of the Securities Act should be applicable to the shares of Common Stock exchanged for the Warrants upon exercise and that, accordingly, no registration under the Securities Act would be required."

If warrants have a nominal exercise price or are exercisable for no consideration whatsoever, why not just issue common stock along with the debt securities? A number of issuers have done just that. In January 1990, a registration statement was filed covering senior subordinated debentures of Sullivan Graphics, Inc. and shares of common stock with limited voting rights of its parent, Sullivan Holdings, Inc. The preliminary

---

8. SEC Release No. 33-6863 (April 24, 1990) (text following note 77).

prospectus stated that the shares were convertible into voting common stock on the fifth anniversary of their issuance and prior to that date upon certain events. The financing was designed to provide for the repayment of a bridge loan incurred in connection with a leveraged buyout, and the offering price of the non-voting shares was fixed at the price paid by the original equity investors at the time of the acquisition.

Warrants offered as a sweetener with high yield bonds can prove to be very valuable. They are designed to provide an incentive to the purchasers of the debt securities, but there have been reports that in some cases they have wound up in the hands of persons for whom they were not intended, e.g., fund managers and others who placed the warrants into their personal accounts rather than into the funds that they managed and that had purchased the debt securities. One such fund manager purchased various high-yield securities for investment company accounts and was allowed to invest for her own account in a Drexel Burnham partnership that owned warrants intended to facilitate the sale of the high-yield securities. Her investment of $13,200 grew to a value of $750,000 in less than three years. The manager was convicted of criminal violations of the "anti-kickback" provisions of the Investment Company Act of 1940 and related charges and sentenced to two months in jail.[9]

• *Units of Warrants and Common Stock*

Warrants are also frequently offered in units along with common stock. In this type of offering, both the warrants and the common stock must be registered, as must be the common stock underlying the warrants. Because the exercise of a warrant is a cash transaction and not an exchange (unless the warrant is exercisable for no additional consideration), Section 3(a)(9) does not come into play, and the issuer must deliver to each holder exercising a warrant a prospectus meeting the requirements of Section 10(a) of the 1933 Act. If the issuer is not eligible to use Form S-3 for this purpose, it must maintain a current Form S-1 prospectus (at least while the warrants are in-the-money) until it is eligible to convert to a Form S-3 prospectus.

---

9. *See U.S. v. Ostrander*, 999 F.2d 27 (2d Cir. 1993).

If an issuer of warrants fails to keep its prospectus current, holders of the warrants may find themselves in the position of having the issuer refuse to honor exercises for fear of violating the 1933 Act. The holders of the warrants could not care less whether they are furnished a current prospectus, for their decision to exercise is solely a function of the market price of the underlying common stock in relation to the exercise price of the warrants. One securities trading firm found itself in a difficult position in 1983 when it built a short position in an issuer's common stock matched by a long position in the issuer's warrants. Although the prospectus continued to meet the requirements of Section 10(a) of the 1933 Act, material developments had occurred that had not yet been reflected in the prospectus.

Counsel for the issuer advised his client to refuse to honor the firm's exercise of its warrants until a post-effective amendment was filed and declared effective. This would take some time, and in the meantime the firm was caught in a short squeeze. The firm retained counsel, who was able to persuade counsel for the issuer to relent and permit the exercise of the warrants on the basis of the following legal opinion dated September 29, 1983:

> Trading Firm, Inc. ("TFI") has a 5,231,017 share short position in the Common Stock of XYZ, Inc. (the "Company") and owns Warrants entitling it to purchase 5,200,000 shares of Common Stock of the Company. The Warrants and the shares of Common Stock underlying the Warrants have been registered under the Securities Act of 1933 (the "Securities Act") pursuant to a registration statement which we are advised became effective on December 2, 1982. We are also advised that the Securities and Exchange Commission has not issued any stop order suspending the effectiveness of the registration statement. TFI wishes to exercise its Warrants and intends to use the shares of Common Stock purchased upon such exercise solely for the purpose of covering its short position. You have requested our opinion as to whether the issuance of 5,200,000 shares of Common Stock of the Company to TFI upon exercise of its

Warrants will constitute a violation of the Securities Act in view of the fact that certain developments have occurred which render the prospectus relating to such Common Stock incomplete as of this time. We will assume, for purposes of this opinion, that the prospectus currently omits to state certain material facts necessary in order to make the statements therein not misleading.

Notwithstanding such omission, it is our opinion that, under the circumstances, the issuance of 5,200,000 shares of Common Stock of the Company to TFI will not violate Section 5 of the Securities Act and thus will not subject the Company to liability under Section 12(1) of the Securities Act. Section 5(a) provides that unless a registration statement is in effect as to a security it shall be unlawful to use interstate commerce to sell such security. We have been advised that the registration statement is in effect with respect to the Common Stock to be issued in that the registration statement was declared effective on December 2, 1982, and no stop order has been issued. Section 5(b) makes it unlawful to cause a security to be carried in interstate commerce for the purposes of sale or for delivery after sale unless accompanied or proceeded by a prospectus that meets the requirements of Section 10(a) of the Securities Act. All that is required by Section 10(a) is that the prospectus shall contain the information contained in the registration statement and that if the prospectus is used more than nine months after the effectiveness of the registration statement, the information contained therein shall be as of a date not more than 16 months prior to such use so far as such information is known to the user of the prospectus or can be furnished by such user without unreasonable effort or expense. Section 10(a)(4) provides that there may be omitted from any prospectus any of the information required under Section 10(a) which the Securities and Exchange Commission may by rules or regulations designate as not necessary or appropriate in the public interest or for the protection of investors. We assume that at the time the registration statement became effective the prospectus contained the required information. Although the prospectus is to be used more than nine months after the effective date of the registration statement, the information therein, including the certified financial statements, is as of a date not more than 16 months prior to its use. In this connection we note that the certified financial statements are dated August 31, 1982.

You have asked us to address Section 10(c), which provides that a prospectus shall contain such other information as the Securities and Exchange Commission may by rules or regulations require as being necessary or appropriate in the public interest or for the protection of investors, and specifically Item 512 of Regulation S-K, which requires certain undertakings for Rule 415 offerings. We are advised that these undertakings are contained in the Company's registration statement. The relevant undertaking requires that a post-effective amendment be filed to reflect in a prospectus any facts or events representing a fundamental change in the information set forth in the registration statement. It is our opinion, based on the history of this undertaking and the release relating to its adoption, that it is essentially procedural in nature and is intended to address the issue of when a post-effective amendment, and not merely a prospectus supplement, is required when a prospectus is to be amended. The importance of the undertaking is that if the prospectus is amended to reflect facts or events which represent a fundamental change in the information set forth in the registration statement, then a post-effective amendment is required, but that if a prospectus is amended to reflect facts or events which do not represent a fundamental change, then a prospectus supplement is sufficient. The existence of the undertaking does not affect our conclusion that the prospectus continues to meet the requirements of Section 10(a) notwithstanding that it omits to state material facts necessary to make the statements therein not misleading.

Prospectuses must be updated to reflect material developments because a failure to do so could subject the issuer to liability under Section 12(2) of the Securities Act. Section 12(2) provides that any person who offers or sells a security in interstate commerce by means of a prospectus which omits to state a material fact necessary in order to make the statements therein not misleading shall be liable to the person purchasing the security. If the Company's prospectus does contain a material omission, then the Company would have potential liability to TFI in connection with the sale to it of the Common Stock, but for the fact that TFI has not and will not incur any loss. By creating a short position, TFI has in effect sold the (common Stock to be acquired upon exercise of its Warrants). TFI has assured us that the aggregate price at which the 5,200,000 shares of Common Stock were sold exceeds the aggregate cost of its Warrants plus the aggregate exercise price. Accordingly, the Company cannot be liable to TFI for any damages. The exercise of its Warrants will merely enable TFI to close out its short position, and the information or lack of information in the prospectus is irrelevant to it.

Calls for Redemption to Force Conversions

There are often strong economic incentives for a company to call for redemption of an issue of convertible debentures or preferred stock with a view to forcing the conversion of these securities into common stock.

By way of illustration, assume that a company has outstanding 2.5 million shares of common stock and 500,000 shares of convertible preferred stock. Each share of preferred stock is convertible into .6 of a share of common stock, and the preferred stock is redeemable at the option of the company at $20 per share plus accrued dividends. The annual cash dividend currently paid on the common stock is $.80 per share, and the annual preferential dividend on the preferred stock is $1 per share. If all outstanding preferred shares were converted, the annual dividend requirement for the 300,000 additional common shares issuable upon conversion would be only $240,000, as compared to $500,000 for the existing preferred stock. The market price of the common stock is $40, and the preferred stock is trading at $25. Under these circumstances, the company might well consider calling its preferred stock for redemption with a view to forcing conversions into common stock.

The success of the call will depend upon substantially all of the holders of the convertible securities electing to convert, rather than allowing their shares to be redeemed. Rationally, this should occur if immediately prior to the expiration of the conversion privilege the market value of .6 of a share of common stock exceeds the redemption price of a share of preferred stock plus accrued dividends. On the other hand, there are sometimes delays in receiving notices that are initially received by The Depository Trust Company as registered holder of the securities, re-transmitted to one or possibly more layers of participating broker-dealers or banks and then re-transmitted in turn to the actual holder. Finally, many holders are "sleepers" who neglect to take any action even after receiving timely notice.[10] Some broker-dealers will take action on behalf of a "sleeper" client to convert the client's securities if it is clearly in the client's interest to do so.

Assuming that the relevant charter provision requires a 30-day notice of redemption, that the conversion privilege terminates at the close of business on the business day next preceding the redemption date, and that once the call is made it cannot be rescinded, then there will be a market risk for at

---

10. If convertible preferred stock or registered convertible debentures are called, a notice of redemption must be mailed to each holder of record on the date of the call. It is customary and advisable also to mail the notice to each transferee of record during the redemption period. In addition, the notice usually will be published in newspapers in major financial centers and in cities where there is a geographical concentration of holders of the called securities.

Although coupon debentures in bearer form have not been issued in the United States for many years, some older issues still may be outstanding. If such an issue is called, the company must follow the requirements of the indenture as to publication of notice. Consideration should be given to more extensive publication if necessary to provide reasonable notice. *See Van Gemert v. Boeing Co.*, 520 F.2d 1373 (2d Cir.), *cert. denied* 423 U.S. 947 (1975); *Van Gemert v. Boeing Co.*, 553 F.2d 812 (2d Cir. 1977). *See also* A.B. Miller, *How to Call Your Convertibles*, Harv. Bus. Rev., May-June 1971, at 66.

least 29 days. If there should be a substantial market decline during the redemption period, so that the market value of .6 of a share of common stock falls below the $20 redemption price of a share of preferred stock, plus accrued dividends (assumed to be $.10 per share), it is possible that none of the called securities will be converted, and the company could find itself in the position of being required to make a cash outlay of $10,050,000, which was not the point of the call. In this example, so long as the market price of a share of common stock (trading at $40 when the call was made) does not fall below $33.50, holders of preferred stock, upon conversion, would receive common stock having a market value greater than the cash that would be received upon redemption. In general, conversion would be advantageous if the common stock does not fall below that price.[11]

If, when the call is made, the spread between the conversion price and the market price of the common stock is sufficiently great that the risk of an unsuccessful call is minimal, the company might be willing to assume the risk of a market decline. But in a more marginal case, as in the above example, or in a period of uncertain market conditions, the company might look to its investment bankers to form a syndicate of standby purchasers to underwrite the risk.

• *Standby Arrangements*

In the case of an underwritten call, the investment banking firms acting as standby purchasers will agree to purchase any convertible securities properly tendered to them prior to the expiration of the conversion privilege at a price slightly in excess of the redemption price plus accrued dividends and to surrender the purchased convertible securities for conversion. In the above example, where the redemption price of a share of preferred stock is $20, plus accrued dividends of $.10 per share,

---

11. In individual cases, tax considerations may be an added factor. Conversion will not result in taxable gain or loss. Gain or loss will be recognized for Federal income tax purposes upon redemption or sale of the convertible securities.

the standby purchasers might agree to purchase preferred stock tendered to them at $20.25 per share.

The effect of such an agreement is that, assuming adequate communication with the holders of the called securities apprising them of the available alternatives, the risk of a market decline is shifted from the company to the standby purchasers. If the price of the common stock should decline during the redemption period to a point at which a holder of preferred stock would find it in his best interests not to convert, it would still be advantageous for him to tender his preferred stock to the standby purchasers and receive the tender price of $20.25, rather than $20.10, the redemption price plus accrued dividends. As the standby purchasers are committed to surrender for conversion any preferred stock purchased by them, the company should be effectively protected against the risk of having to make a substantial cash outlay. The risk that the standby purchasers run is that they will realize less on the resale of the common stock acquired upon conversion than the amount paid by them for the preferred stock purchased from tendering shareholders.

For assuming this risk, the standby purchasers will be paid a fee by the company. The amount of the fee will depend in part upon the degree of risk assumed, which in turn will depend upon the spread between the market price of the common stock and the effective conversion price. The usual arrangement is for the standby purchasers to receive a standby fee based on a percentage of their maximum dollar commitment plus a take-up fee for shares of common stock actually acquired upon conversion. The standby fee might be in the area of 0.5% to 1% or more of the amount that would be expended by the standby purchasers if all outstanding convertible securities were tendered for purchase. In the above example, the standby fee might be $.27 for each share of common stock issuable upon conversion of all shares of preferred stock outstanding on the date of the call.

Where there is also a take-up fee, and this is not always the case, it is customary for this fee to be payable only if more than 5% of the total number of shares of common stock issuable upon conversion is acquired by the standby purchasers. If more than 50% is acquired, then the take-up fee, which, under the above facts might be in the area of $1.20 per share, might either be payable in respect of all shares of common stock acquired or only in respect of the excess over 5%. Under some standby agreements, if the number of shares of common stock acquired exceeds 10% of the number issuable upon conversion, the take-up fee is increased. Some standby agreements exclude in computing both the standby fee and the take-up fee any convertible securities owned beneficially by the standby purchasers on the date of the call.

• *1933 Act Considerations*

As previously discussed, the issuance of common stock upon conversion of publicly owned convertible debentures or preferred stock is ordinarily exempt from registration under Section 3(a)(9). Prior to a 1978 amendment to Form S-16 (the short-form predecessor of Form S-3) which made registration economical for underwritten calls, it had been the universal practice to have the standby purchasers agree that they would not solicit conversions in order to assure that the fees paid to them would not destroy the Section 3(a)(9) exemption.

Historically, the more difficult question had been the availability of an exemption from registration for resales of common stock issued to the standby purchasers upon conversion of the convertible securities purchased by them. In this connection, it should be noted that the SEC has long taken the position that Section 3(a)(9) of the 1933 Act is a transaction exemption rather than an exemption for the securities issued upon conversion. Accordingly, a seller of securities issued upon conversion of an outstanding security (or in any other transaction exempted by Section 3(a)(9)) must find his own exemption under Section 4 or otherwise. The question then is whether the standby purchasers would be deemed to be "underwriters" as defined in Section 2(11) of the 1933 Act in reselling to the public the stock acquired by them upon conversion. This in turn would depend upon whether their sales would constitute a "distribution."

Prior to the fall of 1972, it had been the practice to seek a no-action letter from the SEC in connection with calls for redemption with standby arrangements to provide some comfort to the standby purchasers in reselling without registration shares acquired upon conversion.

The approach that was sometimes taken in these no-action requests was to point out that, because of the difference between the market price of the common stock and the conversion price, it was unlikely that a substantial number of shares would be acquired and resold by the standby purchasers and that, under these circumstances, registration and the delivery of a prospectus should not be required in connection with resales. The difficulty with a no-action letter based on such an assumption is that its effect would be questionable if there should be a substantial market decline and the standby purchasers in fact acquired a large number of shares upon conversion. Nevertheless, until 1972, investment bankers were willing to take this risk and to proceed with redemption standbys without registration, primarily because their experience over the years indicated that the likelihood of substantial acquisitions and resales was remote. Moreover, and perhaps more important, the alternative of preparing a registration statement on Form S-1 or Form S-7 was too burdensome and costly to be justified in the case of a redemption standby.

When it became clear that standby purchasers could be considered selling securityholders for purposes of Form S-16[12] (and, subsequently, for purposes of Form S-3), it became the practice to register the underlying securities to cover resales by the standby purchasers.

Originally, in the context of an underwritten call, a Form S-16 registration statement could be used only to cover resales by the standby purchasers, and not the issuance of stock upon conversion of the outstanding convertible securities. The issuance of stock upon conversion was required to be made under the Section 3(a)(9) exemption, and thus there could be no solicitation of conversions by the standby purchasers.

Eventually, it became possible to use Form S-16 and then Form S-3 to register shares for the purpose of solicited conversions. The prospectus included in the registration statement is mailed to holders of the convertible securities to cover the

---

12. SEC No-action Letter, *Salomon Brothers* (available September 28, 1972).

shares issued upon conversion as well as being used to cover resales by the standby purchasers. Where this procedure is followed, the standby purchasers should be permitted to solicit conversions while they stand ready to purchase any convertible securities tendered to them.[13]

When issuers began to register the common stock issuable upon conversion of securities called for redemption, there was some concern that the customary form of redemption notice published in the financial press might be considered an illegal prospectus in that it did not conform strictly to Rule 134 under the 1933 Act. To avoid this problem, some issuers published their full Form S-16 prospectus in lieu of an abbreviated notice of redemption. In effect, the prospectus was the notice of redemption, and the notice of redemption was the prospectus. There is nothing to say that a prospectus must be in booklet form, and the prospectus filed as part of the Form S-16 registration statement was identical to the newspaper advertisement that would appear as soon as the registration statement became effective. It was all very neat and creative, but the practice never caught on; and, notwithstanding that shares are registered for the purpose of conversions, traditional notices of redemption continue to be published with no ill effects under the 1933 Act.[14]

---

13. In an administrative proceeding involving Blyth, Eastman Dillon & Co. Inc., SEC Release Nos. 34-10565 and 34-10566 (December 19, 1973), the firm and two of its registered representatives were censured by the SEC for alleged misuse of a shareholder list obtained in connection with a redemption standby. The SEC charged that the registered representatives improperly used the list to generate leads for new accounts and commission business, and in making calls to shareholders on the list, ostensibly to assist them in connection with the redemption, engaged in improper selling practices in recommending the purchase of securities. The questions raised in this proceeding as to the proper use of shareholder lists by investment bankers are in no way peculiar to redemption standbys. The same issues are involved if a shareholder list is furnished to an investment banker in connection with a tender offer, an exchange offer or a merger.

14. It should be noted that a redemption pursuant to the terms of the instrument creating or governing the securities being redeemed is not sub-

• *Lay-Offs*

It is customary for standby agreements to provide that the standby purchasers may (but are under no obligation to) purchase convertible securities in addition to those purchased pursuant to tenders in such amounts and at such prices as the purchasers may deem advisable and that all convertible securities so purchased will be converted into common stock.

The take-up fee usually will be payable in respect of any common stock acquired upon conversion of convertible securities so purchased, as well as those purchased pursuant to tenders. As long as the price of the common stock holds firm, there is little reason for the standby purchasers to buy convertible securities in the open market. But if weakness develops in the price of the common stock, the standby purchasers might wish to make short sales of the common stock, purchase convertible securities in the open market and use the shares acquired upon conversion of those securities to deliver against their short sales. Such transactions during the redemption period would reduce the purchasers' risk in a manner similar to Shields Plan transactions effected in connection with underwritten rights offerings.[15]

Prior to the adoption of Regulation M, it was necessary to deal with the fact that Rule 10b-6 prohibited purchases of convertible securities in the open market because these represented "rights to purchase" the common stock being distributed. For many years, the SEC granted exemptions that permitted such purchases so long as they were effected in accordance with Rule 10b-8, which applied to rights offerings. The need for exemptions disappeared in 1983, when Rule 10b-8 was amended to make it expressly applicable to convertible securities called for redemption pursuant to a standby underwriting agreement.[16] Of course, the lengthy history of SEC regulation of "lay-off" activities in connection with rights offerings and standby under-

---

ject to the SEC's going private rule, Rule 13e-3, by virtue of the exception in subsection (g)(4). A similar exception from Rule 13e-4, the issuer tender offer rule, is provided by subsection (h)(1) thereof.

15. *See* Chapter 13.

16. SEC Release No. 34-19565 (March 4, 1983).

writings came to an end in late 1996 when the SEC adopted Rules 101 and 102, neither of which applies to "rights to purchase" a covered security.

Expiring Warrants

Prior to the adoption of Regulation M, the SEC staff was willing to grant exemptions under Rule 10b-6 to permit transactions subject to Rule 10b-8 restrictions designed to facilitate the exercise of warrants that were about to expire.

In 1970, American Telephone and Telegraph Company made a rights offering of debentures with warrants. These warrants were to expire on May 15, 1975. In March 1975, there were outstanding warrants to purchase over 31 million shares of common stock at a price of $52 per share. At that time, the AT&T common stock was trading at a price slightly below the exercise price. Over $1.5 billion was at stake. There were approximately 570,000 record holders of warrants. Morgan Stanley & Co. Incorporated sought from the SEC an exemption under Rule 10b-6 that would permit it to form a dealer group to solicit the exercise of warrants by holders and at the same time to sell common stock issuable upon the exercise of warrants and to purchase warrants in the open market in order to exercise them. Participating dealers were to be paid a soliciting dealers' fee for obtaining the exercise of warrants and were to be allowed a selling commission for the sale of shares issued upon the exercise of warrants. Lay-offs of shares and purchases of warrants were to be made in accordance with the provisions of Rule 10b-8. Offers and sales of AT&T shares would be covered by a current prospectus. Under this particular arrangement, profits and losses resulting from the lay-offs, purchases of warrants and any stabilizing transactions would be borne by AT&T. Therefore, for Morgan Stanley, it was a riskless transaction; its job solely was to get the warrants exercised. The SEC granted an exemption under Rule 10b-6 to permit the contemplated arrangements.[17] Of course, there would be no need

---

17. SEC No-action Letter, *American Telephone and Telegraph Company* (available May 15, 1975).

under Regulation M to obtain such an exemption since neither Rule 101 nor Rule 102 would apply to purchases of "rights to purchase," such as warrants.

Just as an issuer of convertible securities may have a fire sale by reducing the conversion price for a period of time in order to encourage conversions, a company that has outstanding warrants that are about to expire may sweeten the terms in an effort to induce holders to exercise. This might be called more aptly a going out of business sale.

McDermott International, Inc. did just this in the case of its warrants expiring on April 2, 1990. In a notice published in *The Wall Street Journal* addressed to the holders of its warrants, the company announced that its board of directors had decided to reduce the exercise price per share by increasing the number of shares that the holders are entitled to purchase with respect to their warrants. The notice stated that the increase would take effect on March 2, 1990 and would remain in place until the warrants expired. The exercise price would remain at $25 per warrant, but each warrant would entitle a holder to purchase 1.075 shares, rather than a single share, an increase of .075 shares and an effective reduction in the per share exercise price of approximately $1.75. To effect this reduction, it was necessary for the company to file a registration statement covering the additional shares issuable upon the exercise of the warrants.

Chapter 13

TRANSACTIONS WITH SECURITYHOLDERS: STOCK REPURCHASES, DEBT RESTRUCTURINGS AND RIGHTS OFFERINGS

This chapter examines transactions in which corporations deal directly with their own securityholders for the purpose of changing their capital structure or to raise additional funds.

A corporation may wish to reduce the amount of its outstanding common stock. This can be done through open market purchases, privately negotiated purchases or by means of a tender offer. A corporation's management or an affiliate may decide to take it private. A tender offer or statutory merger would be the general means by which such a buyout (leveraged or otherwise) would be accomplished. A corporation may decide that it is advantageous to eliminate high coupon debt securities or to reduce the amount of debt outstanding. It may be possible to do so simply by calling all or a portion of the securities for redemption. If this is not permitted under the governing indenture, purchases in the open market may be the answer, at least if the securities are not widely held. If there is widespread ownership and the corporation wishes to retire all or most of the issue, a cash tender offer may be the best approach. If the corporation does not have sufficient funds on hand or wishes to preserve its cash, it may choose to offer a new debt security or preferred stock, or a package of debt and equity securities, in exchange for the outstanding debt security that it wishes to eliminate. An exchange offer or cash tender offer may be coupled with a consent solicitation designed to eliminate burdensome covenants, or a consent solicitation may be made independently of a debt restructuring. In rare cases, a corporation may decide to increase its capital by means of a rights offering, or, as it is also called, a subscription offering, in which it offers additional shares of common or preferred stock, or in some cases convertible securities, directly to its existing stockholders, rather than to the general public through underwriters.

Stock Repurchases

During the 1980s and into the 1990s, public companies repurchased their own common stock in record amounts. Some went private, deciding that public ownership and the pressure to increase performance in each quarter stood in the way of long-term growth. Takeover fears were a factor during a portion of this period. Companies that were flush with cash were considered prime targets for corporate raiders, so cash was used in stock acquisition programs ostensibly to increase stockholder value and also to make the company less vulnerable to attack.

• *Corporate Law Considerations*

State law must be examined before a corporation embarks on a stock repurchase program. For example, Section 160 of the Delaware General Corporation Law provides that a corporation may purchase its own shares except when its capital is impaired or when the purchase would result in an impairment of capital. When purchased, they become treasury shares unless retired and restored to the status of authorized and unissued shares pursuant to Section 243. Treasury stock cannot be voted and cannot be counted in computing the number of shares necessary for a quorum.

Indentures and loan agreements must be reviewed to assure that the proposed repurchase of stock will not violate any financial covenants. The usual covenant restricting the payment of dividends restricts stock repurchases as well.

Stock repurchases may be made for any proper corporate purpose, and the courts will not second-guess the business judgment of the board. Press releases announcing stock repurchase programs frequently state that the shares being acquired will be used for stock options or acquisitions.[1] Such a statement makes little sense inasmuch as authorized but unissued shares are available for this purpose. What really is being said is that shares are being repurchased so that shares can be issued under stock options or for acquisitions without diluting earnings per share.

One company announced that it was making a tender offer to partially offset the number of shares that would otherwise be outstanding on a fully diluted basis assuming conversion of a new class of preferred stock proposed to be issued to an ESOP. Most amusing are the press releases that state that the shares are being acquired because, given the current market price of the shares, their purchase "is an attractive investment in comparison to alternative investment opportunities." A reduction of a company's capital base hardly can be viewed as an "investment." Perhaps the most straightforward reason that can be given in the usual case is that the board considers the purchase to be "a prudent use of the company's cash balances and debt capacity" while at the same time keeping the stockholders happy.

• *Purchases in the Open Market*

Purchases of common stock from time to time in the open market have an advantage over a tender offer in that they do not require the corporation to offer a premium over the current market price. The purchases are effected on an exchange or in the over-the-counter market at prevailing market prices.

These transactions raise a number of regulatory issues. First, the purchases must be made in such a way that the acquisition program does not constitute a tender offer under federal and state securities laws. The purchases must not be manipulative. Moreover, care must be taken to assure that no purchases are made at a time when the corporation is aware of material

---

1. A corporation should obtain accounting advice before undertaking a stock repurchase program if there is any possibility that it may wish to acquire another company in a transaction that it wishes to account for on a "pooling of interests" basis.

facts that could have a favorable impact on the price of its stock that have not been disclosed to the public. Most of the major brokerage firms have trading desks that specialize in stock repurchase programs. To assure that a program is conducted properly in accordance with all applicable regulations, it is advisable to call upon a specialist to handle the purchases.

• • *Tender Offer Considerations.* If a corporation makes a tender offer for its shares, it must comply with the applicable tender offer rules. Open market purchases, being unstructured, by their very nature cannot conform to the requirements relating to the conduct of tender offers. A stock repurchase program, however, may take on the appearance of a tender offer, and care should be taken to assure that it is not actually a tender offer. For the most part, these programs have been conducted in a manner that does not raise concerns under the tender offer rules.

The 1934 Act does not define the term "tender offer." Attempts by the courts and the SEC to come up with an acceptable definition have been unsuccessful. Consequently, subjective considerations will be taken into account in determining whether or not a tender offer has been made. The SEC has suggested that the courts look to the following eight factors in determining the existence of a tender offer: whether there is an active and widespread solicitation of public securityholders; whether the solicitation is made for a substantial percentage of the issuer's securities; whether the offer is made at a premium over the prevailing market price; whether the terms of the offer are firm rather than negotiable; whether the offer is contingent upon the tender of a fixed minimum number and perhaps subject to the ceiling of a fixed maximum number of securities to be purchased; whether the offer is open for only a limited period of time; whether the offerees are subjected to pressure to sell; and whether public announcements of a purchasing program precede or accompany a rapid accumulation of large amounts of the target company's securities.

The SEC's eight-factor test was first adopted by a court in 1979 in *Wellman v. Dickinson.*[2] The eight factors also were dis-

---

2. 475 F. Supp. 783 (S.D.N.Y. 1979), *aff'd*, 682 F.2d 355 (2d Cir. 1982), *cert. denied*, 460 U.S. 1069 (1985).

cussed in *SEC v. Carter Hawley Hale Stores, Inc.*[3] There Carter Hawley Hale, without complying with the rules governing issuer tender offers, repurchased over 50% of its outstanding common stock in the open market in response to a tender offer by The Limited. The Court of Appeals evaluated the SEC's eight-factor test and found that the repurchase program did not constitute a tender offer, despite the existence of one of the eight factors (i.e., a large percentage of stock was accumulated following a public announcement). It should be noted that the district court arrived at the same conclusion despite its finding that two of the eight factors were present (i.e., pressure on stockholders to sell and a large accumulation of stock following a public announcement). While it is clear that not all of the eight factors must be present for there to be a tender offer, it remains unclear precisely how many of the factors must be present for a purchase program to constitute a tender offer.

In *Crane Co. v. Harsco Corp.*,[4] it was held that a target company's purchase of its own stock from arbitragers in an attempt to block a tender offer was not itself a tender offer by the target company to the arbitragers. The payment of a premium for the shares was the only one of the eight factors present, and this, standing alone, was not sufficient to make the transaction a tender offer.

In *Hanson Trust PLC v. SCM Corp.*,[5] the court held that there was no tender offer where Hanson Trust purchased 25% of the outstanding common stock of SCM Corporation in open market and privately negotiated transactions immediately after Hanson terminated its tender offer for a large percentage of SCM's stock. The court in *Hanson* rejected the SEC's eight-factor test. Instead, its analysis turned on the fact that the sellers of SCM stock to Hanson were knowledgeable, sophisticated investors selling, for the most part, in private transactions and thus not in need of the protection afforded by the tender offer rules.

The fundamental concern of the courts has been to prevent offers that put pressure on stockholders leading them to make

---

3. 760 F.2d 945 (9th Cir. 1985).
4. 511 F. Supp. 294 (D.C. Del. 1981).
5. 774 F.2d 47 (2d. Cir. 1985).

uninformed, ill-considered decisions to sell. If a stock repurchase program is limited to transactions on an exchange or in the over-the-counter dealer market, there is little risk that it will be held to constitute a tender offer, even if a large amount of stock is accumulated in a short period of time.

• • *Rule 10b-18.* The increased demand for an issuer's stock created by a stock repurchase program may result in an increase in the market price. Indeed, this may be an unspoken reason for instituting such a program. There is nothing wrong with issuer purchases that have the effect of shoring up the price of the stock as long as the purchases are not manipulative. At one time, the SEC was rather concerned over issuer repurchases. The sense was that the temptations to manipulate were there, and the SEC should keep up its guard.

A device once used by the SEC to maintain control over stock repurchases had its basis in a rather strained interpretation of former Rule 10b-6. The SEC took the position that if a company had an issue of convertible securities outstanding, it was engaged in a continuous distribution of the underlying stock for purposes of former Rule 10b-6, at least if the convertibles were in-the-money. Thus, if the company wished to purchase its own stock, it would have to obtain an exemptive order. These orders were readily granted, but they were granted subject to a set of standard conditions designed to assure that the purchases did not unduly affect the price of the stock.

In 1982, former Rule 10b-6 was amended to provide that it did not apply to purchases of a security solely because the issuer or a subsidiary had outstanding securities convertible into or exchangeable for that security. At the same time, the SEC adopted Rule 10b-18, which codified the standard conditions and provided all issuers with a safe harbor in which to conduct stock repurchase programs without fear of being accused of manipulation.[6]

Rule 10b-18 specifies the conditions under which an issuer's or an affiliated purchaser's bids for, or purchases of, the issuer's common stock will not be deemed to violate Section 9(a)(2) of the 1934 Act (see Chapter 4) or Rule 10b-5 solely by

---

6. SEC Release No. 34-19244 (November 17, 1982).

reason of the time or price at which the bids or purchases are made or the amount of the bids or purchases or the number of brokers or dealers used by the issuer. The issuer must effect all purchases from or through only one broker on any single day or with only one dealer on a single day. The purchase may not constitute the opening transaction in the stock nor may it be effected during the one-half hour period before the close.

For a listed stock or one as to which last sale information is reported in the consolidated system, the purchase price may not be higher than the published bid that is the highest current independent published bid or the last reported independent sale price, whichever is higher. With respect to unlisted stocks as to which quotations are not reported in the consolidated system but are reported in the automated quotation system operated by the NASD, the purchase price may not exceed the lowest current independent offer quotation reported in Level 2 of NASDAQ. As for other stocks, it may not exceed the lowest independent offer quotation determined on the basis of reasonable inquiry.

There are volume limitations as well. The number of shares purchased on any day, other than block purchases, may not exceed the number of round lots that is closest to 25% of the average daily trading volume in the four calendar weeks preceding the week in which the purchases are made. The term "block" means a quantity of stock that either has a purchase price of $200,000 or more, is at least 5,000 shares and has a purchase price of at least $50,000, or is at least 20 round lots and totals 150% or more of the average daily trading for the preceding four weeks. A block does not include any amount that a dealer has accumulated as principal for resale to an issuer if the issuer has reason to know that it was accumulated for this purpose. Nor does it include an amount of stock that the issuer has reason to believe was sold short by the dealer.

Purchases made for an employee benefit plan or stock ownership plan by a trustee or other person independent of the issuer are not covered by Rule 10b-18. An independent agent can be presumed to be interested solely in getting the best price for the plan and to have no incentive to drive up the price of the stock. The agent will be deemed to be independent of the issuer if it is not an affiliate of the issuer and neither the issuer nor any affiliate of the issuer exercises any direct or indirect control or influence over the times when, or the prices at which, the agent may purchase the shares, the amounts to be purchased, or the selection of a broker other than the agent itself. The issuer will not be deemed to have such control or influence solely because it revises not more than once in any three-month period the basis for determining the amount of its contributions to the plan, or the basis for determining the frequency of its allocations to the plan, or any formula specified in the plan that determines the amount of shares to be purchased by the agent.

Like any safe harbor rule, it is not possible to "violate" Rule 10b-18. The only consequence of a bid or purchase outside the limitations of the rule is that the safe harbor is unavailable in the event of an allegation that the bid or purchase violated Section 9(a)(2) of the 1934 Act or Rule 10b-5. Rule 10b-18 even expressly provides that non-conforming bids and purchases do not create a presumption that there was such a violation. Nevertheless, many issuers try to conform their stock repurchases to the limitations of the rule and require broker-dealers acting on their behalf to do the same.

As noted above, securities that a dealer sells short to the issuer are not considered "blocks" for purposes of the exclusion in Rule 10b-18 from that rule's volume restrictions. Some broker-dealers are willing to offer blocks to the issuer on a short basis. One of the advantages of this technique is that it gives the issuer the assurance of quickly purchasing a significant amount of stock. The issuer may be willing to make the purchase outside the limitations of Rule 10b-18 because of the unlikelihood that a block trade, especially one executed outside normal trading hours, could in and of itself constitute manipulation. Practice is not uniform as to whether the broker-dealer conforms its covering transactions to Rule 10b-18, particularly where the price paid by the issuer for the stock sold short is a function of the price eventually paid by the broker-dealer in its covering transactions. Practice is also not uniform as to whether the broker-dealer considers itself free to continue covering its short during periods where the issuer, because of unannounced material information, would consider itself disabled from making direct repurchases.

In connection with the adoption of Rule 102 as part of Regulation M in 1996 (see Chapter 4), the SEC amended Rule 10b-18 to prevent an issuer or affiliated purchaser from relying on the safe harbor for purchases effected during the applicable Rule 102 restricted period when the issuer or affiliated purchaser is distributing (within the meaning of Regulation M) the issuer's common stock or any other security for which the common stock is a reference security. Accordingly, such purchases by the issuer or an affiliated purchaser are not protected by Rule 10b-18 even if they are entitled to one of the exceptions to Rule 102 (e.g., exception 6 for unsolicited purchases). This does not make such purchases illegal, of course, but the underwriters are likely to be understandably suspicious of such purchases just prior to pricing. Moreover, if an underwriter's price-influencing activity can be illegal (see the discussion in Chapter 4 of the C.O.M.B. incident), why not similar activity by an issuer or an affiliated purchaser?

In the Regulation M Release, the SEC stated that it planned a comprehensive review of Rule 10b-18 "in the near future."

• *Cash Tender Offers*

If a corporation wishes to acquire a sufficiently large block of its own or another company's stock, a cash tender offer may be the best means of accomplishing its objective. In this connection, it is important to obtain the advice of an experienced investment banker. If all of the outstanding stock of another company is to be purchased, a tender offer may be the only way to do the deal. In the usual case, this will involve the formation of a new company to make the offer and to effect the merger that will be used to squeeze out those stockholders who fail to tender. Tender offers can take several forms, and they are strictly regulated under the 1934 Act.

• • *Tender Offer Mechanics.* A tender offer usually is commenced with a mailing of the offer to stockholders and the publication of a summary advertisement of the offer in *The Wall Street Journal.* The offer will specify the maximum number of shares that the maker of the offer will accept for purchase and the period of time that the offer will remain open. The offer may be made at a fixed price representing, in most cases, a premium over the current market price.

A corporation offering to purchase a large number of its own shares may offer to do so at a price determined through a modified "Dutch auction" process.[7] In a modified Dutch auction tender offer, the offeror fixes the number of shares it will purchase and sets a range of prices at which holders may tender their shares. The purchase price will be the highest price that will allow the corporation to buy all of the shares for which it has solicited tenders or such smaller number of shares as are actually tendered. In effect, the market tells the corporation what the price should be, rather than the corporation telling the market. This may increase the chance that the offer will be successful.

In a Dutch auction, the price band usually is relatively narrow. In addition, the SEC requires an offeror to state a reasonable price range for the offer, which the SEC views as no more than 15% of the minimum price. Alternatively, if the corporation's current stock price falls within the range of prices, the reasonable range is determined on the basis of the current market price as the minimum price. For example, Magellan Health Services, Inc. offered on August 15, 1996 to purchase approximately 1.9 million of its shares (subsequently increased to 3.3 million shares) for a price not greater than $18.50 and not less than $16.50 per share. The band in a 24 million share offer by Reebok International Ltd. in the same year was $36 and $30.

A corporation making a tender offer frequently will retain a securities firm to act as "dealer-manager" to assist it in soliciting tenders. During the early to mid-1980s, it was customary to provide that any dealer through whom shares were tendered would be entitled to a fee for each share tendered through it. Letters of trans-

---

7. Traditionally, the staff of the SEC has not permitted Dutch auction procedures for tender offers by third parties. It has permitted these procedures, however, in a tender offer by a company's ESOP. SEC No-action Letter, *Kettle Restaurants, Inc. Employee Stock Ownership Plan and Kettle Restaurants, Inc.* (available February 18, 1989).

mittal contained a space in which tendering stockholders could designate the dealer entitled to the fee. The payment of fees to soliciting dealers fell into disuse during the late 1980s and early 1990s but has more recently been used again as a means of increasing the chances of success of the tender offer without having to pay a higher premium. Currently, the SEC staff's unwritten policy is that a broker-dealer may not receive fees as a soliciting dealer for shares that it tenders for its own account. The staff position is that allowing the broker-dealer to receive a fee would violate the "all holders" and "best price" requirements discussed below.

It is also important for the company to hire an information agent. Firms such as Georgeson & Co. and D.F. King & Co., Inc., which began as proxy solicitors, coordinate the distribution of tender offer materials to brokers, follow up to assure that the materials are forwarded to beneficial owners, and stand ready to answer questions from stockholders.

• • *Transferable Share Repurchase Rights.* One way to effect an issuer tender offer is to issue to stockholders transferable rights to sell shares to the company. In effect, this is a rights offering in reverse. It allows stockholders to realize value even if they wish to hold on to their shares. On May 31, 1989, Vista Chemical Company announced that, for the purpose of purchasing up to one-third of its outstanding shares of common stock, it was issuing to stockholders of record on May 30, 1989, one transferable share repurchase right for each three shares held on the record date. Each repurchase right entitled the holder to sell to the company one share of common stock at a price of $70. The offer was not conditioned upon the tender of a minimum number of shares, but it was subject to certain other conditions, including financing. All shares tendered pursuant to the exercise of repurchase rights would be purchased assuming the conditions were met. As the number of shares that could be tendered was limited in the first place, there was no need to provide for proration.

The company applied to have the repurchase rights listed on the NYSE. To accommodate holders of fewer than 100 repurchase rights, the company made arrangements for a bank acting as its "aggregation agent" to group odd lots delivered to it into blocks of 100 and to sell them on a daily basis during the offer. This was designed to save stockholders the disproportionately high brokerage commissions involved in selling odd lots, but did involve a fee payable by stockholders to the aggregation agent.

• • *Regulation of Issuer Tender Offers.* Tender offers in general and related matters are regulated by the SEC pursuant to authority granted under Sections 13(d), 13(e), 14(d), 14(e), and 14(f) of the 1934 Act. These sections, which were enacted in 1968, are known as the Williams Act after former Senator Harrison Williams of New Jersey.

Section 13(d) requires a filing (a Schedule 13D), and supplemental filings to reflect changes, by any person or group acquiring more than 5% of a class of equity securities registered under Section 12 of the 1934 Act (and certain others). It has no effect on issuer tenders. Section 13(e) makes it unlawful for an issuer that has a class of equity securities registered under Section 12 or that is a closed-end investment company registered under the 1940 Act to purchase any equity securities issued by it in contravention of SEC rules. Purchases by affiliates are treated as purchases by the issuer itself. Section 14(d) governs third-party tender offers and has no application to issuer tender offers. Section 14(e) is a general antifraud provision applicable to all tender offers.

Rule 13e-4 is the basic rule governing tender offers for any class of equity security by the issuer or an affiliate.[8] It was adopted in 1979[9] and was amended in early 1986 to bring it more into line with the rules relating to third-party tenders.[10] It was further amended later that year.[11] The rule governs exchange offers as well

---

8. Rule 13e-1 requires an issuer to make an SEC filing containing specified information if it proposes to purchase any of its equity securities while a third-party tender offer is in progress for any class of the issuer's equity securities.

9. SEC Release No. 34-16112 (August 16, 1979).

10. SEC Release No. 34-22788 (January 14, 1986).

11. SEC Release No. 34-23421 (July 11, 1986).

as cash tender offers, so that if an issuer offered a debt security in exchange for shares of its common stock it would have to comply with Rule 13e-4. The issuer must file with the SEC prior to or as soon as practicable on the day the tender offer is commenced ten copies of an issuer tender offer statement on Schedule 13E-4. It must report any material change in the information set forth in the schedule by promptly filing ten copies of an amendment to the schedule and must report the results of the tender offer by filing ten copies of a final amendment no later than ten business days after the offer terminates. The rule provides that the commencement of the offer is the date it "is first published, sent or given to securityholders."

The filed Schedule 13E-4 must set forth information concerning the security to be purchased, including the exact amount being sought and historical price information; the source and amount of funds required for the purchase; the purpose of the tender offer; other transactions in the class of securities within the preceding 40 business days by the issuer, its executive officers, directors or associates; and arrangements with persons retained to solicit tenders. The schedule must include audited financial statements for the two preceding fiscal years and certain other financial information. Certain exhibits must be filed with the schedule, including the tender offer documents sent to stockholders.

The issuer must publish or send to those solicited a statement setting forth the scheduled termination date of the offer and whether it may be extended; the dates prior to which, and after which, tenders may be withdrawn; if the offer is for less than all of a class of equity securities, the dates of the period during which securities will be accepted on a pro rata basis; and the manner in which securities will be accepted for payment and in which they may be withdrawn. The statement must include the information in Schedule 13E-4, other than the exhibits, although summary financial data will suffice.

The tender offer may be made by publishing the required statement in full in a newspaper with a national circulation. In some cases, a newspaper with metropolitan or regional circulation will be adequate. It may be made by making publication of a summary advertisement meeting the requirements of the rule and by mailing the tender offer statement and a letter of transmittal to any stockholder requesting them. It may take the form of a mailing to stockholders. The customary procedure is to have a mailing along with a summary advertisement.

The rule provides that, if the offer is disseminated by a mailing to persons appearing on the most recent stockholder list, the issuer must also contact brokers named in the clearing agency listing and make inquiry as to the number of beneficial owners for whom they are holding shares. This is done by means of a so-called "brokers' search letter." The issuer must furnish the brokers with a sufficient number of copies of the tender offer statement and must agree to reimburse them for expenses incurred in forwarding the statement to the beneficial owners.

The tender offer, unless withdrawn, must remain open for at least 20 business days from its commencement and for at least ten business days from the date that notice of an increase or decrease in the percentage of the class of securities being sought or in the consideration offered or the dealer's soliciting fee is first published, sent or given to securityholders. The acceptance for payment of additional securities not to exceed 2% of the class outstanding is not deemed to be an increase for this purpose. The terms of the offer must permit securities to be withdrawn at any time during the period that the offer remains open and, if not yet accepted for payment, after the expiration of 40 business days from the commencement of the offer.

If the tender offer is for less than all of the outstanding equity securities of a class, and if a greater number of securities is tendered than the issuer is bound or willing to purchase, the securities must be purchased as nearly as may be pro rata, disregarding fractions, according to the number of securities tendered by each securityholder. There are exceptions to this requirement, however. The issuer may accept all securities tendered by persons who own an aggregate of not more than a specified number which is less than 100 shares, and who tender all their securities, before prorating securities tendered by others. In addition, if the terms of the offer permit, the issuer may accept by lot securities tendered by securityholders who tender all securities held by them and who, when tendering their securities, elect to have either all or none or at least a minimum amount or none accepted, if it first accepts all securities tendered by securityholders who do not so elect.

In the event the issuer increases the consideration offered after the tender offer has commenced, it must pay the increased consideration to all securityholders whose securities are accepted for payment. The issuer must either pay the consideration offered, or return the tendered securities, promptly after the termination or withdrawal of the tender offer.

Subsection (f)(6) of Rule 13e-4 provides that, until the expiration of at least ten business days after the termination of an issuer tender offer, neither the issuer nor any affiliate may make any purchases, otherwise than pursuant to the tender offer, of any security that is the subject of the tender offer, or any security of the same class and series, or any right to purchase any such securities, and in the case of an exchange offer, any security being offered pursuant to the exchange offer, or any security of the same class and series, or any right to purchase any such security. More generally, Rule 10b-13 provides that, subject to certain minor exceptions, no person who makes a cash tender offer or exchange offer for an equity security may, directly or indirectly, purchase or make any arrangement to purchase any such security (or any other security which is immediately convertible into or exchangeable for such security), otherwise than pursuant to such tender offer or exchange offer, from the time such tender offer or exchange offer is publicly announced or otherwise made known by such person to holders of the security to be acquired until the expiration of the period, including any extensions thereof, during which securities tendered pursuant to such tender offer or exchange offer may by the terms of such offer be accepted or rejected. A purchase by a soliciting dealer would be viewed as an indirect purchase by the issuer.[12]

In one of the most hotly contested takeover battles of the 1980s, T. Boone Pickens, Jr. sought to acquire Unocal Corporation by means of a coercive two-step front-loaded tender offer. The Unocal board, deeming the offer inadequate, authorized an issuer tender offer, designed to thwart the Pickens offer, that

---

12. SEC No-action Letter, *MSL Industries* (available September 16, 1971).

was directed to all stockholders except the Pickens group. The Delaware court held that a corporation may deal selectively with its stockholders in making a tender offer, provided the directors do not act out of a sole or primary purpose to entrench themselves in office. The court found that the corporation's response was neither unlawful nor unreasonable given the nature of the threat. The directors were found to be disinterested despite the fact that they tendered their own shares in response to the Unocal offer. The court stated that the efforts of the board to protect the stockholders by providing an alternative to an inadequate offer would have been ineffective if those seeking to take over the corporation had been permitted to participate in the tender offer. In addition, the court noted that the offeror's activities with respect to other transactions justified an inference that its principal objective was greenmail.[13]

In response to this holding, the SEC amended Rule 13e-4 in 1986 so that no issuer or affiliate may make a tender offer unless it is open to all holders of the class of securities subject to the tender offer ("all holders" requirement) and the consideration paid to any securityholder pursuant to the tender offer is the highest consideration paid to any other securityholder ("best price" requirement).[14]

Paragraph (h)(5) of Rule 13e-4 excludes from the rule's provisions any "odd-lot" tender offer by an issuer, i.e., an offer that is directed to holders of a specified number of shares that is less than one hundred. The rule's "all holders" and "best price" requirements still apply, however, except that an issuer may exclude participants in an employee benefit plan and may pay for tendered shares "on the basis of a uniformly applied formula based on the market price of the subject security." With the deletion in late 1996 of a record date requirement (SEC Release No. 33-7376 (December 20, 1996)), the rule now permits issuers to conduct odd-lot offers on a continuous, extended or periodic basis. In the same release, the SEC also granted a class exemption from Rule 10b-13 to permit an issuer

---

13. *Unocal Corp. v. Mesa Petroleum Co.*, 493 A. 2d 946 (Del. 1985).
14. SEC Release No. 34-23421 (July 11, 1986).

conducting an odd-lot tender offer to purchase the subject securities otherwise than pursuant to the offer. Also, as noted in Chapter 4, Rule 102 permits an issuer to purchase odd-lots while engaged in a distribution of the same security.

• • *Going Private Transactions.* If an issuer or an affiliate makes a tender offer for equity securities of the issuer or otherwise purchases them, it will be deemed to be a going private transaction subject to Rule 13e-3 if the purpose or likely effect of the transaction is to cause any class of equity securities of the issuer subject to Section 12(g) or Section 15(d) of the 1934 Act to be held of record by less than 300 persons or to cause a class of the issuer's equity securities to be delisted from an exchange or to be no longer authorized for quotation on NASDAQ.[15] Section 3(a)(11) of the 1934 Act defines the term "equity security" to include not only stock but also any security convertible into common or preferred stock.

In response to perceived inequities and the potential for coercion and overreaching involved in corporate freezeouts and other going private transactions, the SEC in 1974 instituted a rulemaking proceeding that included an inquiry as to whether it should adopt a disclosure schedule for issuers that attempt to go private with the result that they cease reporting under the 1934 Act.[16] The following year, it proposed alternative versions of a rule, one of which would have required two independent valuations and the other the demonstration of a valid business purpose.[17] When Rule 13e-3 was adopted four years later, the emphasis was placed on more meaningful disclosure concerning the fairness of a going private transaction rather than a demonstration that the transaction was indeed fair to the corporation's stockholders.[18]

---

15. A going private transaction also can result from a proxy solicitation or consent solicitation involving a merger, recapitalization or similar transaction, a sale of assets to affiliates, or a reverse stock split involving the purchase of fractional share interests.

16. SEC Release No. 34-11003 (September 9, 1974).

17. SEC Release No. 34-11231 (February 6, 1975).

18. SEC Release No. 34-16075 (August 2, 1979).

A tender offer for less than all of the issuer's shares is not likely to constitute a Rule 13e-3 transaction. An offer for any and all shares to be followed by a short form merger is clearly a going private transaction. Rule 13e-3 refers to a transaction or "series of transactions," and thus open market purchases made in anticipation of or in furtherance of a tender offer or other going private transaction may be caught up under the rule.[19]

A Rule 13e-3 transaction requires the filing with the SEC of a transaction statement on Schedule 13E-3. In the case of an issuer tender offer, this will be filed at the same time as the Schedule 13E-4. The additional disclosures required by Schedule 13E-3 will be disseminated to stockholders as part of the tender offer statement. These disclosures include a statement as to whether the issuer or affiliate filing the statement believes that the transaction is fair or unfair to unaffiliated securityholders. One can search in vain for a Schedule 13E-3 that comes right out and says that the stockholders are being injured, but technically this would satisfy the filer's disclosure obligation.

A statement, however, that the issuer has no reasonable belief as to the fairness of the transaction is not adequate disclosure. The filer must discuss in reasonable detail the material factors upon which the belief as to fairness is based and, to the extent practicable, the weight assigned to each factor. The schedule must state whether or not the filer has received a report, opinion or appraisal from an outside party with respect to the transaction, including any fairness opinion by an investment banking firm. If there is such a document, extensive disclosure must be made with respect thereto, including the qualifications of the organization that prepared it, and it must be made available to shareholders upon request.

• • *Short Tendering of Securities; Rule 14e-4.* If a tender offer is for less than all of the issuer's shares, tenders will be subject to proration. In that event, a stockholder wishing to dispose of all of his shares may not be able to do so at the tender price. He may sell his shares in the open market realizing less

---

19. SEC Release No. 34-17719 (April 13, 1981). This release discusses the principal interpretative questions that have arisen under Rule 13e-3.

than top dollar but more than the price at which the shares traded before the tender offer was announced. The arbitragers will be at work in the market buying shares at prices that take into account the risk of proration.

During the 1960s, in order to reduce the risk of proration, arbitragers and other professional traders developed the technique of short tendering. Tender offers commonly provide that the stock certificates need not be physically deposited prior to the expiration of the tender offer if a bank or a member firm of a securities exchange guarantees that the certificates will be delivered on demand or within a specified time after they are accepted. This procedure originally was adopted to accommodate stockholders who were out of town or otherwise not in a position to get their hands on their certificates prior to the expiration date.

The guaranteed delivery procedure then came to be used by member firms in tendering for their own account shares that they did not own in order to fare better in the proration process, which is based on the number of shares tendered. The procedure also could be used to assist important customers. If, for example, a member firm engaged in arbitrage estimated that only half the number of shares tendered would be accepted on a pro rata basis, it might tender through the guaranteed delivery procedure twice as many shares as it owned. If its estimate was correct, all of the shares that it actually owned would be accepted. Short tendering did not totally eliminate risks. The firm's estimate might be substantially off the mark. Or the bidder might decide to accept more shares than it was obligated to purchase. But it did reduce the risk of proration, and short tendering became a frequent practice.

At the Senate hearings on the legislation that would become the Williams Act, the SEC raised the issue of short tendering and how it could be used "to the disadvantage of the unwary public."[20] The concern was that by tendering a greater number of securities than they owned, and by guaranteeing their own tenders, market professionals were able to secure acceptance of a disproportionately larger number of the securities

---

20. *Hearings Before the Subcommittee on Securities of the Committee on Banking and Currency on S.510*, 90th Cong., 1st Sess. 21–23 (1967).

owned and tendered by them than could be secured by other persons who tendered only the securities they owned.

In its report on the bill, the Senate Banking and Currency Committee made reference to short tendering and concluded that the SEC had "adequate power to deal with the abuse of short tendering under the antifraud provisions of the Securities Exchange Act."[21]

In 1968, the SEC adopted Rule 10b-4 (which was redesignated in 1990 as Rule 14e-4).[22] Applicable to both issuer and third-party tenders, it was designed to promote equality of opportunity and risk for all tendering securityholders. In its original form, the rule simply provided that it was a "manipulative or deceptive device or contrivance" for a person to tender a security unless he owned the security or a security convertible into or exchangeable for, or owned an option, warrant or right to purchase, the tendered security, intended to convert, exchange or exercise to the extent necessary to effect delivery, and upon acceptance did convert, exchange or exercise to the extent required. It also extended the antifraud provisions of the 1934 Act to a tender or guarantee of a tender on behalf of another person unless the security was in the hands of the person making the tender or giving the guarantee, or that person had reason to believe that the other person owned the security and, "as soon as possible, without undue inconvenience or expense," would deliver the security for the purpose of the tender, or such other person owned a security convertible into or exchangeable for, or an option, warrant or right to purchase, the tendered security and intended to convert, exchange or exercise to the extent necessary to effect delivery.

The rule provided that a person was deemed to own a security if he or his agent had title to it; if he had purchased, or had entered into an unconditional contract, binding on both parties, to purchase it, but had not yet received delivery; if he owned a security convertible into or exchangeable for it and had tendered the security for conversion or exchange; or if he had an

---

21. S. Rep. No. 550, 90th Cong., 1st Sess. 5 (1967).
22. SEC Release No. 34-8321 (May 28, 1968).

option, warrant or right to purchase or subscribe for it and had exercised such option, warrant or right. The rule further provided that a person "shall be deemed to own securities only to the extent that he has a net long position in such securities."

Prohibited from engaging in short tendering by what is now Rule 14e-4, market professionals came up with a new device designed to achieve a result similar to that afforded by short tendering. This device, which was known as "hedged tendering," consisted of purchasing the subject securities, tendering them and immediately effecting a short sale. For example, if a stockholder had 100,000 shares and expected a 50% proration, he would tender all of his shares and then sell 50,000 shares short. If his estimate was correct, he would use the 50,000 shares that were not accepted in the tender offer to cover his short position.

This was perfectly legal under the short tender rule in its original form because the stockholder owned the 100,000 shares at the time of tender. The SEC found it anomalous, however, that if the sale had been made immediately before the tender, the tender would have violated the rule, but that the same result could be achieved by waiting to make the sale until a moment after the tender. In two no-action letters issued in 1973, the staff said that, under certain circumstances, a person effecting a post-tender short sale "may be engaged in a course of conduct in contravention of the purpose of Rule 10b-4 [now Rule 14e-4] and may be in violation of other antifraud and antimanipulative provisions of the federal securities laws."[23]

On the basis of certain ground rules set forth in a subsequent no-action letter [24] and informal discussions with the staff, the accepted wisdom became that hedged tendering was permitted as long as the short sale was not made until the trading session next following the completion of the tender and until physical delivery of the securities had been effected.

In 1981, the SEC proposed for public comment two alternative approaches to short tenders: either a strengthening of the

---

23. SEC No-action Letter, *Fred Kolber* (available July 26, 1973); SEC No-action Letter, *du Pont Glore Forgan* (available July 26, 1973).

24. SEC No-action Letter, *Blaine McKee* (available September 2, 1974).

existing rule or complete deregulation. The thrust of the proposal to tighten up the rule was that a tendering securityholder must be "net long" the amount of securities tendered not only when the tender is made but also at the end of the pro rata acceptance period or on the last day when securities may be accepted by lot where that method of acceptance is used. The proposed amendment also prohibited "multiple tendering," i.e., tendering the same securities into more than one partial tender offer at the same time. This provision simply codified the staff's existing interpretation of the rule as applied to multiple tendering, an interpretation that received widespread press coverage in connection with the 1981 competing tender offers for Conoco Inc. by Mobil Corporation and E.I. du Pont de Nemours and Company.

The SEC's Advisory Committee on Tender Offers supported the proposal to strengthen the rule. It stated in its report to the SEC:

> Notwithstanding contentions that short and hedged tendering operate to increase the efficiency of the market and to reduce the spread between the market price and tender price, thereby benefiting individuals who sell into the market rather than tender, the Committee strongly endorses continuation of Rule 10b-4's [Rule 14e-4's] prohibition of short tendering and recommends that the rule be strengthened to prohibit specifically hedged tendering. Because short and hedged tendering opportunities are available almost exclusively to market professionals, they appear to provide a substantial, unfair advantage to market professionals. As a result, the Committee found that these techniques created too great a risk of undermining public confidence in the integrity of the markets. [Footnotes omitted.][25]

---

25. *Advisory Committee on Tender Offers Report of Recommendations* 47–48 (July 1983).

In 1984, the rule finally was amended to prohibit hedged and multiple tendering.[26] It was further amended the following year to prohibit hedged tendering through the use of standardized call options by requiring a person tendering shares to exclude from his net long position shares underlying in-the-money standardized call options written after the announcement of the tender offer.[27]

In *Merrill Lynch, Pierce, Fenner & Smith, Inc. v. Bobker*,[28] a stockholder of Phillips Petroleum Company tendered all of his 4000 shares into a partial tender offer by the issuer. Before the proration date, the stockholder entered an order for the short sale of 2000 shares. When his broker's compliance department canceled the short sale, he commenced an arbitration proceeding claiming that his tender and his short sale were independent transactions. The arbitrators' award of damages was upheld by the Court of Appeals as not in "manifest disregard of the law." In supporting its view of Bobker's short sale as an independent transaction, the court said that it "amounted to a separate gamble." It noted that the rule did not define the term "net long" and refused to grant deference to the SEC's interpretation of the term as applied to Bobker's short sale because it viewed the SEC's interpretation as being inconsistent with the purpose of the rule and as lacking a rational basis.

In response to uncertainties created by the *Bobker* decision, the SEC in 1990 adopted amendments to the rule that defined a net long position in a security as equaling the excess, if any, of a person's "long position" in that security over his "short position" (which included, for this purpose, any shares sold short or that the person was obligated to return to a lender). The amendments also redesignated the rule as Rule 14e-4 to place it among the provisions specifically relating to tender offers. Finally, the SEC noted comment to the effect that multiple tendering did not lessen a stockholder's risk at the expense of other stockholders with respect to any particular partial offer, and on this basis it rescinded the prohibition on multiple tendering.[29]

---

26. SEC Release No. 34-20799 (March 29, 1984).
27. SEC Release No. 34-21782 (February 22, 1985).
28. 808 F.2d 930 (2d Cir. 1986).
29. SEC Release No. 34-28660 (November 30, 1990).

• *Put Warrants*

A corporation that wishes to repurchase its stock but believes that the current market price is too high need not stand idly by and incur the risk that the market price will move even higher before it has completed its repurchase objectives. The corporation can sell put warrants with a strike price equal to or less than the price that it is willing to pay. The premium that it receives for the sale of the warrants is tax-free and will effectively reduce the average cost of the stock repurchase program, whether or not the warrants are ever exercised.

Several issuers have sold put warrants on their stock since an SEC no-action letter in 1991 (*Chicago Board Options Exchange* (available February 22, 1991)), and many of these warrants are traded in the secondary market. A holder of a put warrant hopes, of course, that the market price of the issuer's stock will fall below the exercise price of the put warrant, thus permitting the holder to purchase the stock in the market and then require the issuer to repurchase it at the higher price. The issuer should be indifferent to this result, assuming that it really wishes to repurchase its stock at the exercise price.

• • *1933 Act Considerations.* The *CBOE* letter dealt with the writing of standardized puts by issuers of the underlying stock. The request letter noted that questions might be raised under Section 5 of the 1933 Act because such a transaction might be construed as a "sale" of the issuer's stock, given the breadth of the relevant definitions in Section 2(3) of the 1933 Act. It argued against this result, however, on the basis that the transaction was "an ordinary, open-market transaction unrelated to any effort by the issuer to offer or sell, or to solicit offers to buy, its own stock." The staff took a no-action position without addressing CBOE's arguments under Section 2(3).

Standardized options are, of course, formally issued by the Options Clearing Corporation and registered under the 1933 Act. One could therefore take the position that an issuer writing standardized puts on its own stock was simply engaging in a transaction in another person's security. Would the result be different in the case of non-standardized options? One would think not, since an issuer's writing of a put option remains far from any attempt on its part to offer or sell, or to solicit offers to buy, its stock. The activity should therefore not constitute a "sale" under Section 2(3) of the 1933 Act.

• • *1934 Act Considerations.* The *CBOE* letter also addressed issues under the anti-manipulation, issuer tender offer and issuer stock repurchase rules. The SEC staff granted exemptions under former Rules 10b-6 and 10b-7 to deal with the possible characterization of the puts as "continuing bids" by the issuer for its common stock. (Such relief would not be necessary under Regulation M, which replaced Rules 10b-6 and 10b-7 in early 1997.) In addition, the staff granted an exemption under Rule 13e-4 to make harmless any characterization of the issuer puts as an issuer tender offer. It also took a no-action position under Rule 13e-1 to permit the issuer to purchase stock on exercise of the put during the pendency of a third-party tender offer. CBOE did not request, and the SEC did not grant, any relief under Rule 10b-13 on the theory that the issuer could control its own tender offers so as not to create a conflict with its obligation to purchase stock on exercise of a put.

The SEC relief was conditioned on the issuer's writing only standardized out-of-the-money puts options on a U.S. options market. The puts written by the issuer on any day would be limited to the extent to which the issuer would have been allowed to purchase stock on that day under Rule 10b-18's volume limitation (without regard to the block exclusion). Also, the issuer could write puts only through one broker-dealer on any given day, and it could not participate in the opening rotation for such puts or within thirty minutes before the close of trading in the principal market for the stock. Finally, the staff assumed that the issuer would not engage in any transactions for the purpose of creating actual or apparent trading in, or raising or depressing the price of, its securities.

To the extent an issuer sells puts to a broker-dealer, of course, the broker-dealer may wish to hedge its investment by purchasing stock in the open market. Should the broker-dealer follow any or all of the conditions of Rule 10b-18 in effecting such purchases? Should the issuer require the broker-dealer to follow any or all of such conditions? Should the broker-dealer suspend purchases when the issuer would suspend purchases (e.g., prior to announcements that are likely to increase the stock price)? As noted above in connection with the discussion of the functionally similar practice of broker-dealers' shorting significant amounts of stock to an issuer in furtherance of its repurchase program, practice is not uniform in this regard.

Debt Restructurings

Corporations that issue debt securities during periods of high interest rates may seek to eliminate them or to reduce the amount outstanding through various means, including redemption in accordance with the terms of the indenture, open market purchases, tender offers and exchange offers. If interest rates have declined since the time that the securities were originally issued, they will be trading at a premium over par. But the premium may not fully reflect the decline in interest rates for a number of reasons, including the company's ability to redeem the securities or the existence of a sinking fund provision under which a portion of the securities can be redeemed at par. Under these circumstances, a repurchase of the securities, even at a premium over their principal amount, may be a practical step in the corporation's efforts to reduce the average cost of its debt.

If, on the other hand, the securities are trading below par, perhaps because interest rates have increased, the issuer may make a tender offer at a premium over the market price, thus retiring indebtedness at less than the principal amount with a corresponding increase in stockholders' equity resulting from the recognition of income. Some issuers of high-yield bonds were able to avoid default only through an exchange of new securities with manageable terms for the securities that were about to go into default.

A corporation's objective in restructuring its debt usually is a reduction in financing costs. But other factors may come into play. A stronger balance sheet and a resulting enhanced credit rating may be the goal. The issuer's principal objective may be the elimination of onerous financial covenants, in which case it may seek to acquire the securities through a cash tender offer or an exchange offer and at the same time make a consent so licitation aimed at modifying the covenants applicable to all of the securities, even those that are not tendered or exchanged.

• *Redemptions*

Whether or not a debt security may be called for redemption will depend on the terms of the governing indenture. Some obligations will have absolute call protection, particularly if they have a relatively short maturity. Zero coupon obligations, which are marketed as a means to eliminate reinvestment risk, generally are not redeemable by the issuer. Other obligations may provide limited call protection. They may be nonredeemable for five years, for ten years, or for some other specified period of time. Some debt securities are redeemable immediately upon issuance. If debt is redeemable at the option of the issuer, the redemption price will be structured to protect the holder's yield to maturity. If the securities are sold at par and are immediately redeemable, the initial redemption price will be par plus a redemption premium. equal to the stated interest rate. The redemption premium will be scaled down over the term of the instrument until the final year, or perhaps the last five years, at which time redemption may be effected at par.

Even if a debt security is immediately redeemable, it may be "nonrefundable" for at least five years from the time of issuance, i.e., it may not be redeemed during that period "from or in anticipation of moneys borrowed as part of a refunding operation by the company or any subsidiary" at an interest cost less than the yield to maturity. Nonrefunding provisions have been the subject of litigation, and a call for redemption during the period that a nonrefunding provision is operative must be considered with great care. The courts have been relatively lenient to issuers in construing these provisions and have permitted them to trace the source of funds in appropriate cases.

In *Franklin Life Insurance Co. v. Commonwealth Edison Co.*,[30] a redemption of preferred stock purporting to be funded out of a common stock issue was challenged in a class action as vio-

---

30. 451 F. Supp. 602 (S.D. Ill. 1978), *aff'd* 598 F.2d 1109 (7th Cir.), *cert. denied,* 444 U.S. 900 (1979).

lative of the issuer's certificate of designation, which provided that the preferred stock could not be redeemed through refunding, directly or indirectly, by or in anticipation of the incurring of any debt or the issuance of any shares ranking prior to or on a parity with the preferred stock at an interest or dividend cost less than the dividend cost of the preferred stock. The contention was made that the preferred stock could not be redeemed so long as the company was borrowing more per year than it repaid at an interest cost below the dividend cost of the preferred stock. The court rejected this theory and held that the proper interpretation of the nonrefunding provision required an examination of the "source of the funds actually used to achieve the redemption" without regard to the issuer's other borrowing activities.

A similar result was obtained in *Morgan Stanley & Co. Inc. v. Archer Daniels Midland Co.*[31] Archer Daniels had outstanding an issue of debentures that by the terms of the indenture under which they were issued could not be redeemed from the proceeds, or in anticipation, of the issuance of indebtedness if the interest cost was less than 16.06% per annum. The debentures were redeemed out of the proceeds of an issue of common stock. Morgan Stanley alleged that, in addition to the common stock offering, Archer Daniels had made several recent debt offerings at an interest cost of less than 16.06% and accordingly the debentures had been indirectly refunded through lower cost borrowings. Citing *Franklin Life,* the court agreed with the company's position that the indenture had not been violated as the direct source of the funds used for the redemption was the sale of the common stock. The court also indicated that cash on hand could be used for a redemption without regard to other arguably unrelated borrowings.

An issuer seeking to redeem obligations during a nonrefunding period in reliance on the *Franklin Life* and *Morgan Stanley* cases must take care to segregate the funds from a common stock offering to be used for this purpose or to assure that the proceeds from a lower-cost debt financing are not commingled with the funds on hand used to redeem the obligations. An issuer in this posture is treading on thin ice. It may well be inviting litigation, and the 30-

---

31. 570 F. Supp. 1529 (S.D.N.Y. 1983).

day notice period customarily required for redemptions provides sufficient time for a litigant to mount an attack. The risk of a court fight, even though it ultimately may be defended successfully, may be a sufficient reason to choose another route. Moreover, the issuer's credibility in the debt market is a factor to be taken into account. If a company is perceived to being playing fast and loose with the holders of its debt securities, the acceptance of its securities in the marketplace may be substantially impaired.

An issuer seeking an early redemption of debt must take into account the antifraud provisions of the securities laws. For example, even where an electric utility's redemption of bonds had been held by a state court to have been authorized under the indenture, an appellate court still found itself able to affirm a jury verdict to the effect that the prospectus under which the bonds were sold had "omitted material facts that would have adequately disclosed UE's right to call the bonds, in violation of Rule 10b-5(b)."[32] Moreover, it is probably no defense to such a federal antifraud claim that the indenture or the terms of the security purport to restrict or eliminate the holder's right to sue. Such a provision may be given effect insofar as the holder's *contractual* claims are concerned, but an extension of the provision to the holder's rights under the 1933 and 1934 Act would conflict with the anti-waiver provisions of those statutes.[33]

If debt securities are to be redeemed, the procedures set forth in the indenture must be strictly adhered to. Under the typical indenture, notice of redemption must be given not less than 30 nor more than 60 days prior to the date fixed for redemption. If less than all of the securities are to be redeemed, the selection of securities to be redeemed will be made by the trustee on a pro rata basis or by lot, or by such other method as the trustee deems fair and appropriate. Notice of redemption is given by mail to the holders at their addresses as they appear

---

32. *Harris v. Union Electric Co.*, 787 F.2d 355 (8th Cir. 1986), *cert. denied* 479 U.S. 823 (1986). *Cf. Lucas v. Florida Power & Light Co.*, 575 F. Supp. 552 (S.D. Fla. 1983), *aff'd* 765 F.2d 1039 (11th Cir. 1985).

33. *McMahan & Co. v. Wherehouse Entertainment, Inc.*, 65 F.3d 1044 (2d Cir. 1995), *cert. denied* 116 S. Ct. 1678 (1996).

on the register maintained by the trustee. In the case of bearer securities, notice is given by publication in a newspaper.

• *Open Market Purchases*

Debt securities may be acquired by the issuer in the open market without regard to the redemption provisions of the indenture. These are consensual transactions between the holders and the issuer, and the indenture provisions simply do not apply. The same is true of a tender offer. Thus, if an issuer feels constrained by a nonrefunding provision in its indenture, purchases in the open market or through a tender offer may be the way to accomplish its objective. Open market purchases may be the best and cheapest route if the issuer is not seeking to repurchase an entire issue or if it is known that the debt is in the hands of a limited number of holders. (Some privately-placed debt securities restrict repurchases by the issuer except on a pro rata basis, and the existence of any such restriction should be investigated.)

If the issuer decides to embark on a program of open market purchases, it must take care that its purchases do not constitute a tender offer. Here the same considerations are applicable as those that apply to a common stock repurchase program. Although Rule 13e-4 is applicable only to tender offers for equity securities, Section 14(e) and Rules 14e-1, 14e-2, and 14e-3 thereunder are applicable to all tender offers, including those for straight-debt securities. Rule 14e-1(a), which requires a tender offer to be held open for 20 days, is usually the provision that causes the most difficulty.

In some respects, greater care must be taken to avoid the tender offer trap where debt securities are involved than in the case of a common stock repurchase program. Common stock can be purchased from time to time on an exchange or in the over-the-counter market with little risk of the purchases being viewed as a tender offer, but debt repurchases often require direct dealings with the holders of the securities.

To reduce the risk that open market purchases will be viewed as a tender offer, certain procedures should be followed. It probably will make sense to effect the purchases through the securities firm that managed the underwriting in which the securities were sold. That firm's institutional sales-men are in the best position to contact the customers to whom they sold the securities in the first place. The firm should be furnished with a list of securityholders in order to supplement its own knowledge of where the securities are held. If only a portion of the issue is to be reacquired, the objective should be to obtain that amount from the smallest number of holders in order to avoid the appearance of a general solicitation.

From a compliance standpoint, the firm should limit the num-ber of holders to be solicited in the first instance. The number will depend on the distribution of ownership. If it is necessary to con-tact additional holders, this should be done on a controlled and supervised basis, rather than by simply turning the sales force loose. The sales force should be instructed to apply no pressure on the holders of the securities, to set no limit on the time that the holder has to make a decision, and to be prepared to negotiate the purchase price subject to the issuer's approval.

• *Cash Tender Offers*

If the issuer is seeking to purchase the entire issue and the securities are held by more than a limited number of investors, then a cash tender offer may be the way to get the deal done. The mechanics of a debt tender offer are similar to those for a common stock tender. Generally, a tombstone notice is published in a news-paper of national circulation followed by a mailing or distribution of tender offer materials to all registered holders. Unlike the sub-stantial premium that may be paid in a common stock tender offer, the price offered by the issuer in a debt tender offer usually repre-sents a relatively modest premium over the market price of the securities sought to be acquired. These premiums generally range from .05% to 2.50% of the price at which the securities are trading in the market. The issuer may condition the offer upon the valid tender of a specified minimum aggregate principal amount of the issue.

As stated above, debt tender offers are subject to less strin-gent regulation than tender offers for equity securities. Rule 13e-4 is not applicable, and no filing with the SEC is required. Rule 14e-1 does apply, however, and this rule requires tender offers to be held open for at least 20 business days from the date that the tender offer is first published or sent to security-holders and for at least ten business days from the date that notice is given of an increase or decrease in the percentage of the class of securities being sought or the consideration offered or the dealers' soliciting fee. Prior to March 1, 1986, Rule 14e-1 contained a proviso exempting from its coverage all tenders for straight-debt securities other than those by an issuer engaged in a defensive tender offer. This exemption was eliminated effective as of that date, thus bringing all debt tender offers under the coverage of Rule 14e-1.[34]

This created a problem. Previously, issuer debt tender offers had been held open for a period of seven to ten calendar days. Extending the tender offer period to 20 business days would increase the likelihood that interest rates would increase or decrease materially while the tender offer remained open, thus subjecting the issuer and the securityholders themselves to increased risks.

In response to requests by a number of securities firms, the staff of the SEC has provided no-action relief with respect to issuer tender offers for nonconvertible debt securities.[35] Enforcement action will not be recommended by the staff if the offer is for "any and all" nonconvertible debt securities of a particular series;[36] is open to all holders of those securities; is conducted in a manner designed to afford all holders a reasonable opportunity to participate, including dissemination of the offer on an "expedited basis" where the tender offer is open for a period of less than ten calendar days; and is not made in anticipation of or in response to other tender offers for the issuer's securities. In addition to permitting a tender offer period of

---

34. SEC Release No. 34-22788 (January 14, 1986). *See also* SEC Release No. 34-23421 (July 11, 1986), which made the ten-day provision of Rule 14e-1 applicable to decreases as well as increases.

35. SEC No-action Letter, *Merrill Lynch, Pierce, Fenner & Smith Incorporated* (available July 2, 1986); SEC No-action Letter, *Goldman, Sachs & Co.* (available March 26, 1986); SEC No-action Letter, *Salomon Brothers Inc* (available March 12, 1986).

36. The offer may be conditioned upon the tender of a minimum amount of securities.

less than 20 business days if the conditions are met, the no-action position also affords relief from the requirement that a tender offer remain open for ten business days after the announcement of certain changes in the terms of the offer. In the case of such changes, an extension equivalent to the length of the initial offer would be required.

In taking this no-action position, the staff took into account the economic realities of debt tender offers as represented to it in the no-action requests. Thus, in the *Merrill Lynch* letter it stated:

Issuer Debt Tender Offers invariably involve the retirement of high coupon debt during periods when relatively lower interest rates prevail. Generally, the retirement of debt is closely preceded, accompanied, or followed by a refunding issue of debt that takes advantage of lower interest rates to reduce the average cost to the issuer of its debt. If market conditions render it economic for an issuer to refinance its high coupon debt in this manner, it is generally advantageous for an issuer to refinance as much of its outstanding high coupon debt as possible. As a result, Issuer Debt Tender Offers are usually for any and all outstanding debt of the class or series subject to the offer. In this regard, there may be instances in which an issuer, for economic and financial reasons, may wish to condition the Issuer Debt Tender Offer upon the valid tender of a minimum aggregate principal amount of the debt subject to the offer. The success of the refinancing depends upon maintaining the desired relationships (i) between the principal amount of debt retired in the tender offer and the principal amount of the refunding issue, and (ii) between the cost to the issuer of the debt retirement and the refunding issue.

Based on Merrill Lynch's experience, Issuer Debt Tender Offers are generally held open for a period of seven to ten calendar days depending on a number of factors, including the percentage of debt held by individual debtholders and the principal amount of debt that the issuer desires to retire. Extending the period during which an Issuer Debt Tender Offer remains open increases the likelihood that interest rates will increase or decrease during the tender offer period. Both the issuer and its debtholders will be exposed to additional interest rate risk in those circumstances. Because interest rates can move against a debtholder during the tender offer period and since a debtholder often does not have withdrawal rights, a debtholder has a disincentive to tender his debt early. As a result, if interest rates decline during the tender offer period, the issuer may retire much less debt than it intended. If, on the other hand, interest rates rise during the tender offer period, the issuer may retire many bonds but at a price higher than is justified by interest rates prevailing at that time. In either case, the issuer will be confronted with a substantial potential mismatch between the principal amount of debt it retires and the principal amount of debt it has issued, or intends to issue, in the refunding.

Because an extension of the tender offer period also increases the uncertainty as to the principal amount of debt to be refinanced, an issuer will be less likely to commence refunding operations at or prior to the commencement of its tender offer. This will create interest rate risk on the refunding side of the refinancing. If interest rates continue to rise during the tender offer period, the debt refinancing, if not done in advance, could become particularly costly to the issuer, since the increased refunding costs that the issuer will incur will not be offset by a corresponding decrease in the cost to the issuer of retiring its debt.

There are several choices open to an issuer that is required to hold an Issuer Debt Tender Offer open for more than the customary seven to ten calendar days. An issuer may elect to price the tender offer on the basis of prevailing interest rates and accept the increased risk that the tender offer will be unsuccessful (if interest rates decline) or that the refunding will be more expensive than expected (if interest rates rise). Alternatively, an issuer may elect to increase the premium it offers to debtholders in order to provide a cushion against declining interest rates—thus increasing the cost to it of retiring its debt.

On the other hand, an issuer may decide not to refinance its debt by means of a tender offer and, instead, may elect to engage in an open market repurchase program or request a securities dealer to short debt to it. In either case, purchases of the issuer's debt will be privately negotiated. Under such circumstances, debtholders are less likely to receive equal treatment, and it is unlikely that an individual noninstitutional debtholder will be contacted and afforded an opportunity to receive a repurchase premium.

The staff concluded:

> The Division believes that Issuer Debt Tender Offers for any and all non-convertible debt securities of a particular class or series may present considerations that differ from any and all or partial issuer tender offers for a class or series of equity securities. For example, because of the modest premiums typically offered in an Issuer Debt Tender Offer, it is not clear that participation in the Tender offer by individual non-institutional debtholders would be materially increased by requiring that tender offer be held open for twenty business days.

• *Fixed-Spread Cash Tender Offers*

The SEC took a no-action position in 1990 with respect to issuer cash tender offers for debt securities at a price determined on each day during the tender offer period by reference to a stated fixed spread over the then current yield on a specified benchmark U.S. Treasury security determined as of the date, or the date preceding the date, of tender. The no-action position is subject to the conditions that the offer: (i) be an offer for cash for any and all non-convertible, investment grade debt of a particular class or series; (ii) be open to all record and beneficial holders of that class or series of debt; (iii) provide that information regarding the benchmark U.S. Treasury security will be reported each day in a daily newspaper of national circulation; (iv) be conducted in a manner designed to afford all record and beneficial holders of that class or series of debt a reasonable opportunity to participate in the tender offer, and, in the case of an offer conducted in reliance on the 1986 no-action letter, dissemination of the tender offer is made on an expedited basis; (v) provide that all tendering holders of that class or series of debt be paid promptly for their tendered securities after such securities are accepted for payment; and (vi) not be made in anticipation of or in response to other tender offers for the issuer's securities.[37]

In July 1993, the SEC extended the above position to permit issuers to conduct debt tender offers using a fixed spread pricing methodology in which the nominal purchase price is calculated by reference to a stated fixed spread over the most current yield on a benchmark U.S. Treasury security determined *at the time* that the securityholder tenders the debt security (a "real-time fixed spread offering") rather than by reference to the yield on a benchmark U.S. Treasury security as of a specified time on the date, or date preceding the date, of the tender offer as permitted in the 1990 no-action letter. Real-time fixed price offerings apply a fixed spread to arrive at a series of nominal purchase prices, but the nominal purchase prices do not remain constant but change with any movements in the benchmark U.S. Treasury security.[38] The 1993 letter is subject to the following conditions over and above those specified in the 1990 letter: (a) the tender offer must identify the specific benchmark U.S. Treasury security to be used and specify the fixed spread to be added to the yield on the benchmark U.S. Treasury security; (b) the tender offer must state the nominal purchase price that would have been payable based on the applicable reference yield immediately preceding the commencement of the tender offer; (c) the tender offer must indicate a daily newspaper of general circulation that will provide the closing yield of the benchmark U.S. Treasury security on each day of the tender offer; (d) the tender offer must indicate the electronic reference source to be used during the tender offer to establish the current yield on the benchmark U.S. Treasury security (i.e., Telerate, Bloomberg, Cantor Fitzgerald, etc.); (e) the tender offer must de-

---

37. SEC No-action Letter, *Salomon Brothers Inc.* (available October 1, 1990).

38. SEC No-action letter, *Merrill Lynch, Pierce, Fenner & Smith Incorporated* (available July 19, 1993).

scribe the methodology used to calculate the purchase price for the tendered securities; and (h) the tender offer must indicate that the current yield on the benchmark U.S. Treasury security and the resulting nominal purchase price of the debt securities is accessible on a real-time basis by either calling the dealer manager collect or through an "800" telephone number, if established for the tender offer. In addition to the above conditions, the SEC requires the dealer manager to maintain records showing the date and time of each tender, the current yield on the benchmark U.S. Treasury security at the time of each tender and the purchase price of the tendered securities based on that yield. The dealer manager must also send a confirmation of the transaction to tendering securityholders no later than the next business day after the tender.

- *Issuer Recommendation*

Rule 14e-2 does not contain an express exemption for issuer tender offers. This rule provides that, no later than ten business days from the date a tender offer is first made, the subject company shall publish, send, or give to securityholders a statement disclosing that it recommends acceptance or rejection of the bidder's tender offer, expresses no opinion and is remaining neutral toward the bidder's tender offer, or is unable to take a position with respect to the bidder's tender offer. It can be argued that the definitions of the terms "bidder" and "subject company" in Rule 14d-1 and plain common sense lead to the conclusion that Rule 14e-2 is not applicable to issuer tender offers. It is more prudent, however, for the issuer to state its position or lack of a position, and generally all debt tender offers have contained such a statement. Typically, the tender offer materials will contain a statement that the issuer makes no recommendation that holders of debt securities tender or refrain from tendering and that such holders must make their own decision as to whether to tender securities and, if so, how many securities to tender.

It used to be necessary to obtain an exemption under the SEC's former Rule 10b-6 if an issuer engaged in a "distribution" of new debt securities at or about the same time as it made a tender offer for outstanding debt securities of the same "class and series."[39] As discussed in Chapter 4, the SEC's new Rules 101 and 102—the successor rules to Rule 10b-6—no longer apply to securities of the same class and series unless they are "identical in all of their terms" to those being distributed.

• *Exchange Offers*

As part of a capital restructuring, a company may offer to exchange new debt securities for outstanding debt securities that it wishes to retire. Or it may offer equity securities, or a package of debt and equity, in exchange for existing debt. The exchange offer may include a cash kicker payable to the holder. In making an exchange offer to existing securityholders, an issuer may retain a dealer-manager to solicit exchanges or it may decide to go it alone. If a dealer is paid a fee for soliciting exchanges, the exchange offer will not be exempt from registration under Section 3(a)(9). On the other hand, an issuer that is in financial difficulty or that wishes to reduce its interest costs may be willing to go to the trouble and expense of registration in order to enhance the potential success of its exchange offer by using the services of a dealer-manager. If the issuer does decide to register, the registration statement must be filed on Form S-4.

• • *Section 3(a)(9).* Section 3(a)(9) under the 1933 Act exempts from registration "any security exchanged by the issuer with its existing securityholders exclusively where no commission or other remuneration is paid or given directly or indirectly for soliciting such exchange." For Section 3(a)(9) to be available, both the security issued and the security surrendered in exchange must be those of the same issuer. This is frequently called the "issuer identity requirement." Thus, as a general rule, if an issuer offers its common stock in exchange for debt securities issued by its wholly owned subsidiary, the Section 3(a)(9) exemption cannot be relied upon.

The issuer identity requirement is not absolute, however, especially in the area of guaranteed securities or other securi-

---

39. E.g., SEC No-action Letter, *Playtex FP Group Inc.* (available December 19, 1988).

ties having multiple issuers. The staff has taken a no-action position where a subsidiary proposed to offer its obligations guaranteed by its parent in exchange for its outstanding debt securities that did not have the benefit of a parent guarantee (although the staff concluded that the parent guarantee had to be registered).[40] The SEC has also taken no-action positions under Section 3(a)(9) with respect to small amounts of common stock of parent corporations issuable upon conversion of long-outstanding securities of subsidiaries involving a parent guarantee on the basis of representations that "as a practical matter" the exchange involves securities of a single issuer[41] or that as an "economic reality" the guarantee and the underlying obligation constitute securities of the same issuer.[42] The staff has also acquiesced in the use of Section 3(a)(9) to exempt securities issued by a post-merger entity in exchange for securities issued by a pre-merger entity where the post-merger entity had in connection with the merger become a joint and several obligor on the old securities.[43] The same theory has recently been applied to foreign sovereign debt.[44] And, not surprisingly, the staff has also taken a no-action position permitting the holding company of a savings bank to rely on Section 3(a)(9) in exchanging new debt securities that were joint and several obligations of the holding company and the savings bank, where the securities taken in exchange were also joint and several obligations of the same two entities.[45]

---

40. SEC No-action Letter, *Union Planters Corporation* (available January 10, 1983).

41. SEC No-action Letter, *Baxter Travenol Laboratories, Inc.* (available July 8, 1983).

42. SEC No-action Letter, *American Motors Corporation* (available July 8, 1982). *See also* SEC No-action Letter, *National Can Corporation* (available September 22, 1983).

43. E.g., SEC No-action Letter, *W.R. Grace & Co.* (available July 25, 1988).

44. SEC No-action Letter, *Federal Republic of Germany* (available April 8, 1994).

45. SEC No-action Letter, *First Liberty Financial Corp.* (available July 23, 1991).

The staff also took a no-action position where Norlin Corporation and its essentially "mirror-image" wholly owned subsidiary made a joint exchange offer of Norlin warrants and debentures of the subsidiary for outstanding debt securities of the subsidiary that had been guaranteed by Norlin.[46] There the position was taken that Norlin was offering its warrants in exchange for its guarantee and its subsidiary was offering its new obligations in exchange for its outstanding primary obligations. In another instance, where an acquired corporation's debentures became convertible into cash and debt securities of the acquiring corporation and the acquiring corporation guaranteed the debentures, the staff agreed that Section 3(a)(9) could be relied upon for conversions.[47] Because the acquiring corporation would be liable on the acquired corporation's debentures, it was viewed as the issuer of those debentures as well as of the debt securities issuable upon conversion.

It is not clear whether the word "exclusively" in Section 3(a)(9) modifies the word "exchanged" as well as the phrase "with its existing securityholders." The SEC has taken the position that it does.[48] The consequence of requiring that the exchange be "exclusively" with existing securityholders can be illustrated as follows. Suppose a corporation offers to exchange a new issue of debentures for outstanding debentures and at or about the same time sells some of the new debentures for cash to non-holders of the old debentures. Under the SEC's interpretation, there is a possibility that the Section 3(a)(9) exemption would not be available for the exchange offer. The concurrent cash sale would destroy the exclusivity of the exchange. If, however, the issue of securities to the non-holders could be viewed as a separate "issue," either because of its timing or purpose, then the exchange offer would be exempt under Section 3(a)(9).[49]

---

46. SEC No-action Letter, *ECL Industries, Inc. and Norlin Corporation* (available December 16, 1985).

47. SEC No-action Letter, *Daisy Systems Corporation* (available April 10, 1989).

48. SEC Release No. 33-2029 (August 8, 1939).

49. *Id.*

The interpretation makes little sense. The existence of a concurrent cash sale of securities of the same class and series as those offered in an otherwise-exempt exchange offer does not affect in the slightest the need or lack of need on the part of the exchanging securityholders for the protections afforded by the 1933 Act.

One thing that "exclusively" clearly means is that Section 3(a)(9) will not be available if securityholders of the issuer are required to give up anything other than their securities. An offer of new securities in exchange for existing securities plus a cash payment from the tendering securityholders would not be an exempt transaction. There is an exception, however. Rule 149 provides:

> The term "exchanged" in section 3(a)(9) shall be deemed to include the issuance of a security in consideration of the surrender by the existing securityholders of the issuer, of outstanding securities of the issuer, notwithstanding the fact that the surrender of the outstanding securities may be required by the terms of the plan of exchange to be accompanied by such payment in cash by the securityholder as may be necessary to effect an equitable adjustment, in respect of dividends or interest paid or payable on the securities involved in the exchange, as between such securityholder and other securityholders of the same class accepting the offer of exchange.

In the request for the no-action letter issued to ECL Industries, Inc. and Norlin Corporation, it was explained that the exchange offer provided that tendering holders of old debentures would not be entitled to the November interest payment or any other interest accruing on their old debentures after November 15, 1985. By accepting the exchange offer, holders of old debentures would affirmatively waive their right to receive these payments. Tendering holders of old debentures who became holders after the October 31, 1985 record date for the November interest payment would be required to pay ECL Industries $45 for each $1,000 principal amount of debentures tendered to reimburse it for the November interest payment that it would be required to make to those persons who were holders on the record date but who subsequently sold their debentures in the open market. The request set forth an example of how this would work.

The example assumed that two debentureholders, A and B, had acquired their debentures two days before the October 31 record date. On November 2, B sells his debentures to C. A and C subsequently tender. A thereby waives his right to the November interest payment, but as C was not a holder on the record date no interest is payable to him and he has nothing to waive. He is not entitled, so the argument went, to waive on B's behalf the interest payment due to him as the holder on the record date. Presumably, the price paid by C to B for his debentures was reduced to reflect the fact that they were purchased after the record date, and thus it was argued that it was only fair to require C to reimburse the corporation, thereby placing him on a parity with A, who did not purchase at a reduced price.

The no-action request pointed to two prior instances where the staff had taken no-action positions where tendering securityholders were required to relinquish their right to unpaid accrued interest.[50] It contended that the requirement that certain tendering debentureholders make a $45 payment for each $1,000 principal amount of debentures tendered represented an "equitable adjustment" in respect of interest payments within the meaning of Rule 149. The staff granted the no-action request without commenting on this analysis.

The condition to Section 3(a)(9) that there be no paid solicitation has previously been noted. As originally adopted, Section 3(a)(9) prohibited the payment of remuneration "in connection with such exchange" rather than "for soliciting such exchange." The 1934 amendments to the 1933 Act substituted the present language to codify the interpretation of the Federal Trade Commission that the payment of expenses, such

50. SEC No-action Letter, *Barnett Winston Investment Trust* (available October 11, 1977); SEC No-action Letter, *Geoscience Technology Services Corp.* (available May 14, 1976). *See also* SEC No-action Letter, *NJB Prime Investors* (available May 14, 1976); SEC No-action Letter, *Conrad Precision Industries, Inc.* (available August 28, 1973); SEC No-action Letter, *Wright Air Lines, Inc.* (available August 23, 1973).

as engraving costs, clerical costs and payments to third persons for services in effecting but not promoting the exchange, would not render the exemption unavailable.

The exemption is not destroyed by the payment of cash or other consideration along with the securities issued to the holders making the exchange. This is clear from the language of Section 3(a)(9), as this additional consideration is not paid for solicitation. Rule 150 eliminates any doubt by providing that the term "commission or other remuneration" in Section 3(a)(9) does not include "payments made by the issuer, directly or indirectly, to its securityholders in connection with an exchange of securities for outstanding securities, when such payments are part of the terms of the offer of exchange."

An issuer may rely on Section 3(a)(9) in an offer to acquire its debentures for cash or for new debentures and cash at the option of the tendering debentureholder.[51] If the issuer makes a cash tender offer for its outstanding preferred stock and, prior to such offer, extends offers to certain substantial holders to take common stock in exchange for their preferred shares, the cash offer will not affect the availability of the exemption for the swap.[52]

As in the case of cash tender offers, information agents are retained in connection with exchange offers to perform certain ministerial functions. The payment of the information agent's fee will not destroy the exemption. In the ECL Industries/ Norlin correspondence, the staff of the SEC was advised that the services of The Carter Organization had been enlisted to do no more than to notify debentureholders of the appropriate details of the exchange offer; to confirm the accuracy of their addresses; to ascertain by telephone whether debentureholders have received the offering circular and understand the mechanics of tendering; to answer questions relative thereto; to ascertain what action the debentureholders plan to take and communicate this information to the company; to remind de-

---

51. SEC No-action Letter, *Barnett Winston Investment Trust* (available February 9, 1978).

52. SEC No-action Letter, *Clevepak Corporation* (available March 23, 1984).

bentureholders of deadlines; and to communicate with the back office personnel of brokers, banks and nominees who hold securities for others to make sure that the offering circular and the accompanying materials are forwarded properly and to urge them to check with the beneficial owners to ascertain whether they have received the materials and understand the mechanics of the offer. The Carter Organization was instructed that it could not make any recommendation regarding the tender of debentures and that, if it was asked for advice, it should respond that it was not authorized to give investment advice and that the debentureholder should consult his own advisors or contact appropriate officers of the company.

The compensation payable to The Carter Organization was not contingent upon the number of debentures tendered for exchange, but was based on the number of debentureholders. In approving this arrangement, the staff acted consistently with earlier no-action positions.[53] If, however, a proxy solicitation firm were retained to convey management's recommendations to the securityholders, the exemption would not be available.[54]

Communications between a corporation's officers and its securityholders advising them of the merits of an exchange offer will not destroy the Section 3(a)(9) exemption so long as the communications are incidental to the officers' regular duties and no special compensation is paid to them for performing this function.[55] Also, the staff of the SEC raised no objection where exchanges were to be solicited by the advisor of an investment

53. SEC No-action Letter, *Mortgage Investors of Washington* (available October 8, 1980); SEC No-action Letter, *Hamilton Brothers Petroleum Corp.* (available August 14, 1978); SEC No-action Letter, *Barnett Winston Investment Trust* (available February 9, 1978); SEC No-action Letter, *Valhi, Inc.* (available October 15, 1976); SEC No-action Letter, *The Carter Organization* (available April 7, 1975); SEC No-action Letter, *Georgeson & Co.* (available June 11, 1973).

54. SEC No-action Letter, *Stokely-Van Camp, Inc.* (available April 29, 1983).

55. SEC No-action Letter, *Hamilton Brothers Petroleum Corporation* (available August 14, 1978); SEC No-action Letter, *Chris-Craft Industries, Inc.* (available October 9, 1972).

trust.[56] The issuer may hire an investment banking firm to act as its financial advisor in structuring the exchange offer. But the firm may not solicit exchanges lest its advisory fee be viewed as an indirect payment for promoting the exchange.

The basic authority on the role of a financial advisor was found for many years in no-action correspondence between counsel for Dean Witter & Co., Inc. and the staff of the SEC.[57] Counsel's first letter to the SEC asked whether its client could receive a fixed fee from a corporation offering its debt securities in exchange for outstanding stock without destroying the 3(a)(9) exemption if its services were limited to consultation and advice to the corporation regarding the terms of the offer, including the terms of the debt securities to be issued; advice regarding the preparation of the offering circular, letter of transmittal, stockholder letter, and other documents; the delivery of the offering documents to brokers, banks, and nominees for distribution to beneficial stockholders; the rendering of an opinion concerning the fairness of the exchange to the stockholders of the corporation; and telephone contacts with the stockholders during which the investment banker's personnel would inquire whether they had received the offering materials and during which they would respond to questions asked by stockholders, provided their response was confined to the information contained in the documentation sent to stockholders. The staff replied that it was of the view that the performance of these services by the investment banker, "particularly the expression of an opinion by it concerning the fairness of the proposed exchange coupled with subsequent telephone discussions of the exchange with shareholders," would raise serious doubts as to the availability of the Section 3(a)(9) exemption.

Counsel asked for clarification of the staff's position to determine whether Section 3(a)(9) would be rendered unavailable if its client performed all of the described services, plus being named in the offering circular as the dealer-manager for the ex-

---

56. SEC No-action Letter, *Barnett Winston Investment Trust* (available February 9, 1978).

57. SEC No-action Letters, *Dean Witter & Co., Inc.* (available December 23, 1974 and February 24, 1975).

change offer, but did not have its personnel communicate directly with the corporation's stockholders. Counsel also asked whether its client could perform all of these services, including the limited communications with stockholders, if there were excluded from the offering circular the description of its fairness opinion. The staff replied that the exemption provided by Section 3(a)(9) would not be rendered unavailable if the dealer-manager were to provide all of the described services other than the proposed communications with stockholders. However, the answer to the second question was negative. The staff stated, "In our view, there is an inconsistency on the surface in the proposition that representatives of a firm which has expressed an opinion (whether publicly disclosed or not) on the fairness of a proposed exchange may initiate contacts with the security-holders voting [sic] on the exchange and express wholly impartial views on questions raised by those securityholders."

Counsel did not ask, and the staff did not address, the question whether the investment banking firm could contact stockholders in the limited manner described if it did not render a fairness opinion. The staff limited its responses to the questions asked. In a subsequent no-action letter, however, the staff agreed that an investment banking firm acting as financial advisor could answer unsolicited inquiries directed to it concerning the terms of an exchange offer, within the confines of the information set forth in the offering materials.[58]

In later no-action letters, the staff appears to have relaxed its position to the degree that it has acquiesced in an issuer's financial adviser's participation in meetings and telephone conversations with the legal and financial adviser to a committee of holders of the outstanding securities that were to be the subject of the exchange offer. In one such letter, these meetings took place before the commencement of the offer,[59] and in another the meetings took place after the commencement of the

---

58. SEC No-action Letter, *Mortgage Investors of Washington* (available October 8, 1980).

59. SEC No-action Letter, *Seaman Furniture Company, Inc.* (available October 10, 1989).

offer.[60] The issuer's financial adviser would not be named as a dealer manager in offering documents, would not deliver any fairness opinion and would not communicate directly with any holders on substantive matters. Moreover, its fee would not be contingent upon the success of the exchange offer, and the committee itself would not solicit exchanges.

It is not clear to what extent the more recent no-action letters depend on the issuer's weak financial condition. In any event, many lawyers believe that it is dangerous to have securities sales representatives engage in discussions with customers regarding an exchange offer with respect to which their firm is acting as financial advisor in reliance on Section 3(a)(9). It may be unrealistic to expect these representatives to limit their responses to their customers' questions to the information that is contained in the documents. It is also quite likely that any holder contacted would inquire as to the recommendations of the firm or its representative. If the response must be that the firm cannot recommend exchanges, this could have a negative—and not merely a neutral—effect on the holder's inclination to exchange. Nonetheless, it is not uncommon for a financial advisor to a corporation making an exchange offer, where it has not rendered a fairness opinion, to permit its personnel to perform the services normally performed by an information agent and to refer any substantive inquiries to specified officers of the issuer.

Under the blue sky laws of a few states, an issuer will be required to register as a dealer if it offers its securities directly and not through a registered dealer. To avoid this problem in the case of an exchange offer, it is customary for the mailing to securityholders resident in those states to go out under the name of a registered dealer. If a dealer is paid a flat fee for performing this service and does not make any recommendation or other solicitation regarding the exchange offer, the Section 3(a)(9) exemption will be available despite the dealer's involvement.[61]

---

60. SEC No-action Letter, *International Controls Corp.* (available August 6, 1990).

61. SEC No-action Letter, *ECL Industries, Inc. and Norlin Corporation* (available December 16, 1985); SEC No-action Letter, *Mortgage Investors*

Section 3(a)(9) may be relied upon in a transaction, such as a reclassification of securities, that is effected by means of a stockholder vote rather than through a voluntary exchange. Rule 145 provides that an "offer" or "sale" occurs when there is submitted to securityholders a plan or agreement under which they are asked to approve, on the basis of what in substance is a new investment decision, the exchange of a new or different security for their existing securities. However, a transaction for which a statutory exemption is otherwise available, including one exempt under Section 3(a)(9), is not affected by Rule 145. This is made perfectly clear in the preliminary note to Rule 145.[62]

Even if an exchange offer is exempt from registration under Section 3(a)(9), if debt securities are offered in the exchange, an indenture must be qualified under the 1939 Act. Section 304(a)(4)(A) of the 1939 Act exempts most securities exempted from the provisions of the 1933 Act, but not those exempted by Section 3(a)(9). Section 307(a) of the 1939 Act governs the qualification of indentures covering securities not required to be registered under the 1933 Act, and pursuant to Rule 7a-1 thereunder, the application for qualification is made on Form T-3. As in any other case, the trustee must file a statement of eligibility and qualification on Form T-1. The exchange offer may commence after the filing of the application for qualification of the indenture without waiting for the actual qualification of the indenture.[63]

• • *Tender Offer and Going Private Rules.* An exchange offer is a tender offer. Thus, if the securities being sought in an exchange offer are equity securities, including convertible debentures, the issuer tender offer requirements of Rule 13e-4 must be complied with. In addition, if equity securities are to

---

of Washington (available October 8, 1980); SEC No-action Letter, *Barnett Winston Investment Trust* (available February 9, 1978); SEC No-action Letter, *Western Pacific Industries, Inc.* (available October 11, 1976).

62. *See also* SEC Release No. 33-5463 (February 28, 1974); SEC No-action Letter, *Valhi, Inc.* (available October 15, 1976).

63. SEC No-action Letter, *Mississippi Chemical Corp.* (available November 25, 1988).

be acquired, the exchange offer may constitute a going private transaction, in which case the issuer will be required to comply with Rule 13e-3.

There is an exception to Rule 13e-3 that may be applicable to an exchange offer if the requisite conditions are met. Subsection (g)(2) of Rule 13e-3 affords an exemption from the provisions of the rule if the securityholders are offered or receive only an equity security that (i) has substantially the same rights as the equity security to be surrendered in exchange, including voting, dividend, redemption and liquidation rights (except that this requirement is deemed to be satisfied if unaffiliated securityholders are offered common stock); (ii) is registered pursuant to Section 12 of the 1934 Act (or reports are required to be filed by the issuer pursuant to Section 15(d) of the 1934 Act); and (iii) is either listed on a national securities exchange or authorized to be quoted in NASDAQ if the security to be surrendered was either so listed or quoted. For the exception to be available, all securityholders must be offered the same form of consideration.[64] In essence, exchange offers in which securityholders "are permitted to maintain an equivalent or enhanced equity interest" are outside the purpose of Rule 13e-3.[65]

The substantially equivalent test is met if the security offered in exchange is common stock. Thus, if a corporation offers shares of its common stock in exchange for its outstanding convertible debentures, Rule 13e-3 will not be applicable provided that the registration or reporting test and the listed or quoted test are also met.[66]

A 1988 no-action letter issued to Savin Corporation is pertinent to the scope of the subsection (g)(2) exemption.[67] The no-action request described an offer to exchange convertible preferred stock for zero coupon convertible senior subordinated notes, an existing class of convertible preferred stock and several issues of straight debt securities. Counsel pointed out that the substantially equivalent requirement is satisfied if un-

---

64. SEC Release No. 34-17719 (April 13, 1981).

65. SEC Release No. 34-16075 (August 2, 1979).

66. SEC No-action Letter, *Instrument Systems Corporation* (available February 19, 1983).

67. SEC No-action Letter, *Savin Corporation* (available June 28, 1988).

affiliated securityholders are offered common stock and argued that this was the case because the preferred stock offered in exchange for the outstanding equity securities was immediately convertible into common stock. Counsel referred to Rule 13d-3 under the 1934 Act, which provides that a person is deemed to be the beneficial owner of a security that, within 60 days, he has the right to acquire through the conversion of another security, and to Rule 16a-2(b), which provides that a person is deemed to be the beneficial owner of a security that he has the right to acquire through the conversion of a presently convertible security. Counsel contended that, if the convertibility feature of the new preferred stock is sufficient to make its holders the beneficial owners of the underlying common stock, it was logical to conclude that the requirements of the exemption had been met. Counsel argued, in the alternative, that the new convertible preferred shares afford the holders of the outstanding equity securities not only substantially similar rights but substantially enhanced rights. The staff took a no-action position without specifying which of counsel's alternative arguments it considered the more convincing.

The substantially similar test was found to be satisfied in the case of an exchange offer by Trans World Airlines, Inc. of new debentures for outstanding debentures.[68] It was represented that the new debentures were similar to the old debentures in that both were entitled to annual interest payments, were convertible into common stock of the airline's parent, had sinking fund requirements, were subordinated to senior debt and had the same remedies on default and substantially the same indenture modification provisions. While the new debentures varied from the old debentures with respect to interest rates and conversion ratios, the variations were designed to provide tendering holders of old debentures with a security having a value that represented a slight premium over the market price of the old debentures at the time of the exchange offer.

---

68. SEC No-action Letter, *Trans World Airlines, Inc.* (available November 2, 1980).

• • *Rules 101 and 10b-13.* If an exchange offer involves a "distribution" of the offered security for purposes of Rule 101 (see Chapter 4), then the dealer-manager must refrain from bids for and purchases of the offered security unless they are permitted under an exception to Rule 101. For example, the rule's restrictions will not apply if the offered security is an investment grade debt security or preferred stock or if a common stock meets the $1,000,000 ADTV/$150 million public float standard. In other cases, the rule's restrictions commence on the mailing of the exchange offer prospectus and continue until the conclusion of the offer.

The former Rule 10b-6 also applied to bids for and purchases of the securities sought to be acquired pursuant to the exchange offer, on the theory that these were "rights to purchase" the offered security. As discussed in Chapter 4, however, Rule 101 no longer applies to any "rights to purchase" the securities being distributed.

If the exchange offer is for an equity security, however, then Rule 10b-13 also becomes applicable. This rule precludes any person making a cash tender offer or exchange offer for an equity security from purchasing such security or any security immediately convertible into or exchangeable for such security.

If neither Rule 101 nor Rule 10b-13 applies to an exchange offer, it is now possible for a dealer-manager to assist in the distribution by making lay-offs of the offered securities, against which it may purchase and exchange outstanding securities. This activity was formerly prohibited by Rule 10b-8, which was rescinded by the SEC upon the adoption of Regulation M.

• *Consent Solicitations*

Indentures invariably provide that most covenants may be amended or waived with the consent of the holders of a specified percentage of the principal amount of outstanding securities. But holders of senior securities cannot be expected to agree to an amendment to a financial covenant unless they receive some benefit in return. If a consent solicitation is part of a tender offer or exchange offer, the ability to participate in the offer may provide sufficient incentive. In the case of a stand-alone consent solicitation, however, some incentive must be provided to induce securityholders to go along with the indenture modification.[69]

An example of a consent solicitation tied to a tender offer is the offer to purchase and consent solicitation made on February 28, 1989, for two outstanding issues of convertible debentures of Catalyst Energy Corporation. The offer was made by an affiliate of the corporation that had provided substantially all of the financing for an earlier acquisition by Merrimac Corporation of the entire equity interest in Catalyst. The debentures sought to be acquired were convertible into the amount of cash paid by Merrimac for each Catalyst share. There was a limited market for the debentures, and the consideration offered was based on the rate of return acceptable to the purchaser. The indentures were to be amended to eliminate or modify numerous restrictive covenants, including a restriction on dividends and financial tests as a condition to mergers.

The offer provided that holders of debentures wishing to accept the tender offer must consent to the proposed amendments. The consent form was part of the letter of transmittal pursuant to which tenders were to be made. Under each of the indentures, the consent of the holders of a majority of the outstanding debentures was sufficient to effect the amendments. The materials mailed to debentureholders made clear that holders who did not tender would be bound by the amendments and could be adversely affected by them. In this consent solicitation, as in others, a record date was not set to determine those entitled to consent. Transferees could consent to the same extent as the holders to whom the offer was initially made. A similar offer to purchase and consent solicitation was made by Union Pacific Corporation for the debt securities of Southern

---

69. In the case of any indenture modification, consideration must be given to whether the changes are sufficiently substantial as to give rise for 1933 Act purposes to the issuance of a new security in exchange for the security being modified. Even if this is the case, the "exchange" may still be exempt (as discussed above in the context of exchange offers) under Section 3(a)(9). The supplemental indenture may still have to be qualified under the 1939 Act by filing a Form T-3, and the trustee may still have to requalify by filing a new Form T-I.

Pacific Rail Corporation on September 5, 1996. This offer and solicitation was made in connection with the acquisition of Southern Pacific by Union Pacific.

In the case of a consent solicitation unrelated to a tender offer or exchange offer, there must be some incentive to consent. In a May 13, 1983 request by Fleet Financial Group, Inc. for waivers of a covenant prohibiting the incurrence or assumption of senior indebtedness having a maturity of more than three years unless a capitalization ratio was met, the company agreed that if sufficient waivers were obtained, the rate of interest on all of the debentures would be increased from 8.25% to 9.25%. In most solicitations, however, only those who consent receive the benefits.

In an October 15, 1986 solicitation of proxies from the holders of its 4-3/4% Convertible Subordinated Debentures due 1993 for a meeting to be held to vote on an amendment to the indenture under which they were issued, Eastern Air Lines, Inc. told the holders that if they voted for the amendment and the amendment was approved, then for each $1,000 principal amount of debentures so voted, Eastern would pay, at the holder's election, $125 in ticket vouchers, applicable toward up to 50% of the price of an Eastern Airlines ticket purchased before a specified date, or $35 in cash. The proxy materials stated in boldface type that only debentureholders who voted for the amendment at or before the meeting would be entitled to receive the consent payment in ticket vouchers or cash and that debentureholders who did not vote for the amendment would receive no consent payment even though the amendment, if approved, would be binding on them.

In the case of the Eastern proxy solicitation, the scheduled meeting date set the time frame within which proxies had to be received, although Eastern reserved the right to postpone the meeting if sufficient proxies were not received. Where there is no meeting, but consents are solicited, it is customary to provide that the consent payment will be made to all holders who consent within a specified time period and that, if the requisite consents are not received by the end of the solicitation period, the corporation will extend the solicitation period as in the case of a tender or exchange offer. Alternatively, the corporation may continue to accept consents in the order received and make corresponding consent payments until the requisite consents are obtained or the corporation elects to terminate the solicitation.

For example, Itel Corporation made a consent solicitation on July 3, 1986, that provided for the acceptance of, and payment of the consent payment of $10 per $1,000 of principal amount with respect to all consents received by the close of business on July 17, 1986. The corporation reserved the right, until the requisite majority approval was received, to accept in the order received (on a daily basis), any consents received after July 17, 1986, but on or before July 31, 1986. Consent solicitations made by Catalyst Energy Corporation on February 26, 1987, and by BCI Holdings Corporation on May 21, 1987, contained no outside limit on the length of time that the consent solicitation could be kept open.

Sometimes the issuer and its financial advisor will underestimate what it takes to bring in the necessary consents. In the case of the BCI consent solicitation, the original offer to the holders of four separate issues of debt securities called for a cash payment of $2.50 for each $1,000 of securities consenting to the amendment. On June 15, 1987, four days before the initial termination date, the corporation made a second mailing in which it stated that, on the basis of discussions with certain major holders of its debt securities, it had determined to make changes in the indenture amendments and in the terms of the solicitation proposed in the May 21, 1987 consent solicitation statement, including an increase in the consent payment to $12.50 per $1,000 for its senior notes and $10 per $1,000 for its other debt securities.

Consent solicitations have been the subject of litigation. In *Katz v. Oak Industries Inc.*,[70] the plaintiff sought to enjoin the consummation of an exchange offer and consent solicitation made by Oak Industries to the holders of various issues of its long-term debt. Oak Industries was in deep financial trouble. It had managed to negotiate a deal with Allied-Signal, Inc. for the

---

70. 508 A.2d 873 (Del. Ch. 1986).

sale of its materials segment and for an equity investment by Allied-Signal.

Allied-Signal was unwilling to commit to the cash infusion unless Oak Industries reduced its long-term debt by 85%. In order to complete the transaction with Allied-Signal, it was necessary for Oak Industries to eliminate the financial covenants in its indentures. Thus, the corporation offered to exchange common stock for certain of its debt securities and cash payment certificates for others, the latter being payable after the closing of the sale of the materials segment to Allied-Signal. The offer required that tendering securityholders consent to amendments to the indentures governing the tendered securities in order to remove the financial covenants that they contained.

The plaintiff contended that the exchange offer and consent solicitation was a "coercive" device that, under the circumstances, constituted a breach of a contractual obligation to act in good faith that Oak Industries owed to the holders of its debt securities. The plaintiff argued that no free choice was provided to the holders by the exchange offer and consent solicitation. Under the terms of the offer, so went the argument, a rational securityholder was "forced" to tender and consent. Failure to do so would face a holder with the risk of owning a security stripped of all financial covenant protections and for which it was likely that there would not be a ready market. A reasonable holder, it was suggested, could not possibly accept those risks and thus was coerced to accept the offer and consent to the indenture modifications. It was argued that the linking of the offer to purchase with the granting of a consent interfered with the mechanism for effecting amendments agreed to in the indentures.

Chancellor Allen concluded that the relevant test was whether it was apparent from the provisions of the indentures that the contracting parties—had they negotiated with the exchange offer and consent solicitation in mind—would have expressly agreed to prohibit contractually the linking of the giving of consent with the purchase and sale of the security. The Chancellor placed substantial weight on the fact that the inducement to consent was made on the same terms to all holders of the securities affected and concluded that, while it was clear that Oak Industries had fashioned the exchange offer and consent solicitation in a way designed to encourage consents, he could not conclude that the offer violated the intendment of any of the express contractual provisions considered or that its structure and timing breached any implied obligation of good faith and fair dealing.

The Eastern Air Lines proxy solicitation also was challenged in court.[71] Here the amendment proposed to be voted upon would relax certain financial covenants and thus permit Eastern to pay dividends or make other payments to its stockholders. It would enable Eastern to effect its merger with Texas Air Corporation in a transaction involving the payment, following the merger, of a $1.75 per share cash dividend by the merged entity to Texas Air, which would then be its sole stockholder. The plaintiff claimed that in offering consideration only in exchange for a consent (rather than offering consideration that would flow to every debentureholder if the amendments were approved, without regard to how any one holder voted on the amendments) Eastern had embarked on a course that violated public policy and constituted a breach of an implied contractual term requiring it to deal fairly and in good faith with the holders of its securities.

The first theory asserted by the plaintiff was that Eastern's offer of a consent payment constituted "vote buying" and that vote buying in any context was a legal wrong. The Chancellor found that however wrong vote buying may be in a political context, and despite a line of Delaware cases arguably prohibiting in the stockholder context the transfer of voting power for consideration (except as part of a transfer of the underlying share),[72] there was insufficient authority to support a conclusion that public policy precluded Eastern from offering an inducement to consent and limiting that inducement to those who grant the consent.

The implied contract argument put forth by the plaintiff was given the same treatment as in *Oak Industries*. Again, the fact that the consideration was offered to all consenting holders turned the

---

71. *Kass v. Eastern Air Lines, Inc.*, Del. Ch., Civ. Action Nos. 8700, 8701, and 8711 (slip op. November 14, 1986).

72. *Chew v. Inverness Mgt. Corp.*, 352 A.2d 426 (Del. Ch. 1976); Hall v. Isaacs, 146 A.2d 602 (Del. 1958), *aff'd in part* 163 A.2d 288 (Del. Ch. 1960); *Macht v. Merchants Mortgage & Credit Co.*, 194 A. 19 (Del. Ch. 1937).

tide in favor of the defendant. The Chancellor stated that "had Eastern not made its offer to all bondholders on the same terms, but had it privately paid money to sufficient holders to carry the election, one would, without more, feel some confidence in concluding, provisionally at least, that such conduct was so inconsistent with the concept of voting implied by the amendment provision that it constituted a violation of what must have been the reasonable expectation of the contracting parties."

An attempt to enjoin the consent solicitation by BCI Holdings Corporation likewise failed.[73] Citing *Oak Industries* and *Eastern Air Lines,* the court held that the consent solicitation did not violate any public policy against vote buying nor any implied term of the indenture. The court also noted that a separate ground for dismissal was the plaintiff's failure to satisfy a contractual condition precedent to the commencement of an action, namely, the provision of the indentures that the holders of a majority of the securities must request the trustee to commence the action, offer to indemnify the trustee, and afford the trustee 60 days to comply. The court observed that this standard indenture provision had been upheld consistently as a reasonable restriction on the freedom of action of individual bondholders.

When-Issued Trading and Arbitrage

If a dealer-manager and other soliciting dealers were permitted to sell securities offered in exchange and purchase the outstanding securities sought to be acquired, they would be playing a role not unlike that played by securities firms that engage in risk arbitrage (more recently known as "event arbitrage") in connection with exchange offers, mergers and cash tender offers. In accordance with the SEC's current views, a securities firm may either act as a soliciting dealer in connection with such transactions or act as an arbitrager. It may not do both.

A securities dealer engaged in risk arbitrage will seek to make a profit on the disparity that exists between the market price of a security and the value, whether in securities or cash, being offered

---

73. *Pisik v. BCI Holdings Corporation*, N.Y. Sup. Ct. Index No. 14593/87 (slip op. June 5, 1987).

for it in an exchange offer, a merger or a cash tender offer. For example, in the case of a merger, the acquiring company may propose to exchange one share of its common stock with a market value of $20 per share for each share of common stock of the target company with a market value of $15 per share. Theoretically, the market value of the two securities should come into line if there were certainty that the merger would be consummated. Because of the uncertainties that may exist as a result of regulatory questions, the opposition of the target company's management, the validity of shark repellents, the outcome of a stockholder vote (if one is called for), or any number of other factors, a share of the target company's stock may trade at a price that is less than the share-equivalent of the acquiring company's stock to be issued in the merger. Arbitragers will purchase shares of the target company in the highly-educated expectation that the merger will be consummated and that they will ultimately realize the discrepancy in price. At the same time, they may lock in the value of the stock to be issued in the merger by making short sales or by dealing in call options.

Certain legal questions relating to when-issued trading and the activities of arbitragers are covered in two no-action letters issued by the staff of the SEC for the benefit of certain NYSE member firms that engaged in risk arbitrage on a regular basis.[74] A merger or other Rule 145 transaction, an exchange offer by one company for the securities of another public company, or an exchange offer to existing securityholders using the services of a dealer-manager will require registration under the 1933 Act. The question then arises whether an arbitrager may sell the securities to be registered at the time the transaction is announced and prior to the effectiveness of the registration statement. The answer to this question will depend on whether the securities are of a class that is already outstanding and traded or whether they are of a class that is not outstanding,

---

74. SEC No-action Letters, *Cleary, Gottlieb, Steen & Hamilton* (available February 11, 1973, and March 18, 1973). *See also* SEC No-action Letter, *Crocker National Corporation* (available October 16, 1975); SEC No-action Letter, *King's Department Stores, Inc.* (available March 12, 1975).

such as, for example, a new class of preferred stock or a new issue of debentures.

Under the terms of the *Cleary Gottlieb* letters, where the securities to be issued are of a class that is outstanding and traded, they may be sold short by an arbitrager as soon as the terms of the transaction are announced and before the registration statement is effective, if the following four requirements are met:

- The short sales involved in the proposed arbitrage activities will not be considered or marked "short exempt," i.e., exempt from the prohibitions of Section 10(a) of the 1934 Act and Rule 10a-1(a) thereunder by virtue of the arbitrage exemption under Rule 10a-1(d)(7).

- The arbitrager will not acquire 10% or more of the securities being registered.

- In the case of exchange offers, the arbitrager will not sign a soliciting dealer's agreement or accept any fee payable to soliciting dealers whether or not it executes such an agreement.

- The arbitrager will not have any agreement or understanding with the issuer or any other participant in the distribution.

If the securities to be issued are of a class not previously outstanding, sales in arbitrage transactions will of necessity be made on a when-issued basis. Such sales may not be made until after the registration statement becomes effective.

With respect to when-issued trading in a security to be issued in a Section 3(a)(9) transaction, the Section 4(3) dealer's exemption will be available where the ultimate issuance will be pursuant to an exempt exchange.[75] But when-issued trading may not begin in a debt security to be issued pursuant to a Section 3(a)(9) exemption from registration until application has

---

75. *See* L. Loss & R. Vernon, *When-Issued Securities Trading in Law and Practice*, 54 Yale L.J. 741, 782–86 (1945). *See also* FTC Release No. 33-97 (December 28, 1933); SEC Release No. 33-646 (February 3, 1936).

been made to qualify the indenture under the 1939 Act. It is not necessary to wait until the indenture is actually qualified.[76]

Arbitragers have raised the question from time to time whether certificates borrowed to cover short sales pending completion of a transaction can be borrowed from a person in a control relationship with the issuer. Assume that a company is offering to issue shares of its common stock in exchange for an issue of its outstanding debt securities. An arbitrager wishes to make short sales of the common stock, purchase the equivalent in debt securities, and make the exchange for its own account. Pending the completion of the exchange, it must borrow common stock certificates to deliver on the settlement date for the short sale. There is a scarcity of certificates in the normal borrowing channels, but the arbitrager has reason to believe that it can borrow the requisite certificates from the founder and principal shareholder of the issuer.

The SEC staff is not believed to be inclined to issue a no-action letter on the subject. As a matter of legal analysis, however, if the borrowed certificates are replaced with certificates representing stock of the same class (which may be the certificates received in the exchange offer and need not be the identical certificates borrowed), the borrowing and delivery of certificates provided by a controlling stockholder should not create any problems under the 1933 Act. Although a controlling stockholder may sell his or her shares through a broker in a public unregistered transaction only pursuant to Rule 144, this transaction does not involve a sale by the controlling stockholder. The only sale will be the sale made by the arbitrager acting for its own account. For purposes of the 1933 Act, a distinction should be made between shares and the pieces of

---

76. SEC No-action Letter, *Skadden, Arps, Slate, Meagher & Flom* (available March 12, 1986). This no-action position was based on counsel's analysis of Section 304(b) of the 1939 Act and reversed the SEC's prior position that when-issued trading was prohibited prior to the qualification of an indenture. The letter is also authority for the proposition that when-issued trading in anticipation of a Section 3(a)(9) transaction is permitted under the 1933 Act. *See also* SEC No-action Letter, *Mississippi Chemical Corporation* (available June 23, 1989).

paper that are used to evidence them. After the controlling stockholder has loaned his certificates to the arbitrager, he will continue to own the same number of shares. In this context, the reference in Section 5(a)(2) of the 1933 Act to "delivery after sale" should be read to refer to a sale by the controlling stockholder and not to an exempt sale by another person to whom he merely has made a certificate loan.

Fees payable to soliciting dealers will not be available in connection with a merger. In connection with a registered exchange offer, however, the issuer may agree to pay dealers a fee for securities tendered through their efforts or through their facilities. The practice is more common today than it was during the late 1980s and early 1990s when the practice of paying soliciting dealer fees fell into disuse.

While an arbitrager may not solicit exchanges, when it terminates its arbitrage activities, it may execute a soliciting dealer's agreement, tender for its own account securities acquired in arbitrage transactions, and receive the soliciting dealer's fee with respect to the securities tendered.[77] As previously indicated, however, the Division of Corporation Finance has stated that an arbitrager that receives such a fee may not make short sales of the securities offered in the exchange offer prior to the effective date of the registration statement, even though the offered securities are of a class already outstanding and traded. This makes little sense, but it is one of the conditions set forth in the *Cleary Gottlieb* correspondence. In a 1976 telephone conversation with a member of the SEC's staff, the senior author was advised that this condition had been volunteered by counsel, perhaps in an effort to assure that the arbitrager was not an

---

77. SEC No-action Letter, *OAK Industries Inc.* (available December 22, 1976); SEC No-action Letter, *Hospital Affiliates, Inc.* (available January 2, 1975). As discussed above, the staff's unwritten position is that the "best price" and "all holders" rules prevent a dealer from accepting a soliciting fee for its proprietary securities in connection with a cash tender offer. This position probably also applies to exchange offers. On the other hand, the staff is not believed to have abandoned its previous position that an arbitrager may receive a soliciting dealer's fee in connection with a cash tender offer. SEC Release No. 34-9395 (November 24, 1971).

underwriter, and that pre-effective short sales by an arbitrager should be permitted even if he subsequently receives a soliciting dealer's fee.[78]

Rights Offerings

Thirty years ago, rights offerings with standby underwriters were a preferred method by which United States corporations raised new equity capital. Today they are far less common, with the exception in recent years only of closed-end investment companies. In the international sphere, however, most European and Japanese companies continue to rely heavily on this financing technique. As noted in Chapter 9, a number of foreign companies have registered shares under the 1933 Act to permit their rights offerings to be made to shareholders in the United States.

If the stockholders of a corporation have preemptive rights, the corporation, in raising funds through the sale of common stock, or in some cases securities convertible into common stock, has no choice but to proceed by means of a rights offering. If the stockholders have preemptive rights, the corporation may not sell the securities directly to underwriters for resale to the public, but must first offer them to its existing stockholders and hold the offer open for a reasonable period of time.[79] But

---

78. Memorandum dated January 16, 1976 in senior author's files.

79. A preemptive right is simply the right of an existing shareholder to subscribe for his proportionate share of a new issue of equity securities. Whether or not a particular corporation's shareholders have preemptive rights is a question of state law. Under Section 622 of the New York Business Corporation Law, for example, holders of common stock have preemptive rights as to any new issue of common stock, or securities convertible into common stock, unless the certificate of incorporation provides otherwise. The New York statute contains certain exceptions to this general rule. For example, unless otherwise provided in the certificate of incorporation, there are no preemptive rights with respect to shares offered pursuant to employee stock options, or to effect a merger, or with respect to treasury shares. Under New York law, the certificate of incorporation may deny preemptive rights or may extend them beyond those otherwise provided by statute.

the stockholders of few U.S. publicly-owned corporations have preemptive rights. No corporation wishes to be in the position of being forced into a rights offering as a legal requirement.

• *Mechanics*

Rights offerings of common stock usually are made at a discount from the market. If the market price of a share of common stock is $20 when the subscription offer is made, the subscription price might be $18 per share. The offering is made by issuing to stockholders of record on a specified date subscription warrants evidencing the right to subscribe for one additional share for a specified number of shares held of record on that date. Thus, a company with 10 million shares of common stock outstanding might issue to stockholders rights to subscribe for one additional share for each ten shares held of record, thereby offering an additional one million shares to increase its equity capital by 10%. In our example, a holder of 100 shares would be issued a warrant representing 100 rights to subscribe. As ten rights are required to purchase one additional share, with the 100 rights represented by his warrant, the holder could buy ten shares at the $18 subscription price.

For rights to have value, they must be transferable. Rights will be traded on the exchange on which the issuer's common stock is listed or in the over-the-counter market if the shares are not listed on an exchange. A holder may sell his rights and receive cash to compensate for his diluted position in the company if he does not wish to subscribe for the shares offered to

---

The Delaware General Corporation Law differs from the New York statute in that it provides in Section 102(b)(3) that no stockholder of a corporation shall have any preemptive right to subscribe to an additional issue of stock or to any security convertible into such stock unless, and except to the extent that, such right is expressly granted to him in the certificate of incorporation. Thus, in Delaware there are no preemptive rights if the certificate of incorporation is silent, in contrast to New York where the certificate of incorporation must expressly deny preemptive rights. This provision in the Delaware statute was a result of amendments in 1967 and 1969, and the statute provides that preemptive rights in existence on July 3, 1967 shall remain in existence unless and until changed or terminated by appropriate action.

him at a price below the market. The price at which rights are purchased and sold will depend upon market forces, including the relationship between the subscription price and the current market price of the stock.

In a rights offering, holders of rights will be given a so-called step-up privilege. The way that a step-up privilege works is that if one is issued a warrant that is not evenly divisible by the subscription ratio, in the above example if it is not evenly divisible by ten, if he fully exercises the rights evidenced by his or her warrant, he may subscribe for one additional full share in lieu of a fractional share without furnishing any additional rights. A holder of a warrant evidencing fewer than ten rights would be entitled to subscribe for one full share without furnishing any additional rights. For example, if a stockholder owns 105 shares of stock and there is a one-for-ten rights offering, he would receive rights to subscribe for ten shares, but because he owns another five shares he may subscribe for 11 shares.

Holders of rights frequently are afforded an over-subscription privilege. Where there is an over-subscription privilege, the holder of a warrant who has fully exercised his basic subscription privilege, and the step-up privilege if applicable, may subscribe for an additional number of shares, usually not more than the aggregate number of shares subscribed for by him pursuant to the basic subscription privilege and the step-up privilege. The over-subscription privilege will be subject to allotment, so that if there are not a sufficient number of unsubscribed shares to cover all over-subscriptions, shares will be allotted pro rata among those who exercised the over-subscription privilege as nearly as practicable in proportion to the shares they requested under the over-subscription privilege. Another formula for allotment is the ratio which the rights exercised by each person exercising the over-subscription privilege bears to the total number of rights exercised by all persons exercising the over-subscription privilege.

In almost every case, the record date for a rights offering will be the close of business on the day that the registration statement covering the rights offering becomes effective. At that time, the subscription agent (in all cases the company's transfer agent) will mail a warrant and a prospectus to each stockholder of record. There are no strict rules as to the period for which the subscription offer must be left open. Where there are preemptive rights, state law usually will provide for a reasonable time as determined by the board of directors. The NYSE, however, requires that the date on which rights terminate should be at least 16 days after the mailing of the warrants. This can be reduced to 14 days if special mailing arrangements are used.

• *The Role of the Investment Banker*

A company making a rights offering is subject to the risk that its financing efforts will be unsuccessful if the price of its common stock declines during the subscription period. In the above example, the issuer wishes to raise $18 million by selling 1 million shares of common stock at a subscription price of $18 per share. The issuer may need this amount to finance a new plant or for some other specific corporate purpose. But the subscription offer will be open for several weeks, and holders of rights will often wait until the last day before deciding whether or not to subscribe. They may decide not to subscribe and let their rights lapse if the market price of the common stock declines sufficiently. If the market price of the common stock is on the decline, there probably will be substantial sales of rights. If the market price of the stock were to decline below the subscription price, there would be few, if any, subscriptions and the rights would have no value.

The issuer has two choices. It can set the subscription price sufficiently below the market price so that the risk that the price of its common stock will fall below the subscription price is remote. Here an issuer may be willing to assume the risk of the market. Many issuers, however, in order to assure the receipt of the proceeds required for their particular financing purposes, will retain an investment banking firm to form an underwriting syndicate that will agree to purchase at the subscription price any shares not subscribed for upon the exercise of rights and the over-subscription privilege. Under such an arrangement, the risk of a decline in the market price of the shares is shifted from the issuer to the underwriters.

As compensation for their commitments, the underwriters will be paid a flat standby fee, plus a per share amount for each unsubscribed share purchased by them after the subscription offer expires and for each share purchased by them upon the exercise of rights which they purchase in the open market. The standby fee may be viewed as an insurance premium paid by the issuer for the certainty that all shares offered will be sold.

The underwriters may be required to purchase shares at the end of the subscription period even if the market price remains strong. Although this is not likely to occur where there is an over-subscription privilege, there are always a number of stockholders who will lose their warrants or for some other reason will fail to exercise or sell their rights. These are the so-called "sleepers." In such circumstances, the underwriters will be purchasing at the subscription price, which is less than the current market price, without having to purchase any rights. This will result in a profit to the underwriters. The underwriting agreement often provides that any profit realized by the underwriters upon the sale of unsubscribed shares will be split with the issuer on a 50-50 basis.

• *1933 Act Registration*

A rights offering by a publicly-held corporation requires registration of the offered securities under the 1933 Act. After the adoption of the 1933 Act, there was some question whether or not this was the case.[80] Efforts were made to include in the 1934 amendments to the 1933 Act an exemption for offerings to stockholders.[81] These efforts proved unsuccessful.

Although it is necessary to register the securities being offered for subscription, it is not necessary to register the warrants mailed to stockholders or the rights that they represent, notwithstanding that transferable subscription rights are securities. The reason is that the rights are not offered or sold to the stockholders, but are

---

80. A. H. Dean, *The Federal Securities Act: I*, Fortune, August 1933, at 97. Mr. Dean states that according to street custom and the English precedents, the issuance by a corporation of additional stock to its own stockholders is not considered a public offering, but that language in the conference report would indicate otherwise.

81. A. H. Dean, *As Amended: The Federal Securities Act*, Fortune, September 1934, at 82.

granted to them for no consideration. The only circumstance under which rights might be registered is if a controlling stockholder wishes to sell his rights rather than exercise them. In this case, the requisite number of rights would be registered and a statement would be included in the prospectus that it may be used to cover sales of rights by an identified controlling person.

Securities offered pursuant to rights can be registered on Form S-3 if the registrant has been a reporting company under the 1934 Act for at least 12 months and has been timely in its filing obligations during the preceding 12 calendar months. The instructions to the form specifically provide that if the registrant requirements are met, Form S-3 can be used to register securities to be offered "upon the exercise of outstanding rights granted by an issuer of the securities to be offered, if such rights are granted on a pro rata basis to all existing securityholders of the class of securities to which the rights attach."

If, at the end of the subscription period, the standby underwriters acquire and resell unsubscribed shares, then they must deliver a prospectus supplemented to disclose the results of the subscription offering. Item 512(c) of Regulation S-K requires the following undertaking in a registration statement covering securities offered pursuant to rights:

> The undersigned registrant hereby undertakes to supplement the prospectus, after the expiration of the subscription period, to set forth the results of the subscription offer, the transactions by the underwriters during the subscription period, the amount of unsubscribed securities to be purchased by the underwriters, and the terms of any subsequent reoffering thereof. If any public offering by the underwriters is to be made on terms differing from those set forth on the cover page of the prospectus, a post-effective amendment will be filed to set forth the terms of such offering.

• *Shields Plan*

In 1947, a special committee of the Investment Bankers Association, of which a partner in Shields & Co. was chairman, recommended a new technique to reduce the underwriters' risks in handling standby commitments for rights offerings. This is the so-called "Shields Plan."

The technique involves sales by the underwriting syndicate of the securities offered for subscription (so-called lay-offs), purchases of rights in the open market, and the exercise of rights (or purchases pursuant to the standby commitment) to cover the sales. These activities take place during the subscription period and enable the managing underwriter, on behalf of the syndicate, to place shares with investors prior to the expiration of the subscription offer, thus avoiding the need to wait until after the expiration of the subscription period to determine the number of shares that the syndicate will be required to purchase. If, during the subscription period, the market price declines, lay-offs may be made to protect against further declines.

Shields Plan activities were formerly governed by Rule 10b-8, which was rescinded as part of the SEC's adoption in late 1996 of Regulation M. Rule 10b-8 regulated the underwriters' bids for and purchase of rights and, in so doing, exempted such bids and purchases from Rule 10b-6 (which prohibited bids for and purchases of "rights to purchase" the securities being distributed). As discussed above, Rule 101 no longer regulates bids for and purchases of "rights to purchase" the securities being distributed.

Rule 10b-8 also independently regulated, however, the underwriters' sale of securities obtained upon their exercise of rights. Such sales were expressly permitted by Rule 10b-6, so there was no need to rely on Rule 10b-8 for an exemption. The rule regulated the lay-off price on the theory that the underwriters might otherwise manipulate upwards the market price of the offered security in order to guarantee the success of the rights offering.

The fact that Rule 10b-8 has been repealed does not mean, of course, that the SEC may not still treat conduct formerly prohibited by the rule as a violation of Rule 10b-5. On the other hand, the SEC repealed the rule on the theory that the prohibited conduct was not an efficient way to manipulate the market. This admission would appear to require egregious misconduct in order to expose an underwriter to the threat of enforcement proceedings under Rule 10b-5.

• *Dealer-Manager Plan*

In some cases, a rights offering will be made without any standby arrangements, but rather an investment banking firm will be retained to manage the distribution. The issuer will pay a commission to any broker or dealer whose name appears on any warrant that is exercised. As under the Shields Plan, the dealer-manager may sell shares short and then cover by buying and exercising rights. This is known as the "dealer-manager" plan or the "Columbia Gas Plan."

Chapter 14

ASSET-BACKED SECURITIES

Asset-backed securities are securities the payments on which are derived primarily from the cash flow generated by a pool of assets supporting the securities. The underlying assets are usually financial assets, such as mortgage loans or credit card receivables, which by their terms require payments on a regular basis.[1] The more common asset-backed securities are similar to amortizing debt securities in that interest is payable on a periodic basis and principal is paid from time to time, depending on the structure of the security.

The timing of the payment of principal of an asset-backed security is often dependent upon the timing of collections of principal (or cash flow treated as principal) of the underlying assets. The inherent unpredictability of the timing of such principal collections and, therefore, the timing of related payments of principal of the asset-backed security, is one major feature

---

1. As used herein, the term "asset-backed security" is a security backed by a pool of any type of asset, including first mortgage loans. As commonly used in the market place, the term "mortgage-backed security" means a security backed by a pool of first mortgage loans, while the term asset-backed security means a security backed by a pool of any other type of asset (including second mortgage loans and home equity loans).

that sets asset-backed securities apart from other debt securities. The other major differentiating feature is that the issuer of asset-backed securities is normally not an actively managed entity for which a balance sheet and income statement are relevant to an investment decision. The issuer is rather a passive entity that merely owns the underlying assets and only requires servicing, performed by a third party, to collect the cash flows due on those assets.

Most securities law issues relating specifically to asset-backed securities arise from the fact that the basic framework of the securities laws, having been developed prior to the development of the now considerable market for asset-backed securities, is designed to accommodate offerings of debt obligations and equity securities of corporate and other entities that are actively managed. In contrast, the essential elements of an asset-backed security are (i) the nature and quality of the underlying assets, (ii) the timing of the receipt of the cash flows from those assets and (iii) the structure for distributing those cash flows to the securityholders.

Common to almost all securitizations is the legal separation of the credit risk of the Originator/Servicer (defined below) from the cash flow of the assets being securitized, with the result that the credit rating of the related asset-backed securities is based on the creditworthiness of those assets and the legal structure of the securitization and is not affected by the financial condition of the Originator/Servicer. In the case of an Originator/Servicer that becomes subject to Title 11 of the United States Code (the "Bankruptcy Code"), the transfer of the assets from the Originator/Servicer to the Depositor (defined below) must be a "true sale," i.e., a transfer that removes the assets from the bankruptcy estate of the Originator/Servicer.

Basic Structure of an Asset-Backed Transaction

In order to discuss the application of the securities laws to asset-backed securities, it is helpful to set forth a basic structure and the entities and documents involved. A company (the "Originator/Servicer") with a portfolio of receivables that it has originated, or purchased from another originator, may wish to sell those receivables for any of a number of reasons. It may need the liquidity provided by the sale proceeds, it may want to improve its balance sheet by applying the sale proceeds to pay down debt, it may want to generate earnings or, if it is a regulated entity such as a bank, it may want to remove assets from its balance sheet against which it would otherwise have to maintain regulatory capital. Because the underlying assets in a securitization are isolated from the credit risk of the Originator/Servicer, the cost of funding the assets through a securitization (i.e., the weighted average yield on the asset-backed securities) will often be lower than the cost of borrowing by the Originator/Servicer to fund those same assets. Lastly, many Originator/Servicers with good credit ratings may securitize assets to diversify the types of funding available to them.

In a typical securitization, the Originator/Servicer sells or contributes the assets to a wholly-owned "bankruptcy remote" subsidiary (the "Depositor"), which in turn transfers the assets to a special purpose vehicle (an "SPV"), which is often a trust, and receives in return the asset-backed securities issued by the SPV. The asset-backed securities are simultaneously sold to investors, usually through underwriters, with the net proceeds going to the Depositor. The Depositor in turn uses the net proceeds to pay the Originator/Servicer for the purchased assets. The SPV contracts with the Originator/Servicer to act as servicer of the assets. The Originator/Servicer can be terminated as servicer upon the occurrence of certain defaults in its performance of servicing obligations. Because substitute servicers for most asset types are available to replace defaulting servicers, the financial condition of the servicer is normally not material to the investor.

The basic documents normally involved in a securitization are (1) a purchase agreement pursuant to which the assets are sold by the Originator/Servicer to the Depositor, (2) a sale and servicing agreement pursuant to which the assets are sold by the Depositor to the SPV and that obligates the Originator/Servicer to service the assets on the SPV's behalf and (3) the agreement governing the issuance of the asset-backed securities. The sale and servicing agreement and the agreement providing for the issuance of the asset-backed securities are often combined in one agreement known as a pooling and servicing agreement.

In a securitization, the collections on the assets are applied to make distributions of interest and principal on the asset-backed securities. Many securitizations have multiple classes of securities or "tranches" in the jargon of the market. Tranching may be used to create classes with different maturities or to create internal credit enhancement for a transaction by subordinating one or more classes to other classes. In maturity tranching, Class A receives all distributions of principal until the Class A principal balance is reduced to zero, then Class B receives all distributions of principal until the Class B principal balance is reduced to zero, and so on. Maturity tranching also has the effect of credit enhancing the classes that are paid first. In credit tranching, Class A receives the amount due it on each distribution date. Class B also receives the amount due it, but only to the extent that there are sufficient collections remaining after the required amount has been distributed to Class A. The variations on these basic themes are endless. In addition, classes of asset-backed securities may be structured to pay interest only or principal only or to defer the distribution of interest by adding accrued interest to the principal balance for some period of time. This flexibility allows investment bankers to structure classes specifically addressing the investment needs of their clients. The realization of the intended results of a structure, especially in the case of maturity tranching, often depends upon the payment speeds of the underlying assets.

A large segment of the asset-backed market consists of asset-backed commercial paper. Asset-backed commercial paper is commonly issued by "commercial paper conduit vehicles" which are entities set up to purchase receivables or receivables-backed securities from one or more Originator/ Servicers. The commercial paper is payable from the cash flow generated by this diverse pool of receivables, as well as from bank liquidity facilities backing the commercial paper programs. In addition, the commercial paper often has credit support in the form of either bank letters of credit or insurance policies issued by monoline insurers.

1933 Act Considerations

• *Who Is the Registrant?*

As described above, the issuer of the asset-backed securities is the SPV, and the asset-backed securities evidence either an obligation of or interest in the SPV. If the SPV in a securitization is a corporation, the SPV will be the registrant. On the other hand, if the SPV is a trust as in the basic structure described above, then the Depositor will be the registrant. This position is based on the definition of "issuer" in Section 2(4) of the 1933 Act, which states that "with respect to certificates of interest . . . in an unincorporated investment trust not having a board of directors. . ., the term 'issuer' means the persons performing the acts and assuming the duties of depositor or manager pursuant to the provisions of the trust or other agreement. . . ." This position was established by the SEC in the first registered offering of asset-backed securities, the offering of mortgage pass-through certificates by Bank of America in 1977.[2]

• *What Form Is Applicable?*

Prior to the amendments to Form S-3 relating to asset-backed securities, mortgage-backed securities were registered on Form S-11, which is the form prescribed by the SEC for the securities of certain real estate companies. The form was intended for real estate investment trusts and other entities that acquire and hold for investment real estate and "interests in real estate." While the form clearly contemplates an issuer engaged in acquiring mortgage loans, most of its items, many of which are items from Form S-K, are applicable to an actively managed operating company and have no relevance to an issuer whose assets are disclosed in its prospectus and whose business plan is to service those assets and distribute all of the related collections. In the seminal Bank of America offering, the SEC and the parties to the offering worked to develop dis-

---

2. In that registration process, the SEC rejected the proposition that if, Bank of America were the registrant, then the mortgage pass-through certificates would be exempt securities of a bank under Section 3(a)(2).

closure appropriate for that securitization, the basic substance of which still guides disclosure for asset-backed securities offerings today.

Disclosure in respect of asset-backed securities has, of course, evolved since the Bank of America offering, especially as asset-backed securities supported by assets other than mortgage loans came to be offered in the marketplace. The evolution took place through the process of the SEC commenting on filings and registrants responding to such comments. Prior to the amendment to Form S-3 discussed below, asset-backed securities other than mortgage-backed securities were registered on Form S-1. The same mismatch between what the form calls for and what is relevant to the buyer of an asset-backed security exists in the case of Form S-1. Recently, the SEC announced that it will promulgate rules giving guidance on disclosure required in prospectuses for asset-backed securities.

• *Form S-3 and Common Disclosure Items*

In adopting amendments to Form S-3 in 1992,[3] the SEC made shelf registration available to all asset-backed securities that are rated investment grade (i.e., rated within the four highest rating categories, within which there may be subcategories) by at least one nationally recognized statistical rating organization. Prior to this time, shelf registration of asset-backed securities was available, with a limited exception, only for mortgage-backed securities that qualified as mortgage-related securities as defined in Section 3(a)(41) of the 1934 Act.[4] That section was enacted in the Secondary Mortgage Market Enhancement Act of 1984 ("SMMEA").[5]

---

3. SEC Release No. 33-6964 (October 29, 1992).

4. Clause (viii) of Rule 415 permits the use of a shelf registration for "mortgage related securities, including such securities as mortgage backed debt and mortgage participation or pass-through certificates." While clause (viii) does not refer to Section 3(a)(41) of the 1934 Act, the SEC takes the position that clause (viii) only covers mortgage-related securities within the meaning of Section 3(a)(41).

5. P.L. 98-440, 98 Stat. 1689 (1984).

Under General Instruction I.B.5 of Form S-3, an asset-backed security may be registered on Form S-3 only if it is "a security that is primarily serviced by the cash flows of a discrete pool of receivables or other financial assets, either fixed or revolving, that by their terms convert into cash within a finite time period plus any rights or other assets designed to assure the servicing or timely distribution of proceeds to the securityholders." This definition contemplates assets that require payments to be made over a finite period. There is no requirement that the payments be made on a regular basis or that they have principal and interest components (e.g., a trade receivable is eligible). The definition would exclude an asset-backed security that is supported by natural resource assets, such as petroleum products or timber, since such assets, while they can be sold for cash, do not *by their terms* produce cash flow. The definition would also exclude any asset, such as certain revolving lines of credit, that does not have a maturity date or an amortization schedule that results in full repayment over some period, however long.

The SEC has taken the position that the amount of assets that are more than 30 days delinquent at the commencement of a securitization must be limited (e.g., less than 5% of the pool) in order for the related asset-backed securities to be eligible for Form S-3.[6] While such assets by their terms satisfy the cash flow and finite period requirements, the SEC apparently believes that a higher likelihood of default causes such assets to fail the "by their terms convert into cash" test because, upon default and repossession, the related securityholders are then relying more on the efforts of the servicer to realize on the collateral securing the asset (e.g., the automobile) rather than the obligor making payments.

In promulgating the release that amended Form S-3 to permit its use for asset-backed securities, the SEC took the opportunity to set forth, albeit in brief, the basic disclosure requirements for asset-backed securities:

> By making Form S-3 and shelf registration available for asset-backed securities offerings, the Commis-

---

6. 1 Practising Law Institute, *The SEC Speaks in 1997* at 42.

sion does not intend to change the character or quality of the disclosure that is customary in these offerings. The type or category of asset to be securitized must be fully described in the registration statement at the time of effectiveness. A registration statement may not merely identify several alternative types of assets that may be securitized. In addition, the risks associated with changes in interest rates or prepayment levels should be fully disclosed. The various scenarios under which payments on the asset-backed securities could be impaired should also be discussed.

When asset-backed securities are registered for the shelf, in addition to identifying the assets that will be used, the registration statement must identify the types or categories of securities that may be offered, such as interest-weighted or principal-weighted classes (including IO (interest only) or PO (principal only) securities), planned amortization or companion classes or residual or subordinated interests.

Consistent with staff practice for offerings of mortgage-related securities, when an offering of asset-backed securities includes classes which bear a disproportionate share of the credit or prepayment risks, the prospectus (or prospectus supplement in a shelf offering) must include clear, concise and understandable descriptions of the characteristics of such classes and the consequences of the characteristics. Some of the consequences which may be material, depending on the prepayment pattern of the assets and the characteristics of the offered class, include: (1) past prepayment of principal rates and the factors that affect the rate of principal repayment; (2) the risk that interest-weighted classes bought at a premium may not return the purchase price in the event of rapid repayment; (3) the degree to which an investor's yield is sensitive to principal repayments; (4) the consequences of an increasing prepayment rate in a declining interest rate environment and a declining prepayment rate in an increasing interest rate environment; and (5) an explanation of what an NRSRO rating address [*sic*] and the characteristics the rating does not address.[7]

As mentioned above, the SEC is currently developing disclosure rules specifically applicable to asset-backed securities.

• • *Prefunding Accounts.* In a prefunded securitization, the Depositor sells an aggregate principal amount of asset-backed securities that is greater than the aggregate principal amount of assets transferred to the SPV at the time of issuance of the asset-backed securities, with the intention of transferring additional assets in the amount of such differential to the SPV over a predetermined period (known as the "prefunding period") after such issuance. Net proceeds from the offering in the amount of such differential are deposited in a "prefunding account" and are thereafter applied to the purchase price of assets acquired during the prefunding period. Pending such application, such net proceeds are invested in interim investments that satisfy the definition of financial assets in Form S-3. If the amount in the prefunding account has not been fully applied to the purchase of assets by the end of the prefunding period, the balance is distributed as principal to securityholders.

Originator/Servicers may decide to use a prefunding mechanism for the purpose of lowering the cost of the securitization by spreading the same amount of costs over a larger securitization the size of which has been increased by the amount in the prefunding account or, if they believe that interest rates are rising, to lock in a lower yield for the portion of the asset-backed securities supported by the amount in the prefunding account. The prefunding mechanism is normally available only to Originator/Servicers that have an established record of stable origination standards, as both the rating agency and the investment bankers will require a substantial level of assurance that the assets originated after closing will have terms and credit quality substantially similar to those of the assets transferred to the SPV at the closing.

---

7. SEC Release No. 33-6964 (October 29, 1992).

The SEC has taken the position that securitizations with too large a prefunding account may not satisfy the definition of asset-backed security in Form S-3. In the SEC's view, the "blind pool" nature of a pool of assets that will be assembled after the sale of the asset-backed securities is not consistent with the definition. Currently, the SEC will permit a shelf registration statement for asset-backed securities to become effective if it provides that the amount in the prefunding account for a particular series of asset-backed securities will generally not exceed 25% of the aggregate principal balance of such series and the prefunding period will not exceed one year. The SEC may permit a series to be taken down from that shelf with a prefunded amount greater than 25% if the registrant discusses the proposed prefunded amount with the SEC prior to offering the series, and the SEC is satisfied with the proposed disclosure. The SEC is aware that its position on prefunding accounts may be viewed as being somewhat at variance with the clear availability of Form S-3 for asset-backed securities backed by revolving assets.[8] The relative levels of indebtedness from individual obligors in a pool of revolving assets (e.g., credit card receivables and dealer floorplan revolving lines of credit) change constantly over the life of a securitization, and new accounts may be added to, and existing accounts withdrawn from, the pool from time to time, thus changing the profile of obligors from the profile that existed at the time of issuance of the asset-backed securities.

• • *Credit Enhancement.* The definition of asset-backed security in Form S-3 by its terms contemplates the inclusion in the securitization of rights and other assets designed to assure the servicing or timely distribution of proceeds to securityholders. Servicing arrangements for the underlying assets are part of every securitization. Some securitizations may include (i) external credit enhancement to protect against losses due to defaults or (ii) external cash flow enhancements, which may supplement low-yielding assets in the pool or provide an interest rate swap (e.g., in a securitization in which the assets bear a

8. *Id.* at note 22.

fixed rate of interest and one or more classes of the asset-backed securities bear interest at a floating rate), an interest rate cap (e.g., the assets bear a floating rate that is capped at some level and the asset-backed securities bear an uncapped floating rate, any differential to be covered by payments under the interest rate cap) or a currency swap (e.g., the assets pay in one currency and the asset-backed securities pay in another currency). The inclusion of such enhancements in a securitization raises questions of the appropriate level of disclosure of information about the enhancement provider and whether the obligation of the enhancement provider is a separately registrable security. In the handbook for one of its annual seminars, the SEC staff said:

> Third party credit enhancements differ slightly from guarantees. A guarantee running directly to the security holder is a security within Section 2(1) of the Securities Act and must be covered by a Securities Act registration statement filed by the guarantor, as issuer. A third party credit enhancement is an agreement between a third party and the issuer or a trustee that does not run directly to the security holders. A party providing credit enhancement generally is not a co-issuer. However, if an investor's return is materially dependent upon the third party credit enhancement, the staff requires additional disclosure about the credit provider. The disclosure must provide sufficient information on the third party to permit an investor to determine the ability of the third party to fund the credit enhancement. In most cases, the disclosure of the third party's audited financial statements presented in accordance with generally accepted accounting principles would be required. However, if such financial statements are not available, statements prepared under statutory standards may be acceptable (e.g., statutory financial statements of insurance companies serving as credit enhancers).
>
> The staff considers the following factors in assessing the sufficiency of the disclosure in this area: (1) the amount of the credit enhancement in relation to the issuer's income and cash flows; (2) the duration of the

credit enhancement; (3) conditions precedent to the application of the credit enhancement; and (4) other factors that indicate a material relationship between the credit enhancer and the purchaser's anticipated return.[9]

As is often the case, there is no bright line test for determining when full financial statements of a credit enhancer are required, at least when the related credit enhancement is at a low level. In practice, external credit enhancement is most often for 100% of one or more classes of the asset-backed securities in a particular series and is therefore clearly material, and full financial statements are appropriate.

The determination of whether the investor's return is materially dependent on a cash flow enhancement is more difficult. In the case of yield supplements, the amount of the supplement to the yield on the low-yielding assets is often small (e.g., 5% of the assets have an interest rate that is only 0.50% below the interest rate borne by the asset-backed security) and therefore probably not material. In the case of an interest rate cap, if the likelihood is low that the floating rate borne by the asset-backed securities will ever exceed the maximum weighted average rate (net of servicing and other fees) borne by the underlying assets because of the initial spread between the two rates, then disclosure of the financial statements of the cap provider may be unnecessary. Interest rate swaps and currency swaps provide more difficult analyses since materiality depends upon the direction in which, and the speed at which, the relevant interest rates and currency exchange rates move over a period of time. Because of the paucity of registered asset-backed securities containing these cash flow enhancements, there is little guidance from practice on these questions.

In addition to the disclosure questions that arise in respect of external enhancements, practitioners must consider whether an external enhancement is a separate security that itself must be registered. External enhancements that are themselves exempted securities are not required to be separately registered. A surety bond issued by an insurer is normally within the

---

9. 1 Practising Law Institute, *The SEC Speaks in 1997* at 375.

exemption for insurance policies provided in Section 3(a)(8) of the 1933 Act, and a letter of credit provided by a domestic bank is normally within the exemption for bank securities provided in Section 3(a)(2) of the 1933 Act.[10]

Despite the SEC's position referred to above, most practitioners, perhaps out of caution, register under the 1933 Act any guarantee that is not exempted, even if the guarantee runs only to the trustee in the securitization and not to the securityholders. Occasionally, Originator/Servicers or their parents provide a guarantee of one or more classes of asset-backed securities. In such cases, the guarantor is named as a registrant in the registration statement for the asset-backed securities, and if the guarantor qualifies for use of Form S-3, as is usually the case, the information on the guarantor is incorporated by reference to the extent permitted by Form S-3. Most swap providers take the position that a swap is not a security. This point is discussed in Chapter 1.

- *Asset Concentration—Rule 140 and the Co-Issuer Question*

The SEC's 1992 release expanding the use of Form S-3 states:

The definition [of asset-backed security] as adopted does not include an asset concentration test. Instead, questions with respect to asset concentration will be addressed through existing disclosure rules. For example, if a significant amount of the asset pool represents obligations of a single obligor or related obligors, financial information and other disclosure about the obligor(s) may be required. Similarly, asset-backed offerings with significant asset concentration may involve one or more co-issuers under Securities Act Rule 140. Finally, although an asset concentration test has not been included, the definition does not encompass securities issued in structured financings for one obligor or group of related obligors.

---

10. *See* SEC Release No. 33-6661 (September 23, 1986) for factors affecting the determination whether the exemption provided in Section 3(a)(2) is applicable to the obligation of a U.S. branch of a non-U.S. bank.

In most securitizations, the underlying assets represent obligations of a large number of obligors such that financial information on any individual obligor is not material. However, in some securitizations, most often those backed by commercial mortgage loans, it is possible that there may be only a few obligors or groups of affiliated obligors. In that case, information regarding their financial condition may become material to the investor's investment decision in respect of the asset-backed security. In commenting on registration statements, the SEC has stated that, if from 10% to 20% of the cash flow supporting a particular series of asset-backed securities represents the obligation of one obligor, or a group of affiliated obligors, the registrant must include in the prospectus summarized financial statements for such obligor or group of obligors.[11] If the relevant percentage is 20% or more, the financial information must be in the form of audited financial statements presented in accordance with Regulation S-X.[12] If the obligor is a special purpose entity that is a mortgagor in respect of a commercial mortgage loan, such financial statements may be the financial statements for the related mortgaged properties rather than the obligor. The inclusion of financial information concerning an obligor (or the related mortgaged property) in the registrant's prospectus makes the registrant and any controlling persons of the registrant liable for any disclosure deficiencies in this financial information. The availability of an expertization defense is unclear, even if the financial information is audited.

Rule 140 under the 1933 Act provides in pertinent part:

A person, the chief part of whose business consists of the purchase of the securities of one issuer, or two or more affiliated issuers, and the sale of its own securities ... to furnish the proceeds with which to acquire the securities of such issuer or affiliated issuers, is to be regarded as engaged in the distribution of the securities of

11. *See* Article X of Regulation S-X.
12. The SEC arrives at these breakpoints by analogy to Staff Accounting Bulletins 71 and 71A. *See* 1 Practising Law Institute, *The SEC Speaks in 1997* at 40.

such issuer or affiliated issuers within the meaning of Section 2(11) of the [1933] Act.

Rule 140 envisions an arrangement in which an issuer (the "underlying issuer") distributes its securities by placing them in another entity, such as a trust (the "facilitating issuer"). The facilitating issuer in turn distributes its own securities (e.g., pass-through certificates) that, in effect, represent beneficial ownership of the securities of the underlying issuer and pays over to the underlying issuer the proceeds from the sale of its securities. The effect of Rule 140 on this arrangement is that the securities of the underlying issuer are deemed to be part of a distribution, and therefore, absent an available exemption, must be registered under Section 5, even though only the securities of the facilitating issuer are sold to investors. As a consequence, the full financial statements of the underlying issuer must be included in the registration statement. The rule therefore results in the underlying issuer, as a registrant, becoming subject to the applicable liability provisions of the 1933 Act. Rule 140 applies only to primary issuances of the securities of the underlying issuer and not to securities of the underlying issuer purchased in the secondary market.[13]

---

13. The SEC staff has stated that outstanding corporate debt or asset-backed securities may be pooled and securitized under a registration statement on Form S-3 if the requirements of that form are met. In addition, however, the Depositor must be free to make a public offering of the outstanding securities without 1933 Act registration, *i.e.*, the outstanding securities may not be restricted securities or part of an original distribution. But what is part of the original distribution where an underwriter involved in the original offering is acting as an underwriter in the new offering and is an affiliate of the Depositor for the new offering? In these cases, the staff applies a "bright line" test, *i.e.*, securities will be deemed not to be part of the original distribution if they are purchased in the secondary market at least three months after the sale of the last unsold allotment in the original offering of such securities. Where 20% or more of the pool consists of securities of a single issuer, the staff ordinarily requires that the prospectus include audited financial statements of that issuer; however, a reference to the issuer's 1934 Act reports will be sufficient if the issuer is eligible to use Form S-3 for a primary equity offering and if the depositor's transaction in the securities is "purely secondary." If the securities of the underlying issuer are themselves asset-backed securities, then the staff will permit

In the context of securitizations of commercial mortgage loans, the SEC has taken the position that, if the principal amount of the loans of an obligor, or group of related obligors, equals or exceeds an amount equal to 45% of the aggregate principal amount of the total loans in the securitization, such obligor, or group of obligors, may be a co-issuer for purposes of Rule 140 and therefore required to sign the registration statement as a registrant.[14] Any such co-registrant would have liability for the contents of the entire registration statement and not just the portion thereof that relates to it.

• *Offering Materials*

• • *Computational Materials.* Buyers of asset-backed securities are, for the most part, institutional investors. Many of those buyers require that they be shown how a particular asset-backed security will perform under various scenarios based on different assumptions as to the rate of principal payments on the underlying assets (including voluntary prepayments by the underlying obligors and prepayments as a result of liquidation upon default) and losses upon liquidation of underlying assets as a result of default. The yield and weighted average life of an asset-backed security will change, sometimes significantly, depending upon such assumptions. Purchasers often either create their own "cash flow runs" and yield tables for designated scenarios or require the underwriter to prepare such materials, which are generally referred to as "computational materials." Such computational materials can be voluminous, and therefore cannot realistically be orally transmitted, and may be tailored to the requests of particular prospective buyers. Consequently, they are normally not suitable for inclusion in the prospectus. In some cases, the structure of the pro-

---

a similar reference for disclosure purposes as long as the underlying issuer files periodic reports under the 1934 Act and has outstanding securities in excess of $75 million held by non-affiliates. *See* 1 Practising Law Institute, *The SEC Speaks in 1997* at 378-79.

14. *See* 1 Practising Law Institute, *The SEC Speaks in 1997* at 378. If the relevant registration statement is an effective shelf registration statement, however, there is no procedure in the SEC's rules for "adding" a registrant after effectiveness.

posed asset-backed security will be changed to satisfy the requirements of a prospective buyer after the buyer has seen the requested computational materials. Computational materials used prior to the delivery of the related final prospectus are likely to be considered written materials that offer the related security for sale and therefore a prospectus within Section 2(10) of the 1933 Act, the use of which, absent some relief, would violate Section 5 of the 1933 Act. In 1994, the SEC issued two no-action letters[15] that, in effect, permit the use of computational materials (including information as to (i) the structure of the related asset-backed security and (ii) the assets themselves) prior to the delivery of a final prospectus, subject to the satisfaction of the conditions stated in the requesting letters. One of these conditions is that the computational materials must be filed with the SEC for incorporation by reference into the registration statement covering the related asset-backed security.[16] The effect of the filing is to impose the applicable 1933 Act liabilities for such materials on the registrant and the underwriters. Consequently, a registrant will generally require that an underwriter indemnify it in respect of material inaccuracies in the computational materials created by that underwriter. The underwriter will not indemnify the registrant for information about the structure of the transaction or for any inaccuracy resulting from any inaccuracies in the information about the underlying assets furnished by the Originator/Servicer to the underwriter for the purpose of creating the computational materials, since the registrant is able to verify such information. If there is a syndicate of underwriters in the offering, the lead underwriter often develops one set of computational materials that may be used by any member of the syndicate. At present, there does not appear to be a market standard as to whether the underwriter who develops the computational mate-

---

15. SEC No-Action Letters, *Kidder Peabody Acceptance Corporation I* (available May 20, 1994) and *Public Securities Association* (available May 27, 1994). *See also* SEC No-action Letter, *Public Securities Association* (available March 9, 1995) (providing similar relief for "structural term sheets" and "collateral term sheets").

16. In the case of a registration on Form S-3, the filing may be made by filing a current report on Form 8-K. Because Form S-1 and Form S-11 do not permit incorporation by reference, the filing must be made by means of a post-effective amendment.

rials should indemnify the other underwriters for any material inaccuracies in the computational materials. It is fairly common, however, for the Originator/Servicer to indemnify the underwriters for liabilities arising from any inaccuracies in the information regarding the underlying assets (such as interest rates and original and remaining terms to maturity) on the basis of which the calculations in the computational materials are made.

• • *Access to Loan Files*. In the case of a securitization in which the individual assets have high balances or are not originated on a uniform basis (e.g., commercial mortgage loans), prospective investors may wish to review the related loan files and make their own decisions as to the creditworthiness and security of the assets. Such files, in a technical sense, may be written communications that offer the related asset-backed security for sale. They may therefore come within the definition of "prospectus" in Section 2(10) of the 1933 Act. Consequently, access to loan files prior to the delivery of a final prospectus could be a violation of Section 5 of the 1933 Act. For this reason, many issuers of asset-backed securities do not allow prospective purchasers of registered asset-backed securities access to the loan files relating to such securities.

As discussed below, a particular series of asset-backed securities may have one or more publicly offered classes as well as one or more privately placed classes. In a private placement, the delivery of written materials other than the offering memorandum does not result in a Section 5 violation. An issue arises, however, if a prospective buyer in a securitization with both publicly and privately offered classes is interested in purchasing some of the private classes and some of the public classes. The related loan files are relevant to both the public classes and the private classes. Access to the loan files, while permissible in respect of the private classes, could result in a Section 5 violation in respect of the public classes. In this situation, some issuers have granted access to the loan files only to prospective purchasers who agree not to purchase any of the publicly offered classes.

• *Prospectus Delivery Considerations*

• • *Rule 15c2-8*. The SEC stated in May 1995 that, if no preliminary prospectus is distributed in connection with a takedown from an asset-backed shelf registration statement, then it interpreted Rule 15c2-8(b) of the 1934 Act to require that the final prospectus for the takedown be delivered at least 48 hours prior to sending a confirmation for the sale of the related asset-backed securities.[17] The SEC subsequently provided no-action relief from the 48-hour rule for issuances of asset-backed securities so long as the amount in the prefunding account, if any, is not greater than 25% of the aggregate principal amount of the securities.[18] The relief recognizes that the structuring process for an asset-backed security (which, as discussed above in the context of computational materials, often involves a dialogue between the issuer and prospective buyers) and the assembling of the underlying assets and the related information for the prospectus take place throughout the offering process, even up to a few days before closing, making it difficult to comply with the 48-hour rule. The SEC's relief on this point will, unless extended or superseded, expire on December 15, 1997.

• • *Post-Offering Delivery Requirements; Availability of Materials through Electronic Media.* Because the issuer of an asset-backed security (in the basic structure example, the SPV) is often newly created at the time of issuance and, therefore, not subject to the reporting requirements of Section 13 or 15(d) of the 1934 Act, the applicable prospectus delivery period under Section 4(3) of the 1933 Act is 90 days.[19] During this period, dealers making a market in the asset-backed security will not, absent an exemption, distribute written materials that might come within the definition of "prospectus" in respect of such security without first delivering a current final prospectus.

Buyers of asset-backed securities receive, often on a monthly basis, servicing reports that describe the performance of the related asset pool (e.g., information as to principal collections, delinquen-

---

17. SEC Release No. 33-7168 (May 11, 1995) at note 80.

18. SEC No-Action Letter, *Public Securities Association* (available December 15, 1995).

19. In practice, even issuers such as master trusts, which issue more than one series of asset-backed securities and therefore may be subject to such reporting requirements after the first issuance, use a 90-day prospectus delivery period.

cies, losses, etc.). Servicing reports arguably come within the definition of "prospectus" and could constitute a Section 5 violation if delivered during the 90-day period to a buyer who receives the reports before receiving the final prospectus. The possibility of this occurring was low when servicing reports were delivered in paper form only to holders of the related asset-backed security. Recently, servicing reports have been posted on electronic, on-line financial information services available to the investment community at large. An issuer or dealer with knowledge that servicing reports are available on-line to the investment community could be deemed to have delivered the servicing report to a prospective buyer. Issuers who put their servicing reports on line may avoid this problem by making both the servicing report and the final prospectus available on the on-line service and hyperlinking the availability of the final prospectus to the servicing report.[20]

Servicing reports and other performance-related information are no less important to holders of privately-placed asset backed securities. In fact, dealers may be less willing to bid on Rule 144A asset-backed securities if they are not able to receive this information promptly and on a regular basis. Electronic display of such information runs the risk of being considered an "offer" to non-QIBs in the case of Rule 144A securities or a "general solicitation" in the case of Regulation D securities. A password or other device for restricting access to QIBs or institutional accredited investors would solve the problem, but passwords and similar devices are often cumbersome. It would be more straightforward to use a simple restrictive legend that would state clearly that the information is made available only for use by persons eligible to purchase the related securities, but the SEC staff has not yet confirmed the acceptability of such a procedure.

• • *Market Maker Prospectuses.* The SEC takes the position that the exemption from Section 5 for transactions by a dealer provided in Section 4(3) is not available for transactions in which the dealer is an affiliate of the issuer. The theory of this position is that a dealer, according to the definition in Section 2(12), is a person who deals in securities issued "by another

---

20. SEC Release No. 33-7233 (October 5, 1995) (illustration 15).

person;" an issuer is not deemed by the SEC to be "another person" with respect to its affiliates. While this analysis may be somewhat less than persuasive, there is a policy basis for the position, i.e., when a person controlled by the issuer resells a security of the issuer, the resale by that person may not be far removed in substance from a primary issuance by the issuer, thus requiring the delivery of a current prospectus. Such a prospectus is referred to as a "market maker prospectus." The registration statement will contain a prospectus for this purpose that will state on its cover page that it relates to any resales in market making transactions by the affiliated dealer. No additional filing fee for the market making resales is required.

In the context of asset-backed securities, however, the substantive reason for requiring a market maker prospectus in the secondary trading activities of a dealer affiliated with the issuer is not always present. The situation normally arises in a "conduit" securitization in which the Depositor is an affiliate of the dealer and purchases assets from an Originator/Servicer who may or may not be an affiliate of the Depositor. If the Originator/Servicer is not an affiliate of the Depositor and the dealer, the SEC will not require the use of a market maker prospectus in secondary trades by the dealer in the related asset-backed security. The theory is that because the Depositor and the dealer are not affiliates of the Originator/Servicer, they most likely do not have any access to information about the related asset pool beyond the servicing reports that are generally available to investors. However, if they are affiliates of the Originator/Servicer, the theory is that the Depositor and dealer have sufficient access to information about the asset pool to permit them to supplement the prospectus to the extent necessary to comply with Section 10 of the 1933 Act.

• • *Research Materials.* Rule 139 provides a safe harbor in the determination as to whether, with respect to a security registered or proposed to be registered under the 1933 Act, written information, recommendations or opinions about that security (collectively referred to as "research reports") put out by an underwriter or prospective underwriter of that security will be considered to constitute an offer for sale or an offer to sell that security for purposes of Section 2(10) of the 1933 Act and, therefore, a prospectus. Absent the relief provided by Rule 139, the delivery of a research report about an issuer to a purchaser of the issuer's securities in a public offering prior to the purchaser's receipt of the related final prospectus may constitute a violation of Section 5. Investment banks that deal in asset-backed securities normally distribute research reports concerning particular asset-backed securities, particular types of underlying assets or particular structures used in securitizations. Rule 139, however, only applies to a registrant that is required to file reports pursuant to Section 13 or 15(d) of the 1934 Act. The issuer of an asset-backed security (i.e., the SPV), however, is not formed in many securitizations until the issuance of its asset-backed securities.[21] Consequently, such issuers may not qualify for Rule 139, and research reports distributed prior to the availability of such an issuer's final prospectus may pose the risk of a Section 5 violation. In addition, Rule 139 requires that the publication in which the research report is contained be published with reasonable regularity, and this requirement is difficult to satisfy with respect to a new asset type.

Because of the industry's difficulties in publishing research on asset-backed securities, PSA The Bond Market Trade Association entered into discussions with the SEC staff with a view to obtaining interpretive relief. In a letter dated February 7, 1997,[22] the staff responded with interpretive advice to the effect that the publication or distribution by a broker or dealer of information, an opinion or a recommendation with respect to investment grade asset-backed securities (as defined for purposes of Form S-3 eligibility) would not be deemed, for purposes of Section 2(10) or Section 5(c) of the 1933 Act to constitute an offer for sale or an offer to sell asset-backed securities registered or proposed to be registered under the 1933 Act ("Registered Securities"). The staff's advice was subject to the following conditions:

---

21. In addition, because institutions buy substantially all asset-backed securities and the number of holders of a class or series is usually fewer than 300, issuers often deregister such securities after the end of the fiscal year in which the securities were issued. *See* Section 15(d) of the 1934 Act.

22. SEC No-action Letter, *Dissemination of Research Materials Relating to Asset-Backed Securities* (available February 7, 1997).

1. The dealer must have previously published or distributed with reasonable regularity information, opinions or recommendations relating to asset-backed securities backed directly (or, with respect to resecuritization transactions, indirectly) by substantially similar collateral as that directly or indirectly backing the asset-backed securities that are the subject of the information, opinion or recommendation that is to be distributed.

2. If the Registered Securities have not yet been offered or are part of an unsold allotment or subscription, the information, opinion or recommendation must not identify the Registered Securities.

3. Sufficient information must be available from one or more public sources to provide a reasonable basis for the view expressed by the dealer with respect to the asset-backed securities that are the subject of the information, opinion or recommendation. (PSA's request letter stated that the purpose of this condition was to encourage broker-dealers to publish information, opinions or recommendations on asset-backed securities that are issued by entities affiliated with other broker-dealers.)

4. If the Registered Securities have not yet been offered or are part of an unsold allotment or subscription, the information, opinion or recommendation must not give greater prominence to specific structural or collateral-related attributes of the Registered Securities than it gives to the same attributes of other asset-backed securities that it mentions. (PSA's request letter stated PSA's understanding that this condition was consistent with, and would not by itself prevent, the dissemination of a research piece that focused on a single topic, e.g., on a single collateral attribute, collateral source, structural attribute or market sector.)

5. The information, opinion or recommendation must not contain any "computational material" (as defined in the earlier no-action letters on this subject) relating to Reg-

istered Securities that have not yet been offered or are part of an unsold allotment or subscription.

6. The information, opinion or recommendation must refer as required by law or applicable rules to any relationship that may exist between the issuer or the information, opinion or recommendation and any participant in the offering. (PSA's request letter stated that this condition contemplated statutory provisions such as Section 17(b) of the 1933 Act or relevant NYSE or NASD standards requiring disclosure of possible sources of bias.)

7. If the material published by the broker or dealer identifies a specific asset-backed security of a specific issuer and specifically recommends that such asset-backed security be purchased, sold or held, then a recommendation as favorable or more favorable as to such asset-backed security must have been published by the broker or dealer in the last publication of such broker or dealer addressing such asset-backed security prior to the commencement of its participation in the distribution of the Registered Securities. (PSA's request letter stated PSA's understanding that this condition was limited to "exhortations to purchase, sell or hold a specific [asset-backed security] of a specific issuer, not general comments regarding relative investment merits.")

8. If the material published by the broker or dealer identifies asset-backed securities backed directly (or, with respect to resecuritization transactions, indirectly) by substantially similar collateral as that directly or indirectly backing the Registered Securities and specifically recommends that such asset-backed securities be preferred over other asset-backed securities backed by different types of collateral, then the material must explain in reasonable detail the reasons for such preference.

The staff's letter also stated that in the case of a multi-tranche offering of asset-backed securities, each tranche would be treated as a different Registered Security for purposes of the interpretive relief.

It should be noted that the "PSA understandings" referred to in connection with four of the foregoing conditions were specifically negotiated with the SEC staff. They should therefore be regarded as part of the SEC's response, notwithstanding that they were not referred to in the actual response.

• *Integration*

The principle of integration of separate securities offerings is discussed in Chapter 7. An issuer of a particular series of asset-backed securities containing multiple classes may often sell some classes publicly and some privately. Because classes that are rated below investment grade cannot be sold under a shelf registration, they are often sold privately to avoid the time and expense of registering them under a stand alone registration statement. Occasionally, a particular buyer requires that its purchase of a class be done on a private placement basis. Practitioners are virtually unanimous in the view that the differentiation of separate classes of a particular series of asset-backed securities, by virtue of their relative subordination, their expected maturity dates or any other substantive structural feature, is sufficient to avoid integration of any such classes even though all of the classes are sold at one time.

• *Bankruptcy*

Most rated securitizations are structured so that the insolvency of the Originator/Servicer will not interrupt the distribution of the cash flow from the underlying assets to the securityholders. In the context of an Originator/Servicer subject to the Bankruptcy Code, this means that the underlying assets must not be part of the Originator/Servicer's bankruptcy estate pursuant to Section 541(a) of the Bankruptcy Code. If the assets were part of the bankruptcy estate, the cash flow from the assets would be subject to the automatic stay provisions of Section 362 of the Bankruptcy Code, therefore delaying distributions to the securityholders for some period of time.[23] In

23. For a discussion of insolvency considerations in general in respect of securitization, *see Structured Financing Techniques, by the Committee on Bankruptcy and Corporate Reorganization of the Association of the Bar of the*

rated securitizations, the rating agencies usually[24] require a "true sale" legal opinion to the effect that the assets will not be part of the bankruptcy estate of the Originator/Servicer.[25]

As noted above, the Originator/Servicer often transfers the assets to the Depositor, which in turn transfers the assets to the SPV. The true sale opinion is often given only as to the transfer from the Originator/Servicer to the Depositor, since the Depositor may retain some subordinated interest in the SPV, which may be viewed as a retention of recourse on the assets and, if large enough, make it difficult to give a true sale opinion as to the transfer from the Depositor to the SPV. In many cases, the rating agencies also require an opinion to the effect that a bankruptcy court would not substantively consolidate the assets of the Depositor with the bankruptcy estate of the Originator/Servicer, which would have the effect of nullifying any true sale to the Depositor by pulling the assets back into the estate of the Originator/Servicer and therefore subjecting them to the automatic stay.

Both the Depositor and the SPV issuer of the asset-backed securities are normally "bankruptcy-remote" in that they have no liabilities that are not related to the asset-backed securities and are therefore not likely to enter into bankruptcy.

• *Tax Issues*

The SPV is normally structured so as not to be subject to tax. Any tax at the SPV level could erode the cash flow from

---

City of New York, 50 Business Lawyer 527 (February 1995) and *Rethinking the Role of Recourse in the Sale of Financial Assets*, 52 Business Lawyer 159 (November 1996).

24. In the case of transfers by banks, which are not subject to the Bankruptcy Code, the rating agencies require an opinion that the transfer is either (i) a sale or (ii) a transfer for security, with the resulting security interest being a perfected, first priority security interest. In the view of the rating agencies, in such a case the insolvency proceedings applicable to banks will not interrupt cash flow distributions to securityholders.

25. If such an opinion could not be given, the asset-backed securities might well not be rated higher than the credit rating of the Originator/Servicer, thus defeating one of the main purposes of a securitization, i.e., achieving a higher credit rating for the asset-backed security and a correspondingly lower cost of funds for the transaction.

the assets so that securityholders would not receive the amounts due to be distributed to them. Special, complex federal income tax laws (the "REMIC" and "FASIT" legislation) have been enacted to provide tax treatment pursuant to which there will not be a tax at the SPV level. (The effective date of the FASIT legislation is September 1, 1997.) The transactions' offering materials will discuss these tax considerations at length.

• *Resecuritization*

The Depositor or another entity affiliated with the Originator/ Servicer often retains the subordinated (and usually unrated) class or classes from a securitization. Often, the Depositor or such other entity may wish to liquefy its portfolio of these retained classes by securitizing them (referred to as a "resecuritization"). Investors purchase the higher rated class or classes that are issued in the resecuritization, and the Depositor normally takes back the subordinated class or classes, which provide internal credit enhancement for the higher rated classes. In addition, a broker or dealer may purchase any type of debt security or asset-backed security in the secondary market and securitize those securities.

The SEC takes the view that the securities underlying a publicly offered resecuritization must either (i) have been previously registered under the 1933 Act and purchased in a secondary market transaction or (ii) be freely transferable under Rule 144(k). The SEC apparently rejects the view that the transfer of the underlying security to the resecuritization SPV is a valid private placement, fearing that such a position would permit an end run around the registration provisions of the 1933 Act. It is permissible to register the underlying asset-backed securities in the same registration statement under which the newly issued asset-backed securities are being registered. As a practical matter, this approach is available only when the Depositor is resecuritizing subordinated classes created and retained by it because while the Depositor (or an affiliated Originator/Servicer) would be willing to sign the registration statement in respect of its underlying asset-backed securities, any unrelated issuer of the underlying securities would be understandably reluctant to sign the resecuritization registration statement. As discussed above with respect to Rule 140, the SEC has recently stated its view as to what constitutes a secondary market transaction.[26]

Lastly, the obligor concentration issue and the possible applicability of Rule 140, discussed above in connection with asset concentration, must be considered in structuring a resecuritization.

• *Due Diligence*

The due diligence review for a securitization must always be tailored to the type of asset being securitized and the degree of future activity of the Originator/Servicer (e.g., just servicing a static pool of assets *versus* also originating assets that will be transferred to the SPV from time to time after the issuance of the asset-backed securities). Such a review normally focuses on the following matters:

(i) the underwriting procedures of the Originator/Servicer in originating the asset, including, if applicable, credit checks, appraisal and income verification;

(ii) the servicing procedures of the Originator/ Servicer, including billing and collection methods, pursuit of delinquent accounts and realization on collateral;

(iii) compliance of documents creating the assets with applicable law, especially consumer protection laws;

(iv) proper licensing of the Originator/Servicer; and

(v) procedures for perfecting a security interest in any collateral.

In the case of assets for which the Originator/Servicer is not using form documents known to comply with local law (e.g., first mortgage documents developed by the Federal National Mortgage Association and the Federal Home Loan Mortgage Corporation), item (iii) is often verified by requiring local

---

26. *Supra* note 13 at 879. Resecuritization may be effected under a shelf registration statement. However, as noted above in the discussion of Rule 140, there are no SEC rules for adding a new registrant to an effective registration statement.

opinions of counsel as to such compliance in a representative number of states.

In connection with most securitizations, the underwriter normally requires a comfort letter from the registrant's accountants that reflects the following:

(i) specified procedures performed by the accountants pursuant to which information on the computer tape containing various information (e.g., interest rate, maturity date, type of collateral, etc.) about the underlying assets (from which tape (the "pool tape") the information about the assets that appears in the prospectus is derived) is checked against the same information in the related loan files, and

(ii) (a) comparison of information in the prospectus about the assets to information on the pool tape and recomputation of such information, (b) comparison of loss, delinquency and, in some cases, prepayment information appearing in the prospectus to the records of the Originator/Servicer and (c) recomputation of yield tables and tables showing declining principal balances of classes on the basis of various prepayment assumptions.

The procedures performed by the accountants will vary depending upon the type of asset being securitized.

- *Rule 144A(d)(4) Information*

In transfers of privately placed asset-backed securities pursuant to Rule 144A, what information is to be provided in satisfaction of the minimum information condition found in Rule 144A(d)(4)? As discussed above, balance sheets and income statements are not relevant to an SPV. In the release that adopted Rule 144A, the SEC stated that the financial statements and other information specified in Rule 144A(d)(4) should be understood in the case of asset-backed securities "to mandate provision of basic, material information concerning the structure of the securities and distributions thereon, the nature, performance and servicing of the assets supporting the securities, and any credit enhancement mechanism associated with the securities."

It is also not immediately clear who the "issuer" is for purposes of the information requirement of Rule 144A(d)(4). In the same release, the SEC stated that the "issuer" in the case of asset-backed securities means for purposes of the information requirement "the servicer of the assets or trustee of the trust having title to the mortgage loans or other assets". Also, in connection with a 1990 interpretive letter,[27] the SEC staff was asked to approve an arrangement under which "the issuer (or depositor of the trust issuer) will cause the trustee to deliver" the required information. The staff stated that it concurred with the view that paragraph (d)(4) of Rule 144A does not "preclude the parties by contract from identifying the person from whom . . . [the required information] may be obtained."

1934 Act Considerations

The disclosure forms under the 1934 Act are not easily applied to asset-backed securities for the same reason that the disclosure forms under the 1933 Act are not easily applied. In response to this mismatch, the SEC has provided no-action relief to permit registrants to file information that is relevant to the particular asset-backed security. This has normally resulted in the requirement that the issuer file on Form 8-K the monthly servicing report for the securitization, which will, among other things, show distributions made on the asset-backed securities and losses and delinquencies on the underlying assets. The issuer will file on Form 10-K responses to items 3, 4, 8 and 9 and the annual statement of compliance by the Originator/Servicer and the annual accountants' report as to servicing matters (which is not an audited report) called for by the related servicing agreement. One controversial requirement found in recent no-action letters states that the financial statements of the credit enhancer, if any, of a material amount of the asset-backed securities must be included in a filing. Similarly, the SEC has at times required financial information or financial statements of certain material obligors or underlying issuers in a resecuritization. The inclusion of these financial statements or financial information exposes the issuer to disclosure liability for

---

27. SEC No-action Letter, *Mortgage-Backed and Asset-Backed Securities—Securities Act Release No. 6862—The Rule 144A Release* (November 29, 1990).

information provided by the credit enhancer or material obligor. When this material is included in a prospectus, the credit enhancer normally indemnifies the issuer for consequent 1933 Act liabilities.

The no-action letters are tailored to the type of assets underlying the asset-backed securities, thus forcing both the SEC staff and registrants to spend a great deal of time on a case-by-case basis in the no-action process. In addition, the SEC's positions on requisite disclosure in 1934 Act reports seems to be evolving. The SEC has announced that it will adopt a regulation setting forth required disclosure in reports under the 1934 Act for asset-backed securities.

Rule 10b-10(a)(7) requires broker-dealers to disclose in confirmations for transactions in asset-backed securities that the yield to the investor may vary according to the rate of principal prepayments on the underlying assets and that information as to minimum estimated yield, weighted average life and prepayment assumptions underlying yield will be furnished upon written request.

As discussed in Chapter 3, Section 11(d)(1) of the 1934 Act prohibits the extension, or the arrangement for the extension, of credit by a broker or dealer on a security (other than an exempted security) which is part of a public distribution in which the broker or dealer participated as a selling member within 30 days prior to such credit transaction. The distribution continues with respect to a particular broker or dealer until it has sold its allotment of the security. The staff has taken a no-action position that in the context of the distribution of a multi-class issuance of asset-backed securities, each class of such asset-backed securities is a separate security for purposes of Section 11(d)(1).[28]

1940 Act Considerations

The definition of "investment company" in Section 3(a)(1) of the 1940 Act includes any person that is primarily engaged

---

28. SEC No-action Letter, *Bear, Stearns & Co. Inc.* (available August 29, 1994).

in the business of investing and reinvesting in securities, as well as any person engaged in the business (whether primarily or not) of investing in or holding investment securities (as defined in the Section) and more than 40% of whose assets consist of such securities. Assets that generate cash flow may, at least under certain circumstances, come within the definition of "security" in Section 2(a)(36) of the 1940 Act, which includes, among other items, evidences of indebtedness. Unlike the 1933 Act, the 1940 Act includes as securities even commercial and consumer loans. Consequently, absent an exemption, most SPVs that issue asset-backed securities would come within the definition of "investment company" in Section 3(a)(1) of the 1940 Act because their primary activity of acquiring and holding cash flow assets amounts to engaging in the business of investing in securities. Registering an SPV as an investment company under the 1940 Act is not a practical possibility since the 1940 Act is a pervasive regulatory scheme that is incompatible with the operation of most types of entities other than true investment companies. For example, 1940 Act provisions would likely limit the ability of the Originator/Servicer to engage in certain transactions with the SPV and, moreover, would limit the SPV's ability to issue asset-backed securities at all because of restrictions on the ability of registered investment companies to issue debt.

Prior to the adoption of Rule 3a-7, SPVs issuing asset-backed securities relied on the exemptions provided in Section 3(c)(5) of the 1940 Act. These exemptions worked well for asset types within the terms of the exemption, as long as the assets were whole receivables of specified types (i.e., not participations or other fractional interests in the receivables). Early on in the securitization of mortgage loans, investment bankers began securitizing mortgage-backed securities guaranteed by government agencies. As long as the mortgage-backed security represented the whole pool of underlying mortgage loans, the SEC would apply the exemption by looking through the mortgage-backed security to the underlying whole mortgage loans. With limited exceptions, if the mortgage-backed security represented only a fractional interest in the pool of mortgage loans, then there was no look-through. If a majority of the mortgage-backed securities represented "whole pools," then, subject to certain other composition requirements developed by the SEC in various no-action letters, Section 3(c)(5)(C) was satisfied.

Assembling a majority of whole pools for a securitization was burdensome and expensive. Investment bankers obtained exemptive orders from the SEC exempting securitizations that did not satisfy the Section 3(c)(5)(C) test, but the process was time consuming and the orders had to be amended if a newly developed structure did not satisfy all of the conditions of the relevant order. In addition, new asset types that did not come within Section 3(c)(5) were continually being securitized. One such example was the securitization of credit card receivables. While Section 3(c)(5)(A) excludes from the 1940 Act issuers holding receivables and other obligations representing the sale of merchandise, insurance or services, the exclusion would not accommodate, for example, credit card cash advances.

The "private placement" exemption in Section 3(c)(1), which was historically the only alternative, is basically too confining. Recently enacted Section 3(c)(7) of the 1940 Act provides greater flexibility than Section 3(c)(1) in that it imposes a sophistication test as an alternative to a numerical limit on buyers. However, Section 3(c)(7) also permits only private placements.

The SEC responded to this bottleneck in 1992 by adopting Rule 3a-7, which "was intended to exclude virtually all structured financings from the definition of investment company, subject to certain conditions."[29] An issuer (i.e., an SPV) that satisfies the conditions of the Rule will not be deemed to be an investment company. The Rule provides that:

(i) the issuer must acquire and hold "eligible assets" (described below), may engage in activities related thereto and must not issue redeemable securities. The definition of redeem-

---

29. SEC Release No. IC-19105 (November 19, 1992). As will be discussed in the text, the SEC staff has more recently interpreted Rule 3a-7 in a relatively restrictive fashion. Thus, Section 3(c)(5) is still sometimes used as a basis for an exemption when it is available.

able security has a long interpretive history starting with SEC staff interpretations under Section 3(c)(5);

(ii) the issuer's securities must be paid primarily out of cash flow on its eligible assets;

(iii) the issuer's fixed-income securities that are rated investment grade may be sold to anyone; other types of its securities may only be sold to accredited investors or qualified institutional buyers; "fixed-income" securities for this purpose are securities that have either a principal amount or, subject to certain limitations, provide for the payment of interest on a principal amount (which may be a notional amount) or any combination of such features;

(iv) the issuer may acquire and dispose of its eligible assets only in accordance with the documents governing its securities and only if such dispositions are not made for the purpose of recognizing gains and decreasing losses resulting from changes in market value (i.e., no active management of the issuer's assets as would be typical of an investment company); and

(v) except in the case of an issuer of commercial paper exempt pursuant to Section 3(a)(3) of the 1933 Act, a non-affiliated trustee meeting the requirements of Section 26(a)(1) of the 1940 Act must be appointed and receive a perfected security interest or ownership interest in the eligible assets.

The definition of "eligible assets" in Rule 3a-7 is quite similar to the definition of "financial assets" in Form S-3. With respect to the requirement that eligible assets "by their terms convert into cash within a finite period of time," the SEC has taken no action positions that cumulative preferred stock[30] and auction rate preferred stock[31] do not satisfy this requirement. As a related matter, the securities issued by the SPV must, as indicated above, be based on the cash flow from eligible assets. Securities whose payments derived from changes in the market value of such assets do not qualify.

---

30. SEC No-action Letter, *Brown & Wood* (available February 24, 1994).

31. SEC No-action Letter, *Donaldson, Lufkin & Jenrette Securities Corporation* (available September 23, 1994).

As with financial assets under Form S-3, eligible assets include rights and assets designed to assure the servicing or timely distribution of proceeds to securityholders. This language picks up credit and liquidity enhancements, cash flow enhancements and collateral securing the cash flow asset.[32]

The SEC takes the position that an issuer relying on Rule 3a-7 may only engage in acquiring and holding eligible assets (and in activities related thereto).[33] Consequently, an issuer cannot hold both eligible assets and "hard" assets unless the hard assets are ancillary or incidental to holding the eligible assets, although an issuer holding only hard assets would not be an investment company.

Some issuers of asset-backed securities create classes that may be purchased by money market funds pursuant to Rule 2a-7 of the 1940 Act, a complex SEC rule that governs the operations of money market funds. The remaining maturity of a class of asset-backed securities eligible for purchase by a money market fund may not exceed 397 days. In addition, the securities must be rated in one of the two highest short-term rating categories or, in the case of asset-backed securities having only a long-term rating, be of comparable quality to securities having such a short-term rating. In order to "shorten" the remaining term of a floating rate or variable rate asset-backed security, the issuer may structure the security with a demand feature that allows the securityholder to give notice and thereafter unconditionally receive, at a time not later than 397 days after such notice, its unamortized cost for the security plus accrued interest. In some cases, the demand feature is a put right issued by a third party; in other cases, it is a right to commence receiving principal distributions from collections on the issuer's underlying assets, which collections, in the absence of the exercise of the demand feature, would be applied by the issuer to purchase new underlying assets. The credit of the provider of a third-party demand feature also may be used to satisfy the Rule's rating requirements if certain conditions are met.

---

32. SEC Release IC-19105 (November 19, 1992).

33. SEC No-action Letter, *Citicorp Securities Inc.* (available August 4, 1995); SEC Release IC-19105 (November 19, 1992).

Money market funds must also satisfy certain issuer diversification requirements in Rule 2a-7. In general, the issuer of an asset-backed security is the related SPV. Under certain circumstances, however, the issuer of certain of the assets underlying the asset-backed security may be the issuer for purposes of the diversification determination.[34]

Other Considerations

• *1939 Act*

If publicly offered asset-backed securities are in the form of notes, the notes must be issued pursuant to an indenture qualified under the 1939 Act unless an exemption is available. If the asset-backed securities are in the form of pass-through or other certificates evidencing an interest in a trust that is acting as the SPV, the governing agreement for the certificates need not be qualified under the 1939 Act because either (i) the certificates will be equity securities (i.e., they merely evidence an interest in the trust that entitles them to receive cash distributions to the extent of collections on the underlying assets and there is no default mechanism) or (ii) if the trust contains more than one underlying asset, the exemption in Section 304(a)(2) of the 1939 Act for "any certificate of interest or participation in two or more securities having substantially different rights and privileges. . ." is applicable.

• *SMMEA*

The Secondary Mortgage Market Enhancement Act[35] was enacted in 1984 to improve the marketability of "mortgage related-securities." A mortgage-related security, as defined in Section 3(a)(41) of the 1934 Act, must be rated in one of the top two investment grades and be supported by cash flows from first lien mortgages on real estate upon which is located a residential or commercial structure (including manufactured housing that is personal property under state law and stock allocated to a dwelling unit in a residential cooperative housing corpora-

---

34. Rule 2a-7(c)(4)(vi)(A)(4).
35. P.L. No. 98-440, 98 Stat. 1689.

tion). The underlying mortgage loans must be originated by certain lenders subject to governmental supervision. A mortgage-backed-security that otherwise qualifies as a mortgage-related security but is backed in part by a prefunding account will not be a mortgage-related security until the prefunding account has been entirely disbursed.

The SMMEA legislation made mortgage-related securities legal investments for institutional investors otherwise limited by law as to their investments to the same extent that obligations issued or guaranteed as to principal and interest by the United States are authorized investments under such laws. Such legal investment status could be overridden by states prior to October 4, 1991, and 21 states did so to some extent. In addition, SMMEA increased the ability of federally-chartered depository institutions to purchase mortgage-related securities. It also preempted the application of the registration provisions under state securities laws to the extent such provision was not overridden by a state prior to October 4, 1991.

• *Legal Investment Considerations*

Absent the legal investment preemption in SMMEA, the legal investment authority for regulated institutions investing in asset-backed securities is often unclear. If the asset-backed securities are pass-through securities, the investor may sometimes look through to the underlying assets and determine whether it can invest in such assets. If the securities are notes, many legal investment laws require the satisfaction of historical debt coverage ratios, which may be impossible in the case of a newly-formed SPV. Many regulated institutions may have to rely on "basket" clauses to establish legality.

• *Preemption of State Securities Registration*

As amended by the Improvements Act, Section 18 of the 1933 Act exempts "covered securities" from the registration provisions of state securities laws. While asset-backed securities are not within the definition of covered securities, any securities sold to "qualified purchasers" will be covered securities. The SEC is given the authority to define qualified purchasers. The House Commerce Committee report on the bill states that the committee expects the SEC to craft regulations for qualified purchasers that will implement Congress' intention that asset-backed securities and other structured offerings be regulated exclusively by the Federal government.[36]

• *NASD Considerations*

Publicly offered asset-backed securities rated in one of the top four rating categories are not subject to the public offering filing requirements of the NASD.[37] If the Depositor and one of the underwriters are affiliates, the independent underwriter requirements of the NASD rules that apply to securities of an issuer that are underwritten by an affiliate of the issuer do not apply to the asset-backed security being distributed if it is rated in one of the four highest rating categories.[38]

---

36. H.R. Report No. 104-622, 104th Cong., 2d Sess. at 31 (1996).
37. NASD Conduct Rules, Rule 2710(b)(7)(E).
38. NASD Conduct Rules, Rule 2720(b)(C)(v).

Index

[References are to page numbers.]

A

AAU. *See* Agreement among underwriters

Abbreviated registration forms
F-2, 15, 603, 604, 620, 621
F-3, 15, 159, 160, 161, 217, 471–473, 495, 496, 500, 501, 506, 509, 512, 523, 537, 538, 540, 547, 575, 603, 604, 620, 621, 629, 631, 753, 754
F-6, 603
S-2, 14, 15, 111, 112, 113, 159, 604
S-3, 14–17, 89, 105, 151, 159, 160, 161, 166, 219, 278, 295, 327, 467, 471–473, 492–496, 500, 501, 503, 505, 506, 508, 509, 512, 523, 534, 537–540, 542, 543, 546, 547, 575, 604, 748, 753, 754, 757, 778, 779, 781, 789, 790, 861, 869, 870, 871, 873, 874, 877, 898, 899
S-16, 14, 497, 510, 534, 550, 790, 791

Accelerated debt
stripped Treasury obligations, 704

Acceleration of effectiveness of registration statement, 18, 326 n.23

Accounting treatment
comfort letters, 91, 296, 893

deep discount and zero coupon obligations, 702
derivatives, 290
due diligence, 288
expertizing of selected financial data, 263 n.11
gaap
continuous offering of medium-term notes, 444
foreign issue financial statement, 607
innovative financial techniques, 702
Rule 144A transactions, 426, 428
Schedule B, 623
liabilities, 260, 263

Accounts receivable
commercial paper current transaction test, 660, 666

Accredited investor, 405–411, 435, 436, 438, 439, 443, 445, 446, 457

Acquisitions. *See also* Arbitrage; Merger
and convertible securities, 766
financing, commercial paper current transaction test, 674
and leveraged buyouts, 703, 780, 781
restricted period, 209
and Rule 10b-6, 210
and Rule 145, 35, 36

903